THE HERETIC

THE HERETIC

The Renaissance Trilogy
- Book III

HENRY VYNER-BROOKS

Pravda Press

Contents

PART ONE - 1536

ACKNOWLEDGEMENTS & HISTORICAL NOTE

'The first duty of a man is the seeking after and the investigation of truth.'
Cicero

It is the great privilege and joy of the historical fiction writer to be able to spend long hours in research, which of course usually means plundering the riches of other people's hard labour. So, at the outset, let me acknowledge with profound gratitude the numerous historians, academic writers, web-forum contributors and novelists who have informed and enriched my life, and this book. Writing is a solitary business and they have been like many friends in my mind these last years, like so many Virgils guiding a hapless Dante through the unfamiliar underworld of the 16th century!

The Tudor era is so well known in parts, almost to the point of parody. And yet so many important aspects are forgotten or ignored - the arrogation of state power, the despoliation of the institutions of the poor and the generational landgrab. It was only twenty generations ago and yet the effects of this epochal decade are still with us. I only discovered after the book's first edition that my own Lincoln relations survived the ill-fated 1537 civil war, known as the Pilgrimage of Grace, and fled east to Lancashire. A generation later, under Elizabeth I's reign, they were hiding priests and one, a yeoman farmer call John Finch, was hung drawn and quartered.

But readers need not fear that this book is a thinly veiled apologetic for Catholic grievance, for as the reader will hopefully come to appreciate, my sympathies in this book range across the religious spectrum to all those who are prepared, not just to seek and stand for truth, but also work for the *temporal common good*. These issues might be timeless but even so, they certainly appear more prescient a decade after the book's publication, as the culture wars have been turbo-charged by social media algorithms, Marxian forms of analysis and the ensuing polarisation.

When Britain was remade to suit Henry VIII and his powerbase, many little people fell between the cracks. This book is about them, and even though the main character and many of the sub-plots (murders, assassinations, jousts etc.) are fictional, the great bulk of the settings and political events are based in historical fact. It was on a boating holiday in Norfolk that I first discovered the unique story of St Benet's Abbey - the only monastery never dissolved. From that discovery, and a growing love of the area, the idea for a book began to emerge - and so also, a mountain of research! The Ranworth Rood screen was restored by a monk called Pacificus, who did indeed travel with a dog in a coracle from the abbey to do his work. And that work can still be seen, as can many other locations and details given in this novel. (See: the maps section) The dates, names and events surrounding the northern rebellion are pretty much given as found in the historical record - though Robert Aske was actually executed in York, not London. The smuggling trip to Antwerp is fictional but all the details about Tyndale's Bibles and the Bishop of London's burning of them is accurate. Information given about Sir Thomas Erpingham is accurate, but as his line petered out, it gave me the opportunity to invent the book's central character and his brother. Records from Augmentations still exist for the visitations to the various monastic houses in this novel. I have used them, and the names of the actual monks mentioned, as a base from which to build my characters.

I cannot close this section without once again thanking my wife Ruth and our six children. They deserve awards too for sharing my research, reading drafts & keeping the author caffeinated! Also, I must thank and praise my agents Pieter and Elria at Piquant for bearing with me so long, pushing good books my way and believing in this project. The first edition of THE HERETIC was my first foray into historical fiction. Though it now forms the third in the Renaissance Trilogy, it was written first and published by Lion Hudson in 2014. A great debt of gratitude is owed to Tony Collins and the team at Lion for investing so much in it, and giving me such an experienced novelist-editor in Penelope Wilcock. Sincerely, my thanks to you all for that, and then also for allowing me to retrieve the rights without cost so that a revised edition could be released with this trilogy.

Lastly, I thank the readers and reviewers of this book. Being a second edition, I already have the satisfaction of knowing that this has been enjoyed by thousands of readers across the globe. The reviews have been a greater source of encouragement than any other than an author can know. And the constructive criticism has been a spur to serve an intelligent and well-read audience better. So, the final thanks to the future readers for their investment of time. I hope it will be rewarded with a rich, Tudor feast!

Henry Vyner-Brooks, Loweswater 2022

MAPS & LOCATION PLANS

ST. BENET'S ABBEY & ENVIRONS

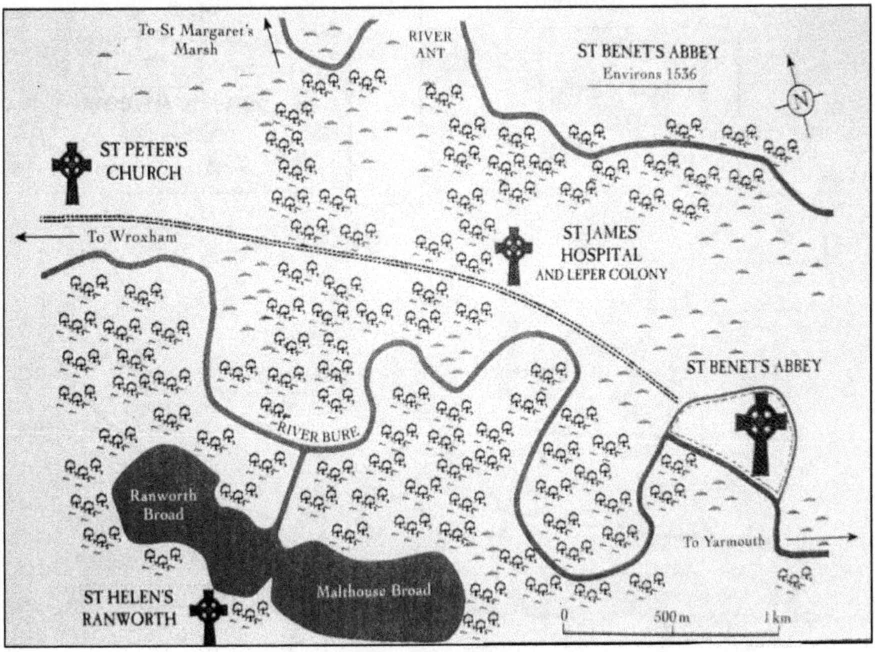

MONASTIC ENCLOSURE

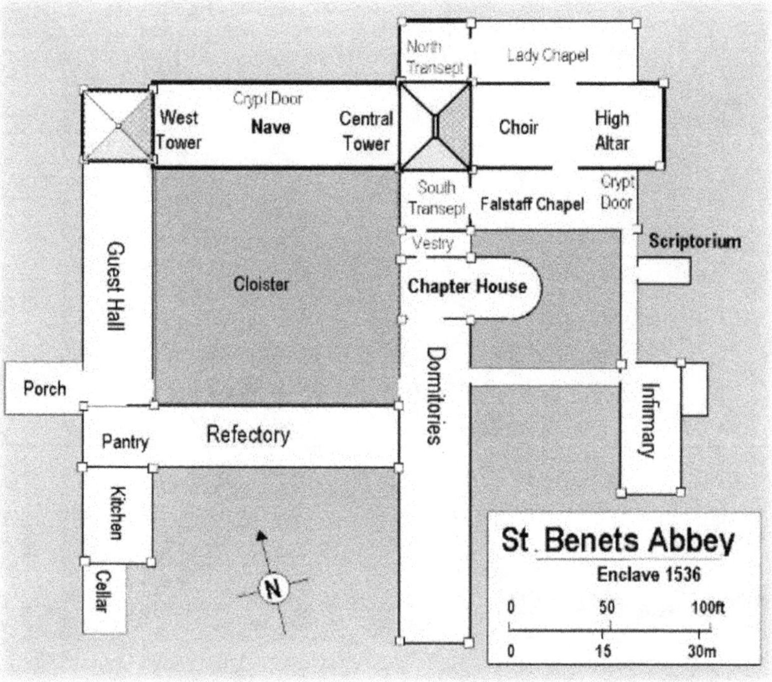
North Transept
Lady Chapel
Crypt Door
West Tower
Nave
Central Tower
Choir
High Altar
South Transept
Falstaff Chapel
Crypt Door
Vestry
Scriptorium
Guest Hall
Cloister
Chapter House
Porch
Dormitories
Infirmary
Pantry
Refectory
Kitchen
Cellar
N
St. Benets Abbey
Enclave 1536
0
50
100ft
0
15
30m

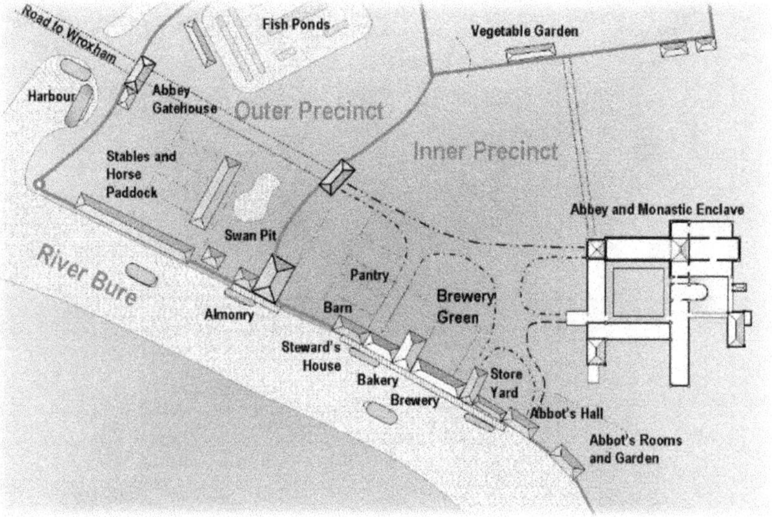
Road to Wroxham
Fish Ponds
Vegetable Garden
Harbour
Abbey Gatehouse
Outer Precinct
Inner Precinct
Stables and Horse Paddock
Abbey and Monastic Enclave
Swan Pit
River Bure
Pantry
Brewery Green
Almonry
Barn
Steward's House
Bakery
Brewery
Store Yard
Abbot's Hall
Abbot's Rooms and Garden

BOOK LOCATIONS NEAR ST BENET'S ABBEY

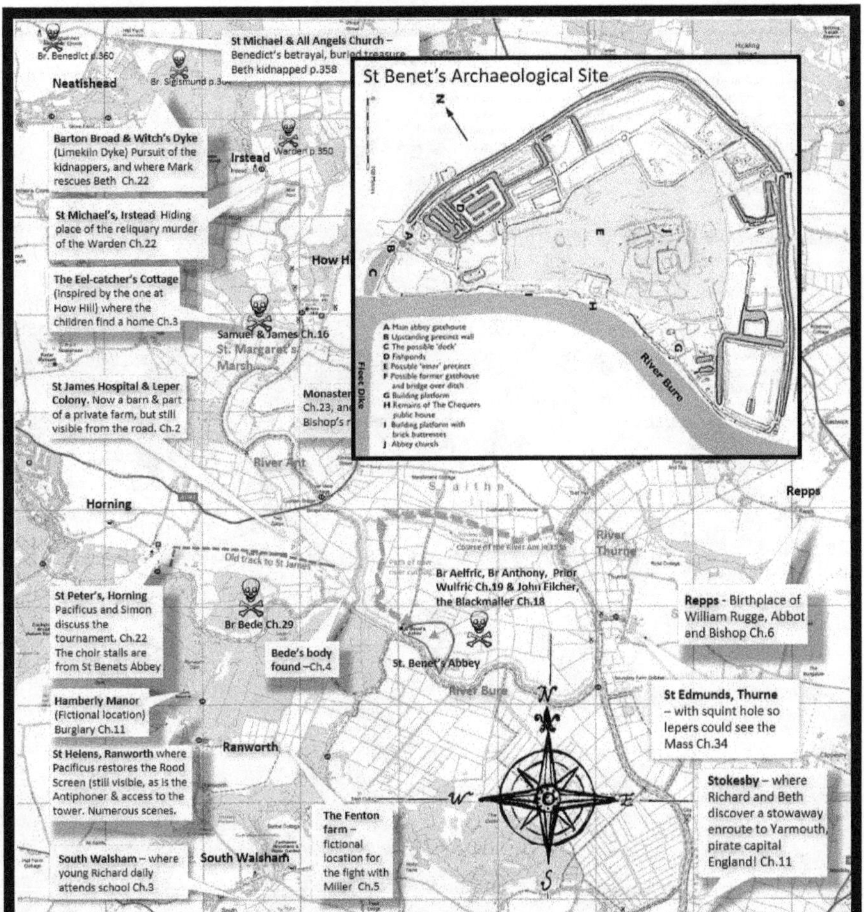
Br. Benedict p.360
Br. Sigismund p.304
Neatishead
St Michael & All Angels Church – Benedict's betrayal, buried treasure Beth kidnapped p.358
Barton Broad & Witch's Dyke (Limekiln Dyke) Pursuit of the kidnappers, and where Mark rescues Beth Ch.22
Irstead
Warden p.350
St Michael's, Irstead Hiding place of the reliquary murder of the Warden Ch.22
The Eel-catcher's Cottage (inspired by the one at How Hill) where the children find a home Ch.3
Samuel & James Ch.16
St. Margaret's Marsh
St James Hospital & Leper Colony. Now a barn & part of a private farm, but still visible from the road. Ch.2
River Ant
Horning
St Benet's Archaeological Site
N
A Main abbey gatehouse
B Upstanding precinct wall
C The possible 'dock'
D Fishponds
E Possible 'inner' precinct
F Possible former gatehouse and bridge over ditch
G Building platform
H Remains of The Chequers public house
I Building platform with brick buttresses
J Abbey church
Fleet Dike
River Bure
Repps
River Thurne
Old track to St James
Br Aelfric, Br Anthony, Prior Wulfric Ch.19 & John Filcher, the Blackmailer Ch.18
St Peter's, Horning Pacificus and Simon discuss the tournament. Ch.22 The choir stalls are from St Benets Abbey
Br Bede Ch.29
Bede's body found –Ch.4
St. Benet's Abbey
Repps - Birthplace of William Rugge, Abbot and Bishop Ch.6
Hamberly Manor (Fictional location) Burglary Ch.11
St Edmunds, Thurne – with squint hole so lepers could see the Mass Ch.34
Ranworth
St Helens, Ranworth where Pacificus restores the Rood Screen (still visible, as is the Antiphoner & access to the tower. Numerous scenes.
N
W
E
S
Stokesby – where Richard and Beth discover a stowaway enroute to Yarmouth, pirate capital England! Ch.11
The Fenton farm – fictional location for the fight with Miller Ch.5
South Walsham – where young Richard daily attends school Ch.3
South Walsham

BOOK LOCATIONS AROUND NORWICH

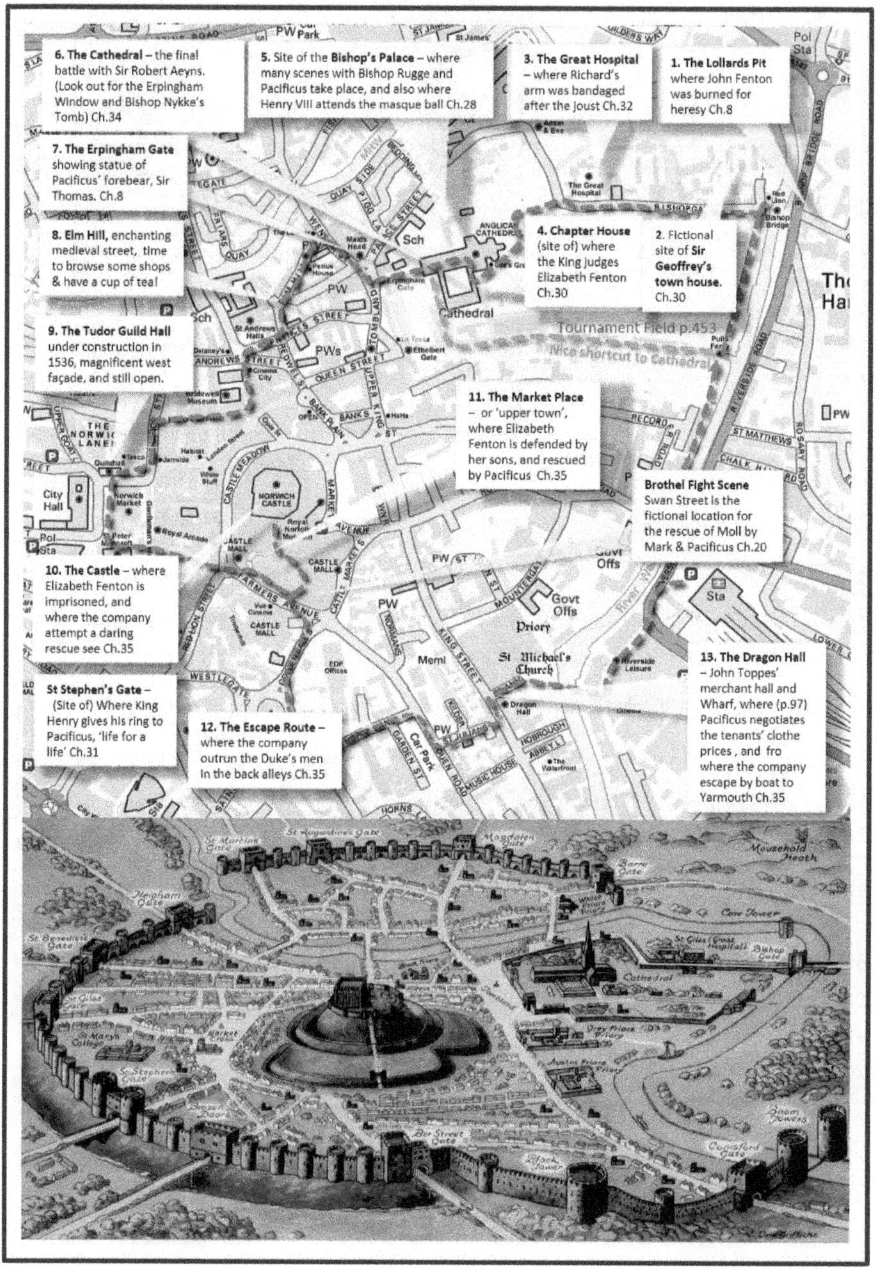
6. The Cathedral – the final battle with Sir Robert Aeyns. (Look out for the Erpingham Window and Bishop Nykke's Tomb) Ch.34
5. Site of the Bishop's Palace – where many scenes with Bishop Rugge and Pacificus take place, and also where Henry VIII attends the masque ball Ch.28
3. The Great Hospital – where Richard's arm was bandaged after the Joust Ch.32
1. The Lollards Pit where John Fenton was burned for heresy Ch.8
7. The Erpingham Gate showing statue of Pacificus' forebear, Sir Thomas. Ch.8
8. Elm Hill, enchanting medieval street, time to browse some shops & have a cup of tea!
4. Chapter House (site of) where the King judges Elizabeth Fenton Ch.30
2. Fictional site of Sir Geoffrey's town house. Ch.30
9. The Tudor Guild Hall under construction in 1536, magnificent west façade, and still open.
Tournament Field p.453
Nice shortcut to Cathedral
11. The Market Place – or 'upper town', where Elizabeth Fenton is defended by her sons, and rescued by Pacificus Ch.35
Brothel Fight Scene Swan Street is the fictional location for the rescue of Moll by Mark & Pacificus Ch.20
10. The Castle – where Elizabeth Fenton is imprisoned, and where the company attempt a daring rescue see Ch.35
St Stephen's Gate – (Site of) Where King Henry gives his ring to Pacificus, 'life for a life' Ch.31
12. The Escape Route – where the company outrun the Duke's men in the back alleys Ch.35
13. The Dragon Hall – John Toppes' merchant hall and Wharf, where (p.97) Pacificus negotiates the tenants' clothe prices, and fro where the company escape by boat to Yarmouth Ch.35
Cathedral
Norwich Castle
City Hall
Priory
St Michael's Church
St Augustine's Gate
Magdalen Gate
Mousehold Heath
Barre Gate
Heigham Gate
St Benedict's Gate
Cow Tower
Bishop Gate
St Giles Gate
St Stephen Gate
Ber Street Gate
Black Tower
Conisford Gate
Boom Towers

DEDICATION

To my father, for teaching me to love History and Art

To my mother, for showing me how to love people

To my wife, for loving me

To the 200 million Christians who still suffer for their faith

To my children, that you may learn to love & endure as they do

DRAMATIS PERSONAE

- THE FENTONS -

Master Fenton (father and stepfather)
Elizabeth Fenton (mother)
Beth (daughter)
Richard (son)
Piers (son)
Samuel & James (infant sons)

- THE ANABAPTISTS -

Pieter (Eel-catcher)
Sarah (Pieter's sister)
Christopher Burgh (Cambridge scholar/reformer)

- THE MONASTERY -

William Rugge (Abbot and Bishop)
Thomas Stoneham (Prior)
Brother William Beccles (Cellarer)
Brother Aloysius (Librarian)
Brother Almoner
Brother Porter
Brother Gerard (Herbalist)
Brother John (Infirmarian)
Bother Pacificus (formerly Sire/Fra Hugh Erpingham)

Mark (Novice)
Simon (Leper and formerly Sir Cecil Erpingham)

- FROM BINHAM (BENEDICTINE) PRIORY -

Wulfric (Prior)
Bede (deceased)
Aelfric
Anthony
Benedict
Sigismund

- FROM HICKLING (AUGUSTINIAN) PRIORY -

Robert Aeyns (Prior)
Eight other Canons

- AT THE TUDOR COURT -

Henry VIII (King of England, Wales, Ireland and France)
Thomas Howard (Duke of Norfolk)
Henry Howard (Duke's son & Earl of Surrey)
Charles Brandon (Duke of Suffolk, King's friend & brother-in-law)
Thomas Cromwell (King's secretary, Lord Privy Seal, Mater of the Rolls. Chancellor of Cambridge University, Vicar General of the King's new church of England)
John Blount (Captain of the king's bodyguard)
Catherine Howard (The Duke's niece & future queen)
Eustace Chapuys (Ambassador to Holy Roman Emperor Charles V)
Thomas Wyatt (English nobleman, ambassador & lyric poet)
Sir Geoffrey de Hastings (retired diplomat)
Thomas Cranmer (Archbishop of Canterbury)
Lady Maria de Hastings (Sir Geoffrey's niece)

- NORTHERNERS -

Thomas Moyne (Lincolnshire lawyer)
Robert Aske (Yorkshire lawyer)
Harry Percy (Earl of Northumberland)
Thomas Percy (Harry's brother)
Thomas Darcy (First Baron Darcy of Temple Hurst)
Maddison and Heritage (the Lincoln envoys to London)
and all northern nobles, clergy and a third of the realm

- THE DEAD -

Richard Nykke (Former Bishop of Norwich)
Catherine of Aragon (King's wife)
Anne Boleyn (King's second wife)
Sir Thomas Erpingham (Hugh's heroic, Lollard forebear)

Ecclesiæ Cœnobialis S. Benedicti
de Hulmo in Agro Norfolciensi, cœnobio
nondum everso delineatæ, et in quodam
codice M.S. in Bibliotheca Cottoniana
repertæ, Figura.

PART ONE - 1536

THE ACT OF SUPREMACY

Be it here enacted by the authority of this present Parliament that the king our sovereign lord, his heirs and successors, kings of the realm, shall be taken, accepted and reputed the only supreme head of the Church of England, called *Anglicana Ecclesia*, and shall have & enjoy annexed and united to the imperial crown of his realm, as well the title and style thereof, as all honours, dignities, pre-eminences, jurisdictions, privileges, authorities, immunities, profits and commodities to the said dignity of supreme head of the same church belonging and appertaining:

And that our said sovereign lord, his heirs and successors, kings of the realm, shall have the full power and authority from time to time to visit, repress, redress, reform, order, correct, restrain and amend all such errors, heresies, abuses, offences, contempts and enormities whatsoever they be, which by any manner spiritual authority or jurisdiction ought or may lawfully be reformed, repressed, ordered, redressed, corrected, restrained or amended, most to the pleasure of Almighty God, the increase of virtue in Christ's Religion, and for...the peace and unity and tranquility of his realm.

Statutes of the Realm, Vol.III, p.142

I

The Orphans

Tempora mutantur, nos et mutamur in illis
Times change and we change with them

Stone columns, dark arches, candlelit pavements, stained glass ablaze in the dying light of Lady Day Eve, March 1536.

"Upon my word, sir, I shall cleave you from head to toe!"

With such ferocious words and a maniacal eye, the knightly Piers brings a broad sword down hard upon his older brother's golden head.

"Aaaargh!" Richard wheels back. "You hit me! You – you – " And turning to his sister: "Beth, I am hit!"

Beth heaves yet one more great sigh. "Why must you always play with those silly sticks? What do you expect but a cracked skull?"

The knightly Piers, all four foot nothing of him, drops his wooden sword. His arms are at once around his stricken brother, "Why did you not block my strike, like I told you?"

"Why must you always do it so hard?" Fourteen-year-old Richard pushes his brother away and drags an already mottled sleeve across his eyes and then his nose. "Why can't you just pretend?"

Piers, two years junior, hair blonde and thick as barley, is hard to resist at the best of times. He crouches beside his brother, laying a comforting hand on his shoulder: "I am sorry – but we're still knights, aren't we?"

"Knights!" Beth scolds, her face scrunched like a merchant's purse, more because of his too ready apology than at their childish obsession with knights – for even at fifteen years, she herself has scarce apologised for anything in her life, much less meant it. "A pretty pair of knaves you are! Fit for nothing, either of you, but the land, or the church."

But now she catches herself; she has said too much, and that too loudly. Suppose the monk hears her talking in such a way? She returns to tending her two youngest brothers, toddler Samuel and the babe James, and wishing the older boys were as biddable. But too late; what with Richard's screams and her unguarded comment about "the church', a monk by the name of Pacificus is advancing down the nave towards them, eyes like thunder, forehead furrowed like a March field under plough.

Like all grown-ups he is very old, perhaps ninety Piers guesses, perhaps mid-fifties his sister thinks. Even so, the children do like Pacificus, for this monk will at least let them play in church if they are quiet (which they never are). And he has never beaten them as the priest has – a man easy to loathe, if you were young.

And so here he stands before them, Hugh de Erpingham, former knight of Rhodes, refugee from the collapse of chivalry. Weather-worn, world-weary and awaiting death, he came here to hide after Rhodes fell to the Turks, and with it his whole life. Thus he who commanded galleons and defended bastions now rows a leaky coracle every morning from Saint Benet's Abbey along the River Bure to this church at Ranworth. The irony, perhaps even narrative symmetry, is not lost on him. But, as he sees it, this insignificant Norfolk broad is as good a place as any to bury lost dreams and a lost life. This small body of water, dug for peat under a license from the Abbey in the reign of King Edward, lies between the great city of Norwich some nine miles distant and the great port of Yarmouth, gateway to the world. The petty local routines and characters are as staid and brackish as the dyke waters that surround it. For a man who has stood before popes and emperors, this abasement - this social flagellation - suits his melancholia well. If humiliation is to be his portion, he will drink it to the dregs just to see how much he can take. If his conceit was to think he could be someone, could be significant, then his contrition would be to fade away, unknown and unremembered. This backwater was as good a place as any.

On this day, under orders from his abbot, he has come to repaint the rood screen. Twenty six crumbling saints to meditate upon, to reimagine and restore. It is supposed to be part cure for his troubled soul, but also partly to get him away from the other monks. He has barely started this work – to which he does not feel equal in the first place – and so is irritable for many other reasons than the children's squabbles, but they are nevertheless a good excuse to vent his frustration. His voice is deep, hoarse, like the chafing of boots on gravel.

"What cavorting and fooling is this?" The monk awaits his answer, hands on hips. But there is none, just hung heads and quivering bottom lips; there is nothing to say after all. Pacificus drops his hands and then his shoulders with a long sigh. "Swords in God's house, eh? Did you not hear the fate of those knights who killed Becket?" He uses a thumb to examine Richard's emerging bruise. "If you would be knights, then first honour the sanctity of God's house."

"But, but he dropped his guard. I meant naught by it," Piers protests.

Pacificus sees the boy's shoulders slump further and Beth's suspicious eye for she has observed the scars on Pacificus' wrists, deep red, almost black in places. Her father has often warned them against friars and monks, for now the smaller houses are being shut and there are all sorts wandering the lanes these days. She observes the monk's face; burnt like a book, bound in tight leather, and telling nothing. The babe strains in her arms; little Samuel has wandered away and is now climbing on the font. She chides him but Samuel gives no heed. She glances back at the monk and thinks she almost sees a smile.

The monk reaches his paint-stained fingers to lift Richard's chin and hold it there. "Second thing lad, never drop your guard, even at play. It is a bad habit, and bad form, particularly against such a wily enemy."

Richard wipes his tears and forces a smile. Piers beams at the compliment.

Pacificus raises Richard's sword arm, helping him into a close-fighting stance. "Feet like so, left arm here, blade here, parry and side-step here; no more sore heads – got it?"

Piers too imitates the move with speed and flow, both boys delighted. Will he teach them more, they ask, and where did he learn? The monk looks back to the Rood saying, "*Multa me docuit usus, magister egregius.*" When he sees they do not understand, he adds: "Pliny the Younger. Know him? He says, necessity, that excellent master, has taught me many things. And so he has."

Beth sighs again, boys are incorrigible. She stoops to pick up baby James as he wriggles free yet again in a bid to pick up Richard's sword. There is no talking to men or boys on these things.

"Is it true you make the black paint from burnt bones?" Piers says.

The monk examines his blackened fingers. "Some have done so, it is true."

"Do you? They say you do!"

"Do they, indeed?"

"Don't you want to know who?"

"Piers, hold your tongue," his sister chides.

"She says so."

"I do not!"

"She does so, and other things – "

"Vile wretch!" she goes to cuff him, but almost before she leaves her seat she halts and listens, for she hears swift footsteps at the gate, then in the porch. Further off down the lane also, the sound of horses, and men barking orders. The oak doors scream on their hinges and a woman bursts through them, near tumbling at the monk's feet, gasping for breath, one hand on the font. "Run children, hide!" she heaves for air, "For the love of God, hide at once!"

"Mother, what is it?" Beth gasps. Baby James strains for his mother, and Samuel runs to her skirts. She hugs him fiercely but then she pushes him back with tears, "No! To your sister now – go child, there is no time to explain! Hamberly comes for you with the law – but go to now; hide! Beth, take them – fly!" Swift and urgent, she beseeches the monk, "Brother, by all you swear holy, pledge me you will spare these my orphans."

"Spare...orphans?" He gapes, appalled. "What business has the squire with you?"

"Mother!" Richard says, his lip beginning to tremble.

"Go, Richard! GO! Hide – I cannot help you now!" She pushes him away towards the door of the bell tower. He starts to well up, he cannot think, what is she doing? Beth wastes no time but clutches James close, hustling Richard through the door towards the steps. She glances back and whispers to her mother, "To the eel-catcher?" Her mother nods emphatically. Piers, waiting for no further command, grabs little Samuel's hand, towing him in the opposite direction down to the altar. The toddler, delighted at last to be included in a game runs willingly. His mother makes as if to stop them, but Pacificus raises his hand, "Best, lady, if they separate," and she at once sees the sense of it, saying 'yes' as a half-spent cry. 'Yes, I see.'

The sound of hooves are in the church yard now, the clink of steel.

She looks towards the altar in the Lady chapel, where she was churched only last spring after James was born. Even in this surreal and terrible moment, Pacificus cannot help but admire the beauty of the steward's wife, quite legendary in those parts, though he has not been so close to her as this before. He sees early signs of age, the lines and some grey amongst the gold, but even so a rare face; and he had seen many. Perhaps it is the fierce meaning of those eyes; fast and blue as a swallow, darting now as they do, this way and that. In the calm before the storm, he knows those eyes, understands them. She looks like the Saint Agatha he has been trying to paint all week; desperate and yet steely in the face of awful providence. What could she have done? He consciously tears his own eyes from her towards the door. And in this brief hiatus of thumping hearts, quickened breath, sweating palms, she murmurs, "Men used to seek sanctuary at the altar."

Pacificus, off guarded by the woman and the moment, finds it hard to say more than, "Yes, in another age." And then straightaway thinks, *Tempora mutantur, nos et mutamur in illis*, but it is too late to impress her that he really is more than the average dog Latin monk. For time is gone and the doors fling wide as her husband's employer, Squire Hamberly, swaggers in, face like a broiled gammon, hair grey and matted like a badger. Pacificus would stand between them but knows it is not his place, not now.

"Promise me," she whispers urgently, touching his wrist. "My children – promise me!"

Her eyes fix him, pleading, but he says nothing. Does nothing. He'll not be cornered by this woman, whoever she is, whatever her plight. Pick your battles, first rule of war.

Then, hot upon Hamberly's heels, comes John the Miller's son, an ambitious oaf with a lithe step and strong arm, and swift behind him, the sheriff's reeve from Wroxham with two men at arms. Ah, thinks Pacificus, she must be guilty of something to have roused that sluggard from the sheriff's house.

"Led us a pretty dance, Mistress Fenton," Hamberly wheezes above a ruff that makes his face look like a boar's head on a platter. "It is no use hiding in God's house when all your devils have forsaken you. We have your husband and now we come for you and that devil's spawn you call your children – or have you sacrificed them to Lucifer?"

Pacificus glances at her. Could it be? Surely not.

"Thank you, Squire." The reeve, a squat creature that smiles too easily, sidles past Hamberly. "We will take matters from here, see the law is served to the letter, so we will." Which is about right, for the villagers say the reeve is so narrow-minded, he can look through a keyhole with both eyes. He clears his throat with a great show of gravity, for this is the part of his work he really looks forward to. "Now then, is this the woman you saw, heard and did testify about, John Miller?"

Miller confirms it with barely concealed glee, "Oh aye, that's her alright!"

Noisome caitiff, Pacificus thinks, sizing the man. I thought Judas was only allowed out of hell for one day at Candlemas to cool himself.

"Very well, Mistress Fenton, I arrest you on charges of heresy and treason. You will come with these good men – you and your family – to a place assigned you by the bailiff until the day of your trial and sentencing."

The guards step forward, but Pacificus moves to intervene: "Prithee gentlemen, I believe in such instances a warrant is usual?"

The reeve retrieves one from his doublet, whereupon Hamberly seizes it and thrusts it at Pacificus, "Read it if you must! The whore is arrested fairly." He turns his gaze on her: "And to think we had so graciously let these vile Fentons manage our estates!"

"I believe – " She draws in her breath and speaks clearly. "I believe my husband's care saved your estates from ruination, and that nothing displeased you until you demanded more than you were entitled to receive." At this she turns the full blue fury of her eyes upon him, but the sally makes little impression, though it is understood by the others.

"Well, that is where you are wrong. You could have stayed on if we had not so timely received confirmation of your infamy from Miller here."

Throughout this exchange Pacificus registers the charges with blinking eyes. He speaks past Hamberly to the reeve: "Serious charges, with evidence I presume?"

"My word, damn you, my testimony!" Hamberly cannot abide being spoken over. "Who are you, monk, telling the Justices their business? Be sure I will speak to Prior Thomas about it, Brother...?"

"Pacificus," Pacificus supplies.

"Indeed, my son, and others have spoken of you." Hamberly scratches the pockmarks on what is still visible of his neck. "Yes, I have heard of you. Well, Brother Pacificus, your Prior often brings his hounds onto my land, and so I have his ear right enough."

"I'm sure he will not mind that I was seeing the law served correctly on this side of the river." Pacificus says. He would dearly love to remind Hamberly there was a time when Squires won their spurs before they won their estates, but he knows his own situation is already precarious.

"The law?" Hamberly mocks. "You talk of the law, monk, and what is this?" He directs the reeve to observe the paint pots and brushes by the rood. "Does not his Majesty's ban on religious art mean anything to this monk? Or perhaps he still thinks the church is above the law?"

"Come now, squire, it is restoration, not creation." And then, rather ill-advisedly for a man of his position, Pacificus says, "And besides, if we were to examine the letter of the law, would not the Sumptuary Laws forbid the silk embellishment of doublets worn by those of the yeoman class, and, for that matter, the carrying of a rapier in public?"

Hamberly is near to exploding with his fists, but the reeve – much to his credit, for he is not used to taking initiative – steps forward. "Pray let us deal with the matter in hand, gentlemen. Mistress Fenton, will you come willingly with these men?"

She nods and steps forward now, hoping by hastening her own fate to spare her little ones. But no sooner has she done so, then the reeve speaks. "And the children, Mistress, the children?"

"They are in God's keeping now, you will not find them." She speaks with confidence.

"What murder, malice and malignity," Hamberly vents on her. "What did I say, Reeve? She doubtless has killed them!"

"Then Squire, if it be so, I have saved the law any further trouble in doing it, or isn't that what you intend for all of us? Prithee let us go now, you have what you came for." Elizabeth says.

The reeve is not sure and even though he would believe anything possible of her, he would not risk his job for want of a little searching. After all, it was to here that she had run from them.

The men at arms are sent to search the nave and Lady chapel. Miller offers to search the bell tower.

The woman is praying, Pacificus can see that, but it cannot do her good now, he thinks; there is nowhere for the children to hide up there if Miller goes all the way – and he doesn't look the sort to stop. I should not get involved, he mutters inside his head, it'll bring trouble. His eyes follow Miller, but when the tower door shuts, they focus on the waning orange glow in the west windows behind him. "The light is fading, I must see to my brushes. Mistress Fenton, gentlemen – "

Hamberly is still too angry to do more than let out a half grunt, half snort. Pacificus does not meet her gaze again as he departs for fear of coming under suspicion himself. But as he strides down the nave with apparent unconcern to all, the mop of golden hair and then the beady blue eyes of Piers emerge from behind the base of the altar. The quick shake of the monk's head sends the boy back to where his infant brother crouches. No one has seen, Pacificus thinks, at which point he realises he has begun to be sucked in. The reeve's men come close to the rood screen and make to go into the chancel.

"You may see behind the screen from here, and you can also see the choir stalls are quite empty, but beyond that you may not go, lest the bishop hear of it." He thinks by these words, said with as much disinterest as he can muster, to dissuade them further. But one of them, Thomas Carter of Aylesham, who has never had a good word for priests, friars or monks, will not be told anything. He steps through the carved arch of the screen while a half-painted Archangel Michael looks on. Carter approaches the altar step, so close now that he will hear the children's breathing if he hears nothing else. Pacificus follows him into the choir, dragging his feet to obscure any noise and very intent to convince this heathen that any sacrilege will not go unreported. "You are at liberty to fetch the priest to search there, if you do not trust me," he adds by way of reconciliation.

"You go, then – to look, I mean," Carter says.

"Very well."

Pacificus genuflects, mounts the step and walks behind the altar, keeping to the back wall, so as not to step on the bairns. He sees Piers feeding James crusts from his pocket – clever lad. But Samuel grabs Pacificus' habit, he wants to be lifted up and cuddled; thankfully his mouth is too full of bread to make much noise. "Nothing here," Pacificus says, slightly louder than necessary. He sees Elizabeth Fenton looking back towards him as the reeve leads her out. Piers cups the toddler's mouth and pulls a funny face to distract him. Meanwhile Pacificus moves round to the other side and follows Carter out. That was too close, he thinks.

He pretends to busy himself with the paints and then to his utter amazement Miller appears from the bell tower empty handed. What magic is this? Impossible, he thinks, unless the brute has done something with them. Soon they are all gone and the place falls silent for a moment as if nothing but good had ever happened within these walls.

Pacificus tells Piers to make no noise and keep Samuel close, while he goes to search outside the church. He hears the horses someway down the road to Wroxham. There are no other houses near them, thankfully.

Back inside he hears steps on the bell tower stairs. A moment later Richard tumbles out, breathing short and fast, white as a sheet even in the fading light. "Our mother?" His eyes alone were enough to break the hardest heart but Pacificus can say little more than, "Boy, how did Miller not find you?"

Richard, distracted for the moment from his aching heart by the cleverness of their scheme, tells the monk how they realised they had no place to hide but one; behind the trap door as it opened onto the bell tower roof. "Really, it is only a half hiding place, and barely enough to cover us all but we did it, and when he opened the door from the ladder, we just kept behind it and hoped that he didn't do more than peep at the roof." He shrugged, "Anyway, he didn't. It was Beth's idea, really."

Beth and James appear at the bottom of the steps. Her face is streaked with tears; she has descended that circular staircase like Dante's cardinal descending into hell. Being careful carrying the baby through that narrow, winding space gave her plenty of time to take it all in.

She came here without a care, a girl on the brink of womanhood. She stands here now with nothing in the world but four brothers.

"Where is our mother, where have they taken her?" She tries to control each word, though begins to feel she is loosing the feeling of her limbs.

"Wroxham, then to Norwich. The charges are serious."

"And Father?" Piers adds, as he joins them.

"Him too."

"But what have they done wrong?" Beth demands.

"You do not know?" Pacificus looks at her carefully.

"Well, I know there was something, something that was secret, that they would tell me when I was ready but not before."

"Do your parents attend Mass?"

"Every week."

"And they take the sacrament?"

"Of course." She puts the baby down on the floor rushes, and then folds her arms. "Why ask of it?"

"Never mind now." He is not sure at all whether she does know something after all. "Do you have other family where you can go now? Who can hide you?"

"Our father's people are from down country, we know not where, he did not speak of them."

"And your mother, child? What of her?"

"Aylesham – though she always said she could not be seen there again."

"Why?"

"I know not, but it is God's truth."

This he doesn't want to hear, but Beth – realising this man is their only ally in the world – has not finished, for there is one understanding her mother has always drummed into her: "But Mother said, if ever anything bad happened to her and Father, if we were left alone, she said we should search out the eel-man, up river beyond Ludham; way up in the marshes, she said."

"Ah," Pacificus says, "I have seen him – the Dutchman. He is sometimes at the monastery to sell his catches."

"That is more than us, then," she says. "We have never met him – or I don't think we have – and we have no boat to cross the river, and we don't know the way to his house." She glances anxiously at the floor. "They say the marsh is very dangerous there."

Silence falls between them as Pacificus looks again at the light through the west window. He could loose the moorings of a boat at the staithe and bring it back in the morning, but the light is going fast, and he must be at Vespers. But he can't let these children wander the marshes alone. She is right, it is too dangerous for those who don't know the paths. But dusk is good for cover, and more than anything else he does not want to be seen with these children – or have anything to do with them in fact. His situation at Saint Benets is not easy already; this sort of thing could finish him. What did Benedict rule? That a straying brother may be received again 'even unto the third time if he promise amendment'. The abbot hoped this painting work beyond the precinct at Ranworth might cool his temper, help him earn his name, but it seems trouble has found him yet again. No, he cannot take them all the way now, but he knows someone who might.

He feels Piers at his right hand, "You will get us there, won't you?"

"Yes. I owe your mother that much at least." Pacificus has made his plan, "You children will split up. Maid, you take the babe – and stop his crying."

"I cannot, he is wet, hungry and needs his – " Her voice trails off in a moment of realisation.

But the monk is not listening now anyway, he is making plans, "And you lad," he says to Richard, "Go quietly in the shadows of the hedgerows to Heron Point. Wait there in the reeds for Piers and me."

"How will we get there?" Richard says.

"You will take Old Man Raker's boat from the staithe."

"But if anyone sees me, or if I can't do it?"

"You make sure they don't, and that no one sees your face, you hear. From now on, no one south of the river must see any of you. Just get that boat, or another, and meet us at the point."

"But if I can't..."

"You'll get, d'you hear, and when you see me rowing up the cutting to the river; follow at a distance. There's a staithe near St James' that I use. See where I put in, deep in the reeds. If no one is watching and no other boat near, do likewise."

"And then," Richard says, "you will take us to this eel-catcher?"

"No, I have no time, I will be missed at the abbey. But I know someone among the lepers who will take you from there."

Beth claps a hand to her mouth. Lepers! She had seen the small colony attached to St James' hospital, but only from her side of the river. Monks may go near them but she would not – not ever. But she then thinks, that was then – before all this. Now we are all outcasts. She lowers her eyes slightly, "I would prefer it if you took us."

"Maid, you cannot prefer now, only take what is offered, the leper Simon can be trusted absolutely, you have my word on it, he knows the marshes up the River Ant. You will be safe with him." He sets his face toward the door. "Gather what you have now. Let's be gone."

2

The Leper

Fallaces sunt rerum species
Appearances are deceptive

The air is laden with damp, ice even. Pacificus hears the twittering of thrushes in the darkness of the ivy-clad hedgerows that flank the road. Thank God for the birds, he thinks, winter won't be forever.

Pacificus separates from Richard by the gate and goes to the dyke where his coracle is pulled up in the reeds. The dog is there waiting, like the aged poor who have grown weary of mere charity and would have alms as a right. Sometimes the dog comes to the churchyard like a suppliant, to endure the affections of the children, but more often patrols the staithe looking for unsuspecting fowl and fights, usually finding the latter without difficulty, for the wherryman's dogs are usually equal to the challenge. It is not a large creature, perhaps lower than the monk's knee, lean, short bodied. At first he tried to shake the dog off, but now has come to tolerate its presence if only to vent his frustration at his current situation – dogs are good for that and this one doesn't seem to mind. Pacificus has named him Gus – after Augustine – for it's plain this mongrel, no less than he himself, loves grace over works, and wild duck more than either. The dog skips into his position at the prow of the coracle, the monk punts beyond the reeds onto the broad. Gus growls at the coots but is cuffed by his master: "Whisht hound, not tonight." Once clear of the reeds, Pacificus looks back to Ranworth staithe, some three hundred yards to the east. He cannot see Richard on the shore yet. "Stupid mutt, come here," he grumbles affectionately. He ruffles the dog's neck fur and waits.

Richard is hiding in the thicket near the boat he means to take. He is not good at doing new things for they never seem to go right for him. He feels more at home with rules, with boundaries. Though it is near freezing he sweats from his brow and feels a cold trickle running down his back. His fists are tight clenched thinking of his parents; he cannot dwell on injustice or unfairness. Tears sting his eyes, he wants to run to his mother, he wants to go home, she said they would eat roast lamb tonight; his favourite. Why did the men take her? It was wrong, he knows it was. Mother is good, why did they take her away? How can such a thing be? He holds back the tears. The boat is in view but he cannot break cover. Some wherrymen not fifty yards away are still securing their cargo and bantering like a pair of drunkards. He daren't move, daren't risk it. He wonders if the other four children have already rendezvoused on the reeds by Heron Point. Wrapped up warm against the cold they might be, but he thinks the little ones will be cold and the babe hungry.

After what seems like an age, the wherrymen saunter over to the far side of their craft to talk to another man. The boy thinks it is the priest, Monseigneur John. They are talking of his own family, he thinks. The men shake their heads, saying they have seen nothing but the world is going to the dogs and they always suspected the Fentons of mischief; and would he buy any more Flemish spirits, as they have some just in? They'll do him a fair price, since it's him – better than last time. The cleric invites them to the house to discuss the matter privately. The minute they are gone Richard sets to work on Raker's neat little boat. The knots go easy but the boat is partly bottomed in the mud. He pushes but cannot shift it. He puffs, pants, pushes, heaves again and again, each time with less conviction. "Won't move, what can I do, it won't move." Tears threaten again, but then he remembers the monk's words. He thinks of the others waiting for him, relying on him. It never mattered before, everything was optional – nearly anyway – but everything is different now. He struggles with his resentment at the impossible weight he must shift and then tries to think what Piers or Beth would do if they were here. In his head he is crying out for help, for someone, anyone. He sits for a moment on the side of the boat and hears – as it tilts – the water rushing into the mud fast area.

That's it, rock some water in! He jumps in and rocks the boat from side to side and then plants an oar into the mud and heaves the prow up and away – he has done it and within minutes he is rowing towards the point, cutting through the inky depths like a pike. He is lean, swift, strong. It feels so good to him to be about something simple that he can do well, so much so that he almost forgets his whole world; and good he might, for the only one who truly understands him is now halfway to Wroxham, and whatever waits her there. He pulls exultantly at the fat oars, as if his strength could pull back time itself.

When Richard arrives, Piers takes the painter and they settle the children. Pacificus leads a good way off but he can't stop Richard closing the gap. "Back you fool, back!" he mutters under his breath, "mustn't be seen near them, damn this leaking tub." Coracles are hardly built for speed, and his barely holds out the water. He should do some repairs, it is the season for it, but he hates maintaining anything, disdains this world where everything is always in decay, always falling apart. He misses a stroke in his haste to keep some space between Richard as they come clear onto the Bure. Water sprays onto a swan who curses him from the reeds, and he curses it back. Why did this have to happen to me – these children, this woman? Can I not be left alone, to have space to do something sublime at Saint Helen's? *Ora et labora*, always *Ora et labora* – pray and work! You've got to admire this about Benedict's rule, but by my oath, the corrupt world is arrayed against the balance. Always problems, always complications, always conflicts; the world always inconveniencing and interrupting the spirit, Martha usurping Mary; the king, Wolsey, now Cromwell and Cranmer – deceived and deceiving. "The world hurries on and speeds towards its end," as that old saint Wulfstan said, "for men's sins, it must worsen day by day." And, by my oath, he survived the conquest, and even had Henry and Queen Eleanor lay their crowns on his grave, promising never to wear them again – or so says William of Malmesbury who is generally reliable. But could any of them have foreseen these days, these new men? Can sins worsen beyond this day and hour, verily I cannot imagine worse, by the mass I cannot. *Argh, will not that boy row slower?*

He raises his hand in frustration at the children, and Piers, observant always with beady eye, recognises the signal and tells Richard to pull back. The boys squabble about it, Beth snaps at them both, the little ones start up their howling again. Everyone else is to blame. Kicks are exchanged and likely fists too, if they had not suddenly come to join the river Bure, and seen the ghostly sails of two wherries appear from behind the alders. The wherries pass before the coracle, their helmsmen unaware of the two smaller craft in the dyke under the shadows of the reeds.

Pacificus crosses to the far side of the river, feeling the pull of the low tide which, even here twelve miles from the sea, can be faintly felt. He works steadily for twenty minutes on the inside bend until he comes in sight of the staithe. He throws a sharp glance back towards Saint James' Hospital and the thin twist of smoke rising from the lazar houses at the rear. No sign of life. He heads for his mooring in the reeds, then signals the all clear with two short dog-like barks, which make Gus's ears twitch. The monk does not wait for the children but trudges up the short rise to this outlier of Saint Benets Abbey. The pasture is already crisp with frost, the monk's heavy breath billows like damp kindling from under his cowl. Glancing to the right he observes faint lights across the marsh at the abbey gate, and hears the sound of laughter cut short as the gate bangs shut.

The lepers' house is shut up against the cold, and there are complaints at the draft as he enters. "Come brother, keep the wood in the hole, won't you," says one nearest the fire.

"Hogging the fire again, Geoffrey?" Pacificus says, "surprised you're not tanned like a Saracen! Where is Simon?"

"The jakes," Geoffrey informs him briefly, "but you're wasting your time, he won't talk to you."

"Aye," says another, "what is it between you two anyway?"

"Our business is our own, and it does not concern you." Or anyone.

"Brother Almoner says he has a cankered heart," another adds.

"He has his story same as you all, best not to pry." If you know what's good for you, you won't.

He sees Simon outside, clothed in wool like himself. He tries to walk away but Pacificus goes to him. "Please don't – I mean, stay." This is hard; their last words to each other were not pleasant, but he is desperate, "I need your help, again, something very serious. I'm sorry for what I said before; well, not what I said but the way it came out."

Simon – not his real name – will not turn, but rather keeps looking away, out towards the marshes. "I care not a groat," he whispers, concealing the emotion. He is taller than the monk, even with a stoop caused by ailing bones. He can walk without a crutch but prefers one; his right foot is slightly lame and the crutch is as good as a pikestaff with the brigands on some of these back lanes.

"Will you help though?"

"Help?" he places the cloth veil back over his lower face. "I thought we were done helping each other, brother."

"Not me," Pacificus says, "but some children of Hamberly's steward, a man called Fenton."

Simon is already starting to say that no child would want a leper's help, when he hears the name. He pauses, turns sharp like a crow. "Fenton? You sure?"

"Well, yes, they are often at the church and – "

"And the girl, I mean, the maid – the one called Elizabeth?"

"You know her?"

"Never mind that. Is she with the others?"

"Yes."

"At the staithe." Pacificus tries to catch Simon's eye to see what his questions mean, but it is too dark.

"The staithe!" Simon gasps but then tries to hide it by turning away, turning deep within himself. He replants his crutch again and again, shuffling with agitation. "And this trouble – you said it was serious?"

"They must make the eel-catcher's cottage on Saint Margaret's marsh; no one must see them."

"I know it, and him too, the Dutchman," Simon tilts his head slightly. "But what of the parents?"

"They are taken, arrested, though we cannot talk of it now," Beseeching, he reaches for Simon's arm. "They must not be seen Simon, their names are on the warrant. Please. Tell this Dutchman they must disappear. And that he mustn't involve me."

"Oh, I see! Not defending widows and orphans these days, are we?"

"Enough', Pacificus restrains himself from raising his voice. "Enough I say. We don't have time for this now; will you help them or not?"

Simon pulls his sleeve free from Pacificus' grasp, saying, "I shall wait behind the jakes – oh pardon, your Worship – behind the privy, bring them round the back." The leper shuffles away, still partially caught up in his own thoughts, in his own past.

"They do not know about us," Pacificus cannot resist whispering after him, but the leper does not respond. As Pacificus watches him melt back into the shadows, he wonders at him. Of all the marvels on this strange day, why did he respond thus?

Following the noises of crying babes, Pacificus finds the children huddled and shivering in the boat. "You'll have to stop the bairns from crying out; its not safe for you," he says, with an ill humour. Beth glares at him, herself frayed and bewildered, "I am trying but they're tired and want their..." She gives up, adding miserably, "Oh, it's just no use." She is on the brink of exhaustion. The babe is hoarse with wailing. Piers tries to distract James with a surprise tickle, but he only wails more. Beth pushes Piers away roughly. Pacificus cannot abide the incessant noise. "Just cover its mouth, do anything. And you, get the other one and follow me, quickly now."

Richard picks up Samuel, folding him into his coat – though it barely covers the little one's sides. "C'mon, let's get going," the monk mutters.

The older children do not forget their manners when they meet the leper, but fear shows in their faces; they stand close to each other at a safe distance from him, clutching the babes tight. They greet him and thank him, but their courtesy is stiff and strained. And for his own part, Simon keeps his face turned away from them.

"Well, let us be gone," Simon says finally, peeling his inky form from the bulk of a gnarled oak, "and pray Saint Margaret will send the moon to light our way through the marsh." He does not go on to say what both he and Pacificus know, that the marsh is no place for children at night and it certainly hadn't done Saint Margaret any favours, for she was raped and strangled in the copse there during the reign of John *san Terre*. The remains said to be her bones lay under the abbey's high altar, though her cult draws few pilgrims. She is no Beckett, no Edmund, and her relics bring the abbey scant wealth. But neither the monk nor the leper regret that anonymity. When two men want to disappear forever, these marshes in Norfolk are as good a place as any.

3

The Eel Catcher

Fabas indulcet fames
Hunger sweetens the beans

"Have you always been a leper?"

Piers is never subtle, but Simon deals with him as straight as he can. He grumps out one word answers as they descend from the relative high ground of St James' Hospital into the darkness of the marsh. But, perhaps overcome by the child's persistence or by something else, he suddenly begins to explain his own circumstances in the only way he can think to express them.

"No man chooses his lot in this life, young sir, that's a fact. Mostly it comes to us."

His voice is refined, Beth thinks; he might perhaps have been a gentleman – once.

He continues, "Take me for example, I would not choose this disease, who would? But it is here, some say because I have sinned, and who among us can say they have not? Some think up other explanations, but howsoever the fact is that I came here; to the abbey, for there is no life for me now anywhere else. They made me lie in an empty grave and confess my sins, take certain vows, then they clothed me and provided for me as you now see. I am part monk, part dead man walking, you understand?"

Piers does not, and is thinking of another question, "Is it far, the eel-man's cottage?"

Simon sighs, "No, but the way is slow, always slow." He sees Beth is stumbling with weariness, and would offer to carry the bairn for her but shrinks from her inevitable rebuff, and dare not even stare her in the face. He knows there is no reason she should recognise him or even know of him, even if he gave her his real name. These things he keeps telling himself over and over, and yet there it is – that gnawing behind all his thoughts, that somewhere out there, hoping beyond hope, some strange divinity has shaped these events, be it for good or ill.

They follow for some time behind the uneven gait of their guide; through fields, then marshes, sometimes on banks, sometimes on boards and tree trunks laid in the wettest parts. The children's feet are sodden and so cold they hurt. Simon feels nothing, the disease had his feet long since. He would give a king's ransom to feel again, even the biting chill of this water.

On they trudge, deeper into the marsh and a thick blanket of fog. At intervals they startle an owl, heron or coot, which in turn temporarily silences the whimpering sobs of the two little ones. After what seems an age, Simon tells them to wait silently, and the older children endeavor to hush the babes.

They smell burning sod, then caustic hints of a byre nearby, then something else – something foul and rotten, the discarded guts of fish. Beth covers her face. But as yet they see nothing, for the reeds are grown high hereabouts so that it seems like some dread maze of the underworld, some otherworld scene from a mystery play. Simon leaves them for several minutes and in the imposed isolation of silence Beth and Richard begin to brood with creeping fear on the vulnerability of their position. They fight hard to suppress each new terror that crowds their minds. Meanwhile, Piers is speaking out his questions with increasing alarm – Will they see Mother again? What about Father? Will he be allowed his toys, his bed? Will the eel-man make them eat eels all the time? Beth cannot think, Richard is too hungry, too cold, too frightened. They snarl at him to do as he's bid and shut up. After that, the silence gives way to the loud sobs of Samuel, whose baleful cries echo upward and remind them all again, that there is no one to comfort him now, and that nothing will ever be the same again.

Eventually they hear Simon's voice beckon them. They feel gingerly along the path in the foggy darkness, until they see the shape of him, then another man tall, thin and stooped like a willow, silhouetted by light from the doorway of a cottage hidden away there in the wilderness of this marsh.

"Come, kinderen," the eel-catcher says, his accent alien, but his voice rich and kindly, "I am Pieter, friends of parents, yes, come!"

They approach him cautiously. Richard observes the long nose, the legs bare up to the knee. He seems to welcome them without reservation and certainly the smell from the thatched cottage, peat smoke and supper cooking, draws him; but he feels afraid for the others – suppose this is a trap. What is safe anymore? What can be trusted? His father has warned him about some of these marsh folk; too poor for the land, but not respectable enough for the parish. Some live by reed cutting and dyke digging, others by thievery and brigandage. No one knows the abodes of half these people, the marshes stretch across vast distances, treacherous and little frequented. No one has bothered to catalogue the paths these grey feet, these bog-dwellers, traipsed to find a home here. Many move from place to place as their needs demand. But this eel-man, he is established, his cottage is sturdy-built, a proper home; yet still Richard is uneasy, gripping Piers by the sleeve to keep him close. Are they all so tall, these Dutch?

Beth turns to Simon. "I thank you for your help sir, when things are better with us we will re – "

He cuts in: "No payment needed maid, only glad to see you – see you, that is, safe here." He wants to offer further assistance if needed but he cannot think how to put it in that moment, so he lets it pass. The children shuffle through into the cottage. When baby James cries out, a woman's voice welcomes them from inside: "Ja, ja! Come in, come in."

Pieter tries to persuade the leper to stay for a bit to eat, but he declines and shuffles back into the night. The smell of livestock hangs thicker now on the frosty air, wafted from byres to the rear of the wattle and daub cottage. They pass through the low doorway into the yellow warmth of the rush lights, the smell of burning animal fat rousing their hunger further, and reminded them yet again of home. For their mother used tallow for workaday candles – but also sweet scented beeswax ones for high days and holidays when guests came - used to come.

Pieter brings the children to the fireside, where an old woman, wrapped in woolen shawls, waits with a wooden bowl in one hand and reaches forth the other. "Ja, come now, kinderen come; come to the fire, hot food, pobs, pobs." She offers shreds of bread soaked in warm milk But Samuel and James are past the point of reason. "He is wet," Beth says, "he needs a new tail-clout, some moss maybe?" She assumes that there will be no waffle-weave cloth here, and that moss will do for him now, it will have to.

"Ja, I have old clout that will do, but no wine for the washing, only the water. Bring him to the hearth, and Pieter, Pieter shut that door!" The woman is called Sarah, the sister of Pieter, she has never had children of her own and the unrelenting crying unsettles her. "The door, Pieter, the door." Beth lays James by the fire, removing his bib, swaddling shawl and gown, then lifting his shirt. His pilcher – an absorbent triangular felted-wool cloth – is wringing wet, and the waffle-weave cloth under is soiled – his skin, chaffed and raw on the inside legs. Beth washes him carefully while Piers brings Samuel to the fire, removing the woolen kerchief across his breast, wet with dribble and tears, and then his apron and pudding cap. Piers's chilled fingers worked slowly at the leading-strings sewn to the back of Samuel's frock – a gathered skirt on a fitted bodice. Standing there in his shift, with blue fingers and lips, Samuel bawls piteously until eventually the pobs are inserted in his mouth by Piers.

While Beth deftly dries and clothes the babe with what Pieter brings her, she is all the while catching glances of the old woman, whose fingers walk through the air towards the cauldron to take the ladle, yet whose eyes stare straight ahead. Ah, she is blind, and that is why her linen coif is so dirty, she cannot see it, and surely a man would never think to point it out. Beth then unconsciously feels for the strings of hers and tucks a loose hair under it. She has so many pretty ones at home.

Pieter encourages the children to the stools, which he pulls to the hearth. He too is old, in his seventies and at this moment wonders how his sister will cope having so many others in the cottage. They grew up in a busy household – who doesn't? – but you get used to your own space, your own routine at their age. And all this noise! But she exclaims, "Ah the poor kinderen!" reaching out her arms, "Po po po, come little one, come." But James hides his face in Beth's skirts and will not be prised away, while Samuel only screams for his mother. So Sarah turns back to ladle the broth, holding out one of the applewood bowls full with steaming potage in their direction, with visibly shaky hands. She squints at the bowls, for she is not totally blind, though in this light it is very difficult. Her eyes have got worse in the last three years but even her blindness is less daunting a challenge than this – how can she, being so old, so set in her ways, be mother to five terrified children? This is a pledge she never expected to redeem. You say all sorts of things to each other when you are reading the gospels and feeling pious, little thinking through the implications. But here it is, five hungry, scared children. The parents will not be back, that much she knows. Maybe next time the bailiff will come for her, and that will be an end of the matter – but five children, and little ones too! "Here now, olders first while too hot, you share the spoons 'til Pieter make more." She chuckles nervously. "Dear me, and bowls and stools too, ja." Her hand fumbles the ladle as she lays it again in the pot. "Oh dear, here we are."

Pieter rests his own hand tenderly on her arm and she acknowledges it. "Ja, we shall be busy, and the roach and bream are spawning, so there is eel enough in the river, what a blessing, and summer will come soon."

It is a good thing that she cannot see the older children's faces as they smell the broth, though to their credit, they start to eat without the usual complaints. Their mother doted slightly too much on the children in regard to food, often remarking with a saintly resignation that if it were a sin, it were but a venial one, and perhaps an occupational hazard for any who love too much. The little ones stop their crying and kicking and, seeing the others with food, nestle in and share the spoonfuls. Even when they finish the food, none of the children ask what they really want to, namely about their parents. It is not shyness so much as the risk of hearing what they cannot yet face. After some awkward silences, Pieter clears a space in the loft for Piers to snuggle down with the little ones. There is plenty of straw but they must share a blanket until more can be borrowed. When they've settle down, Beth and Richard join them by the fire where they turn to practical things.

"You will want learning," Pieter says in an accent oddly mingling the cadence of his own country with the rustic dialect of Norfolk.

Education! Richard's thoughts flash immediately to his career of failure at St Mary's chantry school in South Walsham. His poor, tired shoulders slump as he remembers the twelve-hour days, setting out along the dark, winter lane with Latin Vulgaria in one hand, and a linen bag with food, ink and candles in the other. He was, said Master Pinches, at school to receive a fine modern education. It was one that came with regular birchings. As Pinches right arm grew in strength, so Richard was to become, it was said, *Italianate* – a rounded renaissance scholar, a humanist. His father revered this as a high calling, unthinkable only a generation before, and often spoke of it, only increasing the child's guilt and shame. For Richard, even with all his genteel sensibilities, and all his earnest application, had no calling to the classics;

neither literature nor rhetoric. He envied his sister who seemed to have their mother's aptitude for study, and not just household lore – herbs, medicine, sewing, cookery, household management and the like – no, for Mother had had a tutor of her own when she was young; she knew books, writing, languages, music, dancing. She was forever borrowing books, sharing the great prose romances with Beth, "filling her head with nonsense" father had said, "just make sure they all know their catechism by the time they're eight as the law says, I don't want any fines, not this year the way crops are." How she had ended up wed to a farm steward was not a question that Richard had ever thought to ask, but Beth had. It was a scorching August day when both she and her mother were comparing blisters after haymaking.

"I will tell you one day, but never think unkindly to your father, he is the best of men." That was all she said. Money there was, but not enough for a tutor which would benefit Beth. It was for the oldest son's education, and if Pinches and his birch rod could not make a renaissance man of Richard then it was not the fault of modern education. The boy was plainly a simpleton, no doubt born under the influence of a bad and mischievous star, or at least not Mercury or Sol. This had weighed heavy on Richard, like a deep bruise, and so too had the lesser problems accompanying youth; for he had matured late and his voice is still high. His body, though by no means short, is nevertheless still that of a boy. The other scholars, and even Pinches, have noticed this and long since teased him in their turns. Manhood lies beyond him, through some door that might never open. These and other things stir in the lad's soul as the others talk on, until he is sunk in self-pity.

"Eh, eh," Pieter says, waving the swollen jointed fingers before Richard's mesmerised eyes, "what you thinking lad, I say learning and you look to the fire like this?" Richard comes to, in for a pleasant surprise as the old couple think out loud in the light of their dying fire, "The boy looks strong, he can learn to cut reeds, set eel traps and eel lines, I will teach him to hunt and trap food, to provide for his family." Beth observes Richard straighten up and sit forward, the whites of his eyes now clearly visible. Pieter nods to himself with satisfaction, his eyes lighting with pleasure on the lad. Pieter guesses rightly that Richard would learn quickest without his nimble brother to steal his thunder, but to be kind, he adds: "Perhaps we will let your brother come with us too sometimes? Maybe?"

"Oh yes," Sarah says, "there will be much to do, much to learn, the kinderen will be very good to scare away the birds when we sow the meadow next month. And you, Elizabetta," she reaches an unsteady hand towards Beth and rests it on the girl's knee, "you can help me, my dear, for there is so much to do here too, and these old eyes, ja, so dim now."

Sarah breaks off and gestures around the cottage. "We will bake these hungry men bread, for they are like stubborn oxen when their bellies are not filled. We will cure the bacon, salt the meat and fish, tend the bees, raise the vegetables, milk the cows, feed the animals, make nice pickles, jellies and preserves, ja, ja – and sell them at market!" She chuckles and raises a knowing finger. "And when we have done all this they will need clothes so we must spin wool and make coats for them – and soap for them to wash, and candles for them to chatter by, with a mug of warm ale which we will brew. And then they will want to know what we find to be tired about at the end of the day!"

They all laugh but under it all Beth has the sickest feeling that she has just heard a life sentence passed upon her. She is not a gentleman's daughter but she might have become a gentleman's wife; isn't everyone trading up in England these days? But now, she is robbed of parents, status and prospects in one swoop. Now she will be lower than a serf, attached to no land even, with nothing but these two poor old souls and no future save the drudgery of a peasant's life on the marshes, where the damp carries most off by forty, all except these Dutch, who have willow in their bones.

Beth does not even think to ask how these people have earned the trust of her parents, or what secret agreement has been made, or even what (if any) money has been laid by for the eventuality. Even an hour later, tucked up with the others in the loft, with no feather pillow or linen sheets, she cannot shake off feelings of resentment, self pity, and anger. And then, after these are exhausted and unanswered, she feels a cold wave guilt for not showing greater fortitude like the heroines in her mother's stories. Meanwhile, the boys snore lightly with open mouths. She envies them. She weeps for herself, then for them, then she sleeps. For good or ill, tomorrow is a new day.

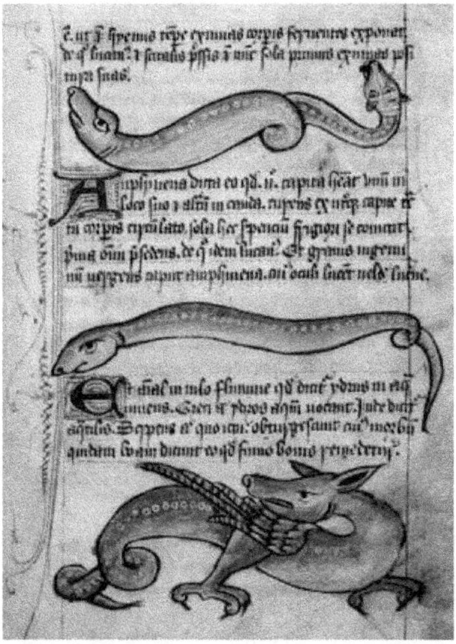

4

The Monks

Respice, adspice, prospice
Think on the past, present and future

On a night like this, Pacificus thinks he would never again curse the Mediterranean sun. But surely spring, though late this year, cannot be far away. Gus sneezes and trots even closer at heel, nearly tripping him up.

His feet are already numb as he hobbles with what speed he can muster along the causeway that runs down from Saint James' Hospital across the marsh to Cow Holme, the small triangular isle at the confluence of the Ant and the Bure rivers. He is late for Vespers, again. He hears the chants rising through the abbey tower, its lead-tiled tower glinting like fish scales in the moonlight. The grand main gate is not long locked but it will nevertheless take an age for Brother Porter to open the postern door, and Pacificus well knows he'll be made to feel suitably guilty for the inconvenience. His loud knocking creates some distant shufflings on the third attempt. On the way down from his upper chamber, Brother Porter's head appears above the wall to Pacificus' left, a wall crenelated after the Bury riots, in the year that Edward III came to the throne. But stone here is scarce and the flint walls before that time were low. So when peasants rioted in Saint Benet's abbey fifty years after the Bury incident, the abbey petitioned the king to allow these meager fortifications. Poor men are dangerous when you take what little they have. Take a man's last groat and he may well be free. He may be free to do things he never imagined, maybe even glance up to see the boot that is pressing him into the mud. What the axe forgets, the tree remembers.

In Bury it wasn't the poor but the burgers who rose up against the excessive power of St Edmund's abbey. But out here on the marshes? St Benet's did well to keep the fires lit and the commissioners at bay. The peasantry burnt deeds and the like outside the gatehouse, and little more – it was not quite time for the meek to inherit the earth. In the end the peasants were all made to buy back their lands, their protest being as ineffectual as these abbey walls they assaulted. Hugh rests a hand on the mullions. He lets his finger trace a cross and his mind wonder at all the things these stones had seen.

"Who's there? Oh its you again, brother, bringing an honest man from his fireside on such a hard night! Oh, I pray the Virgin to send us spring soon, I do. It's a good thing I'm busy, else I'd freeze myself." Brother Porter's head disappears beneath the crenulations but his voice is still heard listing his chores, as he comes to the gate. He's the sort of man who is never so busy that he won't delay you ten minutes telling you how much he has to do. It is not so much that he talks so much but more that he won't let you stop listening. The iron hinges grind and his sow-like features peer out of the gloom. "Now, they says I's gotta ask, brother, if you've seen Brother Bede, only he's been missing all day, I's not seen him pass the gate but then why should I with all the extra work they gives me? And then today a fire in the infirmary store – rushed off me feet, I am that."

"Bede?" Pacificus is not really thinking, more willing the man to open the blessed gate and get out of his way.

"Yes, Bede; you know, one of them six what come down from Binham, the young friendly one, nicest of the lot too, I'd say. You tried talking to any of "em? No, don't suppose you have. Well, I'll tell thee; they're keeping "emselves to 'emselves, won't look you in the eye." The door squeals on its hinges and the dog slides through, going to find some food and warmth.

Unwillingly Pacificus forces himself to think and sound like a Christian, "Oh yes, of course, Brother Bede – voice like an angel."

Binham Priory is, or at least was a smaller sister house to Saint Benets, some thirty miles to the north-east. It was sacrificed at the first Act of Suppression, Prior Wulfric and five brothers coming to St Benet's with their white faces and sunken eyes. "The people cheered when the Augmentations men had the bell tower dropped," Bede told them with tears. "To think they hated us so much even after all we had done. Beams, statues, bells, slates; all sold before our eyes and carted away. The work of centuries, gone in a week."

It's not good to think on. Pacificus thumbs the greying bristles on his chin. "Maybe he's run home to his mother." But on reconsidering the thought – no, not him, that stripling had a true vocation and a tender heart, Jesu, I envy him that much. Perhaps he is lost on the marsh, or fallen ill somewhere in the precinct? This cold damp is miasmic, puts many an ague in the air. Concern for what may have befallen the young monk bothers Pacificus's conscience, but this will have to wait. He dare delay no longer and so thanks the porter and heads past the fish ponds to the inner precinct gate, beyond which the abbey buildings loomed large and grey against the dying eastern sky.

He enters the choir by way of the Lady chapel to avoid detection, but soon notices Hamberly's son glaring at him from under his cowl. The lad's lips curl at the edge with a sort of perverse satisfaction; he will tell the prior for sure. Little wretch – ruddy faced, impudent, he has all the makings of his father about him. Roger, now Mark, was grudgingly given as an novice to Saint Benet's by Hamberly, no doubt as an insurance policy for his many less venial sins – sins where a quick confession and a groat in the offering will in no wise suffice. He has been given the name Mark after the Evangelist.

He certainly has no vocation for poverty, obedience and chastity, that remains plain. He hunts most days after Chapter with the prior; the two of them thick as thieves.

Pacificus's thoughts are far from his prayers for the remainder of Vespers that evening, partly they are on Mistress Fenton (for which he blames the devil) and partly he has a bad conscience over the children. She did insist they be left in the care of the eel-man, but Pacificus now begins to feel he may have acquiesced to her choice too quickly. As his voice falls in rhythm with the plainchant, his thoughts wander. Might not the children have been better brought to the abbey, where at least they would be under the wing of the church and so maybe less vulnerable to the penalty of law should they be discovered? Would they have been accepted by father abbot? Perhaps not. And by then, of course, it would have been too late; they would be discovered.

He recalled with a shudder the ten-year-old boy who had recently been consigned to the flames for possessing the merest fragment of the New Testament in English. No, he thinks at last, no, let them stay where they are for now and have such childhood as they may. Off my watch at least.

He notices the white scapular of an Augustinian at the end of the row of black Benedictine habits. It's that giant prior again from Hickling Priory, another local house under threat of suppression, and perhaps another lot of mouths to feed. And what a goliath mouth too. He's head and shoulders above any other on the row. They are not generally esteemed or trusted, those Augustinians - least not here and now in such tense times. Pacificus glances the other way and observes the émigré-Benedictines from Binham. They have spread along their row so that for a moment he does not see Bede's empty place.

True to form, Brother Mark approaches him after Vespers – Prior

Thomas will see him at the Abbot's lodgings, he says, and sidles off without waiting for a response. Pacificus barely acknowledges him, but moves off in the opposite direction. One day he will lose his temper with that novice and teach him a lesson, Heaven help him, he will.

Pacificus takes the long way round through the nave, sacristy, chapter house and dormitory. He kicks the jumble of boxes and crates cluttering the corridor near the dorter, he will complain about these when Abbot Rugge comes; and why can not at least one light be lit in the dorter, it's a miracle no one has broken their neck getting up for Matins. He walks slowly and reluctantly, wavering at each door – it is not the fear of punishment, more that he might let himself go again. Heading out of a side door he pulls his cowl close to descend the small slope to the abbot's hall and lodging. He's wondering how Abbot William fares, down there in gaol at Norwich castle. No doubt he has made himself comfortable – he's a survivor is William Rugge and he's no fool either, no matter what men say about his luxuries. The prior's hounds yelp and whine from a yard just over the wall, and beyond that, the wind charges through the reeds like the phalanxes of Alexander, drives all before it. The reeds bow and the alders shake. There is a storm coming.

Brother Mark answers the door, "Ah, brother, you came after all. Prior Thomas will see you when he is ready."

Pacificus says nothing, and presently he is called for. "Pacificus, good, come in." The prior, Thomas Stockhole, is standing to the left of the fireplace, fingering lightly the mannequin upon which hangs the Abbot's pontificalia, the sandals, the dalmatic with its voluminous sleeves. The velvet gloves, mitre and signet ring are lying in ceremonious state on top of a linenfold oak chest nearby. "Keep 'em out and well aired Tom," the Abbot had said, "I'll be back before the swallows." The prior, a man *lang and lythe* as the serving girls in the village say, is not much older than Pacificus. Son of Yorkshire gentry, he is determined to replicate the gentleman's life denied him by an unfortunate position as fourth son. Set on squat neck square shoulders, his face glows ruddy from outdoor exercise. His eyes are a penetrating blue, his hair sandy, and his tonsure small, in fact the barest concession to the rule –

perhaps more the thinning of age than the result of the razor. At the last visitation they had complaints against him, about his fine linen shirts and eschewing his sandals in favour of those fancy boots, also that he often missed Matins too, or if he did attend, it was only to go hunting after in the dawn hours before Lauds. He's wearing the boots tonight, tanned and scuffed under the habit. They let him keep them when he pleaded an undefined infirmity in his shins. And even though he had imprisoned others like Brother William Bynham for similar but less flagrant violations, Bishop Nykke of Norwich seemed to have overlooked the rest of the charges.

Abbot Rugge doubtless stood up for him, forgiving his offences. The prior is good humored on the whole and keeps a tight reign on the money, for he is chamberlain and sacristan too – something else which produces grumbling in the ranks. But, as the abbot pointed out, the accounts and inventories are always in order when presented at the Michaelmas Synod. The abbot does not, however, mention the continuing six-hundred-pound debt with such relish.

Theologically Prior Thomas is happy enough to let other men bicker about indulgences, transubstantiation and papal supremacy. He is not of *the lean and hungry sort* that Caesar feared, nor did he wish to be, and perhaps that is why the abbot preferred him as prior – a safe pair of hands for the storms ahead – and storms there will be.

"Of course we all miss Father Abbot," the prior says absently, caressing the embroidery on the purple gloves. Perhaps he's not so sure that he would like the responsibilities of the abbacy himself. Certainly the private lodgings next to the river, his own servants, a house in Norwich and London; all sounded grand enough. But then there were the extra duties, offices, crown grants, endless meetings in the house of Lords, squabbles to settle, tenants to listen to, barons and dukes to appease. How much time would he have then for the field? Not much. Even so – did you ever see anything so fine as these red Turkey satins?

Pacificus interrupts the prior's ruminations: "No word, then, from Norwich?"

Prior Thomas shakes his head and returns to the table where a new cookery book lies open next to a brace of partridge, soon to be dispatched to the kitchens with new instructions, new demands for herbs they don't have. He shuts the book. "I don't see why he doesn't just give Henry his way on it, let him be Supreme Head if he wishes, and let us alone to our business."

"Some say we'll not be left alone – not now, nor then, none of us." Pacificus sidles to the fire. The only places with heat in the Abbey precincts are the kitchen and calefactory – so this feels good, but he knows this giving in to the flesh will only make it harder to face the drafty dorter later.

"Some say? I take it you mean Prior Wuflric? That lot from Binham are touched, something not right with them – and that reminds me, their Brother Bede is missing, you've been about I dare say. Seen him?"

"No – er – no. I came back late...by Saint James'..." he lingers fatally and the prior, that keen huntsman, senses a chase.

"Saint James'? What were you doing there when you should have been at Vespers?" He's been told to keep a tight rein on Pacificus. The abbot never said why.

"Oh, nothing – just visiting the afflicted." Then, hoping to deflect further questions: "Anyway, the Brother Bede, where was he supposed to be?"

"Counting our swans – in and without the precinct, so Wulfric tells me – simple enough job," the prior glances towards the window, "though God alone knows, its been no weather for bearing signets this year."

"There's a freezing mist tonight, the upping cut we use on the swans is slight. It's hard to spot from far off."

"Yes, I know – I know. If he did stray into the marshes, it'll be the worse for him. Anyway that was all, brother, just remember to ask around when you go across the river tomorrow. And don't be late again; it is such a bad example and brings some of the obedentiaries out in rashes – and frankly I could do without any more strife right now." He returns to his chair, and slumps into it as he waves Pacificus out. But before he reaches the door Prior Thomas calls after him, "Oh, and that dog of yours – "

"I have no dog."

"Oh, very well, the dog that follows you about. Don't be obtuse, man. He took a bone from one of my best hounds and then lamed him in a fight. If I see him I'll set the pack on him. Be kind and tie him in a sack and toss him in the Bure tomorrow before I see him." Pacificus leaves without answering either the prior's comment or Brother Mark's smug grimace as he moves from behind the door where he'd been listening.

The next day, after a fitful night with little sleep, Pacificus is talking to Brother Justin the almoner, near the main gate, looking down the pathway to the almonry: "You look overburdened, brother, on this Lady Day."

"I could say the same for you, brother."

Pacificus pauses to watch the queuing of the poor at the almoner's store in the outer precinct; frostbitten fingers and hunched shoulders waiting patiently for grants of clothing, food and the like. The almoner sighs deeply, and with almost a breaking heart says, "it has been a cruel year, many of them are freedmen, but that doesn't fill the belly when the harvest fails, and how are we to help them keep body and soul together when this east wind persists like a scourging whip across the fens? What do I have to give them, pray? Precious little."

His ruminations are interrupted by the clatter of Prior Thomas sallying forth on horseback with his retinue. They burst forth from the stables near the abbot's lodging and thunder across the precinct green toward the crowd. Brother Mark is at his side, whip in hand. The hounds are yelping and jumping like mad things. The mass of beggars scatter quickly to make a path, though some make no disguise of their disdain. Pacificus smiles to see Gus keeping out of sight behind the stack yard – clever dog.

"And see all this," Justin laments, pointing at the disappearing hounds.

Pacificus places his hand on the bony shoulder of his friend. "Come brother, *errare humanum est*; to err is human. This here is a place for ordinary men, not saints." But Pacificus can see from the other man's face and fists that he is not appeased.

"True. Judge not and so forth..." Justin shakes a weary head. "And yet we must feed the prior's dogs while the poor starve. And did not Bishop Nykke, God rest his soul, say at our visitation four years back, that there were too many dogs? Is it right, I ask you?"

Pacificus is caught for a moment. Yes, he agrees; but he has seen what discontent can cause in the precinct, and the camp as well. He dodges the matter. "Spring will not tarry forever. Take heart, brother; the Lord is a father to the widow and orphan."

"And they multiply daily, as do we! These six from Binham priory, and probably the Augustinians now, too!" Justin's bushy eyebrows rise high with anger; but they fall again, defeated, the creases with their rivulets of tears collapsing into their accustomed places. "I'm sorry, Brother Pacificus, to put it upon you; only I'm so vexed. I would do any other job, this year, than this."

"I think you are where Christ would have you be. We shall pray for more alms, and when Father Abbot returns I will speak up at Chapter on the matter, too."

"You're a good man, Pacificus." Justin takes him by the arm.

"I only wish I were."

They walk across the stable yard in the direction of the almonry. "But tell me, Brother Justin – you mentioned the Augustinians, and I noticed one among us last night?"

"Ah!" Justin's face darkens again. "Thus comes our tender prior this morning to see his horse, and tells me to be sparing with the food as we may have to feed Hickling Priory too before Lent – and if they're all as big as that prior of theirs, the one who stopped last night, we may as well turn the poor away now."

"But why are they here?"

"That he did not say, though I do know six of them at least made confessions of laxity when they were visited by Doctors Layton and

Leigh from Augmentations." Justin gives a knowing nod. "Perhaps they will be suppressed too, like Binham. These are strange times, brother."

He rests his hand on the doorframe of his storehouse, now mainly just empty crates and shelves. Another pained sigh and he turns back to the poor gathered by the hatch like so many tattered reeds blown by the hard wind. "Do you think the king's coffers will be satisfied with just the small houses? Wulfric says they are but the first course, that the main course will be – "

"Justin – brother!" Pacificus places an unconvincing hand on the almoner's shoulder. "*Timendi causa est nescire*, don't be guided by Prior Wulfric's fears. Our Abbot will not let Saint Benets fall, and there is no prince in Europe that could cross him and come off better! Why he's Wolsey, More, yes and even Cromwell, under one habit – Saint Benets could not fall under such as he." His humour works and Justin smiles, but as he walks away Pacificus is fighting the forbodings in his own gut – things too dark to contemplate.

All that day he struggles to focus with his brushes at Saint Helen's – but, oh, the times, *the times!* Would any man know when he is living in the Last Days? Suppose the old world is changing forever? Was it not always? Could twelve hundred years of tradition be swept away for good? Perhaps, but it doesn't do to think on it overmuch. Old Brother Anselm in the infirmary is ill-advised to say the usurper Antichrist reigns on the Plantagenet throne, but then he is not long for this earth anyway. Let us look to the living!

On his way home that afternoon, Pacificus leaves the coracle as usual at Saint James' staithe and is halfway across the causeway when he hears the sound of hooves from behind. It is Prior Thomas at the head of a cavalcade, horses snorting great billows of steam, their hooves shaking the earth. Gus trots tactfully into the reeds to sniff out some fowl. The Prior's face is pained and resolute, passing without even a nod. It is only after they pass that Pacificus sees the body slung over the back of the last horse. He hurries through the gate and catches them all dismounting in silence in the stable yard. Pacificus is long used to this but the corpse is nevertheless a mess. "So that's the poor lad."

"Dogs got to him." The prior tries to sound calm but Pacificus can see he is unmanned by it, and no wonder, they must have been on the lad several minutes before they were beaten back. "Don't look at me like that, they're as hungry as the wretches at our gate, and don't know any better. Fetch someone to...to...to lay him out in the infirmary – and call for the reeve. Back you lot, stop your gaping. Back, I say."

Pacificus examines the tide mark of mud on the deceased's shoeless feet, knees and face. "Where was he found?"

The prior is on him in a moment. "Well you may ask, brother! We found him not twenty yards from your precious staithe at Saint James, face down in the river among the reeds."

"Or perhaps you knew that already?" says Brother Mark, standing behind the prior with hands on hips.

"It is a wonder, boy," Pacificus replied, the whites of his knuckles visible, "that you speak thus to me if you think me capable of such a sin."

He starts to sidestep the prior to get to the impudent youth, but Prior Thomas fends him off. "That's enough, brother. We need not suspect foul play at this stage. You will answer to the sheriff and no doubt we shall all answer to Doctors Leighton and Leigh the more, for they will make as much of this as they possibly can. Now, off with you both!"

Later that evening, and then again in the refectory after Compline, Pacificus notices the looks and whispers, even from monks he counts as friends. There are no stalls or seating in the choir so it is only too apparent when the brethren wish to avoid a man. Pacificus' usual corner near the chancel is occupied only by himself this evening. The vapour from his plain-chant billows forward into the frosty void where once cowled figures stood. Still, can he blame them? In all likelihood there will be a murderer or two among them, these are times that find out men.

No end of discussion erupts after Chapter next morning, mostly morbid and unworthy. The sheriff will attend them and examine the corpse by eventime and all must be ready to answer what they are asked. Pacificus says nothing, enduring the suspicious half-glances, every attempt to look at ease further raising his temperature and discomfort. He feels a bead of sweat run down his forehead onto his nose, but he doesn't wipe it away. They want to convince themselves it is an accidental death but no one is sure. It certainly isn't, he thinks. He will inspect the reeds, look for the dead man's shoes even, on his way to Ranworth where he is eager to start his Saint Agnes on the rood.

Halfway across the causeway, the next day, he is hailed by a dolorous voice: "*Pax Vobiscum*, brother!"

It's Prior Wulfric, the gaunt ex-prior of Binham. "I see the Augustinian is on his way, they say he is hairy all over like Satan." He points a willowy finger back down stream at the departing Augustinian prior, whose boat is pulling out into midstream from the granary staithe. Even from a distance of fifty yards Pacificus can marvel at the sheer thickness of the man's neck.

"*Pax Vobiscum*, brother." Pacificus turns back to observe the prior, who but lately joined them at Saint Benet's, and now has so grievous a loss to bear in the death of his novice. Wulfric, lean and taut as a bow of yew, was named after the man who re-founded Saint Benet's monastery after the Danish slaughters. A great name to live up to. He has been prior for thirty years before this, all at Binham, a small Benedictine priory two days' journey to the north. Pacificus judges him to be about sixty years old. In the hollow eyes, sunk with despair and red with tears of honest grief, Pacificus sees some latent fire that he recognises but cannot quite identify. The man's hand trembles slightly, his fingers clenching and unclenching incessantly about the cuffs of his habit, or even just thumb on finger.

Pacificus takes all this in while trying to console with clumsy humour: "Rumour is, the Augustinian will be back before Whitsun with the rest of his house, another six of them, by which time Brother

Cellarer and Brother Almoner will have pulled out what little hair they have left." This finds no response. He tries again. "It...well...it is a long time until grain harvest. Oh, I'm sorry, brother, I did not mean – "

"No, no, it is true. We are a burden. I know it," laments Prior Wulfric, "but the Danes are back and what can we do, any of us? And look at that, will you?" He points to the place where winter floods have exposed the shingle foundations under the outer precinct wall. "I don't know what's worse, that we are ruled by heathen barbarians, or that Rome builds her houses on this shifting shale bank."

Pacificus smiles, for they have interminable settlement and cracked walls in almost all the abbey buildings nearest the river. Where's the bedrock in anything?

"And now all this dreadful business with Bede, the poor boy!" After a few more steps Wulfric half-exhales, as one too overwrought even to breathe. "I thought to visit the site where he fell, I did not want to go alone and I knew you would be passing – " He breaks off to apologise and bite his lip. "You – you don't mind, do you?"

"No, no, not at all," Pacificus says, glad that someone at least does not suspect him of foul crimes. "I will be what help I can."

They soon come to the site, where the dogs and horses have made a terrible mess; all is mud and furrow, the reeds offer no clues for they were all but quagmire now. The two men stand there, for some moments silenced entirely. Somehow neither one of them has foreseen the ugliness, the sickening tale too plainly told by this trodden ground churned by the milling feet of beasts and men. It is not easy to stand there and remember the dead with any equilibrium.

Wulfric, wild-eyed and struggling with emotion recites what snatches he can remember of the *Ars Moriendi* – concluding somberly: "He died a true son of the Holy Church, of that I am sure. He was a devout youth." And then wandering into Latin: "... a heart truly confessed, with contrition and repentance for all his sins, by the most holy sacrament through Christ our Lord."

Pacificus leaves a suitable pause for reflection after the Amen, then tries to probe with delicacy concerning any possible sins aforementioned, but Wulfric turns on him with glaring eye, like a different man: "He was the best of us, d'you hear me? The best of us! And that is an end of the matter, brother!" He stands there breathing hard, blinking at the broken reeds. "Forgive me. My humours are quite outbalanced by this. We are all on edge. But now I've seen the place, if you will excuse me I must visit two of our number who took the journey badly from Binham."

"Oh, I'm sorry to hear of that."

"I thank you – but your infirmarian has them well seen to." His quick glance back towards the abbey betrays something like apprehension. "Sigismund and Benedict are strong as oak, where it counts," he remarks. "Some rest is all they need."

After their odd conversation, Pacificus comes back to something again and again throughout the day: *so the Danes have returned.*

When evening comes, back in the abbey he answers the sheriff as best he can, afraid his account must sound vague to the man, perhaps even evasive. He does not want to implicate the children, and he has no alibi for the morning journey – though it seems that everyone else does, even the new Binham monks who will be the most likely suspects.

They sit in the abbot's lodging, Pacificus staring sometimes directly at the sheriff, sometimes past him at the Flemish tapestry. The sheriff still has the ruddiness of youth about his cheeks; self-consciously he pushes the fur on his sleeves so they do not appear too long. The oil of youth, Pacificus scoffs inside his head – sending a boy to a man's task! The sheriff does not believe the novice died naturally. Nor does Pacificus, but he keeps quiet for fear of arousing suspicion. If murder is confirmed, the sheriff will be under pressure to find a culprit, and speedily too. For one thing, these young men in office are always wanting to prove the efficiency of their generation, the new learning, and so on. But beyond that, the powerful will want a quick conviction, for if it goes unresolved, who knows where it may end – clerics one day, landlords the next.

The sheriff keeps saying with heavy implication that he 'had heard it said Bede was a fair youth' – just to get a reaction, impudent fellow. Rugge dealt short and sharp with pederasts, even if he let other things go. The sheriff pushes, but he learns nothing from Pacificus. He says nothing about the tide lines of mud that he had seen on Bede's legs and face, but he does mention the missing shoes. "The shoes, have you found the shoes yet?"

The sheriff hides his shock. He tugs at the sparse moustache he is cultivating, then to cover the oversight, thinks to belittle the monk, "You think someone took them, perhaps murdered him for them?" He turns grinning to the reeve who plays his part in supporting his superior with mocking laughter.

"Perhaps," the reeve adds derisively, "he went for a swim?"

Pacificus adopts his stoniest stare until they recover from their jest. No one murders for shoes, not even in these times, yet a corpse found without them is a strange occurrence. They content themselves with telling Pacificus not to travel anywhere in the next few days, a thing unlikely in any event, and then he is free to go. As he leaves, he is thinking about the shoes.

5

The Millers

Proprium humani ingenii est odisse quem laeseris
It is human nature to hate a person whom you have injured

Spring comes finally to the marshes and is all the more valued for the long absence. Browns give way to lime greens and the hammering of wind and rain, to the chatter of new life among the reeds. Spring, yes, but not Easter, at least not for the children on Saint Margaret's marsh. Only Beth and Richard notice but, they say nothing, for the feast and fasts of the Church seem irrelevant to them now. The stirring of new life in the fens all around speaks of joy and calls to them to play; but beyond the innocence and beauty of this place they think often of the ominous grinding of the law at work, the mechanisms of an indifferent world; of lock and key; manacle and chain; judge and jury; faggot and flame. They await news of the assize, but still there is no word from Norwich.

Despite the sombre recollection of these shadows, within these few short weeks the Fenton children have settled well to their new life. Better perhaps than old Pieter and Sarah, now discovering just how set in their ways they are – they remember wistfully the quiet of the hearth and space at the table. But with the warmer weather coming little by little, they are all, even blind Sarah, more outside the confines of the cottage and daily life feels less cramped.

While they are out setting eel-traps, Pieter and Richard talk of extending the cottage. And though the marshes are their playground even in wintertime, there is hardly space to sleep or sit of an evening, so crowded is the cottage. They have considered the out-houses, but with more mouths to feed they need another cow – there is no space to spare. Even one more room added to the cottage, two if it might be, would make all the difference. So Richard helps Pieter measure out the space in the yard, and they talk of the materials they will need for the building; hazel and thatch to cut, clay and manure to gather and store. It seems like too big a job for one old man and a boy barely with a whisker to his chin, but they dare not risk involving outside help. When he returns from the field with his two sibling bird scarers, Piers says at once, eagerly, that he will help. He bares his arm proudly to show them the muscle coming on. Sarah smiles affectionately as he guides her hand to his biceps and pumps them up as best he can. 'Can lift as much as Richard, nearly anyway.' Beth merely rolls her eyes and turns away to lay up the table for dinner.

As the migrant birds return to broad, dyke and river, and fluffy chicks appear nestled on the backs of the grebes afloat, so too does God's warmth return to the world. Marsh marigolds, wood anemones, Lords-and-ladies bloom, and the hedgerow trees are laden with blossom. But new life everywhere else does little to fill the children's senses with hope. Whites, lime greens, yellows and pinks seem merely to mock what dwindling hope any of them have. Baby James is taking his first unsteady steps, and reaching for the bowls on the table now: "Ma-ma," he says: "Ma-ma."

"Whisht, button, whisht," she says, at first pushing him away, but then turning tearfully to kiss his head. "Yes. Ma, ma, ma. Yes, button."

Twenty yards away, the small wooden punt is moored in their dyke and a little further on, just out of site beyond the bend, the River Ant moves lazily along. The cottage, built in a small clearing, is mostly hemmed in with willow and reeds. The paddock, vegetable garden and field enclosures lie behind the house and outbuildings, with one field – the one for oats – being half a mile off on some raised ground. Up and down the riverbanks through the reeds, Pieter has constructed walkways to easier stretches of the river or to join up paths and tracks. Some evenings, but only as a treat, Richard and Piers are allowed to take a boat and inspect the nearer eel traps on their own. To their credit, the boys have grasped the connection between their own survival and a bagged eel. Hand over hand, never releasing their grip, they bring them into the security of the holding nets, and ready for transport to the Abbey or the town. With every day that passes, the children become more at home in their new surroundings, and their initial reserve relaxes into trust of the good people who have taken them in with such kindness.

Perhaps caught up in the happy atmosphere of dinner outside by the river in the last sunshine of the day, or perhaps just because he thinks the children are ready, Pieter reaches into his inner breast pocket for a folded and re-folded page with print on both sides, the page of a book. They watch, intrigued as he opens the precious page, such reverence on his face. It is a fragment of the New Testament – the only one he has, a portion of John's Gospel. And now he does what neither of their parents ever dared do: slowly, stumbling here and there, but with the meaning of the words clear enough, he reads to them in their own mother tongue the words of the Holy Gospel: "They will put you out of the synagogue; in fact, a time is coming when anyone who kills you will think he is offering a service to God, they will do such things because they know not the Father or me."

Beth has seen similar parchments among other papers in her mother's oak trunk. Though they kept them hidden to protect the children and themselves, Beth knew more than she cared to say, even then. She has read some too, as much as she could, and the words are still etched on her mind – *deny yourself, take up your cross.* This parchment Messiah, this *man of sorrows*, promising that *in this world ye shall suffer loss*, had proved to be true to his word in the most costly of ways. Look at them now. Even back then, her mother tried to engage her, but Beth would always stave her off, like two wherries caught on a tight bend in uncertain winds. What, be like that poor child burned in Norwich for having just a fragment of the Bible in English, who screamed even as the blood burst on the crowd from his black, blistered limbs? Or those six parents burnt in Coventry for teaching their children the ten commandments and the Lord's prayer in English? No, this was not for her, this she knew. What God would want it, nay, demand it?

Pieter has read on by the time she returns from her thoughts, and come to the end. He folds the page carefully away again. He clears his throat, his face sober. The three older children, silent, give him their full attention. Pieter tells them: "They have set the date for your papa's trial. It will be before George's day."

"Papa come home?" Samuel looks up from his brother. "Papa?"

Beth strokes the back of his head, "Papa is going to stay with Jesus." Beth and Pieter exchange glances. Richard and Piers stare down towards their soup.

"There is," Pieter continues shakily, "no news of your mother, but I thought I maybe take some smoked eel to the castle market next week, perhaps get some news, ja?" Both boys look up at once, saying instantly that they will come too, but the old man shakes his head. "No, no. Too dangerous for this. Your mother would like this, eh? And, of course, Sarah needs help here. Maybe you will stay here for me, and take care of her, eh?"

Next week comes slowly for the children, but soon after Pieter leaves, Beth reveals her plan to Richard. "Look, Pieter is gone all day and we are all to be outside at our work."

"So?" Richard says, stroking Prudence their cow, behind whose shed they hold this secret meeting.

"So, if Pieter will not return until very late, why not go back home and collect all those things we left behind?" Her eyes burn with the same dangerous blue that her mother had turned on Hamberly.

"Well, I don't know, Beth." Richard squints at her anxiously. "It's a long way, and you heard that monk; we're not to go south of the Bure. If we were recognized..."

"We could be back for dinner if we leave now. We... we... we could bring presents for Pieter and Sarah. She needs some new coifs and aprons, and we have lots. And just think, sheets of our own when the extension is done, and books!"

Nothing on that list tempts Richard out of his caution until those last thoughts. For there are certain items at the house, items that belonged to his father, that he wishes very much to have. Beth sees the squint go and knows she has him, but before she can say anything there is a shuffling from the hay-store beyond Prudence's stall and Piers emerges well decorated in the dried grass.

"I shall come too," he says, with the characteristic impishness that makes Beth want to box his ears.

"Why you noisome little – !" She tries to cuff him, but he ducks. "How long have you been there? What did you hear?"

"Everything," he says. It is a lie. "Anyway, enough."

"Well, you're not coming, you or your big ears – and you'd better not tell."

He appeals to Richard, who intercedes on his behalf. His brother and sister exact from Piers solemn promises that he will not antagonize his sister; and so with resignation, bordering on the most heroic martyrdom, Beth gives in.

They leave a note for Pieter on his slate and tell Sarah. They say that they will not be back until late, and not to "fret for them till supper time." The day is promising to be fine and Sarah doesn't seem to mind.

They dress with floppy felt hats hats to hide their faces and row down the Ant as the morning mists lift from the marsh. A sedge warbler serenades the start of their great odyssey and Richard, now skilled and powerful with the oars, takes them swiftly past the coots, geese and river craft in the direction of the abbey, which they pass when they have joined the River Thurne. After an hour they find the mouth of the Bure, even as the last of the mist lifts to reveal an pale blue sky.

It is a long and indirect route compared with the footpath, but they must have the boat for bringing back all they hoped. Richard does the bulk of the rowing, Piers and Beth doing shorter turns. He rests every twenty minutes to tend the baited horse-hair lines they are trailing from the boat. They catch two bream and one perch before they lose the line to a pike near Thurne mouth. Not until mid-morning do they reach Saint Benets' wharf. The crenelated wall runs the length of the frontage, and every now and then they pass a thatched building, a staithe, a barn, a moored wherry. The abbot's lodging has its own staithe, as does the abbey brewery by the storehouse. There is a small harbour also, dug beyond the westerly limit of the water frontage, near the main gate.

They see Brother Pacificus on the wharf as they pass, and he is jolted out of his heated conversation with a trader (who sold ochre pigment at an exorbitant price), to stare after them amazed that they would show themselves so openly on the river near their home. Piers, quite forgetting to pull his hat brim down, beams at Pacificus from the little boat as they pull by. Another half-hour and they are safely pulled up in a dyke just off South Walsham broad, it giving them better access to the house than Ranworth broad, and better cover too.

It feels strange to be back in familiar waters, here in the fields and woods they imagined would be theirs forever. Richard can see his old school next to Saint Mary's church beyond the broad. He wonders what his friends will be doing and the thought of them seems odd, like another life. Was it really only a few weeks ago? Being here, now, so close to home, their new life starts to feel like ill-fitting woolens, that they might even now cast off. They eat the bread and dried fish which they have brought, leaving the fresh ones for supper while discussing the best approach to the house. They decide not to take the track but rather the fields. There is a copse near the farm where they wait before advancing further. It is a cloudless day and so far they have seen no one.

The farm sits along the easterly lane from Ranworth village and there are no other properties within earshot of it, Hamberly's manor being a mile hence on Ranworth broad itself. Hamberly's father got the whole estate cheap, and more besides, after the battle of Bosworth field, though himself little more than a yeoman farmer. Some said he and his sons roamed the lanes near Norwich to catch vagrants and thus claim them as their own property according to the law, and so it was by man-stealing he had acquired his wealth.

Others said old Hamberly was a usurer who sold his soul to the devil to get the estate, even though by the standards of the day it was a small one – just the manor, two farms and the tannery near Panxworth. But however he came by it the title was his, and before he had half run it into the ground, the Fentons came up from the south and turned the whole business around as his estates manager.

In the fullness of time old Hamberly went to his rest. His son, "another pharaoh who knew not Joseph', as the Old Testament story puts it, inherited a situation of which he had only hazy knowledge. When rumour reached him of his estate manager's religious bent, a damnable Lollard under his own patronage, his first thought was to use it to his advantage; with the mistress if he could, but failing that, to escape his debt to them – for he owed Fenton substantial unpaid wages from as far back as harvest the previous Michaelmas. Having no luck with Fenton's wife, Hamberly struck a deal over a flagon of ale, with John Miller's father, for both the farm and the sultry maid Mary his serf, whom he gave to Miller for a wife. And so it was in this manner, and with little thought beyond his belt and his purse, that he betrayed the Fentons.

The children tread breathlessly along the line of the old hedge and then the dyke where they have played so many times that almost every inch is know to them. It brings them right near the house, though they pay for the route they have chosen with feet thoroughly wet and cold. They are not heard on the approach, for John Miller is arguing in the farmyard with his wife – their old maid – whom conjugal bliss had in no way beautified. It had ever been the domestic trial of Beth's mother when Hamberly forced Mary onto them. Beth recognizes her shrill voice snapping and sniping at Miller across the yard.

The banging of doors and clatter of chairs on the flags announce that the Millers are taking their argument into the kitchen. The children, keeping low, steal under the window to listen, where they can scarce keep from laughing at Piers's fine impression of Mary's hatchet face and finger wagging. They must wait this out, listening to the sultry squabbling and foul oaths of these usurpers who so entirely deserve each other.

He, so his wife's accusations run, is a poorer farmer than ever he was a miller, and no fit manager either. She, who connived in intimate ways with Hamberly to become mistress of the farm, was by her husband's account a lousy cook and as bitter-tongued as aloes, and foul of breath as a sewer.

Soon the shouts turn to shrieks of vengeful hatred. He says he would be minded to beat her to teach her a lesson but dare not, lest he render her visage even more hideous than it already be. But after the answers she gives him back, some scorning his manhood, Miller changes his mind. The children hear the thud of fist on bone, a clatter of furniture and then no more sound from Mary at all. "That shut you up, didn't it. All your prattling and nagging. Well, sleep it off and let a man have some peace." A moment later, the children hear a door slam and Miller's boots crossing the yard to the brewery shed to crown yet one more argument with their Father's winter ale.

Rising to peep through the kitchen window, Richard and Beth exchange a glance of white-faced shock. To hear such things, see such things, in a place they only associate with the tranquility of their mother's voice; to see Mary unconscious in that grotesque position upon the hearth where their mother's new iron cauldron stands. Beth has her hand to her mouth and Richard is breathing hard, pupils dilated and hands visibly trembling. Piers is alone in his mirth, and hearing Miller leave, he chortles, "Are they not a pretty pair?" And then, in puzzlement: "Why such a face, sister?"

"Shhh! Quiet, you," Beth chides. They form a plan below the window; Richard will go in and pass the things out, Piers will watch the yard in case the brute returns.

The first part is easy; with a leg-up from Piers, Richard is in like a ferret down a hole. But he finds their room is bare, most things have been sold; spare shirts, shoes, toys even. Richard stands aghast when he opens the oak chest in their room; everything gone but the linen sheets and an extra blanket. He wants to cry, to clothe himself in pity, but then he remembers where he is, who he now is. The back bedroom window opens and he flings out such as he can find. Beth gathers their booty, the blanket serving as a carry-all. Pointing to her head, she hisses, "Coifs, Richard, coifs!" Then, remembering he never did more than he was told, "and smocks, and my bodice, my blue skirt, spare sleeves – oh, and aprons for me – and Sarah too!"

But Richard cannot find all these, so in exasperation Beth is soon getting a leg-up through the window to see for herself. Mary lies still, her pale face blooded and bruised. She half-breathes half-snores on, as her stealthy visitors help themselves to the cupboards and larder shelves. Richard lets his sister go to work, for he now remembers just what he came for. First his father's cane fishing rods and net go out of the window, then the Misericordia – a long dagger – that was his grandfather's from the last war; then his other grandfather's sword, damaged handle and all; also his great-grandfather Fenton's longbow which had been put to good use on Saint Crispin's day, though little since, more a hallowed relic. Quickly they are dropped from the back window and thence to the ground. But without Beth being there to handle things, the long bow clatters against the pewter plates thrown out by his sister. For a moment he freezes and she glares at him, eyes wide as a noose. They stay motionless for a minute, then they hear Miller swearing from across the yard – rousing himself from his drunken sulk.

"Quick! We must go!" She grabs her mother's sewing box from the cupboard by the hearth.

They hear Piers in agitation at the back window, "Hurry, he's coming now!"

Richard runs to the front to glance from the window there, and sees Miller staggering unsteadily across the yard, eyes red from the drink, face dark as the broad's water. They have only moments, if that.

Richard reaches above the front door to retrieve his father's matchlock rifle, along with wad and the pouch containing the sixteen bore matchlock balls. It is still too heavy for him. His hands tremble and he almost drops it; the smell of the waxed wood leads to a split second remembrance of the only time he ever saw his parents argue. It was here, in the kitchen. The matchlock was an "extravagance', his mother had said.

"Hurry!" Beth grabs at him. "Richard, hurry!" They go for the window but are just too late, the door swings wide and Miller stands stupefied in the entrance. His head goes back and eyes slowly refocus at what he cannot believe or process.

"What? Villains! My matchlock!"

"Liar, 'tis our father's – you – you – " Richard's eyes well with rage.

Miller lunges forward, banging his head on the lintel as he enters the kitchen. He cries out and clutches it with his left hand, his right groping for them. Beth, seized by the assurance of last resort, takes an iron pan from the shelf and lunges at him while Richard stands frozen with fear. Miller fends the light blow easily and returns the favour, cuffing her broadly with a tight fist. There is a sickening hollow thud as Beth falls against the table and, without even a scream, crumples at Mary's side.

Miller, well tutored in brutality by a drunken father is on home ground here. In the village very few think it possible to knock him down – though some have tried.

At this moment Piers, who has heard all, is trying in vain to reach the window. So quick to get into scrapes usually, he now feels the tendency rise in him to escape, to run. What can I do, how must I get in? He thinks, but it is too high for me.

Meanwhile Miller glowers at Richard and then the matchlock. "Give it to me," he pants, raising his left hand, clenching his right. "I don't want it damaged when I give you your medicine, little boy." Miller's eyes suddenly widen and he screams, "GIVE IT TO ME NOW, CAPON!"

Richard shrivels inside, terrified, shoulders drooping, eyes filling with tears. But then he sees Beth on the flags, blood oozing from her mouth in a pool that cries out to him, cries to heaven, almost. Fixing both eyes on the approaching brute, he swings the matchlock butt at his head. But Miller again fends with his right hand and though the impact breaks two of his fingers, he feels no pain for a moment. "You worthless runt of a heretic whore." Miller yanks at the matchlock, closes with Richard, forces the wheellock hard against his face. The impact numbs Richard's skull and lips. The cartilage in his nose crunches, warm, iron-tasting liquid gushes into his mouth and down the back of his throat. An inch higher the lock would have been through his eye; blinded, perhaps dead. Miller likes the effect. He grins, all sparse yellow teeth and black gums, then bears down on Richard with a maniacal glee, ready to lay a second stroke on him, harder than the first. He swings the matchlock back and is just putting his shoulder into the blow when his eyes and mouth open impossibly wide, like in the stories when demons come out of witches. He then releases a high-pitched squeal, freezing for a moment in the agony. Richard then sees the reason. It is Piers with a pitchfork. When Miller had moved back to take a stronger blow, Piers had been there, fork in hand. The handle was wedged against the wall, the fork itself was embedded deep into Millar's buttocks. With his muscles in spasm, Miller relinquishes the matchlock to Richard and twists to grasp the fork.

"I'll kill you!" Miller roars: "As God's my witness, I'll kill you all!" He draws it out, hissing and drooling heavily, his face scarlet red, contorted and veined like ivy on an oak.

Piers begins to back out of the room and Miller goes after him. Richard, without even wiping the blood from his eyes, swings the matchlock a second time and crunches the heavy brass ends on the man's skull. Miller reels for a moment under the blow and then in staggering, trips on the iron pan, falling heavily on the hearth. On the way down his head makes contact with the edge of the mantel shelf, and he is rendered senseless next to his wife and Beth.

Richard stands over him and raises the matchlock, ready to cave in the man's skull with the butt of it. He lingers for a moment, his breaths deepening and quickening but eventually he drops the weapon to his side. He cannot do it.

Piers, rooted to the spot, stares with trembling limbs, first at Miller, then at Richard. He tries to smile between deep breaths but tears overwhelm him. He steps over the tangle of fallen bodies to his big brother for a comforting hug, but Richard will not have it. "No! We must see to Beth, Piers!" The pool of blood has now spread to the size of a large pancake. Richard stoops to feel her jaw, already blue and swollen.

Piers bends down, "Is she dead?"

"I don't think so. Fetch some water, the pitcher on the table."

They drag her away from the other fallen bodies, propping her up against the dresser to sponge the blood from her face, her hair and clothes. "Beth, come on Beth, come to now, won't you." The blow has made her bite her tongue, it is a deep cut but its not hanging off or anything beyond recovery. She comes to with a start, coughs out some more blood and then gazes with small pupils at the bodies by the hearth. She blinks and shakes her head slightly: "I'm all right...I'm all right..." But, as she struggles up, Piers supports her all the same. She tries to repel him but in the end he manages to save her from falling again.

Piers tells her rapidly all that had just happened, while she squints and nurses her jaw. She looks at her brother's broken nose and listens on. Eventually her face hardens with something of a dark resolution. Solemnly she walks out into the yard, the boys following and calling after her.

She trudges across to the woodshed, takes water buckets and fills them with sewerage from the cesspit. Her lips are tight, her breathing quick and shallow, she says not a word to either of them. She plods doggedly back to the kitchen, pouring the excrement over the new master and mistress of the farm. The boys look on in astonishment, for she appears not to do it with mirth but a quiet, simmering hatred.

Piers soon joins her, using buckets from the brewery to empty filth from the jakes into the brewing vats. By the time Beth is well into her third bucket, which she pours on the stored foods, Richard remembers that the piss-pots in the bedrooms were unemptied and so he takes delight in pouring both solids and liquids liberally over the pillows and bedding. After no less than five minutes – and without a word said between them – the children have saturated the entire house, its occupants and stores. They stand together at the end, breathing deeply the satisfying stench as if by this triumph they would be avenged on their enemies; as if by it they would have back their parents, their home, their lives.

"That's that, then," Richard says.

"Yes, that's that," Beth replies.

There are tears as they bundle the goods, and pains too from their injuries as the adrenaline subsides. This is goodbye to home, and as near as they will likely come to saying goodbye to their parents. It is a slower journey home and little is said beyond rehearsing the deed – they are in no doubt that they have just fought for their very lives, and it does feel good to win, though the coots seem unimpressed. They feed on the story, laugh at it, suck from the memories all the marrow of comfort they can.

For now revenge seems enough, later it will seem a hollow victory, cold comfort. None of them stops trembling until they are well out onto the Bure. Each acknowledges the others' contributions. Beth even kisses and hugs Piers. She also tries, despite her own pain, to arrange Richard's nose; though after several, excruciating attempts, he gets back to the oars. No, he won't let Piers experiment on his nose either – but as ever, it is a struggle to dissuade him.

The boat sits low in the water under the weight of goods retrieved – all their own, nothing stolen, they assure themselves. They salute no one and hide their faces as before. As they pass the abbey, no one cares or notices.

Not sure what to expect, they approach the staithe with a mixture of triumphant exhilaration and guilty apprehension. Pieter has travelled back by wagon and is home earlier than expected. He treats the children as if they were his own and would have beaten them, but he had never done it before and was, in any case too angry, too despairing. "You went to this house?" he shrieked, "No, no, NO!" Again and again he asks who saw them, again and again frets that that they must now leave the area, that they will all be taken. It could mean the severest reprisals if anyone has seen them; life is hard already, he says. Sarah fixes Richard's nose without mercy – at least it is now straight, even if swollen like a beetroot. After sending them all to the loft without food, and listening to some more forecasts of woe from her brother, Sarah makes a fluttering gesture with both hands about her forehead, "Ja, ja, enough, brother, enough. God sent them here."

"And?"

"And he will keep them, besides – " she straightens her shawl.

"Besides what?"

"Besides, I am not moving again, and the kinderen need a mother."

"But – "

"They stay with me."

It was the last word spoken on the subject.

6

The Abbot

Exitus acta probat
The end justifies the means

Late April is bright and dry, but still often cold. When spring comes, it is always like the first time, Pacificus thinks as he wanders across the abbey green. Though verily, I would like it better if the abbot was released, and the damoclean sword of Cromwell were not hanging above our heads. And then there are the debts, and the other matters. He looks across the yard towards the ravens picking at the soil on Bede's grave. The sheriff and reeve have done precious little. Maybe they think we'll be closed soon anyway. Pacificus keeps walking, breathing deep draughts of air that bring forth new and sweet scents. The pussy willow is in full bud, plum and pears flower still above the dewy orchard grass, and even the apple are boasting red buds. They have not given up, and better late than never. A wet autumn and cold winter it may have been, but they are not moved, there will be a crop again, seed time and harvest like the book says.

Who is that now? He hears his name whispered from across the cobbles. He turns to see two monks talking privily, and looking his way. Like Herod and Pilate, Brothers Eustace and Anselm seem to have forgotten their usual jealousies to unite for once around a common victim. Let them talk, what care I? He cares more than he would admit.

All the way along the river, and during that morning he wrestles with it. Pacificus has borne two weeks of whispers and suspicious glances. His art suffers for it too. And today he is painting the Archangel Michael trampling Satan underfoot, but he cannot concentrate. He keeps huffing and puffing, breaking off and pacing about. What does Lucifer look like anyway? The nun Elizabeth Barton said that he visited her – mind, she said a great many other foolish things besides, dragged in by people who harboured ill feeling to the king, got her to speak against marriage to the Boleyn whore – all had their necks stretched at Tyburn for it too – more's the pity, I could have asked her what he looked like.

He looks across at his Saint George on the other panel, made up as he is in white, shield buckling under the dragon's breath was all his own; at first he thought it clever, but now he is not so sure. Someone has already complained that the elaborate linen scarf of the helmet makes him look like a Saracen. As if they'd know. And anyway, how does one paint a seraph? He remembers that first ineffable sensation when reading Dante's description for the first time. His eyes close to recapture it, but when he opens them again and sees what he has painted, he knows that he has failed. Too much anatomy, too much armour –

more like the gods of Homer and Virgil. He sighs and comforts himself, at least they have decent swords – not like these effeminate rapiers so popular of late.

It was not easy painting out of a dry bank of experience. He heaves a big sigh again and bows his head, half in prayer, half in exasperation. Saints help him, he cannot paint angels today. Perhaps demons are easier, they're everywhere. He moves his pots and brushes to the side, fixing his resolve to give the dragon under Michael's feet six heads. Each one he sketches thinking about his own accusers; snarling, petty, ambitious. Malice comes easier than virtue to his brushes today, and feels better too. He senses his own demons more acutely than ever on days like this. At one point in the afternoon, when a strong shaft of light pierces the stained glass, Pacificus even throws himself to the ground where the light falls, and holds his scarred wrists heavenward with piteous groans from the deep ravines within an even more scarred soul. The manacles are tight as ever! Jesu, will you never have pity?

He sought the cowl to find peace, to leave strife behind. But that was before his temper flared – it seems Benedictines will forget anything but fisticuffs during Chapter – anyway, it wasn't him who started it, not really. It was the Welshman, Brother Oswald; his way of accusing and finger prodding would make anyone feel violated. The king had just banned the Welsh language that summer and then, referring as far back as the outbreak of the Black Death thirty-odd years before and also to an outbreak of the sweats, he had said that was God's judgement for it, on the English. Typical Welsh. One shove led to another, it wasn't pretty. But Oswald recovered quick enough, and next time he'll mind his manners when passing judgement about God's country. Pacificus tries to paint into that last serpent-head Oswald's little, bovine, beady, Welsh eyes. He stands back uneasily to observe the dragon's heads at the end of the afternoon. He sniffs, cocks his head, squints and tries to imagine Michael complete. Not really a very virtuous day's art for a monk. The accusing voice of his conscience rings loud – still, he consoles himself, a monastery is a place for men, not saints. It is a phrase that has become thin with the wearing.

It is the beginning of May and Pacificus is requested by the abbot to be the one who brings his meat to Norwich. It is a strange request – yet more knowing glances around the Chapter house when Prior Thomas announces it – but Pacificus nods his assent and hopes for dry weather on the morrow. It is over ten miles to the castle jailhouse, a goodly distance with a laden donkey who has little interest in the destination.

Brother Cellarer questions him the next day, "Poor Father Abbot, what a winter to sit in a castle dungeon, will he be alright, brother? Still, the spring will put some warmth in him, and these few things we have prepared."

Pacificus views the "few things': cured and smoked hams, venison, and fish among other things. "Good brother, your sympathy, and affection does you justice, but I fear 'tis misplaced on his account." He watches the brother's reverent face jolt back with shock. 'Nevertheless," he continues, "our beloved abbot will be, as ever, well furnished if I know him; the king would not have it otherwise for a Lord Spiritual."

Brother Cellarer decides his downturned face might as well stay down at the mention of his sovereign. "The king!" – he nearly spits the words – "and his *praemunire* charges! All codswallop! It's the p – '

"Brother! I would surely imagine that our Lord Abbot would not have you speak ill-advisedly at such a time about our prince; you are too needed here."

The words and knowing glance sink in and Brother Cellarer's face returns to an expression of blameless piety. Everyone needs a virtuous cellarer, no one has any use for a heretic on a gibbet. The abbot, not the whole convent, has been asked to acknowledge Henry as supreme head of the English church. He has refused, for which bishops and other monks have been hung. Abbot Rugge will not sign – a strange way to hold out for a deal. Cromwell will want as many bishops on side and as early as possible, but it wouldn't do to test a man like that, not too far, not if you want your abbey and your innards intact. Surely it must be a time playing game, or Cromwell would have had him at London in the Tower. Pacificus knows the abbot as well as anyone, he would have been a superb general, he thinks. Even so, there is something strange going on here; he feels it.

The journey through the villages is uneventful, though people are less friendly these days; too many monks and friars without homes, so they all fall under suspicion.

The cathedral spire looms from a five mile distance; from then on a blind man could find the city, for the wind is in the west and carries the smell. He makes no stops but goes straight for the castle; bare Norman walls rising like a monumental fist against liberty in the midst of the realm's second city.

The keep is reached through two other levels; each higher than the last, and the higher the smaller, with a bridge across the separating ditch. He is waved through the keep gate, but the watchman has espied the food before Pacificus has even made the drawbridge, so he reluctantly surrenders a small ham to avoid difficulties. The inner courtyard is all a-bustle; special arrangements are being made – an event on the morrow, the gossips say. He spots a ragged boy stacking fagots against the wall near the gate. Heretics then. He wonders why no word of this has found its way to the abbey. Straight away, though he's been trying to forget them, he thinks of the Fentons, especially her. He leaves the donkey with a lad at the stables, and Pacificus shows him the food inventory – not that he expects the lad to read, though it turns out he can just a little.

"It's all written here, take it to the cellar, anything goes missing and you'll face the sheriff; but if you guard it well, there'll be something good for you." The boy scratches his arse almost constantly; it is not endearing. Pacificus advises washing it daily and applying goose fat. The boy nods, sniffs, then uses the same hand to wipe his nose.

"What do men call you?"

"Tom Short. My father is the stable master and blacksmith here, but he don't like monks."

"Has he met them all?"

"Dunno," he shrugs. "But I for one ain't gonna be no monk – all that prayin'n'singing."

"Oh, yes."

"Not me!" The boy leans forward confidentially, and whispers, "I'm gonna be a knight!"

"Really?"

"Aye; me dad can make armour, you know. Trained at the Royal Almain in Greenwich, he has."

Pacificus glances over to the forge at a vulcanesque figure silhouetted against the furnace, hammer in hand. "And yet he is here shoeing horses?"

The boy shrugs. "Says Germans is ignorant, and other things what I'll not say before your tender ears."

"Does he now, does he?" Pacificus raises his finger in admonition. "Be that as it may, armour maketh not the knight, and never did."

'You've met one then, 'ave yer?"

"That I have, boy, and according to the old way, to be knightly always starts first here." He pats Tom's heart. "Be noble and virtuous in here, serve your father well, protect the poor and you shall have Saint Michael's armour against all devilry in the hour of danger."

The lad looks curiously at the ghosts in the monk's eyes. Then, very knowingly, he says, "Oh aye, that all?"

Pacificus' eyes wander for a moment longer. Does he really believe all that, now? The boy prompts him again, and this time he answers – though more as one who is both speaking and examining almost his very soul. "No, by no means all, a knight ought to be fervent in prayer for the love of Jesus Christ, have reverence and devotion towards the Church, be humble in himself, have reasonable knowledge, be stable in perseverance and constant in execution, honest in conversation, secret in consultation, discreet in speech, courteous in receiving strangers, liberal in gifts, magnificent and noble in actions, magnanimous in enterprises, continent in purity, abstinent in sobriety, amiable in all good qualities, incomparable in clemency and invincible in patience. And other things I cannot now remember."

"Alright, alright! So there's even more than that."

"Aye, lad – like washing between your legs more than once a year! That enough for you?"

Tom grins. "You can read books, you monks can. I can read too, me."

"Good for you, lad. Now tell me, where may I find Abbot Rugge?"

The lad straightens his shoulders and points him towards the steps of the north tower.

"You'll be lucky to catch him in, on his way to the bishop's palace he is."

Pacificus mounts the stairs with speed; *is there news?* He passes men carrying boxes, some with rugs and plate. Gaining admittance, he finds his abbot sitting at his desk surrounded by his seal, inkhorn, parchments and folios. It is a spacious room with a commanding view over the city from two windows with dog-tooth mouldings on the round arches. Even with half the furnishings heading for the wagons in the courtyard, the accommodation is much as Pacificus had expected. Abbot William Rugge insists, in the manner that Wolsey would, that the trappings of station are just that, trappings. For all any knew, there would be a hair-shirt under the abbot's garments same as there was under Beckett's – though somehow he doubts it. Even so, the winter here – and the strain, perhaps – has aged him. He does not see Pacificus at first, busy with his papers, surrounded by scurrying servants; and so Pacificus has time to observe him. Of an age, fifty perhaps, well fleshed, large temples and grey hair in full retreat. The squareness of his jaw seems squarer than he remembers and the nose fatter, like a blacksmith's hammer. His hands move deliberately from page to page, everything has purpose, everything can be used, ordered, made to serve. Pacificus knocks gently and the Abbot raises his finger for pause, his index finger and sleeve are inked; he has been writing much this morning.

Presently he looks up, "Pacificus! Brother, my dear fellow, come to the fire! How good to see you in health! How are the lanes? You had good weather? I am glad."

Pacificus hangs his traveling cloak on the back of a chair and they greet with the kiss of peace. Quite forgetting to kneel and kiss his abbot's hand, he responds, "Pax vobiscum to you too, Father." His eyes water. He is touched by the show of genuine affection, in a world where there is so much suspicion and hostility. His abbot, shrewd, sees it, smiles at him. "Now, come to the fire; we have much to talk about. Johnson! Johnson! Some warm ale up here, please! Oh, I swear this place is never warm!"

Pacificus moves a velvet cushion to the rear of an oak chair and hesitates, unwilling to sit before his superior. "I see you are moving. I trust all is well?"

"Indeed, yes it is, things move apace here. Sit you, sit you – there is much to do." Rugge fidgets and glances from the bookshelves to the half-filled chests. "Yes, much to do." He scratches the mole next to his left nostril. He is agitated about something.

"They said you're to go to the bishop's palace?"

"Yes, yes. Look, let me shut the door." He walks over to it quietly, an ear cocked as if to hear who is about. When he returns, he speaks quickly and deliberately, "I requested they send you, for that reason. I have had a visit this morning from Archbishop Cranmer and Lord Cromwell, no less. I knew what it would be about, and Cromwell is nothing if not plain in speech. Aye, and I knew what I would say too – what I would sign to, what I would not."

There wis now a pause. Rugge looks to the side, puckers his lips; it is confession time. Eventually, a log shifts in the fire, almost falls out; but Pacificus, with adept speed, knocks it back with the tongs.

"See? You are quick as ever! Now where was I? Ah, yes," he continues, securing Pacificus' eyes, "if I have taught you nothing else you will know at least that I am a pragmatist. England is changing. By the holy rood, the whole world is changing – new learning, new continents, new universe even, if that Polish priest Copernicus trumps Aristotle."

"You are to be bishop?" The second bishopric in the country, he thinks, how can you afford that?

"Yes, of course," Rugge squares him, he is matter-of-fact, his mind always on the next matter, the next deal, "I know every abbot and bishop in the realm; there is not one who sees where we are headed, not really. I do, Pacificus – believe me man, I do. I saw it in Master Cromwell's eyes this very morn, though I knew it before Michaelmas. But I was waiting for them to come to me and they have. I taken the king's oath and have asked for pardon. I suppose you wouldn't? Not knightly enough for you, perhaps?"

"I judge no one my lord, verily, I do not." He is sincere too, and humble enough not to think himself a saint or martyr. "You must act as your conscience dictates."

"And the times, brother – and the times," he almost sighs but then brightens. "Mercury's in the ascendant; a time for men of action!"

Aye, and *Mercibus praeest* is the patron of profit too, thinks Pacificus.

"I am told Cromwell doesn't hold with celestial bodies," he says aloud.

"Yes, but doubtless they hold him! Born under Saturn, if ever a man was!" Rugge heaves a long sigh, shutting his eyes for a moment. "Our day passes – our usefulness in their eyes."

"You mean...because of the printing press?"

"No," he dismisses the idea with a wave of his hand. "Though the scriptorium certainly loses much revenue without the government contracts. No, I meant us – you, me, the brothers." He walks to the window and stares down on the crowds milling in and out of the shambles: clerks, ostlers, joiners, chandlers, farriers, lawyers, peasants. "By our mettle we bent a barbarous world into what it has become and now they do not need us. Though..." he pauses and glances back, "though perhaps they would like our lands."

Pacificus frowns, "I am not with you, my lord. Who bent the world?"

"We did! We did, long, long ago when Rome fell to the barbarians, the heathen. We used to be the revolutionaries, we were the reformers back then, or preservers at least. The most impractical men in an age of bare necessity. Men who wouldn't carry swords for their own safety, only a staff. Men who clothed the naked and housed the lepers, yet went barefoot themselves; who fed and educated the poor, taking the son of the humblest serf for the cowl and allowing the least to vote for or against those same abbots!"

The abbot spins round, that old fire in his dark brown eyes, the sort of passion that has made men follow him so readily. "Think of it, Pacificus! In a sea of heathen barbarity, we men who wouldn't mind our own business became the businessmen of the age. But, alas..." He rests both white hands upon the back of his chair and hangs his head briefly. "Yes, alas, that age is passing or has passed."

"But, my lord, we are still here – a force for good, surely?"

The abbott shruggs. "The day, the hour when Rome began to decline was not known; not to Julian, Constantine or Theodosius. They passed the curve of the hill without perceiving it. And I fear, my friend, that is true for us too; what light remains is but the afterglow of the setting sun, the wilting of already cut flowers. Do they not say that the fingernails and hair grow on a dead man for three days? This new world order, this protestant order, this pagan Calvinism, this rising of the rich – whether it is the sin, or the punishment, I cannot tell. Perhaps both? But it will not wane now. Leviathan is awakened."

"You think the king too strong?"

"Too weak! No, I mean your lot – the aristocrats – they see the day coming when they may rule without restraint, without God and his church. They forge ahead to appropriate everything, to bring forth Antichristus, as blessed More said, *sheep are eating men* – there is no moral to their lust for monopoly, only the endless insatiable avarice of Lucifer. Be it done ever so slowly, the masses will one day live under the few, with no church or king to fight for them. Mark my words, and mark it well, we may live to see it yet! And meantime," he says, more brightly, first examining the folios on the desk, then tossing one aside, "we, brother, must pass into that sunset like lambs to slaughter, or else be wise as serpents and robe ourselves with cunning – there can be no other way."

Pacificus waits perhaps too long to agree. He wants to, of course and this man above all his current acquaintance has his esteem, but to bow to the king in this way is to forsake the Pope, surely. "I am certain," he starts slowly, looking at the specks of mud on his toes and sandals, "that whatever you have done, it is for the good of the church and our abbey." Is it overmuch sloth to lamely defer your spiritual and moral opinions to another? Certainly it is easier than thinking for yourself. And is he not pledged in obedience to accept his abbot's good judgment?

Rugge waves away the compliment, saying, "*Bonitas non est pessimis esse meliorem* – it is not goodness to be better than the worst - most bishops' hearts are more in tune with the vaults of the Star Chamber than with the vaults of heaven these days. Aye, and most are happy to save their own necks in days such as these; they will not stick them out, or have them stretched on behalf of the great houses, let alone little Saint Benet's! No Pacificus, my good brother, if we are to come through this great dissolution then we must operate from a position of strength. We cannot know every turn of nature but at least from here in Norwich we can steer the ship favourably to the cause." He purses his fat lips, thoughtfully, adding: "*Non semper erit aestas10* – it will not always be summer." But mind brother that none of this goes any further for now."

"Of course, my lord, but does that mean you have found a way to save Saint Benet's?"

"And others I hope. Cromwell reckons the church has a third of the nation's wealth. I think he's mad; but he means the crown to have it, whatever the actual figure. If it comes to much less perhaps he will pillage the parishes too; perhaps even the guilds, the common lands – who knows where you stop once you start with this sort of folly? And remember this, it was Wolsey who started it; twenty nine small houses dissolved for his Ipswich school and Oxford college, all with the Pope's blessing, aye, remember that! The church made the tools for its own destruction, or at least Wolsey did."

Pacificus screws up his face in pain, "Oh, why must it all end like this?" It is rhetorical.

"What, the money? The King must have it for his defenses against Rome, against emperor Charles' mighty armada that would have been here years ago but for all the trouble he is having with the Mohammedans. So we must have these coastal forts that Henry plans; so numerous, so ingenious. Well, they don't build themselves."

"They are a waste of money. That fall at jousting this winter must have left him witless, or else, who in God's name advises such intemperate nonsense?"

"Oh yes, of course, naval strategy is more your bag," Rugge tilts his head slightly, he sees once again the confident man he had first met, resurface momentarily from under the cowl. Ah, he's still there, somewhere! Good.

"And to think," Pacificus leans forward, "if he had kept troth with Queen Catherine, none of this would have mattered anyway; there'd be no threat." He's annoyed as much for the waste, lives, money, time, all of it - diplomacy is always less costly than warfare.

Rugge has not heard, he is distracted by other thoughts, new plans. He formulates his next phrase carefully, pacing deliberately to the other fireside chair. "Prithee hear me this once; I cannot command it, as you will see."

He squeezes his eyes shut for a few seconds. This is unlike him, in fact his whole manner today is unlike him; the self-assured *maître contrôleur*. "You were aforetime a man skilled in other arts than painting – no need for that black look, brother, I have told no one about you; but...you see – well, that is to say...I might have more need of a soldier than a painter in the days to come..."

"My lord abbot?"

"I will have – that is, I do have – many enemies, and now many more inherited from my predecessor. I...er..." He pauses awkwardly and starts to pick the braiding on his velvet overcoat. He is not used to showing his fear. "I do not believe Bishop Nykke died a natural death," he blurts out.

"But surely he was very aged and the winter hard?"

"Aye, aged, blind and stubborn too! Refusing the king, and scorning the archbishop to his face! That sort of prating doesn't go down well – I mean, you of all people know the game. You give them the choice; for us or against us, choose silver or lead, and be quick about it."

"Men of his age aren't likely to be ambitious, my lord. You can't bribe a man on the brink of the next world with lands and provinces."

"Exactly my point, and of course, he was old enough to know Cranmer as a penniless undergraduate with a pregnant barmaid and bastard in tow, he didn't suffer fools gladly, but even so – " Rugge scrunches his eyes tight shut again for a moment. "Even so, he knew not how to play his cards; these men must needs preen their feathers – he should have known that better than anyone. *More are flattered into virtue than bullied out of vice,* and so forth. They got ten thousand marks from this diocese to secure his bail from Marshalsea, ten thousand marks! What I wouldn't do for that money now; the bishop's palace is a dank, miasmic hermitage, we'll need thousands."

It is always *we* with Rugge, Pacificus thinks, he draws you into his confidence with silken cords, if not, you'd become a *they*. A friend for the abbot is always someone who has the same enemies and interests.

"But that's not all Pacificus," Rugge continues, "for once they saw him isolated, and found him writing to the Pope, they could not but notice the bishopric lands, they dredge up that Bilney nonsense – you know, where he had the heretic burned at the Lollard's pit without proper authority from the state – but still he would not sign the bishopric lands over, not Nykke, you know what these old saints are like; all backbone and the rest gristle."

"And the king grew impatient?"

"Yes impatient, for the land or a more willing successor." Rugge comes back to his chair, which now creaks under his weight, "He...he...well, he feels entitled. No doubt he will appropriate them for the help of the poor." He manages a chuckle.

"And you have agreed?"

"Ah well," Rugge eases back, then stretches his legs out towards the fire. His italianate silk stockings and leather boots glow in the soft light. "I was not specific, and I'm sure it will not come to that but let us say that for now they think they have assurances."

"But if we play for time...?"

"The future may be anyone's, Pacificus; the king might die, they will rise in the north in any case, the emperor even may come, who knows, but either way it would be prudent for me to keep someone exercised in arms – someone I can trust."

Now he is shocked, flattered, and not a little tempted, "But my vows – my vocation?"

Rugge opens both hands liberally, "Poverty, chastity and obedience; it changes nothing. Besides, did you really think God put you on earth to paint pictures? That Ranworth would be your legacy?"

"Well, I..." Yes, he did actually.

"If what your Grand Master says of you is true – " Rugge leans forward and takes Pacificus's wrists, as if to prise apart his hands in consent. "If it is true, I say, then you may well have been sent by God into the kingdom for such a time as this."

"You have not spoken of me to others though?"

"No, no, I have kept my word. You and your brother have my protection as ever, but..."

Rugge releases his wrists, raising his own palms in barter. "But to whom much is given – "

"We are grateful, you know that," says Pacificus quickly.

"Avaunt, you have my protection freely!" He waves his hand generously. "And besides, yours was not the only family to suffer loss after Bosworth, our fathers knew the risk, we are sworn to help each other in such times, I think?" Rugge raises his eyebrow. "And that is why I come to you now. We have a mutual understanding – do we not?" But it's not a question; never is, with him.

"But when I took my vows, it was you who gave me the name Pacificus – "

"Ah yes, the disciple of – "

"Yes, yes, Francis of Assisi!" – enough bonhomie – "You said that I could now be a man of peace, here in the cloister – the name, the vow! That I could find peace!" He is near pleading now; it cuts very deep, this does, for surely after these fourteen years he's not found either. Just of late, even before the brawling in Chapter, Pacificus has felt a gnawing anger usurping the better angels of his soul, like slowly losing his mind, drowning in frustration while nobody notices or cares.

"Yes," says Rugge, still at his machinations; his friend's state of mind is not of primary concern. "But there is more than one way to bring peace to a realm, and to a man. You have been a shield to Europe in times past; now England needs you. And where better than here, the places where Alfred Magnus and Edgar Atheling of old held out against tyranny?"

"I hung up my spurs!" He feels his cheeks flush and his finger is stabbing the air in that old familiar way. "I broke my oath to our Langue, to the Order, to Rome; all that for this king, this England!" It is only partially true; other more personal reasons combined to lead him home incognito. "I would that you mention it no more, no more I say."

Rugge pauses, choosing his response carefully. He knows he can win Pacificus, but not when he is angered. A bruised reed is this one, he remembers, bruised but by no means broken. Rugge flicks lightly through his unfailing memory to the stored image of the tanned Cavaliere that he won over in informal debate at Gonville Hall. The debate was against the White Horse set, men like Latimer, Barnes, Bilney, Frith; reckless reformers who met at the White Horse in Cambridge – euphemistically called Little Germany back then. Rugge had taken them on single-handed, never stood, nor even sat forward when he spoke – just reclined and brushed the floor with all their arguments. Age and experience trumping youth and enthusiasm.

"You sir," he had said confidentially to the man that Pacificus was – a curious enquirer – "You sir, have missed your vocation among these coxcombs. Methinks we should talk privily and apart. Peradventure some position more substantial can be found you." He was nothing if not a persuader then, and he still is now. Standing here in the cell, looking at his flushed protégé, Rugge knows how to reel him in, how to tension the line just right.

"I will do as you say, of course," Rugge persists, "but there are not many good men who will readily admit that the king is badly advised and" – carefully now, carefully – "and you – that is you and I – may still keep our vows to the temporal and spiritual authorities..."

"Aye, the king and the Pope."

"Quite so, quite so, these are difficult times, perhaps the last days and who knows if we – you and I, that is – have been brought together by the hand of providence?"

"I understand well enough." He sighs, wearying of resistance.

"Then you will pray on it?"

"That I will – and so should you!"

"Yes, yes of course – but you see how it is."

"I do, my lord. That I do."

Johnson's foot is soft on the steps, Rugge has caught it first, "And brother – *vir sapit qui pauca loquitur est - The man is wisest who talks little.*"

He nods just as Johnson enters. Don't fret yourself, he thinks. In matters of sedition even fools keep their mouths shut.

7

All The King's Men

Qui tacet consentire videtur
Silence presumes consent

Pacificus has agreed to nothing yet, though he will stay on for an extra day, dine with Rugge, Cromwell, Cranmer and the Duke of Norfolk at the palace that evening. He is surprised at the invitation but perhaps Rugge wants to break him into his new scene, and have his opinion on the men.

The abbot has been ever one for ruling by consent, then somehow getting his own way on all things. And every man in power needs enforcers; Cromwell was Wolsey's strong arm and now the king's. Men would have rules, or else rulers – it is regrettable but these are the times. "We should know what we are dealing with, weigh up the players," he'd said. Perhaps Rugge thinks to revive *il gladiatore* in Pacificus; perhaps rouse him by luxuries, or perchance the pride of being with great men.

To be what he had once been would be too easy; it is weakness surely to bully and shed blood. It is to go back, and is this what God requires of him? These things he ponders during his afternoon in the town.

He has business to transact on behalf of the abbey with a merchant called John Toppes on Kings Street. Toppes and others from Saint George's guild are driving down the price of worsted cloth, which they export to the lowlands, and in so doing are bringing some of the abbey tenants to penury. Pacificus is indignant at it. The merchant class has grown so strong, so insolent even in his own lifetime. Kings Street is heaving as usual, many of the great mercantile families are holding court in their yards; Pastons and Heydens among them – the new families. He draws near the entrance of Toppes "palace', the grand exchange where they are all inordinately proud of being seen – these busy men and their trade. Pacificus is focusing on its inner ogee arch as he approaches the entrance. He had not noticed its shallow, inverse curve before – how cosmopolitan. He knows the shape well from Venice and beyond; it is Moorish influence, when we were on better terms – how strange to be touched by such things so far from the war.

And it is just as he is thinking this when, from the Augustinian priory – which stands adjacent to the trade hall – that an enormous, black, cloud-like form passes to the corner of his eye and then behind him down the street, and with it a chill down his spine. He wheels round and sees none other than the prior from the soon-to-be-dissolved Hickling priory, striding up the street as if he had a good dinner before him and the bailiff after. Robert Aeyns, they called him, that much he had got out of the cellarer – not a local name. Wonder why he could not find lodgings for his six monks here in Norwich? Something in Pacificus withers at the sight of him. And this he cannot credit; perhaps it is his size, nearly seven feet; or is it the mass of black habit? For though it is the same as his own, somewhere further back in his memory perhaps he will always instinctively spring to battle readiness at the sight of black robes, that being so often the garb of the elite Janissaries of the Saracens. Fearless, merciless; captured Christian children, indoctrinated and brutalised like Spartans, then turned loose on their own kind – a sight of them pouring over the battlements was the stuff that still woke Pacificus up in colds sweats.

He thinks of this when waiting upstairs for his interview. He also examines the dragons carved into the wooden ceiling vaults of the great hall. He thinks of amendments he might make in his painting of Michael trampling down Satan on the Ranworth rood screen. These dragons have something intentional and malevolent in the eyes, or perhaps it is the whole facial expression. Perhaps the artist had seen the devil or had someone like that Elizabeth Barton to tell him? Either way, they are better than his. He sighs and consciously tries to capture these in his memory, which is hard amidst the din and bustle. He disdains them, these merchants, their peascod and peplum doublets, their gaudy silk sleeves, their meanness, their single pursuit of Mammon. Look at the coins they vaunt, a king's head where there used to be a cross.

Never trust a man whose whole eye is prudence – where self-interest alone is the bottom line – his mother had always said, and she was right. He knows that some of these upstanding pillars of the community will be secret usurers, many whoremongers. He has heard that Cromwell is a usurer of old, that he fornicates with half the moneyed men of Europe, that he acts as banker to many a great family in England too. He tries to imagine the end of all things, where the church is replaced by the men of commerce and usury. What a thought! Perhaps banks will set the holy days in the future – though not too many, for that would affect trade. But even with fewer holidays than the church gives, which is a lot, perhaps the new serfs of their mercantile dreams would even then learn to be grateful.

Is that the utopia Cromwell imagines? Lord knows, the king has scaled down the feast days to a mere handful. Saint George's is still allowed, so they'll be happy here in Norwich. On George's day the guilds turn out with a life-size dragon and players; this he remembers from his childhood, and happier times. It was his dearest dream to be a knight like Saint George, to slay the dragon – any dragon. In those days he had never doubted dragons existed beyond England, nor that they could be overcome by good knights. But that was a long time ago, before Rhodes fell to the Saracens.

But these holy days, why deprive the working men of so many, what manner of new world are they thinking to build in cancelling all but a very few from July to September? And then it comes to him; *they* – he's even thinking like Rugge now – *they* hate men's rest. Yes, that's it, they hate it; for a man at rest is a creature of God, not a slave as they are to Mammon. In resting, a man is rest-ored to his creatureliness before God, the *Imago Dei* common to all humanity, God's indelible imprint on the human soul; what a defiance of mere Mammon-worship is that!

He watches an apprentice cuffed and scolded near the stairway, then looks round at the faces of the merchants sitting nonchantly behind their money at tables, all dukes and earls in the making. He had seen where this all ends during his years in Italy; those Strozzi, Pazzi, Medici, extortioners and brigands in one generation, usurers and king-makers in the next. Venetians, Genoese, Lombardians, Florentines – they'd sell their mothers for a half crown. When Constantinople fell – and that only by the guns sold to Mehmet by Hungarian Christians – the Venetian ships made port to trade with the Mohamedans before the gunpowder had scarce left the air. The Great Whore that trades upon many waters!

Presently he is drawn out of his morose meanderings by the sight of Alderman Toppes on the hall stairs, remonstrating vehemently with wool-mercer Isaac Timms, so much so that others begin to look their way.

Toppes is shouting, "You cannot do this, we had an agreement – well, an understanding at least –between men of discretion!"

Timms is unmoved. "Fellingham says his four-master is quicker and I need this business transacted with haste, without delay."

People are interested now; the competition between Fellingham and Toppes is a standard joke. Fellingham's new ship The Genoese could cripple Toppes' Antwerp run, and they all know it. In the past he has blamed the winds and tides, but next Thursday they sail together so the matter will be known once and for all.

Seeing the other merchants gather, Toppes disputes no further, but rather takes the man by the arm, gently leading him to a quiet corner. It is the same corner where Pacificus sits and listens.

"But Fellingham's rates are so much more. Be reasonable. I would not lose your business and send out my Pelican half empty for a few marks; let's talk terms, my fellow."

Timms is shamefaced now, but Pacificus sees he has caught the modern way. "I'm sorry for it Toppes, we have dealt a long time you and I, and our fathers. You would perhaps do well to invest in newer vessels yourself..."

"Fellingham is in this with Cromwell, as you very well know. Not just in the finance but a cut of the profits too. I cannot work like that, and I won't."

"Well, there you have it. Perhaps another time, then." Timms bows. "As you would say yourself, business is business."

"Aye, and when they have cleared the competition, your children and granchildren will not find their rates so competitive, I fancy."

Timms does not trouble to reply as he retires. Toppes gives a long sigh. He catches sight of Pacificus as he turns, and this provokes a further sigh. "Oh. You again, brother. What is it now? More alms for the needy?"

And so begins the begrudged interview. Toppes will not hear that he has taken advantage of the poor over the price of worsted cloth, though the reddening at the top of his loose cheeks say he is a liar. Pacificus lets him know it, too, by a hard stare. Then, being led beyond his brief by the snobbish pride that will get the better of him, he even tells him what would be a just price this summer. Toppes' eyes nearly drop from sockets already loosened by too many hours picking over his ledgers – no doubt all done in the new Italian double-accounting system; *oh, so modern.* He removes his cap and runs inky fingers through his grey thatch: "We cannot compete at those rates."

"And they cannot fill their bellies. You must pay a fair price."

Toppes looks fit to burst, those reddening cheeks and flared nostrils, but he won't cross the abbey, not when the prior and abbot are in the habit of buying so many of those little luxuries he back hauls from Flanders. After all, there are plenty of merchants to choose from in Norwich and Yarmouth with silks and spiced wines for sale. Toppes has heard about the abbot's turn of affairs, that he will now be bishop. He says he will act as a Christian in this matter and hope that, when Rugge is bishop, that his lordship will think kindly of him. Pacificus smiles. He gets to his feet, wishing with all his heart that money everywhere could come from fishes' mouths and not from business done like this. He is glad to leave the place.

That evening, the fires bristle to capacity in every fireplace at the palace, even so Rugge's comment about the damp air proves true. The dismal miasma is impossible to ignore. Pacificus notes the pomanders of dried thyme and lavender hanging on every spare nail in an effort to freshen the space and somewhat dispel the fetid pall. He takes one from a hook by the chimney breast to his nose, and the smell takes him straight back to the fields of Aquataine. He closes his eyes briefly, never doubting in that moment that such fragrances ward off plague and other airborne maladies. He catches the aroma of oakmoss on the burning logs, and the scent of that too takes him miles away, conjuring a thousand Ottoman spices, and so many memories. He hangs the bag on its nail again, but the beautiful sweetness stays with him.

He is waiting for a servant to take his cloak but the lad seems too flustered to remember. Would he like ale or spiced wine while he waits for the others? Was he hungry? No, take my coat first, he thinks. By Saint Agnes, it must have been a long time since they'd had guests here! And no wonder the lad's a bag of nerves, considering tonight's pretty company. The boy takes his coat eventually and Pacificus tries to bless him with a thin smile. The lad must be about the same age as Piers Fenton. This gets him wondering how the children get on with that eel-catcher. He takes his spiced wine by the fire, all alone. It is a very rare luxury, his toes are stretched towards the flame while no one is watching. How alluring these temporal blessings appear on cold nights. In the abbey the cold is seen as part of their purgation – to mortify their earthly members. If he capitulates to Rugge, it could be like this every night; think on that. He does, but there is much to consider besides. He wishes his brother were here to talk things through with.

Rugge has already been in private conference with Cranmer, Cromwell and Norfolk before dinner and so the group is already formed when Pacificus first sees them. They stand in the linenfold-paneled dining hall, in a semicircle round the fire, half orange, half black in the firelight. They have stayed on to see the heretic dispatched on the morrow. There is nothing like the sight of their duke in town to bring the crowds to the Lollards pit for the spectacle – and to have an archbishop and Master Secretary too; they will be spoilt for choice.

They do not see Pacificus approach but he sees Norfolk's head and face well, so bony and shrunken amongst the magnificent roundness of his ermine-edged velvet cloak that it looks like the stalk on a furry apple. Frail, skeletal fingers massage some holy amulet, the sort of thing Cromwell abhors. Being nearest, Norfolk turns first to see him approach but does not appear to recognise his face – which is good – even though Pacificus must look like his father by now.

First duke and earl of the realm, the Lord Marshall of England does not deign to acknowledge this lowly monk – just make sure he wipes his knees on the way in. Old Norfolk looks him over and leaves Rugge to make any introductions. But the abbot is deeply embroiled with Cranmer on some theological minutiae regarding predestination and "that heretic in Geneva', so it is Cromwell who speaks first.

"Brother Pacificus?" He extends a hand like a shovel, warm even for a devil; he grants him that. Introductions are made and Pacificus bows where necessary, which tonight is almost everywhere. He has no fear that Cromwell will recognise him, though they have met a quarter of a century ago in Milan. Back then he had been an honoured ambassador and Cromwell, a cockney chancer working for the French. He had shown him to the workshop of Leonardo da Vinci. How the great wheel turns! Since then his star has risen, a man suited for the times. And look at him now, legs planted apart like two great oaks. Cranmer, on the other hand, seems ill at ease, those frog-like eyes reddened, intermittently looking away from conversations to the fire or to the window, those effeminate fingers pinching and tapping, that mouth sighing from time to time, as restless like a sheep with colic.

Over dinner they exchange pleasantries. Cromwell wants to know where the monk has been, what the traders are saying. He knows them all, keeps them in his head, and their continental partners. He escaped the fists and boots of his blacksmith father for the Antwerp trade at sixteen, thence to Italy. The king's secretary has been all things necessary for the times; even a mercenary, before ever he came back to these shores to study the law.

Those eyes, Pacificus thinks, had ever a man such small eyes for such a head? Hard as cannonballs they are, he thinks as he observes them dart to and fro, quick as a lizard's tongue. He doesn't miss much. He appears to descry everything.

Norfolk picks over his venison like a fussy buzzard. "Physician says I should stay away from venison; brings on melancholia," he observes pessimistically. He mutters *paternosters, aves* and *credos* between every mouthful to counter the ill effects. Rugge muses on the events of the morrow; Norfolk resents having to attend, and says so.

Cranmer says nothing as their host strings them along. Indeed, so adroit is the abbot in articulating why this type of lollardy should be stamped out, that Norfolk murmurs into his wine, "He'll prove a better inquisitor than Nykke ever was – and he used to say he could smell hell's flames on an anabaptist – *ils sentaient le fagot*."

"He'll need to now," Cromwell eyes Rugge carefully, then picks his teeth with a thumbnail.

Rugge pretends not to notice. "Yes, these radicals are a worse scourge than any Lollard, they'll have Norwich as ankle deep in blood as Munster, you mark my word."

"They hold everything in common, these bigamists – wives and all," Norfolk says. His manner changes and he waxes ebullient, seems to grow and almost come alive as the thought of the bloodshed takes hold of him. "No respect for private property, secret conventicles in caves and dark woods at night – you can't reason with 'em, they only quote scripture at you. What did Pope Leo say – sorry Cromwell, bishop of Rome – " Anyone who touches the mountain should be thrust through with a dart." Saint Louis said the same; thrust the hilt in up to the belly, he said; don't argue with them."

Cranmer is trying to enter the conversation but Norfolk has the wind in his sails now and carries on over the top of him. "I wondered whether Gonville Hall might turn a few of them out some years back – you were with "em at Cambridge, weren't you Archbishop? When you were not wenching with that barmaid. God's blood, England has seen some strange happenings, I'll say!"

Content to have exercised his position to cause maximum offense, the duke diverts his purple lips back to the venison, but not before telling Cranmer not to take his past so seriously, nobody else did, and would he stop hogging the wine, drinking as he does like a man happy to be away from his wife. Norfolk hits close here; Cranmer frets daily that the foreign woman he has secretly married will be used against him with the king – who probably already knows, but pretends not to in order to keep things straightforward.

Cromwell stirs to protect his vexed friend, but Pacificus is already there, which seems to please Master Secretary a great deal.

"H-how many, Your Grace?" Pacificus asks.

"What?" Norfolk barks, resenting the interruption.

"How many die, tomorrow?" He sounds more confident this time.

"I'm sure I know not, nor care less. Rugge?"

"I am told it is just the one, a farmer from up our way, right under the nose of the abbey, would you believe it? He could not be persuaded to give the names of others, I hear. They hold the wife over, hoping that her husband's ordeal will persuade her to see sense. No one wishes to be inclement in these matters."

"Indeed not, the king would not desire it, if it can be avoided," Cromwell says. "She could say she was misled, confess before the sacrament, amend her ways and return to her children. Are there children?"

"Yes, there are," Rugge says, his face now alight. "They disappeared on the day this farmer Fenton was taken, only to turn up feral a month later, attack the incumbent tenants, steal what they could, and cover the rest of the property with – well, you know – the contents of the farm privy! Can you imagine, Pacificus?"

While Pacificus tries to look the picture of shocked innocence, Norfolk almost chokes on his food. "I told you! What did I say?" Brandishing his knife, he bellows, "Heretics' spawn! No respect for property! They should be found and made an example of! *Ils sentent le fagot*, they smell of the very fagots, the lot of them."

Cromwell brings his fist down hard, and then a second time more gently, on the table. He raises an admonishing finger at Norfolk. "They are children!" He is affected, then, which is to his credit. Perhaps he is not a demon after all, perhaps only half devil? Pacificus hears the news with sinking heart.

The lute player returns to playing in his shadowy corner. He purports to have been trained in the court of Urbino. No one believes him, but it sounds good to tell important guests. Urbino is just a name to Rugge and the others, but Pacificus remembers being there at that court in its noble twilight. He remembers that evening on the terrace with its soulful widow, the Duchess Elisabetta, and the radiant Vittoria Colonna, Bembo, Castiglione and the rest. And remembers the dinner that went on until daybreak, debating so many matters that ended up in Castiglione's book *The Courtier* - so popular now in the northern European courts. Urbino is no a word to bandy around for profit. What happened to Duke Frederico's Urbino, is no less tragic than Cromwell's despoliation of the monasteries. The Antichrist Cesare Borgia despoiled that noble library and violated its precincts leaving a pattern for people like Cromwell to follow.

Pacificus glances down the table only to see Cromwell placing his goblet down in order to speak: "Many of these people merely groan for a Bible in English; they resent the condescensions of some." He glowers at Norfolk and then at Rugge. "But my lord Archbishop will have one for them soon, one we trust will not be outlawed for its seditious inaccuracies like Tyndale's."

"Oh, yes. Cranmer, how is your bishops' Bible coming along?"

Norfolk only asks because he knows the bishops are all unwilling and have not filed their papers when required.

"Like a goodly many worthwhile things, Your Grace, slowly." Cranmer has had to accept it is a project that will need Cromwell's force to drive it. Besides, he has enough on already; things are at breaking point between the king and Queen Anne. She miscarried a male child after the shock of Henry's jousting accident in January. Edward Seymour has been given an apartment near the king's so that he might visit his sister Jane privily – things do not look good.

Pacificus is surprised Cromwell and Norfolk can seem so at ease in such a time. Norfolk has nieces to spare, he supposes, and some of those Howards are very fair. He knew their families, particularly those ambitious Boleyns – Blickling Hall being not four miles from their own estate. He'd had a liking for Mary Boleyn since early childhood, though their father had his sights set higher than the son of one of yesterday's old families. He'd raised his matchlock high, Boleyn had, and now they are all to fall, like lightening from heaven: incest, adultery, sedition, Cromwell will see to it. And Cromwell himself?

Perhaps not so easily disposed of, he thinks. He alone has the cunning to break the monasteries and lay their wealth at the feet of their new Peter. But after that? Maybe even he, the fixer, will have nothing to offer. Pacificus hates being here, he has so much to say, to accuse them all with, but he is bound in secrets. Rugge looks at him every now and again, such delicious pleasure in his smile; to know all the play, to able to create possibilities for the future under their very noses. He'd have me as Samson in the camp of the Philistines, Pacificus thinks, bring the roof down on the lot of them. Can't help admiring the rascal but I'm not yours yet Rugge – not by a long shot.

Cranmer calls for his retainers before the evening is out. He is plainly out of sorts, and Norfolk has not helped. Cromwell is not long after – he has work to do and eighteen-hour days don't happen by supping wine, even this Italian wine which he likes. Norfolk alone stays for a private conference with his new bishop. Pacificus, taking the hint, retires.

8

The Heretic

Facta non verba
Deeds, not words

His parting words to William Rugge after morning mass, regarding their conversation, is that he be given some time to consider the matter in his cell. Rugge agrees. In the meantime Pacificus has suggested one or two gentlemen of his former acquaintance and profession who might serve well in the household. He will make inquiries.

Grey skies and drizzle; not the best day for a burning, but the officiating clerics – Doctors Reading, Hearne and Spragwell – have promised bread for any who bring faggots. *Panem et circenses*, bread and circuses, nothing much has changed. It worked for the old Caesars and the new. Pacificus passes what they call the Lollards Pit on his way back to the castle to check his animal. He remembers well the day his own father brought him here as a lad to watch the heretic Peke burn – part of his education. In those days indulgences were offered for children bringing faggots to start them young. "Recant Peke, and believe the sacrament," they'd said, he remembers it like it was yesterday. "I despise thee and it also," Peke had replied, already black as pitch, when the flames blistered his skin like the crackling on pork. They kept prodding him with a white wand and offering him forty days indulgence to recant but he only spat blood in their faces. He went slowly, too slowly for the crowd. Eventually even Baron Curzon and John Audley used their swords to cut ash branches. But even so he was an interminable time dying.

Pacificus wears his hood up, against the drizzle, when he leaves the cathedral close. He passes under the gate built by his great-great-great-grandfather. He glances back for a moment after passing through, for there is a statue of the old man kneeling, set above the arch. Him, Sir Thomas Erpingham, the hand that helped Bolingbroke crusade with the Teutonic knights across Europe to Jerusalem and thence back to England to grasp the very stars. Him, defender of Norfolk's peace, patron of the arts, warrior, statesman, hero of Agincourt. His grandfather said it was a poor likeness, but there he is, the old rascal, gazing piously across Norwich. Wonder what he would make of today's execution, him being a one-time supporter of Wycliffe – seems I have both reformer and usurper in my blood, Pacificus thinks, God knows how much of each, no doubt we will see soon enough.

He passes the Lollards Pit on his way to the castle. A new oak stake is being fixed, ragged children with pitiful bundles of kindling have arrived already, but there is no sign of the bread. Pacificus does not tarry and he has no interest in seeing the event either. *God delighteth not in the death of the wicked*, though many others, who shouldn't, do. Either way, no one is sentimental; and most prefer a burning to a hanging for there is nothing like a bloody spectacle to make you feel alive, if nothing else will. Fenton has done well to escape a traitor's death, and that only because Hamberly wanted his possessions – a traitor would forfeit them to the crown, by the new Acts of Attainder. If he had to choose between the two himself, he'd rather be burnt than hung, drawn and quartered.

On entering the castle yard he sees the smith's lad go to fetch the faggots out of the drizzle. Seeing the boy, he thinks mainly of the young children for whom this will be the first one. He asks the lad his name – Jack, he's told. The boy confides, excited, that he will be allowed to the front, so his dad says, if he keeps the faggots dry. What a world. It would be better that Fenton go quickly, for these children's sake as well as his own.

He asks to be shown to the cellarer, for the abbot has no need now of the provisions he brought. Pacificus suggests they might be shared at the prison. Rugge is not a mean man, and can even exhibit a tender conscience – on occasions. The cellarer agrees readily.

At Saint Benet's they gave more than the usual five per cent to the poor; but now as bishop, his alms giving is best done in public, that all men might see and glorify his Father in heaven. He has a position to maintain for one thing, and for another, he would always want to be known as a friend to the widow and orphan, for he will need their prayers – that he will.

The cellarer is happy to oblige if he can have "what is his' – his cut. Going back though the vaulted underworld, Pacificus does not realise that he is passing by the cells until the head jailer Andrew Bates, a man of round countenance and humour, hails him.

"I thought you'd never come, Father – and he is to be called any minute!"

Pacificus begins to explain that he is no priest confessor but Bates, notoriously deaf, swings wide the cell door all in a hurry and hustles him across the flags.

"Here Fenton, your confessor has come, be quick now," Bates magnanimously fends off Pacificus' objections, mistaking the muffled sounds for an apology really not needed. Why should he care, after all?

In a second, the door shuts behind him and Pacificus finds himself alone with Fenton in a generous cell with enough room for a straw bed, bucket, stool, and a small table which he had lined up under the little window looking north towards Ranworth.

Fenton, standing with his back to the window, is the living image of his son Richard. For a moment Pacificus is taken aback.

"Show me your hands," comes a weary voice from the prisoner.

"My hands?"

"Show me." Fenton, stepping forward, takes them in his own and turns them over, "No, monk, you are not my priest. Mine has nail scars. "

Pacificus pulls his hands back and massages them nervously. "There was a misunderstanding. I came to deliver provisions for the prisoners. I think the jailer doesn't hear too well."

"Oh. Forgive me." Silence falls between them, awkward, frozen.

"Your children – "

"Do not tempt me with them, monk! I will not change my confession!"

Then his vehemence melts in an instant at the thought of them, his wife and what lies ahead of him this day all crowd upon him. "I pray thee, be merciful, do not thou tempt me also."

"They are safe with the eel-catcher. It was I, there at Saint Helen's, when they took your wife. All is well with them. I saw them only last week."

"You are Pacificus?" He exhales, more gasp than sigh, and drops to his stool. "Oh, praise God, praise God! What providence. It is well with them, you say? And – and thank you, also. Do I owe you anything for your trouble?"

Pacificus shakes his head, marveling at how mighty and yet how frail is this thing called man. Such a small wind that shakes the barley.

He bows his head awkwardly and there is another silence, into which Fenton breathes deeply before asking: "Is it true you feel no pain after the fire has your legs?"

"No." He cannot lie to him.

The man shuts his eyes, constantly biting his top lip, every now and again letting out anguished breaths. Eventually he stands, and removing his doublet and jerkin, says, "Richard, the oldest, will be a fine boy, though God knows he has no head for Latin, or the New Learning."

"It may be no sin to him," Pacificus answers. There is much in current scholarship even he cannot abide.

"No. I know." Fenton smiles for the first time, "We put a lot on the boy – wanted too much for him perhaps. He'll no doubt be just as happy with what Pieter can get for him – even happier perhaps; though how he shall look after the others..." he breaks off, shuts tight his lips, his eyes, holding back the flow.

Pacificus thinks to say something consoling about "the God of widows and orphans', but in the end he does not; it wouldn't sound right from the enemy. Anyway Fenton probably knows that much himself.

"No matter, God will judge aright. Perhaps, of your charity, you could pass these on to him? I dare say he'll fit them soon, and I shall not need them after today." His face is set firm now, but his hands tremble as they hold out the clothes.

Pacificus takes them, and probably a few fleas in the bargain; the price you pay for charity.

Fenton pats the clothing now in Pacificus' hand, imagining his sons as young men, wearing them in turn. "They are fine boys," he whispers distractedly.

"And a fine daughter too, I warrant."

"Oh, yes, to be sure! Though little Beth came from another union, e'er her mother met me."

"I see. Well, these will be safe with me. I shall pass them on, when I can." They both stare at the leather jerkin, but still he does not leave. There is something strange in this unmeant meeting, he thinks. And then it comes upon him to ask, "You have peace? About today, I mean?" It is a strange question and he doesn't even feel it was he who asked it.

Fenton's brown eyes look him full in the face. "Aye, but not in myself, nor even in my doctrine, but in Christ. I know whom I have believed. There is peace in that, monk, and I do feel that, even today." He turns away to the window, gazing the way Ranworth lies. "But, of course there is so much still to be done – my wife, my children ...it is planting season now ...but, howbeit, I trust God knows when to harvest each soul. I have wronged no man, nor the king, and my conscience is clear. If he pleases, let it be now."

It is one up on Thomas More, Pacificus thinks. Surely all men say their conscience is clear, but to have no blood on your hands at a time like this must be more assurance than all the indulgences in Christendom. God knows, he envies Fenton that much, and all this assurance without any penance. "I wish I had what you have," he says. And where did that come from?

"But you can!" Fenton is urgent. "Though you must trust Christ, and abandon all else!"

Ah yes, faith and faith alone, make it easy why don't you - *credo quia absurdum?*

Fenton is about to press him, but a key rattles in the lock, heralding the gaunt form of Doctor Spragwell, come to confess the heretic.

Fenton takes Pacificus's arm. "Remember what I have said," he pleads. "Also – please take word to my wife that all is well with me."

"He shall not!" Spragwell exclaims, ruffling out his black robes like a crow. "You are here to confess, not send men at your behest hither and thither! Good morrow, Brother...er...?"

"Pacificus, from Saint Benet's. He is all yours." He bows and retreats before any further questions can be asked, though he does give the condemned man a small nod to reassure him.

He finds Mistress Fenton's door ajar, with none other than Master Cromwell himself inside, his ox-like features softened and speaking kindly to her. Cromwell's own wife had been called Elizabeth too, she and their two daughters both carried off in one summer by the sweating sickness. Pacificus has a moment to observe them both, unremarked by Cromwell as he stands there in the doorway.

The weeks in jail have taken their toll, he sees. She wears the same pale blue bodice and skirt she had worn that day at Saint Helen's, but the bodice is stained and creased now, the lower parts of skirt and chemise dark with filth from the floor. She is thin too, and greyer in the face than the woman he has been idealising without admitting it until now. She stands next to a stool amidst the squalor and stench, in a room half the size of her husband's. It is three steps lower too and the mildew and green mold creep on every wall. Her eyes widen as she catches sight of the doublet and jerkin. Cromwell, seeing her look beyond him as though beholding an apparition, swings round.

"Why, Brother Pacificus, what brings you here?" Cromwell demands.

"I..." He tries not to look discomfited, which is hard, even when His Majesty's Secretary is being gentle. "I bring word from her husband – that all is well with him."

Cromwell's face falls. Bad timing, monk.

"There, my lord! What did I say?" She straightens up, heartened. "He will not recant –and nor will I."

"I see your mind is made up," Cromwell sighs, then carefully positions his hands, joining his fat fingers, as a butcher might lay out his prime pork sausages. "Well, then. Is there anything we might do for you here?" He likes her, this strong woman, that much is plain.

"I am often hungry and I have nothing to read," she ventures. Perhaps she does not think martyrs would complain to their tormentors of anything else.

Pacificus says, "The abbot has sent his own gifts from the abbey here for the prisoners."

"Has he? Has he? How generous of him," Cromwell says. Rummaging in his deep pockets, setting the keys a-clanking, he fetches out a small red leather book. "Do you speak Latin? I thought so. Well, here is a New Testament for you." He passes the compact Vulgate, adding: "If Spragwell thinks it injurious for you, tell him I will it. And," – he moves to go – "if you hold out here 'til doomsday, I might even send my friend the archbishop with his English version!" She thanks him, finding the spirit for a gracious smile, and what a face, even here and now – what a face!

"And perhaps," Pacificus makes bold to say, "she might be given a room with less damp. I know of one becoming available this morning." He gives a small cough.

"Ah. Yes, I see. Very well. I will mention it on my way out, and these clothes are the condemned man's I suppose?"

"Yes." Pacificus hesitates, seeing Cromwell's lawyer's mind at work. "For...for the poor."

Cromwell's features crease in a small, tight smile, not especially warm. He is going for the door but then pulls back momentarily, raising a stout index finger to indicate the intervention of a sudden recollection. "Last night, a mutual friend of ours took delight – after only one glass of wine – in front of Norfolk, in telling me His Majesty's plans to build coastal forts are – what were the words he used? Ah, yes – *intemperate nonsense.* Said he had it on the authority of probably the most experienced naval tactician in England. Of course *who* he would not say, after he had scored and sent Norfolk into a fit; only I wondered what you were doing dining with us last night. And now, this morning, I notice you have the skin of a sailor. Yes. Your scarred wrists I noted at table last night too, but I had you for the criminal type so prevalent in the great houses of late – anything for sanctuary. Today though, I wonder – " He moves closer until Pacificus can feel the warmth of his breath and smell the milk he drank for breakfast – " Perhaps not a criminal, for there is no branding on hands for theft or murder. No. I fancy these are the manacles of...hmmm...peradventure, a galley slave? Aha."

Pacificus stands unflinching under his immense gaze. It feels like coming nose to nose with a bull. He wonders how on earth he would handle him in unarmed combat. All the while he is cursing Rugge too; what a mocker is wine, to loose such pride and vanity from discreet lips. A gift of strong wine is an old trick; clever of you Cromwell.

Now Cromwell in turn is weighing the matter, weighing him, waiting for his eyes to water over, see the pupils dilate, waiting for the signs of fear, of weakness. Master Secretary is at work now, and amidst the immense cogs of all his machinations, these are the thoughts that now form. Should I press this matter now, ask more questions? Cromwell thinks it through. No, let him simmer awhile. Suppose he is one of those errant Hospitallers? Yes, just suppose he is, better keep him where you can see him, and Rugge too. Either way, he will wait, we know where he is – always half the problem. "Take my advice, brother; tread carefully, and take to your cell to pray. It might seem to you that your friend Rugge has risen very high – nay, but it only seems thus; and that only by my leave. How does Bonaventure render it? Ah, yes – like an ape that higher climbs, *plus apparent posteriora eius* – yes, exactly. And the more we may yet see his arse, too." This he almost whispers, and then finishing with one more backward glance, says, "Mistress Fenton, I bid you a very good day." He bows genteelly toward her and then squeezes through the door, his furs sending loose mortar to the floor as he goes.

When his steps are away from the door, she whispers: "My children?"

"Safe." He peers out, to check they are as private as it seems. "Do not fret yourself."

"Oh, thank God! And bless you, bless you!" The hair falls over her face and she brushes it away quickly. "But you must be careful with those!" She lays one slender, white hand and then the other on the clothes. She pauses to steady herself. "They are still warm. Oh, you...you must not risk the children's safety. He will have you followed I think." So pragmatic, women are.

"I will see to it." Best not to promise more.

"Thank you. God bless you, sir." Her hand is touching his. She is not aware of it, he thinks. The jailer is approaching. She looks to the clothes and lets the fabric linger on her fingers, smoothing it as if she had found a crease. "My husband is a good man. Do not let them use him ill, if it is in your power." It is not.

An hour later, even though he had wanted to be on the road, Pacificus is standing at the Lollards Pit, surrounded by urchins gnawing at old bread and jeering.

Cromwell, seated in state on a platform, flanked by Norfolk, Cranmer and Rugge, has not allowed her to be present: "I don't want her fair form garnering public sympathy."

As he is taken from the cart, Fenton sees Pacificus, they exchange a glance, the slightest nod in acknowledgment. Surely here is a righteous man, he thinks, led astray by others though.

Cromwell observes all, a finger drawing back and forth across his lips and chin. Fenton is led to the stake, while the churchmen prepare to summarize the charges for the benefit of example and suspense. He does not resist the high manacles and, as they are fixed, Pacificus feels a spasm in his own scarred wrists too. He massages them under his sleeves, and remembers. Fenton is gagged with a wooden bit, necessary since so many on the continent have been led astray by the fiery sermons of burning Anabaptists – one way for sure of winning an audience. It will not happen here.

Children are allowed forward to spit but he reaches out and stops the lads in front of him from going. "Where are your parents?" They do not answer, glowering resentfully, defiantly – *monks!* They wouldn't have done that a few years ago.

The city clerks call for peace, then Doctor Hearne in his black cap and with a still blacker look on his face, brings his list, and it is long.

"The charges read as follows. That first, he has acted contrary to the mandate of the king. Secondly, he has taught, held and believed that the body and blood of Christ are not present in the sacrament. Thirdly, he has taught and believed that infant baptism does not conduce to salvation. Fourthly, he has rejected the sacrament of extreme unction."

There are pauses throughout to allow for people to tush, tut and cross themselves.

"Fifthly, he has despised and condemned the mother of God and the saints. Sixthly, he has declared that men are not to swear before the authorities. Seventhly, he - infamous sinner - has admitted taking both the bread and wine for the holy Eucharist; eating and drinking the same. Eighthly, that he is found with illegal and heretical books banned under the laws of this realm, namely one by the heretic Tyndale. Ninthly, that unlawfully and unlicensed he has preached that our gracious sovereign king, may no more be head of a church than a Pope or a magistrate."

This last charge sends Doctor Spragwell quite purple. Whether it is genuinely felt, or whether just for a show of piety before the illustrious guests, he springs to his aged feet and cries out so that all can hear: "You desperate villain and arch-heretic! I tell you if there were no faggots here, I would hang you myself, and think that I had done God service!"

But there *are* faggots, and they are quickly lit. There will be no last words from the condemned today, no chance for recantation. Even the smallest watch intently, without too much ado, their faces flickering orange as his blackens and blisters. He screams hideously all the time, braying like a donkey, his head back and forth on the post. There is no divine deliverance for him - no delivering angels. In between times, his desperate gaze fixes straight ahead to one spot. It is old Pieter, standing midpoint in the crowd, staring steadily back at him, nodding occasionally and, no doubt, praying too. Pacificus is moved in a way he has not felt since boyhood. Is it something from then, how he saw Peke die? No, not exactly. Since that time he has stood on many a field of battle, drenched to the skin in the blood of his enemies, and not felt a thing. And yet here, this man and his heretic religion, his eyes, this peace he claims to have; *oh this peace!* Would I be a heretic too, for one good night's sleep?

9

The Whore

Deos enim religuos accepimus, Caesares dedimus
The gods we inherit but the Caesars we created ourselves

It is his longest journey from Norwich. Not the ruts and mud of the road but a journey of a thousand thoughts. How all things conspire against him, the children's plight, the father's words, and now the mother's face – is he to have no peace?

Fenton's courage moved him, but he has seen infidels with courage on the field to shame all of Christendom; you can be wrong and still bear yourself like a man. No, it's not the courage but the tranquil serenity in the face of death that really sticks in Pacificus's throat. He sees nothing of the birds building nests, nor hear the larks. Even the heady fragrance of the hawthorn fails to reach him; his senses only yearn towards the peace that Fenton had. He's like a man who doesn't know he is hungry, forgets what food can be, until the smell of dinner greets him. Fenton had something, but can it be trusted – is it real? How is a man this side of eternity to really know? To serve God was his earliest and most earnest wish, his purest vocation. The knights had warped that, and the fall of Rhodes had dealt it a fatal blow. He staved off more drastic measures by donning a cowl at the abbey. Abbot Rugge had been beneficent it seemed, but now look – he's turning the tables, he wants paying out for his loyalty and his silence on my behalf.

Perhaps, he thinks, Rugge was sincere enough in the beginning; it's only the times have turned him. What did Grand Master Villiers say? "Judge no man 'til thou hast trod his ramparts, fought his battles"? Is this what God requires of him, then? To stand with Rugge against the king, against this new world order, for what? The old world, the Pope, to save St Benets? Certainly as a younger man he might have seen it no other way than this, but now, now he stands beyond a river of blood, an ocean of gore, which baptises every question, colours every motive, sullies every simple pleasure that might have been on the other bank. Damn Rugge! Damn Cromwell! Yes, and the king too.

He is late, past Vespers and supper, only just in time for Compline. Others have heard already about their abbot, that he has acknowledged Henry, that he is released, that he shall be bishop and abbot, all in one. Even through the customary silence after Compline, Pacificus can see they are all buzzing with the news, its all over their faces – dying to ask him for more detail now he is back from Norwich. But he will not break silence, let them wait till Chapter. He eats nothing, even after the walk and sleeps ill, rising for Nocturne in the small hours, doing his best to purge the memories of all he's heard in the last two days.

The psalter is good for clearing the mind. He is comforted to hear the lusty but flat singing of his friend the almoner. Pacificus begins once more to think that he could go on like this forever, forget the world and its troubles, shut them all out; the heroes and covetous men. But then he remembers that the world and its troubles will not forget them, and that no matter how clever a web Rugge spins, it is probable that the old ways and the world they have known will not survive the decade. What was it Rugge said? Ah yes, the

afterglow – that's what this was, still the sun, still round and warm, still beautiful even, perhaps even more sublime as the horizon nears, but a setting sun nonetheless.

Later on at Chapter the prior gives them the news in person. An act of parliament will have the bishopric of Norwich surrender its ancient lands to the crown – old Bishop Nykke will turn in his grave, Pacificus muses – and that in its place Saint Benets and Hickling Priory and its possessions will given to the said bishopric *in commendam*, and divine service thereby maintained. From henceforth the Bishop of Norwich will also, and hereafter be Abbot of Saint Benets too. As Prior Thomas reads the words, a look of releif spreads from face to face like a incoming spring tide fanning out over the saltmarshes. Few are thinking about what it cost to secure such an unprecedented assurance from the state; for now all that is in their minds is; he's done it, bless his soul, Father Abbot has done it, we are spared.

These things, along with the turmoil of his recent, vivid experience, Pacificus thinks on all that next day at his work on the rood screen. Rugge's big gamble, his only hand in the game has been dealt. And it appears that he didn't need kings when he had aces. Or perhaps it was knaves? For how will they word that act of parliament? The devil is in the detail; how many monks will stay on? How many men does it take, for example, to maintain divine service? Ten, twenty? Surely not the whole sixty something now in residence. He knows these lawyers, these courtiers; there is usually malign intent behind vague wording. Why did it not say to keep a thriving house of prayer, a just economic community, a bulwark for the poor, the widow, the orphan and the leper against a sea of troubles? Why just divine service? There is mischief enough here. And how, with their £585 income, will they cover the outgoings of both the abbey and the Norwich See? The bishop's palace alone would swallow two years income without any trouble at all, let alone cathedral repairs.

Today he will try to finish his Saint George panel. He starts filling in the detail on the dragon under Saint George's feet, remembering the lively dragon's head from Toppes' hall. He is not pleased with the eyes but makes a good start at George's face. The parish clerk clutching the chalice and primers, says he thinks George looks like Richard II in his youth, before he was corrupted. They have a brief exchange, but Pacificus does not look away from his work.

"Why must kings always become so?" Pacificus goes on painting as the clerk muses aloud. Is he luring me into something here? Perhaps he's in Cromwell's pay, setting me up, just to denounce me later – it pays to be paranoid sometimes.

He makes some quip about his coracle, says he wishes someone would stop it corrupting, or else one day he'll sink before ever he makes Saint James' staithe. The clerk goes his way, but Pacificus still thinks on his words; it is a good point well made. Richard failed to exert the people's rights against the high born – surely a monarch's prerogative. He was strong enough to face Watt Tyler, but not strong enough to reign in the aristocracy. Pacificus' own grandfather had told him so repeatedly. "In my grandfather's time," he'd say – meaning their illustrious forebear, the great Sir Thomas Erpingham – "the earls and barons had a limit to how high they could ascend. In those days the king was anointed, untouchable, the defender of the poor. But that was before Bolingbroke rose like Icarus towards the heavens and took all unto himself." He always omitted to mention it was Thomas Erpingham more than any other man that helped Bolingbroke establish the house of Lancaster. Its a detail that spoils the narrative, for, in the intervening years, the family had all become good Yorkists. "Since then the curse of God is on our realm – the curse of God!" Perhaps he is right; now we have a grasping Bolingbroke and a Watt Tyler rule from the same throne. Yes, Henry had dealt with his father's henchmen in the star chamber when he came to the thrown, but if anyone had thought that this meant a less centralised state, then that delusion had long passed. If a man was deluded enough to think he could dissolve something as divinely sanctioned as marriage, then what hope could there be for the lesser institutions like the monasteries? He thinks of old Spragwell's purple face at the Lollard's pit as he'd read out the charges. Its not enough for weak and ambitious men to buckle under the lies, they always insist, at the point of sword and flame, that everyone else must also confess what no sane man could believe true. Damn them.

Later that day, he stops by the Bure on his return, to bail out the coracle. Gus disappears into the reeds after fowl. While tethering at the staithe later, Pacificus sees a young peasant girl, thick auburn hair and ragged clothing, trudging along the road from the causeway to the hospital. He has seen her this winter among the poor at the gate. He watches closely while following her on the same rise towards Saint James, for he cannot get the thought from his mind that something about her is not quite as it should be. And then he knows; it is her feet. She is not barefoot but wears turnshoes, simple leather shoes notable for being in the older style, but also far beyond her purse, or foot size. In a trice he remembers his suppressed envy at the monks of Binham, for having an able cobbler in their precinct; and how, being only few in number, they had arranged brass buckles rather than laces for their shoes – which were turnshoes too.

"Prithee, damsel!" He catches her before they reach the hospital. "How do mén call you?"

Her freckled cheeks are crimson from the walk, and with a saucy lilt of the head she says: "Margaret, though no saint, if you're buying." Gus sniffs her and she bends to ruffle his head.

"Maid, I am not!" He knows others of the order have done so. Dear Mother of God, she cannot be older than twelve or thirteen.

She smiles, then indicates towards the staithe. "You're the one who paints the saints at Saint Helen's. I expect they visit you, the saints?" He shakes his head but she continues as if he were talking about the weather or the harvest. "They came to me once, there at Saint Helen's, in the Lady chapel."

"You? What...what do you mean? Visited you? Who, child?"

"I cannot say. When I was of an age for my first communion, me and the other girls took turns to keep the light for the Virgin – that it should always be lit. I was there on my own one evening, summer last; it was a week after my mother took ill with the sweats and died. I was about my work when I felt a burning warmth all over, and a light behind me – not so much to see with the eyes, but to feel, if you can understand my meaning. It was like being immersed in love and comfort. If heaven is like it, it shall be well."

"There were no voices?" he says, but she shakes her head. "And yet you remember clearly this comfort?"

"It was for my mother's passing I thought, now that she was gone and I was left on the parish. The priest took me on as his maid."

"I've heard tell he has a short temper," he says, meaning nothing much by the remark except to set her at ease. Yet instantly her face clouds over and she exhales painfully through clenched teeth, and then in a shudder, says: "Aye. And he has no wife." Her eyes stare across the marshes south to where Saint Helen's spire pierces the skyline. "So I ran – ran away across the river."

"It's not too late, you know; not for anyone."

These words he attempts with little conviction and she, detecting the staged piety, shoots back: "Oh, you would save me! What, join a nunnery?"

"They've had worse, child." He meant himself, but she's in no mood for humour and doesn't take his meaning, thinks he considers her beneath him, something unclean.

"Don't 'child' me! I have wits at least, and I know there'll be no nunneries or monasteries in a year or two – no alms for the poor neither, so we must look to ourselves." Her defiant glare subsides to a hollow smile. "At least the priest showed me what men like, so I'll not starve."

Pacificus tries hard to clear his mind. All right. Back to business. He points to the shoes. "How came you by these?"

"I ...er...I have...that is...men pay in different ways."

"Think carefully before you answer this." He looks at the buckles, and gambles on a bluff. "Those shoes belonged to the monk whose body was found just down there. Are you telling me that Brother Bede gave these to you? Speak fairly to me now, remember a dead man's reputation is in your hands. I'll do what is in my power to protect you, and him if he lapsed, only I must have the truth." But he need not have cautioned her, for he can tell instantly by her half-open mouth that she did not know it. "Ah, very well. Then tell me how you came by them."

"I found them, by the river, but there was none to claim them, I swear it."

"Here?" He points to the staithe and the area where the body was found.

"No, and I didn't filch them from no corpse neither."

"Whence then, if not here?"

"Up river, not far."

"Up river?" This is strange news indeed. "You will take me?"

She nods. "If I can keep them."

"You're in no place to barter, Margaret, just take me there, now, if you will."

"Suit yourself, monk, if you don't mind being seen with me going into the woods." She raises a cheeky eyebrow and vaunts her lips, the sapphire gaze at once drawing him, for she is a beauty in her bedraggled way, yet angering him that such a one has been so corrupted. He tells her to wait past Saint James settlement in the copse by the road to Horning and that he will attend her presently. She asks him for food, if he has any. He says he will bring what he can, and Gus approves with a sneeze – surely it is time for a little something. She sets off into the trees, and Pacificus goes to find Simon the leper. He finds him working on some weaving behind the lazar house.

"You again."

"You have not lost that bile on your chest. Do they treat it?"

"What is it, brother? Be brief. For you see – " he lifts his basket – "I am busy with making amends for my life, *adjusting to my new destiny*, as you once so eloquently put it."

"I must needs speak with you Simon."

"Again? What this time?"

"Away from here," he whispers. Simon sits out of earshot of the others but even so. He hesitates, and Pacificus presses his case. "Please. I'm begging you."

They walk to the copse, Simon slowly and wheezing, his distemper of the lungs not shaken since the winter, Pacificus explaining about the girl and the shoes. They reach

the copse and see the girl's pale face looking out for Pacificus and the promised food. Catching sight of Simon her face drains of colour.

"I will cover myself, child," the leper calls out to her. He buttons the linen napkin across his lower face and then continues, "Are you not afrighted of this monk, then? They say he killed poor Bede!"

Pacificus does not rise to this, and Margaret takes him by surprise with her reply: "I know what they say, but the same people would swear the prior a virgin; they know nothing. Besides he has not the face of a murderer."

"You're the first person to say so." Simon laughs. "And me? What of my face?"

There is a hush, and then she says to Simon, with more tenderness and sympathy than Pacificus would have imagined from such a one: "My mother said that if I believed the sacrament, and said my Aves and Paternosters, there would be new bodies one day. When these..." she looks at her feet, "when these ones is used up."

"And all sins will be forgiven," Simon adds.

"You're making a mock of me," she says.

He mutters in response nothing more than: "No. I wasn't thinking of you."

Then Pacificus intervenes: "Now, about these shoes you took..."

She leads them down through the woods to a place where the alders give onto the reed banks hiding the river, sometimes fifty feet of reeds before the open water on this stretch, sometimes only ten or twenty. It is little frequented because the road is near and direct.

She says she came here collecting wood – why should she not be telling the truth? She points them to an area of mud bank between the reeds and the alders, about fifty feet long. It lies just opposite the cutting joining Ranworth broad to the river Bure. If tall enough, it's possible to see straight down the dyke to Saint Helen's from there, for it runs straight. Pacificus interrupts her: "You have not been back since?" She has not. So he and Simon go forward slowly, scanning the ground. Albeit smutched by rain fallen over the last three weeks, small barefoot prints are still clear enough to see, indenting less than an inch.

"You came this way, I see, but what is this?" Another set of prints enters the place from the alders. They match the shoe size: Bede's, for sure. "So he comes here, a strange spot for spotting the abbey swans – they usually go downstream if at all, but perhaps he didn't know. So – what does he do next?"

Simon points his crook to the broken reeds: "He walks into the water!"

"But he takes his shoes off first," Margaret says hastily, pointing to the place where there is a jumble of her prints and his. "That's just where I found them, set neatly side by side. But then – where did he go?"

"Into the water – look at the reeds, all snapped as they are."

"To swim on an afternoon that cold?" Simon sounds sceptical.

"No. No, obviously not." Pacificus thinks back to the tide marks of mud around Bede's knees. "No. I think he went in to kneel and pray."

"But...a strange place to come, withal?"

"It's quiet here. Perhaps he was desperate to find the damned swans and get in out of the cold, sank to his knees to implore the help of the Virgin? Or maybe he was doing penance for some sin, and wanted peace?"

"Plenty of places nearer." Margaret looks unconvinced, bending to touch the place where the shoes had been. "Even the reeds in a hundred feet of the abbey can hide a man's sins, I should know."

It is a point well made and Pacificus knows it, but now Simon is getting impatient. "So. He kneels up to his waist in water to pray, freezes his humors and dies, and is swept downstream."

"But...how can he?" Pacificus looks perplexed. "There are still ten feet of reeds. If he died here, he would have stayed here. And another thing – his mouth was filled with mud. No. His face was held into it until he drowned. Mayhap, someone forced him to kneel. They launched him elsewhere, but where?" He steps slowly, always looking, along the shore, for all the world like a bittern on the lookout for fish, until at last he sees the indents in the sand that tell a stranger tale still. Something is dragged along, leaving a double trail – a man's feet, he thinks. But who – or what – does the dragging?

Simon points at the prints with his crutch: "This is strange indeed, deep, almost triangular ruts, almost like the hooves you would see on a devil in the old paintings."

Hugh stoops and looks closer. Whatever in heaven or hell it was, it made deeper imprints because it was dragging the added weight of the dead body. "Hmm," he says, "this is...odd."

"Demons?" Simon says.

"No. I think not."

"But verily – you do still believe in their doings?" Simon says, wrapping his cloak about him tighter, and glancing anxiously around.

"No, I did not mean that," Pacificus hedges, pausing to examine the mysterious hoof-ish marks again. Does he believe in devils that walk in our world? Many books attest their existence, not least the scriptures, he thinks. Layamon's Brut shows he believes in daemons and spirits; but for all that, not as a savage believes in them, for he has learnt these things from Wace, who in turn had what he knew from Geoffrey of Monmouth, and he from Apuleius. And who did they all track back to then, these tales of mystery and legend, the stories of Arthur and the times of old? Perhaps Plato's phenomenology of the life-world; and perhaps Plato had met Epicurus – and certainly Epicurus was on the side of the devils, whether he knew it or not. But then, I suppose most of the devil's men serve him unawares, and perhaps do it all the better for it, too.

"Well, what prithee did you mean?" Simon says with growing agitation after the long pause.

"What? Oh!" Pacificus comes back with a start, from his rambling thoughts, "I meant...er ...that the trail leads to where the reeds are almost non-existent – where a body would more easily catch the tide."

"But...why not conceal a body here? There could be nowhere better." Simon looks in puzzlement at the place.

"No, his body was *meant* to be seen – a warning perhaps?"

Simon shakes his head, unconvinced, "I still say they look like the hooves of devils." Prodding at one of the deep prints with his crutch, he adds, darkly: "They say 'tis the Antichrist reigns; why not have his ghostly minions murder good monks and send them floating past their abbeys?"

"It's not a jesting matter. You don't believe that, Simon!" Pacificus speaks sharply. He doesn't like this talk, especially with the girl almost within earshot.

"Well, I don't know. Diabolic hoof prints that appear from nowhere and disappear without trace – it is an omen of some sort, or perhaps a portent of things to come."

"Avaunt!"

"Well then brother, you tell me. If they are the prints of a man – where does he come from and where does he disappear to, eh?"

"You forget the lass, her prints are here too." He whispers, though he judges her not near enough to catch their words.

"Her? She has neither the strength nor the passion – "

"To drown a half frozen monk with a pair of good shoes when she is barefoot? She does indeed have a choleric temperament along with that hair, believe me; and you should have seen her eyes when she spoke of the man who wronged her."

"Oh, yes, but Bede? Pacificus, can you really imagine him taking advantage of a woman?"

"Who's to say? We all have failed women one way or another, at some time in our lives."

"What? Meaning? Why did you say that?" Simon clutches and reclutches his crutch. He's caught on the raw.

"Later, man, later – first this damsel." She is wandering closer now, the dog sniffing about her feet. Pacificus gives her the promised food from his scrip, but he charges her straight to tell no one about any of this for the moment. She is glad to go, and Gus trots alongside her, the little Judas – seems even dogs cannot resist the warmth of a female spirit.

As the two men turn back into the copse, Pacificus feels Simon's eyes on him. He must tackle this with care and diplomacy. It will not be easy. They retrace their steps in

silence as far as the road, and as they rise from the marsh, a chill easterly wind catches them. The alders shudder, their catkins fall like stars. How to start? How to begin this?

"Cecil – "

"Don't play up to me, brother! My name now is Simon. Let's not complicate things."

This is not going to go well. "Forgive me – Simon. I...I suppose you heard, Fenton was burned this week."

"They gagged him I hear," Simon answers tersely. "Even the Lutherans and Swiss do so to many of his sort, that they may be dispatched at night – you know, avoid an outcry."

"Yes, I've heard it is so, though his end was nothing secret. Well, anyway, I spoke with him before his ordeal. He let slip that the oldest child was not his, and then I remembered what you said when we had spoke last – when I mentioned the maid Beth. You...well, you behaved yourself in such a way as I could not forget. I knew she hailed from Aylsham, so close by us. I had not thought to know all the business from home after I left for Rhodes, but I am surprised you never mentioned this matter, particularly because – "

"Because what? Because it would affect my oath as a knight? Or cast doubt on my vocation?" Simon turns and stands sideways on the path, struggling to face his brother. He was speaking quickly now, as if he knew this conversation would one day find him, as if a good defense could ease a man's conscience. "Or is it because a true knight never runs from difficulty? Like you, I suppose!"

"Cecil? I joined the order with a clear conscience! My vocation was from boyhood – you know that."

"Oh yes! And nothing to do with running from the marriage father wanted for you!"

"Oh!" Pacificus waved the thrust aside. "You know our father – always some scheme to restore our position, but uniting with the Howards was never going to happen. The Duke would never have consented. We're yesterday's family – it was just a fancy."

"Really?" The leper's voice rises in sarcasm and rage now. "Father's oldest dream – planned from your cradle – mother's dying wish?"

Pacificus grabs a fistful of cloth at the man's chest and raises his fist in fury. "Don't you dare speak of her like that! You leave our mother out of this, or we are no longer brothers, so help me we are not!" His face contorts, saliva running through gritted teeth onto his chin. "I sought a *heavenly city* and *incorruptible crown*, Mother knew that!"

"And so you abandoned us all for a patch of Mediterranean dirt instead, to become – become what, pray? The great Sir Hugh?" Simon now grabs him likewise and the two stagger unevenly in the trees. "So, don't you judge me then about the girl's mother! What have you ever loved but bloodshed and your own glory? Yes, all right then, I wronged her – and I carry that, and I pay for it! Mary and Joseph, brother – look at me! I am paying now." His voice breaks into an anguished cry, repeating it, "Look at me!" He brings the scaly, white fist down before both their eyes and the heavy sobs convulse him forwards. Little by little they disentangle fists, and then embrace – a long, heaving, crumpling embrace. And even with the anguish, with all that has gone sour and died, it feels good to be close again, even like this. For until these last ten years, these two had been close, had fought alongside each other and seen many winters. But since Rhodes, Simon's slow, inexorable deterioration, and Pacificus' agony of mind had locked them both away. They had both been, as the Italians called it, *uomoni rispetatti*, honoured and respected men. Now they are alike lay in dust and ashes, brothers of ignominy and quiet despair.

Eventually they sit side by side with their backs against the alders, spent, vulnerable. Simon scrubs the tears from his face with the linen cloth, and lets it drop. "Father threatened to disinherit me when I told him of Elizabeth's condition, for we were betrothed, secretly. He would not have it. Not good enough for us, the noble family, *sans terre*. He said he would disown me!" He breaks off at this point, tearing impotently at sparse weeds under the trees with his clawed fists. "I couldn't face myself afterwards – or think of any other woman. I couldn't. So I ran to you – to take it out on the Saracens, some penance that was."

Some more ripping at the undergrowth, more choking breath. And Pacificus stares sightlessly towards the reeds, the broad, the sky, wondering at how things could ever have played out as they did. He remembers the broad-shouldered, cheerful seventeen-year-old he left on the quayside at Yarmouth all those years ago. Who could have foreseen what life would hold in store? So many threads, such a large tapestry.

Eventually he hears the abbey bell ringing out and remembers the present with its duties and obligations. Getting up stiffly, wiping the last traces of his own tears away, he says, "You say you lost interest in women? Even mine intended fair lady Howard?"

Simon's ruined face twists into a grin. "What? That sour-faced pudding? No fear Hugh! And you were well away from that, too!"

10

The Spy

Cave quid dicis, quando, et cui
Beware of what you say, when, and to whom

Simon is leading Pacificus to the eel-catcher's cottage. They go to deliver the clothing to the children from their father. Simon would not go alone, he needs support, not that they will say anything, or not yet anyway. The afternoon is blustery but dry, the geese, coots and ducks seem unhurried by it, or anything else; for them it is business as usual. Pacificus is uneasy; he would rather not have come, he may be missed. He feels eyes everywhere these days, and there are, even now.

They emerge into the clearing by the cottage but there are no signs of life beyond the wisp of smoke coiling this way then that, as the wind makes up its mind. The children have been sent to the field to work, only the bairns are left, and they are shut inside with the adults. Doors are shut and barred for good reason. A stranger from Yarmouth has come. He goes by the name John Smith – not his real name but best for everyone's safety to keep it simple. Today the door is closed and the children away, for there is grave news from the coast and grave decisions to be made. Those closeted indoors do not hear the brothers approach because of the little ones playing and the whirling wind in the alder and birch. What a day to do a surprise visit!

Thinking at first there really is no one present, Simon and Pacificus go to inspect the extension Pieter and the boys have been building. It is then they overhear: "Yes, Brother Smith, all six men captured in port and held for Cromwell's agents – they will hang at the least. Only pray God they hold out and say nothing of our whereabouts before they die."

"And the ship?" This is old Sarah's voice. "And the men at Antwerp? They have been warned, ja?"

"That's the worst of it, Sister Smith, I am told Cromwell will send spies on the same ship in hope of trapping more honest men in Antwerp – but what can we do?"

Suddenly there is a commotion. "What, who is that? Beth! What are you doing there listening?"

In the commotion and shouting that follow, the visiting Mr. Smith, who is not really cut out for a life of espionage and already in fear for his life, turns abusive and threatening; "she is a spy perhaps, how long has she dwelt with you? How well do we really know her anyway? Suppose she is in Cromwell's pay too – she looks old enough for sure!"

Pacificus is thinking it might be a good time to leave. But, as he turns to go, he sees Simon go for the front door – she's his daughter, after all. The ensuing minutes of explanation and argument are not easy. Sarah insists they all – Beth included – sit round the table on their odd assortment of stools and home-made chairs. "I cannot see so well, you must sit down, all of you." She is not the sort of woman you can easily deny. This is her home after all and these children, this late fruit of providence if not the womb, has awoken in her all the fierceness of a mother's love.

Smith of Yarmouth is beside himself. First the girl, now this papist and a leper – who will be next, the Duke of Norfolk? As it happens, the next through the door is Richard and Piers, both wide-eyed at so many visitors, and at the sight of a leper standing near. But there is more to Simon than leprosy, and it is he who talks most and best. He has an interest in the children's safety, as does the monk, and they must be privy to the whole story, says he grandly, so that he may discern how they might "effect a solution."

Smith, whose face grows more pale and moist wit every word, scorns him. "Even if we told you more, how could you prove yourselves trustworthy? And how can a monk and a leper be of any help in this?"

Pieter was thinking it could have been put a little more gently, when Simon speaks up again. "I see time is of the essence, and we know these children, as you see, are every day in danger. Very well, I will tell you what only a handful of men know in England, knowledge that you will see renders us at your mercy, even as you are at ours."

"Simon!" Pacificus cannot believe his ears. He gestures urgently to silence his brother who ignores him and plunges on: "We are Sir Hugh and Cecil Erpingham, Hospitaller knights of Saint John, who have faced Saracens a hundred to one and seen them repelled on land and sea. Yes, that's right, this really is Sir Hugh, scourge of the Barbary fleet, who made Barbarossa himself appear before him without sword or dagger – "

"Stop prating like a fool! Enough I say – Simon!" But his brother goes on all the more, trying to impress his daughter by these incautious words. The adults seem to freeze in open-mouth astonishment and the children's eyes are nearly popped from their heads. Can it be that the kind monk with the paintbrushes was really a holy knight after all? Don't you have to be tall to be a knight? They look at him and he at them, resigned, and he thinks, tell the whole world why don't you? He sighs. What's said is said, now let the poor creatures have their father's clothes.

He lays the bundle of clothes on the table, and begins to explain. "I was with your mother, and your father on the day of his death." He passes the jerkin and doublet carefully with both hands. "He bade me give you these, Richard. He wanted you to know he loved you – all of you – but especially he said that if he was over-harsh with you, Richard, he was sorry for it; he meant not to bruise you, lad."

There comes on them a double hush now. Richard, and soon Piers too were handling the clothing. There were no tears now, just sober nods. They had not taken it so the day Pieter had brought home the news from Norwich. Then – even knowing it must happen – they had raged in bitterness of soul against the world. Both boys had taken to the marshes and wept till their eyes burned, then both, quite independently had vowed a bloody oath that they would not let the flames have their mother too. Beth had wept much too that day, but she did so cuddling James and Samuel. She loved her stepfather, though they had vied daily. He was all she had ever known, and he had never treated her less than the others. And now he was truly gone, she felt the loss of his censure as much as a less sulky girl might feel the loss of a father's affirmation. A river must needs banks, and Beth had been like a spring torrent. Today she bears the news and the sight of his clothing with a silent gulp, and a tingling coldness all through her body. Beth lifts up the bairns to touch the garments for themselves. Samuel says "Papa," a number of times, and this undoes her. She cannot hold back the hot tears. "Yes, darling one, it is Papa's. Now come away and play."

At this point Smith starts again; he cannot see why these two strange men would busy themselves with the children's welfare, what business should it be of theirs, whoever they are.

"Call it providence," Pacificus almost groans, his head is in his hands. "I am sworn to help them, and – "

Simon takes it up, "And by reason of another matter, that cannot be discussed."

'John Smith' is only barely satisfied, and now Pacificus, losing patience, is curt with him: "My brother has shared information with you – and Saint Stephen alone knows who else, beside you – that I'd rather he had not. And yet, sir, we know nothing of you; though if we were spies as you imagine, we would have enough on you either way, for your complicity in this act of piracy, smuggling or treason is manifest. So please, unburden yourself of this information, before I lose my patience."

And so, reluctantly, and even in front of the children, Smith recounts the whole tale. He tells them that Cuthbert Tunstall, Bishop of London, and the man notorious for seeking and destroying Tyndale's Bibles in London, is now sent to the continent on official business for the king. His way passed through Antwerp, where he learned of English New Testaments for sale. He reasoned that if he could purchase and destroy them in Antwerp, at source so to speak, he could slow the flood of Bibles entering England. In the course of events, he met Augustine Pockington, an English merchant, who reportedly knew where copies of the Scriptures could be located. Pockington was no Lollard, just a shrewd businessman and a friend to any who brought him trade and Tyndale was one such man.

Pockington agreed to sell the New Testaments to the Bishop for four times the normal rate, and Tunstall agreed, thinking he had God by the toe when really he had the devil by the fist. He bought the Bibles and had them burned in Antwerp, not knowing Pockington had these Bibles from Tyndale himself, who welcomed the finance for the revised edition. So the Bishop got the old edition, Pockington got the thanks, and Tyndale got the money, with which he was able to finance the printing and distribution of his new edition.

It is a consignment of this revised edition that now waits shipment from Antwerp to England. The six men from Yarmouth were bound on Fellingham's new four-master that very Thursday but now they are arrested, held at the tolhouse by turnkey Jacob Eames, and it is rumoured by people who know these things that Cromwell will send spies in their place on his and Fellingham's four-master. Mr Smith wrings his hands until Pacificus thinks the man's finger bones might pop out and drop to the floor.

"So why have you come here?" Pacificus asks him. "Your presence is a threat to this whole house, surely?"

But it is Pieter, quiet this long time, who now speaks. "He has come to me, I was a sailor a long time ago, and because maybe I know someone who can help, but I do not."

"And you Smith, you have nothing more to report, nothing more to offer?" Simon demands, as the worry-stricken spy shakes his head. "Very well then, you are best out of here, my man. And tell no one where you have been, or what you have heard here today, or believe me, I will find you."

Smith of Yarmouth seems eager enough to leave and when he is gone there is silence once more. Pacificus weighs the options. "Will the men in Yarmouth talk under torture? Have they more than their own lives to lose?" Pieter nods.

"And this house, these children, they will likely be exposed?" He nods again and Pacificus slams his hand on the table. "God's teeth, man! And all this over some heretic books!"

"The word of God," Sarah corrects him.

"With two thousand mistakes in it, More said, so don't lecture me, woman! For one thing, we read the Scriptures every day at the abbey."

"Ja, ja – but from Jerome's Latin, with the papal stamp and the papal meanings." She's a plain speaker is Sarah; Pacificus ought to beware, Simon thinks. Perhaps they all are, these Dutch. He smiles behind his facecloth.

"And you cannot wait for the Bishop's Bible? You have to get yourselves hung for this one?"

Sarah, unruffled, says the two are not the same thing at all, and if he's going to do nothing more than insult Master Tyndale's scholarship in the original tongues, then he knows where the door is.

More silence but Pieter is smiling. "When I pray," he says slowly, "I will beseech the good Lord to send his angel to release these six men, so they can disappear – say, to Holland. And I will ask him to send another, faster vessel to Antwerp to warn our friend Mister Pockington and retrieve those Bibles. For if we do not tie a knot in each end of this rope, I cannot see how we, here, will escape loss or harm."

Simon steps forward. "We will need a light vessel, but big enough for the cargo. Is there much?"

"Oh – wait a minute, I prithee! Wait a minute!" Pacificus raises his hands, then he takes his brother outside to talk. As soon as they are far enough away from the house, he snaps: "By all the saints, have you lost your mind? Life might not be all it used to be for you since – well, since we returned – but...but this ...this is...it's lunacy. Or is your judgment clouded because you are fixed on winning the affection of your daughter?"

"Not at all. The eel-catcher is right, Hugh. Can't you see?" Simon retorts stoutly. "If there are any *loose ends* Cromwell's men will get more names than they know what to do with – and yours among them, I dare swear. No, I say we get to Yarmouth and do as he suggests."

"Oh, I see. Break men from prison, commandeer a vessel, outrun Cromwell's spies – which, if you missed it, ride a four-master – and perhaps even his Majesty's fleet, and...and then smuggle contraband back into a Cinque port without being caught? You make it sound like a day's hawking."

"If anyone could do it – look, Hugh, don't walk away, please!" Simon has his habit by the sleeve, pleading. "I've just found her again."

So, after some quick discussion, and more than a little cajoling and pleading, the two men return to the cottage. No one has moved from around the table; Piers is so far forward on the stool he is virtually falling off it. Beth is down on the floor, occupying the little ones with pebbles and Pieter's whittled animals. Pieter says nothing, he sees the hand of God in all this, and he's not the only one. Pacificus feels a net tighten; he should have seen this coming with the children, the trip to Norwich, the conversation with the merchant John Toppes and the one he overheard. One, two, three, four, bam! Got you! He feels like the Pharaoh looking at the locusts and frogs – you couldn't invent a God like this. Want to make him laugh? Then tell him your five-year plan! Maybe it's Sir Thomas Erpingham's Lollard prayers being answered a century late, maybe his own inarticulate cries to heaven in Fenton's cell, but dear Christ, what a way to answer a man whose only prayer is for peace in his soul.

Simon gives Pieter and the children a nod as if to say, 'watch this'. A moment later his brother breathes out in a laboured and anguished way, then buries his head in his hands on the table. Well and truly caught is he now, well and truly. There is an old saying among his former comrades that in love as in war, it is the man who despises his life in this world, the one who sallies forth with reckless abandon that is more likely to keep it. He will do this thing, and do it as if his life depended on it, which it yet may. He rests there for a few seconds then raises his eyes to Beth, risen to her feet and watching him. She looks at him, startled. It's like a different man, energy and intensity burst from every ounce and crease in his face. The man Rugge lost and looked for – is back.

"Maid, go catch up with that man, Smith of Yarmouth, tell him to get word to the jailed men's wives, if they have them."

"What message?"

"Prepare to sail on Toppes' ship, the Pelican, this coming Thursday on the evening tide, with their husbands, *deo volente*." She nods, and goes.

"Master Eel-catcher, you can gain us access to this Merchant Pockington in Antwerp?" Pieter nods. Pacificus spies Fenton's matchlock, sword and knife atop the mantel. "Good. Then, you be at Yarmouth too, and bring your weapons."

"But I am sworn to lift a hand against no man, as the Gospel commands."

"I see." He stares now at Simon, his big mouthed little brother. "Well, that's a fine thing, isn't it? The first privateers on the seas without arms. Let's hope Cromwell's agents have turned Anabaptist too, and we can all hold hands together, wait to see who is predestined to swing first."

"Hugh!"

"All right, never mind. But bring them for me, at least. Have you shot and wad?"

"Yes, sir!" Richard pipes up, though Pieter frowns at him.

"Good. Well then, eel-catcher, you must go tomorrow to Alderman Toppes in Norwich with this message, and see that he alone hears it.

Tell him Brother Pacificus says, “The bishop remembers your kindness to the poor and wishes to reward you – that is to say, reward you secretly. He has heard of honest merchants suffering from Fellingham’s pride and Cromwell’s avarice. He wishes to covertly redress this by sending a gentleman to Yarmouth this Thursday, to ensure the Pelican makes Antwerp and back before ever Fellingham’s boat looms on the horizon. In recompense, let the Pelican transport some poor Christians on their way to pilgrimage, and bring back a small tonnage of goods from Antwerp as the said gentleman will direct. This, my lord bishop enjoins you to perform to the gentleman by way of a payment for his services to you and your guild. You may send permissions for your captain with the bearer of this message, but nothing more, not by any means. Furthermore this business must never be mentioned in my presence or to another living soul, if you wish my palace in Norwich to benefit you again. What almsgiving we do, we do in secret, that our father may reward us openly.” Now. Have you got that and how does that sound? Or are you going to tell me now the New Testament enjoins you only to tell the unvarnished truth?”

“You...you are well connected, sir.” Pieter does not rise to the thrust. “This is wondrous indeed, though I fear I will need to write such words down.”

“Very well man, but the living minute they are committed to memory, burn all trace. That much is crucial.”

“Yes, yes, as you say! But – who, pray, is this gentleman?”

“Them, for there shall be two,” Hugh says glancing at Simon, “must be conjured from these marshes.”

“Aha!” Simon had barely laughed more joyously these four years together. It was good to hear it again. “And you think that you will even make gentleman of a leper?”

“Oh, we can find clothes to disguise you. Cesare Borgia had a leather mask to hide his syphilis, it is a thing almost respectable in Paris and Rome. But this – ” he pats his tonsure in jest – ”this will need one of Hamberly’s velvet caps, with all its bilaments, its ribbons, its feathers and its pearls! Outfits will be the least of our troubles, but yes, a trip to Hamberly's when he is at Mass might be beneficial to our enterprise. Can you wear calf boots, Simon?"

The leper rubs his calves and shins, but he feels only a faint tingle. "Riding boots would be better, then I could strap them tight to suit."

There is more to discuss than this, and still more that the brothers plan on their walk back through the marshes. Three days is not long, for sure, but it will suffice. Any longer and the six men might yield. As they set out Simon catches sight of his Beth returning from her errand to Smith of Yarmouth. He leaves his brother and walks across to wait for her. "He understood the message?"

"Yes, well enough."

"I hope he can be trusted, then. The man's as jumpy as a bag of ferrets." He frowns, pointing to the bruising just visible around her jaw. "You are happy here? You are treated well?" He's heard all sorts about these heretics. She explains about their trip back to the farm. He begins to scold her, but then wonders whether he should, whether she knows who he is. She has heard his name now – did her mother never mention the name Cecil Erpingham to her? He looks at her face, but cannot read it; the way she heightens the eyebrows when she listens, the easy but straight smile when he gives up on his

reproof. She waits a moment, but he says no more, only looks at her so she curtseys and turns to go, giving him no hint. Perhaps, he thinks, she does know but I am odious to her, dead to her; I deserve no more. He watches her step down the path, the hem of her blue cotton dress tugging on the grass. *Oh, tug harder grass, tug harder.*

She vanishes round the corner of the cottage, out of his sight. So he does not see her walk behind and run up-river to her quiet place, the place where she can think. She reaches the hemp swing at the water's edge, the one she made just for herself, and there she stands clutching her stomach and then her heart, and then her stomach again. She paces this way, then that, not sure which way to turn, where to run. "My...my father," she whispers, but then straightaway covers her mouth, then her eyes, as the hot tears roll onto her cheeks. Yes, of course her mother mentioned his name, the man who left her with child and ran away. And now he's alive. A leper. A wraith, walking dead. She sits on her swing ever so slowly, and then stares sightlessly across the murky waters.

Pieter takes the message, as agreed, to Toppes. The merchant is taken aback but, spurred on by his good fortune and the good favours of the bishop, he quickly makes a note in his own hand for one James Cobbe, the Pelican's captain, telling him to work with the bearer of it as if his livelihood depended on it – as indeed it does – and thereafter have the commission burnt.

Come Tuesday, Simon takes the coracle to the westerly end of Ranworth broad, where the waters come closest to Hamberly's manor house. From the deep reeds there, he watches the family process with all regalia and pomp for the Saint George's day mass. Hamberly is followed dutifully by all his servants, even the farm hands – not that Hamberly is pious, but rather he can't bear to think of them at ease while he is at prayer. When they are fully gone from sight Simon steals across to the house. He makes slow work of the locks, listening carefully beyond the ticking clock and birdsong, in case there is anyone inside.

In the bed chamber and closet, his eye lights on a fine pair of ebony masks, no doubt from some tawdry country ball. He had thought to make something from linen or leather to cover his visage, but the man's one here is full face and quite malevolent in appearance. It will render him both an enigma and an object of terror to his enemies, he thinks.

I'll have that and with a high-necked linen shirt, my long hair, and riding gloves, nothing of my affliction will be visible. But, to the clothes, what a pretty closetful this man has! I wager old Norfolk himself is not arrayed better than this fellow. How does this man Hamberly wear such garb without arrest? It would never have been so in Father's day. For myself, I think black, in keeping with the mask – even at the risk of being mistook for a Spaniard, or worse, a lawyer. Black suede breeches with silver brocade and matching doublet, very fine, but with wool stockings, for it will be cold on the journey. I'll have a pair of those for Hugh too. Jerkin on top, wool or leather? Best take leather, for there is bound to be trouble if Hugh's there – and besides, look at the embossed roses on the edge, and even the Beaufort portcullis on the epaulettes. By heaven, this man Hamberly knows how to play the game! And I – he holds it before a glass – I will look every bit the patriot. Leather boots as desired, studs and straps that will have kept a cordwainer busy for a week or two, and look at this double lined gown! Wool and velvet with silk edging in the Burgundian style, though a few less feathers in the matching cap would have been more tasteful. Now, what else for my brother, let me see...hmm...I think buff and brown. It always suited him well and besides most of the rest here is too brash for his tastes.

He bundles up his selection and goes downstairs to see what arms are available. He is not disappointed here, either, procuring two basilard daggers and rapiers, very modern, with belts and scabbard to suit, a fine pair of new matchlocks all the way from Augsburg in Bavaria, and a short blunderbuss – good for clearing the decks.

Simon leaves Hamberly a short note that his brother and he had devised, saying that all his secrets and sins were known to God; that all these objects had been borrowed by angels, and that if he breathed a word to anyone he would be murdered in his bed, or something worse. He reads it through with satisfaction, then leaves it on the man's desk for him to find.

Pacificus is busy too, his greatest challenge is absenting himself from the community for a period of days without arousing suspicion – well, no more than usual. He sends to Abbot Rugge, tells him he will be away on Wednesday on matters relating to "all we discussed in Norwich last week." He begs, would he "send word to Prior Thomas," to smooth things over when he is missed. This is not the sort of game a man can keep up indefinitely. *Mendacem memorem esse oportet, liars do need a good memory,* he mutters into his cowl, shuffling back to the bed with the others after Nocturne. Yes, yes, and a lot more than a good memory withal. How about the very devil's luck as well, to finish this business with my innards intact. After this long flight from his past, Brother Pacificus of Saint Benet's will be a holy privateer once more, when he gets up in the morning. Wakeful in his bed, he resigns himself to it, all of it, this refuge from blood and danger such a fleeting, brief hiatus.

Tomorrow he will step back into that other world without difficulty, without pause, for he knows how turn a result in this business better than a midwife knows how to turn a baby. It will not be hard for him – and this most of all he fears, that it is no hardship, that these years in the cloister have been not so much God's will as his own fabrication. And he wonders whether, if he resorts to sword and buckler once more on God's behalf, will this finally bring him peace? Or will he forfeit whatever tranquility he has found here, in this drafty dorter – one foot in purgatory, the other tortured in the lower circles of hell? What part of his course does a man truly choose anyway? He has been taught that a wise man overules the stars, but maybe it is the planets that rule after all? He struggles to sort what is needed in his head against the next day, but is sound asleep within a minute, so deep that Matins and Lauds come as a cruel interruption.

11

The Privateers

Lex non distinguitur, nos non distinguere debemus
The law makes no distinction, so neither should we

Even great doors turn on small hinges, and sometimes even the greatest of them by a light wind. It is two days after the feast of Saint

George on Saint Margaret's marsh. Pieter lies struck down with a flux of some sort; it is in his stomach and he cannot move. Sarah fears the worst – he's always had too much black bile, she says, but would never give credence to the doctors. The bairns keep her busy, the older children stand by helpless. Sarah hears Beth summoning Richard to walk out. She hears them slip out and so moves her knitting to an open window. She hears them clanking on the boards at the staithe, their low murmuring occasionally breaking into high-pitched exclamations and then shushings. Sarah knows what they are about, for she has kept a close guard on them since their trip to the farm. She allowed them to keep the sheets, one dress for Beth and sundry items for the bairns, but nothing more. The rest she puts by for the poor. Now she sees that Pieter is in no fit state to take the boat down river to Yarmouth for the evening rendezvous – she is well caught between two opinions as well. Pieter, or someone must deliver Toppes' note to the ship's captain, and what about this Pockington in Antwerp? Who could gain his confidence if not Pieter? Perhaps one of the prisoners when freed, she thinks. Still, the note must go down river.

Outside Beth and Richard discuss all this too. Who else can take Pieter's place now but them? They debate the alloyed nature of their own motives, for there is the obvious element of self-preservation in it all. If this venture fails at any point then what little safety they enjoy on the marsh is forfeit. But then there is something else beyond their own safety that soon enters their conversation. It is an uncomfortable question: do they share in their parents' religious convictions enough to hazard such an enterprise? Richard says yes, but perhaps he is trying too hard and too late to please his father, to make him proud, fill his shoes. This is what Beth thinks, but as for herself she is undecided. Risk something like this for the God who took her parents? Or do it just to protect themselves on the marsh? Or do it to keep Richard company? After all, he's not the sharpest knife in the drawer and will likely do something stupid.

In the end they are all saved the decision. Sarah calls them in and herds them to Pieter's pallet where he lays half-doubled in pain. "You will take the weapons the brother requested." Pieter speaks through gritted teeth and hissing intakes of breath. "And this letter from Master Toppes. Deliver them to Joseph the tanner of Stokesby. It's – oooh." Pieter twists on the pallet, and then shakes his head back and forth as if to refuse the pain its complete mastery "Halfway to Yarmouth. He can be trusted, you can tell him all, everything, you hear. He will go for us, to Yarmouth. And you wait for the tide, ja, before coming back." He falls back, pale and sweating. The exertion brings on such violent cramps that he cannot help crying out.

Sarah wants to argue, she is anxious for the children's safety but knows there is no other answer, for the ships sail that evening on the tide. If the monk's plan fails, all is forfeit – their home and likely the lives of every one of them, too.

She gathers food for them and mutters prayers in her native tongue. Her own father and eldest brother were soldiers, veterans of many campaigns with the Burgundy Duke, but now both long gone. She tries hard not to look upon the blurred forms of the children, as she sees them, otherwise she might hold them too close and never let them go. She remembers hanging on to her brother Franz's jacket, that last time he left with her father, but you cannot tell men anything; and besides, wasn't the Duke's pay better than weaving? That's what they had said so jocularly. And now these children, barely here a month and she feels like Abraham offering Isaac all over again. And so she loads them, not with wood for the burnt offering but bread and cheese, smoked eel and small beer. And all the while in the back of her mind she supresses the voice that accuses her God – even tyrants leave children out of their wars, but not you. But they are not children this Thursday morning, any more than her God is a tyrant.

Richard reverently handles the weapons, placing them on the folded sail in the stern of the boat. Samuel and James are screaming for Beth. She goes to kiss Pieter's sweaty brow. She tries to pray for him but her words seem hollow, without power. He caresses her face, "*God zegene*, bless you, pretty Lizabetta." He can no longer marshal his thoughts, the pain is too much. He wanted to bless her again, tell her to trust in

Christ as he and Sarah do, but the spasms take him again, like being bayonetted. And, for herself, Beth knows that she must leave with no further delay. Here, sixteen miles from the sea, a low tide still makes the river flow fast and the sooner they get to Stokesby, the sooner they can return.

When it comes to leaving, Piers is not there to see them off. Richard, Beth and Sarah had explained why he could not go too and he had stormed off in a sulk. Nothing is ever fair when you're twelve. They imagine him to be in the byre, or up in the field. They will be back soon enough, so they do not bother to look for him.

Richard helps Beth settle in with the food basket, and never thinks to go back to kiss Tanty Sarah – probably as well. She is bearing up bravely, Reminding them one more time where the tanner's house is, to lower their hats, to stop nowhere else, to hail no one on the river – to come back as soon as they can. The sight of Sarah, James and Samuel standing close together waving from the shore choke Beth up – but not Richard, for now he is taking hold of the oars; a man's work for his hands, and a man's responsibility on his shoulder. He pulls smoothly down the dyke and out onto the river Ant. The clouds billow and furl under the silent heavens.

They join the Thurne within the hour, the Bure soon after that. Beth sees the spire of Saint Helen's Ranworth and points it out for Richard. Somewhere in the woods on the flat lands is their old farm, like someone else's life, it seems.

Upton and Acle dykes pass them, and still Richard pulls without a break, great beads of sweat running down his brow. His sister marvels, though silently so – it wouldn't do for him to be a big-head. Neither does Richard speak, but he puts his back into the rowing as he wonders whatever he would do if they met Miller again, or anyone else who would welcome the bounty on their heads.

Their father believed it wrong, as Pieter does, for a man of God to put a sword into the hand of the Bride of Christ – a sin to do violence in Christ's name and for his cause. But the monk Pacificus seems to have no qualms, and are they not fighting for their lives not their parent's religion? His conscience is tender, and this is the only means he has for quietening it. His instinctive compulsion to finish off Miller with the matchlock butt that day at the farm affected him deeply then and does still. It made him so ashamed that he has barely prayed since. To hate a man in your heart is the same sin as murder, so says Christ, and he has heard his father say it too. Then, he reasons, we all must be murderers, with no hope unless God forgives as much as Mother said he did – though how this is possible he doesn't know. He could never forgive the murder of his father; in fact, this is the only way he can make them pay. If they don't want English Bibles, here comes a flood of them.

A wherry has just cast off from the staithe at Stokesby as they round the last bend and the village finally comes into view. Richard fends with the oar and Beth leaps to the bank, making fast the boat. She sets off alone to the tannery while Richard rests, her heart beating hard, following the acrid smell with no need to ask for directions. But there is no one home. She tries the house next door where a maid tells her Joseph is away delivering.

"Delivering!" Beth replies, her light smile falling heavy in despair. "But when will he return thither?"

"I'm sure I don't know. He's sometimes away for days. Besides, it's not my business to keep tabs on't neighbors. Stokesby ain't like Thurne for tattle and eaves-dropping you know, folks is respectable hereabouts. Eh, what's with you missy, you've turned white as a sheet?"

Beth does not wait to explain. How can she? She turns on her heel and runs back to tell Richard as fast as she can. But when she arrives at the staithe, Richard is already shaking his head. Can there really be even more bad news? He lifts the sail to show her Piers lying fast asleep and now snoring loudly under the gunnels – with their grandfather's longbow held close as if he were nursing a treasured toy.

Pacificus and Simon are having a better time of it in the herring capital of Europe. Trade with the Low Countries and the Baltic brings more ships into Yarmouth's docks than London's, more wealth than any other Cinque port – more even than Norwich. This piratical metropolis is a teeming warren of smokeries, taverns, markets and crowded wharves, a heaving sea of humanity right through from Candlemas to Martinmas. Most of the ship owners – some admirals no less – expect to make up their tax money from privateering, and the pickings are good. But now with the Tuckett Fare in full swing, everything is herring and plaice, the next two months they'll be busy with the Shotnett Fare for mackerel – but once that passes they'll look to French ships and even raids on the other Cinque ports for sport and luxuries. If there were ever a den of pirates and cut-throats, it's here in Yarmouth, the place where the sheriff will never call a curfew because the warders can't enforce it. The brothers don't mind it though, they've seen worse; in fact, Pacificus is trying not to enjoy the way it fires his belly. There is nothing like a town half-filled with men-stealers and brigands to make a man feel alive and fully alert – his hand is never far from his weapon.

They have been here since noon, not in their finery but walking about the place separately in their usual clothing, looking, listening. Simon watches the baggage on the wharf, shuffling up and down the quay in sight of it and listening to the sailors. The harbour is silting again, it's a problem, the men of Lowestoft say it's God's judgement, but many men go without work when they could be digging it out. Foreigners just off wool ships offer themselves for a pittance, undercutting the locals, it's not right, not right at all, something should be done. Perhaps the city fathers will put another levy on the herring or the wine, perhaps they will cut another port entrance?

Pacificus – with cowl up, and eyes open – is heading for the Tolhouse where the prisoners are held. The streets in this quarter are old and so notoriously narrow as to barely let two fishwives pass without a tussle. The smell is worse than the worst tenements of Norwich, which is saying something. Eyes down, watch every step, breathe through your mouth so you don't wretch at the acrid stench of fish guts and sewage.

Yarmouth's Tolhouse is part gaol below, with stairs rising to assize court and old council chamber above, the assize being held on Mondays usually, though daily at the height of the fares, when complaints sprout like a pox. Its steep-thatched roof looms above the stench and on the front walls the statue of Justice with sword and balance gazes vainly across the town to the sea. There is a large open window at street level with thick iron bars, so the ragged souls inside may reach from the dungeon to passers by for scraps of food and news. It is cold Angevin logic – cruel bastards those Francs – why waste the jailer's time with visiting and keys and so forth, when this barred window on the street is stocks, almoner and jailer all in one. No wonder the warder is an infamous drunkard, he has nothing to do but chase the wastrels who use the window for a public convenience.

Pacificus waits to see whether the place is watched. Not so – or not from the street anyway. He sidles up to the window and holds bread towards the darkness between the bars. A hand shoots out for it but Pacificus grabs the wrist: "Good morrow, friend. How do men call you?"

"Jameson, good brother, it's Jameson, and I thank you for your charity. My hand?" Two sunken eyes peer up from the darkness, and there are grunts and scufflings as two others scramble to see who it is. "It's all right, brother, I will share the bread you give."

A likely story, knave, he thinks but then he hears that the other men inside agree. "How many are you here?"

"Six honest men and true, brother." Good, he thinks, they are alone.

Pacificus whispers, "Would you be bound for Antwerp?" More eyes now appear. Their women had been with news, but they had not been believed any more than those women on Easter morn. Now comes this monk – if monk he is and not a spy – and they begin to wonder. They are not chained, that much is good news indeed. They tell him about the jailer, his habits, his routine. He tells them to be ready against the evening, and if they be praying – which they assure him they are – to pray some Paternosters and Aves for him, to which they make no definite reply. He smiles at this, at which point a man from the very back comes to the fore: "Hugh?"

"Not so loud!" Pacificus squints into the darkness, "Prithee, Christopher! I wouldn't have known you! How come you here?" He has not seen him since the White Horse days, when Christopher was a divinity student, the youngest and most fired of all of them.

"Well, after Cambridge I...er – prithee Hugh, are you a monk in truth? We heard you had become a knight – "

The jailer is passing back to the tavern and Pacificus pulls clear of the bar to hail him, "Good Warder Eames!" The corpulent turnkey near trips over his belly when he twists to see who calls him. Sixty, built like an outhouse, this man's bloodshot eyes say he's spent the morning in bed and the night before in high fashion. He has this job for the free lodging since his wife threw him out. He's been a drunkard, malicious gossip and bullying thief since his youth, but he's a talker too, and give him five minutes and he'd help you see that he is one of the most honest men in the port, which might be true. The aldermen of the wine guild got him this post as jailer to keep him from brawling in the taverns. The magistrate acquiesced, saying it was better he was employed gainfully at the Tolhouse than always being in it without profit.

Pacificus approaches in as fretful a manner as he can muster, "Oh good warder, good warder, I perceive this be a place of much wickedness," to which he agrees and would gladly name a few travelling friars to prove the point, if only this monk would pause for breath. "Yes, yes, just as I thought, and here also I see these men in your charge – *your* charge, good warder – have gone without a confessor these three days."

"But they will take no confessor, they be heretics, brother – sons of Belial, all. Not my doing."

"But I think they are ready to recant. I have just had words with them even now, and I think mention should be made to Lord Cromwell's men when they come of *your pious influence*, once they have fully confessed. Yeah verily, look not so astonished good gaoler, for I will testify that you have worked wonders on them. They are ready to repent, I say. It is a miracle, almost." Hugh then takes Eames' soiled woolen sleeve and shakes it in joy. "Oh, it is good news indeed to turn a sinner from the error of his ways, is it not? But you see for yourself I am no confessor, just a humble brother. Still, I know six good confessors come from Norwich this very day, so let us confess these wretches one and all this eve, that the town may rejoice with us – and toast you, too, and perhaps even reward you with some bounty for your goodly work. Eh, eh?"

The warder blinks rapidly, one blink to absorb each word. He strokes his stomach, anticipating his rising reputation and credit perhaps even. Pacificus helps these pleasant thoughts go down with a coin pressed into the ruffian's palm – for "some strong Flemish beer in celebration." Eames sets off cheery to the tavern and Pacificus relays details of the plan to the prisoners before returning in search of his brother.

It takes Richard, and more particularly Beth, a good half hour to scold Piers. "What were you thinking? What will Sarah be thinking? Who will help her if James runs off? Boys don't think; foolish, impish child. I should throw you in the river and let you swim back!"

Through it all, a crestfallen but largely unrepentant Piers is trying to point out the obvious – that they had better get the message to Yarmouth without delay – but he is shouted down by the older two. Richard keeps casting a nervous eye down the broad river. It's a long way down there, and dangerous too. They would as likely be pressed on a foreign ship before they ever even found the monk. For a time, it seems easier for the older ones to compound the misery of their situation by shouting a Piers. But after that is all done, there is no more to say. The tanner is not there, and without admitting anything to Piers, they acknowledge quietly that they must go on with the note before it's all too late. But, Beth says emphatically, she does not want to see the leper, is adamant she will not see him. Richard thinks it is disgust at the man's condition, and that she is unfair to speak so about a man who had offered them help, but does not argue. He has hours of rowing before him and, even with Piers on one oar and mouthful's of Sarah's victuals in between strokes, it is as much as he can do just to face each new challenge without thinking what will come after it.

The tide is still with them as they near Yarmouth's great wharf by early evening, the same time Pacificus is returning to the quayside. For Richard, Pieter's sailboat had always looked small enough compared to the wherries and red sailed tilt-boats on the river, but now it felt truly dwarfed by the hulking mass of the crayers, the rigging and masts of the ballingers and the walls of cannonade on three gargantuan carracks, merchantmen, slavers and men of war. From down below in the ever turbid flow, this all looks to the wide-eyed children like a vast, wooden city of its own, beside which they are mere flotsam. Richard pulls closer and closer, his heart beating out of his chest, oars greasy in his sore, sweaty hands. Men are shouting, jeering, laughing overhead. There is nowhere to put in. His oar hits a dead mastiff, bloating and rolling in water. He doesn't know what to do, so he keeps going. More giant boats, sometimes with foreign voices, sometimes singing. He wants someone to tell him what to do, but there is no one. He looks behind him and then at Beth and Piers. He sees their faces which, like his no doubt, are stricken with panic. He wants to turn and flee for the safety of Sarah's cottage. Its only the remembrance that if he fails, there will be no cottage and no Sarah to go back to, that he him grimly rowing on. This is really it for them. They are in this up to their necks now, in it together – like the dog-sized rats that swim near the hulls to his left.

Then a passing wherry is suddenly on their starboard. A deck hand fends them off roughly with a long pole and an even longer string of curses. Richard's cheeks are flushed crimson, but to his credit, Beth thinks, he does not cry. Piers has covered up the weapons with the sheet and is pointing out obstacles for Richard to avoid. Richard is just saying for the tenth time that he has already seen all these things when Beth cups her hands to her mouth and calls up to three idle cabin hands on the carrack: "Good morrow! Pray tell me where we might find the *Pelican!*"

To her surprise she is amiably directed to it by an eager boy about Piers' age, a lad who is captivated by the beauty she is unaware of still. The older lad at his side leers down in a way that makes her skin crawl. They find the *Pelican*, putting in just alongside. She was formerly a Spanish carrack, whose name was kept to add insult to injury, about twenty feet in the beam with three masts, the largest rising to ninety feet. The boys gape at her guns fore and aft; she needs them, too, for these are no times to be without defense. Beyond the harbour is 'nought but salt, devils and death,' as their father often said. But adventure too, Piers now thinks as they draw up behind her and he scrambles like a bilge rat up the ladder on the quayside with their rope. It is low tide and the big vessels are now fully grounded, though not their little boat. The rope just reaches, and when they are all up they see Simon sitting by the baggage, talking to some unemployed Flemish sailors, just as Pacificus asked him to.

Simon is shocked and not pleased to see them, but hears them out and softens when they explain. Beth stands behind Richard, looking the other way. She makes no eye contact with Simon, and she will not reply when he greets her. The blackguard has no right to civility, the way he treated my mother. She has settled finally upon hating him, hating everything about him, anything she can find. Lepers smell like the French cheese, did you know that? It's the pustulant sores, it's in their clothing. Of course, they are past detecting it, but they stink like the foul matter that comes from behind the corner of your big toe-nail, or the seeping mucus that comes from your ear when you have an infection. She cannot bear to be near him, in fact if it were not for the crowds of drunkards, she would run a mile.

Pacificus joins them soon after this, and after his initial shock at seeing them there, he talks them quickly through their current options. They will take the captain's note and the weapons, even though they now have their own, and the children will stay to help them until they sail, for there is much to do. But thereafter they must return with all speed and await word from them. First they must look to the *Pelican*, already being loaded for the journey, sack barrows of wool tods and horse carts of the same arriving by the minute.

Pacificus approaches Captain Cobbe, a man smarter in his own eyes than his ship is clean. He is good with the men, which is to say he is as hard as a November storm on them. They need it, to be sure, but it is clear to Pacificus the man has lost interest in the business. His position is guaranteed for life, for he and Toppes have done too much *extra* business to be parted without acrimony or worse. Cobbe examines the note, dragging a cracked and course finger over his briny lips. He recognises his master's hand, but these are irregular dealings, as he protests to the monk: "Aye, I can see its Toppes' hand alright, but it's a queer business is this, brother. Indeed it says nowt about a monk here, either!"

"It says enough for you to know," Pacificus says gravely, "and for the rest you are best minding your own business. There are four hours before sail, you should have men scrubbing the barnacles exposed by the tide, and what are these ropes doing all affray about the mizzen? Does the carpenter have wood for two spare masts? No? Well, he must have them too, and two mizzen sails before we leave this wharf? That is what we need."

"Hey, hey! But, this is *my* ship," Cobbe replies affronted, "Mine to sail at any rate. What is Toppes about to have you give him orders?"

Pacificus observes the sallow eye, the tightened lips, so takes the man by the arm and says confidentially, "You are still captain, and days from now you will never see me again, but unless you and I work together there will be more than cargo lost on this voyage. Moreover, if you do well in this, then your name will be known in England as the captain who outran Cromwell's four-master."

"Outrun the *Genoese*? You jest, monk! Have you seen her?" Cobbes now unfolds his arms a moment to stick a thumb out in the direction of the *Genoese*. Men scurry like ants on her mainsail rigging, and that all-important fourth called the Bonaventure mast, hers crowned with castles high as cathedral towers. They're not so new, Pacificus thinks, he's gone up against a few in his own day when they were, but she's in good order nonetheless, and under a good captain.

"I have seen her all day, and her captain too, but we are fifty hundred tonnes lighter by my reckoning, *and* we also have some tricks up our sleeves too. Now send your men to the chandlers and let's have this timber and sail."

"And these barnacles – "

" – Will give us a quarter knot more speed, would you not agree?" The captain's sour face breaks into something of a smile, "Aye, it would that, if speed's our thing. Leave it with me monk, you'll have your masts and'all." So saying, Cobbe then goes for his men like a curfew dog and soon enough they are all soon thigh-deep in the mud removing the barnacles as the children look on amazed.

Back on the wharf, Pacificus leaves them once more to speak to some Flemish sailors. Yes, he says, it is true he will give them a lodging for one, maybe two nights; yes, there will be food and drink, plenty of the latter. They are already too well juiced to be suspicious, even though their mothers told them never to trust friars, monks or priests.

This dressing up of sailors in Benedictine habits is a goodly joke. He makes them change in an alley just off the main drag, but warns them solemnly that they must be reverent and quiet from now if they want more ale than what he has already given them. They agree, meek as lambs. He leads them in procession through the back alleys pausing several times to stop them sniggering. One can barely walk straight but his fellows help him. As they come near the Tolhouse he insists on quiet – cowls up, heads down, no laughing or no beer. "See that window there? I will pass you ale through those bars in just ten minutes, if you keep your heads." As it happened they didn't, but the warder, not knowing his Latin from his Flemish assumed that was what they mumbled. After the lower cells are opened, Pacificus waits outside with the warder, at all times keeping his eye and flattering him within limits of the man's pride, but not so much as to make him suspicious.

Once inside the cells, the prisoners take over the talking. "We have come to confess you', "Are you ready to recant', all loud and clear. His old friend Christopher Burgh plays his part well, though Pacificus thinks the others are hardly convincing, but the warder is too consumed with contemplation of his reward to notice. The lowlanders are only too happy to be rid of the habits and wait for their reward. The prisoners are dressed and ready within three minutes. The light is waning now, and the lack of it, helps no end when the new monks finally re-emerge. As he passes, Christopher even makes the sign of the cross at his former jailer, with not a flicker of recognition in response. Pacificus is last to leave, handing Eames a sealed note as he passes out through the doors. "This is for the magistrate when these men come for sentencing. You have done good work here, my man. God reward you."

The note reads "*Your Honour, Pray pardon these happless, lowland revellers, for, to a man, they had no knowledge of this crime, but were tricked by a cunning Englishmen who begs leave that they be not chastised beyond that which their drunkenness may require, whilst also remembering that the ill treatment of Dutchmen in Yarmouth would doubtless adversely affect our trade if it were noised abroad.*"

He knew that this last point, and only this last point, would sway the justice of Yarmouth. Their pride will be injured surely, but at least the townsmen have been saved further expense in hosting dignitaries for trials, feastings – and the burning. True to his word, Pacificus has quarts of ale brought to the jail bars. He has Beth and the boys collect the clothing in the same alley, so the six prisoners board the *Pelican* not as monks but as men carrying a tod of wool apiece; faces barely visible amid the shaggy white fluff of the bales. Below deck, the men find their wives and their children; then, and only then, do they breathe as men not dreaming. Simon too is below deck, in his own cabin at Cobbe's insistence, to get changed. Cobbe watches in amazement from the deck as Pacificus directs the shipwright to fix iron rings into the hull, he's never seen anything like this one, doesn't know how to take him. "Said you could travel with us, not make us more work!"

"Oblige us in all particulars and it will be well Captain. Remember these orders are from Toppes." Pacificus is too busy inspecting the work to look. "You have some good men, captain, one or two of them!"

He casts the man a merry eye, and Cobbe's face softens, "Aye, well *them what's born to hang is best kept on the water*. Likewise, I'd surely like to know who you are – no more a monk than me, that's for sure."

"Don't flatter yourself Captain, there is still time for you to take the cowl." Leaving him with a wry smile Pacificus observes the light is going fast in the east and the tide rising beneath them. The children will need to leave soon if they want to make use of it on their long journey upstream. He leaves Cobbe and returns to the quay to pay one last visit as a monk before they embark. He hurries to the harbourmaster's house, all puffing, and out of breath. "Master of the harbour, is it true?"

"Is what true?" The harbourmaster approaches the window, clutching a reed and parchment. "Out with it brother, you can see I am busy here."

"Forgive me, I have been summoned to attend a dying man on board a ship called the Genoese but I cannot find it in this light. I came as quick as I could, on Saint Michael's wings, as the reported symptoms sound of plague to me. Of course, these ships from the continent you know; ports with bad air, miasmic vapours, it is little wonder."

It is like a taper lit; the harbourmaster calls for his retinue with great oaths and clatterings. As they proceed with lamps toward the unsuspected four master, Pacificus slips away to his own ship.

But back at the *Pelican* he finds a new commotion on the dockside. A tall man, standing on the gangplank, swears at the top of his voice, "By Saint George, I tell you straight sir!" He's bellowing while the captain stands astride the top of the plank to bar him entry, "I have seen the three children of Fenton from Ranworth, Fenton the heretic they burned in Norwich a week gone and I *will* come aboard, or fetch a constable." Beth peers again from behind the rigging on the steps to the poopdeck, and she shudders. It is Miller, come here to Yarmouth, for no one will lend him money in Wroxham and probably not even Norwich. They saw him come out from the chandlers on the wharf and they ran on board to hide. The boys linger on the stairs, listening above their thumping hearts to what the stern captain will say. Richard fingers the hammer on his father's matchlock but it is not loaded. The other sailors gather round their captain, but Miller is not put off, not him. He's calling to the men outside the tavern, saying so that all can hear, "There's illegal stowaways on this here ship, lads, ones what have prices on their heads! That's right lads, rewards for them what hands 'em in!" He points to the deck. "But this 'ere captain don't like the king's justice it seems! Thinks he's better than us! But mark me, I'm Miller of Ranworth, I farm for Hamberly and my word is good, ask anyone. I know about this business, and I say we go aboard." It does the trick. A small crowd gathers to him at the foot of the plank and even sailors are murmuring about the reward, one or two glancing behind them, to see if they can spot the children. Cobbe thumbs the white bristles on this chin, never taking his eyes off Miller. It is a pity this noisome caitiff had not mentioned it privily, for they might have done business, but now this crowd – well, it would need another course. "Back to your work, men," he growls from the corner of his mouth, "or by God you'll feel the quartermaster's lash." But what will he say to this Miller and this mob? Beth, trembling, closes her eyes and begins to pray, very sincerely for once. The next thing she knows, a great, broad gentleman, appareled in black and silver, leather and steel is walking behind the captain. Cobbe is about to repeat the order to get back to work, but when he catches sight of Simon – or Sir Cecil as he is now refashioned – and particularly that ebony mask, it is all he can do but to stand aside himself. Now it is Simon facing Miller, a man he had wanted to meet. Despite the infirmity of his feet and the stiffness in his left shoulder, he approaches the gangplank steadily giving no hint of either. The quay falls near silent at the sight of him.

"You may come aboard and search, any of you, but you must come past me first."

Miller's left eye is twitching. "What's all this?"

"No trick. I will even give you my rapier. Here." Miller catches it and Simon takes another step towards him. Miller holds the sword with his strong right hand, Simon observes and draws the basilard dagger with his left, then raises his right index finger to caution him. "Make your strokes count, Miller of Ranworth, say your prayers, for by my oath, I may not spare you."

In the next instant Miller is at him, swinging the rapier at Simon's head like a switch, but it is all over in an instant. Simon ducks back to dodge the first stroke, then closes with the drunkard at the point when he is over-balanced most. He catches hold of Miller's right arm and brings the basilard up hard under his armpit, jerking it up and twisting it until it appears out of the top of his shoulder. "Clipping your wings, sir."

Miller, paralysed and gasping with a mouth and eyes as wide as china bowls, stares helplessly back. The rapier clatters onto the gangplank as his body hunches with the pain. "That," Simon, whispers into his ear, "is for striking the maid Beth. You will find your arms less useful for hitting women after this." He pulls out the blade none too gently and leaves Miller sprawling at the feet of the mob. "If I see you again," he levels the dagger at him, "I will not be so lenient."

But in the crowd behind Miller are ten or more veteran soldiers, all the more interested in the rumour of bounty money now that this lone, masked gentleman has confirmed it.

"Now, then," says the oldest of them, fingering his pike staff, "he was well dealt with but I don't think you will fare so prettily against me and these boys here, it being ten to one."

But the words are barely out of his mouth before the ringleader feels the cold steel against his jugular. It is Pacificus, also out of his habit, by now, emerging as a gentleman in his finery. "Ten against two, friend, and you will die first – then you." He raises a matchlock to the face of the next keenest man. Everything in his face, his silent eyes, says 'You don't want to mess with me.'

"I wouldn't play with this one," Cecil says blithely, retrieving his rapier and stepping on to the quayside. "He won't stop until you're all ribbons! I suggest you take these coins and drink to a lucky escape." He tosses a bag of coins to the leader, a mercenary and veteran fighter of many foreign campaigns. The bounty for fugitives would set him on nicely compared to this sop of coins. Perhaps he should risk it, he has before and he's always got through. His eyes move to the man who holds the knife and matchlock, searching for any pretence, the slightest sign of hesitation. Many so-called gentlemen like to style themselves as knights, but most are no more than women in real battle. He adjusts his grip on the pikestaff and looks carefully at Pacificus, whose breathing is stilled for the thrust, and his eyes like stone, the blade not at the windpipe, rather pointed to the side at the jugular vein. No, he knows his work, this one, he thinks, and he'll do it without blinking if I tried anything. Damn him.

"All right, very kind of you, my noble lord," he says, snatching up the bag. "We shall drink to the king's justice." The other men make this their cue to stand down. At least they will get a drink out of it, Hugh thinks, better than a grave. Always let a man save face, retreat with honour. Well done, Cecil. Diplomacy is cheaper than war. You'd think it would be more popular.

He watches the crowd clear slowly, keeping a careful guard, just in case. When they have gone he looks at Simon with a long hard sigh of relief. "I would love to know what you are thinking under that new mask."

"Oh, just how much the brown cloth becomes you, perhaps more than the cowl. Nice beret!"

"I removed some of the feathers. Anyway, just hope I wasn't recognised. Come, go yonder and guard the children in case the crew get ideas – it seems that they'll have to come with us now."

He glances towards a bystander on the wharf. "You there! Fetch a woman to bind this man's wound!" And then, to Cecil making his way back aboard: "No dead bodies, no trouble! And *you* – " he walks over to Miller, still lying on the wharf, and gives him a kick, " – cease to pursue these children, cease to even think of them, or I will pay you a visit at – where did you say? Ah, yes, Ranworth."

Miller nods and hisses some more, slavering, red as a beetroot, rolling back and forth, clutching his shoulder. Pacificus ascends the gangplank, nodding to Cobbe who has only just recognised the identity of this mysterious *Cavaliere* under the brown velvet beret, "Captain, make ready to set sail; they may be back when the money is spent."

"So – you are no monk after all."

"It does not concern you."

"And the children, the reward?"

"They are under my protection. You *will* be well rewarded," he makes sure Cobbe has his eyes, "but you once cross me, by heaven, you will feel it." The captain smiles and nods. Make me famous, will he? Cobbe thinks, get me hung more like it. Nevertheless, he gives the order, and the crew put the *Pelican* out into the midstream and from thence to the roaring ocean.

12

The Smugglers

Aut viam inveniam aut faciam
Either find a way or make one

The port is behind them, the sea black and orange under the setting sun. Winds from the south-west have them tacking across the seas towards the Baltic at six knots. "It is a goodly speed, is it not, Gentlemen?" The captain is standing on the poop, hands on hips and decidedly please with himself and his vessel. Pacificus nods but his eye is on Cobbe now, and he and Simon will sleep in watches.

Simon talks with Beth on the foredeck, his cloak around her shoulders. She did not want it, but he insisted. He does not stand close to her and she, in turn, does not move away. She does not hate him quite so much this evening, not after he dealt so with Miller and rescued her.

She has seen the way the crew looked at her, and still do. This man and his brother are all that stands between them and capture. He is her only defense. It's hard for her to despise him under these circumstances. In fact, as he stands so tall in his mask and costume, he seems like a different person, someone else entirely. In her mind, she has hated a ragged leper in a lazar house on the marsh, not a mysterious *cavaliere* in black leather and velvet. She steals a surreptitious glance at him when she thinks he isn't looking.

Simon breathes the salt spray through the mask. It is like a cleansing balm, even though it stings. He had forgotten how much he loved it out here, how big the skies, how much space to think, to recover the horizon and forget all that happened on land. The captain had said that *men who were fit to hang were best kept out on the water*. In truth, men have always escaped to the sea like Narcissus went to the fountain pool. They go to look at themselves reflected in the deep, to see what manner of man they are against that fathomless abyss. The temptations of the pool are one thing, the ocean is quite another, and the seas around Rhodes, worst of all for finding out men. When the ancients marked the maps 'there be dragons', they might have been seeing no more that their own reflections - the abyss staring back at them. Simon found dragons of doubt, despair and cowardice out there in the Levant that made him only too glad to skulk back home with his tail between his legs. He needs no sermons or catechising, for he knows well enough what kind of man he is. No wonder Christ *did not entrust himself to the mob, for he knew what was in man.*

These are things he is trying to forget as Beth stands quietly by him, clasping the cloak to her breast. He tells her various unconnected things about the sea, the ship and the heavens. In truth, he feels a solemn joy and does not know quite what to say. "Since my father first took me as a boy to the coast, almost from that day until now, I have dreamt about the ocean almost every week."

Her heart misses a beat. Him as well? It is exactly her own experience. Should she tell him? The trail of their talk is interrupted by the sound of Piers acting the goat in front of Richard and the crew, rolling round on the deck, pretending to be Miller, whimpering, pleading. Richard kicks him and tells him to get up. The sailors look on, sulky at the intrusion on their deck but will say nothing if their captain will not. And Cobbe won't while this strange monk – or whatever he is – is sitting there, surrounded by them; Piers, Richard, three other boys and two girls of his heretic cargo. The sight of the Anabaptist children make Beth remember Samuel and little James back home on the marsh. Her eyes fall momentarily and Simon asks her if she is alright.

She nods and smiles politely at him, but now the thought that she might never see her little brothers again overwhelms her. She confesses it, and he is quick to comfort her as best he can with faltering reassurances. He knows nothing of fatherhood, but suffering has made him tender. Beth mumbles her thanks and then glances back at Piers, who is now clutching the bow and talking to the other Anabaptist children. For a long while, it seems, she and Simon follow the gulls dipping and squabbling. Sometimes he talks, sometimes they are silent, neither saying what they really want to, though neither leaving the chill air to go below either. Does he have the right to be her father now – to claim paternal fealty, just because he is lonely and she is the only thing of beauty to come from his whole life? The more the urge forces itself into his mind, the more unworthy and selfish he feels his claim. Let her alone for now, he thinks. God watch over her. It is enough that she exists and that I can serve her in some way.

Meanwhile at the forecastle, Pacificus is being adored by the other youngsters. Richard and Piers are too excited to feel yet what they are involved in; they creep about behind him, one holding the matchlock, the other the long bow. They all want to know about his days with the knights, his sea battles, his sieges. He tries to be stern, in order to keep the respect of the crew who are secretly listening. But when the crew are out of earshot he makes them sit down out of the wind. "Tell us!" they demand, "Please tell us!"

"*Dulce bellum inexpertis;* do you know what that means?"

"Oh, I do." Richard's eyes brighten suddenly; "War is sweet to those who have never fought!"

"Ah, so the Latin was not wasted after all," Pacificus gently lets his eye fall past Richard to the middle distance. He crouches down with them, so that his sword catches on the rail. "Good. So if you really know what it means, then you will not ask me to talk about what I once was, and I pray you will never see it either."

When he thinks they look penitent and downcast enough, he takes them about the ship, telling the crew to tighten this, loosen that, tidy the other. Piers lingers near the small canons, as if he might be able to take one home if he is good. Pacificus crouches beside him and pats one reverently: "Now, these are your Perieraes, two-pound shot, close range – have as many as you can get your hands on, stick them everywhere." He points to a similar gun with a longer barrel. "These Falcons are for longer range, but still two-pound shot. But these," he says, laying his hands on the largest cannonade, "these are your Minions, your persuaders; four-pound shot, can rip through the hull of any ship afloat. Have as many as you can afford, even have them on the forecastle if you have a spare, helps clear the way ahead when things get busy."

The children mill like bees, they want to fire them, or else ride them like horses. Cobbe is scowling. Pacificus says he'll make them all good sailors and they are ecstatic. He has a crew member bring them all water and scrubbing brushes and sets them to work on the poop deck, which seems even to bring a smile to old Cobbe, and at least keeps them busy before his old friend Christopher calls them below to their mothers. Pacificus finds a place for the Fenton boys with them on wool tods in the cargo hold, where they can be watched over, for the twenty or so crew are a mixed bag and still eye the passengers with unconcealed avarice. The Fenton children will be worth two years' wages each, and well they know it.

When the children are settled, Pacificus and Christopher go back on deck to see if they can see any sign of the *Genoese*. "This is a marvelous deliverance, Hugh. I had never thought to see you again after Cambridge, and surely not in such circumstances."

"Think not on it, friend." Pacificus' raises two hands in resignation. "I have my own reasons, sure enough. And as for the rest, I feel a powerful providence at work against me. But this I cannot discuss." Both men fill in the years; where they have been and how they chose the religious path they now walk. Christopher, eyes riven and weary, clutches a grey blanket about his shoulders, dark curly hair flicking in the breeze. He is honest about the difficulties of being an Anabaptist, but then you can be honest at sea, away from land – no church commissioners, or constables out here, just waves and the far horizon. "I did not know then that to choose Christ in this way would mean so much hatred from the world." Pacificus starts to remind him that it was for smuggling contraband that he'd been arrested, when Christopher speaks across him. "No, I didn't mean that. I mean in every other matter, how we fall beyond all the usual protection, barred from every position, every advancement; it is these things I did not fully consider. I was naïve, really."

"And yet you chose re-baptism Christopher, an act condemned by state and church alike. If you're looking for pity, my friend, you'll be hard pressed to find it here. Think of your wife, your child!"

"I make no windows into men's souls Hugh, God will judge aright; only I am convinced by the Scripture – "

"Convinced about what?" Pacificus raises his hands in incredulity. "That you should rend the church to justify your interpretation of Scripture?"

"Not rend the church asunder but rend the church from the state, as Tertullian answered Origen: *"Quid est imperatori cum ecclesia?"* He saw what Origen could not, and neither can you, I suppose."

"Tertullian? 'What has the emperor to do with the church?' Then you would...would – "

"Rend her from Constantine's sword! Yes, of course. Surely you can see that? Restore her to her virgin state as in the days of the apostles; part of society, not the entirety, winning men voluntarily – not by coercion and force of law."

"I see. And you think Henry or any prince in Europe would allow this? Why, not even Luther or the Genevans would allow it."

"Christ does not seek their permission."

"And what of the state? We are to leave it in the hands of godless men?" Idiot, Pacificus catches himself, you walked straight into that one, does it need an answer? "All right, Christopher, I know what you are going to say but even if all the Popes and bishops were antichrists, as you no doubt say, even then their power to restrain the petty ambitions of Europe's princes has been beneficial. Look at England, about to descend into a bloodbath at home and with the emperor."

"There will always be bloodshed between nations while men have their say, you of all people know that, but we are not traitors to the king, we argue only for freedom to practice religion as we see it in the Scriptures, without interference."

"Hah! Apply that across the board and it would be the death of religion."

"No Hugh, don't you see? It is rather this religion held together by kings and Popes that will die – you can't make a silk purse out of a sow's ear. In arithmetic you cannot make a calculation right by going on, only by going back."

Pacificus is trying to interject but Christopher raises his voice: "Besides, do you think this *New Learning*, this *humanism* will forever stay within the church's skirts? It won't. With their Plato and their Aristotle, they will set up an independent world, free from the interference and petty tyranny of your state religion."

Pacificus tries again to disagree but Christopher won't have it until he's done. "No friend, let me finish, our way will be the flowering of true faith among hungry men – or do you think they come to mass now because they have true religion?"

"And now you presume to judge men?"

"Judge men's *actions*, Hugh, as is commanded by the Scripture, it is *by their fruit* that we know whether men belong to Christ, not in word only – or church attendance. But I'll not play pedagogue to you Hugh, you know all this already, and methinks already see it to be a truer way."

"Oh! So you *do* judge me after all!"

"I only know that you are not at peace," Christopher rests his hand on the leather glove inside which Pacificus' hand clenches the gunwhale banister with white knuckles. "You did not find it with the knights, or at the White Horse, nor at the abbey."

He does not pull away, but exhales with a shudder. "All right, all right, I will admit that I have struggled, and that the man Fenton has unmanned me. I just...just..." Pacificus drags his beret off and scrunches the velvet against the handrail. It distracts his attention and for a moment he looks down at it with an ironic smile. It is the sort of beret worn by men like Erasmus to symbolise free thought. Free thought, dear God! Did Simon choose this for him on purpose? Can a man have free thought? Free from what? He scrunches both eyes tight into his head for a long moment. "Christopher, pray what is it that Christ demands of a man, for surely I have given him body and soul, and blood too these thirty years, he cannot still ask more?"

"You plead an offering of Saracen blood for your soul, Hugh?"

"Oh, a fine reply! And I suppose your sect would sit by and let them overrun and destroy Christendom!"

"And I suppose you would defend with a sword him who said to turn the other cheek, him who told Peter to put his away?"

"It's different, when you have an aggressor nation – "

"Then fight them to defend your nation, not Christ's church. For surely it is an abomination to him to shed a man's blood to please him who commanded you offer your enemy bread, water and clothing, not your blade."

Pacificus is already countering this last point by listing his good deeds, even to the Mohammedans, but it sounds lame, like merely sending up smoke. He groans inwardly. Damn them. Christopher and his sort are such proud expositors of the Scriptures that they set their opinions – for that is all they are – above the combined wisdom of the church fathers, embodied in the holy mother church. Could there be more arrogance afloat than that? Hugh follows this line of reasoning but Christopher won't let him off easily. For all his airy idealism, he's no lightweight when it comes to church history. The church fathers contradict themselves on major points he says, the church has always cherry-picked and interpreted what they wanted from each source to support their latest corruptions. "Hugh, he who marries the spirit of the age today must be widowed tomorrow. There is only one solution, one source from which to argue."

"Yes, yes, we know, your blessed Bible, Christopher!" He is suddenly reminded of his conversation a quarter-century before with Erasmus on a scaffold under Michelangelo's fresco in the Sistine Chapel. It was Erasmus who had this idea to compile the best Greek New Testament texts – this is all his fault. "I know, I know. Well, here we are risking life and limb for it, and the lives of your family too, so say no more."

They part friends still: "I'll make a heretic of you yet, Hugh," Christopher says. He thanks him again and goes below.

Pacificus goes to the Captain for news. They are making good time, Cobbe says and on the present course will make Antwerp by tomorrow afternoon. Pacificus tells him to make use of the current winds and run the ship due south until they reach the channel. Cobbe is not happy, it will take them off course – he's been his own master mariner these last three years, done this run a hundred times. But Pacificus insists, "you must trust me captain, when that strong north-westerly is in the channel I want us as far south as possible, if I'm not mistaken the *Genoese* will be close by then and I have something up my sleeve that will leave her standing.

He was not wrong, for the next morning at first light, the *Genoese* is sighted on the horizon. It is far enough away, the first mate says, but Pacificus disagrees. "No, she will be on us before ever we make port. Send me the carpenter and let us be busy."

With almost everyone's help, including the women and children, the new masts are secured like the wings of a great swan, outstretched at right angles to the ship. The bases of these wings are each lashed to the main mast then to the gunwhales, so they rise out over the ocean like giant fishing rods. The ship's carpenter works hard to fix the pulleys and ropes, and finally when the new sails are unfurled by the crew, everyone sees what Pacificus has secretly been about.

"It's a fantastical arrangement monk, I'll grant you that," Cobbe says. "So, I take it we run straight – north-west with the wind?"

"Aye, captain, and then we can rig these new wings. If we rig her before, while she's across the waves, we risk a wing dragging in the water and turning the boat. Once we're running with them, we'll have as much sail as the *Genoese* and more, per tonne."

But Pacificus' smile turns pensive as he walks to the gunwales. He knows that the next task, that of threading the ropes through the iron rings on the lower hull, is dangerous. He mentions it to Cobbe in front of three of the men. It takes only the briefest hesitation on the part of the crew for Piers to volunteer, and then Richard too. Beth says they should not. She looks to Pacificus, expecting him to see the sense of it, but he merely nods at Cobbe. "Prithee Captain, I think they should be allowed to earn their spurs – that is, if they don't mind a ducking."

"I see. And what say you, lads?"

"We'll do it just fine," Piers says. "Won't we Richard?"

Richard, feeling the encouragement of Pacificus' smile, replies, "Yes, like he says. We'll do it."

Richard has half got the rope through the ring when the ship lists to port, and sure enough he is plunged right into the green surf. The salt water bites his flesh and floods his mouth, has him choking and gasping. He emerges to the cheers. He has to try five times, with everyone watching and some laughing, but he heeds them not, holding onto the shouted encouragement of his knight: "Keep at it! It will go through! Again, again, lad!" With each ducking his fingers and body are more numbed as he struggles and struggles to get the rope through the rings. He can't do it, there is too much movement. Everyone is watching. Beth would have had him pulled back after the third and forth attempt but Simon gently holds her back, saying quietly, for her only: "No, the boy ought to earn his spurs," and so she lets it be.

With Pacificus urging him on, at last Richard succeeds. It is the same story for Piers, though he has it through in two attempts and pretends that the water is just the right temperature for a swim. He's not saying that three minutes later though, when his sister is rubbing down his shivering body below deck. Nevertheless, they are all back up on deck for the final hoisting of what the crew is dubbing the "*Pelican*'s goose wings."

"And what a speed she goes, Cap'n, what with the turning down wind and all," the first mate bellows, "eight knots and more!"

"He's right too," Cobbe says, doing his best not to look too impressed.

"You and I, captain, will take our lunch in port after all," Pacificus says, "and perhaps you will have the quartermaster let my squire here handle the whipstaff? I dare say he's not been to sea before." Richard is beaming. To steer a great vessel like this is something he has only dreamed of.

"And you," Cobbe says to Piers, who is about to ask for a turn on the whipstaff too, "can warm up those skinny limbs by climbing the rigging, just to the yard arm and back, and mind you do it quickly before your sister sees you."

Pacificus raises an eyebrow, "Going soft Captain?"

"Well," Cobbe says slowly, then shaking his head, "Might as well be useful while they are here."

Richard takes to his lessons at the helm with great sobriety, and by sun-up he is looking almost at ease, even though the running with the wind requires quite a rhythm to keep them straight; a quart to port then starboard, then port again, for the swell is always tending to bring the back of the ship round on them. But he gets it so well that the quartermaster leaves him with Able Seaman Jacques of Caister for ten minutes, while he goes to break his fast. By mid-morning they have lost sight of the *Genoese* and can see the flatlands around the point of Vlissinglen, where they enter the five-mile-wide estuary leading to the great port.

They are yet forty miles from Antwerp but that westerly wind from the Channel is still gusting them straight towards their destination and there is no need to take down the goose wings yet. Richard marvels at the estuary, the numbers of ships passing each way, the sheer width of the last reaches of the river. He never conceived the largeness of the world and the almost miraculous courage and ingenuity of these traders who circumvent it to ply their wares. It makes the approach to Norwich on the river Yare – a journey he made with his father twice a year with the barley – seem like a domestic or provincial affair. With a sudden stab of longing he wishes his father had been there to see him. He wonders how large this city can be, that it should be served by such a river.

Soon after midday they come within site of the great spire of Our Lady's Cathedral, and a half hour later Richard is relieved of the helm by the crew when they turn the final corner and the great port comes into view. By now, the goose wings are packed away and the children gathered on the forecastle, pointing out the various ships, the steep-roofed town houses and the great castle.

The men of Antwerp have built landing stages to take ten ships at one time. The captain points to the wharf where they must unload and where Pockington's offices and warehouse are located. Pacificus says he wants the boat facing upstream for a quicker departure in case that is needed, and also that they bring four of the starboard perieraes onto the port side – and have them loaded and ready for action.

"You expecting an army then, are you?" Cobbe says.

Pacificus smiles, then shakes his head. "Always imagine the worse and you are rarely surprised. You cannot press a man that you cannot say no to."

"Or a man standing between four perieraes."

"Exactly."

He calls a meeting of Christopher, Simon, Beth, Richard and Piers at the captain's table. He is stripping and cleaning the matchlocks, then reloading them while he describes how the next hour will run. Even if they themselves are not being watched, Pockington certainly will be. They nod. He has thought of everything. He makes them repeat their moves, to be sure they have remembered all. No, Piers, you don't get to take your fathers long bow. And what will he, Pacificus do? "*Quis custodiet ipsos custodies,*" he says – he will *watch the watchers.* This is the town where Tyndale was finally betrayed and caught last year; he won't let it happen to them.

When the *Pelican* is finally secured and the gangplank fixed, it is Pacificus and Beth who leave first; he in his finery, Beth on his arm. They look in at the cluttered market stalls and barrow sellers, argue the toss over linen and spice, wine and almonds, and then stroll on, all the while moving closer to Pockington's warehouse, and all the while watching for the watchers.

And then he sees them – the ragged boy on the corner of the alley, and the beefy fellow in the jade cap and muddied travelling cloak. Both these are taking note of any entering or leaving Pockington's counting house, or his warehouse doors. The big one will need seeing to, but first the boy. He wanders near him, leaning in to Beth with a charming smile, for all the world like a loving relative sharing a joke or a compliment. But, in reality, he is whispering into her ear that she must not make eye contact. The boy is staring at Pacificus with his fine clothes and weapons and doesn't see Beth pull the large white feather from her pocket and let it fall on the street, but Richard, who follws thirty paces behind with Piers, does. He's has his hand on his father's basilard dagger, sheathed in his hose. Anyone messes with you or the lad, wave it in their face, Simon had said. The boys take to the narrow alley behind the ragged boy, and proceed to unpack the food bag. The ragged boy assumes, as they intend, that the food is stolen, and is greatly pleased to be offered a share of the spoils. He forgets his post instantly at the sight of English beef pie and plum pudding, joining Richard and Piers in the half-light. Why work all day for stale bread when you can eat like a king for free? The small beer they share is Sarah's own – how fantastical, Richard thinks, and who would believe us back home that we shared it with a spy in a foreign land?

Meanwhile, back on the main street, Pacificus whispers to Beth, "remember what we talked of. You pass him slowly and give him that peevish glance we discussed. Then head straight for the alley." She nods then saunters on, unsteadily at first, but then boldly. She passes to the spy's right hand and smiles with all the coyness of a regular strumpet, masking well her growing horror at the man's grizzled heft and odour. With one look, she has netted him and soon her echoing steps in the alley's half-light are matched by heavy boots. It's a warehouse alley with a double height brick wall at one end and not another soul in sight. When she is far enough down she turns to look at him again, and then shudders in earnest as the brute loosens his belt. His bovine physique near blots out the slender form of Pacificus, who is pacing lightly behind him. How will the kindly monk she has known at Saint Helen's church – the one fussing over brushes, egg whites and ochre – fare in this dark, narrow alley, against such an opponent? Pacificus is wondering the same thing. He walks light as a sparrow, bobs his head, squinting in the shadows, weighing the man in front for vulnerability – a point of attack. This one's a brute, bristled neck as thick as a capstan, scars which tell of skirmishes survived. Don't look my way, girl, keep at him with your mother's eyes. She does well, but he can see her fingers and thumbs fidgeting nervously. He had better get this right. Providentially, the man is too big to be cautious, over six-and-a-half feet of him. It would be easier to kill him, than restrain him – let's hope he doesn't like the wheellock. It's time! One – two – three – big breath, all or nothing! He rushes him, kicking the brute's legs from under him, and dealing him such blows with the brass butt of Hamberly's wheellock that the man goes down like a baby. Pacificus bludgeons him once more, just to make sure he's not faking it. The hollow sound of wood on bone make Beth wince. The man's arms and legs go limp as his face sinks into the dirt. Pacificus binds him hand and foot while Beth stands over him with the matchlock, ready and primed. She can hardly breathe for nerves. "He...he's coming to," she quakes.

"Don't fret, he's secure."

"Maitre Cremuel?" the concussed man keeps saying.

"Aye, and there's joke for you, maid." Pacificus says, "He thinks all Englishmen work for Cromwell." They drag him across the cobbles to a woodshed, stick a rag in his mouth and tell him that he is lucky to be alive.

They return to the wharf and Pacificus sends Beth back to the *Pelican* for Christopher. She finds Simon stands guard over the gospellers. He says that one of their number has gone to town to seek out friends where they might lodge. Christopher soon emerges onto the quayside, dressed as a monk with the hood of his cowl pulled low over his face. He is known here and must not be recognised. Pacificus nods when he passes, and the two of them go into the counting house to see Pockington. The clerks make way for them, all eyes on the monk – this is out of the ordinary. Pacificus asks for a private audience with Pockington, mid-fifties, squat, decked in red velvet and the most shocking pair of red silk stockings he had ever seen. The trader recognises Christopher Burgh, dismisses the clerks to their duties and scuttles like a crimson beetle through to his back office where they can talk in privacy. Christopher explains the complications and the imminent arrival of the *Genoese*. Pockington is unruffled, he knows his trade. There is no paper trail to him, besides he pays Maitre Cremuel's spies to inform for him too. The money is dealt with, the stock is ready. What is it? Pacificus asks to know. It is almond crates, the extra merchandise wrapped in skins and buried within. How many? One hundred and twenty two crates, he says. "Good; we'll take a hundred, but leave the rest for the *Genoese* – we must leave Cromwell's men with something to take home, no point robbing them of their dignity as well as their prisoners. No, let them have some Bibles to parade about at Smithgate and burn as they will, keep them from disgrace. Can you deliver straightaway? We hope to leave this evening." Pockington agrees, glad to be rid of them. They shake hands and part well content.

Two hours later the *Genoese's* four masts are spotted on the river. Cobbe's men haven't stopped since arrival, first with their regular cargo to export and then the new cargo to bring on board. Stevedores, cranes, pulleys and every member of the crew, all fly into action to unload and reload cargo. Once Piers is back safe on board, he marvels and chatters like a monkey to see the pulleys on the yardarm and the wine kegs being brought on. Pacificus bids farewell to Christopher Burgh and they talk a while, on the quay, with a roving eye out for trouble all the while. Where will he go, Pacificus wants to know. After the Leyden fiasco, where there was riot and bloodshed, his sort are about as welcome in the emperor's territory as they are with Luther – *ils sentent le fagot!*

Christopher dismisses this, saying that the Munster Anabaptists were a lunatic fringe, just as the Circumcellions were to the Donatists in Augustine's day. "No, Hugh," he says, "the devil only counterfeits what is genuine, don't be fooled."

"Well, why not back down just a little. Eh? Even for the children's sake? You have learning, languages, you could become a Lutheran or a Genevan pastor."

But Christopher shakes his head again. "No, no, Hugh, not me. Sinner though I am, I will not for filthy lucre join those evil priests who work hand-in-glove with the kings of the earth. Their conduct speaks for them; they have no king but Caesar."

"How charitable! Well, how will you work, support yourself?" But Christopher has the same insistent confidence in his Anabaptist God. 'The Lord will judge aright' seems a popular sentiment among them, though his wife looks like she won't last long, and the poor children – what a life for a child! No bed, a father with no living. And here's Christopher still trying to persuade him to read Tyndale's scripture, to convert; says he'll find true faith and lasting peace for his soul. You'd think he'd be more worried about his own body and soul – and his family; *a price on your head* means just that – deliver just the head and get your reward. But, he supposes, it's like old Norfolk said, there's no talking to them, these Anabaptists. He says he'll think hard on what Christopher has said, but really, why would he wish away thirteen centuries of Christian tradition? And why would anyone opt for a noose?

Pacificus is glad to be under sail again and mid-channel. He wonders whether he might have stayed a while longer and gone to the *Genoese* by night, to fix a net – or better, an old sail – to the underside of the hull. He did so once before, to the ship of a Teutonic knight – should have seen his face when he couldn't pass three knots! But this time he accepts it will be best to capitalise on the speedy turnaround and a constant wind, and not risk being caught. They pass her as she is putting into dock on their way out. Pacificus guesses the six who are spies, twitchy and nervous on the forecastle, waiting for the plank to be lowered. They will not go empty-handed. Twenty two crates is enough for them, and should be enough to throw Cromwell's men off the scent. The way *Maitre Cremuel* glared at him the other week at the castle was enough to make anyone look guilty. Hugh sighs uneasily and grips the rail tighter. He only hopes that when Cromwell hears his proud new four-master was beaten by Toppes' old barque on the Antwerp run, he doesn't start to think too much about it and get suspicious.

13

The Visitation

Castigat ridendo mores
One corrects customs by laughing at them

The *Pelican* makes fair progress to the Channel from Antwerp. Pacificus shows Captain Cobbe how to tack tighter and longer, how to lose less power in each turn by a gradual regulation of the sails, and they deploy their goose wings at an angle once back in the Channel.

They make Yarmouth six hours ahead of the *Genoese*, a pyrrhic victory, but Toppes' business is guaranteed for a while longer. The problem Pacificus faces now is where to store the contraband. He and Simon, convinced the Stokesby tannery will surely be watched if the tanner is a known gospeller, settle on the most unlikely place of all – Saint Benet's almonry.

This is initially Simon's idea; he can see his brother would sooner dump the cargo at sea than have them discovered in Norfolk, thus bringing down more spies and trouble on them. Pacificus begins to think his brother is suffering from his family's latent Lollard tendencies. At first he thinks Simon is jesting about Saint Benet's, but soon he sees the real benefit; not just that in spring the almonry is the least visited dry store with river access, nor that it would be the last place on earth anyone would search for heretic Bibles if it came to it, but that with each of the hundred cases there is half a crate of almonds and Italian chestnuts. If Brother Almoner could keep the body and souls of his poor together before the early harvest with these fruits, then he might be persuaded to misplace the key for a few days with no questions asked.

And so it comes about that some Yarmouth wherrymen, men who often deliver to the abbey, are approached on the Saturday by a monk offering them a fair price for the transport of a hundred crates. The proviso is that they will take him in one wherry and the leper in the other. Pacificus cannot risk losing sight of the contraband. The wherrymen object at first, they don't like the abbey's obsession with helping lepers and would rather have it any other way, but in the end they won't risk losing the Saint Benet's' patronage.

The children say their goodbyes, Beth saying to Simon that she wishes he would visit them again on the marsh. He says he will, with all his heart. The boys want Pacificus to come too. He feels for a moment what it might have been like to have his own children. He smiles and says he will come, but not for a while. Not for a day or two, the boys take this to mean, so they happily take their leave of the crew to bail out Pieter's little boat. While they are busy with this and chatting about their adventures, Pacificus keeps watch over the cargo and the alleyways. Simon has a gift for Beth before they part, "I took the liberty of wrapping some almonds, and this book for the old man, your guardian." It is one of Tyndale's second editions.

"I thank you sir. That is very kind." Beth places the gifts guiltily into her bag.

"You would like to read it too, I think?" Simon says.

"I don't read so well as my brothers." It's not quite true.

"I could teach you, perhaps? We could read it together, perhaps, anon."

"You are not afraid of the king, sir?"

"I'm not afraid, nor yet too old for new ideas, besides what can they do to me now?" She looks up into the man's eyes above the old linen cloth. He has been a knight again for a little over two days and now he returns to the lazar house. How can she deny him, when he saved their lives?

"That would be very kind," she says, "I'm sure my guardian will not object."

After a slow and fretful journey up river, the boats finally pull alongside Saint Benet's wharf. Pacificus steps off first, casting his eyes left and right. This matter must be expedited quickly and quietly. He finds brother Almoner in one of the storerooms and explains what he can. Later on, while the wherrymen are unloading, Pacificus catches a glimpse of Prior Robert and the Hickling brothers approaching and then entering one of the stores. The stores and barns that straggle the length of the wharf, are often partitioned sparsely with latticed planks, so as to aid ventilation. Pacificus slips into an adjacent barn and silently moves to the far end. Soon he hears the urgent whispering of conspirators: "I say the time is now – we all say so, for verily we have waited here long enough. I – I – I say that we should screw our courage to the sticking point, and let his guts out." There follows a silence, an uneasy one. Have they not heard him open the door? Pacificus doesn't think so, it is well oiled, and besides, he can see the crown of Prior Robert's head between a slat, and his lips in a crack below it. His head has not moved, is still not moving. Pacificus' own heart starts to thud unevenly in his chest. But then the prior's lips move as he answers the other speaker. "You have spoken freely, nay you seem to have spent ample time in conference one with another, so hear me privily then the matter will rest. We stay here 'til I say. Any man declare against that, then – " There follows an ominous pause in which Pacificus can hear naught but the nervous shuffling of feet next door, and then the menacing tones of the prior concluding all: "So – we understand one another. Good. Now, to your work!" And that is the end of the meeting. The men go their separate ways leaving Pacificus alone with his crates, asking himself whose guts they are plotting to spill, and why.

Brother Almoner is indeed happy with the delivery, eyes rolling white in wonder, hands raised in praise. The almonry lock on the abbey wharf almost needs oil to loosen it – " Why, we've not had provisions coming for the poor since harvest! Bless God, Brother, this is marvelous indeed – just look at it!" Pausing to wipe the perspiration from his forehead, he sees the mark on the crates now being hauled off the dock into the almonry. "Ah! I see this business for the bishop has taken you far away to Antwerp."

"Yes, but between you and me," Pacificus runs a modest finger through his stubble as he draws close and then says, with as much humour as he can muster, "these gifts are like Elijah's bread from the ravens, so to speak, they are to be wondered at and used with thankfulness, but not enquired after, not talked of, you understand – else the gifts to the poor may end up on the tables of the less deserving."

"I see, I see, brother." They exchange confidential nods.

"You know the way with these old saints! The bishop's alms-giving must be done in secret, if he is to win God's blessing. So distribute these as you can, but privily, and let the poor also have the crates for kindling. It is all for God's poor – we are to keep back none."

Pacificus then moves the talk on, enquiring closely what news since his journey – who has been in or without the enclave; what events have passed?

"There is none but this," Brother Almoner says, his face suddenly turning grave, "but only yesterday at Chapter, Brother Prior says that the Augustinians from Hickling will be offered hospitality pending a decision by the bishop, which seems strange when so many others from the dissolved houses must wander the lanes, finding work as chantry priests and tutors, and yet these men from another order are taken in. What's wrong with their own friary in Norwich, that they can't go there? There is something bothersome in it, brother. Of course, it may be the good bishop wants to heal the breach, seeing he has Hickling's lands now: but even so ...it gives me a distemper in my bowels!"

Pacificus has usually no time for idle talk or gossipers – though he forgives it in Brother Almoner for his great heart towards the poor – but in this case, he too wishes to know more. The Hickling prior, Robert Aeyns, strikes him as an oddity. There is something in his manner, a bearing more soldierly than clerical – something you cannot hide from those who know what they're looking for.

"And does anyone say why they were dissolved?"

Ah, here it comes; Brother Almoner knows a man who knows a scribe who, only last week, made copies of the *scandalous comperta* – the findings of Cromwell's commissioners Legh and Ap Rice – for the Norwich records. And, he says, this man – who is honest and has no favour in the matter either way – copied the names of six canons in Hickling Priory confessing *incontinency* in their offices, but before the matter could be gone into – puff! – it cannot be investigated because their entire house is dissolved. "What are we to make of it, Pacificus? We are a house with three priors!"

He waits for the conspiracy to sink in and then pulls closer to say, "Now tell me, brother, what could they have been up to all alone out there on the fens, that would have them moved before they are properly investigated? Someone high up is involved – pulling the strings I mean, protecting them. You see what I mean, don't you? I mean who is high up enough to do that?"

Pacificus does see, indeed, but he does not supply an answer – they came *here*, that's the point, so it must be Rugge. But then again, perhaps it is not so unusual. These Augustinians *are* a tough lot, but even so, some of their number, like the Williamites in Italy, have left to become Benedictines. Indeed, if it were not for his timely meeting with the abbot all those years ago in Cambridge he, Pacificus, might himself have become an Augustinian. For they had this one thing to his mind that trumped other orders: they alone were founded directly by the Pope, for which reason they were avowed, above other orders, to defend him and the church. In this they were the ecclesiastical mirror of the Knights of Saint John, whose oath he had taken, so what easier transition could he have asked for? But as things turned out, Rugge was a better persuader, and it is not good to go over things too much.

Brother Almoner is about his stores again, busy like a bee in summer. Pacificus waits for an opportune time and, while the almoner has the wherry men arrange the crates and no one is looking his way, quietly takes the storehouse key from the lock and slips it into his sleeve. "It is so good to see the shelves full again," he remarks conversationally, as he does so. But the almoner hasn't heard, for even now he is filling a bag with chestnuts, "it will not wait until tomorrow and I don't think I could sleep if I thought that widow Smyth of Horning and her children went to bed with empty stomachs again. I will go before Vespers."

Pacificus waits with bated breath. Another few handfuls might have revealed the bibles. After the brother has left on his errand, Pacificus quickly removes the contraband from the crates, and stores the books in a dark corner of the loft, well out of sight. Simon will send word where the key is hidden, and Pieter, if he still lives, will see to it that the heretics collect them within the week.

The children receive what Sarah calls a Lazarus welcome – back from the grave. Their boat has barely entered the dyke when James and Samuel see them and cry out. At first Sarah cries, unwilling to believe the sound of the wooden oars on the rowlocks and the bow rustling through the reeds is anything more than a cruel trick of her memory. When the sound she has yearned for is finally real, she can hardly take it in. But when she hears Piers' voice too, she drops her knitting. "Richard? Beth? Is that you? Bless me! Piers? Answer me!"

She, carrying James, rushes into the water before ever the boat has landed, and they too leap to her arms. Wet feet, wet eyes; Samuel beaming like spring sunlight, James' cheeks rosy as apples.

Pieter is mending too from his fever, and they are able to eat their evening meal together once more. The boys vie to regale them with stories of tall houses, steep roofs, wide rivers and mighty waves, tales they will be living on for weeks as they work on building the extension and going about their chores. Tonight, only Beth is quiet, sitting with Samuel, curling his golden locks, blending soft whispers with kisses on his cheek. She looks at the crackling alder log and the deep red of the burning peat beneath it. She thinks of her mother in prison, her step-father's grisly death, and of the arrival in her life of Sir Cecil. She is still conflicted, both repelled and attracted at the thought of him. This conflict extends in strange parallel to her feelings about her parent's religion too – this God who they say loves so much, but who demands so much in return. To embrace that narrow way is as risky as embracing a leper; it is courting Lady Poverty and even death. Would God really ask it? It is a question she does not even try to answer that evening. For now she is simply glad to be reunited with the little ones and Sarah.

In the coming weeks she will be visited, mostly by Simon but sometimes both brothers together. Sometimes Pieter will sit with Beth and Simon off at a safe distance, to hear the Bible being read, commenting hear and there, asking questions. Pacificus, hearing of these *illicit conventicles* – his name for it – worries that his brother is unguarded, weak even – perhaps because of guilt regarding the girl. A man looking for a clean conscience will go to great lengths. That much he knows himself. He, on the other hand, allows himself the small deception that he is there to deliver alms to the poor, when the truth is that he misses the boys' company. Richard and Piers revel in every visit, not least for a welcome break from the routine work of the household. They treasure their self-given status as Pacificus' page and squire. When he says nothing to forbid them such talk, they take it as encouragement and start to claim their 'rightful training.' It is mostly horseplay, but Piers – who is an inveterate tease – always brings it up.

It happens like this one day when they are all together round the table. Pacificus sees disapproval on Pieter's brow, but nothing will distract or deter Piers. "Oh, prithee, Sir Hugh, you will train us, won't you? You will? You said you would!"

Pacificus wonders how he can diffuse the tension, for apart from this, they have enjoyed a blithe afternoon. He has no wish to usurp the old man's authority with the boys in his care, here in his own house.

"Whisht lad, surely you know that no page or squire can train with arms unless he first learns the code of blessed Adrian Fortescue? Has it by heart, I mean." Confident it is beyond them, he thinks himself safe. He gives Pieter a wink, but the aged man's tawny eyebrows move but little.

"We're good at learning things, aren't we Richard? Oh, do tell us how it goes!"

"Very well," says Pacificus, glancing cautiously again at Pieter. "If you are sure you want to learn it, well then, I've had it been emblazened on my mind this many a year.

Above all things love God with all thy heart.

Desire his honour more than the health of thine own soul.

Take heed often with all diligence to purge and cleanse thy mind with confession, and raise thy desire from earthly things.

Receive Communion with entire devotion.

Repute not thyself better than any other persons, be they never so great sinners, but rather judge and esteem yourself most simplest.

Judge the best.

Use much silence, but when thou hast necessary cause to speak.

Delight not in familiarity of persons unknown to thee.

Be solitary as much as is convenient for thine estate.

Banish from thee all judging and detraction, and especially from thy tongue.

And pray often.

Also enforce thee to set thy house at quietness.

Resort to God every hour.

Promote not thy words or deeds by any pride.

Be not too much familiar with servants, but show them a serious and prudent countenance with gentleness.

Be in the habit of kindly rebuking frivolous and wanton people.

Encourage all persons in well-doing.

Love wholesomeness in thy house, especially before young people.

Show thyself a sore enemy to vice, sharply reproving all vile and decadent language and deeds that are not honest.
Be not partial for favor, lucre or malice, but according to truth, equity, justice and reason.
Be merciful unto poor folk, helping them as far as thou canst, for there you shall greatly please God.

Speak courteously to all persons, especially the poor and needy.

Also be diligent in giving of alms.
In prosperity be meek of heart, and in adversity patient.
And pray continually to God that you may do that is his pleasure.
Also apply diligently the inspirations of the Holy Ghost whatsoever thou hast therein to do.
Pray for perseverance.
Continue in awe of God, and ever have him before thine eyes.
Renew every day thy good purpose.
What thou has to do, do it diligently.
Establish thyself always in well-doing.
If by chance you fall into sin, despair not; and if you keep these precepts, the Holy Spirit will strengthen thee in all other things necessary, and, this doing, you shall be with Christ in Heaven, to whom be glory, praise and honour everlasting. Amen.

"Yes, yes – *above all things love God*," Richard said. "I almost have the first part, but will you write it out for us?"

They learn it in two weeks, both of them – he should have seen that coming! And so for his part, well away from the cottage in deference to Pieter's scruples, he shows them the use of the rapier, buckler, basilard and matchlock – though in the case of the bow he thinks they will not have the strength, and besides, he tells them, it is yesteryear's weapon.

Richard spots the inconsistency, "But you said only this afternoon that you prefer the heavy broad swords – and aren't they are yesteryear's weapons too?"

"Yes, well, that is because, at least, that is to say, clever clogs...I - I prefer to see effort rewarded and not just the cleverness of skill and chance – it is unseemly somehow, *unknightly*. The broadsword and, yes, the long bow need a combination of strength and skill, and the exertion they ask of us are consonant with the gravity of war. To take another's life in war is a solemn thing, not to be held lightly, accomplished casually with a flick of the wrist or subtle teasing of a trigger, at least to my mind anyway."

"I'm sure if you were being killed you wouldn't care of the method," Beth says dryly from the sidelines.

"I would – and methinks you would too." Pacificus challenges her at once. "The rapier and matchlock are the weapons of today, I grant you, they mark the times, but in my heart I feel they offend against chivalry, making it easy to kill a man, and thus we honour him less. But – " He concedes with raised hands, "we must take the world as it is given to us, and be the best we may in it."

Piers stoutly clutches the long bow that was his father's, the one treasure from his former home that no one else covets. There is something in what the monk said that rings true with him too. His resolve to master this weapon is knightly in its way, more than just a boy's enthusiasm. Pacificus sees them both standing there, so innocent, so eager. It would be well for them to stay like that, but the world is not well.

He takes the bow in his hands and looks from that to the matchlock. "This will send an arrow one hundred and eighty yards, when your matchlock could only manage a hundred. But then again, at thirty yards, that matchlock could smash a ball straight through a man's body, splintering any bone in its way."

Pacificus approves Piers' attachment to the bow, telling the boy that if it really has been at Agincourt as they say, then their great-great-great-grandfather would have been under the command of his own forebear, Sir Thomas Erpingham. He might even have seen this bow with his own eyes, talked to your kin – nay, even trained them – think on that! They do, greatly taken with the idea. Piers announces his determination to master it by the time he is Richard's age and, he lets slip, "When I have, I will go to free my mother."

There is still no word of the date of her trial, Pacificus thinks. Poor lad, it gives him a child's hope, and a forlorn one at that. After an uneasy silence, in which Pacificus fails to frame an adequate response, they hear Sarah calling them in for a drink of beer. It is a day remembered in hindsight too for 16th May is the date of Queen Anne's execution, the day that her dainty corpse – the one that had made Henry ransom his soul and kingdom for – was buried in an arrow box at the tower. Hugh remembers her as a girl. If his own father had not had his way, Anne would have been his sister in law. Her brother George is executed too, and the king's friend Henry Norris. What a business. News is that the emperor would have had the King marry the infanta of Portugal – with 400,000 ducats – but no, Henry Tudor wanted little Jane Seymour instead. He took her two weeks later to wife, poor girl.

Ten days later, on 26th May, Bishop Rugge's first official visitation of Saint Benet's, and first time back since he was arrested on charges of praemunire the year before. Pacificus observes the fine white charger he rides, stately and elegant. Is he triumphant in his own mind or does he now feel a pinch of conscience at his recantation? It may well be that he does. Pacificus knows for himself how a man must bend with the wind to save being completely uprooted. He is received as both bishop and abbot now, with all due deference, but it is clear from the very first evening that this will be no easy visit. Generally the brothers knew how to uphold their conspiracy of silence at such visitations – after all, Rugge himself had trained them well. Doctors Leyton and Leigh managed to extract no more than four confessions of laxity at their visitation the previous winter, a thing that had greatly angered Cromwell.

On this occasion, the good abbot enjoys the affections of the brothers, many of them genuine, and he does not seem inclined to push too deeply during the interviews – at first, anyway. He hears minor grumblings about impudent novices, Mark included, and that, along with lapses from silence in the choir, looked to be as dark as things would get. The cellarer William Beccles gets in his complaints about Prior Thomas' hunting dogs, as if that would rank highly in Rugge's mind, when all the time he's wondering how , by the motions of the heavenly bodies, he can make this abbey yield enough to support itself and shore up the bishopric as well.

But then the more he goes through the accounts, the more his mood changes. Pacificus expects to be sent for at any minute, something he dreads for he has no final answer to what his abbot has asked of him. Time goes by and still he receives no summons, though they exchange nods of greeting during Compline. Next morning after Chapter – and a restless night for Pacificus – the brothers from Binham go in singly to see Rugge, then together with Prior Wulfric, then Wulfric on his own – something that seems odd to Pacificus. Perhaps it is about poor Brother Bede, though by now his "death by misadventure' is all but official, pending the final inquest at the assize in June.

When Pacificus is finally called to the abbot's lodging, he is surprised to see all nine canons from Hickling, including Prior Robert Aeyns, descending the stairs from the upper hall. Had they too been in conference with the bishop? To what end? They return his "*pax vobiscum*' reflexively, as he waits at the bottom of the oak steps for them to pass.

Hard, grey, sullen, cruel; what do those faces mean? He has not yet been introduced to a single one of them, and he – not the most sociable man in the abbey – has never made any effort to befriend them.

Prior Robert completely obscures the window on the stairs as he descends. The oak treads creak under him and he lets his great hands gently tap upon the banister as he comes down. His rounded shoulders slope down from his head like the prow of a ship, his eyes aloof, disdainful. A dense fleece of curly black hair extends down his neck. He smells badly of sweat, not the usual odour but the acridity of a man whose humours are out of balance. His bold nose and chin look Irish or Norman but the deep accent is English, though not local.

"You are Pacificus?"

"I am." Pacificus unconsciously squares his shoulders and draws himself up to his full height, which is not much by comparison. Aeyns gives an amused tilt of the head, but on reaching the bottom step, Pacificus notices him wince slightly, and let out a rough sigh of discomfiture. He is not old, perhaps only forty, but Pacificus knows that tall men are plagued by agues of the back and legs.

"Your leg is troubling you, prior?" Pacificus looks at him in concern. "Our infirmarian, Brother John, has a balm that – "

"No need, no need!" Eyes opening wider, Prior Robert says: "We Augustinians do not put *our trust in princes, nor in the sons of men, in whom there is no help*; the Almighty is our strength and healer. That is why we will succeed where you Benedictines fail." The prior carries on walking as he speaks, so that he is almost out of the door as the last words are uttered.

Pacificus' brow is furrowed deep; did I miss something? It was like joining a conversation halfway through. What did he mean about the Benedictines failing? And the reference to princes, was that significant? He was only offering some simple medical advice. God knows, Brother John's comfrey balm has eased his own aches over the years. Its a poor substitute for a mother's soothing words, but comfort is in short supply these days.

Pacificus continues to turn these things over in his mind as he climbs the stairs. He pauses to watch the swans avoiding the wherries coming into the abbey wharf. One signet follows its mother between two converging boats, like Jason dodging the clashing rocks. Pacificus puts his knuckles on the window ledge and lets the tension drain from him in a long breath. Oh bird, I envy you I do. Would I could follow as deftly as you do between my own Symplegades!

His contemplations are brought short by Rugge's voice from the open door to the upper hall. "Is that you Pacificus? Pray do not tarry."

He enters the upper hall, kissing the abbot's ring, proffered regally on a velvet glove across the oak table. Rugge is decked in pontifical white Bruge satin, his voluminous sleeves draping across the many papers spread before him. He is blinking more than usual and his ear lobes are brightest red – the last meeting has excited him, perhaps. Behind the bishop stand the light oak panels he had installed on Saint Clement's day three years back. Linenfold ornamentation on the lower panels, shields in relief on the top panels, then, in the middle, relief roundels of men and women from Scripture and other classic texts – Caesar, Alexander, Penelope, Medea. The Norwich merchant who sold them to him said they had Italian provenance, which Pacificus doubted; but Rugge could not resist this little luxury in his lodging – for his guests' sake, of course. Anything broadly classical makes a place feel less like a backwater. Pacificus had never liked them, or any modern incursion into the religious seclusion that he had believed cloistered life to be. Indeed, he now imagines the prying eyes of Caesar and Alexander exercising a malevolent influence upon his abbot – perhaps he has been too long fancying himself more than a mere prelate. Perhaps the sorceress Medea has whispered great things to him, as she did to Jason. Perhaps Rugge fancies himself more like the Prince Bishops of old Northumberland.

They talk of the month past: the death of the Queen, things move fast at court, this way and that, the visitations due in Norwich in the autumn – but then Rugge stops, as if in remembrance. A small, sharp intake of breath, two index fingers joined in a pyramid go to set a guard over his mouth; his words become fewer, his nods more frequent.

"And Prior Thomas tells me of your trip away earlier this month – fruitful, I trust?"

"Aye, my lord." Pacificus wills himself to meet with steady gaze the shrewd eyes watching him.

"Somewhere near, was it?"

Pacificus half nods and smiles.

"I suppose Antwerp could be considered near by a man of your former profession." Ouch. Pacificus shuffles uneasily under the hawkish eye of his master. "It's all right brother, no need to flinch so – and no, I don't need to know the details either. Just as long as we know where we stand – that we can trust each other, that is."

What does he mean by that, and, more important, who has been his eyes this time, Pacificus wonders, hardly knowing where to look. Eventually his gaze lights again on the carving of Medea. Rugge, seeing him distracted, says "something ail you? Why do you stare thus?"

"Medea, the carving."

Rugge turns to see. "A remarkable woman that – single-minded."

"Hmm," is all Pacificus can muster. She was single-minded enough to kill her own children. Is he making a point? He tries to keep his expression neutral, wondering how to change the subject. "I trust your lordship finds the abbey in good order?"

"Well, let me see." The bishop narrows his eyes. "Apparently the altar cloths are not clean enough for some, and there is a lack of service to the sick, and five novices have no grammar, and even less respect. And what was the other thing? Oh yes!" He looks very hard at Pacificus. "A mutilated monk outside our gates – know anything of it?"

"I...er...I do not believe it an accident."

"Nor do I but let it be for now. Keep an eye on Wulfric, where he goes, who he talks to."

"Wulfric? Is something amiss?"

"The matter is delicate." Rugge puckers his lips. The old rascal is uncomfortable; see how he fingers that ruby ring. "Just observe and report to me, understand?"

"As you wish, my lord." But he is not happy – that look he just gave me, like a wounded and spiteful child. Does he know about the heretic Bibles? He's looking at me as he would look at a leper.

"Some have mentioned that Brother Mark is distracted in his offices by his devotion to Prior Thomas; would you agree?" The velvet fingers form a pyramid once more and he lets the stitching caress his pursed lips.

"He is more page than novice, my lord." You know my mind on this already, why ask again now? Pacificus hates all this. When people like

Rugge ask for advice they are usually looking for an accomplice. He can almost hear the creak of a trap.

"Perhaps you're right. Perhaps you are." The gloved fingers come back down to the table, each still meeting its opposite. A brief smile – a victory. "And perhaps as God has ordained you to see this need, you yourself would take Mark as an assistant after I leave?"

To spy on me, *custodiet ipsos custodes*, checkmate. "As you wish, my lord."

"You can bring him on in his devotions."

I might strangle him.

Before Pacificus is dismissed, the bishop also mentions that a young nobleman may pass a night at the abbey this summer.

"A nobleman, my lord?"

"You will know soon enough, only make sure *you are here* and that you remember your allegiances and render him your services."

"I see, my lord." Pacificus bows. As the old saying goes, if you can't be kind, at least be vague.

And so when it comes to it, there is no question of allegiance or position; he is to serve the bishop blind after all.

14

The Conspiracy

Facile largire de alieno
It is easy to be generous with things of another person

"You have fixed it!" Pacificus, drop-jawed, stands hands on hips by his coracle. "You have actually fixed the leak?"

He has sent the novice Mark away from Saint Helen's with a flea in his ear, indeed he found it hard to speak one civil word to him since the bishop left four weeks ago. His only comfort is that the lad seems to hate, or least feel chastised by, being the assistant of a man who paints pictures. No riding, no sport, he's bored, nothing but Latin primers now with the novice master, prayers and – of course – leaking coracles. But here he is now, the stripling he cursed out of the building but two hours hence, and seemingly without tools, he had mended his coracle. For a moment Pacificus looks from it to him in astonishment. Who have I been hating these past months – a real human being, this lad no older than that Richard Fenton, or a figment of my imagination? He is brought to by Brother Mark's offhand explanation about the top-weave still needing to be replaced before next winter. "Yes, yes," Pacificus says, "but it is mended for now at least, which is near enough a miracle for me."

Mark shrugs. "Easy enough. I needed something to do." The shock of it knocks Pacificus into his more affable self for the next hour. Mark said that he had borrowed the tools from old George Wheeler at the Ranworth staithe, says he always liked George, always went there to learn about fixing things when he was a boy. And he's no fool or poor judge of character is that Master Wheelwright, Pacificus thinks.

They scull up the dyke to the Bure, no splashes from the paddle, Mark can do it like a true native. He talks about his family, his older brothers, how he'd hated being sent to Saint Benet's at first, how he would have done anything else. He says he could improve the oars another time, remake them even, indeed everywhere he looks he sees and mentions things he either did or would like to do. So much so that Pacificus gets the impression the lad must needs use his mind and hands for something constantly, or else – well, you know what they say about idle hands. That's why he favoured the prior's life and perhaps why the prior favoured him; he proved an eager accomplice, if nothing else. And now he is sent to spy on me by Bishop Rugge. Pacificus asks him as much that same day in the boat but the lad does not break his stroke.

"Oh! Is that what you think?" He grins so that the freckles stretch on his cheeks, "No, though I suppose I'd have to tell him if he asked; maybe that's what he meant by it."

"And Prior Thomas?"

"Oh, he's finished with me alright, now Brother Martyn stepped up and him having a duke for a second cousin."

"No, not that. I meant did he ever get you to spy on me?"

"Oh yes, a few times. Said you had a big secret only the abbot knew. He didn't trust you. Frightened of you, he was, I think."

"Was he, now!"

Again the big grin; it is all just a game to him, "Don't worry, I didn't tell him everything, you know."

"What, prithee?"

"Ooh... about your trips up Saint Margaret's marsh with that leper."

Pacificus is stunned. Unthinking, he grabs Mark by his throat. "And what did you see there? Tell me, knave!" The boat lists towards the reeds at a dangerous angle.

"I – I meant nothing by it! Like I say, I didn't tell anyone," he splutters.

"What did you see?"

"I saw that leper reading with the maid, that's all. I swear it on Saint Margaret's bones."

He loosens his grip, "And why not tell Prior Thomas?"

"Well...er...well, because she was – "

"I see. She was very fair; and what of your vows?" He releases Mark, now gulping hard.

"No, it's not like that – well, not really. It's...you see...I know who she is. I grew up with Beth and her brothers about the place, and I didn't want them arrested on account of what their parents did, or because I betrayed them."

"I see, I see, very noble, that is." Pacificus gives a penitent cough. "I'm sorry I misjudged – that is to say, well...I hope your throat is not hurt."

"No, it's all right, only I thought for a moment you were going to do me in and toss me into the river." He shudders. "I think I need the jakes."

"Don't use that sort of language."

"The prior does."

"We don't though, all right?"

"All right! *Magister dix.*"

"Magister does say so, and it's "*dixit*' Fool! – *magister dixit.*"

Pacificus has almost forgotten the mystery visitor promised by the bishop. Then one day soon after Corpus Christi – it coming late that year on account of the lunar cycle – he hears the distant clatter of hooves on the lane. As if by some intuition or premonition, the abbot's words come back to him. But, busy with his brushes and bowls, he pays it no heed.

Outside on the lane however, a lithe nobleman in his mid-thirties approaches from Norwich, attended only by his gentlemen and two servants, not in livery. He holds a goodly countenance full of noble intent; forehead high, hair in half retreat but by no means surrendered to baldness, beard thin with hints of ginger among the brown, and markedly long ears and nose, though not unbecoming. Not that Sir Thomas Percy, brother to the sixth Earl of Northumberland needs fine looks, being heir to the largest seat of the noblest title in the northern realm. His elder brother Henry is ill – very ill, and moreover, very childless. Poor Hal came down for the annual Chapter of the Garter knights, but is now coughing into his sheets at the Percy house in Stoke Newington. But on this breathless summer day, his brother and heir has come to the middle of God-knows-where on a deep business. Sir Thomas may be riding as if he has no care in the world, but his gentlemen mark that he never takes his eyes from the road, not even to admire the maidens harvesting marsh hay for winter fodder, and thatching corn stacks, on every side. They are lightly armed, yet vigilant.

Minutes away at Saint Helen's, Pacificus is in no cheerful humour this day; nay, not one wit. So used to mixing his pigment in an egg-based tempera, he is finding the vegetable oil based variety – better for that durable and translucent colour blend – too thin, and now running hither and thither on Saint Helen's gown. Above his own grumblings he barely even notices the door open and the verger and clerk escorting someone outside. Only when all is quiet and the clink, clink of spurs and riding boots echo louder down the nave, does he finally turn to see the visitor. Taller than him, as most are, but broad of shoulder too and slender of waist, Sir Thomas is as fine a specimen as the aristocracy has produced. The gold silk edging on his doublet, the bejewelled sword and dagger, speak of wealth – rank even, Hugh thinks. The boots are worn down on the insides, he's been about of late, been busy. And those brown eyes, that swift step; this fellow has urgent business, and a world on his mind.

He does not introduce himself at first, just stands looking at the Tudor roses decorating the reredos, little ornaments Pacificus paints on bad days when his mood is out, or perhaps when he has slept ill and cannot tackle a larger section. Pacificus, brush in hand, follows his visitor's eye.

"These are – " Sir Thomas draws a word carefully down from the air " – very patriotic."

"Our abbot is a loyal man, as everyone knows."

"Yes. Of a truth, I know it." But then he gestures with his crop towards Thomas à Becket. "Though I fancy you will be called on to paint over Becket before long; replace him with Saint Thomas Cromwell, mayhap. Many of yesterday's saints are today's traitors."

The two men stand for a moment beholding the martyr, until Percy places both hands on his hips saying: "The question is, which are we, and which shall we be remembered as, Sir Hugh Erpingham?"

"Ah." Pacificus raises his head and looks at him, man to man, as his father always taught him. "I see you have the advantage of me, Sir...?"

"Thomas Percy. I have sought you out at Bishop Rugge's request." Sir Thomas takes the priest's chair, sitting cross-legged and casually removing his gloves. "He thinks you may be useful to the cause."

"You come at your brother the Earl's request?" Let's test the waters.

"My brother?" He uncrosses his legs before they are barely crossed, leaning forward and glaring hotly. "My brother has no stomach for anything but his sleeping draft and his bedchamber. But I tell you something else – there is not a noble, abbot, yeoman or peasant in the north that shares his apathy."

Pacificus keeps his eyes upon the rood screen. "You have pledges from the great houses, the nobles – men who keep troth?"

"We have, and will have more."

"Enough to stand against Norfolk, Suffolk and Shrewsbury? They will bring five or six thousand a piece, and Cromwell will not hesitate to bring mercenaries over if the outcome tarries."

"I think you mistake the strength of feeling north of your own shire; these men are boiling with fury, the common people too – "

"Come my lord, let us not speak of fury. Think you not that they will melt like wax before a real army, a real cavalry, real artillery. I don't say that numbers are all, but untrained men are a forlorn hope."

"Yes, yes, which is why we need to train men now." Thomas gets to his feet again and approaches Pacificus from behind, while he continues to busy himself with the *tempora* and brush. "That is why you must come north with me. Think on it, Hugh: there's not a man from Lincolnshire to Berwick who would not put a thousand to flight if he knew you led the field. Look at yourself, man! You're a soldier through and through, this is no fitting end for the great Knight of Rhodes, the scourge of the Sultan." Sir Thomas draws closer still. "You are near legend to them, man."

Ah, beware the flatterer, Hugh muses without turning to reply. Pompey Magnus was more legend and more deserving too. And what happened when he stamped his feet – did all Italy rally to vanquish Caesar? Most men are fickle as the spring weather. They weigh their lives like grain, assessing how much oppression they can stand while still remaining comfortable, then they choose accordingly. And what if it is misunderstood that Hospitallers have sprung up in England? What sort of diplomatic problems would that cause? Besides, the order is sworn never to fight against other Christians. "And your intentions?" Pacificus still faces Becket – what a man to look to at a time like this.

"We are not talking of treason, if that's what you think. No, our terms would be that the king has been badly advised and should lay off the pillage of our great houses and traditional religion."

"I see." Pacificus glances slightly to one side. "And suppose he does not agree, or his advisers outflank you in his affections? Will you call on the emperor, drive Norfolk into the sea, send Cromwell back to Cheapside? Replace the king will you? And with whom?"

Pacificus knows that Sir Thomas' elder brother, the Earl has made the king his heir; all England knows it, this might colour things somewhat for Sir Thomas.

"It will not come to that, and no, we want nothing for ourselves, only the preservation of traditional piety – a man's life here is short."

Pacificus wanders away towards the painting of Saint Helen. He has painted her so proud of her son Constantine, but now wonders whether later generations might think the pious smile ambiguous. Perhaps they will think her embarrassed? He wipes his hands on the rags and points to her, "It was the actions of her son, you know. It was Constantine who first put a sword of steel in the hands of the bride of Christ." That is Christopher Burgh inside his head, confound him. "Tell me Sir Thomas, do you think Christ is pleased that we make his bride so bloody?"

"You ask this? I mean, you of all people."

"Yes, me of all people, more bloodied than David!" He gestures towards his painting of Paul on the rood screen, "You will notice that in ancient times we only painted swords in the hands of the church's persecutors."

Sir Thomas walks round in front of him. "God's son, Hugh! We fight for the very liberty of England!"

"But we don't, do we? As you have said, we fight first for the old religion."

"The two are one in my mind, and our cause just. Now enough of this – are you with us or not?"

Pacificus looks up at the crucifix high in the rood loft and heaves a great sigh. "Yes. I am." But, he wonders, is Christ – looking down from his cross as we fret and strut, fast in this mortal coil? Ants we are, with too much to carry and too much to lay down. "For the sake of my old order I will go – anonymously, mind – just to advise on strategy and training."

Thomas agrees reluctantly, and Pacificus also makes him pledge to keep his name from the others for now. There under the rood, each man silently takes the other's arm, as if to seal a covenant, or else bind God to their cause. Pacificus is numb; this feels like sinking into death, yet somehow inevitable, like when his father made him wear a coat of mail and his mother disapproved because he was still so very young.

As they walk together down the aisle, Pacificus says, "I am sorry to hear of your brother's illness. We knew each other."

"Yes, I know. I thank you."

"If perchance you are alone and there is no one to hear, you might say that I am yet alive and that I pray for him. He was a fine soldier; do not be hard on him. I say that as much for you as for him; it is not good to have regrets. He may not be long for this world."

Sir Thomas nods penitently, and Pacificus continues, "I hear that he took it hard at Queen Anne's trial."

"He collapsed after the verdict, doesn't go down well when a peer of the realm has no stomach for the king's justice when he's on the judge's bench." He releases a tense sigh, remembering the monk's advice go easy on his brother, then adding, "you knew they had been close once, I suppose?"

Pacificus nods. Of course I knew. All England knew.

The Feast of the Transfiguration, 6 August – High Mass and many local worthies in attendance, including the sheriff included – whose wife is wearing peacock feathers in her hat – most unsuitable, someone ought to say something. They have news that Erasmus of Rotterdam died three weeks ago, and Pacificus is saddened. He feels that the scholar's mantra, *reform from within*, was the only sane voice in the wilderness of these last twenty years. He will be missed, though not in the English court.

After mass, Pacificus wanders away from the abbey to think on these things, and somehow weigh the sense of them against the madness of Christopher Burgh and his Anabaptist schismatics – how could anyone make the church stronger by dividing it?

He passes through the inner precinct gate, heading down to the fish ponds which are cut like an acre-sized maze of shallow dykes. Something about them has fascinated him since childhood, something about mysteries below the surface, other worlds we can only observe from above. The carp coast the pond in random patterns, leaving smooth streaks in their wake.

He looks up to see men busy at work beyond the abbey walls, for he is still on elevated ground. It is the month for clearing the dykes of mud and weed, ready for transporting marsh hay to the river staithes. Towards the marsh he can see others, women and children among them, cutting rye grass that they will use for finishing thatched roofs.

He wonders how the children are. He has not been to see them for three weeks and thinks he must do so soon, for he expects any day the promised visit of Thomas Moyne, a lawyer who will escort him to Lincolnshire to see what may be done for the rebellion.

As he turns all this over in his mind, he detects strained whispers coming from behind the wall to his right. The vegetable garden and herbarium are not large affairs, this spit of land at the forking of the rivers, means acreage is sparse. Most of the produce is brought in by the abbey tenants and from the abbey farm at Ludham, and certainly he thinks on this feast day there should be no one working there. He draws closer. One man keeps cutting another off when his companion tries to speak, though he cannot make out any words as yet. Pacificus steps lightly on the grass at the edge of the path, now making out not two but three whisperers or more. He is now six feet from the wall, and the closed door not more than twenty feet to his left. The garden is rectangular, two hundred feet in width on the side which Pacificus stands, and half a furlong in length. There are gates at each end, with the orchards, and then poorly drained pasture beyond. The whispers hiss louder.

"It's right enough," one says, "Bede knew the consequences. We had common cause, he was avowed, was he not?"

Another chips in piously, "God will judge aright."

Then still another, warning: "Shhh! Someone is coming."

The hinges on the oak door grind open on the farther side of the herbarium. Pacificus has almost reached the small door by now, but thinks it prudent to move away again to a more neutral distance and await developments. He sits himself down under the shade of a cherry tree and takes his rosary to his hands, half-closing his eyes, waiting to discover who might come forth.

He is not long waiting either, no sooner settled than the door in the far wall opens and through it come Prior Wulfric and his four remaining obedentaries from Binham Abbey – Aelfric, Benedict, Sigismund and Anthony. Their faces show nothing worthy of note but Pacificus does see Wulfric hang back for one last glance through the doorway before closing it firmly. The others meanwhile pass by, led by the lean and intentional faces of Benedict and Sigismund, who walk in front of the others, speaking one to another casually about the feast day and the weather.

"Brother Pacificus, what brings you here?" Benedict says with a nervous smile. They have had cause to talk before this, though not in any depth, when Pacificus had visited another brother at the infirmary and seen Benedict in the next bed.

"I am gathering my thoughts, such as they are. I see you have both recovered your full strength."

"Indeed we have," Benedict replies. "Your Brother Andrew in the infirmary is a credit to the abbey – marvellously gifted."

"Marvellously busy," Pacificus says, "but yes, a gifted man. He was an apothecary once, you know. Between them, he and the herbalist Gerard can fix anybody."

While they exchange these insignificant pleasantries, Pacificus cannot help but notice Brothers Aelfric and Anthony lingering at a distance, with a deference that puzzles him. Then as Prior Wulfric approaches, Brother Benedict murmurs a polite farewell, and then heads off with his three companions towards the precinct. This leaves Wulfric and Pacificus alone.

"*Pax vobiscum*, brother." The prior parts his hands in greeting and forces a momentary smile, all the time observing the doorway from the corner of his eye. "May I join you? It is a fine day for the feast, is it not?"

"Indeed it is. And how goes it with you, Wulfric? You and the brothers are settling in here, I hope?"

"Yes, yes," Wulfric says, sitting on the grass, slightly apart from him. "At least well enough for men who have renounced the world." He sighs like a man who has been holding his breath in pain. "And you, brother? Have you been here long?"

"Long enough." He pauses. Ah! Now I have your attention. "That is – long enough to see how the carp are faring; we have a goodly stock this year, despite the long freeze."

"The carp? Ah, yes – no doubt we will be dining on some tonight, celebrating Our Lord's feast with all the guests here today."

The fish squabble and push, rolling over themselves in clumps like boiling oil. "Yes, and swan too. For myself," Pacificus continues conversationally, "I always found something unnatural in carp, that they harass a weakling in the way they do, picking the flesh off his back "till he dies."

Until this point Wulfric had been smoothing the course wool of his habit round about his lower legs. But now he stops momentarily and his eyes narrow to weigh the comment before relaxing and continuing to smooth the fabric. "Aye, like these barons and bishops who conspire with the king to despoil the church." Wulfric looks from the door to the now upturned palms of his hands. "None of us is safe, certainly not you, not me. They have had a taste for flesh, and now the frenzy will begin in earnest."

"You seem very certain of it, prior?"

"It is written that Antichristus will war against and lay waste the church, does it not?"

"Really?" Sitting next to you as you rock back and forth like that, it is not the Antichrist I'm concerned about. "The writings of Saint John can surely be taken in various ways. And besides, Wulfric – " here Pacificus places a restraining hand on the man's arm, who in turn gives a little jump " – you ought to beware to whom you say such things regarding the king."

Wulfric's face tightens. "I will speak what is true; unlike our *brave* abbot, bishop and whatever else he has secured for himself."

"Surely you judge too harshly. Besides, when Cromwell's Office of Augmentations sends men to make us swear to the king – as assuredly they will – will you be braver, or have better reason than our abbot? Remember those six Carthusians last year at Tyburn? Men must spill their guts if they would stand by their consciences these days."

"Well, I will swear nothing, I will take refuge somewhere. Does it not also, in Revelation, say a place of safety will be given the elect of God?"

"Something like that, I cannot recall exactly."

"Well either way, we should be like our founder Benedict, judging the times and making preparations, as wise as serpents just as our Lord commanded."

"Benedict was not seditious, if I remember."

"Benedict saw all the world in decline. He saw the barbarians on the frontier, nay, the barbarians in civil office and he withdrew to preserve moral civility and Christian piety, as did Cassiodorus. What he did not do was wait lamely on the promises of impious princes and godless clerics. No – he acted, brother. He struck out and made his model society."

To these points he gives emphasis by stabbing the air with his finger. "And it was men like he, Ninian, Patrick, Hilary of Poitiers and Martin of Tours, whom posterity will remember if anything be remembered at all – certainly not Esau and Judas, or abbots who sell their faith for a bishopric, a pension, or any other mess of pottage."

Wulfric wipes the saliva from his lips and tries to control the involuntary twitch in his left eye by blinking. Pacificus observes it, and admires this much in the man. After all, he has been through a parcel of trouble in the last six months, and what is there not to admire in views honestly held, ideals yearned for.

Wulfric apologises for speaking with ill-considered haste, and he gets up to leave. Pacificus says that it is all right but again cautions the man that he ought not speak such things too openly. He watches Wulfric wander back to the precinct, mulling over their conversation. He had taken the man for a melancholic; how wrong can you be? Clear waters may look shallow, but are sometimes deeper than those splashing in turbulence. Perhaps a man of such passion ought to join the Anabaptists, for surely they are all choleric utopians like him, even if in theology on the flip side of the coin.

But what can Wulfric hope to accomplish here, now? There is no room in England for new monastic orders; above all not men that acknowledge a Pope and might court the interests of the emperor. No, if salvation is to come to England it will have to come, however regrettably, by force of arms, by civil war. The rights and wrongs of taking such a course seem beyond evaluating, no matter which way he argues and chews it out. Nor can he fathom what conspiracy these brothers from Binham are into either, whispering in there among the beet and the berries. What was Bede avowed to? Do they think his death was punishment from God? Are they in it together? No, for there was only one set of extra footprints in the sand, prints that came from nowhere and went nowhere. And above all, who as that Wulfric was watching for just now with such fear. Pacificus shakes his head; too much to take in, to assimilate. This will need time to digest.

The day following is the feast of the Holy Name of Jesus, and while Pacificus is going in for High Mass, there appears Mark, flushed of face and out of breath: "There – you are! You must come quick! Prior Thomas would speak with you."

Prior Thomas is out of sorts – these feasts always keep him from his hunting. He sits in the abbot's lodge behind the table staring at a small letter, while another gentleman with a lawyer's black robe and cap sits at a chair in the window, perched like a crow. Pacificus is about to dismiss Brother Mark, but the prior says he should stay. And so there they are, the four of them, while outside the swallows are dipping on the Bure and the abbey bell ringing for Mass.

"Well Pacificus, let us be brief, for I must away to Mass," he holds the letter up, "Our lord bishop and abbot commands that you and Mark go with this man of the law – this Thomas Moyne – to the north, and that I must destroy this writ as soon as I am satisfied it is his hand." The prior's tone is ironic and amused as he finishes surveying the note and looks up to Pacificus. "I suppose you know something about this?"

He gives a nod.

"I see. Well, I'm sure I can make nothing of it; which is probably best." He sniffs and gets to his feet. "Go then, and God be with you. See the cellarer for what you need. You may take a mule each – no!" He pauses on his way through the door. "No – better take my charger Percival. And you, Mark, that game little courser Arundel, that we broke this spring. Yes, a charger and a rouncey, might be just what you will need, if the game in Lincoln is as rough as I've heard – who knows but you may even get some hunting in." Ah, so he's guessed then.

"Thank you Prior, that is very – "

"Foolish, no doubt. Just make sure you bring them back if you can – and yourselves, too." He bows to the visitor but does not glance back again as he leaves. Moyne, who has up until this time not said a word, approaches over the oak boards at speed, extending a slender hand with a markedly strong grip – another keen lawyer; no doubt he fancies himself Chancellor or Master Secretary if the rebellion is successful. "Well, well! My clients in the north are most desirous to make your acquaintance."

"Brother Pacificus? Why him?" Mark says.

"Oh," Moyne says, "oh, I see, the lad is not privy as yet, well there is time on the journey no doubt, eh, Sir Hugh, eh!"

Pacificus is silent a moment, his eye on the commission that the prior has – whether on purpose or not – left lying on the table in neglect of his instructions. "Tell me, Thomas – " He leans over the desk and retrieves the letter; it might come in useful one day, *semper letteris mandate* – how many men know that you have come here, to this monastery, to seek me out?"

"He called you "Sir Hugh –"

"Silence, Mark!" Pacificus's voice rises like a tempest. "How many, sir?"

"Well, I…er…that is to say – just me. Only this day has passed since I visited the bishop."

"Well hear me, man of the law: if you ever use my name again, or breathe one word of where you found me, by God's own blood I'll see to it that you and your family pay for it." Even Mark's face drains at the tone of the words.

After Moyne has absorbed this, he gives his pledge. "Yes. Yes, I see there must be no links back here."

"Not so much as a whisper, and upon your silence rest the lives of all at Saint Benet's."

"Yes. Yes." Moyne has beads of sweat now on his pale forehead and the sides of his hooked nose. "Yes, I quite see. If the King hears – "

"My man, do not even *breathe* what is planned until you are among your own people! *And* – " at this point Pacificus lays a finger twice upon the man's heart, " – you remember what I said. Not *one word* – not even if they rack you or put you under the board, for it is *nothing* compared to what I will do to you and your people."

"Aye, my Lord –"

"'Brother'! Just 'Brother'. I go as I told Sir Thomas, as a monk to advise, nothing more. Mark and I will attend Mass, you will return to your shire and we will follow on tonight. Take not the king's highway, for it is sure to be watched – where shall we meet?"

"Oh, my house at Willingham, on the ferry road to the east of Lincoln."

"Expect us within the week." And keep your mouth shut, lawyer.

And so they leave that very afternoon, and all the while Pacificus keeps his eye on Mark, watching that he speaks to no one before they pass the great gate, perhaps for the last time. He will not visit Simon on their way north either, for they have long discussed this and have disagreed. And if he had been of two minds about aiding a rebellion before, he fears his harsh dispute over the matter with Simon – who daily seems to manifest a most willful lollardy – may serve to solidify a militant position to which he had been far less inclined in the first place. He blames Tyndale's bible. Simon reads it too much and, being untrained in theology, speaks a lot of nonsense about it.

Simon sees him that afternoon, knowing well enough what it means when his brother rides out on the Wroxham road past Saint James' Hospital, fully provisioned – on horses, no less. They wave from a distance one to another, each silently praying this will not be the manner of their last meeting on earth.

15

The Rebellion

Vox populi vox dei
The voice of the people is the voice of God

Whatever Mark expected, the journey to Lincoln is not an easy one. Still, as he says, even the open road is better to his mind than the cloister. Pacificus has loaded the horses with food enough that they need never spend so much as a groat on the road, or at an inn. They travel by the back lanes and over fields, hoods up when passing strangers and never talking to anyone – which is easy enough in these days when dispossessed monks are two a penny and much distrusted. They sleep in the fields far away from any dwellings, only ever asking directions from the most destitute of persons. There will be no trail for anyone to follow, they will simply arrive in the north from nowhere – and hopefully disappear once their work is done.

For two whole days Pacificus does his best to stave off Mark's questions – mainly through getting him to improve his dog Latin by reciting passages from Ovid, and putting him through his paces in the seven liberal arts – or as much as he could remember of it himself.

"Must we, again?" Mark laments with heavy steps.

"Yes we must. For without education you are in grave danger of taking educated people seriously - its your best defense. Now hear me and repeat: as with the seven heavenly spheres, so too the seven liberal arts: grammar; the skill of speech, are you listening to me? Grammar; the skill of speech, dialectic; proving by reason for proofs historical and experiential."

No answer.

"Rhetoric?"

No response again, just passive eyes gazing up the lane.

"Mathematics, geometry, astronomy and music." Pacificus sighs. The Latin has stupefied the boy's brain. He himself can still recite Ovid with ease from his own boyhood, the verses live in his very bones, and even though his own geometry and mathematics are weak, nevertheless it grieves him to see that the boy has little hunger for any of it. Though when it comes to learning the worthy stories, it is another matter entirely. "Twelve worthies there be, Mark, and well you should learn them, if nothing else. Three ancient; Hector, Alexander and Caesar, three Hebrew; Joshua, David and Judas Maccabeus and three Christian; Charlemagne, Roland and Godfrey of Bouillon." And so he would always start before each story, and so he developed the pattern of their lessons, often also reminding the novice that Saint Francis, himself once a knight, modelled his order partly on Arthur's round table - Christ's chivalric knights serving Lady Poverty. "When you are enhungered later today, think on that."

"Yes, master, I will, but tell me again about Charlemagne's sword. Does it really have the lance of Longinus in the pommel, and how so? I should like to work in metal myself one day. Have you seen it with your own eyes?"

And this is how it is with the novice, all he needs is some practical application to capture his imagination. And glad too is Pacificus for the lad's bent, for whenever they are to pitch camp, or get a fire going or build a prop for the pot, it is Mark who leaps eagerly to the task, even after a long and weary day on the byways. One day he teases a shard of flint from Percival's foot, another day he constructs a dry shelter from ash and sycamore boughs to keep them from a rainy night. By day three Pacificus so trusts in him that he sees no way round including him in all the details.

When he first hears about their commission Mark is excited, but later on the realization grows in him that there really is no riskier business. Poking the fire that night

Pacificus tries to reassure him: "If we are perchance taken, you may quite truthfully confess – before the rack – that you were sent to spy on me by your superiors, and nothing more."

"And do you think the North can really win?"

"Depends on how many stand up, and for how long. The lawyer says there is support, but we shall see. God knows I'm no politician, but if there is a chance that we can bring sanity and peace, rid the king of these evil advisers, then we must do something or hereafter always regret it."

"Speak for yourself. I was happy where I was."

"Nonsense. You, boy, said you were bored at your prayers. Perhaps heaven heard you."

Mark makes no reply, but tilts back his head to look full up at the night sky, which tonight is like diamond-studded velvet. "Look at them. So many stars."

Pacificus looks up and breathes in deeply. "Chalcidius said no man would seek God, nor aspire to piety, unless he had first seen the sky and the stars."

They are bright tonight, blessed be God; bright as pins in your very soul.

"This is Saturn, I think. This one more yellow that blue-white in colour."

"So it is, who taught you that?"

"Brother Anselm."

"He is a good man." But then Pacificus broods over the star, and has thought upon it often. The ancients called *Infortuna Major*, the bringer of melancholy to men and calamity to human affairs – a portent?

There follows a long pause in which the fire crackles and sparks fly heavenward. Eventually Mark shifts his sitting position and leans far forward near the flame. "What is beyond Saturn?"

Pacificus observes the eagerness on the lad's face. "*Stellatum*, fixed stars."

"And beyond that?" Marks head now tilts so far back that his voice strains in wonder.

"Beyond that is the *Premium Mobile*, though this you cannot see for it hath no luminous bodies, even though it moves all the others in their turn."

"And us, does it move us?"

"A wise man overrules the stars lad, though most do not."

"And beyond that?"

"Well now," Pacificus drinks deeply of the damp air so that the very essence of the dewy grass and the night pervade his senses. "The ancients say that outside the heaven there is neither place, nor void, nor time. Hence whatever is there is of such a kind as not to occupy space, nor does time affect it."

"How could they possibly know?"

"It is reliable learning, in books I hope you will read one day."

"Aye, but how can they know what is really beyond – beyond – well, beyond all this." Mark thrusts his hands skyward.

"Because they studied books, as I say. Now, don't be impudent. Bernardus calls that part *Caelum Ipsum*, the very heaven, which I like. And Dante calls it *that heaven which is pure light, intellectual light, full of love.*"

Mark, whose flitting mind had already lost the scent of debate, firstly by the whims of youth, but secondly by the majesty of the sky, merely says in a voice full of yearning, "So vast out there! Does it not make us all so insignificant?"

"No, not necessarily. All things here – and I mean all things, from stars to stones – kindly incline from their love for God. And who does he love?"

"Christ? And the Virgin?"

"Aye, boy and you too, if ye can believe it." Which he knows is always the harder thing - for it is a truth easier to preach to others than to reserve for home use.

Mark is silent a while, but then asks if they might say the night office. This they do, and for Mark it seems more real and fitting than all his time under the tutelage of Prior Thomas Stoneham, even though he had formerly held the prior in high esteem as a very great man, to be emulated. Tonight he feels close to heaven, a veil has been lifted somewhere. Partly it is the prospect of war, for no man is impious when he thinks the immediate future uncertain, and Mark is above all things a practical youth. But partly also he has the real quiet knowing, or at least a faint new suspicion of something *kindly inclining* in him too.

These peaceful awakenings are interrupted however when the wind gusts and sparks are scattered towards them. Mark brushes them away from his cloak, Pacificus does the same. For a moment there is the pungent smell of burnt wool, and in his mind's eye Pacificus sees the gaunt head of Norfolk, his pallid lips moving – *sentir le fagot.*

They arrive safely at Willingham and are well catered for in Moyne's modern house and new stable yard. He is not married but his housekeeper sees to their comforts. From Willingham they journey on to meet with supporters in the towns north and east.

They find that it is not the great and good in the shire, but more the aspiring mercantile classes and the common people, who speak openly in the streets and taverns about bringing an end to *the king's evil advisers*; which to them include Cromwell, Cranmer and the bishop of Lincoln, who has cooperated far too heartily with the commissioners.

Pacificus attends meetings with sympathetic landowners too – though not all who show an interest, for it is not certain if many can be trusted. But even with the sympathetic there is equivocation;

after all, they have more to lose and well they know it. The fifty-one Acts of Attainder – raised mainly against the Yorkist pretender, and one time benefactor of Sant Benet's, Richard de la Pole – have already been effective in transferring vast estates from traitors to the crown. Sedition is a grey area, as everyone knows. The cautious magnate of these informant-ridden times will think twice before sneezing near a portrait of the king.

After three circuits of the shire about Lincoln, visiting all and sundry in places like Louth, Horncastle, Caistor and Market Rasen, Pacificus hits upon an idea initially inspired by Percival, the prior's horse on which he rides. Their problem is that no landowner dares to stick his neck out too far; but supposing – and here is their guile – supposing word came to them of a rising at some particular place, there would be nothing to stop them from being out hunting that day, with their retainers equipped for the sport – this is, armed to the teeth.

They could therefore see the mass of the common people and – more importantly – which of their fellow nobles had declared for the cause, and stay to see the matter through if they wished. These things he is discussing one night with his host after dinner – it is a goodly plan, is it not? Another useful aspect to this scheme, which Moyne's legal mind swiftly identifies, is that common people will – from their vehemence to the cause – persuade any uncertain gentry to their cause by a bloody oath. Pacificus does not like this suggestion – a gentleman should be free to choose his side – but he agrees eventually, partly because of the vacillations of many they had spoken to, but also partly because such a forced oath might exonerate them later if things do not go as they hope.

In this way the scene is set within eight weeks. Pacificus is kept so busy that he barely senses the deadness in his soul, the calluses that canker his heart. He plays through arguments with his brother in his head, and he does not pray with feeling - and worse, is not even aware of it. The heavens are as brass – what is new? The men of Lincolnshire will fight for their relics, the wealth of their cathedral, and their practice of the old religion, but what is he, Pacificus, fighting for? He clings to some distant fragrance in his mind, like a memory that he knows but can't quite summon, much less articulate. He will fight to defend this fragrance, this whatever you call it – truth, true religion, some heraldic conception of Christendom that probably never existed – but he feels it slipping from him, feels it might just be the lingering perfume of an empty bottle. He acknowledges he has changed. He expected to be more alive, purposeful, vital. Instead he feels numb, detached, melancholic - perhaps the influene of *Infortuna Minor*. But come the end of September, it is too late for questions anyway.

The abbey at Louth Park had been dissolved that summer, and an inquisition among priests and monks is still underway. It is conducted by the bishop's chancellor, Doctor Raynes – a man universally detested for his gross arrogance as much as any reforming zeal he professes. As numbers of priests and monks are hauled to Bolingbroke for inquisition, tempers begin to flare among the commoners. Moyne gets wind of the Augmentations office dispatching commissioners to assist Doctor Raynes in his work. One of these is none other than Cromwell's aide; a man ironically called Thomas Wolsey, though he is no relation of Cromwell's illustrious-but-now-fallen benefactor.

This news is passed to a Fulletby man, William Leach, and with this extra oil for the fire, the rebellion begins. Leach fans the flames around Horncastle on the Monday,

pressing men to the cause, and with this boiling mass of humanity he marches on Louth, to protect Saint Mary's church from being spoiled by Cromwell's jackals.

The day following is 2nd October, by when Pacificus and Moyne arrive to find the men of Louth already numbering over five hundred, sitting about the church yard, some stern and surly, others jovial. The priest preaches blood and thunder against the greedy reformers. Women dispense small beer and vegetable broth from their cottages, and children run in and out of the matchlocks and pike staffs, thinking it no more than a village fair. These would-be rebels have done little more than burn the commissioner's books, and are hungry for greater insurrection now Louth is saved from the despoliation that Rayne's intended. They are led by the priest, William Leach, Philip Trotter, Robert Sotheby and William Bywater, reporting to Moyne that Raynes has fallen sick, so cannot meet them.

"Oh, aye? And you believed him too, fools," Moyne says. "Best get back to Bolingbroke and bring him to Lincoln before he escapes. The rest of you, agree your routes to Lincoln, and take who you need to spread the word. We want every man old enough to bear arms there before Friday – and the gentry too, aye, do not forget them."

After some discussion about how to divide up, and who would go where, the seeds of Louth blow in all directions across the ripening grain and second hay. In their wake, from as far as Caistor and Market Rasen in the north of the shire, to Spilsby in the south, men converge on Lincoln. In Caistor they find the Kings commissioners, bringing them down to the cathedral as instructed. But further south, in Bolingbroke, under the angry hands of John Hawnby and Gibson of Keal, Doctor Raynes is dragged from his bed to face an assembling mob in a field near Horncastle – all contrary to Moyne's instructions. As ever, it is easier to summon a dragon than to ride it. And it is there, among their own trampled grain, that the mob haul Raynes from his horse chanting, "Kill him! Kill him!" Brian Stanes, William Hutchinson and William Balderstone, three men who had certainly not thought that they would become murderers the week before, drive their pike staffs again and again through the man's body until their fury is spent. This same Tuesday, Cromwell's aide Wolsey is hung by the neck also. Other nobles, like Sir Francis Stoner escape the same fate only by swearing, what is being called, Moynes' oath - or the *Oath of Honourable Men.*

Leviathan is awakened and is gaining strength by the day – a monster that can only be gently led. By the time the men from the northern shire arrive, the others are assembling an army on Hambleton Hill which is near twenty thousand strong.

It is Friday and the northern men are late for the action in Lincoln. By now they have already conducted meetings at the chapter house in the cathedral, drawing up articles for the king to sign. Lincolnshire has over a hundred and twenty religious houses, and the people will not suffer them to be touched, not by any means. Nor will they keep paying heavy taxes in peace-time and neither do they favour the 'Ten Articles' or "The Statute of Uses'. These and other terms are sent to London in the capable hands of two local worthies, Maddison and Heneag, while a crowd nearing fifty thousand heaves about the city and surrounding countryside awaiting an answer.

Pacificus has but a small role to play in all this; plenty of monks, nobles and men of law now swell the throng of voices with their own eloquence and desire for prominence – pre-eminence, even. As with commerce, competition is bringing out the best products from the worst people. The sheer numbers and strength of feeling have swollen their pride. Fifty thousand men could walk over the combined forces of Norfolk, Suffolk and Shrewsbury with sweeping brushes let alone hoes and rakes, even supposing the other dukes wouldn't join them, which they still may. This is what they tell Pacificus, when he tries to entreat the assembly at the cathedral chapter house. What need they of discipline and training? Their numbers will speak for them loud enough, before the king. It will not come to war now. The crown and nobility would not risk it. Pacificus waits patiently in Chapter while puffed-up prelates and the local *magnati* prophecy victory and laurels. His groan is met with a glance from Moynes, who whispers, "Is all well? Do you not agree, brother."

"Indeed, no. This kind of political forecasting makes astrology look respectable. I must be allowed to speak."

Moynes arranges for Pacificus to address the company. He stands at the rostra and calms them with his hands, "My lords, friends, brothers, fathers, our numbers are indeed great and our cause just, but let us not be naïve and ill prepared - " He was going to put it a lot stronger and, when about to follow with a call for a greater supply of arms and ordinance, he is suddenly shouted down as a near unbeliever by a local abbot.

"We trust in the holy rood, in Michael and the Virgin, not the counsels of a Benedictine from who knows where, if Benedictine he be, for certainly we know him not."

Pacificus is never more tempted to divulge his identity than at this point, but that would be foolish. Thomas Percy is not there, but further north, and he begins to see how much his anonymity is working against him. In the heat and fever of the afternoon, he is soon forgotten and others take his place. He slips away but while crossing the cloister garth in despondency, he hears the voice of the lawyer Moyne, full of apologies.

"Prithee brother, I do apologise. Committees, committees – twisting alleys where good intentions are lured and strangled."

"I think not of myself in this matter, Thomas, believe me, I do not. But I beg you do not be over-confident. Henry will play for time. He will vacillate, demoralising and dividing you. Take my word for it, this multitude will melt as quickly as it came, if you do not press your superiority on the king's men."

Moynes nods but Hugh can see that he does not heed the warning, not really. And even if he did, how much power does he have to ride this dragon? Indeed, how much does anyone have when it becomes a creature of its own? They part on good terms. Pacificus leads Percival back through the crowds across Cathedral Yard to Pottergate, where he and Mark are lodged in Chancery Cottage, a dwelling not as grand as it sounded when they agreed to it on entering the city gates. He's insisted Mark keep his face away from all this, there will no doubt be spies in their midst. This cottage, only stabling and one dark room, has been just what they needed. The mercer had wanted one groat per night but Mark laughed him off and offered him sixpence. The doors are double-locked and there has been no trouble yet, but so many men in such confines tends to mischief.

"We're leaving already?" Mark says.

"We're heading north, to see what young Percy has mustered. They think they have no need of me here, and pray God they're right."

A glance tells Mark further conversation may be less than welcome. "I'll pack our things," is all he says.

After the assembly is disbanded and the cathedral locked, the keys are in the hands of Nicolas Melton – whom they call Captain Cobbler, after his profession as a cordwainer. He stands on a horse cart on the green, holding the keys aloft to the crowd, waxing loquacious as if he'd been the author of all English liberties. Burgers and bailiffs, mercers and masters, villeins and journeymen, all stand round the precinct and cheer.

But Pacificus is groaning on the sidelines, yet again. Happy the man, he thinks, who has nothing to say and abstains from giving wordy evidence of the fact. It is one of the enduring sights of the rebellion in his mind; the image of a new world which both entrances and repulses him. He has an aristocrat's yearning for noble knights clad in steel and holy fervour, making speeches before a pious and biddable populace. He knows that they are to blame: they, the aristocracy. The rich have not regarded the poor, but increased their power against them. They have betrayed their responsibility. The chivalric ideal collapsed centuries ago, for all Saint Francis had tried to revive it in a purer guise. And the knights of Rhodes? God forgive him. Whatever the ideal he'd held had been quickly lost. Sir Gawain bore the cut on his neck and the green baldric around his waste to remind him that all flesh is dust. As the scripture says, *there is no help in man*, not ultimately. Arthur gave a green baldric to all the knights to remind them of this, yet even the Round Table eventually failed. They, their green girdle, me, my scars. It is to remind me to hope in the one man who did not fail, in Christ.

He mounts Percival with this more comforting thought and glances once more at the crowd. Where this would end he cannot begin to guess, but one thing he does know, it will take more than a lawyer, abbot and cobbler to ride this dragon. Even as he and Mark are setting out along Ermine Street towards the north, the Lincoln envoys, Maddison and Heneag, are arriving in the capital with their articles for the king.

Star Chamber, London, 9th October. Its raining hard and torrents of water batter the glass and drum on the leadwork. His Majesty's leg is flared. Master Secretary has been warned by the new Master of the Stool: "tread carefully Cromwell, he's peaceable as a wasp in a firkin this afternoon."

The king mauls the northerners' petition with his eyes and fingers. "It says here there are fifty thousand armed men willing to take to the field against my enemies and evil advisers; have you seen this Master Secretary?" The king hands the vellum to Cromwell. "They want your blood, man. And who, prithee, leads this mighty host, eh? I'm sure I don't remember any worthy knight in that poultry shire."

Cromwell's eyes bulge slightly as they race through the document looking for the names of individuals whose necks he will surely stretch for this. But identifying a figurehead becomes a matter of pride for the king; who is this man daring to lift a banner against him, I'll geld him. Surely the mob is led by someone? Unsettled, the king picks, pulls and pinches the silk chemise poking through the slits in his red velvet sleeves. He is worried. By God, fifty thousand men! He will have all the leaders' names. He can imagine taking the field against another prince or duke, but he cannot conceive of anything as abstract as all England in revolt. "By heaven, Thomas, I will know who it is!" They leave the Star Chamber and summon the northern envoys. Maddison and Heneag squirm under the king's questioning.

"Well, your Majesty, I believe your loyal subjects are aided by diverse nobles, abbots, burghers, lawyers and, so we were told, generaled by – well, by a monk."

"A monk? What name and what house?"

"We have not his name, Majesty, for it is kept secret from us, all we know is that he hath long experience in military matters."

"Does he now – does he?" The king sniffs and then shifts uncomfortably on his regal stool. "What know you of this Thomas?"

"I know naught Majesty, not yet at least," Cromwell says. Then, turning sharply on the men as a thought races through his mind, "A monk you say? What of his countenance? Is his visage much weatherbeaten, like a seafarer?"

"We know not my Lord – that is... we have not seen the man ourselves." He can tell they're lying.

The envoys are dismissed and promised word within the hour. When they are left alone, the king gives Cromwell one of his 'Well? Would you like to tell me about it?' looks.

"Your Majesty?"

"This monk, Thomas. You suspect someone already? Ah! God's blood! If Wolsey were here he'd know! He knew everything that farted from here to Berwick. Well? Come on, man – tell me!"

Cromwell could easily have given Pacificus' name at this moment to satisfy his pride, but to his credit he will not do it. "Your Majesty will forgive me but I would not name a man of such heinous sedition without grounds. Though, the instant I am sure, Your Majesty knows I will not hesitate to act swiftly."

"I see! Then what of this rabble? Would you set Norfolk on them? For, upon my honour, I will have none of their demands, no more than they can have this crown my father gave me! This is a Yorkist plot, mark you, that's what it is! We must be subtle with them."

"No, Majesty – no disrespect to His Royal Highness, but I think the duke's sympathies might be aroused by these papists, particularly papists in such numbers."

The king doesn't approve of the insinuation. Cromwell contemplates adding: 'If indeed there is a Yorkist element, then perhaps His Majesty might also remember where the Howards fought at Bosworth,' but he rejects it as too risky a suggestion. So instead he clutches the letter tighter in his fist and moves on. "No, your Majesty, with your permission, I would rather send a delegation to meet the rebels and refuse their terms, at the same time gathering all the names of the leaders. Then I can send Brandon hot on their heels with the loyal Suffolk men, to bring them to the tower."

The king agrees and everything goes the way Cromwell plans. The men of Lincolnshire rose against the king's evil advisers, not the king himself, and when they hear that the king upholds the cause of his advisers, there is confusion. Men melt away like summer snow, some to their homes, some further north for there is ferment there too.

When he arrives, Charles Brandon, Duke of Suffolk has little difficulty finding the leaders – for there are many to denounce them to save their own necks. Moynes, Melton the Cobbler, the Leach brothers, Brian Stanes, Roger New, Robert Sotheby and Phillip Trotter are all in Brandon's consignment for the tower. Will they swing? Like as not, but time will tell. News of this will not travel north for many days.

None of these events have yet reached Pacificus and Mark. If Pacificus felt like a spare part in the Lincoln rising, the more would he feel redundant in York. By the time he arrives on the fourteenth of October, the Pilgrimage of Grace has already broken out the day before and is all that men talk of from castle to tavern. York has fallen to throngs of people, no less in number it seems than those in Lincoln. Monks and nuns are returned to their houses, Catholic worship is once more enacted in the city and the new occupiers – those restless rich, moneyed mercers, who bought up the convents and priories cheap, those strutting *arrivistas*, those profligate whoremongers, sons of horse gelders who thought they would ride the crest of the new world order, summarily are evicted and openly disgraced.

Pacificus finds Sir Thomas Percy at the castle in conference with the foremost northern nobles and abbots. They sit at table in the great hall like hungry relatives waiting to hear the division of a will. By the heraldic signs on their retainers it appears that no one of note is missing; here are the Tempests, the Constables, and the Hamiltons. And there are the Nevilles, the Lumneys and the Bulmers. Sir Thomas immediately rising from his chair leaves the heated discussion to greet his visitor.

"Ah! Good, you are here!" He sweeps a blue velvet cloak from his shoulders and offers Pacificus a hand. "I am told Lincoln was a success! Well done."

"Time will tell. I see you have quite a council of war here too."

"Yes, indeed we do! Even old Darcy has thrown his lot in – see him over there?" He points to a distempered old man with a whisping white beard, dressed all in black silk from head to foot, with one of those large white linen collars in the old style. He is as aged as he is revered, and hunches over them all like a Medici counting his florins.

"Things have moved on apace since we last spoke, Hugh." Percy's voice is hushed. "The baron has passed word to the emperor via ambassador Chapuys – "

"The emperor!" Pacificus draws Thomas into a small chamber away from the main hall.

"Dear God, my lord! What sort of message was that, prithee?"

"He has invited Charles to...well...to restore order."

Pacificus clenches his eyes tight shut, while Sir Thomas carries on: "He does not believe for a moment that Henry will listen to anything but bare steel – says he's known

him from a child and it was ever thus with him. Hugh, I'm sorry, I knew none of this when we spoke in the summer. Still, Darcy may yet be right; he has known Henry a long time. I suppose we'll see soon enough when we hear how he handles things in Lincolnshire."

"I see." Pacificus is pinching his eyebrows, eyes shut, deep in thought, painful thoughts. "This changes a lot of things; do we believe kings are ordained by God anymore? It was what we were taught, but now this – what will the emperor do? Hang the king for treason?"

"Hugh – Hugh!" Percy tries to prise Pacificus away from his thoughts. "You are still with us, aren't you? Come, man – this is no time for half measures."

Apparently not. A simple protest one day can be full-blown civil war the next if one old baron sees fit. "I prithee, Thomas – I need some time to think."

"I see. Well, before you do, at least tell me you will dine with us here tonight? There are men who wish to meet you, and one I particularly want you to instruct."

"Oh yes?"

"Yes, indeed, he's fallen into our lap from heaven, and if you can imagine the north's answer to Cromwell – but without the black bile – then you've got our man."

"Really?" Not another wretched lawyer, thinks Pacificus in despair, hasn't the world got enough already – going round in black robes calling each other brother and fleecing the innocent; anyone would think they'd miss their true vocations. "I see," he says aloud, "and who, pray – who is he?"

"The son of one of our old families." At this he draws back to the stone archway and points through towards a man near old Darcy. "You see him there? Robert Aske, a fellow of Gray's Inn, though originally from Aughton, which is Selby way. The man is a as sharp as a barber's blade, but devout with it. You'll like him I think."

Dinner is served late at the castle, Pacificus and Mark along with many other monks who have attended Compline being among the last guests to arrive. Again, when Pacificus examines the badges on the saddles he sees all the great monasteries have sent their abbots for the rising; it was Rugge's dream come true – Fountains, Sawley, Bridlington, Barlings, Bylands, Jervaulx, and Rivaulx among the number. Up here the ferment is stronger, he feels – more deep-rooted. Here they had not pressed the gentry as unwilling participants like the Lincolnshire men; here the foremost nobles would lead the field and the negotiations. At dinner Pacificus is seated almost directly opposite Robert Aske, just under the red banner of the Holy Wounds with which Aske had marched on York just a day before – with nine thousand men.

"Why are men looking at you?" Mark whispers from behind him where he waits to serve. Why indeed. It appeared Percy – or perhaps Rugge – has not been able to keep his mouth shut. Someone was even leaning to whisper in old Darcy's ear and pointing their way. So much for anonymity. Pacificus tells Mark to mind his tongue, but not before Aske hears it and realises this weather-beaten monk must be the man Percy had mentioned.

"I have heard about you, sir, from Thomas Percy." He offers his hand over the table.

"And I you." He grips the proffered hand for a moment, shrewdly observing this man who had risen so swiftly through the ranks of dissenters. Still young, in his thirties, with a square, honest face and sandy hair. No ostentation or embellishment to his clothing; not from any studied stoicism, Pacificus thinks – rather because such triviality never gained the attention of a man bet on meaning and purpose. When their eyes meet, Pacificus thinks of Jesus looking into the eyes of Nathaniel – *an Israelite in whom there is no guile.* How rare a thing is this. As they release each other's hands, Pacificus says, "You fared well yesterday, sir. Have you considered how you will meet the king's men when they come?"

"Do you think the king will sue for peace? Darcy does."

Both men refuse wine when it comes.

"I think the king will send Norfolk, Shrewsbury and Suffolk with no more than six thousand each. If they are met with a crowd such as we had in Lincoln, they'll not lift a matchlock. Besides Norfolk wants what we all want, and he's the only real warmonger among them, well, him and Suffolk."

"And your advice?" Robert leans over his venison, putting his knife down.

"The more you sweat in peace, the less you bleed in war." It is a trite response that comes easily to his lips. As soon as the words are out of his mouth Pacificus stops, closing his eyes and breathing deeply. "I'm sorry, Robert. This is not easy for me, you understand. I came here not to replace the king but for a return to the old religion."

"Yes, and I too – and we have no reason to suppose the emperor has the strength to leave his other campaigns for our cause. Besides, our pilgrimage will be over long before he could assemble an invasion force."

Pacificus smiles. "You're not just saying this because Sir Thomas put you up to it?"

"No – certainly not! I mean what I say. I believe the king is a faithful son of the Church at heart but needs rid of his advisers. And from all I hear, you are the man to help put the fear of God into them."

Pacificus nods noncommittally and then says quietly and very deliberately, "Very well. I will assist Sir Thomas in organizing whoever comes into a fighting force – and you, my friend," he leans across and thrusts a finger into the quilting of Robert's doublet: "prepare yourself for battle!"

A month later, 13th November. Aske is meeting with the Royal delegates, including, as he predicted, the Duke of Norfolk, with Shrewsbury watching over his shoulder. The first snows fall gently around them like angels in attendance. A light but chill north-east wind bears down upon the king's men in their grey stockings, shod in the court pantoufles. They are met in a tent at Scawsby Leys near Doncaster, chosen by Pacificus to showcase the forty thousand pilgrims in battle formation. And they are not going away either, Norfolk's spies tell him.

The whole force is fed, not by scavenging but by a general quartermaster, funded by the northern lords. *Nervos belli, pecuniam infinitam.* Pacificus had insisted.

Musketeers and pikemen in the forefront, flanked by the flower of the nobility mounted well on goodly steeds, blades drawn. Let Shrewsbury see their northern steel, and, by God, let him tell the king to repent his folly. Just the sight of them, bristling for war and well-disciplined is enough to allow Aske to demand what terms he wished; a reprieve for pilgrims – which by now they knew was more than the Lincoln rebels got – and the promise of a parliament to be held in York within the year, to discuss the complaints.

For once shaky, Norfolk observes Aske leave the tent in triumph and cross the field to where the chief nobles and captains surround a hooded figure – a Benedictine perhaps?

Fingering a holy amulet, Norfolk broods at the tent door while the clerks pour sand onto the vellum to dry the ink. He hates reform as much as any of the pilgrims, and in some ways he is as pleased with the day as any, but he also hates this new consciousness among the people; hates it and fears it more than ever he hated that upstart Cromwell or that coward Cranmer. Lawyers making terms with nobles. He, Norfolk would surely have Aske's head for this high-handedness. And monks on military councils with no sight of an abbot? The world has gone mad.

For Pacificus and Aske, this day is a final farewell. "They will grant me safe conduct to present these claims unto the king."

"Aye, if you disband the army," Pacificus smiles.

"It is what we expected; some things must be taken on trust." He rubs his arms against the bitter wind. "I have the oath of the king – the same oath as upholds all laws in the realm. I cannot ask for more."

"There is a lot more, as well you know." Pacificus says.

"What? You trust not the word of a king? Why, brother, you should be a lawyer and no monk!"

"Aye, and you are fit for naught but the cloister if you think Cromwell will not look for any reason under heaven to depart your head from its shoulders once you travel south."

"We have a just cause and I trust in God – well, in God and this host, a host in such good order, for which I thank you, brother."

Pacificus motions towards the tents of the northern lords, "And I expect none of them will be going to London with you, leave their castles and enter the lion's den?"

But Aske's shrewd smile shows it all; he understands the game they are in, and he doesn't seem to mind his part, "You are afraid that they will use me ill? 'Tis no matter to me."

Aske takes Pacificus by both arms, he is going to miss this monk who has taught him so much in so few weeks. "Be not sad for me brother, for when has life ever come to us neatly packed? For myself, I rejoice that I see what is right and can find some strength to stand by it. That is enough for any man, and besides – " He shakes Pacificus' arms for one last time with a broad Yorkshire grin, " – a youngest son has few other ways to distinguish himself in the world!" They embrace and that is an end of it. The pilgrims of Grace return happy that day to their homes and farms, the lords to their castles, the abbots to their monasteries, the priests to their livings - for now.

Pacificus leaves with Mark even before the royal delegation has quit the field. There is no more for him to do here. After many farewells, he loads Percival and Arundel with provisions, striking south on the king's highway. He heads for Norwich to convey the news directly to his bishop, hoping in so doing to redeem himself in his old master's eyes – though when the moment comes he feels unexpectedly indifferent to Rugge's approbation. And this detachment is driven deeper by one more dark thing in his soul – not a thought, or at least not one that he had allowed to surface yet – but a morose brooding and groaning against the Almighty himself.

This first surfaces in his conscious upon leaving the bishop's palace to pass through the gateway where the statue of Sir Thomas Erpingham stares down upon him. He is at once filled with both righteous indignation – nothing new – but also a heaving and morbid self-pity. There you are, God! I have delivered England from heresy and preserved the true religion without plunging us into a civil war. What more can you ask? May I not have some peace now? May I not find rest in my soul, one goodly night's sleep?

He stops just short of calling God a cheat and deceiver, but he knows the lead and wad are already in the barrel. God's teeth, what is a man to do? He squints for a time as if his eyelids were thrice strong mortar to dam an ocean of pain. Mark stops to ask what is wrong but he shakes his head, eyes still shut. When he finally does open them, Pacificus sees the turrets of Norwich castle crowning the rooflines of a hundred lesser dwellings. What is a man to do? He cannot answer, but thinks he will – for the children's sake – visit their mother Elizabeth Fenton at the castle jail and see if she is yet alive.

Mark waits with his horse on the castle green, while Pacificus leads Percival to the forge to be re-shoed. He falls in with the smith's son, Tom, as he crosses the yard.

"Where's the mule?"

"At the abbey, this here is Percival."

"He'd be fine at the tilt yard. My! Just look at his flanks!" The boy slaps the horses' thighs with gusto.

"He needs shoeing. Is your father busy?"

"He'll do it for *you*."

"For me?"

"I told him about you – that you were a knight."

"I never said that." Pacificus tugs at the sleeve of his habit.

"Didn't 'ave to." The boy grins with yellow teeth and then takes Percival's reins. "Now you've got the "horse and all."

Tom leads the horse towards the forge and Pacificus walks to the jailer's door.

Mistress Fenton has not improved in health during seven months' incarceration. She is thinner, the shape of her skull delineated clearly now beneath its shroud of pale skin. She is not in her cell but attending other prisoners in the lower dungeons. Pacificus watches from the door with the under-gaoler.

"She does this a lot?" he asks.

"Aye, brother, they call her *the angel* down here, and my master does not much mind, for she has never tried to run. And, as you see – " he points his keys to the compliant prisoners sitting like children on their straw " – she has made 'em stop fighting, which is good for everyone."

Elizabeth looks up, with a small but noticeable intake of breath as she recognizes her visitor. For a moment he flatters himself that she thinks of him, but then he remembers the children. She gathers the linen strips and water jar and joins them at the door. The under-gaoler grunts a little and says, "Here Mistress, another visitor for you, and he's definitely not the marrying kind, so don't you worry none."

She does not acknowledge the joke, but bows her head slightly to Pacificus and he to her. There are one or two more grey hairs, he thinks; and what was all that about "the marrying kind'? He enquires after her health as they climb the stairs, and asks her if she has enough to eat. She says God provides for her needs very well, to which the gaoler snorts. "Unless God's angels is now wearing Mercer's company livery, I'd say you've got friends in the guilds, my lady, not in t'heavens, and is it any wonder with you know who calling by here each time he's in town? Ain't for the air, y'know."

To this she replies not one syllable, though Pacificus sees her cheeks are slightly flushed in anger. Neither does she reply to the gaoler's further insinuations all the way down the corridor to her cell, though her silence does nothing to restrain him. Only when they are alone and the footsteps have receded does she clasp both hands to her chest and open her mouth. "The children?" she whispers.

He nods. "They are in health, last I saw them."

"Oh, thank God!" She sinks down onto her stool under the window. "Thank God!"

"They are very comfortable there, the small ones are thriving; you need not fret yourself."

"And my Beth?"

"Quite the little mother from what I have seen." Pacificus sits on the other stool.

"She has settled well with Sarah?"

"Aye, and is as happy as can be expected. And the boys too, they have great affection for the eel-catcher. They are...well, they are good people."

"For heretics?" She catches his eyes with a twinkle.

He nods back, that's exactly what he meant. She tells him that she has been worried sick since she heard from the gaoler that her children had been seen in a ship bound for Antwerp from Yarmouth, and that John Miller, in trying to apprehend them, was injured by two gentlemen, one with a mask. She hadn't known whether to believe it or not, only she knew Miller, and also thought it possible Pieter might take the children somewhere safer, nearer his own people. Pacificus is unsure how best to answer and she sees it.

"Brother?"

"Mistress Elizabeth, this is no safe place to speak of these things, only your children have been at sea, yes. It was not planned that way but Miller's arrival made it judicious to take them aboard for Antwerp. Still, they are safely at home again now, and no harm has come to them."

"You seem well informed of all this."

"So I am, but it was not my doing I assure you, and I'd rather we did not talk about it here."

"No," she says, lowering her head again and looking to the flags. "No, I suppose we ought not, only I have been much vexed by it all. But now I am quite at rest again, seeing you."

She turns back to him, asking in detail about each child, mostly things he cannot answer. But when he does, she closes her eyes and drinks in the images until she can remember their faces again, hear their laughter, feel their skin. She gives him little messages and admonishments for each child. But so glowing is his account of the older boys that she eventually opens her eyes and looks straight at him with an expression of half-enquiry, half-admiration. Like all mothers she thinks too highly of her boys and approves of anyone who shares her imbalance. He notices this look and breaks from speaking. After a telling silence, she concludes, "Their father would be very proud of them."

Pacificus nods, "Yes. Yes indeed." And then, after the shadow of his ghost passes over her eyes, he adds, "He died well, Elizabeth, very well. I don't know if anyone told you." Her eyes are closed now, but she nods. He notices how her thumb rubs at the place on her finger where her wedding band would have been. These have been doubly hard months for her, he thinks, was that a wrong thing to say? Two tears are now coursing down her cheek, so he gets up to go, though God knows he doesn't want to. This woman, with all her virtue and fading glory, makes mockery of men's vows. A wave of powerful feeling - a breaker so strong that he had scarce felt possible - surges deep in his breast. He tries hard to avoid her eyes and leave silently. But as he moves toward the door, she sniffs and blurts out: "It is Cromwell."

"He comes here?" Pacificus says. Well, that explains the Mercer's company supplying food for her, Cromwell never forgets a favour.

She nods. "He says that he has feelings for me, that he could help me."

"The blackguard!" he says.

"No, its not like that at all. And that is why I wanted you to know – because of what the gaoler accused me of before. It is not true. Thomas is a kind man at heart. He has suffered loneliness after his wife and children were taken by the sweats."

"And he asked you to be his wife?"

"I told him he ought to think of someone more advantageous for his position."

"Than a heretic?" *Touché*. "And what did he say to that?"

"Ah, well." She smiles and tilts her head in reproof. "That is none but my own business, brother, only I mention it for I didn't want you to misunderstand my position."

"And so you refused him?"

"I'm sure you aren't interested in the affairs of a woman's heart, but I thank you for coming here, and for taking these messages to my children. I really am very grateful to you."

She stands watching him turn awkwardly between the doorway and this, her whole world. She has known men and how to deal straight with them all her life. This her father had taught her – for such is the lonely portion of all truly beautiful women; to be seen but not seen, known but not known. She has boxes for amorous men, covetous men, ambitious men, but no boxes for papist monks who have rescued and loved all that is precious to her own heart. This man, this strange, awkward man, him she cannot quite place so easily, and yet she has prayed for him often. She stands up for the parting, wiping the tears from her cheeks with the side of her hands below the thumb. "I do pray for you." He acknowledges it as if it were a light thing, but she continues, "for I feel there is so little else I can do to repay your kindness, and you always seem...well...you seem so troubled."

"Please! There is no debt, but I thank thee for thy prayers; these are troubling times for us all." He holds his breath rather too long, letting it out at the end in that uneasy way that men with colic do. He feels a strange desire to tell her about his exploits in the north; who he has been with, how great men deferred to his skill and experience – no wit behind Cromwell at any rate. But he seals it in – heavens, what is he thinking? “Anyway, I will take my leave, and do as I have said regarding the children. There is no word of your trial?” She shakes her head. “Perhaps your suitor holds it off until he has your final answer.” How romantic.

She raises her chin. “I am not afraid to die, if that’s what you think – nor do I hold off justice by playing games with a man’s heart!” She flushes crimson. “And you should not judge harshly those others who – like yourself – have shown kindness to me!”

“He would save you, madam, as he has saved others.” His voice rises with indignation at this. “To win their gratitude, their troth – men with insecure tenure in life always do as much.”

“I see. And you would condemn me for accepting such an offer? Accepting a man who would ruin your monasteries, even if I could save my children from penury?”

“I...” Why did I not leave earlier? “I...would have you keep your conscience unsullied. The children will be safe, in any event.” She says nothing back, so he presses on. “Please forgive me for presuming, madam. I have spoken too freely, when in truth my own conscience gives me enough to struggle with. Anyway, I must be back at the abbey before the light goes. I bid you adieu.”

PART TWO - 1537

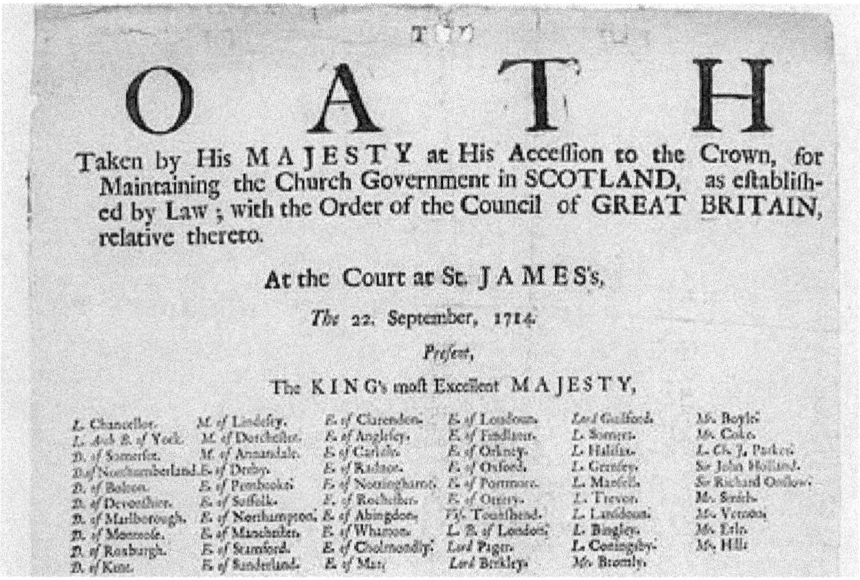

THE

OATH

Taken by His MAJESTY at His Accession to the Crown, for Maintaining the Church Government in SCOTLAND, as established by Law; with the Order of the Council of GREAT BRITAIN, relative thereto.

At the Court at St. JAMES's,

The 22. September, 1714.

Present,

The KING's most Excellent MAJESTY,

L. Chancellor.	M. of Lindsey.	E. of Clarendon.	E. of Loudoun.	*Lord* Guilford.	Mr. Boyle.
L. Arch B. of York.	M. of Dorchester.	E. of Anglesey.	E. of Findlater.	L. Somers.	Mr. Coke.
D. of Somerset.	M. of Annandale.	E. of Carlisle.	E. of Orkney.	L. Halifax.	L. Ch. J. Parker.
D. of Northumberland.	E. of Derby.	E. of Radnor.	E. of Oxford.	L. Gernsey.	Sir John Holland.
D. of Bolton.	E. of Pembroke.	E. of Nottingham.	E. of Portmore.	L. Mansell.	Sir Richard Onslow.
D. of Devonshire.	E. of Suffolk.	E. of Rochester.	E. of Orrery.	L. Trevor.	Mr. Smith.
D. of Marlborough.	E. of Northampton.	E. of Abingdon.	Vis. Townshend.	L. Lansdown.	Mr. Vernon.
D. of Montrose.	E. of Manchester.	E. of Wharton.	L. B. of London.	L. Bingley.	Mr. Erle.
D. of Roxburgh.	E. of Stamford.	E. of Cholmondly.	*Lord* Paget.	L. Coningsby.	Mr. Hill.
D. of Kent.	E. of Sunderland.	E. of Mar.	*Lord* Berkley.	Mr. Bromly.	

THE OATH OF THE HONOURABLE MEN

Ye shall not enter into this our Pilgrimage of Grace for the common wealth but only for the love ye bear to God's faith and church militant and the maintenance thereof, the preservation of the king's person, his issue, and the purifying of the nobility and to expulse all villein blood and evil counsellors against the common wealth of the same.

And that ye shall not enter into our said pilgrimage for no peculiar private profit to no private person but by counsel of the common wealth nor slay nor murder for no envy but in your hearts to put away all fear for the common wealth. And to take before you the cross of Christ and your heart's faith to the restitution of the church and to the suppression of heretics' opinions by the holy content of this book.

Oath sworn to by all supporters of the Pilgrimage of Grace, Oct 1536

16

King Death

A fronte praecipitium a tergo lupi
A precipice before, wolves after

Black, coiling, seeking. 1537 brings death through England like the spawning bream brings the eel back up the rivers to every dyke and every pond. It is a year they will all want to forget. No sooner is the winter reed-cutting finished than a bloody flux comes into many homes, carrying away those already weakened by the winter. The carpenter at Wroxham is caught quite off guard and cannot produce enough coffins to meet demand; many are buried one or two weeks after death. It is an ill omen. Then comes news soon after Candlemas of the judgement on the Lincoln rebels. That fiery priest of Louth, and Nicolas Melton the cobbeler who so proudly banded about the key of

Lincoln Cathedral, both hanged at Tyburn. The Abbot of Kirkstead – a very noble and even-handed man from what Pacificus remembers – along with three faithful monks, hanged at their own town of Horncastle. They say it was the women, not the men who went beserk when the king's monks were brought out to die. As ever, *last at the cross, first at the tomb*. Pacificus wonders if there would be anyone to bury him if he'd been caught like they were – things like that matter more to him now than he ever thought they would. Other ring leaders are hung drawn and quartered at Guildhall; including the ambitious lawyer Thomas Moyne of Willingham; the brothers, Nicolas and William Leach, Philip Trotter, Robert Sotheby, Roger New and Brian Stanes.

All this Pacificus hears aghast on the abbey staithe, from a wherryman, from whom he was supposed to be buying more pigment. At first he cannot believe the high-handedness of the king, or Cromwell, or whoever. Lincoln alone has brought fourth fifty thousand souls as suppliants before their king; does that count for naught? If he kills their mouthpiece what does that say but that he would hang them all if he had the rope. Damn his weakness, what is a monarch for but to protect the people against the nobles? And I didn't notice any of *them* swinging at Tyburn this spring! But the wherryman isn't finished.

"They says, brother," he confides, so *sotto voce* that many nearby will make the effort to hear it, "that even the crowd what watched it had had their fill of blood by the time they drew the fifth man – that they did groan at the sight of the innards such that the executioners feared they would be lynched, and that they did cling to the ankles of the other prisoners to make sure they was dead before they was taken down to be drawn. What d'ya say to that - evil business?"

"Nothing Jack, and nor do you." Pacificus looks at the old gossip sternly, "And don't you speak, or even think, against the king's justice – else you'll be praying someone'll be there to pull your ankles too, before you know it!"

At that, people on the abbey wharf start to go about their business. The walls have ears, and Cromwell has eyes everywhere. A groat can be made these sad days for a bit of tittle-tattle. Pacificus leaves for Saint

Helen's today with a heavy heart. What ill omen was this for the York lawyer, Robert Aske? The oath of a king, is that what he had said? Yes, that was it – all the laws of England are held together by the oath of the king. Dear God, what a poxy thread that has turned out to be for the Lincoln men – a king who cannot even keep troth with the wife of his youth, nor even his mistress.

His fears are justified, for Henry does break his word to the northern nobles too. Robert Aske is taken that very spring on the pretext that the Cumberland earls – chiefly Sir Francis Bigod – have rebelled and so broken the truce. Caught in the trickery is almost every man who led the field with Pacificus at Scawsby Leys: Sir Thomas Percy, Sir John Bulmer, Sir Stephen Hamilton, Sir Nicholas Tempest, Sir William Lumley, Sir Edward Neville, Sir John Constable, Sir William Constable, Sir Robert Constable, Adam Sedbar, abbot of Jervaulx, the abbots of Barlings, Sawley, Fountains, and the prior of Bridlington. At first most people thought it was just the lion roaring; these after all, were the great northern families of the realm, the voice of a third of the kingdom. Surely it was meet, at the very worst, that they should appear with nooses around their necks, for the king to condemn them, and then the queen to win them back with a suppliant's tears. That, at least, was tradition. But Pacificus now sees a regime that has lost all bearings on hereditary and moral rights. There is no past now, only the future. There is no history, save what can be marshalled to serve mammon and power. By force or by stealth: everything and anything is permissible. *Inter arma enim silent leges, for among arms, the laws are silent* – it's like having that lunatic Machiavelli reincarnated on the English throne. That book he had discussed with Hugh, Bembo, Guicciardini and others so many years ago at Santa Croce, is now *de rigueur* with the princes of Europe - its poison giving license of the vilest pretensions within the breasts of the most virtuous of rulers. Truth and troth are trodden in the dust, even as pragmatism and power are hailed as the new virtues.

Pacificus visits Mistress Fenton three times before Easter, as time and chance allow. They are polite meetings and he does not again venture to offer her moral or marital advice. They find a common interest in literature and so he is able to supply her with rare editions borrowed from Saint Benet's' library, as well as his conversation. Once, he stays for two hours discussing Boethius before either realises the time. The sixth century author had himself been imprisoned at the time of writing and so his *Consolation of Philosophy* seems a fitting book and almost, a temporary salve for Elizabeth. He also visits the children on average once a month, with Mark now in attendance. It has taken a while for Mark to gain the children's trust, for certainly Beth had never liked him when they were growing up – the puffed-up squire's boy who bragged he would one day be her master. But eight-year-olds say all sorts of careless things. There are traits of his father in him for sure, Pacificus thinks, but we – none of us – are our past only. Only God can give a man his name. Every saint has a past, and every sinner, a future. If that isn't true, then nothing is worth being true, nothing matters. This squire's-son-turned-novice has his faults and blind spots as anyone does, and yet is also a young man of ability and sense struggling to keep his head above water in a strange world, and strange times.

Pieter's health has never fully recovered and it is Mark who helps overhaul Pieter's two boats, and Mark who shows them how to get the best edge on the scythe for the reed-cutting that winter. And where would they be without Mark when it comes to clearing the dykes and slogging it out with a scythe among the reeds? Beth sees a different side to him, but cannot help still despising him as somehow complicit with his father in their own family ruin.

The boys on the other hand, particularly Piers, come to regard him as an elder brother. When Mark is there the two of them work harder, more efficiently and with less argument. And of course, if they have their work done early, there is always time for matchlock drill and rapier fencing when Pacificus or Simon is there.

Richard is filling out now; partly because he works hard but mainly because the boy is growing into a man. Pacificus enjoys his company, loves teaching him. Piers will be a natural swordsman in five years, there is no question. Mark will be adequate, if a little ham-fisted to be elegant with a blade. But it is Richard whose developing skill delights Pacificus most of all. He is so diligent and exact, so earnest and grateful for encouragement – so eager for the approval of a father.

Simon, meanwhile seems to be slipping further and further away, Pacificus thinks. The more he reads the Tyndale New Testament with Beth, the more distant he becomes. They argue now about things they once took for granted: the Real Presence, papal authority, even the need for priests. He seems to Pacificus like a different man, as twisted in his theology as his face is physically, as if he would let all Christendom burn if only he could have his own private interpretation of the Scriptures, with no reference to church tradition or the early fathers. *Sola Scriptura, Sola Scriptura,* he bleats like a recalcitrant Lutheran when Pacificus tries to persuade him with reason or history. Unless it is Paul or a gospel, there is no arguing the point, he will not listen. When eventually the thing descends into name-calling, they give up and stop talking about religion altogether. Once Simon apologises for being too argumentative and not peaceable, but no more than that once. And Pacificus remembers that day well, for it comes just before death strikes the household.

King Death comes to the cottage soon after Corpus Christi. It is the time when Pieter, Beth and the boys are working hard to bring in the marsh hay – fodder so necessary for the cattle's winter feed. The day starts like any other, the same sun, the same birds, same wind in the reeds and same chores awaiting them in the kitchen or river, or field. A day like any other – would God that it were! No one knows how it finds them, cut off as they are, but they all get it. Waking up a little shivery, a tad achy, the older ones think it is no more than a summer cold. But soon after the early chores are done, and it is time to break their fast, not one in the eel-catcher's cottage can stand at all. Sarah is the last to collapse, which is a mercy, for she manages to strip the children, making them drink as much as they can. She opens the shutters, but even then, it is hardly enough. They lie like fevered corpses, sweat pouring from every gland, delirious and helpless. Beth has Samuel whimpering and sighing near her. She dreams ten times an hour that she is making him drink, or wiping his brow, only to come round for half a second to realise that she cannot, that she has not even moved. It goes on until they lose track of time; the splitting head, the racing pulse, the lips and mouth parched like a desert, the limbs and torso burning like a furnace.

It is Simon who saves most of them. He's heard word of a small outbreak in Wroxham, and he's come near to the cottage to call to them, so that they'd be warned. But when there is no answer he comes closer. Then he sees the chickens wandering in and out the cottage door, and he knows there is trouble. He goes straight to work when he sees them all lying there; strips of wet cloth for their brows, water to moisten their mouths.

Beth remembers him there. When she looks back later, she recalls his voice speaking kindly, gently, remembers him holding the cup of cool water to her lips, fortifying her in the struggle for life. She does not remember him taking Samuel's body from her side, to lay him out for burial. Neither does she see him do the same for little James, golden hair and pink cheeks now as pale as a sheep's bladder.

It is enough to break his heart, he thinks, to see both bodies laid out there, looking so peaceful on the kitchen table – the jaw bound, a candle at the head and feet. Poor mites! What will the others say, if they survive? The fever breaks for all but Beth somewhere in the early hours of the morning, by which stage Simon has been able to get word down-river to Pacificus and Mark. Exhausted by now, Simon is only too glad to sit with Beth, while Pacificus and Mark arrange fresh bedding for the others. The last stage of the sweats – for those who survive – is a long, deep sleep. As they come through, Pieter and Sarah are able to talk for a short time, but nothing is told them of the bairns.

"You sleep now," Pacificus says, "we will tend them."

At the foot of Beth's bed, where Simon hunches motionless, Mark sits and prays, so fervently that Pacificus begins to feel concerned. "Come lad! You've done enough of that. God has heard you. Now, what about – " he whispers it " – coffins for these two poor children. There is wood in the barn." He nods and goes to it, like the labour of love it is.

When Mark is gone out, Pacificus lays a hand on his brother's shoulder, and Simon crumples, "Oh Hugh, to think that I had just found her too!"

"She still has strength, do not fret," Pacificus says.

"So much to say to her ...so much I wanted for her, so much she might have become, said, done...I didn't know this was how it felt – to be a father, I mean."

"Peace man, she may yet mend, even now. But get some rest yourself." Simon does rest, and is thankful when Mark wakes him two hours later, to let him know that Beth's fever has broken and she is sleeping well.

They buried the little ones four days later when the others can stand. Sarah and Beth are inconsolable, weeping for hours at the coffins, crying until there are no more tears, just retching guts and bent backs heaving in time with impotent sobs. The house will never be the same again, can never be, they all know it. Those joyous laughs and mischievous, beautiful, earnest, loving, trusting little faces - gone. No more. Never again. It is too much to take in. The boys are very quiet for many weeks after, exhausted from the sweats and stunned with grief.

Two little lights have gone out in Sarah's heart - it is like flesh ripped from the bones. How can you refill such a void? God has made her, old as she is, their mother; and she couldn't even nurse them through their first serious sickness. It feels to her like having someone pitchfork her viscera. The ache is so unbearable that often all she can do is sit and clutch her inwards.

And what of their real mother, so far away, how will she take the news? It is Pacificus who carries it, with two locks of golden hair, one week later on his way to see the bishop. She takes it with a pathetic sigh, then a near total faint. Their hair is lighter than she remembers, but then of course it is summer now. She is not well herself. She has been sharing the food the mercers have brought at Cromwell's command with the destitute in the lower cells. He suspected as much at his last visit. But now, weak though she is, she will hear every detail of their passing – a mother's last duty. Pacificus tells her all he can remember of the informal funeral, and it seems to give her comfort. They had been laid out in new clothes, their bodies washed, their hair combed.

She pushes down the voice inside her mind condemning her for not being there – and even worse, whispering that she has, by her confinement, become surplus to her children's needs. She enquires after this kind leper and novice who did so much. He wonders whether he should tell her Simon's identity, but he has sworn not to. What had his brother said? "Better she hate a whole man in her memory, than pity what he had by sin become." He tells her Mark is Hamberly's son and she smiles unaffectedly, "Yes, I remember him. God bless him for his kindness. Did he, too, not get sick? Nor you?" Pacificus shakes his head, but will not say what he is thinking. This month Mars is in the ascendant and, as all know and fear, *Infortuna Minor* produces martyrs – and he wouldn't lose her too. She makes him go over the funeral details again. What did they sing, who said what? How is Beth, Richard, Piers? Are they eating well? Tell them to take majoram, lavender, sage and just a touch of rue with their food. Have they smoked the house yet? He answers as best he can, and omits to mention that he and Simon almost came to blows about the propriety of burying children in unconsecrated ground, without a priest. He feels profoundly relieved that Pieter, Sarah and the children were not present to see them quarrel. In the aftermath of the conflict, while still nursing his bruised ego, Pacificus has had a nagging doubt; that while arguing for the traditional position of the church, he was betraying some more universal law of love. In a way he cannot fully explain, it helped Pacificus see how involved he has become in their lives, all of them. In the uncertainty that pervades almost everything else in his life, nay in all of England for that matter, this at least feels right – common kindness, ordinary faith, protecting the small, the vulnerable, the abandoned.

From Elizabeth's cell he goes to Bishop Rugge, who is excited about a forthcoming trip to London where he will meet with his fellow bishops. "I want you there Pacificus, need you there!" he says while

Pacificus is still kissing his ring. "Come – take a seat and let's talk awhile. This meeting of bishops will be all important in determining the *Ecclesia Anglica.* We of the old religion will need strength of both wits and numbers if we're to win any ground from men like Cranmer and Salcot – did I tell you Salcot never even moved to Salisbury after he was made bishop – without papal authority? Good God, man, what *is* the matter with you? You look like a bulldog chewing a wasp! It's not that unhappy business of the Lincoln faithful? We still have some hopes for that northern parliament the king promised, you know."

Pacificus explains that, yes, it was that – the arrests of the northern nobles – but other events as well; an outbreak of the sweats had left some dead near the abbey. The bishop offers condolences and orders some wine. They sit in a private drawing room away from the comings and goings. Everyone needs space to think, not least Rugge with all his schemes and plans. Click, click, click, its like clock mechanisms. The bishop chews his bottom lip and then grinds his jaw while clearing his papers. Round and round like millstones, grinding the affairs of men as small as dust before the winds of time. He has barely sat back before he starts again. There is the possibility of a rising in the west country, and perhaps a rising even here in Norfolk, he says. "Mind, those west country Cornish are a breed apart, hardly Englishmen!" Pacificus lets the remark go, he's not here to bicker. Besides, the bishop grew up in Repps near Yarmouth, where they have more truck with the Flemish and the continent than with Englishmen in the western reaches of the realm.

The bishop waves the air as if he were shooing a fly. "The fire smokes like the upper reaches of Hades, and you never get the sun here at all, but at least there is room to think," he says as it billows again. "And don't worry about that ghastly tapestry with all the mildew, I have a new one coming from Calais next month – friend of a friend you know, in touch with certain useful men in the French court; might be beneficial soon."

Click, click, click; wheels within wheels, doesn't he ever tire? He's excited today for some reason, his fingers scuttling over folios, letters and parchments like gilded mice, never still, never resting for a moment. Behind the desk, a rail on the panelling carries his correspondence, all tucked in line like feathers on the wing of an albatross. The table is spread with a red and black rug, and on that are set his pewter ink pot and quills, a glass vase with dead flowers and some chronicle of the Wars of the Roses, its binding near completely gone. So he's reading up, too. After the briefest pastoral chat regarding the sweats, he's back on to the details of his trip to London – where he'll stay, who he'll need to meet first, with whom he'll dine on night one, night two, and so forth, who must be watched, who must be leaned on.

"You will go on ahead of me, make sure the rooms are suitable – and safe. I do say it's a scandalous business that Henry took our London house on Bishopsgate and gave it to some minor courtier! But don't worry, Pacificus, we'll have it back, no doubt, when there is a reckoning."

There he goes again; *our* house; *we'll* get it back; does he really think I give a cottar's gong for his London house?

"My lord, perhaps I might visit Robert Aske and Thomas Percy, while in town?"

"What! Why? You will do no such thing! Have you lost your mind?" He rises from the desk and leans over it on his knuckles. "We are no use to them, nor to the cause, if we are caught; you may depend on that! No, brother – distance, distance! We play the game as we can, and carry it forward by what means we many. Visit them, indeed! They may get a reprieve, they may not, but either way, there are bigger things at stake here than individual lives – they know that, and so should you."

Ah, amputate and quarterise; Rugge would have made an efficient general but a bad captain. And then, finally comes the bishop's feverish plan, the reason for his excitement. He has a scheme to remedy the bishopric's financial trouble, namely pilgrimage.

"Now as you know," Rugge starts, fingers tentatively caressing a copy of the abbey's ledger while looking straight at him, "we never had any relics worth visiting at Saint Benet's, not like Bury's or Canterbury's. No one bothered to come on account of Saint Margaret, poor girl. But supposing there were? Supposing we had a relic so famous, so efficacious – with genuine provenance – that men and women would flock from every part of the realm to make votive offerings!"

The bishop leaves the question hanging while he arises and takes a seat by the fireside. He extends his ankles toward the heat and then raises a knowing eyebrow at Pacificus.

"But, forgive me my lord, the injunctions of last year were not favourable to pilgrimages, relics, nor yet the use of images."

"Nonsense Pacificus, you have no eye for detail. The injunctions stated the *misuse* of pilgrimage – people shirking their work too often and worshipping, rather than venerating relics and images. No, Cromwell has spent his shot on this one and made the position clear; the door is still open for us, and," he is whispering now, "God has all but placed in our hands a reliquary that will secure us a goodly future!"

"And this relic?"

"*That* you will know in good time my friend, but be assured it is of impeccable provenance and international acclaim – and not far away, I wager. Now – tell me about the Binham brothers and how they settle, how Wulfric seems to you? You have been watching them as I asked? There is a connection between them and the relic. More than that I will not tell you now, but prithee, how seem they to you?"

"Well, they seem to keep close, they hold private conferences, and I would say they are distanced from the other brothers by some matter of their own. It might help if I knew what I was watching for. Are they connected with this reliquary in some way?"

Rugge suddenly retracts his feet and leans forward, frowning his most serious frown and whispering with urgency. "This is a delicate matter and we cannot use any coercion, or we'll likely lose everything. Watch them all, but particularly him – Wulfric. See where he goes, whom he corresponds with; we are not the only interested party – here or abroad, we can't be sure who he knows."

Rugge then leans back with a broad, optimistic smile. "For my part, I will make sure among our brother bishops that pilgrimages have their prominence in the bishop's book. All this is a side matter, I know, but we cannot march, nor yet dream, on an empty stomach. The abbey's debts and the bishopric's fiscal needs are pressing. They must be met, or it is all over for us. I can rely on you?"

Pacificus nods mechanically as he tries to fit a new Flemish tapestry in the category of 'fiscal needs'.

Pacificus arrives in London as instructed, to ready Rugge's rooms. He has barely unpacked his spare cowl when he hears aghast that, just like the Lincoln rebels, the northern nobles will be hung, drawn and quartered for treason, within the week. You'd think that the northern pilgrims would amass and descend in fury on London to put the king on a gibbet. But Cromwell, wise as a serpent and innocent as a wolf, has decapitated the whole uprising so that there no one to lead reprisals – two hundred and sixteen souls will swing for the north. Lords, knights, half a dozen abbots, thirty-eight monks and sixteen parish priests – and of course his friend, Robert Aske. Part of Pacificus would like to think, if he had remained a minor lord, his serfs and freedmen would rise against tyranny to rescue him, but his romantic and chivalric naiveté is fast wilting under the scorching duplicity of these modern times. Perhaps they remake all of us in their own image – cynical, deceitful, unworthy of God and each other. The executions are spread out between Tower Hill, Tyburn, the Guild Hall, and Smithfield Market – it's always nice to have a side show when you've done shopping.

"You should have seen the Strand! I counted over fifty-two goldsmiths," Mark says, tumbling through the door of their personal lodgings at Ely Gate. The novice spills the provisions from the market onto the broad oak table in the upper chamber. "I never imagined there was so much silver in all the world!"

"You're late." Pacificus has been in a foul mood, waiting for news but not wanting it. "And I suppose you forgot about the other thing."

"No, I'm afraid not," his face falls for shame at letting the wonder of silver distract him, forgetting that this, Wednesday, 12th July, is an evil day.

"Well then, don't stand there like a limpet – spit it out."

"The date is brought forward because of the Queen's birthday."

"To when?"

"Today, brother, today. They say old Darcy, Percy, Robert Aske and many others will be executed this very afternoon at Tower Hill. Master, master! Don't look at me like that; it frightens me! Where are you going?"

In truth, he hardly knows himself. He has kept his word to the bishop and not visited the tower, but feels an overwhelming sense of loyalty to the condemned lawyer. He walks swiftly in the shade of the old houses in Shoe Lane, crossing the Fleet at Ludgate Hill, and passing Saint Paul's on Paternoster Row. At every turn it seems there is some small friary, priory or nunnery being dismantled under the watchful gaze of some self-made man or his clerk, each remaking the old enclaves after their own uses, some for slum housing, some for townhouses.

But for these busy reclaimers of the old world, all of London has forgotten their business today. It is not often you will see so many great men meet their maker at Tower Hill, or indeed, how substantial a portion of the northern nobility could be wiped from the earth for raising an objection to the current ideas of a handful of southern men.

Beyond Watling Street the crowd becomes like a living thing bound for Budge Row and then Candlewick Street, the stream fed all the while by yet more bodies from Dowgate and Walbrook. Here come the proud city people, some with liveried servants in attendance, some in litters, yet others heading for the river boats to avoid the throng. Pacificus is left among them; the velvet chamberlains, the clerks with inky fingers, clothiers with gauche doublets made from offcuts, constables with large keys hanging from belts under even larger paunches. Some of them seemed unlikely spectators for such events; they must have made an exception for such a spectacular line-up.

Here are the wisest men in all England, the men who know for sure which way history would turn, for they would never themselves lift a finger to make it otherwise. Even a gambler at the king's new racecourse in Newmarket, yes, even he risks something on the outcome. For surely no man ever backed a winning horse, but a contending one. Jesu, even

Norfolk's father eventually declared for the crown at Bosworth, but this rabble are like the Stanleys who wait until the battle is half won before they choose sides. A plague on them, they are worse, for at least Stanley fought, but these merely appear at the winning post and serve the first across the line. And look at them now – none shows the least shame or embarrassment, yet all go in the same direction, shoulder to shoulder, quite as large as the thousands who rose in York or Lincoln. Here is the king's real arm; the practical and complacent men of the new world. Damn them. Any violation of liberty is made possible when the populace has no greater value than their comfort, not greater god but mammon. These are the pilgrims of pleasure, voyeurs of someone else's history - denizens of the new world order, where might is right. On and on they mill, picking up a second and third class of rabble from Cheapside: bakers, barbers, blacksmiths, bottlers, bowyers - all fresh from work and all eager for a spectacle to discuss in the taverns later. What a marvel he thinks, pilgrimages are frowned upon because they take men from their work, but it is permissible for a nation to have a full holiday when they hang yesterday's saints and today's traitors. England will make a new virtue of it no doubt, with new saints too.

Candlemakers, chandlers, cooks, cobblers and cordwainers. Ostlers, ewerers, farriers and fowlers. And in every nook and cranny between there are children – laughing, shouting and crying, most not knowing even why they are there. Pacificus sees the Tower turrets up ahead, and squeezes off from the crowd to walk quickly up Hart Street, that he might come round the back of Tower Hill and so hopefully get closer. But the throng is already a thick mass by the Augustinian house of the *Fratres Cruciferi* – in process of being demolished for the mere price of the building materials. Crowds pour through the rubble like rats, some scrambling up to an elevated position atop an arch or half-demolished stairway stopping in mid-air, twenty feet from the ground. Pacificus pushes through the groundlings and despite their cursing and occasional raised fist, he eventually fetches up before the very scaffold and butcher's tables.

Sir Thomas Percy is making a short speech; he says he was ever the loyal subject of His Majesty – always a wise thing to do if you have any family left. Perhaps it had been well for him and England if he had not been, Pacificus thinks, not so loyal and trusting. What, with even forty thousand men behind him, he could have swept Norfolk and Shrewsbury from the field, taking London within a week. God's blood, this monarch is not worthy of this line-up of subjects! He can see Robert Aske in a cart behind the scaffold. There will be no more speeches after Percy; once the knife work begins, the screaming will drown out all.

Old Darcy is taken from the noose half strangled, and then they place it round Percy's neck. Francis Bigod takes the scaffold while Percy is raised up, and Darcy is handled onto the butcher's block and sliced from his navel to his chest. His screams come high-pitched and breathless. He turns his face sideways, he can't bear to watch his intestines being wound on the large bobbin. A minute later, Percy is dragged past with a purple face and rope-burnt, bloodied neck. His eyes widen at the sight of old Darcy, or what is left of him. Poor Tom, Hugh thinks, its a wonder he can stand at all. Courage, friend, courage. Hugh can see that the poor man is choking out his *Ars Moriendi* in Latin. Soon he, too, is being drawn. You can tell he wasn't expecting it to be so protracted, so painful. Oh, God help him. There are no words for it. It is a charnel house, an anti chamber of hell, made worse by the insatiable bloodlust and jeering of the crowd.

Next they hoist Sir Francis, and after him the three Constable brothers. Robert Aske is waiting behind them. Darcy's quartered carcass - jagged, white ribs and steaming, pink flesh - is carted away in a barrow to the groans of women on the edge of the crowd, and the Constable men go one after the other like lambs to the slaughter. Bigod is keening with intolerable pain as they burn his organs in a brazier before his eyes. Pacificus' and Aske's eyes meet as he ascends the scaffold. Aske tries to smile but brave as he is, he cannot hide the terror, much less walk without assistance – his breeches are stained. The crowd is cheering in the main, they are all worthy subjects of their monarch, adherents to *the divine right of kings* even when this is what it eventually means. This metropolitan mob and the king are made for each other, but this lawyer, he shouldn't be here, oh Jesu, he should not. Oh God, let the rope finish him, or if you'll not act, I will. Aske is hoisted but his neck is not broken; he is still moving when the constable stretches out his hand to untie the rope. Pacificus will not let this happen; he will not let them butcher his friend while he is alive to watch it. He will put a stop to it or die with him. Between him and the scaffold is a tight row of soldiers with horizontally criss-crossed poleaxes, then twenty feet and then an assortment of executioners, clerks, clerics and nobles, including Norfolk but not Cromwell – though today must be a personal triumph for the latter more than the former. Norfolk looks, as ever, like a corpse freshly dressed from a mortuary; today burgundy is the cadaver's colour of choice. If he had loved honour more than power this whole travesty could have been avoided: nay, if he'd loved his religion more than his position, he could have saved England from this tyranny, this butchery.

Pacificus has no trouble raising himself with a hand on the shoulders of two sturdy crowd members, and from there he slides his feet between two soldiers, using their poleaxes as a step to jump into the open space before the scaffold. The whole movement is quicker than a breath. The violated soldiers give a shout, but are so enmeshed by their poleaxes they cannot get free to grab him. The stewards and clerks scatter at one look of the monk's face, but there are two tower guards and one courtier who gather their wits enough to draw their steel– though even then, they are hardly quick enough for this maniac. Pacificus closes with the first in an instant, pivoting his body round a hundred and eighty degrees along the length of the drawn blade until his left elbow breaks the man's jaw. His object is to stay the constable's hand, to buy Robert more time in the noose. Better die there than face the butchers. He barely takes his eyes off him, or Roberts quivering ankles. He reaches down and removes the guard's truncheon, in one movement lets it fly towards the constable's head. It strikes true and the man stumbles back off the scaffold onto the mud below. But Pacificus is too late; the rope is undone and Robert is crumpling on the deck. What now?

Pacificus has the first guard's rapier in his right hand and does not wait for the other two assailants, but rather, rushes between them like a wild boar. The first soldier is parried in one blow and his nose broken by Pacificus' forehead. He falls like a baby. The next is a courtier, whose rapier's classic Italian-swept hilt indicates to Pacificus, along with his stance, just how he will fight. True to form, the velvet gentleman over-extends his blade, according to the Italian school. Pacificus overbalances him and, grabbing his immaculate blue velvet cloak with his left hand, swings him violently into the scaffold. He has barely recovered his beret before Pacificus pummels him unconscious with the hilt of his own sword. This takes no more than eight seconds, and by now the uproar has started in earnest. He has moments to do what he came for. He takes the courtier's long dagger, and springs onto the scaffold. Two aghast priests stand aside to the corners of it, with their new prayer books, as Pacificus goes to work. Robert is lying on his side, hands and ankles tied, panting, and spluttering: "What are you doing here?"

Pacificus cuts the cords on his hands, the tears now coming like hot springs from the depth of his bowels. "I came to pull your ankles. Spare you." He's heaving his sobs and trying to talk through gritted teeth. What now? He has done this before, and swore he could never do it again. And yet here he is. It is called the mercy stroke – the *Misericordia* – a soldier will give it to a fatally wounded comrade to speed his end; left arm raised, straight through to the heart. He presses Robert's forehead against his own: "God save you, Robert! God save you, and God speed." He will not wait for a response less his own heart fail him. Robert winces and clutches Pacificus' shoulder as the blade finds its mark. He gives a long, whispering sigh as life leaves him. A moment later he is limp. Pacificus lets out a prolonged wailing at the same time, as if his whole soul were being torn asunder. He is tempted to make a bloody end of it right here and now, murder Norfolk and tear his black heart out. He can hear the old goat bleating orders to other soldiers. *Oh to God that Cromwell were here, then I'd know my course, then I would act for certain - cut his inwards for all his villainy.* But when he final staggers to his feet and sees the duke, flanked by the pathetic priests, he forgets it all. What are men, but grass? It is God he curses and would kill today, for allowing to exist such rotten men in such a rotten world.

He has not thought as far ahead as escape, but no sooner is he up than he sees the empty tumbrel cart arrayed like a ramp to freedom. The Tower guards are rushing to the scaffold now in force and so he takes his chances with the cart. He jumps onto it, getting as much speed as he can in the twelve feet of its boards, and then at the end vaults his body from the small railing at the back, over the soldier's heads and crashes headlong into a crowd of foundry workers from the Billingsgate works. Two of them, a father and son, help him up and steer him through the crowd. No one stops them and, within a miraculous minute, Pacificus is through the priory ruins and away. From there he takes a long route back to Ely Place, crying in the alleyways and cursing at every church.

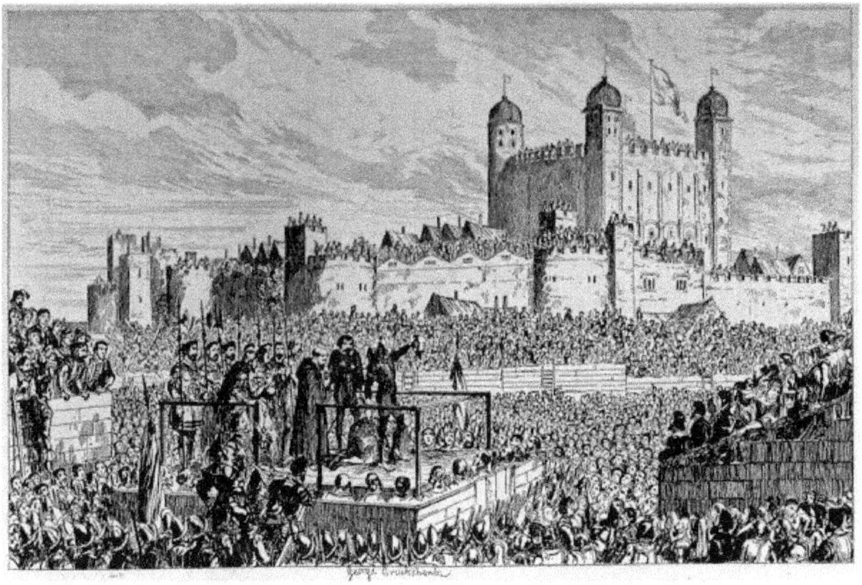

17

The Players

Scire tuum nihil est, nisi te scire hoc sciat alter
Your knowledge is nothing when no one else knows that you know it

Rugge is in a foul mood. The council of bishops has removed most of the sacraments from these new articles of faith. Pacificus barely registers it under the numbness of his desolation at the pilgrims' deaths. In his head, he's ranting at heaven again.

The God he has served all his life does not exist; is that not now true beyond dispute? This God of his imagining, this robed deity of his childhood training, has refused Catholic England, though it be delivered to him on a silver platter. The north would have risen in arms to defend the traditional religion of England, but this God – whoever he is or was – would not have them, would not own them. Yes, perhaps there should be martyrdoms and the intermittent triumphs of wickedness over virtue, but his intuition is that this defeat, this rejection, is different by kind, not degree.

In this despair, Pacificus feels as if he is reliving the fall of Rhodes all over again. For many men the defeat of four hundred knights and four-and-a-half thousand regulars to two hundred thousand infidels, after an eight-month siege, would seem an inevitable result. But to Pacificus, the knights were God's elect, garrisoned by angels, fortified by the Holy Spirit. They never turned, never armed their backs, so to speak. For them to lose the last of their fifty-six cities was to lose divine sanction. For if there be *no shadow of turning* in the Almighty, then everything they had believed was a lie. For eight years the knights had been homeless wanderers, feared and misunderstood by many monarchs in Europe. They had sworn first allegiance to the Pope, they were had strength of arms and great possessions within most countries of Europe and yet were also under oath never to lift a sword against another Christian. In the great age of the emerging nation states and wars of religion, these Hospitallers were antique curiosities, refugees from the collapse of chivalry, out of place and out of time - and perhaps even out of friends. Worse, in the eyes of some, they might even prove useful to papal interests and a genuine threat to the emerging protestant order. If the Pope were to say that the Lutherans and Genevans were *no true Christians*, the knights might find themselves in a very new and very bloody crusade. And so for eight years, Europe watched distrustfully from the sidelines until the emperor had finally relented and given them a windblown patch of rock called Malta. This he did for the simple reason that these knights were such effective pirates in draining the coffers of Suleman the Magnificent. Pacificus had long since resigned to the fatal conclusion that, for all their sacrifice and long tradition, God was no longer with them. It must be this same predicament that the king, this same double confirmation that God is not with him; no heir by Catherine and then none by the Anne, even after all the theological posturing and make-believe pontifications that everyone had to go along with for fear of the gibbet. Now what? An abandoned man with tare the realm from heaven and damn it to sword and flame.

Surely this, Pacificus thinks, must be the meaning of the northern rebellion's uncomely defeat. He does not for one minute think God has metamorphosed into the brutal, conniving God of Cromwell, or the regal puppet of Cranmer – damn them to hell! But neither can he now have such an overarching confidence in his own papal God; his own Constantine church, his church triumphant – what did Christopher say about a sow's ear? Easy to jump ship when the wind's contrary, too easy. And it's not that he is so base or so blind as to overlook the church's vices or crimes, for in this matetr he is a realist. The church is a place for men, not angels. And men are born to sin, as the sparks fly upward. And if he loved the church of the living God, it was always more for what she was intended to be amidst all that she ended up becoming – the valiant bride of Christ, as tender as a dove in fledge, yet also terrible as an army with banners. He loved her, or the idea of her, as men should love, with faith in the beloved's full and eventual loveliness. For surely everything that will be lovely must be loved beforehand to make it so? Men loved a patch of swampy ground near the Tiber, and it became Rome. A mother buys a new bonnet for her baby not to make the baby beautiful but because to her – even if to no one else – the child is what she adores above all. And through her mother's love, the child becomes lovelier than the bonnet.

Men like Cromwell and Cranmer have no right to criticize what they have not loved, and Norfolk, damn his caprice, has no right to breathe the same English air as men like Percy and Aske. Norfolk had Aske's body hung by chains from the walls of York Castle, as Saul's and Jonathan's were hung by the Philistines from the walls of Gath. In those days the valiant men of Gilead travelled all night to steal back the bodies for proper burial, but no one does it for the lawyer, nor is it even expected in this day and age. Pacificus takes his black thoughts back to Saint Benet's during what is an oppressively humid July, for he is about to receive two very different visitors.

The cool cloisters of the abbey bring him little comfort for, if there is glory here, he knows now that it is certainly the glory of a setting sun. Lincoln and York were the test of that, and even though in all ways right to his mind, they have utterly failed. In this light he can not now look at any of the monastic routine without prophetic nostalgia mixed with cynicism. For he cannot be sure anymore what God wants from men. This monastery is not his whole life as it has been for others. He has travelled, seen the world. He could travel again, perhaps rejoin his old order at Malta, or a quiet house among the Angevin Benedictines. But it is precisely in this that the deepest wound aches most; he does not now believe that even this will please whatever deity is left in his cosmos. He is like a moth drawn to an unknown light through a maze of cobwebs, a moth whose wings now had no more strength to struggle free and find the way. Worse, in the exhaustion, he now doubts he ever did see the light.

One Tuesday afternoon, he is eating his bread – or more accurately, pulling weevils from it – in the porch of Saint Helen's at Ranworth, when an aged gentleman, unattended yet well mounted on a grey gelding, approaches the porch. He is certainly old enough to be Pacificus's father – though he dismounts without obvious stiffness or complaint. He wears his collar in the old style, without ruffle or ornament – and certainly no foolish codpiece as is popular among those mercantile *arrivisti* and coxcombs he saw in London. His face is kindly, and almost familiar, Hugh thinks, His clothes speak of the faded glory of a gentleman once loved; his doublet well styled, but jaded at the elbow in a way no wife would have countenanced, and his hose almost worn to a thread at the crotch. His grey beard is long like an Athenian stoic, though perhaps less densely populated, for he is clean whatever else he may be. No sweat or stain in the collar, no grit under the fingernails.

"Good. You are alone," he says matter-of-factly, casting a hooded grey eye about the churchyard, "you are the monk Pacificus, are you not?"

Pacificus nods, tilting his head slightly as if to say, and you are? But the gentleman merely smiles expansively, striding past him towards the church door. His face grows more familiar with each moment. Pacificus abandons his crust for the dog and rises slowly to his feet.

The gentleman pats the dogs head, then straightens up to look him in the eye. "I am minded to see what you have been up to in here. I've heard you are a queer fellow, as delightfully out of step with the times as am I."

Pacificus follows him in. "Heard from whom, sir?"

"Hah! From your bishop, for one." He does not look back to answer, but continues walking with purpose down the nave. "But I'll tell you now, brother, it was poor Tom Percy who mentioned this rood screen, and, as you probably noticed, he is – or was, God rest him – not the sort of man to take time over little things like painting. Ah." At this point he stops and views Pacificus' work. "Ah, yes. He was right to mention it, yes. Yes, indeed."

And so here he stands to take it in, before moving forward and across the individual works which by the summer of 1537 are beginning to form one grand panorama, not just at the east of the nave, but also to the two smaller altars at the east end of the north and south isles. In the middle range, the twelve apostles. In the south aisle chapel, the three Marys with Saint Margaret. In the north aisle chapel, Saint Etheldreda, Saint Agnes, Saint John the Baptist and Saint Barbara. But it is the side chapel reredose, that catch his eye most and make him almost grab at his own beard. "Yes, yes! You have it here, brother! Dear Saint Felix – yes, you have him!"

Pacificus is resisting the urge to point out where he has not finished, and what he hopes to add. On the north side, Saint Felix and Saint Stephen the Martyr are joined by Saint George. Similarly, opposite, Saint Thomas of Canterbury and Saint Lawrence the Martyr are joined by Saint Michael. "Ah, the three dragon killers! God help us, how they are needed in our time. Did ever a saint sit more foul of the polity than you, dear Becket? Your bones cry out against the very age. But tell me something, brother, I am not long returned from the continent and there I met a Senior Buonarotti – "

"Michelangelo? You met Michelangelo?"

"You know him?"

"Yes, very well, but many years ago, fifteen years before the sack of Rome even, when he was doing the ceiling of Sixtus' chapel and other things..."

"Well, in my opinion he is very ill favoured and self-important – and he has painted his Capella Sistina in a way I cannot fathom. He has," he turns aside and almost whispers confidentially, as if not to upset Saint Barbara, "employed the use of pagan sibyls in his Christian themes!" He raises a knowing and bushy eyebrow. "And his Last Judgement! Pah! He fain would have Christ judging us quite naked, if some sensible man had not restrained him. And all this business of realism, this *New Learning*, this pissing in the wind...have you heard of anything more naïve and foolish?"

"I do know," Pacificus tries to sound as humble as he can, "that Michelangelo could not make even his cartoons without a model, but - "

The old man slaps his thigh and waggles his finger. "Exactly! And did the Evangelists ever sink so low as to give us a mere physical description of Christ?"

"I believe that reality is too deep a thing for paint. I acknowledge the limits of art, most particularly my own, and am resigned to paint symbolically, for the little facts of nature may mislead us into thinking they are all there is."

"As I see *here*, brother!" The old man paces the rushes once more, one finger pointing to the rood screen and another waggling in the ether against the sons of Vitruvius. "I tell you, sir, these new men take upon themselves a burden that will unhinge us all! Can a man, for all his studies of the human form, really show in oil or pastel the glory of the saints, let alone the glory of the Son of Man – nay, any man? I tell you, they have lost all humility – some have even desecrated human bodies in their lust for *la gloire*. But also I tell you, brother – and I mean it – that I have seen the frescoes of Fra Angelico, Lippi, Duccio and that godly man Francesca, and you are not in the least behind them."

Pacificus has seen their work too when he crossed and re-crossed Italy in search of Marcantonio Vendramin, and he assumes the old man's eyes must be failing. He wants to join the old man in scoffing, in thigh slapping; wants to pour scorn on these latest *geniuses*; the 'Divine Michelangelo' and 'Divine Raphael and Leonardo' – Italians are as comical as the rest of Europe is drab. There are no 'divine geniuses' in England, thank God. At least they have not sunk that far yet. We used to have many goodly words to describe those type of people, usually Saxon words not best fitted for church. But now we flatter these coxcombs by saying they are *men ahead of the age*, or *practical men who know how to get ahead.* God help me, Pacificus thinks, I preferred the Saxon equivalents. But then, even as he is thinking these thoughts, he groans inwardly, knowing – or at least suspecting – that it is *he* who has dug in his heels on the wrong side of history's curve. *He* is the relic, *his* the image and not theirs that will be forgotten, discarded. He tears his mind away from these morose speculations to this other archaic character before him.

"I did not catch your name, sir."

"I did not give it." He looks Pacificus over, head to toe once more and then, drawing breath as if he had been a runner unable to talk until he had drunk water, says, "Jeffrey de Hastings."

"My Lord Hastings, of course!" Pacificus makes to bow.

"Come, Hugh, no need for that here. Yes, of course I remember who you are dear boy, but do not worry, your secret is safe with me. That is why I have left my retainers in Norwich and sought you out privily. As a friend of your father, God rest him, I must say that you look ill, boy. Do you not have red meat at your house, or is it all carp, eel and oats?"

"My humours are out since God abandoned us to despotism and slaughter." Pacificus puts a brave face on it, and stares towards Saint Michael, but where was he when it mattered?

"Tush, what talk! The blood of the martyrs is the seed of the church, it was ever thus!"

But Pacificus does not answer, he is too weary for optimism now. Do not all men claim to have God's approval, or claim a martyr's crown for their dead, these days? How can you validate his backing, when he himself is so silent? By his silence he makes fools of us all.

"But let us not talk of that now, for I have a reason for being here. I am travelling back to my estates which, as you know, are fast to the former lands of Binham Priory." Hastings begins to scrunch his velvet cap between gnarled fists in a way that rouses Hugh's attention. "This is a delicate matter Hugh, but Bishop Rugge says you may be depended upon." He pauses and screws up his face like a man about to make a grave confession.

"Would you like to sit down?" Pacificus says.

"No my lad, I will stand. As perhaps you may know, Wolsey had me in the Papal states some twenty years ago, all through that terrible war that engulfed the continent and brought Christendom so much disgrace." Pacificus realizes he means the French-Muslim alliance forged by King Charles' mother after he was captured by the emperor at the battle of Pavia. Every nation and canton forgot its own broken treaties and rose in high indignation when one mother's treachery fractured the Christian world.

"As I fear God, it was a sorry business and, as you will see, I had no honorable part in it. You see, Hugh, when King Charles came over the Alps, all Italy was in an uproar, his forty thousand seemed to be unstoppable, and so many efforts were made to deprive the likely conqueror of his spoils. And so, I won't bore you with the detail, it came to my care by the hand of a papal legate – for we were leaving by sea – the reliquary of Saint Helen."

"*The* reliquary?" Pacificus' mouth drops open as he begins to join the dots. No wonder the bishop had high hopes.

"The very same, kept in the same chapel since the fourth century, perhaps the most valuable reliquary in all Christendom, fashioned to the design given by her own son Constantine at her death."

"And you are about to tell me this is the great secret kept by Prior Wulfric and the Binham brothers?"

"God forgive me, I broke the trust of the church, bringing that and a huge quantity of gold coin home on my return, even after I heard of Charles's defeat at Pavia."

With drooping shoulders and sunken eyes, Hastings walks slowly under the statue of Saint Helen on top of the rood screen. "Ambition makes scoundrels of men, Hugh. My father was Lord Chamberlain to King Edward, before Richard and Buckingham had his head. I was only a young man then, and the doors of preferment were suddenly closed to me – it is hard when you have certain expectations, I think you understand that."

There follows another pause as Hastings feverishly thumbs the edge of his cloak. "God alone knows what I intended, for I did not. My wife Catherine, God rest her, would have no part of it. Women are so sensible, so immune to ambition - save perhaps the late queen, Anne, I mean. Anyway, I entrusted them to the secrecy of Binham priory. Wulfric knew, and their priest Jary, as did your abbot of course, but no one else. So the matter was closed for a time until I could decide what to do, never thinking the king would start searching out every cellar and crypt in every holy house. God's teeth, could any man predict that?"

"But Augmentations never found it at their first visitation?" Pacificus says.

"No, quite, and I was abroad at the time when I heard of Jary's sad demise."

"The priest at Binham – dead too?"

"Oh yes, didn't you know? Bludgeoned to death in front of his own altar, like Becket, poor fellow."

"And was Wulfric suspected then?" Pacificus says.

"Well, why would he be? The sheriff was out looking for thieves, for many of the chalices and plates were missing from the vault too. But now – well, now it looks very different. We must assume Prior Wulfric has made some of the other brothers aware of the gold and the reliquary."

Pacificus nods. "I have observed them, seen their private conferences. It would explain a great deal."

"And this poor novice, Bede? Got cold feet?" Hastings says.

"Perhaps," Pacificus says with a smile, though Hastings does not notice the pun. "But, what did he get cold feet about? I mean to say, what could they hope to achieve with such a relic in days like these?"

"Oh, I know exactly what they intend – well, almost exactly. Wulfric shares your pessimism; he has written off England, and petitioned the emperor to set them up on the continent in their own monastery, where they can be the keepers of the relic."

"You know this for sure?" Pacificus says.

"I am not without my contacts where it matters. But if they think the foreign court will treat them fair, they are mistaken. It is far more likely – for all their piety – that some cardinal or abbot will seize the relic, and make them disappear. I have it on good authority that the Emperor's ambassador, Chapuys, has hired men to *negotiate with them*, and who knows where that will end? So we must hurry, Hugh."

"Hurry to do what? I cannot but see that you and the bishop are at odds here," Pacificus says. "You, presumably, want to ease your conscience and return the saint to her true home, whereas the bishop wishes to have her work miracles for Saint Benet's."

"And you are the bishop's man?" Hastings asks wearily.

"I am my own man in matters of conscience."

"Really? You are aware that these relics could save your abbey?"

Hastings is a strange one, Hugh thinks. Even against his own expressed intentions he would look for any excuse to have his spoils remain in England. Pacificus' countenance takes on its stormiest aspect, shadowed by memories of the bloody scaffold on Tower Hill, "My lord, if God will not save the monasteries by his grace, nor good men, should we ask the devil to do it with mammon?"

The old man might have been affronted, but at these words, casts his eyes downwards in shame: "No, indeed, my boy, quite right. But you will at least help an old man ease his conscience then, and perhaps save the lives of some of your own brothers? It gives me no sleep to think of Chapuys' spies lurking about your precincts with their long knives and continental morals."

Pacificus says he will do what he can, and the old man seems happy with that.

That same afternoon Pacificus revisits the riverside sandbank where Bede had been murdered. Simon is with him and things are still awkward between them after the fight. Pacificus relays to him all he has now come to know about the matter. Simon says he remembers old Hastings at their house one Michaelmas, how he swung him round and round by the fireplace. Pacificus cannot remember these happy times nowadays. His childhood memories lie dormant like forgotten bulbs under long ages of winter. He lets Simon reminisce about their father, so different from his own memories, as the firstborn – could almost be a different man. He died less than a year after their mother, the house was sold to cover the endless remortgages and relentless taxes. Nothing is left, no property, and even the title will die out with the brothers.

"Would you want to go back – be a child again, I mean?" Pacificus asks him.

"That, and many things," Simon says, "but time slips away from us, does it not? They say you never stand in the same river twice."

"Yes. I see that." Pacificus gazes, lost in thought, across the sparkling waters, down the dyke to Ranworth broad and the spire of Saint Helen's.

"What was that novice doing here, that afternoon when he met his end?" He points to the reeds. "He knelt here in the water – we assume from his own free will, because he left his shoes on the sand. But, why? And why here?"

"Well, we know he was a tender youth," Simon says.

"So?"

"So, suppose he happened upon this place while he was out counting the swans."

"This place?" Pacificus says, trying not to let the impatience of an older brother sour his tone.

"Yes, *this place*; the first point at which the vista leading to Saint Helen's opens up."

"Saint Helen's ...of course!" Pacificus exclaims. "He was kneeling and praying to her, asking the saint for aid his forgiveness."

"And perhaps too loudly, for if I'm near my mark, someone else heard him praying."

"In a boat perhaps – sound carries that way, and it was misty." Pacificus says.

"And that would explain the footsteps coming from nowhere."

"Yes, yes! But the strange triangular shape of them?" Pacificus says.

"Ah, well, I've been thinking about that," Simon glances at him, his eyes bright, interested. "Let's say Bede is overcome in the reeds and drowned there, and then the murderer drags the body down the beach where he can launch it. He's facing backwards, so we only see his heels raking up the sand. They're at quite a depth because the body is heavy."

"No return footsteps though?" Pacificus ponders, but as soon as the words leave his mouth he grasps what that must mean.

Simon, seeing the change come over his face, nods grimly, "Aye, brother, there was more than one in on this. An accomplice brought the boat round to pick him up."

Meanwhile on the River Ant another conversation is taking place. "Caught much?" Beth is at her thinking tree up-river when Richard and Piers row past on their way back from the nets.

"Some, but not much. Give you a ride home?" Richard calls back.

"Why such a long face?" Piers asks impudently, mimicking her expression and, earning himself a clip on the ear.

"Shut up. I've got something to tell you." She sits on a sack at the rear of the boat, arranging her dress just as their mother would if she were about to tell them a story, and begins to explain how Simon – that is, Sir Cecil – is really her father. She sketches out the events that led to her birth. Richard stops rowing, goggling at her in amazement.

"But...why did mother never tell us?" Piers says.

"You will understand when you're older."

"But – but – you're still our sister?" Piers eyes are starting to fill with tears. A few years back he didn't want to marry anyone else but her, despite all the arguments.

"Of course I am, silly boy!" she says. "We have the same mother, only you have a new uncle."

"And, and Sir Hugh is our uncle too – sort of," Richard points out. "Have you told Pieter and Sarah?"

She nods. 'Yes, I told Sarah."

"What did she say?" demands Richard, all agog.

Beth shrugs. "Not much, you know Sarah, just gave me a hug, that's all, said it didn't change anything."

Pacificus asks at the abbey gate for information about any strangers in the outer precinct – foreign types – but Brother Porter is as helpful as ever. "What? You wants an inventory now, brother? By the saints, I wonder you don't think I's got better things to do!"

In truth, the outer precinct is a daily throng of tradespeople and visitors. If spies want to find a foothold, it will be no hard thing. He makes the mistake of adding, like some clueless under-sheriff: "So you haven't noticed anything you thought suspicious?"

This was enough to get the old boy ranting a full ten minutes, during which monologue Pacificus happens to glance up at the spandrels in the vaulting of the gatehouse where the coats of arms of the abbey's original baronial benefactors are carved, among them De la Pole, Beauchamp, Clare, Valence, Warren and Arundel. He sees his own family shield next to the Hastings shield – what a strange thing is providence! But Pacificus is jerked back from his wandering thoughts by Brother Porter who, like all those sent to try the saints, is famed not so much for his prodigious ability to hold forth, as for his insistence on being heard. And amongst his tirade on the suspicious types that frequent the abbey precincts, he makes mention of a travelling troup of players only just arrived.

"Suspicious? By my soul! I've never trusted players, nor yet mimers and *jocatores*, no – not far as I could spit! If I had my way, I'd let happen what they did let happen in my father's time – have all them cozens and caitiffs arrested and made useful somehow."

Pacificus detaches himself with difficulty, but an hour later the porter's words come back to him, prophetic indeed. In the lavatorium, washing his hands before joining the brothers in the refectory, Pacificus notices a guest lingering near the door – no doubt with the players, they do have a certain look and smell. But this lusty, long fellow waits until they are alone before taking a few steps closer from the doorway. Pacificus observes him from the corner of his eye, his pulse suddenly quickening. Breathe slowly now, he thinks, probably nothing. It is only when he stretches his hands into the sink, thus exposing his wrists that the man exclaims, "There! I knew it was your face, old comrade! Though for a surety, it's the wrists that gives us all away."

Pacificus shakes the water from his hands and faces the stranger. Who on earth could this be? The doorway light is behind him. "Do you not recognise your old rowing partner, Hugh? Neptune's beard! I had not thought to see you again – and so comfortable too."

Pacificus heart missed several beats as he remembers the face and the voice. "Nor I you, Filcher." He spent many months chained to this horse thief on a Barbary galley. Back then, both of them were naught but a sack of bones, though Filcher's bones had been considerably thicker than his own. Now he was fleshed and toned like a wrestler.

"I see you and De la Valette got ransomed, then." Filcher forces a malevolent smile. He has no love of the rich. Pacificus nods. He and his comrade from the French langue, an ebullient knight, John de la Valette, had been ransomed by Dragut – pirate and naval tactician par excellence, second only to the infamous Barbarossa. If there was any etiquette of the sea, this alone was it; the knights and the Mohamedans would always trade well for their own. Even Dragut had been a galley slave for the Genoese at one time; business is business. If no one traded for you, then you were dead in a few months, simple. Which makes Pacificus wonder all the more. "How did you escape?"

The man takes a step forward, walking on the balls of his feet like some courtly dancer. "Ah, well, now that would be telling, would it not, my noble lord knight?" Filcher's eyes have that demoniac and predatory gleam about them, hungry to grind any opportunity for a coin. He leans forward, and the cunning leer is not pleasant to see. "The question I asks myself is how one such as yourself is hiding out here."

"I'm not hiding."

"Oh! So they know you was a knight sworn only to the Pope, do they? No, thought not! And that being the case I's a-guessing that someone with your past is up to no good in England, and that the secret of your identity is worth a great deal to you." He gives a condescending cough. "Not that I think a godly monk would withhold worldly goods from a destitute player who has fallen on lean times."

"So you are one of the players?" Small talk seems better at this point than knocking the teeth down his throat. For one thing, it would not look good if he were discovered doing it in the abbey, and for another Filcher is a big fellow and likely to be armed.

"I'm their captain, and though there's not so many gold angels in it, we do get to meet people, see things – like you, for example." The whites of Filcher's eyes are jaundiced yellow, and from this distance the veins in them do not make for pleasant close viewing.

"You got the wrong man for bribery Filch, I'm –"

"What? Just a lowly brother what's renounced all worldly possessions? Oh, very handy! But see, I know your sort, you rich boys, snouts never far from the trough and all that."

He now closes with Pacificus and jabs his index finger into his chest as he speaks. "You used to say, on those long nights at the oars, that your people had lands hereabouts – yeah, I ain't forgotten – and wealthy friends no doubt too. Now suppose you tap one or two of them for a favour, cross my palm with some gold..."

To hell with it. Pacificus is having a black day anyway, a black year for that matter and there's only one language a man like Filcher understands. He clips the man's pointing finger upwards with his left hand, and delivers a hard right into his belly, putting his whole shoulder and body behind the blow so that Filcher first heaves into mid-air, then crumples to his knees. Weren't expecting that, were you? Filcher reaches for the concealed knife in his breast pocket but Pacificus has anticipated him and – moving swiftly behind him – closes his own hand on Filcher's. A bent arm like that is in its weakest position, and a good thing too, for Filcher is strong.

Yanking his head back by its greasy hair, Pacificus forces the blade arm up tight to Filcher's own jugular vein, his voice low: "You don't know me, you never saw me, you will never speak to me again."

Filcher is struggling all the while to get to his feet – he gasps and splutters like a sick pig. But Pacificus knows his own business too well and keeps him down by kicking his legs away. "Ever! D'you hear me?" Whatever reply he might have given is interrupted by the sudden arrival of Prior Wulfric, whose hands rise up in horror at what looks like a murder in progress.

He almost shrieks as he falls back against the doorway. "Brother! Brother! Brother Pacificus! Jesu! What is this?"

Filcher is not slow to grasp his advantage. 'Brother – dear brother – oh, help!"

"Silence, knave," Pacificus says.

"This monk attacked me, a guest," Filcher whines, "he is deranged."

Pacificus rams Filcher's head against the wall to distract him, twisting his knife arm behind his back until he releases the blade. Pacificus recovers the weapon, drops the man with a final kick, and shows the knife to Wulfric at the door. "You will notice that he was holding the knife, not me."

"Well, I...oh ..."

"Liar! He attacked me!" Filcher is quick to his feet, his fingers feeling that his neck is not cut. "You saw him yourself!"

"Well, I don't know...I mean to say, this is all very vexing – we must report it to Father Prior – "

"No," Pacificus cuts in sharply. "No, that won't be necessary. This man had grounds for his hostility. He mistook me for another villain, that's all. No harm done." He let his eyes bore into Filcher's. "He is our guest after all, and will be gone on the morrow."

"Well...I – er, I don't know. Is this true, friend?"

Filcher sniffs and gives a sulky nod. Pacificus goes his way, hoping he has laid this to rest. He does not see, a few moments later, the rogue also following Wulfric to talk to him in a quiet nook in the abbey court.

Pacificus does not attend the players' performance that night. He wants some space and time to calm his nerves, and takes refuge in the quiet of the library. Mistress Fenton has requested any Langland, Gower or Marie de France he can procure for her. He told her he does not approve of Marie de France. She had smiled coyly, admitting there is much amiss with that lady's moral views, but little to rival the breathless ease of her diction and characterisation. It makes the time hang less heavily. At this he felt more prudish than an Anabaptist, and said that perhaps he would look at her work again. Right now, in front of Father Aloysius's disapproving stare, he's feeling a mite hot under the cowl himself. He takes the books quickly to a window seat where the evening sun pours onto an elm table in liquid bronze pools made more surreal by the window tracery. He sees diagonal cracking to the left of the mullions and remembers – or at least tries to forget – that he sits, as does the abbey – and everything else – on a shifting sand bank between two rivers. Trapped between Rugge and Sir Geoffrey, the king and the emperor, nay, celibacy and marriage, and even between faith and unbelief, he cannot escape the poetic irony of everything he sees and touches these days.

He opens the *Lais* of Marie de France, and although his Anglo-Norman French is as dusty as an Angevin attic, he is nonetheless guiltily rapt by the poems that so easily draw forth memories and that inner yearning so habitually suppressed. That forgotten voice; that soft, low murmur of sensuality that draws his mind back to her – her in the castle cell. And it's times like this when his vocation to the celibate life sags under the pressure of other forces. It is easier as a knight, he knows that; living by your sword and nerve will make you forget everything else – even food for a time. But it's when the arms are laid down and the drama of action is spent that the longings arise. The need to be held, to find the comfort of another, fragrant, soft – *pah!* Almost had me. Pacificus shakes the feeling off, and casts the book down as if it were a bewitched and unholy thing.

His best defence is to gibe at the passion of this poetry, and Marie de France gives him every opportunity for such easy diversion. Her love poems at once condemn yet then somehow condone infidelity. "When the deceived partner has been cruel and merits deception, and where her lovers are loyal to one another," she says. What in God's heaven is that supposed to mean? Is that the measure by which the French break covenants? No wonder King Francis' mother could betray Christendom to the Mohammedans with such a clear conscience. He is wrapped up in the uneasiness of such disturbing thoughts and vague hungers when he hears the bell for Vespers echoing louder and louder down the halls.

The evening offices are fulfilled in all peace and propriety. Not until a short while after Nocturne does the cry go up - first as a nightmarish disturbance in their dreams, but then louder and more real as the monks abruptly awake.

Murder, murder, come quickly all! Murder most foul. Saint James and Saint Jude, help us!

18

Maitre L'Ambassador

Sapiens nihil affirmat quod non probat
A wise man avers nothing he cannot prove

William Beccles, cellarer, is pacing the granary floor barefoot. He clutches his stomach like a woman in labour, all the while declaiming in his broad dialect on the evils of the age and the wickedness of godless men in general. Pacificus elbows his way into the centre of the torch-lit cluster to see the corpse. Blood, gore, entrails spilt like tripe. He is more used to this than most but even he is unmanned by the sight. Prior Thomas, no stranger to carcasses, is white as a sheet. He is ordering that it – he – whatever it is – for in truth it is difficult to tell – be taken down for examination. Pacificus places a reassuring hand on his shoulder, "We should leave all for the coming of the sheriff, no?"

"But we cannot even know who it is!" the prior objects.

Pacificus takes a torch from the hand of one of the brothers, and approaches the blooded carcass. It is suspended two feet from the floor by ropes attached under the arms which have themselves been bound tight. Guts and many quarts of blood form a pool underneath – he has been opened at the navel while still alive. Skin is flayed from the back but these wounds have already partially scabbed, whereas the sideways slash across the belly is still dripping. The naked, blooded corpse hangs forward but it is impossible to find any identifying features, such is the beating it has taken, seemingly on all sides. Pacificus brings the torch close to examine the head wounds.

"What is it, brother?" Beccles says, his voice trembling with horror and dread.

"This man has – " Pacificus says.

" – then it is a man," Prior Thomas says, still keeping his distance.

"Yes, he's been gelded, with his parts stuffed in his mouth."

"Not another of our number, surely?" Prior Robert again.

"I don't think so," Pacificus replies, trying to push out of his mind the suspicion forming there. "He's too tall – and by the looks of him, he's been tortured first, though I don't think they ever intended him to live."

"Holy Mother of God!" William Beccles exclaims, glancing around him as if for help.

"Tortured?" This time it is a white-faced Prior Wulfric whose voice gasps from the edge of the darkness.

"Oh yes, brother, tortured for something he knew, brutally and for some time before they let his innards out."

"Oh Jesu, no more!" Wufric steps back, his hand clapped to his mouth.

"Oh, there *is* more, prior Wulfric." Pacificus' eyes blaze red at him in the firelight. Somehow, he knows it, this thing is linked to him and the Binham monks. "For I'm thinking they did not get what they wanted. Do you see with what rage they bludgeoned his brains out? This was an instrument heavy as a fuller's club, but with deep, sharp edges. A mace, perhaps?" He has seen such wounds often on the field of battle.

A great groan of horror now issues from those assembled but, before discussions flare up, Prior Robert sends them back to their dorters. "We will leave this charnel house to the sheriff's men. Brother Porter, you will stand guard from without. And God have mercy on us all."

Pacificus breaks his fast in the refectory when morning comes, his mind in turmoil. The cadaver is Filcher, and he examines the mystery, probing its possibilities. Suppose Filcher had other enemies at the abbey? Suppose he was followed – or more likely, supposing he was tied up somehow in this business with the relic and the gold. What better guise for carrying out his negotiations than as a travelling player? On the other hand, he might have found someone else to bribe and run foul of, but how likely is that? No, he was brutally tortured – and it must have been more than one man – for something he either had or knew.

The sheriff is as thorough as a man can be that whole week long, but without anything to show at the end of it, save several rolls of vellum with his witness statements. He can be forgiven this time, Pacificus thinks, there are wheels within wheels here.

Pacificus himself has an alibi for that night, but he is also not slow to notice Prior Wulfric has mentioned nothing of the scuffle he saw in the lavatorium. That by itself lends credence to his suspicions about Wulfric, yet the prior seems squeamish about the gore, and genuinely so. Perhaps another elaborate facade? *Wheels within wheels.*

The brothers from the disbanded Hickling Priory still maintain a detachment from almost everyone else. Their Prior Robert Aeyns is, if possible, even more aloof and solitary than the Binham brothers. But whereas these Hickling Augustinian canons stride about the enclave as if they owned it, the Binham men, like sheep, are never seen in less than threes. Pacificus knows well what this means; these men are in mortal fear of something or someone. He meets Prior Robert of Binham one night on the night stair to the dorter. He is ascending after Nocturnes, having stayed behind a long while to meditate after the others had gone up, and there is the Augustinian coming down. Pacificus is half asleep and backs down, for he has only just started. Aeyns does not acknowledge it, nor even make any attempt to explain where he is going at such an hour.

Pacificus raises these things with Prior Thomas the next day. "Are they part of our house or not? They eat with us, but will you find them one time in ten at Vespers or Terce? And work? Or do they – "

"Brother, things are complicated here, and I am prior," is all he says at first. But when pressed he acquiesces somewhat under Pacificus stare. "Yes, yes, alright brother. You have my word this is all noted and reported to the bishop, but I cannot act beyond his authority in this matter – trust me, you must just leave them be for now."

Aye, I will, Pacificus thinks, *but that's not all. This business effects us all. They'll not find me unarmed in this precint again.*

Then strangest of all comes the news, towards the end of the week, that no less than Eustace Chapuys, ambassador for the emperor, has departed from London for Saint Benet's. He visits ostensibly to escape an outbreak of the sweats in the city. Bishop Rugge has offered him lodging at the palace in Norwich but he has refused. "No, Saint Benet's out on your marshes, my dear bishop, this will be just the thing, tranquility and contemplation."

Rugge understands exactly what it means, and tells Pacificus as much, "Watch that magpie like a hawk, if he's not after our eggs than I know nothing. Watch him, watch Wulfric too – he will make treaty with us now, so I've heard."

"Heard from whom?" Pacificus leans forward to the edge of his chair in the bishop's small dark study with its smoky fire, a place where he seems to spend more and more time these days.

"Now then, Pacificus, you can't expect me to reveal all my sources."

He leans forward at the desk and gives a knowing smile. "Don't worry. You'll know all you need, when you need, only we must close this reliquary business with Wulfric before Chapuys reveals his hand."

"And you are sure he will speak with us now?"

"Oh, yes. Particularly after that grisly set-to with the player in the granary. A bad business, that; wouldn't be surprised if Chapuys had a hand in it."

"And he will talk with me? But not your *other sources*?" Pacificus doesn't like this one bit. Who in hell's teeth are these others, anyway?

Rugge mutters something whimsical about velvet gloves and iron fists. "For once you are my soft solution Pacificus, so bring him in, we'll give him what he wants – an abbacy even – so long as it is at Saint Benet's and nowhere else. Wulfric knows where he is safe, he knows."

More than the rest of us then, Pacificus thinks as he nods unconvincingly. As he gets up to go the bishop holds out his ring for yet another kiss. Pacificus frowns at the imposition, thinking of Cromwell's ape again – *plus apparent posteriora eius,* but even so he complies with the courtesy. Does he need all this reassurance of fealty now? Does he think he can no longer rely on my conscience?

Rugge interrupts the internal monologue of resentment. "Remember, brother, Chapuys is a talker, the sort of player who'd get you to save your castle by surrendering your bishop. Just warning you ahead of time."

Pacificus arrives at the castle prison in a less than congenial mood. Why have a velvet glove and an iron fist working separately? He feels vulnerable and exposed, and this, he does not like. It shows in the brooding, lowered brow, which Elizabeth Fenton sees and questions him about it.

She is looking well, and she has new clothes – no doubt from you-know-who. He does not mention it for fear of sounding jealous. The thought crosses his mind that it would be a pleasant thing for every man to have someone like her to talk things through with, but he says that he is not at liberty to discuss it. He gives her what news he has of her children, and when she is done wringing from him every last detail, with return messages following, he then also produces the books from his satchel. She clasps her hands to her breast in delight, then places both sets of fingers over her lips as each volume is laid upon the table. She is as excited as a young maid at her first rush-bearing festival, and for a moment Pacificus imagines her to be twenty years younger.

They talk together of Langland and Gower, compare favourite verses, though never do they coincide. Eventually they talk piously about Marie de France's *Lais*, though the intimacy of the subject matter gives him a dry mouth and a beaded brow. He must swallow hard as he talks. She thinks this modesty fits him well, and later admits that she has never discussed these things with another man save her father and brothers. "My husband was the best of men, but he did not approve of any worldly books – only the Scriptures."

"And you disagreed?"

"It was not my place to say," She looks down to her lap, but he can see the corners of her lips catch in a smile. She lifts her eyes and gazes past him to the window. "But if I had a disagreement with our sect," she says, "it was this way they shunned the whole world; not just its sinful ways but also its art, its literature, its philosophy. As if an un-Christian man – even though he were made in the image of God – could not produce anything worthy to be studied, admired or discussed. By cutting ourselves off from the world, I fear many of our number will not be salt in it."

"*Come out of her my people and be ye separate, less you partake in her judgments.*" Pacificus is aware of the dilemma. As a monk, how can he not be? They forget this, these schismatics.

"Ah, so you know the Scriptures, brother, but I cannot think it means we should leave the whole world to go unsalted. God says, by Moses in Deuteronomy, that the pagan cities he would give them were *beautiful cities*, and were not they wicked nations? I fancy they were."

"We," he means *we monks*, "have managed to be separate, but, I hope, also integrated. Perhaps you have missed your vocation." He is teasing her and she smiles coyly. Even so, he could imagine her as a wonderful abbess.

"It is easy for you monks, you are hand in glove with the state – at least you were. You will find it different when you are hounded about as we are, and perhaps that is why our people so scorn the world in its entirety – "

"What, that they are excluded?" Pacificus says.

"Yes, they have no leisure perhaps, but maybe someday there will be a place for them, a country of their own, where men may worship and believe as they choose, perhaps then they will be free to write, to sing, to paint beautiful things."

"Maybe, or they might stay the same, or force everyone to be as they, or perhaps it is God's will for them to stay and change this isle, for surely it's all change here now."

She does not think it could be so and they talk of the possibilities of new lands, as if he himself were a heretic like she. When they touch upon the Spaniard's New World, he feels his heart rise, unusually so, but perhaps it is just her. Maybe everyone yearns for a new promised land, no rules or rulers, no gibbets, no scaffolds no dark history. Luther looks back to Augustine, Zwingli to Origen, Michelangelo to Arcadia, Rugge to the bishop kings of the old time – even he himself, to some vague chivalrous past, when pious kings deferred to yet more pious Popes, a time before all these schismatics – a past he now suspects never existed. Then perhaps it is Eden they all seek, perhaps that is the danger. A famous Umbrian poet went once to visit his sister at a convent. While there, he heard Saint Francis preach and was so struck by the simple appeal of the gospel, that he cried out, 'Brother Francis, rescue me from this world, so I may be God's alone.' He became a lowly brother and to him, that man of restless heart, Francis gave the name Pacificus – the peaceful. It is a story that Hugh often thinks upon. One word, let alone a sermon full of gospel words, is a dangerous thing to give a man whose life is starved of meaning, and bereft of peace and joy. Christ's words are a beggar's last hope, he thinks. If they are not true then nothing else is worth being true, isn't that what I used to believe before all this trouble? Being with her - now, in this cell - verily I could believe it all again. All through the ages, each generation of drowning, starving humanity, has groped after those words to prove them true – to receive the peace that comes with forgiveness.

And now, at the end of this procession of fugitives, comes these lunatic Anabaptists – and what do they want? Only the lot of the early church, a small remnant in a pagan society, struggling to convince a sceptical world that they are not seditious but the only answer to the deep needs of the entirety. He knows the argument all too well by now, had it hammered into him good and hard by his brother, and is by no means won over. If anything, Pacificus sees the unlikeliness of it all, a small possibility illuminated for the briefest moment in the rays of late afternoon sunlight against the darkened gritstone of her cell walls. How small and fleeting is an idea, a possibility. How easy to ignore or dismiss a dreamer. Prophets are always without honour – they are too practical in a world where the thirsts of most are so easily satiated.

They talk easily, their conversation ranging over many things – poetry, art, music. When it comes to art, Pacificus cannot resist telling her of his own work. He hates himself for it – it is not humble, it is vainglory – but he does it nonetheless.

"I...I – er – I have come to believe – nay, hope – and I only speak from experience – that when I paint, I worship God by it – my painting, that is." He is fishing for a compliment and he knows it, so he adds, "though many times I fear that it, and everything else I have done is not much, and may not be acceptable to him."

She says that without faith it is impossible to please God. Why does she always say things like that? Always *faith*, always something amorphous and unattainable. Worse yet, she goes on to admit she cannot in conscience look upon religious art in the style which he paints, without some pain. He questions her further, pushing down in himself the personal rejection and the feeling that he need always justify himself to her.

"It is all part of the world that murdered my husband and orphaned my children." She is holding back the bitterest of tears and gives him a stare he will never forget. And then she says, perhaps to repay him out a little, he fancies, that she thinks there is much to commend the new art.

Things start to warm up, he will not be told about art, not by her. Has she been to Florence, Rome, Ferrara, Venice, or Mantua? *He has.* Has she seen the way these Renaissance men think, how reduced their view of reality is? To what madness it may lead? *He has*, or at least thinks he has.

"In the old days, our fathers – nay, even the ancients like Plato and Aristotle – looked back and knew things had been better, and they worked to improve the world without hoping for too much. But these dreamers will make us all mad with their talk of the limitless possibilities for ourselves and our society. They want to give the world back to man, and man back to himself. He is no longer a sinner. Now he is the 'measure of all things,' his body to be unclothed and celebrated, no shame, no shame at all."

She lets him go on and have his little rant, observing with a coolness, his head cast back with disdain and his forefinger stabbing the air. When he has said his piece, she is ready with her quiet but withering rejoinder: 'It maybe as you say, that things were better of old, but that does not perchance count against these *Umanista*, but surely may against those who are content to keep the old order unchanged because it suits them – no matter how many lives it may destroy."

Pacificus blinks, stunned for a moment as she straightens the creases of her dress. There is nothing more to say. Celibacy weighs light again as they part with cold courtesies – he, licking his wounds and she trying to seem busy.

He punches the wall at the top of the stairs. The law was clear enough, she and her husband knew the risks. There is no point blaming him, when the apple cart tipped. Pacificus nurses his bruised fist and shakes his head with incredulity as he descends the stairs. *Blame me, me of all people – the one who risked his life for your children, the one who stepped into the breach to save you from the results of your own reckless actions. What as I thinking of her – must have been bewitched.*

Two minutes after he has gone, Elizabeth relents and wishes she could have apologised. It's because the monk is so frustrating and confusing to her. How can he see so many things, feel so many things and yet remain a eunuch of such a system? Would a man who had been a slave all his life know he was a slave? Would a man love his chains though they were of gold? Thoughts crowd in on her, redoubling her fury, reaffirming her own prejudice and grievances. She feels the knotting in her bowels, but then stands up straight, treading the paved floor with clenched fists – kicking the straw. If he had defended the church by saying thus, then I would have said thus, and thus. And if he had tried to counter with that, then I would have – her eye alights on the books. Ah, but he did not say *anything*, only slunk away like a wounded puppy. Men are so frustrating! She lays her hand on the Langland, the other on her breast, then sits, restively, once more. He had been kind, very kind, she thinks, then adds quickly - to the children.

Back at the abbey, the precinct is all a stir with the coming of Ambassador Chapuys, eyes and ears of the Holy Roman Emperor. A fatted calf is slaughtered on the Thursday afternoon, as if the Frenchman had been a returning prodigal. But Pacificus knows, or thinks he knows, why he has come and has not been idle. If Rugge is to be believed, the reluctant Wulfric has been scared – by the murders – into opening negotiations with the bishop through Pacificus, but not until the other main contender for the relics is virtually at the door. Wulfric is either the cleverest negotiator or the maddest gambler Pacificus has yet come across. He approaches him on two occasions on the preceding days, both times making clear the extent of the bishop's offer, but neither time getting an answer. "I will think well on it," is all he says, "and I will give you my answer presently."

Pacificus sees what is happening; the fellow is holding out to weigh both offers. What should he do? Shake the answer out of him? Rugge said he must be gentle with Wulfric, and he usually obeys orders. Nevertheless the sands are almost drained through the glass in this case, and it is always easier to better a known offer. Tenure of any English monastic house is uncertain in the present hour, so anything Chapuys offers under the emperor's protection is bound to look more attractive.

And then, of course, there's old Hastings and his guilty conscience; Pacificus doubts anything could be done to help him, even for old times' sake. His own conscience is by no means unsullied either. In times past he maintained a clear rationale for bearing arms against the Ottomans. But this – this intrigue over bones and pilgrimages, just to save one religious house? It smacks of abominable self-interest and he knows it. What should he do? He decides to suppress his doubts and act for the bishop, rather than relinquishing the responsibility of questionable acts to someone in authority. It is easily and painlessly done.

Perhaps what is less excusable is the way he involves the Fenton children as accomplices. What he needs is more eyes and ears. Simon is not there when they agree, but makes his mind known soon after. The Fenton children on the other hand, along with Pieter – though not Sarah – had been only too happy to repay Pacificus for all he had done for them.

The children take up positions around the abbey in accordance with his instructions on the Thursday evening at sunset. Pieter patrols along the abbey wharf and outside the abbot's lodging in his flatboat pretending to catch eels; Beth, Piers and Simon in the outer precincts and amongst the fishponds, herbariums and gardens; and Richard, Mark and Pacificus in the inner precincts. If anything is said, any private meetings are held in the cloister, wharf or gardens, they must see and hear it. Mark shadows Wulfric as closely as he dare, as does Pacificus. Richard is dressed as a visiting page with the ambassador's party, but the other children are not so fortunate, having muddy rags and little else.

Chapuys stays with ten retainers in the abbot's lodgings. Prior Thomas has graciously given way to him, laying on a special banquet with roasted beef, swan and three other poultry dishes. He proves an excellent host, all teasing and bonhomie. Chapuys is obviously impressed by him, and perhaps it is as well Prior Thomas knows nothing of the skullduggery going on all around him.

Pacificus is invited by request of none other than Chapuys himself, sent for after Vespers to join them for a dish of strawberries – and Sack, the strong, sweet Spanish wine Chapuys has brought as a gift. The cook marvels about it as he leads Pacificus up the stairs, "three shillings and fourpence a gallon that, and I've heard tell he's got some *aqua vitae* to follow! Not short of a shilling, these Frenchies!"

They pass the ambassador's retainers in the hall and on the landing. No courtiers they, Pacificus thinks; you can dress a man in silk stockings and velvet, but the face of a soldier remains unmistakable – the hardening of the brow, the coldness in the eyes of one who has spilt blood like pouring water. He looks each one in the eye and thinks there are at least three here he would be glad not to meet in a dark alley.

Chapuys is nursing a large glass of Sack by the fire. He is wearing a dense fur travelling cloak over his grey silk doublet with its bright silver buttons. Pacificus bows stiffly and observes how the small, deep-set eyes brighten as he rises. "Ah, *bien*! *Bien*! Frère Pacificus, you will forgive me, I have your English summer cold, and nothing worse, *mon Dieu!*" He does not get up but rather sniffles into an embroidered handkerchief. "Ah, *insupportable*! But better than your sweats! Ah, forgive me, please sit with us!"

It is just them, the prior, and Chapuy's wiry retainer – a hawkish *cavaliere,* his hair jet black and smooth as a cat, keeping his own council by the door. Pacificus observes him carefully, to see how he is armed, before giving Chapuys fuller attention. He only has a sleeve dagger, good – that makes two of us if it comes to it.

"You must not mind François; he cannot help his face, but he is very helpful in other ways on occasions, *n'est pas*, François?"

The man bows slightly, as a bull might if you yanked his nose ring. Pacificus had not thought Chapuys even noticed where he had been looking. Those little Savoy eyes of his are sharp ones, he'll be more careful next time. "I cannot eat fruit now, they will unbalance my humours, Frère Pacificus will have mine."

He gestures for Pacificus to take the bowl but he refuses. God, these French are rude – wearing that Florentine velvet hat at table! No, I won't eat your strawberries, poisoned for all I know. He raises a hand of gentle refusal.

"Oh, but you must." The smirk and raised hands of mock offence.

"Tout à fait délicieux, et je vous remercie; mais non, monsieur."

"Ah, so you have a little language – but of course you have." Chapuys raises his eyebrows above the brim of the glass. His lips purse tight in a deliberate consolidation as he does so, and for a long moment the two men stare at each other across the fireplace.

The prior tries to lift the atmosphere with an anecdote about strawberries and the bishop of Wells, but he knows no one is listening to him by now. Chapuys waits until he finishes and then raises a finger to command attention, "My dear prior, you have been a host *par excellence ce soir*; but I would like some minutes alone with this brother, if you would oblige me."

"But of course ambassador, in fact there are some matters I must attend in the abbey."

"You are very kind, and have my thanks."

When the door is closed, Chapuys replaces his glass on the table and joins his fingers together, brooding. "*François aime bien les fraises, n'est ce pas?*" François walks round the table and takes a chair beside Pacificus. "*Oui, je les adore.*" He starts to eat them, his face close to the bowl, like a peasant. But what will he do when the bowl is empty? Pacificus cannot watch his front and back at the same time.

"You know why we are here?" Chapuys mumbles through his steepled fingers, "But of course you know. You want the same thing."

Pacificus has had enough games. He swivels round and kicks François' chair from under him, at the same time drawing the basilard dagger tied to his own arm. Before François can even remove the spoon from his mouth, his face is pressed hard into the half bowl of strawberries and a blade is prodding his jugular. When Francoise does not appear to appreciate the seriousness of his predicament, and tries to stand, Pacificus brains him twice with the hilt until he is half senseless.

"*Mon frère*!"

"Command him to stay still. I mean it. Do not cry out, or I swear you will both die. Reach for that blade, François and it will be the last thing you do."

"*Mon frère* – " Chapuys mouth is gaping, his eyes wide as eggs.

"What I want, Chapuys? You know naught of *what I want* but I will tell you. I want justice for the men who murdered a novice here last March, and the player who was butchered within these sacred walls last week."

"But wait – wait! The man Filcher was *our* initial negotiator. It was not we who did this, I swear it upon the Virgin. In fact, we thought it was you – this is why we have come with such an escort."

"And the novice, Bede?" Pacificus tightens his grip as Francois bristles under the blade. "What of him then."

"I represent the Holy Roman Empire! What need have I to murder novices? The emperor has personal reasons for wanting what you have here, and he is prepared to treat generously for it, even though it was wrongly taken from its original resting place. There is no question of murder – really. *Mon frère*, please!"

For the second time that week, Pacificus is speechless. The cogs need more time to turn than the situation allows. Chapuys is telling the truth, he thinks. That does not leave many other candidates. He wishes he could even now be watching Prior Robert and the Augustinians. God, how could he have been such a coxcomb not to see what was under his nose?

"Please, *mon frère*, release François, and let us speak together as gentlemen." Chapuys removes his hat to reveal a thinning head of grey hair. He is the same age as Pacificus and looks it.

Pacificus releases François but cautiously and not before having his weapon. "You thought those acts of unspeakable violence were committed by me?"

"But of course, you are the bishop's man, it is known to us, and with your past – " Chapuys shrugs, turning down the corners of his mouth in that particularly French grimace, as if to say, *Well? What can you expect?*

"My past?" Pacificus is feeling ill disposed towards his bishop, but without reason on this occasion, for the information has come from another, more illustrious source.

"But of course. You did not think you could simply disappear? Your Grandmaster Phillipe Villiers de L'Isle-Adam was a favourite with the emperor, as I'm sure you know. He spoke of you often."

"He was a noble knight, a great soldier."

Chapuys nods. "I knew him too, though not closely."

Pacificus releases a pent-up breath, placing his basilard on the table as he does so. "And so the emperor wants the saint?"

Chapuys leans forward, "Look, I know your bishop has ideas for her, but he is behind the times. The big houses will fall – the Cluniac house at Lewes is in negotiations even now – *c'est l'inévitable*." He gestures in resignation. "I did my best for Queen Katherina, God rest her, against that Boleyn whore, and I will do what I can for Princess Mary, but you see the times, *non*? I have it from someone at court that a new act to ban the veneration of relics altogether is being drafted even now, and then where will the saint's holy bones be? Maybe cast into the heretics' fires! No, you must obey the emperor in this, it is your duty as a true son of the church. We will find a way to make it up to the bishop, but we must act in the wider interest. *Alors*, as Mary is the mother of Christ, so *Helena is the mother of the Church Triumphant*. If Cromwell should get her..." Chapuys makes a swift sign of the cross then, half-throwing his arms up in despair, or at least as much as he can muster with his summer cold, exclaims – "*Merde*, we shall not think of it!"

"And Prior Wulfric and the brothers?"

Chapuys waves his hand again – they're good at this, the French – this time dismissively. "Strange man. He will get some of what he asks – you know he will treat with none but me?" He now begins to gesticulate with his free hand – Pacificus has forgotten how much the continentals do this – "Bringing me all this way when I am unwell! Yes, yes, he may be near the saint, but as for a new *Order of Saint Helen*, or his plans to see the mother of Constantine raise up another *church triumphant* from her bones to renew Christendom – well, we must let the emperor decide later."

"And God."

"Yes, but of course – and God." He gives Pacificus a steady stare. There is a difference between polity and piety, *mon frère*.

"And these injunctions against venerating images – you are sure?" These ambassadors didn't get where they were by telling the whole truth.

"Oh yes, *absolument, ami*, and pilgrimages too; little by little these filthy varlets nibble away at true religion like rats. They will not stop, I tell you, not until they are as godless as the Lutherans." He picks the glass up once more, swirling the contents as if conjuring a solution. "I am told many hundred pious friars, priests and monks have starved to death in Newgate, the Marshalsea, and other places this summer – there is no law in this land, you are under the hand of pagan despots. We must stand together, *non*? Or else be divided, and fall." When he sees Pacificus nod, he continues carefully, "You will not, I hope, stand in our way? We have come prepared to take it back with us – you understand?"

Pacificus sighs "No. I won't stand in you way – "

"*Ah, bon!* This is what I wish to hear!" Chapuys sits back in his chair. "I have so little good news for the emperor these days, but this at least is something."

"But take heed of the Augustinians," Pacificus cautions, "for they are in this business up to their elbows – "

"Yes, I see. My men will see to it. François!" He turns to his retainer – who by now has cleaned his face and is standing back at the door, "*Allez! Vite!* Take Armand, Jacques Touland, and those three fat ones; fetch me Wulfric. Take no excuses, and watch out for these Augustinians. *Allez! Maintenant!*"

"I will go too, Ambassador. I am afraid that if there be mischief abroad in this cloister – "

"Not quite yet! There is one other matter we must discuss first."

He waits while Pacificus reseats himself. "That concerns me?"

"*Oui.*"

"My past?"

"Your future." There is a pause to allow Chapuys to savor his drink once again, which he does, with a winning smile. "You will know the emperor is occupied with the menace in the east – that matters are acute?"

Pacificus is blunt. "He should have had a mind to it sooner."

"Yes, yes; there is much, as we say, *chagrin* at court, that His Holiness went unheeded, and no force was marshalled for your aid during the siege. It is regrettable."

Pacificus sets his jaw; they had another word for it on Rhodes, when two hundred thousand Mohameddans were breaching the citadel for eight months. Chapuys' playful smile sobers under Pacificus' stare, and he raises suppliant hands in half-surrender. "Yes, yes, all right Hugh, it was a disgrace. But neither was the in-fighting ameliorated by your king and his whore, so let the past be past. We learn from it *avec des remonstrances douces et tranquilles, n'est ce pas*? And *doucement*, that is, with meekness, and *entre nous-mêmes.*"

Yes ambassador, Pacificus thinks, his teeth almost grinding together, we can all twist the words of Saint François de Sales if we want.

"But to my point," Chapuys coughs, "we are having this conversation. L'Isle de Adam, de Ponte, de Saint-Jaille are dead, and after this debacle in Tripoli, the emperor does not have confidence in Grandmaster de Homedes. The times being as they are, he needs a tactician, someone *consciencieux* – "

"You may tell the emperor that I am flattered, but I cannot."

"But surely – *la gloire, l'honeur* – to be Grandmaster?"

"Ambassador, please!" Pacificus spreads his fingers, trying hard to control his blood, "I answer as Achilles did Odysseus, that *I would rather be the slave of the worst of masters*, yes, even this Tudor king, *than rule down there among all the breathless dead.*" It is not the first time he has turned down great honours. If he wouldn't be gonfalonier of the papal forces for Cardinal Cornaro, then by God, he won't be brigand in chief on a windy rock called Malta.

"But the Barbary Corsairs grow in strength and impudence, the seas must be swept!"

"I repeat: I cannot."

"*Mon frère*, think about your reputation, the survival of Christendom. Vienna might have been another story, the emperor knows that, we are not as strong as we were – please *mon frère* – "'

"The answer is still *no*. By my oath, if God wants a *church triumphant*, let him fight for her himself! I have slain my last infidel." Damn him, should I show him the scars on my arms, my back, my chest, my soul? We buried the flower of the European nobility – nay the bravest men in Christendom, during that bloody summer – while they held their masked balls.

"I see, I see! And if they order you?"

"Then they should come with more than just pretty commissions."

"But why? You could be Grandmaster?"

"Because – *because* – I am *not* that man anymore!" What else can I tell him that he would understand? Tell him about Rhodes, about Lincoln, about York, about God? Jesu! Tell him about Darcy and Aske at the scaffold? Better that, I suppose, than that Anabaptists are making my head soft, or worse – a woman.

Chapuys can see that the conversation is about to become unnecessarily heated, and that he will get nowhere in any event. So, with a magnanimous gesture with a hand freed from his glass, he smiles once more and bows slightly from his chair. They part amicably, Pacificus returning to the yard to find Richard. But the lad is nowhere to be seen in the courtyard, and it is now dark. Pacificus walks towards the precinct gate with swift steps and increasing pulse. Where is he? Where's the lad? I should not have brought him here. Then he hears the slap-slap of sandals on the abbey path. Richard appears at the gate, breathless and trembling, "Oh, thank God! You must come quick – but hurry!"

"What is it?"

"There were screams from the abbey – the most horrible screams!"

Pacificus loops up his habit and makes all speed towards the great doors. Other monks appear from the guest hall, milling about the abbey's west door. There is no sign of François and his friends. They dodge past the gathering brothers, darting through the great doors into the cool, damp gloom of the abbey nave.

Pacificus lays a cautioning hand on Richard's arm, and they pause to listen above the beating of their hearts. There are no more than a few lights burning in the sconces, but even so, they see well enough to satisfy themselves there are no signs of trouble here, and no screams can be heard now. Through the gloom and the small pools of light, they see Prior Thomas standing near the altar with a few others who have come from the dorter and through the south door. But they too are searching for the source of the disturbance, they are not part of it.

"Quickly now," Pacificus says, towing Richard along by the arm, skirting the abbey interior, taking the shadows of the left ambulatory. They are only halfway down when a hand reaches from the blackness of the crypt doorway, and fastens firmly on to Richard's arm.

19

The Crypt

Facile omnes quom valemus recta consilia aegrotis damus
When we are healthy, we all have advice for those who are sick

Richard lurches backward. It is Mark, thank God. He fights the loosening of his bowels as Mark leads them from the darkness of the recess into the pallid, orange glow of the abbey's candlelight.

"Mark, what are you doing?" Richard says.

"Shhh," Mark hisses. "Down there!"

"What is?" Pacificus whispers.

"I followed Wulfric as you said."

"And?"

"Well, he came as far as here, then...er..." Mark's voice tails off, his eyes big with fright.

"You were afraid to go any further?"

"That's right, and a good thing too, for not long after that I heard those screams."

Pacificus peers past him, discerning a faint glimmer of light at the bottom of the steps. "All right, stay behind me, but for God's sake watch your step, stick close; with all those little chapels and passages, it's like a badger's sett." He descends slowly and breathlessly quiet, dagger in hand, one ear cupped to listen. At first there is nothing, then as he nears the bottom he hears harsh, fast whispering, reverberating off the cold, damp walls. "Come with me."

The floor of the crypt is a mixture of sandstone and silted sand. It is hardly used for burial now because of the regular flooding, though there are still plenty of alcoves and miniature chapels, where the sarcophagi of forgotten dead await the resurrection. Light leaks from a side chapel at the far end of the crypt, somewhere just beyond the foundations of the great pillars supporting the main tower. Pacificus inches slowly down the corridor towards the light, towards the voices. The boys follow behind, clutching each other with white knuckles. The voices are clearer now: "You would betray the saint to our enemies, fornicate with the emperor's vassal, even when the bishop still holds out such an offer? Traitor! Traitor! Villain!" It is too hard to make out the whisperer's identity, but the subject is surely Wulfric.

Again the shrill voices reach them, this time rising in volume and intensity. "Damn you! You – you feckless, faithless vacillator." Pacificus increases his pace, blade forward, even as the stream of curses, oaths and threats reach him. "Tell us where you and Bede hid her, or join him in purgatory!"

"I – I will not betray Saint Helena, not ever, d'you hear?" Now, he thinks, this is definitely Wulfric. "Your hearts have cankered and – oh Jesu! Put that thing down!"

"Tell us! Or it will go in, to the hilt! It's your choice – there's no water mixed with the blood yet."

"Please! *Please!*" The voice rises in intensity and volume "No! Oh, stop, I beg you..."

As Wulfric's pleas disintegrate into shrieks of agony, Pacificus breaks into a jog, shouting with a lusty voice, "Come, men! They are down here!" Richard and Mark stumble over the flags, chasing to the side of the monk's swirling garments, only just in time to see, the blur of two other monks darting from the side chapel and off down another corridor. The three of them pile into the chapel to find Prior Wulfric tied to the altar by his hands, blood pouring from his right side. Next to him though not tied, the two other Binham brothers, Aefric and Anthony lie slain in a pool of gleaming, viscous blood.

"Help him! Stem the blood! Here, put your hand here." Pacificus barks out, pointing at Wulfric. And then to Mark who had spent two weeks barrowing silt out of the crypt the previous spring. "Mark – where does that lead? Is there another exit?"

"Yes, in the Falstaff chapel, but wait, don't leave us here, wait – "

Pacificus moves swiftly into the blackness, making what haste he can groping along the wall.

Richard, who has not been able to obey Pacificus stands rooted to the spot, aghast at the bloody sight, his breath short, his frame shuddering. It is Mark who unties the prior's hands.

"Oh Jesu... oh Jesu..." Wulfric keeps saying over and over, looking up at Richard with wide yet twitching eyes. He is still breathing, but sounding more and more like a man drowning. "Oh Jesu... oh, prithee help me, boy, this was not to be... all of it... not to be at all..." He reaches out his hand, shaky, as if he might rise again, but the gaping wound wells copiously, and he presses his hand again feebly to the place. His legs begin to judder and scrape the ground.

"Help me," Mark says desperately, looking up at Richard. "I've got to try and get this plugged with ...something."

The two go to work, Richard holding the man's wet head, Mark ripping off strips from Wulfric's cowl and bunching them to pack the wound. They lay him flat on the top step, under the altar. His breathing worsens, gurgling. They try to prop up his head, but nothing seems to help. Wulfric raises a hand to grip his chest, his fingers scrunching the coarse wool. His eyes open wide with the intensity of the pain, he knows his life is ebbing fast. His head twists to the side and he sees the cadaver of Brother Aelfric slumped and contorted against the wall. He moans and turns away. The sound of sandaled steps approaches. The boys strain their eyes into the darkness, tensed to defend themselves, but – to their relief – it is Pacificus who appears.

"I got close, but they bolted the door against me. Is he yet alive?"

"Just," Mark says, still vainly trying to stem the blood.

Pacificus crouches and assesses the location of the wound. He feels it, probes carefully with his fingertips for the width and extent. "Pierced in his lung. You can tell by the sound. We must sit him up, try to drain it." As they are doing this, Pacificus says to Mark, "Go up top and raise the alarm – first with the prior, but then also with the ambassador; they must find those Augustinians and put them under the charge of the night watchmen. They must do it *quickly*, too."

While Mark feels his way back towards the stairway which leads to the nave, Richard gets his arms under Wulfric's shoulders, lifting him.

"Will he live?"

Pacificus shakes his head. "Wulfric, can you hear me?"

He nods very slightly.

"Did they murder these men to make you talk?"

Again he nods and begins to sob. He hasn't betrayed the saint into cruel hands, he says.

"Now you must listen very carefully, there is little time. I know you think I'm the bishop's man, but in this case the relics are better going with Chapuys, for Cromwell is set to destroy them all. We cannot allow this to happen to Helena's bones, do you understand?"

He nods, more slowly this time.

"Do Benedict and Sigismund know?"

He shakes his head with slightly more vehemence.

"I see, then prithee, you must tell where she is."

He opens two doleful eyes and stares at Pacificus. "Wanted to do something good – new – better." It is barely a whisper and yet even then he coughs blood with the effort.

"I know," Pacificus says. 'We've all done that, believe me."

"Who will confess me?"

"I will fetch a confessor, but first the saint?"

At this point he jerks in a final spasm of life, and as his spirit departs he grabs at Pacificus' clothing. "Find her in confession – in *confession...*" It is his final breath. He flops back heavily into Richard's arms, staring at him blankly face to face. "He's...he's gone," Richard says, between great heaving breaths, "he's dead." The lad scrunches his eyes shut, he will not see anymore, cannot see it. The blood of this man is on his hands, his legs; the blood of a man who only moments before was living – a real thing, like himself. His skin is still warm, the scent of onion from his last breath still evident in Richard's senses. The lad crumples and sobs, while Pacificus searches each of the corpses. He pulls Richard to his feet. "Come lad, no time for that now, let the dead bury their own, we've murderers to catch."

They leave the corpses there and head back to the nave, where torches are lit and a full-scale hunt for the Hickling canons is underway. Pacificus heads straight to the outer precinct, fearing for Simon, Beth and Piers. There is a commotion to the left of the main gatehouse and the sound of hooves in the distance, but perhaps only as near as the rise to the hospital across the causeway. They find Simon behind a cottage near the stables, with Brother Porter standing over him.

"What's all this? Simon, is that you?" Pacificus pushes past the porter, and drops to his knees at his brother's side.

"Found him like that, brother," the porter says. "There was a terrible carry-on near the stables, so I came out to see."

Simon is still breathing, but unconscious. "Who took the horses, porter? Did you see them? How many?"

"I cannot say, not for sure, but I knows they led 'em out of the side door near the main gate, for I heard the bolt."

"But you didn't think to look?"

"I was a-bed, brother, in my lodge, and I ain't paid to be nigh watch and all, am I?"

"Six." Beth's voice comes from the direction of the stable. "There were six, all monks, or at least dressed as them."

"But Simon wouldn't let us try to stop them!" Piers is with his sister. "He said we had to hide in the hay loft – oh! Is that him?"

"Yes. He's all right, but he's been hit hard."

"Beth! Piers! You're safe – oh, thank God!" Richard embraces them both like a man clinging to a rock. His hands shake and his face is white with shock. All around is the continuing and anguished neighing of horses.

"Can we go after them on the horses?" Piers says eagerly. He is fearless, this child.

"No lad, find Pieter and get thee home. Those horses won't be for riding again, I know that sound." It takes a harder man to hamstring ten horses than kill an adversary; Prior Robert Aeyns has them well trained.

Mark escorts the Fentons to the west staithe where they see Pieter sculling up river.

"You'll be all right from here?" Mark says to Beth.

"Yes, except poor Richard. He looks like he's seen a ghost."

"He's seen worse than that tonight; we both have. Help him get cleaned up when you get back." Mark wishes he could go with them, escape the precinct. How can he stand in the cloister in a few hours' time for Matins, then Lauds, while the butchered bodies of monks still lie in the crypt beneath their feet? As she goes to leave, Mark tries to control his own shaking body by hiding his hands in his cowl.

"Will *you* be all right?" Beth says, the pale moonlight picking out the contours of her cheeks and neck.

"Suppose, and I can't think anyone has cause to come after me." He attempts a smile, and she attempts to return it. "Anyway, go to now Beth, you look cold, and the sooner you're away from here the better."

As he returns to the gate he sees Simon emerging with Pacificus.

"He's a big one, their prior is!" Simon ruefully rubs the side of his head with a bandaged fist. "Came at me on horseback. I tried to introduce him to my pike staff but he grabbed it, just like that! And, oh, I am so slow when this cold damp is in my bones, and my feet, I cannot move lithe as I once did..."

"No more of that now, you did what you could, and it's a good thing he was in a hurry or he might have finished you off altogether. Now, are you sure you can get back on your own?"

"Yes, yes – but bring me news tomorrow if you can, and make sure that porter keeps his mouth shut." He hobbles slowly along the silver causeway towards the lazar house. He's not going to tell his brother that he hid and feigned unconsciousness, because he was afraid to take them on six to one – and he a knight! At the sight of their leader the strength had ebbed from Simon's body, just as it had at the great siege on Rhodes when a wall was breached by the suicidal hordes of Janissaries. These elite Ottoman troops of captured Armenian Christians had been brainwashed from childhood into fanatical, relentless fighting machines. Simon had been guarding a small parapet with a militia of local men when the breach occurred, and saw the Janissaries cut the militia to ribbons. To his shame, terror and love of life prevailed. He abandoned his post and fled, forsaking the knightly resolve to stand firm even when death was certain. It was something never mentioned by his comrades afterwards, not even his brother, though he thinks every one of them knew. The leprosy appeared during the knights' withdrawal, not long after the eventual surrender made for the sake of the native islanders. Again no one said anything, especially not his brother, but they all knew.

And none saw what he had done and called it cowardice more candidly than Simon himself, for which reason he accepted his disease as the punishment of heaven. It is no less than I deserve, he thought,

God is just. He has run from responsibility as a second son; run from honour, with regards to Elizabeth; and now from the field of duty before God, angels, demons and men. But this night he thrice hates himself, for what life is he trying to preserve now; the life of a half-dead, half-decayed cripple? There's no running from *that*, at least. He's been a skilled shot and swordsman in his day, perhaps even having the edge on his brother, but what is a knight without honour, courage and without chivalric virtue?

As he makes his slow and painful way home, Simon stops on the causeway and looks into the black waters of the dyke, overcome with horror at himself. As he moves to the edge, the moon appears on the water and his ragged, wraith-like frame is reflected back to him. *What am I, in God's name, what am I? What is my life?* Hugh would have never turned his back on the enemy, it just wasn't in him – so consumed with devotion to the cause. Perhaps that's why he finds it harder to turn his back on the old faith now? Perhaps that's why I find it so easy – why the talk of a new start for cowards and sinners every morning shines so bright. I'd like to believe, nay better yet, *experience* all Beth reads me from Tyndale's bible. About being "*washed from sin*', the "*promise of a good conscience towards God*', dear heaven, a good conscience! And about there being "*no condemnation to those that are in Christ Jesus.*"

But truth is easier to believe about someone else, anyone else, but yourself. It smacks of injustice anyway; why make a way easier for turn-coats and caitiffs like me, and hard for good men like Hugh? Surely Luther's faith and Calvin's grace will populate heaven with scoundrels? Can a man do nothing to earn salvation? Must we all come like cowards, beggars and lepers? It is monstrous unfair to my mind, though I'd be glad of it for all that. *Oh, Lord! Wilt thou not ease this burden of righteousness from Hugh, that we may come to thee together, beggars and lepers all?*

The sheriff, reeve and a company of soldiery are in attendance the next morning. Chapuys is cleared of all involvement and allowed to leave with his men. He speaks to Pacificus before mounting his horse: "So! He passes from us with no word for my master, poor man."

"Nothing monsieur , only that we might *find her in confession.*" Pacificus folds his hands inside the sleeves of his habit. "But seeing that we were already talking about getting him a confessor, I think, well, those were no more than the confused words of a dying man, God rest him."

"Yes, I heard what you told the sheriff." Chapuys observes the patches of red forming at the top of Pacificus' cheeks. He's a bad liar. Chapuys waits for a confession, but nothing is forthcoming. Eventually Pacificus relents and smiles at him. "It is just as I told him and I say it in truth to you too, because I did make the precaution of checking around the abbey confessionals and the small storeroom near them in the Falstaff chapel, but there was nothing – nor any suitable hiding place either."

Satisfied with this answer, Chapuys heaves a sigh, shrugging. "*Eh bien, ça va. Tant pis*, uh? You did your best. Even so remember, *mon cavaliere*, if anything further comes to light you will send word, *non*? The gold, you may give to the poor, it is of no concern to the emperor, but the saint must be saved. You will watch the other monks that hid – "

"Sigismund and Benedict have sworn under oath that they know nothing – "

"Ah, but even so, where there is a carcass the buzzards gather. You are a sensible man, you understand. The Augustinians might return for them, or others perhaps."

Pacificus nods, and helps the ambassador up onto his mare. "I am glad your horses were kept at the abbot's stable."

"Yes! Oh, a ghastly affair! But the Augustinians won't get far, unless they have help – which we might reasonably expect, perhaps?" He's angling for a hint. Pacificus remembers Rugge's warnings about Chapuys, so keeps his counsel. Rugge will need talking to, this has gone too far; there is blood on his hands now surely, no matter what he intended.

Chapuys stops for some more bonhomie with Prior Thomas as he moves towards the gateway. He says they'll hunt together next time, but both men know there will be no next time. He will not risk being implicated in scandal. How ironic, Pacificus thinks, as he surveys the bustling precinct of Saint Benet's, the one abbey where there really *is* murder and scandal is the only one given *in commendam* to the Bishop of Norwich – bet it makes Cromwell livid.

Pacificus walks back to the abbey where he passes the sheriff, who eyes him with suspicion. Why is this monk always so near to the trouble? Two graves barely grassed over, and now three more to join them. Pacificus has told him nothing of the relics, only that he followed the shouting. Mark is the witness. If he wants to know more he'll have to find the Augustinians; perhaps easier said than done. The surviving monks, Sigismund and Benedict are more than vague – they say the Augustinians surprised the five of them at prayer, but they escaped. They know nothing more than that. The sheriff would have them put under the board for contempt, if they were not clerics – the sooner these places are torn down the better, is his opinion.

But even if he could read minds, Pacificus would not give a groat for the opinions of a man in his position who lets his wife appear on holy days dressed like a peacock.

Even today when his head is full of dark matters, he cannot forgive her the gaudy, feathered bonnet she wore. For him aesthetic violations are worse than violations of the sumptuary laws. His latent patrician contempt would fain have new laws framed against bad taste, or something near like it. Make me lord chief justice and I would hang a man for slashed sleeves and any use of orange and silk, and for women - tush, enough prating Pacificus, you fool. Once these old demons are exorcised through grumbling introspection, he repents his folly and goes again about his business. He walks through the abbey, around the cloister to the scriptorium, where he finds Mark dismally failing to learn the new italic style of calligraphy. Brother Aloysius, his frog-like eyes and cheeks more puffy than usual, hovers about Mark and two other novices with obvious dismay. The late September sun may be streaming in on them but the muses are not.

"Well, I don't see why everything has to be Italian," Mark says, trying to scrape away yet another smudge.

"And nor do I," Pacificus adds, making his presence known. "The purpose of script is like the purpose of art, to show the meaning and make nothing of itself. Mary and Joseph boy, even when it's done well, it's barely legible."

"Now then brother, many say it is more so," Aloysius says with a glint of jollity, "besides, you would not keep these subtle young minds from progress, would you? It is the abbot's express desire."

"I would stop a great many things, as you well know, brother," Pacificus says, for this conversation they have had many times. He sighs affectedly. "But, be that as it may, I would borrow this novice for some other improving work, if it please you?"

"By all means for, by the rood, he has no head for letters old or new," Aloysius says. "But, faith, it's hardly surprising he is distracted, seeing we too may be murdered in our beds this very night."

"Fret not, brother! Verily you will die of progress and Italianate letters, before you ever die of villainy."

Mark gladly tidies his vellum and reed under the desk, to the jealous glances of his fellow novices. Pacificus glances through the door to the library. "I'll be back later for some more books."

"Not until you've brought back Marie de France and Gower!" Aloysius is a good *Umanista*, as the Italians say, loves all learning, all good books and cannot rest until all his children are on their shelves. If he knew they were in Norwich Castle jail, his eyes would pop out altogether.

Pacificus nods deferentially and takes Mark to the monastery gardens. The novice gets few answers to his many questions, at least, not until they are clear of the buildings. "We are going to pay a visit to Sigismund and Benedict, see how they fare, before anyone else does."

"You think they are in danger still?"

"Most definitely, now watch your step and mind what you hear. We must know what they know."

The brothers are working with Gerard the herbalist. They are harvesting and drying chickweed, and groundsel for his spacious stores. Gerard is in a high fever of excitement today because bees, not their own, have formed a swarm on one of the pear trees at the edge of the herb garden.

"Ah brother! Come, see this, I will show you something wondrous!" Gerard beckons with arms, his face and eyes, wide as the heavens to share this thing with someone.

Pacificus approaches warily when he sees the swarm, hanging like a huge riving blanket laid over a branch to dry. "You've not got special clothing, brother." Pacificus hesitates, "Heavens, there must be thousands!"

"About thirty thousand," Gerard nods enthusiastically, beckoning Pacificus closer. "Come nearer! They're quite safe, you know, for they have no hive to defend. You can touch them, see."

"*Touch them?*"

Gerard puts his hand under them and bounces the swarm. "Nothing like it to touch in all the world! Come on, you do it."

Pacificus does not, as a rule, have any affection for small, fast-moving insects. He hates spiders for example, but bees somehow have always fascinated him – their wisdom, their industry – so he steps closer, then closer until he is finally within arm's reach. "And they will not sting?"

"Give me your hand, man, and close your eyes." He does so, and Gerard lifts his hand under the swarm, gently bringing it up. "Relax, will you? By my oath, you look like a man on the scaffold."

And then it happens, the strangest, most beautiful sensation he has yet experienced; the bees are piping hot and fluttering their wings and moving their tiny bodies against his palm. It is as though he has never really touched anything else before in his life. In the span of that small moment he thinks of the many other things he has touched – the swords, the matchlocks, the canon – the skulls he's cracked, the limbs he's severed. He feels the shame of it all in one instance, these hands of his, these bloody hands. Could these hands of his ever do anything beautiful, say at Ranworth? Or would he be like King David, who was not permitted to build the temple because his hands had shed so much blood. He still believes that to shed blood in war is not murder, yet even so, he had aforetime killed Saracens for Christ, for Christendom. Pieter, Christopher, and now his own brother are telling him this is a grave sacrilege.

When he feels the beauty of these bees on his palm, vibrating every nerve and sinew, he feels persuaded more than ever. But then also something else, something greater yet, for they also feel like the extended hand of a God he has never known, pure as honey, gentle as a shimmering wing, hot with love, vibrating with a cleansing forgiveness. Am I *imagining* this just because it is what I have sought for so long? He tries to resist – *depart from me, Lord for I am a sinful man!* Yet still the feeling is there, the waves and ripples of love flowing through his body. He knows he could stay there, in that place forever but, shaken, he pulls his hand away.

"Brother, what is the matter? These tears – are you quite well?"

"Yes, nothing amiss." For the next half minute Pacificus remains standing there, feeling his palms, aware only of his breathing and the nearness of that unseen presence. Eventually he turns to the herbalist, looking him straight in the eye, "Thank you, Gerard – thank you indeed. But now we must to business; we are looking for your two helpers."

"Ah yes, I see. Well, as you wish." He knows more than he lets on, does Gerard, he has the healer's heart and is loved and revered for it far and near. What will become of him and his trade when they close the abbeys? Gerard touches Pacificus' arm gently, "All will be well, brother and, as our own Julian of Norwich says, *all manner of things will be well.* You may call back anytime, you know that." Gerard then he points Pacificus towards the thatched byres. "They'll be in there, shirking again no doubt! So, when you're done, tell them to hurry back here for rain is forecast."

"Thank you brother, I will. And – and...thank you."

"What happened back there, with the bees," Mark says when they are out of earshot.

"I don't know," he looks down at his palms once again, "I don't know, but no talking now, we are near the building." They approach the building quietly. Mark waits by the entrance as Pacificus enters the half-light. He can see nothing at first but gradually his eyes match the pungent variety of scents with their origins. Hanging in the rafters are mallow, shepherds' purse, sweet woodruff, bugle, and clumps of red clary. Down below, spread on tables and shelves as well as stored in a variety of baskets, are the stalks and seed heads of white saxifrage, yarrow, lesser hawkweed and trefoil. And there at the back are the two monks, staring towards the silhouetted figure in the doorway, arrested in mid-conversation.

"Good morrow, brothers. I am glad to see you in health!"

"What do you want of us?" Benedict demands, both of them rising and moving to the far side of the heavy table. Benedict reminds Pacificus of old Norfolk, something of death about his drawn and skeletal features. Poor man, he'd been through it all right – they both had.

"Upon my word, brothers, you have nothing to fear from me. I came only to enquire after – "

"We said what we had to say to the sheriff," Benedict says sharply, moving his slender form nearer his more well-fleshed companion.

"But I fancy you did not mention the relics, eh?"

"How could we?" Benedict answers for them both again before Sigismund can speak, and this time his left eye twitches involuntarily.

But Sigismund adds, "Perhaps we should have told the sheriff who the Augustinians work for – set the cat among the pigeons, mentioned you too!" He waggles a nervous finger at Pacificus. "Yes, brother, we know you are Rugge's man – like they are."

"Ah, but you will not say so I think, for you would implicate yourself in theft and fraud, not to mention wrecking any possible chance of recovering the reliquary and gold."

He's keeping an eye on the two sickles on the table, which are now in reach of the monks' hands. They are cornered and frightened of him, why wouldn't they be, but he doesn't think he should be worried.

"Yes, Rugge did ask me to negotiate with Wulfric, but he held off for the emperor's offer – a better one in my opinion." He notes a flare in both their eyes and tightening of Benedict's lips at this. "But now I must ask myself, have you also done this because you know where the saint is?"

Both men immediately shake their heads with something of an honest and embittered frustration. "There's no use asking us more questions," Benedict says, "besides, we've seen the way you and all the bishop's men negotiate – blood and butchery! Still, either way you'll get naught from us, for we were not privy to the hiding place."

"You truly do not know it?"

"Oh yes, didn't you know? The prior decided that he and just one other should know the hiding place," Sigismund says. "He judged it safer that way, in case – well, in case of any accident."

"Bede."

"Yes, and after he was gone, Aelfric."

"And you did not object? You did not see it as favouritism? I mean, he could have used lots."

"No, we trusted our prior, and we were obedient. Why shouldn't we be?"

There is more than a tinge of sarcasm here. Why indeed – the gold for one thing. Wulfric obviously had his reasons anyway.

"And so," Pacificus says airily, "you know – "

"We know nothing!" They say it in unison.

"Which is what Wulfric told me last night, but I just wanted to check."

He spoke with you?" Benedict's voice is suddenly softer and his eyes more alive. "Pray, what else did Father Prior say?"

"Naught else, except – " he watches them very carefully now, "where I would find the saint."

Both men start visibly, staring at him.

"Where?" This time it is Sigismund who finds his voice.

"He was cryptic."

"Well, tell us," Benedict says, "perhaps we can-er-we can help."

"What? Would you become the bishop's men too?" That's got them.

"We – we want to put this business behind us, now it is known," Sigismund says quickly, eye twitching again.

"Yes – to be rid of the suspicion, the threat of harm," Benedict backs him up. "As soon as the treasure – and the saint – are recovered, the sooner we can forget another visit from Prior Robert Aeyns."

Were they telling the truth? Did it matter? Pacificus had the scantiest information and no leads at all. He thinks, they look like men who have endured a sleepless siege under the battery of a thousand Turkish guns. Perhaps sleep is all they now desire – or peace, like himself.

"He said I would find her *in confession*. Mean anything to you?"

It did not, or if it did they both showed remarkable restraint in their identical blank-faced response.

"We will give it some thought," Benedict says.

"And you will share what you have with me?"

"Of course."

Somehow he doubts it. "Then I will speak to the bishop on your behalf."

He leaves them and returns – unwatched, God willing – to the abbey with Mark, pulling him to stand close, behind a pillar in the Lady chapel near the north door, from where they can see through the choir to the confessional. A shaft of dying light shines through the west window right down the nave into the chancel. It is always empty in the hour before Vespers, this is a good time.

"What are we doing here?"

"Just watching. Keep well back, here they come!"

But it was not they, but just Benedict, alone and scurrying fast as a rat from the arch leading to the night stairs and up to the dorter. Pacificus whispers, "He's done well to get here so quick!"

"What does he want?"

"Watch."

Benedict is in and out of the confessional boxes behind the choir and also the storeroom nearby, even checking the floor, lest any slabs have been disturbed. Suddenly, Mark grabs Pacificus' arm, pulling him down out of sight, murmuring, "Look to the nave!"

Pacificus raises his head just enough to see that it is Sigismund, walking towards them down the south side of the ambulatory. But as he creeps behind a pillar at the transept, it is not them he is watching by stealth, but Benedict. Pacificus and Mark keep very low. What does this mean, then? They seemed so united in purpose only a few moments ago. Mark's expression almost says as much. Pacificus is still thinking on it, there is something about these two that he does not like – *lupus est homo homini.*

As he crouches lower, Pacificus begins to wrestle with uncomfortable counter-thoughts. So, each does not trust the other, yes, but would their failings and resentments, nay, their ambition, run far enough toward even murder? Here am I pinning all on the Hickling canons, and yes, they did run. But, in truth, we do not know who it was in the crypt that night. We saw no faces and there maybe more in these men's faces than just fear.

"Are you alight master? You looked vexed."

Aye, he thinks, that is one world for it.

20

The Brothel

Mendacem memorem esse oportet
A liar needs a good memory

Confession? Or was that plural? *Confessions* perhaps? Wulfric had been slurring towards the end. Did he mean anything by it at all, this one word?

It is nearly two weeks after the last murders and though they have had correspondence, Pacificus has made excuses for not attending the bishop in person, that is, until he is summoned by Rugge in a curt letter and a high-handed tone that has set him in a black mood. But though he is simmering with rage against Rugge, he is also wary; he knows more than enough about his abbot to bury him – he knows that this knowledge makes him a liability, and he is beginning to think he does not know his old master as he once thought he did. Rugge has changed with the times – steeped so far in blood, he may think nothing of severing any who can incriminate him. Business as usual, or Sever and quarterize. What will it be? The Augustinians in some dark corridor of the palace? It is more than a faint possibility, but if he's bound for purgatory this afternoon he'll not go alone. He flexes his lower arm muscles for the comforting pinch of the basilard dagger near his skin. He'd wish for a pair of Hamberly's wheellocks today, and even more to live in a world where he needed them not. Is that why monks of old refused a sword but carried a staff, bend the times rather than let them bend you. Perhaps old Pieter is more Benedictine than I? God's teeth, the times have bent us all – nearly all.

He begins to regret bringing Mark. The lad walks at heel, deep in thought. Across the meadows beyond the causeway some brothers are finishing the thatching work on the outlying farm buildings, that they started on Our Lady's day. The sound of their singing drifts on the wind like the autumn leaves. *Ora et labora*. He takes a last glance at the abbey, just in case. The Michaelmas feast of the Angels has been banned now, but it is the Feasts of St Jerome and St Honorius of Canterbury in a week, and then comes the winter. Aye, he whispers, and so comes the winter. The sun is weak when the fast clouds allow it to shine. He feels for the novices up to their waists in the dykes, removing the small bushes before the reed harvest. They're not singing!

They make the palace by mid-afternoon. "Take the mule to the stable and wait there," says Pacificus when they near the porch. "If I do not return or send word within the hour, take yourself home. Do not look for me, and do not delay."

Rugge is seated in the great hall with his luncheon and three guests from Saint George's guild. On seeing Pacificus he lays down the morsel of bread in his hand. The guildsmen do not pause in their conversation but Rugge starts to move his tongue round his mouth to clean his teeth. He stares at his protégé in the doorway. He sniffs and touches the tablecloth to his lips . "You will pardon me gentlemen, I have an urgent message to attend to."

He pushes back his chair and gets to his feet, passing through the doorway without looking at Pacificus, merely muttering, "Follow me."

They pass the building work – a new wing for a court and entertaining. Rugge never even points to it. In his hasty wake comes the mingling smell of lobster and incense. Pacificus is watching every arch, every doorway. He keeps within reach of his master in case he needs insurance. Eventually they come to the far end of the palace and to Rugge's damp, dark drawing room with its smoking fire.

"I see you have the Flemish tapestry." Solomon judging the two whores, how appropriate.

"Are you going to shut the door?" Rugge is facing away towards the window. He sees three journeymen not at their work on the masonry. He's mumbling something incomprehensible with a fist clenching and unclenching. Pacificus takes one last glance down the corridor, listening hard as the door closes.

At last his abbot turns back from the window. "You alone?"

"Aye, my lord."

"I see Hamberly's son down there at the stable."

"I meant alone in the palace, my lord."

"Oh, very well, I see. Good." Rugge's smile is too late, and too forced. "And you have been cautious, prudent, er, you know, guarded in giving information to the reeve over this business in the crypt?"

"Aye, my lord."

"But I thought it was the sheriff?"

"It was both." Pacificus holds Rugge's clever eyes as he would the bead on a matchlock. "And if you have something to say, my lord, I would that you come out and say it."

"No need for offence, brother! No need in the world. Just deal straight with me, it's all I ask – all I've ever asked." Rugge moves towards his desk. "Have some sherry? You spoke with Chapuys, I hear." Rugge points to the glasses.

"I thank you, no. He invited me in for strawberries."

"Strawberries?"

"I let his retainer have them. I wanted to give Chapuys my full attention."

"And what was his tack?"

"It is as I wrote; he feared the relics would be confiscated and burned before they ever left England, that your plans for a pilgrimage centre here were not realistic."

"Did he now!"

"M'lord, not even the bishops included pilgrimages in the articles – "

"Yes, yes, I know all that now, don't teach me, man! I do know my own business at least."

Rugge's fingers are jittering about his papers, he's hurt.

"And I suppose you agreed with him? Slimy savoy weasel that he is. And you didn't stop his men at their butchery in the very abbey itself, I see – very loyal!"

"My lord, those were not Chapuys' men, that much I know; all mean assumer that they were your Augustinians."

"You saw them did you? Which ones?"

"I could not say who, in the light as poor as it was – only that they were monks."

"Pah! *Dressed* as monks! Chapuys has deceived you – you did not heed me, did you? He probably has the relics even now and is laughing up his braided silk sleeves at us! A nice little jewel in his cap this will be."

"No. The assassins got nothing from Wulfric, I heard that much. Surely this was your *iron fist* grown hasty."

"No, no, and don't speak of what you do not know; it was Chapuys tying up loose ends, you know these foreigners – "

"Aeyns ran away and hamstrung nine horses!"

"Don't raise your voice at me. That was all your doing. You raised the alarm against them, they did what they had to, and don't use his name again, certainly never here." Rugge throws up his hands. "Confound you, man, their work is far too important for them to be taken."

"The relics?"

"What? No, nothing to do with them, but forget I said that, back to the matter at hand." Rugge sits down heavily, clearing his accounts, nearly upseting the ink horn. "Take a seat, won't you, and tell me what these other two, Benedict and Sigismund have said."

"They don't know where it is, I've been watching them closely. Wulfric kept it between him and one other."

"You are sure? You trust them?" He's stroking his chins, and blinking less madly.

"I am sure, for I tested them by a subtlety, but no, they are not to be trusted – neither of them."

"So the trail runs cold."

"Aye, my 'lord, it has."

"You will keep me informed if there are other developments? Of course you will, and in the meantime you will help me with somthing else."

"I will do what I can." Pacificus answers warily.

"And aren't you going to ask me about it?"

"I'm sure you will tell me when you are ready."

"Pacificus!" Rugge is now suddenly merry and blithe as a prince, the dark cloud inexplicably lifted. "Upon my word you are a churlish fellow at times! Come and cast your eye upon this." He rolls a parchment plan of the castle and environs out on his table. "Hold this corner will you? Yes, move those books; yes, and those papers. Any ideas yet?"

"A tilt yard? You are having a tournament?"

"Aye, but for whom? And not just a tournament, my friend, but a royal pageant! Masked balls, feasting, speeches, gifts – "

"The king?"

"Oh yes, Pacificus, the king!" Rugge beams and presses his stubby index finger down three times onto the royal box, where he has sketched in himself alongside the king. "Next summer, after the Newmarket season finishes and he has forgotten the court and Cranmer and Cromwell, yes, when he is bored of horse racing and bored of reforms, *we'll* revive his chivalric, Catholic heart with the noble preferments of the lance and pageant."

"You say 'we'?"

"You've got your mind on the money again, haven't you? Yes, you have! I should have made you a chamberlain."

"It would bankrupt even a rich city."

"Oh, be at ease, this is old Norfolk's idea – well, his with a little encouragement. He needs to regain some ground from under Cromwell's nose, after his niece and nephew fell from favour. Well, you can see that, can't you? Anyway, he will front most of the money and bleed the guilds for the rest."

"And you?"

"Hah!" Rugge claps his hands, letting the map roll back. "That's the best of it. I've persuaded the Duke of Suffolk to be the king's champion once again. Nay, more than that, he's persuaded the king they will – together – challenge all local contenders who enter the lists. Just like they used to!"

"But the king's no age for that sort of tomfoolery, not after his accident last January! And Brandon's no spring chicken, for that matter. I know they used to do this ten years ago, but really...if they want to recover their lost youth, I can think of safer ways."

"Ah, but they cannot. The king leapt at the idea. Pacificus, I did not think you would be so careful of the king's person?"

"My lord?"

"No matter!" He brushes it aside hastily. "Let us dwell on the detail some other time. Think you that I should perform a visitation soon?"

"I think it would be well for you to be seen managing the abbey on a tighter reign after recent events."

"Good, then I shall come." Rugge gives one of his affable smiles. "You see? I do trust your judgment, Pacificus. Now have some of my Spanish sherry."

Pacificus nods. The devil he does.

He leaves the palace with his head still on his shoulders, glad to be away. Pacificus glances up as he crosses the courtyard to rejoin Mark, still patiently waiting for him near the stables. He chances a look backward and sees that Rugge is still watching from his window. *The devil he does.*

His time with Elizabeth Fenton is short on this visit. She is darning the woolens of other prisoners and wearing a new, sage green dress. Her face is fuller again today too; perhaps she has been outside for her cheeks show some colour. He is able to watch her for a few moments while she is unaware of his presence, or how beautiful she is to him.

He points at the woolen clothing. "The winter will be soon upon us."

She is embarrassed and covers the work on her knee. "I have no eye for embroidery, but no one minds my rough stitching here." She puts it to one side, then stands and curtsies.

"A new dress," he says, eyeing it, then realises too late the comment must sound like an oblique criticism of her suitor.

"Oh! Save us! More marital advice?" she snaps back, then bites her lip.

"No." He tries to smile. "Only that it suits you well. I have no more advice."

"Forgive me." She stares down at the floor for a moment, then looks up at him, clearing her throat in determination, for now comes the speech she has been working on in the weeks since their last visit: "I regret the manner of that last parting of ours those months back, and I, I did not, nay have not – for our talk of books – adequately expressed my gratitude for all that you have been to the children and I this last year. You must think very ill of me."

Pacificus smiles, and she feels the warmth of his kindness. "By no means," he reassures her, "and besides, I was presumptuous to speak to you on a matter which did not concern me, though...if I did, you know it was only the concern of a friend – that you should do nothing to compromise your integrity, Elizabeth, nothing you might later regret."

"I am sensible of it and I thank you."

In the awkward pause that follows, she realises he is still looking at her dress.

"Yes, it is from him," she says frankly, "indirectly of course."

"The...um – that is...the colour suits you well." What should he say?

At the sight of him blushing, a little chuckle bubbles up, reminding him of how she used to be, and she twirls, smiling, her arms lifted, to show him. "The style is very old, but I confess I do think it's pretty – it puts me in mind of one of those old damsels in the French prose romances, trapped in a tower and awaiting her prince."

Pacificus lowers his eyes from her hips to the stone flags of the floor. Perhaps that is why Cromwell gave it. This is dangerous territory. He can feel it in the very air. So, he moves on to tell her how Piers said he would deliver her, just as soon as he had mastered the long bow. She sits back down with her hands now on her belly. "I am getting too old to rescue."

"You should not say so." Pacificus says, seeing that the joy has gone now from her answering smile. Her gaze goes beyond this place, this prison and she looks lost, forlorn. "I did not mean my age – but you are very kind nonetheless – I meant that my sentence will soon be announced."

"You...your...what?"'

"I refused him."

"But...but..." The sudden dizzying rush of elation unsettles him, going beyond the relief a family friend might understandably feel.

"I could not marry a man with whom I differ so much in religion."

"I thought..." He has got his equilibrium back now. "I thought you were both reformers."

"It seems we are different in kind, not degree. In all conscience I could not be part of a church hand in glove with the state, yay, a church that suppressed dissent and difference in doctrine, and compelled men's conscience in matters of religion. What would Christ say to me on that great day, if I had been party to that? Besides, it is you I thank for steeling my resolve, for it was you that brought me Chaucer's *Troilus and Cressida*. I would not be as unfaithful to my Lord Jesus as Cressida was to Troilus - so I refused him."

"I see. And how did he take that?"

"Very calmly. He looked down into his hands and said he expected as much. In fact he said that he could not have felt so deeply for me if

I had been otherwise – and that he was more the fool for wanting to destroy the very thing he loved."

"Very chivalrous." He says, but seeing Elizabeth does not catch his sarcasm, adds, "No, I mean, it was well said - er, by him, that is."

"I know! Wooed like that, I was almost ready to change my mind!" But her playful grin now barely hides the sorrow. It fades from her face as she reflects on the situation. "No. I will not betray my Lord, or my husband's memory, nor what I know to be true from Scripture, not even for the children, or all the fair dresses in London."

He tries to smile, but now faced with the appalling prospect of her inevitable execution, Pacificus is at a loss to find anything comforting to add. She steps in and fills the silence, asking for news of the children with the obsessive energy of a woman trying to avoid other matters. She is pleased that Beth is reading Master Tyndale's Bible. She asks whether he notices any change in her conduct by it? He says he is too little about them of late to answer with accuracy. It is this Simon the leper who must be thanked. Will he do that for her? He will. She is curious about him, but Pacificus gives her little more. They talk of the boys, of Pieter and Sarah, their cottage and their lives on the marsh. He does not mention that Richard all but witnessed a triple murder, and that her daughter and her other son were inches from being attacked by six escaping Augustinians. He produces Chaucer's *Parliament of Fools* and Bocaccio's *Decameron* from his scrip, explaining, "I must have the Malory, and the other, back." He will not mention the *Lais* of Marie de France by name, and there is mischief in her smile as she brings it with the others from her shelf.

"I'm sorry, I could not get Chrétien de Troyes – would you believe it, Prior Thomas will not part with it!"

She hands him Malory's *Morte d'Arthur*. "Chrétien says that "love is not as it was in Arthur's day". Do you believe that?"

He stows away the books uneasily, and places the new ones into her hands. "I believe a great many things are not as they once were. Take care with Bocaccio, the binding is quite loose - in truth, take care of Bocaccio altogether, for his morals are even looser than the binding."

She handles them reverently, holding them close to her breast like a beloved child. "I fear your librarian will discover us," she says with a smile.

"Brother Aloysius does not even know they are out of the abbey. Anyway, I am more likely to be chastised in Chapter for having that *other* book of yours for nearly eight weeks, than anything else!" They both laugh like children over the joke, and it is only later she realises she has never seen him laugh before. The laughing subsides three times only to start again until both are gasping for breath with tears in their eyes. It is there, leaning against the wall in order to draw wind, that he suddenly feels the weight of her plight crushing him like a falling mountain. He swallows hard and looks full at her, "Do not you lose heart Elizabeth, your God will not forsake you, and nor will I, so long as it is in my power."

She gazes back into his moist, slate-blue eyes, wondrous at the manner of his words. It is only for the briefest moment, yet in it passes more meaning than she can comprehend. He strengthens my hand in God, and also says he will not forsake me so long as it is in his power? And that, after I have turned down the second most powerful man in the realm! What should I make of him? What can a monk on the borders of eviction offer me now, except these few small comforts, and his friendship?

All her life, she knew what each relationship meant to her - how each fitted within the narrative schema of her life. But this awkward man, this well-intentioned monk - what category was there for him, except enemy? Yes, he had been an arm of divine providence to her and the children, but what a strange arm! For the first time in her life, at perhaps the most crucial time, she cannot fathom what it all means. She wants to say something to him but she cannot find the words. He is mumbling something else and bowing as he steps past the threshold and out into the corridor. Supposing it is the last time I ever see him? Supposing he is the last kind face I ever see? As his footsteps recede and she is once again left in her unpeopled solitude; Elizabeth Fenton, arch heretic, clings to his books and his words.

Outside in the castle yard, he sees Mark's eyes are straining beyond the gate. "What is it, lad?"

"Just saw someone I know. 'Tis no matter."

"Oh yes?"

"A girl from Ranworth who I once knew, Margaret Smythe."

"I see." Pacificus stops adjusting the mule's bridle, but his voice betrays no surprise. He had not seen her in the outer precinct or in Hoveton since last year. "And how did she seem?"

"I barely recognised her – she just walked away, down there, like she'd never known me." Mark kept gazing outward with that vacant expression of a practical soul engaged in fixing a problem.

"Mark!" Pacificus lays a hand on the novice's shoulder and gently tries to turn him round. "Our road is to the north, to the abbey."

"It shouldn't be, though, should it?" Mark answers him stubbornly, his eyes still fixed on the road leading into the town.

"She has chosen her way to live, we can only rescue those who want to be helped."

Mark shakes his shoulder free. "You shouldn't say so! Besides, you don't know her. She was just...she was only a *child*."

"Mark, we're going home."

No reply.

"Mark, I will leave without you and you know how disobedience is punished."

Still no reply.

"Mark – "

And this time the novice turns on him with swimming eyes. "You want me to be like you, isn't that right?" And this time it is Pacificus who makes no reply. "Isn't it? Well, you laid aside the Rule, laid aside obedience – nay, even the law, to do what was right, what was merciful – and so will I." With that he leaves the reigns hanging loose and runs through the gate.

"Mark! Mark!" Pacificus kicks the dirt in frustration, and mutters, "Oh, you fool!"

Mark knows where to look, Swan street was well known to his father. Close stacked and close thatched, the houses, ale houses, brothels and tenements are packed together tight as a cluster of pustulent sores on a corpse. You didn't come down here without a stick, a stout one too. Mark tries in vain to counter the dryness in his mouth. Gulp after gulp, each time ingesting acrid smells issuing from the sewers and windows alike.

"Looking for the first time, my darling?" A gross bawd entices from an overhanging upper window. "Be real easy on ya." Her cackling is joined by others on the street when they see he is not buying. Some jostle him, a lurching drunkard gropes him between his legs, "Come on, little horse: lets see what'ya got!"

Laughter erupts all around him.

"Oi! Leave 'im be!" A girl about his own age takes him by the arm and draws him further into the street. "You never mind them – let Sal show you some real love, eh?"

He resists her. "I'm...I'm looking for someone."

"We's all looking for someone, lover, and you've just found all you'll ever need."

But it is then he sees Margaret, sitting on a sack on the pavement, leaning against the wall of what is clearly a brothel. Her auburn hair is matted with filth, her bare feet black.

"That's her!"

"What, *Molly*? You don't want *her* quinny, stud, she's got the rot – "

But Mark pushes her gently aside and goes down to where Margaret's is sitting. "Margaret, it's me, it's Mark! You can't stay here!"

"Oh, be gone." Her voice is dead, mechanical, not really hers at all.

"I will not." He tries to touch her arm but she knocks him away.

Her lips purse tight then, with her dull stare hardening against the opposite wall, she says. "A shilling for an hour."

"Margaret, you must come away – "

"You heard me. A shilling for an hour," she insists, opening her hand.

Mark tries to enfold the hand in his, but he is grabbed by the scruff from behind and swung around. "What's this? More homeless friars?"

He finds himself face to face with Jack Thatcher, journeyman roofer and master pimp. "Troubling my girls? You wanna play, you gotta pay – *me*, not her."

"I'm – I'm taking her away from here." Mark tries to wrest his cowl free but Thatcher keeps a tight grip.

"Oh! Hear that, boys?" His gaze sweeps a circle round his drinking companions, who have tumbled onto the street, a scruffy dog at their heels, "He's taking her away from all this! So genteel! Who are you then – her mother in that dress?"

"No, I'm her...her brother – well, half-brother."

The pimp focuses his bleary eyes on Mark's red hair and freckles, then hers. "Really? Well, you shoulda asked for family rates, my lad." He pulls him so close Mark can almost taste the garlic and French gin. "Very good of ya to come over, very nice." He gestures with his iron tankard towards the girl slumped on the floor. "Only snag is, Moll don't wanna go, do you sweetheart? No, see? She don't. And why? 'Cause she owes me for her rent and vittles, and she likes the work – you wanna see what she can do!"

"She's not staying here."

"Oh, is that so?" Thatcher pulls Mark's cowl tighter. "Really? You sure about that?" he says through yellow teeth.

Mark's breathing is rapid but he won't back down. He grabs Thatcher's arm in order to release himself, "Yes, really, now let me go!"

Thatcher's eyes harden, like stone. "You pushing me, boy? Down here in my own patch? That's not very clever, is it?"

Mark knows what will come next, Thatcher's like his own father. He grits his teeth and gives the brute his best right fist in the ribs. But he's on the back foot and he can't get enough force to make Thatcher release his grip.

"Oooh," the pimp bellows in mock torment, then without warning yanks Mark towards him in a sudden motion that brings their heads together, Mark's nose crunching under the impact. Thatcher holds him close: "You like that, do ya?" He head-butts him again, and then again, until Mark has all but lost consciousness, his blood running down

Thatcher's forehead and beard into his mouth. "Tastes like *chicken* blood to me. Shouldn't have come 'ere should ya? Shouldn't a hit me before these 'ere witnesses, should ya? Cause now I gotta defend myself – with me boots, so down you go!" He swills the last of the gin from his tankard and then uses it as his bludgeon, hammering Mark into the sewer. The rim cuts a gash into his cheek as he goes down. His last memory is seeing Margaret's black feet and then her hands over her ears and her eyes tight shut. And then darkness. Thatcher, pausing for breath before he really sets to work on this impudent boy, catches sight of yet another monk at the end of the alley. The cluster of harlots lets out a whoop at his approach. Thatcher, not quite sure what this should mean, hesitates, standing over Mark's body like a bear. "And who are you? Her father?"

One look at Pacificus' face and no one is laughing this time. He walks straight into the centre of the scene and stops by Margaret, his eyes on Thatcher. He motions to Mark. 'The novice was troubling you?"

"You – what?"

"The boy, was he troubling you?"

"He assaulted me."

"I am sorry for it, but I see you have taught him his lesson. Mark, are you awake?" Mark mumbles and eases from his hunched, defensive position in the sewer.

"Right. Well, get up, apologise to this man, then go tend the mule tethered back there in the market." One less liability.

'What?"

"Do it!"

Mark gets painfully to his feet, the blood still dripping. His face turned aside, he mutters the apology. Pacificus, meanwhile is looking at the dog. *Gus, you little traitor.* The dog whines and goes to Margaret's side. Her hands are still on her ears, but now her eyes, cautiously opening, see the sandalled feet in the gutter beside her. She has heard this voice before.

Thatcher wipes his mouth and cocks his head. "She's a shilling an hour, if you want her."

"Is she?" Pacificus crouches beside her. He speaks gently. "Is that right Margaret, just a shilling?" She will not look at him, but he sees her nod. "I see, and how much for longer?"

Thatcher takes a step closer. He can almost taste the money. "Well, what were you thinking? Two hours?"

"I wasn't talking to you. Margaret, how much for longer? Say the rest of your life. A bag of angels?"

"Hey, listen monk! You deal with *me*, right?"

Pacificus traces his finger along the cobbles, but keeps on looking at her, "Angels, Margaret? Or a home with other children and people that love you? It's your choice."

She looks up now, to see whether these are just more words, more *man*-words. She reads his eyes with her own fierce hostility. Her, trust yet another man?

"Maiden, you can walk out of here today."

To his side, Thatcher is looking round at his peers, and then back to the monk. "Oi, listen! I'm warning you! If you want what the boy got, there's plenty more just for the asking."

The other harlots are gathering in the street, the word is going round, other pimps lean from upper windows and shout abuse: "Go on Thatchy-boy, don't take any lip from him!"

But Pacificus is still with her, in their own hollow of calm. "You only need to tell me that is what you want."

"Right, that's it!" Thatcher is all out of patience.

"A nod Margaret, that's all I need."

She does it, at first timidly but then, as she makes her affirmation, an old fire rekindles in her heart. "I...I will," she says, her voice tremulous. Then louder, as she scrambles to her feet: "I will. I will go."

This stops Thatcher in his tracks, his mouth ajar. And at the sight of her, the whole close street now strains to hear the next words – and the response.

Pacificus nods slowly and straightens up, looking Thatcher in the eye. He speaks quietly but deliberately. "We're leaving that way."

"She ain't leaving with you," the pimp spits out the words with a low, seething rumble, then points with his tankard at Pacificus, "And you my friend are a long way from your cloister."

Pacificus sees Thatcher hold his breath in anticipation of landing the first punch. He considers the dagger but thinks it would be a poor day for him if he couldn't take down a drunk only a few pounds heavier than himself. Here he comes. Thatcher aims a blow with his tankard. Pacificus side-steps, blocks with his left arm and uses his right to take hold of the tankard, wrenching it back in a series of violent jerks until he hears the celery crunch of three fingers snapping. Thatcher shrieks like a woman and pulls his fingers free, using his left to retrieve his blade. Pacificus rams the tankard into his belly and, before he's even seen it coming, into his mouth again and again, until Thatcher, spitting out teeth, heads groundward. The women throw their hands up at the sight of him, and the men stop leaning on the walls. It is over in the blink of an eye, and they're all caught off guard.

"Right, then." Pacificus is breathing hard as he throws the tankard to one side. "You go first Margaret, and I'll follow." She stands slowly to face the wall of onlookers. Women she has worked with, men who have used her often. The women are a mixture of disgust and delight, for most had forgotten even the smell of hope. The men are looking at one another. Pacificus makes it easy for them by drawing the basilard from his sleeve and pointing it at them individually. "This one goes free. Make a space for her now, you men, or I'll cut a way through."

He whispers to Margaret. "Walk. Now. You're free." She looks round at him with trepidation – won't he take her by the arm? Her eyes meet his and she sees her answer; this is something she must do alone. She licks her lips and takes the first steps of her redemption, with unsteadied breath. He falls in behind her and they walk together towards the sea of faces.

"That's right, keep you straight," he reassures her. Then, making sure his eyes meet those of the man he considers the greatest threat, whispers so he can hear, "And the first hand to touch you, I'll take off at the elbow." The crowd begins to part, begrudging and unwilling at first, but the more people squeeze back, the more easily others follow suit. Insults are still thrown at them from the upstairs windows, some at him, some at her, but they're not listening now. No one cares about words – not now, not when you're leaving Swan Street. The dog follows on behind them, sneezing every few paces as if to exorcise the ghosts.

Where the street meets the market, they find Mark is nursing his nose. Margaret nearly collapses on him when he greets her. They give her water, and bread, and put her on the mule. "Your sister, then."

"Yes, my father...well, you know. I'm sorry for what I said, going off like that."

He nods. "I too. We're all someone's kin. I spoke in haste. But now let's see your nose."

This is a painful business but once Mark's anguish has subsided, he tries to apologise again more fully. Pacificus will not have it. He's never been one for open shows of forgiveness; *forgiving* should be done like *giving*, so secret that your left hand does not know what your right does. In the deep things, words can be liars and deceivers. It says as much in Benedict's rule: *We must know that God regards our purity of heart and tears of compunction, not our many words*. Margaret herself neither speaks, nor unclenches her fists. It will be a long time before she can put any of this into words. Mark takes the mule's bridle and leads the way out of the city, Pacificus watching them, and every alleyway too, until they are clear of the gates. Like Joseph and Mary, he thinks. She says nothing, but raises her face to the raindrops when they pass through a strong shower. Where will she go? Who will have her now? Mark has said nothing but he doesn't need to. There are still favours to be cashed in at Saint Margaret's marsh. Looks like Pieter and Sarah will get a dog in the bargain.

As they near South Walsham that evening, the girl is asleep with her head on the mule's neck.

"How did you persuade her?"

"A clean start, that and a bag of gold angels."

"Avaunt, where are you going to find that sort of money?"

"Oh, you'd be surprised where people leave money lying about."

"But the trail is dead, we only had one word to go on – "

"Ah!" He gives a knowing smile. "*Verbum sat sapienti* - one word is enough for a wise man."

21

The Scriptorium

Verbum sat sapienti
One word is enough for a wise man

Just one word – confession. He has played it through his mind a thousand times. What did Wulfric mean?

On the evening they return from Norwich, as they are nearly at South Walsham, Pacificus sees the spire of Saint Helen's rising in the distance, and remembers all that he still had planned for his painting there. He has been putting it off far too long – he knows that, but he needs a scaffold to finish it and there has been so much else on his mind. Even so, sooner or later he must press on; next to be done must be the four Latin doctors – Ambrose, Augustine, Gregory and Jerome. How will he portray Augustine?

Augustine...And that's when the two thought-streams merge in his mind. Augustine...confessions ...*The Confession of Saint Augustine*! And didn't it sound perhaps like the Latin *confessio* when he said it? Perhaps there is a message inside the book – a map, a code? The library has at least two copies of the work, all the brothers read it. Energised by the thought, Pacificus finds his mind racing eagerly through the possibilities. Best say nothing to Mark as yet, it may lead nowhere. I only hope the books are there. He visits the library the next day, straight after Chapter. Shafts of sharp, morning light illumine trails of dust drifting from the rafters. The scriptorium is empty, save for Brother Aloysius and a novice he is teaching to bind books. They don't see him approach. When he does eventually announce his presence with the word 'brothers', they pay him little heed, for the work they are doing requires all their concentration. Aloysius deals with his request without taking his eyes, or fingers, from the spine of the book under his repair.

"What? Augustine? Yes, we do. Better than that French tripe you've been reading these last weeks." And then to the novice: "No boy, no! Put the pressure here, your finger – your finger! Saints preserve us, that will never do. Now the thread – the thread, lad. Pull it. Yes – yes, tighter, and again. No – no, closer to the edge; they will want to actually open the book, not just look at it – that's better." And on they sew while Pacificus waits as patiently as he can. Aloysius is just reaching for the glue when he asks again: "The book, brother?"

"Eh? What? Oh, yes." But then Aloysius pauses, straightening up. His brow furrows, and his eyes narrow in thought. "Actually – no. Both copies were taken out yesterday."

'By whom?"

"Ooh...ah...let me see...Ah yes! Those two lonely fellows from Binham."

"Benedict and Sigismund?" It can be no one else, but he has to be sure.

"Yes. Quite separately they came, too. Does them credit, that they study even at a time like this. We all deal with grief in different ways, though. Perhaps it's something that reminds them of their poor brothers and prior."

"Wulfric studied Augustine while he was here?"

"No, not to my knowledge. At least, he never had Augustine out of our library." He leaves the bench for a second to stretch his back. "No, if anything, I'd say Wulfric leant more to the Celtic than the Latin fathers – I had to fetch Saint Patrick from his bedside – " he points to a book on his other desk, " – spine bent back and writing in the flyleaf – can you believe it? I dare say he thought no one would notice his puerile attempts at poetry, but I do check the books, I mean to say, it is my job and I'm no slacker like some brothers we could name. And I know we shouldn't speak ill of the deceased, but what kind of monk does a thing like that?" And then, turning back to the novice who has been a little overzealous with the glue, "Heavens, lad! Not all over the page – get a cloth – a cloth, quickly now! Oh, these novices, they get worse year by year. Yes, yes; well, just give it to me, will you."

Pacificus moves to the other table and picks up the volume. A tingle runs down his spine and smarts in the tops of his cheeks; it is *The Confession of Saint Patrick*. But of course, Patrick, the youth who returns to the land of his former slavery to bring a monastic revolution transforming a pagan society – how appropriate. What did Wulfric say? *The Danes are back, Antichrist reigns*; he'd become the new Saint Benedict, the new Martin of Tours, the supreme Ninian or Patrick – here to rescue Europe from these heretic schismatics, with a new monastic order.

Aloysius has already started work on the book. "It'll need rebinding; I mean, look at the spine."

"The poem? I should like it."

"A remembrance?" Aloysius smiles, he never had Pacificus down as sentimental.

"Something like that."

"It's in hell, if you can find it." He points to the back of the desk. The expression is from Aloysius' days as a cordwainer, hell being the receptacle for the scraps and offcuts of leather. Pacificus tries not to look too eager as he bends to rummage under the desk. Fortunately there is not too much rubbish, as Aloysius is as fanatical about cleanliness as he is about his books. He finds the flyleaf within seconds, sees the writing, gives it the once over and then slips it into his scrip. As he goes, he thanks Aloysius, adding casually: "Best not spread it about that Wulfric wrote in one of our books. As you say, it's not right to speak ill of the dead, and it's probably best not to put the idea into people's heads either – you know how sloppy some men can be, no idea how to care for a book."

Incipit confessio sci patricii epi·
EGO PATRICIUS PECCATOR RUS
ticissimus & minimus omium fideliu & con
tēptibilissimus apud plurimos patrem habui
calpornium diaconē· filium quondam potiti
presbiteri· qui fuit in vico bannavem taberniae·
Villulam enimpe habuit ubi ego capturam
dedi· annorum eram tunc fere sedecim· Dm

He can't think of a better way of ensuring Benedict and Sigismund hear nothing of this. Aloysius pauses from his task, nodding sagely and agreeing some things are better committed to silence. Pacificus thanks him again, and then leaves for the guest hall, the less visible route to the outer precinct.

Through the lead glass of the guest hall, Pacificus can make out the shape of Mark patiently waiting for him by the gate, ready for a day at Saint Helen's. He increases his pace, penitent at being so tardy. He reaches the outer door in its musty recess, and is just twisting the iron handle when he feels a bony hand upon his arm. "Why, Brother – " it is

Benedict – "I declare, you are walking with a new spring in your step today. Do you have any further news about that matter we spoke of this week?"

Pacificus tries to look dour and disappointed, shaking his head with a grimace. "You?"

Benedict looks at him hard. "It's only – I thought I saw you coming from the library just now."

"I see." And what were you doing near there, I wonder? "Yes indeed, brother. I had a few books to return. Listen, if you're still worrying about the Augustinians coming after you, I think you can rest easy. I have spoken to the bishop, he knows you know nothing."

"It – " Benedict hesitates – "it is very kind of you."

"Yes, well," he observes Benedicts' beady eyes move towards the scrip, his lean thumbs and forefingers rubbing each other greedily, "I'll be away then."

Pacificus walks through the yard to where Mark is waiting. "What did he want?" He motions up to the entrance of the guest hall where Benedict, arms crossed, is still watching them.

"Never mind him. How's the nose?"

"It's better. I think. Well – better than it was." Mark strokes the blue, swollen skin and the scab where Thatcher's tankard had gashed him. "Don't know which was worse, his head or you straightening it."

"You'll thank me in a week or two. And your cheek is looking better too. How did you do with Margaret?"

"Well, they took her in. I don't think the old woman was too happy at first, and I suppose you can't blame her really; that's quite a houseful stuffed into one little cottage. But they're good people." He sniffs painfully and observes the precinct where monks go about their work. "So, we're going to the church?"

"No, boy. Today I think we'll visit the poor."

"The poor? But won't Father Prior object – "

"He has other matters to worry about. Come, now."

They cross the causeway as usual but, instead of heading to Saint James' staithe, they call in to collect Simon and then walk slowly up through Saint Margaret's marsh to the eel-catcher's cottage. Before heading into the woods, he glances one more time back across the fen to check that no one is watching.

"So, she's Hamberly's bastard is she?" Simon says, as he ducks awkwardly under a willow branch. He sees Mark look back with a frown, and adds, to amend it: "I confess I liked the girl; she has spirit."

"Father is not all bad, you know. If he'd known she had nowhere to go, he'd have done something."

Simon calls ahead to his brother, "You should pay Hamberly a visit, lean on him. I'm sure he thinks sowing his oats around the shire is a mark of his ascent into society, but it wouldn't hurt to make sure he'll provide for her – "

Now it is Pacificus who turns in anger. "You're a fine one to talk, you are! Enough now, the girl needs more than a house and money, she needs a family." Aye, and not just her, we all do.

Simon is silent and Pacificus starts to regret what he has said. They need a distraction. He suggests they take a break, have a rest.

"No need to for my sake," Simon says in a huff.

"Just sit down here and look at this, will you?" Pacificus retrieves the flyleaf from his scrip.

"What is it?" Simon says.

"You remember what Wulfric said, with his last breath?"

"Find her in confessions?"

"Confession, that was what Wulfric said, "confession", *minima maxima sunt* Mark, remember, the *smallest things* often carry the greatest importance. Guess which book was by his bed? The Confession of Saint Patrick, with this," he hands the paper to Simon, "written, by him, on the flyleaf."

Simon holds it on his lap, and reads, "*A second Madonna, though no Virgin, am I, laid beyond the mortal eye, In Saint Michael's arms we trust, in two locales we have been thrust* – great saints, he was no poet, this Wulfric!"

"Never mind that, he was in fear of his life. Just read on, will you?"

"Behind the serpent's coils and eye,

in darkness do my bones now lie.
But if seek ye treasure less sure,
then west ye must rove some more;
o'er Norfolk's broadest water,
upon which pilgrims walk and take no harm
in the quiet half world, under th'eternal thorn,
At the place –

Simon looks up from the page, aghast, "Oh great, he hasn't even finished his *magnum opus*."

"Yes, but what do you make of it?" Pacificus says.

"I'm perplexed, that I am," Mark interjects. "If he was trying to make sure no one found the bones, he was doing a good job."

"No, he wants this to be a guide to the saint's whereabouts, but at the same time throw the ones he doesn't want to find her off the scent. Come on Simon, this is more your sort of conundrum. The first stanza – "

"*If* you can call it that!" Simon objects. He looks down at the verse, reading in a sonorous voice: "*A second Madonna, though no Virgin, am I, laid beyond the mortal eye*, well, it has to be the relics of Saint Helen, that they're hidden out of view, as if we hadn't guessed."

"Why Saint Helen?"

"Because she gave birth to Constantine and therefore the Madonna, the mother of the Church Triumphant, besides, it must be, they are her bones after all," Pacificus says, "don't you ever listen?"

"Sorry for asking."

Simon continues, "*In Saint Michael's arms we trust, in two locales we have been thrust* – what, he's split the bones up?"

"Possibly, but I don't think so, look at the next two stanzas, I think the bones are in one place, *behind the serpents coils and eye*, and the *treasure less sure*, that is the gold, is somewhere else, further away."

"Yes...I see that, and it makes sense too I suppose; less conspicuous, less chance of both being discovered, but behind the serpent's coils and eye, in darkness and in Saint Michael's arms? That doesn't give us much to go on."

"Wasn't it Saint Michael who..." Mark hesitates for he doesn't wish to be chided again.

"Go on boy," Pacificus says.

"Well, he fought the dragon, like on your painting, and that is a bit like a serpent isn't it?"

"He did, true enough."

"Could it be at Ranworth?" Simon ponders out loud.

"I doubt it, my Saint Michael is on a wooden partition, there is naught behind it but the Lady chapel. No, somehow I think he must mean somewhere else. Both the treasure and the relic in some way rest in Saint Michael's arms, and I think he means under the saint's protection somehow, but beyond that I cannot reason."

"And the treasure?" Mark asks hopefully, looking over Simon's shoulder at the scrap of verse, "What else does he say about that?"

"Stranger still, let me see, *o'er Norfolk's broadest water, upon which pilgrims walk and take no harm.* Don't know which pilgrims he means but I've seen none walk on water, and this other business about *the quiet half world, under th'eternal thorn,* could be anything."

"Perhaps it would have been clearer if he'd finished it." Mark says.

"Perhaps so," Pacificus replies in resignation, "but that is all we'll get. Anyway, let's get going, for I know you would not miss dinner, Mark, on Sarah's baking day. We can think on this further as we go."

Meanwhile, at the cottage, Sarah has sent Margaret and Beth into the barn to refill the mattresses with some of their new, fresh-cut straw – so she can talk to Pieter alone. It is not that she would be un-Christian in her attitude to this new girl, but unless he hadn't noticed, there are boys of a certain age in the house. By now Richard is fifteen, with his voice finally in his boots, and Piers getting more grown-up every day. Besides which, she's heard only bad things about this girl.

Pieter says he will talk to the boys, and then adds in a comforting tone, that, "Perhaps we should pray later, ja?" He crosses to the boat where the boys are waiting with the nets and wicker eel traps. He waves to Beth who is at the barn door pulling out the old straw. She waves back and then says to Margaret, who stands under the shadow of the loft, "Now at least we shall have some tranquility for the morning. And you and I shall have the fattest, softest mattress ever. Who'd have thought that, one day, you and I would be sleeping in the same bed?" She starts for the straw loft and Margaret follows on the ladder. Beth has a half-romantic notion that Margaret will be the sister she had always wished for. As time has gone on however, she is realising that it might be a long time in coming, if ever.

"Do you miss living on the other side of the river?" Margaret says.

"Sometimes, well, perhaps more than just sometimes. You?"

"No, not since my parents died." Margaret bends down to help stuff the mattress. Her face is drawn and pale, her skin clammy, even before she starts work. "Do you think you'll see her again?"

"Mother? I don't know. I – I hope so."

"I always liked your mother, she always smiled at me. I suppose you miss her."

Beth nods. "You?"

She nods too. "The Dutchman seems kind."

"Sarah too, when you get to know her."

"She won't want me to stay." Margaret stuffs harder and harder. "There's no need for more womenfolk here, another mouth to feed."

"Don't say that, you don't know her! They took us in – all of us – when we had nowhere else in the world, and we're not kin either. What they do, they do in Christ's name."

"Oh. Like the priest – "

"The priest at Ranworth?"

"Aye. All charity, him. You know he took me in, I suppose?"

"I did hear, yes, I'm sorry if he wasn't kind to you."

Margaret turns on her with a spiteful retort: "Don't know much of the world do you?"

"Well, I – I know enough, and anyway, why are you looking at me like that? You can make a new life here Margaret, if you can put up with my brothers!"

But the jest doesn't bring Margaret round. She has knelt back, and is sulkily looking through the upper barn door towards the river. Tiny specks of dust, sent up by the straw, glisten in the shaft of shriven morning light. "No one will hurt you here."

Margaret continues to stare out of the window, but now tears form in the corners of her eyes; not from repentance, or self-pity, but disappointment with herself. She had raised her fists against heaven, and thought she could go on indefinitely in her revolt. Today she feels like a hypocrite, a failure; she couldn't even make a living by the worst means. Now she is forced, not onto the parish, but onto the charity of people who would give everything to her and ask for nothing back. Worse, they'd do it in the name of the God who would not answer her when she prayed under the merciless hand of that priest for all those months. She expected to fight to the end, to force her way past Saint Peter, even give God a piece of her mind, curse him for making a world where such things could be – she felt entitled to that much at least. But this turn of events had crept up from her blind side – is this how God gets people to surrender? Seems underhand. Well, he's not got me yet.

She wants to say something neutral to Beth, but somehow it comes out wrong. "We don't know what tomorrow will bring, not you, not me. Could you have known that morning they came for your parents? No, of course not. It's all part of God's little tricks. Keeps you on your toes."

"I don't blame God; it was men who wronged us, not God." Beth tries not to look hurt. "He gave us a new home."

There is a long silence and eventually Margaret joins Beth to finish the stuffing.

"Thank you for sharing your dresses, and your bed."

"Our bed."

Margaret smiles for the briefest moment, "Yes, all right, our bed. I just hope I didn't disturb you too much last night."

"Were they very bad dreams?"

Margaret nods, she had cried out several times – always the same sort of dream; of being alone and small, as tiny as one of those specks of dust she can see today in the air, but then help and comfort come in some form, usually a man, and then it invariably goes hideous after that and she wakes up in a cold sweat, screaming for it to stop, or for a mother who never comes. Just thinking of it makes her shrink and sweat all over again.

"They will get better now, I think," Beth says. "Anyway, don't worry about me, I'm a heavy sleeper. With Piers' snoring, you have to be."

It's not quite true, and Beth had awoken fitfully just before dawn to find Margaret out of bed. She heard splashing in the dyke, and went to open the shutters. And there she saw Margaret standing up to her knees in the cold waters, washing her naked body in a mechanical yet vengeful manner – pressing fists of wet moss hard into the skin between her legs. Had she been asleep, Beth had heard of such things – distressed souls walking in their sleep. Margaret dare not say that she is late with her period this month, they'd throw her out for sure.

They hear the voices of men arriving in the yard and Margaret freezes with terror, "Who is it? Have they come for me?"

"No, it is my father, and his brother, the monk Pacificus," Beth goes excitedly to the opening to see, "Oh look and your brother too."

"But your father was executed, wasn't he?" Margaret says, joining her at the opening. "What, the leper?"

"That was my stepfather." Beth says, but then nods excitedly towards the window. "My true father was a gentleman and a great knight who fought the Turks; so was his brother, the monk."

"Oh well, I've seen that one fight, makes sense now. My, aren't we both full of secrets, you and me?" Gus trots out to welcome them as if he'd been here all his life and Pacificus bends down to ruffle his neck; stupid dog but no traitor. Margaret sees it and smiles, she would have gone mad if it were not for that dog.

"I did not know until recently, but you must not say anything, for he does not know that I know. He knew my mother before she met my stepfather, I suppose he didn't know about me when he went away."

Or perhaps he did, Margaret thinks, and that's why he went. "D'you mind him being a leper?"

Beth shrugs. "I suppose we'd all like things different."

Sarah brings small beer for the men to a table in the yard. The young women leave the mattress in the loft and join them. Beth curtsies and Margaret copies.

"You look well in that dress, sister," Mark says, "I thank you, Beth."

"Ja, ja," Sarah says, bustling about with the tankards and cloth, "there is time enough for nice talk when everyone has somewhere to sit, now go to girls; fetch the other stools from inside for the menfolk." And when Margaret has gone back inside, Sarah says more quietly, "I suppose you bring us news from Norwich today, and not just more work, ya, more mouths to feed?"

Pacificus moves uneasily on his stool, he hadn't quite reckoned on Sarah's Dutch forthrightness, even though he guesses that it is mostly just *her way*, as Pieter says. He sees that she is smiling under the bustle. She loves their visits, loves news, loves to feed them – in some ways it is like having her big brothers back from the war, from the grave. "Yes, I have seen the children's mother. Are the others near?"

"Back soon. Have your beer and I'll see to the food."

"Come, brother!" Simon says, "if my nose does not deceive me, by some miracle we have come on bake day again. And who in these parts bakes as fine as you, eh?"

"You can't get round me Sir Cecil, I am not soft." She's rubbing the table twice as hard now, but a smile is appearing at the corners of her mouth. "I might poison you yet!"

"Avaunt, I wager you'll not risk poisoning even me, when the punishment is boiling alive in oil."

"Ja? Well, we will see." Sarah turns to see Margaret with two heavy stools. "Don't just stand there, put them down; and Beth, bring us some apples from the loft, the good ones."

"No need, I'll go," Margaret says, leaving Beth to sit near her father.

"And how is Beth today?" he says.

"I am well, thank you. And pray, brother, how is our mother?"

"She is in goodly health and sends her love to you all."

They talk on like this for twenty minutes until Pieter and the lads are heard coming down the dyke. The afternoon is warm so long as you are in the sun, for it is that time of the year when they will make every opportunity to ignore the onset of winter. The harvest has been good, despite Sarah's concerns, and the boys are now so well used to their work with the eel traps that Pieter has more time to maintain the building and smallholding. For the first time in a long time, he can look forward to a comfortable winter, with seasoned alder and ash for the fire, and sod too, and a growing company of young people to amuse them both, perhaps even care for them when they are old. When the boys arrive and have greeted the visitors, Sarah hustles them to their seats. Pieter, who by now is standing at the head of the table, raises his goblet, carved by his own hand from apple wood, and toasts the months ahead. Could a man be any richer, really? Can any man be happier at the onset of winter, than to have a good fire, good woolen socks for the hearth-side, good hedge wine and good companions for the long nights. They had suffered cruel blows, all of them but even so, Pieter feels a profound gratitude this day as he observes this strange community of misfits that gather about his table. Pacificus, on the other hand is eager to divulge the contents of Wulfric's fly leaf message. When they are finished eating he reads it to them and they pass it round.

"I will read you what I have found, but prithee, make no answer before I have finished for it is a deep business is this -

'A second Madonna, though no Virgin, I,
am laid beyond the mortal eye,
In Saint Michael's arms we trust,
in two locales we have been thrust
Behind the serpent's coils and eye,
in darkness do my bones now lie.
But if seek ye treasure less sure,
then west ye must rove some more;
o'er Norfolk's broadest water,
upon which pilgrims walk and take no harm
in the quiet half world, under th'eternal thorn,
At the place ' –

"And that is where he left off. We take from it though that the sack of coin and the reliquary are hidden separately, and that both locations have some connection with Saint Michael – at least that much we can divine from it, and for the rest..." Pacificus raises his palms slightly above the plate. "And the rest might well fall into place after that."

"Or it might not," Mark says. "Well, it might not, the prior, God rest him, never finished his riddle and the vital information might well be missing."

"You forget," Pacificus says, "that he told us where to look – to which book – so that means he expected us to be able to work it out."

"Where it says about the serpent's coils," Margaret ventures, "I remember when the priest took me to the church at Irstead, to say the Mass when their priest was ill." She doesn't know whether to go on but Richard urges her with an encouraging nod. "Well, there's this carving above the church door, a really good one, of a man wrestling with a serpent that coils all around him. He has it round the neck, I think it was an angel." It had struck her because she knew how the man or angel felt.

"It sounds like Saint Michael," Simon says.

"It is," Pieter replies, "I know this, for Saint Michael's at Irstead is not more than three miles hence by water. The lads and I often set our traps at Barton broad just beyond."

"Yes, I know the church. What are we waiting for?" Piers exclaims. "Let's take the boat now!"

"Wait, my page," Pacificus says, thinking this must be too good to be true, too easy. "Tell us about the place Pieter, I have not been there."

"It is a quiet place, near the mouth of Barton broad, you know, ja, it is quiet though, not so many houses."

"And it would be near enough when they came down from Binham," Simon says, "and near enough to Saint Benet's too."

"Tell me Pieter," Pacificus says, "where is this carving?"

"Well, now," Pieter crinkles his brow to recall. "The carving is above the porch door, it is a small porch, I do not remember any upper windows."

"There is no school there, I know that much," Richard says, "because the boys round here either go to Barton or Ludham."

"Well, perhaps we should let Piers conduct a few of us there after lunch when Mark and I have completed our prayers." Noon was the time for Sext, and to pray through the "Little Hours." Simon shoots his brother an exasperated glance but he takes no notice. Ah, Simon thinks, poor Hugh is just making a point, still trying to make his way to heaven with his good deeds and multiplication of prayers.

Simon is brought back to the present by Richard, as he gets up from table. "I will row you, there is no time like the present."

"Very like, young squire. And we can sleep off our cakes, eh Sarah?" Simon says.

"I'm staying right here, and so are you two!" Sarah points at the girls, whose expressions immediately fall, "These men off gallivanting! They'll want to be fed again when they get back, no doubt, and there's the animals and the house to see to."

After Pacificus and Mark have fulfilled their office, the party depart. Simon stays behind to help the girls, and no doubt to read with Beth, while others take to the boat. Pacificus and Pieter sit back in the stern as Richard pulls them swiftly up the Ant to Irstead, and Piers stands on the prow above Mark, taut as a bow string and expecting great adventures. They put in at Irstead staithe within the hour and from there it is but a stone's throw to Saint Michael's church. A few thatched cottages stand some way off on the lane to Neatishead, but there is no one around to see them as they enter the churchyard. The sun fights its way through the curling leaves of a beech tree and as they walk, Pacificus is aware of the noise of crunching beech nuts under his feet. The porch, and the church, like almost every other permanent building in these parts, is constructed of flint and lime mortar. The sculpture of Saint Michael and the dragon is a rare one, he thinks, as they stop to gaze up at it, and certainly not like anything he has seen before in England or abroad.

No wonder Margaret, and perhaps even Wulfric, remembered it, for it depicts a vast writhing, coiling serpent, so big that it spills from the alcove and almost overpowers Michael. Is it too much to hope that this could be it? He hardly dares to hope, even though his spine tingles. And why does he care anyway, she is not his patron saint, and surely it is not just to please Rugge, is it? He used to think doing everything right would be enough, get him where he needed to go, but now he's running out of optimism.

His introspections are broken when a crow caws from the soil of a newly dug grave. He looks from it to the side of the building and sees a large crack in the southern transept. This building is built on shifting foundations like the abbey, like everything – too close to the river.

"Look at this!"

"What can you see?" Pacificus says to Piers who is already in the porch with Richard.

"There's a room up there, all right."

"But no windows," Pieter says, "how strange."

Pacificus sees the conical bulge in the wall to the left, showing where a spiral stair must lead to this mysterious little dark room. Perhaps it is a sacristy? Or perhaps a store. "Look for a door to the left," he says.

Piers lifts the heavy iron latch and they enter into the coolness and silence of the church. They smell the incense, the damp, the mould in the thatch, but also the fainter odours of leather and waxed oak. The others follow and see Piers waiting at the bottom of a narrow stairway.

"Well then?" Pacificus says.

"Well, there might be bones," Piers says, now suddenly embarrassed for all his forwardness, "you go first, Richard."

Pacificus sees Richard hesitate and, perceiving that perhaps their recent brushes with death have affected them, takes the lead up the winding stairway. It is so narrow that his shoulders touch both sides as he ascends. At the top he comes to an oak door on worn iron hinges. Curious, he thinks. No lock, nor latch, just an iron loop for a padlock, but no padlock attached. It pushes open into near complete darkness, but for the slivers of light let through the edges of the thatch. It takes him a few minutes to adjust his eyes, and stave off Piers' interruptions, but eventually Pacificus can feel his way about. The room is a store, as he suspected, perhaps six foot square. Near the door is a broom, a scythe and the grave-digger's shovels. Further in are crates of various sizes and two beehives stacked high, and in one corner there are ropes, stays and greasing. He moves round the back of the bee hives and lifts up some sacking in the far corner. At first he does not believe his eyes, though there is certainly the glint of metal; but slowly he runs his hands in the half-light over the object; yes, it is a box, nay, a reliquary, finely carved in bold relief. It is not big, perhaps two feet long, he lifts it reverently and carries it to the door so to be properly visible to himself and the others, who through various contortions, are able to peer in from the entrance and stairway.

"It is, you know," Pacificus catches his breath. "It really is her, I can't quite believe it. Wulfric took quite a risk – a room unlocked! I mean, anyone could have found it. But clever too, don't you think, to hide it in plain view."

They spend ten minutes at the bottom of the steps admiring the gold relief castings and ornate designs around the lid. It is quite mesmerising even in this light. The scenes depicted the life of Constantine, including him as a child on his mother's knee, and one curious design showing Constantine giving the key of the empire to Saint Miltiades, the then bishop of Rome. It is then that the thought comes out of nowhere into his mind: *It was not the first time the kingdoms of the world were offered thus.* So sharp was the thought, so poignant to all he had been wrestling with these last months, nay, these last years, that he does not hear, nor respond to Piers' many questions. He remembers what Elizabeth Fenton had said about the church being hand in glove with the kings of the earth. That was where it all started. There was a time before Constantine, when the church was despised and persecuted -

our *long lost* brothers of the primitive church, we call them. Primitive, yes, but now I begin to suspect which of us was long lost.

"Brother, *brother?*" Piers prods.

"What?"

"What are you going to do with it – shall we take it to the cottage?"

Pacificus glances at Pieter, whose Anabaptist face is already frowning on the idolatrous object. "No, if you were found with this, it would go ill for you. No one knows it is here, there is no link to this place except the riddle which we alone possess, so no, we will leave it here for now. I'll put her back under the sacking." He does so and moves the wicker beehives about her as sentinels, leaving the door shut exactly as he found it. Mark makes sure no one is watching the church before they leave, and when at last they are away from the hamlet, Pacificus is relieved. If he'd not been so giddy at the thought of finding the saint, he would have come alone, with less risk of arousing suspicion. But they've got away with it. He sits back with Pieter once more at the stern as Richard pulls them steadily through the water.

"So," Pieter says, "you only have half of what you seek, let us look again at this riddle."

Pacificus looks in his scrip and takes out the paper again, "I am glad to see this amuses you Pieter; I suppose it is a departure from finding eels."

"Ja," Pieter says affably, "but, try me, for even eels can be slippy as riddles."

Pacificus chuckles nervously as he begins again to read.

"But if seek ye treasure less sure,
then west ye must rove some more;
o'er Norfolk's broadest water,
upon which pilgrims walk and take no harm
in the quiet half world, under th'eternal thorn."

"Now look you," Pieter raises his finger, "this is what I thought. Barton Broad is big, ja, but not the biggest broad, nothing like it, and it is more north than west of Irstead."

"And anyway," Mark replies, "what does it mean? Pilgrims can walk on it and take no harm. Who can walk on water?"

"Perhaps it is figurative," Pacificus says. "He means a bridge, or some boarding or some such."

"Or perhaps," Pieter suggests. "He means a marsh, like our one only bigger, where only those who know can cross."

"Yes, but is there one west of Irstead?" Mark says.

"No, not at all, the ground is higher there, that's why the duke has bought it up for his sheep," Pieter says. "It was a big wheat area, you know, I did good trade when I took my eels there. In those days, we didn't need to worry trying to grow our own as we do now."

"Why did the duke not grow wheat?" Piers says.

"Shh! Don't interrupt," Richard says, almost losing a stroke.

"Because," Pieter says, "wool was worth more."

"But you can't eat wool," Piers counters.

"And you can't wear wheat," Richard chides again, "now stop interrupting." Pacificus chuckles to himself. Not until much later does he see the significance of their remarks.

22

The Graveyard

Non teneas aurum totum quod splendet ut aurum
All that glitters is not gold

They made their plans well, did Benedict and Sigismund. *Fortuna*, bitch-goddess of all pagan chancers, smiles on men who lay their plans with cunning - or, with what they call, prudence. Benedict had followed Pacificus after Chapter that morning. He found out from Brother Aloysius about the so-called "poem' in the flyleaf of Wulfric's book. It was only minutes after Pacificus had left the scriptorium. He knew about it when they met in the doorway of the Guest Hall. Oh, how he had wanted to have that note when he was within feet of it. Would that God had made him stronger so he might have taken it by force, or that Sigismund had been there to help him.

He didn't trust this monk with the scarred wrists; he wasn't Rugge's man, or anyone's man for that matter – you could see that in his eyes.

The caitiff was a loner; it takes one to know one. You can't bring a man like that in on a deal, he'll turn on you in the end. He knew all about that sort of thing too. No, better keep it just him and Sigismund, at least for the present.

Benedict has been shaking like a leaf all day, not with fear, but excitement. It tells on his nerves, a smile spreads and contracts on his face without his knowing, and his thoughts have begun to resemble multiple opinions competing loudly in his head. As afternoon draws on they coalesce as one voice and he senses the time is at hand, that the relic will be his, with the new beginning it promises.

Wulfric failed – men like him always do in the end, they cannot see what's necessary, cannot read the times, cannot even remain under the authority of their own abbot, treating with the emperor behind their backs – always stumbling about in the dark, always wandering like an ass on heat. They vacillate, procrastinate and dither to their own destruction. Wulfric was dealt as if with by the hand of God, as all faithless men ought to be. It was God who saw fit to move Wulfric to leave clues, and only the pure in heart would see what they meant. He must have that note, or the knowledge of it at least. When he sees Pacificus and Mark return late for Vespers, he is quick to notice that they seem jubilant about something. The spring in their step is unmistakable. He sees Pacificus almost smiling – the villain! Has he found the saint already? God's blood, I'll know of it by some means! Dear God, let it be today, this week, *no; let it be tonight, yes, tonight.*

Mark is on his way down the night stairs for Matins. He is long after the last monk because someone hid his sandals. He hurries, for being late is something the sub-prior takes careful note of – could get him a flogging. Then as he reaches the bottom step, he feels a hand on his shoulder and cold steel at his neck.

"Quiet, now. Quiet, Brother Mark. One word and it will be your last."

He cannot see the face but he knows Sigismund's voice. He moves his arm up slowly, but it is seized by a hand, smaller but still firm. "I'd listen to the good brother, if I were you." It is Benedict. "He's a butcher's son, you know. He's forgotten more about knife work than you'll ever know, my lad."

"What do you want with me?"

"You're going to take us to Saint Helena's bones, and the gold coin – tonight." It's a calculated bluff.

"But I – " Mark shudders at Benedict's uneven breath in his ear.

"Or I'll start by cutting your freckles out, then your eyes," Benedict pushes Sigismund's blade deeper so that Mark rises higher and higher on his toes to avoid an incision.

"Argh, prithee, all right! But we only found the bones, the gold coin is somewhere else."

"Don't play games with us." Benedict takes a tight hold of Mark's cowl and pulls him down on the blade. "Don't you dare, see, or I'll not protect you from Sigismund, will I?"

"I swear," Mark gulps and gasps, he knows the blade has cut his neck but cannot feel how deep. "Please don't, it tells you in the riddle."

"Good lad," Sigismund hisses, "and do you have it, this riddle?"

"No, Pacificus has it."

"Do you remember what it says, the location of the gold?"

"Yes, I remember."

"Good lad, you can tell us about it on the journey, come on now," Benedict says, the frenzy of exhilaration barely suppressed in his voice. "And be quiet about it."

Benedict leads the way to the staithe, then Mark with Sigismund. Benedict is now muttering and the echoes of it reverberate around the the cloister vault like they do in his head. "A riddle! Wulfric was a half-wit, we'll soon have it solved, a riddle indeed." When Mark struggles and begins to call out, Benedict strikes him hard on the skull with the butt of a wheellock pistol. It had belonged to old Jary, the priest from Binham Priory. That had been his first murder, the beginning of his descent to this half world. He had not intended murder, who does? But Jary wouldn't talk so he kept on beating him until he told them where the key was, and then the fooled died, damn him – damn them all. Tonight he's glad to have it more than ever; a great leveller is a wheellock, and these days those who live by the sword get shot by those that don't.

Fortunately for Mark, this blow was not as forceful as the ones dealt Jary. He lurches forward and clasps his throbbing head.

It is after Matins that Pacificus first notices Mark is absent. He walks about the cells and sees neither him nor the Binham brothers in their beds. No one saw them at Matins, is everything all right? Of course it's not, how could he have been so foolish? He starts for the door – but then pauses to gather his wits, eventually calling out in a loud voice,

"Rouse the prior! Have the sheriff send men to Saint Michael's Irstead!"

The silver forms of the thirty or so monks appear in the doorways of their cells, like ghosts summoned to judgement.

"Dear Lord! Not *more* bodies – " It is brother Aloysius.

"Aye, more bodies!" And by God, I'll add Benedict and Sigismund to the tally if they lay a hand on that boy.

"What did I say? We shall all be murdered in our beds! Brother, BROTHER, where are you going?"

"Just fetch the sheriff, as I say..." Pacificus' voice trails away as he descends the night stairs.

Richard wakes to hear the banging at the door. Pieter calls out: "Who is it at such an hour?"

"It is Pacificus and Simon, Mark is taken, we need help."

Richard opens the door in a trice: "Taken by whom?"

"Never mind that now, get your hose on, and fetch your father's matchlock and sword. Pieter, which is the quickest way to get to Irstead, on foot or in the boat?"

"Through the marsh, if you know the way, and if you run." Pieter looks back to where Sarah is rising from the bed, "I cannot run, ja, as you know and Miss Beth is the only other who knows that marsh path, but at night – "

"I know it well, with my eyes shut!" Beth is descending the ladder in her nightgown. She was often up that way for it was near her thinking place. "Is Mark in trouble?"

"For his life, maid," Pacificus says, "for his very life, I tell you. Quickly now."

She looks steadily from his face to her father's, "Be down in two shakes of a duck's tail." She disappears up to the loft, where Margaret and Piers have now stirred and are sitting up, bleary-eyed, and starting to ask questions.

"Pieter, bring Simon and the boat to Irstead, and think on that riddle again, we may be too late – "

"Brother," Pieter takes Pacificus' itching fingers, "Trust in God; the boy shall yet be safe."

"Aye, and I'll see to it, only don't delay. Richard, come now lad, I'll carry those. Come, quickly now."

A harvest moon, full and yellow, reveals the set of three, bounding like deer across the open marsh, with naught but the sound of their feet in the shallow water to mark them. Pacificus has the match-lock and balls, Richard the sword and powder. Beth is fleet like a hind and never misses a turn. Through dense willow, sprawling alder and over fallen birch, she runs without asking for rest. On and on into the dense darkness of woodland bog and ten-foot high reed beds, on and on over dykes, fallen trees or half-collapsed makeshift bridges. Sometimes there is no path at all, just a general direction through the reeds, always north, always up river. She never talks as she goes, only the word *please* is often heard as a whisper, trailing behind her as a prayer on the wind.

Richard takes the rear, looking as best he can towards the river whenever they are within view. Sometimes the moon is kind and they can see, sometimes the clouds take almost all vision away and they are forced to go slower. Pacificus is watching too. How much head start did they have? An hour? Don't be a hero Mark, just give them what they want, and run, run away if you get the chance.

Beth stops in a copse of sycamore trees. They smell of woodsmoke and catch the sound of cattle and dogs. "Irstead – the church is beyond those cottages."

"Take us, quick as you can!"

They meet a track and run swiftly along the central verge to avoid making noise. Even so the dogs bark as they pass, which sets the cattle and sheep off even more, then some poultry. It strikes Pacificus as ominous that they were even making a din before they arrived. They come within site of the church green, the stonework temporarily lit silver, then darkest grey as scudding clouds cross the moon. He moves back out of sight and loads the matchlock.

"Keep down low; we'll go along under the church wall. Beth, wait when we get to the gate. Richard, carry both blades and be my rearguard – be ready to give me the sword you understand, and keep yourself free from any sword play. Don't let them take you as a hostage too, or be in reach of any moving blade, especially mine. It will be too dark to tell out there. If I am struck – "

"You'll not be struck – "

"Don't interrupt, just listen. Mistakes can happen and my eyes are not good at night, so – if I am struck, you let them away with the relics if need be; it is not worth your life. Remember, we're here for Mark, not bones."

Richard draws his grandfather's blade from its sheath with trembling hands and sweating palms. Beth takes the sheath from him with a stern look, and then she lays it on the grass. "God go with you, brother."

"Aye, and you too."

"Come now, and quiet."

They run crouching, heading straight for the low wall that surrounds the church yard. Pacificus waits a few seconds to listen, then moves swiftly along, the matchlock in his left hand, and his right trailing against the stonework, steadying his balance every now and again. The wind billows and the clouds pass at speed, sending projections of light and creeping shadows on all sides. The cattle are quiet now and only a dog's whining can be heard above the rustling leaves. They come close to the gate, where Beth crouches still lower against the wall, but very much against her will. If Mark needs her, she should be there. Pacificus is keeping a careful eye toward the porch when, for the briefest second, the moon casts a beam right inside to reveal a body on the floor. Is it? Jesu, it is! Dear God! "Quick now," he whispers, "up here."

Pacificus pulls back from the gate and scales the wall to approach the church doorway at an angle under cover of the gravestones. He doubts they have matchlocks, but he'll not risk walking up to that black hole of an entrance in full view. Richard stays at his back, momentarily looking back to see that Beth is out of sight. She is, but before he has turned, Pacificus is sprinting the last thirty yards to the door's edge. Richard is after him like an arrow, heart leaping out of his chest. He hears the controlled breaths of Pacificus, whose back is now against the wall, with the matchlock barrel on his lips. He wants to be ready. One, two, three.

He nods at Richard and then swivels round to the front of the porch, raising the matchlock as he goes. He doesn't look at the body, he daren't, but quickly steps over it and moves in one quick motion through the open door into the church. There are tools on the floor, tools from the upper store, but no one in sight or sound. Richard rushes behind and trips on the body, clattering to the floor with his weapons. Pacificus steps past him and goes straight to the body, willing it to be anyone, anyone on earth but the novice. The robes are dark, he cannot say, but no, wait, there is a long beard and bald head. Thank God, it is an aged man. "Thank God," he cries out, a surge of relief and tears rushing into his eyes, "Oh, thank God!"

"Who is it?"

"Probably the verger – likely disturbed them, poor soul. He is dead. But oh, thank God."

Pacificus rolls the body over and feels until he finds a warm wet patch. "Fifth rib, they wanted him shut up quickly and the killer knew what he was doing."

"Poor man," Richard crouches and starts to lay down the blades.

"Don't do it! Stand guard and I'll search the store." But it is as he suspected, the reliquary is gone. The tools must have tumbled down the stairs as they fled in haste, or perhaps Mark tried to be clever? He sends Richard to the staithe to see if he can see up-river at all, but there is no sign. They sit at the staithe and wait for Pieter to bring the boat, desperately playing the second part of the riddle through their heads – for now everything rides on them deciphering it.

"But this at least we know," Beth says, "that they came by boat, and they left by boat, and they left up-river not down, else we'd have seen them. We know they are headed west, for the riddle says so, and the only way west by boat is round by Barton broad, and then on through Witch's Dyke to Neatishead."

"But to where?" Pacificus paces on the water's edge, back and forth. "That's the point, *where?* And where are the others? We're wasting time here."

"You said back at the cottage this afternoon that Saint Michael was the key to both locations."

"But of course I did, the chucklehead that I am; I've been thinking of just the second half of the riddle."

"Is there another Saint Michael's church?"

"So close, it's unlikely. Let me see, I've been on the Stalham road out of Hoveton, there was a church that would be west of here, but no, it was Saint Lawrence, yes that was it, Beeston Saint Lawrence. I just don't know the country hereabouts, our estates at Erpingham were near twenty miles north of here, best wait for Pieter. God, speed them safe and sure to us."

"I hear a boat!" Richard eventually says, some time later. He is craning his neck out over the water from the edge of the staithe.

"Careful!" Pacificus says, pulling him back, "best hide yourself here with us – could be anyone."

But after five more minutes Pacificus sees Pieter's mast swaying above the reeds, so they prepare to board her.

"Quick, now! Away to Barton Broad!" Pieter and Piers tighten the sail, while Pacificus tells what they have seen.

Margaret is there, and so is Gus – "Well, he's my brother, ain't he? And the dog wouldn't go without me, and he'll be useful at night."

"I see," Pacificus says, casting a glance at Simon and then to Piers. "And you let the page come too – a handsome boatload."

"Now then, brother," Simon says. "You know the boy, there's no stopping him when he has it in his head to help."

"And – and – and I've been practicing every day with the bow, just as you said! I can hit an apple at a hundred yards, honest I can!"

"Once. You hit it once in twenty arrows," Richard corrected, "and it was more like fifty yards."

"Was not!"

"Was."

"Shush the pair of you and let the men talk," Beth says. "Pieter, what churches are west of here, apart from Beeston Saint Lawrence?"

"Well now, ya, I see what you are thinking. Ja, there is Saint John's at Coltishall."

"Too far." Pacificus says.

"Hoveton then, again Saint John."

"More south than west, anywhere else?"

"There's little Saint Peter's on the road north, that would be west."

"But not Saint Michael's."

"Wait, wait, there is another, just across the new fields from Neatishead, a lonely place on a small rise, but I cannot recall the name."

"Well then," Simon says, "if there are no more, we must at least try there."

"But is there a broad water there?" Richard says, taking the bench with Pieter and one of the oars so that they can pull together. The wind is sporadic down on the river and every bit of power helps.

"There is none, but nevertheless we should go," Pieter says, "for we have nothing else to go on." He hears Richard sigh with anxiety, and indeed it does seem to him a hopeless, blind odyssey. He rests a hand on the lad's shoulder and whispers, "Let us do what *we* can do and trust in God for the rest, ja? Just row hard, lad, until we reach Barton

Broad. God will judge aright, you will see." Richard puts his shoulders and back into each stroke to match the wiry strength and rhythm of Pieter, whom it seems that age and illness have barely weakened at all. Sometimes the gusts of wind catch their sails and rowing is not necessary. Other times, under the thick darkness of the spreading alders and willow, there is barely a breath, and Pacificus urges them on. Once out on the broad itself they feel the full power of a westerly wind and run goose wing along the southern reaches of the water, where it curls round towards the west. At this point, the broad narrows to a few hundred feet wide, the Lime Kiln Dyke, yet even here the wind carries Pieter's flat-bottomed sailboat, rousing coots, swans and moorhen in the reeds in her wake. At the end of Lime Kiln Dyke the open water vanishes once more into the darkness.

"Where to now?" Piers says from the tiller.

"There lad, aim just left of that tall tree that breaks the skyline. Ya, that's it, a little more, good, now hold that course, and girls, let us have the sails down, and the mast, brother, if you will; Witch's Dyke is long, twisting and overgrown these days."

"How far to Neatishead from here?" Pacificus says.

"About a mile."

"Would to God we were there. I'll take the mast and use it to pole from the back," Pacificus replies, "I can't abide doing nothing at a time like this."

They do as Pieter says, and the girls store the sails in the stern, where they sit quietly with Simon, who now holds the matchlock forward. He is half-expecting to hear or see the boat coming back, hear the flash of another matchlock in the dark, feel the familiar bite and punch of the ball, in his arm or worse. As they enter the narrow, wooded confines of Witch's Dyke, the thick, dense blackness envelops them, extinguishing stars, moon and conversation. The long boughs fold round them and over them like fingers; like a tunnel. Behind them, they leave open heavens above open waters; before them the uncertainty of a night from which some of them may not awake.

"Hush now," Pacificus says to Piers who is shifting nervously on the gunwales, "and listen."

The rhythm of the oars, the hooting of owls, the sounds of night creatures scuttling and scattering from the boat. Pacificus uses the mast to prod the banks more than once to get them unstuck when they do not see the serpentine twists, which are many and sharp. Sometimes it feels as though they go in circles, the twists never unwind. Twice they end up in a blind alley of a dyke that ends abruptly, and have to reverse out. But slowly and surely they come within the sounds and smells of the cottages of Neatishead – whose dying peat fires greet them well before the final turn.

They find the abbey boat at the village staithe, oars left in. "They intend to return then," Simon says, as they moor a short way off.

Pacificus recovers the reliquary from under the rowing seat and, with Richard's help, moves it a short way off into the undergrowth. That done, they move silently through the village and ascend the short distance to the great new open fields of the Duke of Norfolk.

They soon reach a small rise above the settlement, and there, beyond their feet, stretches a vast, silver sea of grass as far as the horizon to the north and and west. The dawn is only just now pushing back the darkness in the farthest east, but even so, the close-clipped dewy grass, of the east-facing undulations, glistens and ripples into the distance. No one calls a halt but they all stop nonetheless. The scale and beauty takes the breath from each soul; it is magical, mythical, like something Dante might have dreamt and written about.

And in all of it, the only black among the silver and grey are the trees and church on another small rise to the north.

"It is the church," Pieter says, grim faced, as if he were a guide welcoming Orpheus to the underworld. "And now I see it, I remember the name, ja: Saint Michael and All Angels."

Margaret bends to run her hand over the grass. "That's it, of course; *the broadest water, upon which pilgrims walk and take no harm.* I suppose *the half-world* would be the graveyard, and *thorn* would be a tree to mark the grave – a hawthorn?"

"Holly perhaps," Beth says. "Though I think we will know when we get there. Ought we not to go now, and quickly?"

"Not all," Pacificus says, "Pieter, you stay with the women and Piers here until we return."

Margaret is starting to raise an objection but Simon pacifies her: "It is senseless to risk so much life, for we will be approaching with few weapons, and in full view of theirs - if weapons they have."

"He's right, Margaret, we will wait in the shadows of this wood and pray, come now." Piers is furious to be left, and even more so because Richard is trying to take the longbow and arrows from him.

"It's mine! You only want it because they have the sword and matchlock, it's not fair."

Beth wrenches them from him and passes them to Richard, "Feckless child, Mark's life hangs by a thread," she scolds, "these are not toys."

The four start towards the church across the silver ocean. The clouds sail like ships to the east, never stopping to see the foul deeds happening over Norfolk's land this night. Pacificus cups his hand towards the knoll where the church stands out like a galley, but nothing yet can be heard above their clothing and breathing except the occasional sounds of sheep coughing, then giving off a grumbling sound. Grumbling! They've got no reason to, Pacificus muses in a strange, detached moment, with grazing land fetching two shillings an acre, almost a quarter more than it would under the plough, and with wheat about to rise to twenty shillings a quarter, it is the people who cannot grow their corn and oats his year who'll be grumbling at the abbey gate. And next year, will there even be an abbey to keep the flesh on their bones? Will Norfolk feed them? No, not he. And Parliament? The Poor Laws were rejected by them, every man for himself now, let the weak go to the wall, and the dead bury their dead. *Sheep are eating men indeed*, as Thomas More said. Clever of Wulfric to have noticed it. Perhaps there has been no breaking up of the fields near Binham for these modern farms. Perhaps this seemed to him an oddity. Indeed it it is, *sheep are eating men.* Perhaps the squires thought they got a good price from Norfolk, but a people who rely on others to grow their grain should beware. The Duke won't go without oats, nor will his horses, but the men of Neatishead well might.

"Get down!" A sudden flash in the darkness bursts from the church yard, and a second later the thud of shot. A matchlock? No. A wheel-lock, then. They drop to the grass and bury their heads.

"Aimed at us?" Simon says.

"Don't think so, listen – "

They hear an anguished voice howl and groan. "Why? But why – " the voice is saying.

"Come," Pacificus says, "give me the matchlock, brother, I'll run it."

"But – "

"There's no time, Mark may be hit. Richard, stay in my wake, we mustn't present more of a target to them than necessary. Come."

Simon passes him the matchlock and he and Richard move as fast as they dare towards the shadow of the trees which border the graveyard. It is only a few hundred yards but it passes like a flash. There is no stopping now, just swift hearts and oft stumbling feet, heading inexorably towards the moment – somewhere in there, the place they cannot yet see.

Pacificus enters the churchyard first, sword in one hand, matchlock in the other. If he sees either foe, he'll not hesitate now; one shot, one thrust – they'll die in their sins, these two villains. He rests against a yew tree and beckons Richard in. Beyond the darkness of the outer bushes and tree-line, they look carefully towards where action has been, where sporadic shafts of moonlight illumine gunpowder smile in the churchyard. They catch a glimpse of another body slumped against a tombstone in the far corner, still moving, and then another next to it lifeless. *Dear God, two more! Oh Mark, I'll not forgive myself....* He forces despair back down his throat, scanning the shadows near the church and then the edges of the graveyard. Where's the third, God's blood, where is he?

"Richard," he whispers, "draw the bow but stay here, I will draw him out, do what you can."

He does not wait for the reply. Three deep breaths and he is gone, dashing in a zigzag across the graveyard, looking this way and that. But there is no shot, nor any movement, only the two bodies, getting closer and closer. Another shaft of moonlight from behind a shifting cloud. Pacificus moves quickly to the bodies and sees that the one against the tombstone is Benedict. He feels about the gurgling corpse, finding a warm wet patch on his back. He has been shot between the shoulders, from the back; a ball aimed for his heart but which shattered his two ribs and is now in his lung – a lung filling with blood, just like his poor prior. It is just, poetic even. Benedict gasps and splutters. He has had time to look at the stone sarcophagus in front of him under the holly tree, time to consider the body of Mark on the grass before him, and time to remember the others who died by his hand, time for *momento mori*. Pacificus sees the other is Mark but grabs at Benedict first, whispering, "Where is he? Where is Sigismund. Tell me!" He holds the rapier against his throat. "Tell me!"

Benedict's eyes stare ahead, not blinking, not feeling. "Gone," he says, then splutters blood from the corners of his mouth. He never expected the oaf to have enough wits for such treachery. Like Julius Caesar, he always suspected those with the lean and hungry look, like himself - and certainly not the well-fleshed butcher's boy, cunning as he was. Pacificus throws him back and then trains the bead of the matchlock about himself in all directions, yet nothing moves. Richard too, from behind his tree, strains his arm and bow taut, the cord biting into his fingers, waiting, watching for the slightest sight or sound. But there is nothing. Should he go to them? No, he said stay here, so I'll stay. He can hear Simon coming nearer in the field, but nothing else above the thump, thump, thump, thump of his chest.

Pacificus steadies his breath and then, still crouching, shoves his hand heavy on Benedict's chest so that he cries out. "Did you kill him, did you? Villain!" He shoves again, harder still; by God, his grey hairs won't go down to the grave in peace. "Did you take Mark's life like you did Bede's, Wulfric's and the others, did you, villain?"

"For the church, *pro fides*." Benedict wheezes. "God knows I did it for – "

"For ambition! You did it for yourself, knave." He raises his hand as if he'll gouge his eyes out at any moment.

It is only then that Pacificus hears the shuffle of grass behind him. It is Mark, he is moving, he is alive. "My head," he half-moans, half-whispers.

"Mark!" Pacificus moves over and rolls him face upward, "you're alive, lad!"

Mark pushes up heavily on his elbows. "Sigismund shot Benedict with his own wheellock, then struck me with it. Oh, my head."

"Oh thank God, you are well." Pacificus holds the novice close. "Thank God, lad. Thank God. But why shoot *him?*"

"He didn't say, just did it. Oh, my head!" Mark cradles his temples.

But while this conversation ensues Richard is now seeing a different scene: Benedict scraping across the grass with his knife, and then – in one last exertion before death – throwing himself towards Pacificus. For Richard, it is an easy shot but a hard decision, which must be made in an instant nonetheless. The arrow sings across the tops of the tombs and strikes Benedict in the chest bringing him to ground. Pacificus wrestles the blade from him and holds him down.

"You were working for the bishop, weren't you? Answer me!"

Nothing.

"It was you all along, Rugge's iron fist! What did he promise you, an abbacy?"

Nothing.

"Fool, knavish fool! You sold yourself to the devil. Speak now. Confess it."

Nothing. His eyes are obscured in shadow like two empty pits, his mouth open like the grave, the teeth revealed either in a demoniac grin or a pain-riven grimace. But of a word; nothing whatever, just his final drowning breath in the silence of the half-world that he now enters. Perhaps if Binham had never fallen, nor would he. The times find us out, of what mettle we are. It is like Elizabeth Fenton said of Cressida; she might have been a noble and faithful wife had not war come to Troy. 'To Diomede, I will will ever be true' she had said, selling virtue for safety. God help us all, but it's a fool's business to think of what might have been.

Pacificus cannot tell anything more from him now, not even if he repents his sin. Benedict has minutes – aye, and eternity – to think on it all, to blame Sigismund, Wulfric, Cromwell, the king, whoever. But Pacificus will not wait any longer. "Come, Mark. Leave him to God, and let's get after the other knave while there is time."

But even as he is saying it, Simon, still on the edge of the graveyard, calls over, "Brother, come quickly! They are shouting back in the woods!"

The four dash back out into the field and across towards the position where they left the others. Margaret and Piers run out to meet them with Pieter close behind.

"What is it, what has happened," Simon shouts, "where's Beth?"

The groups close in the open field and Margaret points back to the darkness. "It was the monk – he held a wheellock to her head."

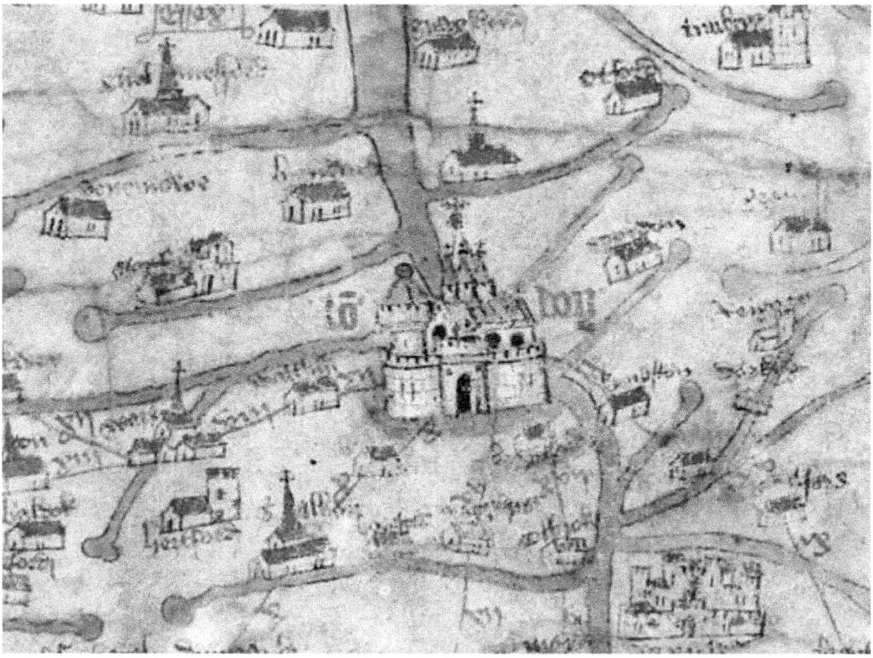

23

Kidnap

Radix omnium malorum est cupiditas
Lust for acquisition is the root of all evil

"God forgive me," Pieter says, "we did not hear him 'til he had her, he said if we follow, then she will die."

"If I'd only had my bow – "

"Silence Piers!" Richard says. "Have your stupid bow." He thrusts it at Piers and then turns to Pacificus. "What can we do? He has already shot his partner, surely he will think nothing of killing Beth if he hears us?"

"He will not hear us, only the sound of his skull cracking." Pacificus lifts Pieter's chin: "Do not despair, God will judge aright – isn't that what you people say? Well then, let us do what we can. You, Simon and the others bring the boat back to Barton Broad, and we'll find our way there through the woods and so be waiting for Sigismund to appear from Witch's Dyke."

"I should go with you..."

"No Pieter, you will be too slow in the wood; take the others."

"And then?" Pieter says.

"If we don't get him now, at the centre of the web, we may never find him or her again."

"Only ...only...dear God." Simon has a thumb and forefinger on the bridge of his nose, deep in thought, then looking this way then that – but what other way is there? "Only, aim sure, brother, keep your powder dry." And, dear God, he groans inwardly, bring her back to me.

Pacificus takes his arms. "Pray for me brother, won't you? *Pray.*"

Pacificus turns to go but Mark and Piers won't leave him.

"I must be there, near as I can," Mark says.

"And you'll need me because I can climb those willows near the waters edge and keep a lookout."

"Piers!" Richard says.

"No, let him do as he says," Pacificus replies, "only let us go quickly."

They separate and Pacificus leads the boys towards the woods east of them, where he hopes that somewhere further on will be Lime Kiln Dyke, the wide stretch of water leading to Barton Broad. It would be there or never, for in the open water of the broad it might be impossible to do anything with a matchlock. Down they go from the fields into the dense undergrowth, and on and on they push through birch, hazel and then alder and willow as the ground becomes wetter, then bog, then marsh. Mark and Pacificus tuck their habits into their belts, but even so, on occasions they sink in deep water above their knees. Piers keeps up and never once complains.

Pacificus thinks they have been going in the same direction, he's done his best not to deviate but he knows how easily it can happen. After half an hour they appear to be lost, surely they should be at the broads, or be able to at least see some light beyond these infernal, creeping, twisting willow trees. "Can't be sure," Pacificus says between breaths, "just can't be sure, damnation."

"Send me up that tree, the light dawns, I will be able to see," Piers says, "give me a leg up, Mark. And hold my bow."

Mark does so and Piers is up like a squirrel. The higher branches bend as he goes, but they do not break. He's barely up for a moment when he scrambles down again in a feverish hurry, "Nearly there! I can see Irstead, you know, the church spire, just a bit more to the right." He takes the bow from Mark. "And I heard the sound of oars in rowlocks somewhere near; it must be them."

"Come then, or we'll be too late." Pacificus says, pushing yet another branch to the side and wading out once more.

Soon they all hear the sound of water fowl dabbling, and then the sound of a boat. "Quiet now," Pacificus whispers, "and don't shake the branches, they must not expect us." But it is to no avail, for the wind is dropped now to a whisper for the dawn, and as they approach the reeds at the water's edge, a family of moorhens scatter in all directions. A short way off, perhaps no more than a hundred yards, and happy at his oars, this commotion alerts Sigismund. He leaves the oars and stands behind Beth, whose hands he has tied about the mast. "Up woman, on your feet." He tugs at Beth, who is sitting on the lowered mast and sail. She stands unwillingly, sliding the rope as she rises. Sigismund holds the wheellock to her temple.

"Who's there? That you Pacificus? Oh, yes it is! Shouldn't have come, you shouldn't. Couldn't keep away from the gold, eh?"

Pacificus already has the matchlock leveled at the monk's head. "That's right, brother, do what you want with her, it's the money you'll have to share, or I'll take the head from your shoulders, so help me I will."

He says this, all the while wading out into the clearer water so that the reeds and trees do not obscure his range. Mark looks first at Pacificus in horror – does he mean it? – and then back into Beth's eyes.

Once or twice she tries to look away from the two different barrels aimed at her, but eventually she can only stare back towards Mark and her brother who wait in horror in the reeds.

"You're a bad liar, brother," Sigismund grips Beth tighter and grinds his lip, "I've seen your sort before, the bishop even said as much, all chivalry, piss and wind, that's why he set me and Benedict to work; he knew you'd mess it up."

"And that's where you're going now – to the bishop?" He draws the hammer back, click, click. Steady now, steady.

"What? That coxcomb? Pah. Beaten him at his own game, I have, and I'll not beg, nor be lackey to any like him again. He'll soon fall like the rest of them, like the abbeys – and when he does, I'll not go wandering for my bread, pensioned off for five pounds, like you. I was a butcher you know, so no scholar's stipend for me; not ordained, so no cosy Chantry job neither – a man must fix his own stars, Pacificus, you should know that!"

"Worth all that blood is it, your soul?" Pacificus must take his chance soon, as the boat is drifting slowly further from him. He blinks the sweat from his eyes and re-tightens his grip on the trigger. Come on man, do something, expose a bit more of that fat head for me.

"Wasn't me that did the killings, Benedict saw to that – he had a taste for it, and anyway, there wouldn't have been any if Bede had not been so stubborn."

"How did you do it without detection?"

"Easy, we started that fire in the infirmary store when we heard Bede was alone counting swans up-river, and we slipped out to the abbot's staithe while everyone was busy. Just a shame the lad wasn't more forthcoming with the information we needed, we never intended to do more than just frighten him, get what we wanted and leave. But you know how straight these young people are."

"And Jary?" Come on, *come on, just a bit more.*

"Oh, that were Benedict, I only found out later, he was a touched one, was Benedict."

"And the player?"

"Us? No, that was those Augustinians, sick dogs that they are, doing that to a man."

"And your brethren and prior?" *Move, damn you.*

"Course we did them, but Wulfric had it coming; he was going to cut us out, like Benedict would've too like as not. As I see it, it was them or us – me."

"And – and your deal with the bishop?" It is weak and he knows it.

Sigismund laughs. "Wouldn't trust Rugge as far as I could throw him myself, even if Benedict did. Known his sort all my life; soon as piss on you as keep troth in matters of money. He'd have had us both disappeared. Probably would've asked you or Aeyns to do it – we knew too much, just like you, brother, now there's a thought. So lower your weapon, be content that you have the saint, or this maid's blood will be on your hands. I mean it, I'm in blood too far now to care one way or the other."

"Last chance to negotiate." Pacificus' breathing is down to nothing at this point, the last air being released from his lungs and his heart stilled as the words leave his mouth.

"Hah," Sigismund cocks his head back in mockery, "you can negotiate over my dead b – "

My pleasure, click, thud. Bang. The head movement gives Pacificus the only opening he was likely to get. The powder flares and an ear-splitting explosion of flame and smoke fly from the nozzle. Beth strains forward at the flash, pulling Sigismund with her so that his head passes behind the mast just as the ball strikes the side of it, sending splinters in every direction. When the smoke clears, Pacificus can see what Piers has already seen from his position on the bank. Sigismund has recovered his balance and is spluttering his revenge.

"Very well, you had your shot, now here is mine if that's the way we are to play. On your head be it."

He is repositioning the wheellock to her left temple, but before he can fire a shot or Pacificus do more than cry, "No', the air is cut by the twang of a bow. Beth has seen him, Piers in the tree, and now sees it – coming like fury across the water. It will hit her surely, so she yanks away from his grip on her arm just as the arrow strikes his shoulder. It is the arm which holds the wheellock, and Sigismund flings the weapon away in a spasm of agony. In so doing, he overbalances the boat, dragging Beth – and with her the mast – towards the water. The boat topples with a slapping and spraying of water across the calm and silent deep. They hit the water struggling, she for breath, he for the two leather saddlebags with the gold. The boat is on its side, and the more Sigismund pulls and scrapes for the bags, the more the boat starts to turn over – taking Beth down with it.

She's straining at the rope and kicking her legs, but there is little she can do to save herself. "She'll be drowned! Quick!" Pacificus says, frantically stripping down to his undershirt.. But Mark is ahead of him, already naked and plunging into the cold waters, going at it like an otter. Pacificus follows with the basilard dagger, starting out just as the boat lurches when one of the saddlebags is displaced by Sigismund. He is only just above the water now as he holds the gunwales, but when his fingers finally do move one of the bags it slides quickly towards him. He instinctively slings it over his good shoulder just as the boat finally flips on him. But the opposite gunwale strikes him unconscious, so that under the weight he sinks to the peat bottom some twelve feet below him, never more to rise.

"Beth," screams Mark, who is only halfway.

"Go down, take her air in your mouth," Pacificus shouts from behind, "quickly now."

Mark rushes on with his head down, ploughing through the water until he sees the mast, not facing totally down, yet with the familiar blue dress, suspended and billowing in the murky half-light like a flag in aspic. She is still tugging at the rope with all that is left of her last breath. Mark takes a last breath above the surface and then descends. She sees him come, with eyes wide and terrified as her own. She's offering him her hands but he goes straight for her mouth, taking her by the head, and hair and closing his lips over hers before releasing the air. Her lips are cold and their teeth rub together, but when he returns with a second breath from the surface, they do it better, eyes wide open, and more calmly, his arm round her waist.

After that Pacificus is there with the knife, but even so it is Mark who takes her back to the surface, and Mark who keeps her afloat as she regains her breath, and perhaps even a little longer than he should as Pieter's boat comes into view. Meanwhile, Pacificus is busy loosening the other saddlebag from under the seat. Let Rugge have his bodies, but not all the gold. There'll be enough round Sigismund's neck to finance his tournament and palace extension. No, but let at least some of it go to the poor, some of this tragedy be redeemed. It is what Marcantonio Vendramin would have done, he muses, remembering that other knight errant he had pursued half way across Italy as a younger man. Yes, let the poor have it.

It takes them little over half an hour to retrieve what they must. He passes each item to Richard and Mark in the boat. Mark is doing his level best not to catch Beth's eye. After the initial explanations, she gives him her thanks in as formal a manner as it is possible, which is more than she does to Piers, though she treats even him differently from this day on. Yes, the shot was foolish but saved her nonetheless. Pacificus says as much. He sits on his own at the end of the boat, knees under his chin, the bow lying beside him.

He does not look up as Pacificus sits next to him. "Hit an apple at fifty yards can you? It's a good thing your sister moved when she did."

Piers sees the monk smile. "Well, *you* did no better."

"I would've had him if she hadn't unbalanced the boat." He laughs but Piers does not, his face now frowning with earnestness. "You said killing is not a sin in wartime – "

"It was the gold that killed him, not your arrow, likely thought he could make the near bank with it, but you can't swim laden down like that, can you?"

Pacificus lays a hand on the lad's cheek, then his shoulder, speaking softly, "It would have been a sin to let your sister be murdered, when you had the power to act, which you did. There is no wrong, no sin in that – you did well." He puts the bow back in Piers' hand and as he does so, he's thinking on it; strange, this old bow from Agincourt, and perhaps even older things besides are not spent yet.

"And my mother? Would it be a sin to let her be burnt while – "

"But *if* she is condemned," he knows she will be, "if, *if*, then it will be for breaking the king's peace, not – "

"But aren't there better laws, higher laws than the rules of men, it's what you always say." Piers has that fierce look in his eye again, like he would damn the very heavens to justify what he feels in his heart to be true. Pacificus knows that look, has known it his whole life. The world is crooked, the boy is right. "We'll talk about it later," is the best he can do for now. He hears Piers blow through his nostrils in discontent, but what else can he do for the lad? Why does everyone make me the solution to all ills in the world?

Pacificus sends Pieter, Beth, Richard and Piers with the reliquary and the gold, a long way back to the cottage. "Keep away from Irstead, for the sheriff may be there by now. I will take the boat there with Mark, and we shall meet him. Simon, you go back through Horning, but brother, you must take the fields. People will be about their work soon and none of you must be seen." He will not compromise them, not after all this.

He and Mark arrive at Irstead just after the sheriff and the reeve with their men at arms. Prior Thomas is also there with the outrider William Hornyng, a monk responsible for the outlying granges and abbey farms.

Pacificus chooses his words carefully, trying as often as possible to put the onus back on the bishop. It was the *bishop* who learned of a theft of gold from Binham Priory, goods not recorded in the 1535 *Valor Ecclesiasticus*; the *bishop* who had set Pacificus to discover which of the Binham monks was the thief; and the *bishop* who could verify all this. The truth is that all six were thieves, and all six now dead, killed by each other, the last drowned with the gold.

"You will find him on the bottom, near the upturned boat at Lime

Kiln Dyke, he has the gold – or perhaps more exactly, it has him – and also an arrow in his shoulder."

"An arrow?" The sheriff looks older than last time by ten years at least; it has been a harder job than he thought. He hasn't bothered to do half the buttons up on his doublet.

"He took the novice, Mark, as a hostage, the arrow did not kill him, be assured of that, it was the weight of gold."

"I see." He observes Mark's bedraggled appearance. "He floated and the other sank. If this was trial by ordeal, we'd have a pretty mess wouldn't we?"

"All the same," Pacificus tries to sound confidential, "I'd imagine the bishop would not want mention of the arrow in the report."

"I answer to the justices, not your bishop." He answers to the duke more like, everyone knows he's in Norfolk's pocket. But at least it will clear up what is turning into an infamous string of unsolved murders. Get these tied up and he might rise in the shire, get his wife that small manor she has had her eye on, more feathers for her silly bonnets.

Pacificus is there for the salvage, he doesn't want the sheriff or Norfolk getting the money. Rugge sends people from Norwich to mediate at the assize. It is a strange business, but eventually he and Norfolk dedicate the money towards the tournament, with a small part going on the palace. Rugge is grateful for the duke's largess in the matter, and promises him over dinner that, "if anything should e'er befall the abbey, and if materials became available," he will remember the duke – who is always building something grand. It is the most the bishop has ever spoken about the future of the abbey; by now he has given up the idea of Saint Benet's becoming a pilgrimage site. Chapuys was right, Pacificus was right. Rugge had gotten wind of the new injunctions which Cromwell would bring out in the following spring: *no relics or veneration of images*. But without that extra source of income, Saint Benet's will never make him more then £600 per year.

It is a problem that will not go away, for much of the revenue is spent on the upkeep of the monastery buildings and the monks. In olden times, copying documents brought in revenue, but the printing press has put paid to that. The farms and tenants could pay their money straight to the bishopric, but for the abbey. It is an acute and imminent dilemma. He has played every card in his hand – well, almost.

Queen Jane has just given the king his first living son, Edward, but then she has died two weeks later, poor girl. But this means a Protestant succession at any rate, not good news for Rugge. The large Cluniac monastery at Lewes has surrendered to the crown just last week, others will follow. There is an air of political resignation from many priests and bishops, nay, even condemnation from the Calvinist persuasion; *you cannot fight God's will* is what they are bleating these days. God's breath, he hates that sort of pious apathy. He'd publicly debated all that tripe with that heretic reformer Tom Bilney back when he, Rugge, had been doctor of divinity at Gonville Hall, Cambridge. It was a *Trialogus* between him, Bilney and Hugh Latimer, and written down by the Carthusian Thomas Spencer so others could read it. Fat lot of good it did, and here we are facing the same errors two decades later with the stakes ten times higher. Spencer is dead, Bilney was burnt five year gone, at the Lollard's pit and Latimer's heading that way if he doesn't watch his mouth. And then there is me, and what can I do now. No relics, nay, no veneration of relics allowed anyhow, and now all these bills for my palace. I hate to sound like one of those Calvinists, but if God wants the abbey to survive then he'll have to do something himself at this rate.

His next proper meeting with Pacificus that October is strained. That "Binham business' is barely even discussed. Amazing, all that blood and intrigue for nothing. Pacificus will hardly broach the subject himself for fear of losing his temper. Why didn't you tell me Benedict and Sigismund were working for you? He knows the answer – Rugge doesn't trust him. Perhaps he is right about me, that much anyway. He thinks of the great bag of gold angels they took, what Rugge wouldn't give for it - for his palace, his new tapestries, velvets and Bruges silks.

The most said is that Rugge never intended there to be blood over it, and that if he had known that Benedict was so unstable, or Sigismund so avaricious, he'd never have spoken to them. As ever, it is easier to summon a dragon than ride it. They are standing together in the walking gallery on the south side of the palace, gazing out across the grass. His two gardeners are doing their best to stake out a maze from a vellum plan ready to be laid next spring, which they keep turning this way then that. Rugge rests his stout knuckles on the window ledge so that his ruby ring scrapes awkwardly on the glass pane.

He draws a long breath, sifting careful words from the air. "It was a goodly sum of gold, though I confess I was hoping for more." He turns his head slowly to observe Pacificus' reaction.

Best to look straight ahead and not seem concerned. "Did not Lord Hastings tell you the sum?"

"He is abroad, yet again. But I shall ask him. Oh, just look at those idiots, will you?" Rugge bangs on the window. "No, not sideways – hold it long-ways!" They cannot hear him, but he nevertheless gesticulates and shouts as if they should. "Two fools, can't even get it right when the plan is in front of them!" What – not like us, you mean?

They spend the afternoon talking over the events for next summer. "It will do the king good, methinks. He is sore grieved at the queen's death. He needs to be away from court, all that miasmic, Protestant air – let him celebrate his son and heir with us, let him see some good, Catholic pageantry – he's no damned Lutheran, that's for sure, just needs to remember the old ways, see it, hear it. Will be goodly medicine for him."

But Rugge is also using the tournament as a remedy for himself, to stave off the decision he'll be forced to make about the abbey. He does not mention this to Pacificus of course; no need to risk problems sooner than need be.

Business done, Pacificus pays a visit to Elizabeth at the castle with some keepsakes from the children and more books. He finds her out of sorts and her cell cold. What comfort is Wace' poetry, or moral Gower, or even Langland, what comfort is anything in this world, now she will die? Oh, that she might have the scriptures in her own tongue! And oh, that she could calm herself amidst the gnawing despair and hear God speak words of comfort to her once more. The date for her trial is announced already; she will be tried at the feast of the Visitation along with other heretics and treasonous persons, as part of Rugge's 'pageant' for the king. What could be more fitting than to show His Majesty the loyalty of the bishop, of the duke – nay, the whole shire – by the execution of the king's real enemies, these radical reformers, these step children of the reformation - these Anabaptists and Lollards, unloved even by Lutherans and Genevans? It's where it will all end if Henry is not careful, once the cat is let from the bag – London will become Wittenburg one day, Geneva the next, then Munster. After that God alone knows what mischief and anarchy will ensue. Let the king's justices try these heretics at the tournament but the king himself, like an Angevin monarch, sentence them. He'll like that and so will the people.

Now, in the jail, face to face with a real, unrepentant heretic, he is less sure. Abstract conceptions of theological triumphalism and Angevin pageantry all fade before her face, her tender fingers; a real, feeling, breathing woman, who now shifts so uneasily at his entrance. Pacificus places the few gifts on the table and then sits in silence. What can he say to her, he of all people? Does he believe her sort should be allowed to go free – to smash Christendom into a thousand shards? Soon he himself will be forced to make an oath to the king's sovereignty in religion; it is already happening. Can he take this oath now in good conscience, a pinch of incense on the altar, say Caesar is lord? But if the king's church is too little a thing, then maybe even Christendom is too small. Maybe it is these heretics, in having the smallest conception possible of the church, their internal kingdom of conscience, that have found the biggest thing of all – perhaps the only thing. His thoughts run in a perverse progression, but only as a man who travels abroad in order to convince himself that his own town is the best. But today, on returning, Pacificus will not dare look at his own town, let alone his own heart. He has not done so since the failure of the rebellion, since Aske's death.

So he sits at table with her, observing her hand on the book, his own near it, her slight fingers reaching for life, his for truth and meaning.

"When..." He clears his throat. "*If* they find you guilty, you may still plead with the king; he can be merciful."

"You are kind sir, but I think the summer too far spent." She smiles half-heartedly but does not look at him, rather at the worn skin on the back of her hand. But when she finally meets his gaze, the movement loosens some hair from her coif and it trails like a golden waterfall down her cheek.

"If the queen were alive, I would plead as the men of Calais did before Queen Philippa, plead as a mother – I would not be so proud as you think, but I have little with which to appeal to the king. I don't think he is *that* merciful."

"But...you will try, won't you?" Dear God, even I'd forgive you murder! And why do tears come so readily these days when I'm near her? "I mean, you will do it for the children's sake? That much at least would not be a sin for you, would it?"

"No," she whispers softly, "it would be no sin." And then she takes his hand and squeezes it hard. "Promise me you will not let them see me be put to pains, you will keep them away – promise me. They should remember me as I was."

He stares at her hands for a moment, speechless. Why are women so practical? The words on his lips, though he dare not utter them, are that she will not die at the gibbet while he has breath in his body; he will not permit it. Should he say it, is it right to? Should she be one more exception to the rule, just because Piers, or indeed he would have it so? The words would sound knightly, for sure, and would flow naturally from his sanguine humours when their skin is touching as it is now, but is it more the influence of courtly love – the romances he was fed on his mother's knee, rather than the harder truth of the true church - if indeed it even be true? He closes another hand on hers, her skin is quite cold. Poor woman, she is not as strong as she seems.

"Of course, I will do as you ask." He leaves his hand there on hers, savouring the guilty moment. He shouldn't take advantage of her pain. God knows, life would be simpler if she were not here, but what life would that be now? Could it even be called life? How many hours have they sat in this cell talking, knowing each other. These few books they have shared, these jokes, these tears. He can feel her hand shake slightly. He wants to warm them in his but dare not squeeze. Oh, dear Lord, he thinks, I have been even as Bede's sparrow, flying through a winter window into the warmth of Edwin's great hall and then out again without knowing what I was doing. In and out of this cell I have flown, hour after hour I have warmed myself by her light. Could even matrimony be better than those hours? I cannot imagine it possible. And now must I imagine it should cease? Without knowing it, the fullness of this woman seems to call forth a greatness in me to which I am not equal. And yet perhaps, as in the old tales, maybe the divine enabling will come in obedience to the summons. Look at her, so strong in the face of adversity. And look at me, always acting on the dictates of other men's consciences. All my life I have strained at great things, yearned for them, given myself to them; the knights, the *cause*, Christendom, Ranworth, the northern rebellion, on and on, on and on, each smaller and frailer than the last. The bishop, the grand master, the pope, the cardinals and emperors; all wanting me to spend my life, bend my conscience for them. But to be a father? To love one woman, any woman, make her happy, nay, just to look at a woman; is that a small thing or a great thing? Everything about these Fentons turns the world on its head.

When he reaches the point where he feels his heart would burst within him, he steels himself inside to tear away by presenting the only secret that now strands before them. "Before I leave you, there is one more thing that you must know."

"Say on."

"I am not who you think, nay, not whom I appear." He swallows hard. "This is difficult, prithee bear with me, for I am not altogether unknown to you. That is to say, one time long ago you knew my brother – "

"Your brother!" She almost jumps. "Upon my word, you are Cecil's brother! I should have guessed it – the eyes!" She straightway withdraws her hands towards her breast. "And where is he? Is he yet alive? Is he well?" She cranes her neck to catch his words, his meaning but, when she sees his face crestfallen, says, "Ah, so he did not fare as well as you with the knights. Poor Cecil. I did hear tell of the Great Siege; I am sorry. But did he ever talk of me? Our parting was...well, it was unexpected."

"I – I – er, I cannot say – " This is trickier than he thought, she has taken that he is dead, and perhaps that is best for now.

"Well, either he mentioned me or not while you were abroad."

"He did not, I have known only recently." That much is the truth.

"And so all this kindness is a guilt offering of some kind, a brother's debt mayhap?"

"Why no, by no means – "

"Or peradventure to step in where the brother left off, then?" Her voice has become sharpened with the pain of very many nights of anguish on this abandonment.

"Elizabeth?"

"Do not use my name thus, and do not look at me thus either, your family has done me a great wrong, a very great wrong."

"Prithee – "

"Go now, anon, leave me!"

He lingers a moment longer until he sees her rage turn to grief. "Just go," is all he hears her whisper through her tears; words that follow him down the corridor. He feels he is in the right – at least he thought he was – wasn't he? Why couldn't they talk it out, argue it out, like men? These thoughts go with him out of the keep, along with a secret resolution that he has made despite it all. For in the space of just four steps Sir Hugh Erpingham has hatched a plan. He passes guard-after-indifferent guard, locking door after door, and then down twenty steps in the inner keep, along the crenellated wall, and down ten steps to the castle yard at the back of the smithy. Tom Short brings him his mule. The lad has grown like a bean stalk this summer, but he has lost none of his peevish wit for all that. "That was quick, would she not see you?"

"Mind your manners," Pacificus glances across to the forge. "Your father busy?"

"Not busy enough with winter coming, and rents up again. He says I'll need to look for work in London. Mother ain't happy."

"I would speak a word with him."

They enter the orange glow of the forge where Vulcan stands astride his craft, sparks scattering on the dirt floor. Beads of sweat fly from his forehead to sizzle on the anvil at regular intervals. His face is fixed as he hammers away with no evident love for it, or so it seems at first glance. Pacificus discerns in the pinching of the mouth, that all too familiar melancholy. Will Short catches a glimpse of Pacificus when he turns briefly to plunge the shoe in water. He raises an eyebrow to his son, and then turns back to his work: "The one you talked about?"

"Aye, he would talk with you."

"I heard you were trained with the Almains at Greenwich," Pacificus begins.

"What of it?" He's putting the shoe back in the coals and applying the bellows.

"I'm surprised you left, *for this.*"

"Had my reasons." The bellows send the coals into a flare and flurry of sparks.

"Perhaps you weren't up to it."

The smith turns with the red-hot shoe in mid-air between himself and the monk's face. "What the hell would a monk know?" His eyes twitch with rage. "Perhaps they were jealous." And then, sardonically, "Why, are you buying? Of course not, so get you gone before you get yourself a beating." He takes the shoe back to the anvil and starts to beat it again as if it were a thousand German faces.

"Can you acid etch and fire gild?" Pacificus waits for the reaction, but the smith merely stops hammering. It's been years since he'd even heard those words spoken inside his own head.

"Aye, and blueing too, if I had somewhere to get the heat right."

"Aye and the rest," young Tom says, "they used to say Pa could make a knight blaze like a phoenix in the sun – hands of an artist and fingers of a clockmaker."

"Silence boy," Will Short snaps gruffly, but he turns to Pacificus with a proud eye. "What do you want from me, monk? State your business."

"Suppose you could have armour that you designed and built, at the tournament next summer?"

"What?"

"You heard me, the best you can make. To go up against the best Almain armour, nay, the king's at that."

He looks to his son for a moment and then back again. "For you?"

Pacificus shakes his head. "For another, but it must be done privily you understand, none should know of it."

"But – " he's starting to breathe heavy now, blinking and licking his dry lips. "But where would I get the steel, the silver – "

"Gold. The inlay will be gold. I will see you have all you need. But not so much as a word to anyone." Pacificus looks at him steadily, "this knight will blaze like a phoenix from the flames." By my oath, he'll have to.

PART THREE - 1538

Where divers and sundry abbots, priors, abbesses, prioresses, and other ecclesiastical governors and governesses of divers monasteries, abbacies, priories, nunneries, colleges, hospitals, houses of friars, and other religious and ecclesiastical houses and places within this our sovereign lord the King's realm of England and Wales, of their own free and voluntary minds, good wills and assents, without constraint, coaction, or compulsion of any manner of person or persons, since the fourth day of Feb, the twenty-seventh year of the reign of our now most dread sovereign lord, by the due order and course of the common law of this his realm of England, and by their sufficient writings of record, under their convent and common seals, have severally given, granted, and by the same their writings severally confirmed all their said monasteries, abbacies, priories, nunneries, colleges, hospitals, houses or friars, and other religious and ecclesiastical houses and places, and all their sites, circuits, and precincts of the same, and all and singular their manors, lordships, granges, manses, lands, tenements, meadows, pastures, rents, reversions, services, woods, tithes, pensions, portions, churches, chapels, advowsons, patronages, annuities, rights, entries, conditions, commons, leets, courts, liberties, privileges, and franchises appertaining or in wise belonging to any such monastery, abbacy, priory, nunnery, college, hospital, house of friars, and other religious and ecclesiastical houses and places, or to any of them, by whatsoever name or corporation they or any of them, were then called, and of what order, habit, religion, or other kind or quality soever they or any of them were reputed, known, or taken; to, have and to hold all the said...voluntarily, as is aforesaid, have renounced, left, and forsaken, and every one of them has renounced, left, and forsaken.

That the King our sovereign lord shall have, hold, possess, and enjoy to him, his heirs and successors for ever, all and singular such late monasteries, etc....And it is further enacted by the authority aforesaid, that not only all the said late monasteries...but also other etc....which hereafter shall happen to be dissolved, suppressed, renounced, relinquished, forfeited, given up, or by any other means come unto the King's highness.... All monastic lands shall be within the survey of the court of augmentation except such as come by attainder.

From the *Act of the Dissolution of the Great Monasteries*
Statutes of the Realm vol. III

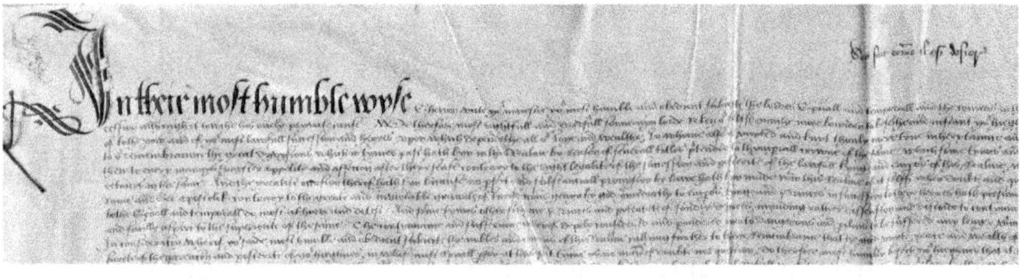
In their most humble wyse

24

Lord Hastings

Sedit qui timuit ne non succederet
He who feared failure, sat still

January 24, 1538, cold morning, bright as a pin. "My, this is an unexpected honour!" The aged Lord Hastings embraces Pacificus tenderly. They are standing by the moat in front of Bindringham Hall. He is returning from walking four greyhounds as the Benedictine is dismounting at the gate.

"I heard you had returned, sir, and I would speak to you – before others."

"Our lord bishop, I suppose. Hmm. I see." He runs a thumb along the beard which by now is even longer and raises his eyebrow in an irreverent manner.

"Well, you've braved a lengthy journey for the time of year. I expect the roads were all but impassable. Howsoever, Hugh, come to the house and we'll get a lad to see to your mule."

They start towards the house, which lies at the end of the short cobbled drive. The red brick coins that contain the flint walls burn with the warmest orange available for the time of the year. Candlemas is soon upon them, and from there the hope and expectation of spring. Pacificus says that he would prefer to be called by his Benedictine name. The old man apologises but then adds, "Have you taken thought where you will go when the big houses fall?" After the pause, Hastings rests his hands on Pacificus' shoulder. "Dear boy, we all wish it were otherwise, but you must look to the future; there'll be no monks soon."

Pacificus nods, and looks up to the windows on each gable. "It is a fine house, my lord."

"A hen roost, my son says. Do you remember Arthur? You played together on this lawn."

"I came with my father." He words the reply carefully, thinking: yes, I remember the brat! Pacificus listens as Sir Geoffrey tells how his eldest and dearest has already secured large quantities of building material, timbers, features from the dismantled Binham Abbey. "All to make improvements, enlargements after these old bones rest in the earth," adding sardonically, "and not for a mausoleum!" The monk does not return the old man's grin, it is an unpleasant thought for a father. Well might Arthur Hastings scorn this hen roost when the Hastings family had held so many great estates about the country in the times before Bosworth – Whitefield, Stratton and Cundover; Wigginton and Wolverhampton in Staffordshire; Bromesgrove in Worcestershire; Bolsover Castle in Derbyshire; Owardbek and Mannesfeld in Nottinghamshire; Blunham in Bedforshire; Nailstone and Burbage in Leicestershire; and Fillongley in Warwickshire. They had always been on the wrong side, these Hastings, not just in the last civil war, but before that too. It's not that you can't get the estates back, some of them at least, its just you've got to be a brown-nose like old Norfolk to do it, and even then there are no guarantees.

"It was your first ride – first big one – the day you came."

"Oh, yes," Pacificus says, squinting slightly, partly to remember, partly to shield his eyes from the sharp mid-morning light when he turns back to the lawn.

"I remember you both clattering through that gate, as if it was yesterday. Some things I remember so clearly – other things, alas not so well." Hastings draws a breath and then sighs. "A serious child, you were."

"Yes, I suppose I was," Pacificus says, remembering that the visit was soon after the burning of the heretic Peke that he had witnessed in Norwich. "Poor Father, things did not quite work out for him."

"You mean the estate?"

"Aye, that, but us too; Cecil and me."

"If you were both stubborn, it was all from him, not your mother, God rest her." Geoffrey sees that this does not lift the monk, so he adds, "I dare say he never put it in so many words to you, God knows we fathers don't do many things we should, but he *was* proud of you both, for what you did I mean – who wouldn't be? He always spoke of it."

"But never the Erpingham title, I warrant."

"No, he did not, I grant thee – but all men carry burdens, and I said to him on more than one occasion that a great name is better than a lasting one. The two are not the same. Great saints, I've enough grandchildren in London all as foolish as their fathers. I'd have been glad of sons like you and Cecil, men with better things on their hearts than trade – it's like a sickness with my kin."

"I am sorry for you."

Hastings tries to wave it off, but he finds it far less easy to be the diplomat at his own home. "Oh, don't think on it, Lord knows I am not ungrateful, and besides, they learnt the greater part of their folly from me." He stands for a moment, trying to undo the fastening of his cloak, which eludes his juddering fingers. "And it's for that folly I assume you attend me today?" He sees Pacificus nod. "Aye, well, we'll speak away from the house then. Johnson – Johnson!" A groom appears from the side of the house. "Ah good man, take this poor mule and show it some kindness for its troubles. And tell Maggie we have a guest until tomorrow."

They walk about the side of the house and round to a smaller bridge to the rear. The bridge leads over to a topiary garden with a colonnade of naked fruit trees running down the centre. As they enter the dappled tunnel, he rests an equally gnarled hand upon the trunk of the first Pippin tree. "I bought these apricots here with me from France twenty years hence at Catherine's insistence; she said it was not seemly for ladies to walk out in full sun. In truth I think I filled her head with too many a story from Italy." He pats the trunk as it might have been his favourite mare. "Poor Katerina never really did see it in its glory – it is quite a picture in the summer, you ought to come again to see it."

"And I think you have a goodly orchard too, perhaps more diverse than the abbey even."

"That I doubt, and I would not let Brother Gerard hear you say so! How is he these days?"

"He is well. Worried about everything, of course, but otherwise well."

"Ah, I see. Hmm, well he would like it here – many of these were from his cuttings you know. Yes, they were; the pears, walnuts, bullace, damsons and apple for sure. The others are from hither, thither and yon, I forget. My filberts are particularly fine, and the plums. Mind you, the walnuts have done ill there in that corner, it is the shade I think. Oh, and listen to me rattling on about my garden, I sound like the emperor Diocletian. I suppose you know he resigned public office to raise cabbages? Ah, well he did. And I confess it does do something for a man to be back with the land after all the machinations of foreign courts."

Lord Hastings stands awhile, chewing on his few teeth, lost in thought. Pacificus glances about him at the seasonal skeletons of plants trained about willow frames in the shapes of men, women and animals. Where yew is used, the body of dark foliage, though sometimes tinged with brown, make the figures look like rooted, evergreen gods, awaiting the flute of Pan to summon them to life. Where hawthorn has been used, and the leaf died back, they look like skeletons. *Momento Mori.* But by far the most ghostly are where dead rosemary plants still inhabit the willow framework of a man or maid. For they are doubly silver by colour and by the frost which still clings to them, glistening as the sun struggles above the yew trees beyond the moat.

"It is my one little consolation this," he says, pointing to the topiary and the arbours, "I have no more stomach for courts and intrigues – wearied of it all. Of course, a man tries not to be cynical but it gets hard at my age. But enough of me; you came with news of Santa Helena?"

"I have her safe, and half the gold."

"Ah, so you *are* thinking about the future."

"Aye my lord, but not for myself. I would spend the money for the poor when the abbey can no longer do it – if you agree, that is."

"It seems right enough, for God knows no one else will."

"And there is a family I would speak with you about particularly."

"I see. Don't be awkward about me, Hugh. I am very much in your debt, as you well know. So say on, my lad."

Pacificus explains the situation of the Fentons, his brother's relationship to Beth, and the upcoming tournament, and lays out the request he has in mind. "She is my niece," he explains: "and the boys – well, if I had ever had sons – you know..."

"I see. So, if I hear you aright, you wish me to take these orphans – heretics that even the Lowlanders and Lutherans burn – for four months and transform them into – what? One page, one lady of court and a knight capable of challenging – nay, bringing down – the king's champion?"

"My lord, he is a strong and noble youth, and will have his own armour – "

"Aye, well I hope that's so, for I'm sure I've nothing here these days but my man Hobb's old Almain rivet."

Pacificus takes Hastings by both arms. "My lord, there was a time when Brandon or even Henry would have gladly carried your lance, just to see you in the lists. You have a goodly yard here still I believe, and time too; you know what they need more than I do. God's teeth, I had little enough time in the tilt yard – I was up to my armpits in Saracen blood before e'er my beard was thick."

"Aye, they were sorry times, mind, so are these."

"These are times," Pacificus insists, releasing his grip, "when good men do what they can, for whatever's in front of them. If I've learned aught in these sorry months, surely it's been that – there's no gospel command to love the world, but only thy neighbour. These children, heretic or no, must have the opportunity to win their mother – surely you can see that?"

"She must be a very fine woman indeed, this lady, my lad."

Pacificus does not at first catch Hastings' meaning, or the raised eyebrow. "Aye, my lord, she is that and more." It is only now he sees Hastings' grin. *"My lord?"*

"Nothing dear boy, only pleased that you do have an eye on the future after all." Pacificus is about to defend himself but Hastings, moved by love for this man he knows of old and his father's memory, commits himself to the venture, concluding, "Yes, very well, I will do it. Perhaps I make some amends, perhaps assuage the innocent blood that was spilt because of my folly. And Lord knows, a man of my years has little enough to kindle his own fire. Perhaps my retirement may not be so uneventful as I had imagined; be it so."

That night they discuss the difficulties of repatriating the reliquary to Rome. If it is seized in England, the bones will be burned in one of Cromwell's crowd-pleasing fires. If she makes it across the channel there is a chance the emperor will take it and use Helen's cultus to add to the growing ferment against England. The emperor certainly won't surrender it to the Pope if he has any use for it himself. The rumours already abound that the Pope will call for a crusade against England at any time. It is an inconclusive conversation, both men unwilling to contrive a reason for moving her.

"Perhaps the times will bring greater stability,". Hastings says, as they are retreating to the house. "Until then, surely our duty is to keep the reliquary safe? Upon my oath, I agree she should return, but the timing cannot be now – perhaps you could deal with it? I would not need to know, perhaps best that way." Pacificus nods. What else can he say? Hastings has just been generous to him. Perhaps he'll just bury the reliquary under the rood at Saint Helen's; yes, that would be fitting. Just for a season, of course. He thinks of Anne Boleyn's bones, in an arrow box under the flags in St Peter's chapel at the tower, surrounded by traitors, all under their own flags, rotting in lime and sand. He shakes the grisly thoughts from his mind, as he follows Sir Geoffrey back towards the house.

By late afternoon the day following, Pacificus is sitting with Sarah and Pieter at their fireside while the others are at work in the far field or at the eel traps. He puts it the best way he can, but Sarah won't have it. "God brought them to us, they are happy here!" She picks threads from her apron in her agitation. "This will throw them back onto the mercy of men that have none – they will be arrested."

"They will be known as Erpinghams, not Fentons; besides, they are much altered, and shall be more so when Lord Hastings has finished with them."

"You don't listen, monk," Sarah blusters while Pieter tries to calm her. "You will build up their hopes, risk everything when God has set them safely here – and for what, pray? A dream, a fancy!"

"Sarah, Richard has grown strong and he has courage, the – the – the king can still be magnanimous." Pacificus is biting his tongue, trying not to reply in kind to her. "Besides, it would be wrong to say God has determined a thing when really we have not the courage to act in faith. Surely you cannot deny them a chance to save their mother – "

Sarah is about to boil over but Pieter stills her straight-speaking Dutch tongue, with his familiar *whisht*. "Whisht, sister, you will always be their Tanty Sarah. They will not forget you or me; we have been here for a time, but they are not ours – and besides we are old, you and I." He reaches his arms and bony fingers around her shoulders. "Come now. Ja, ja, I know. But do not make the children choose between us and their mother; there should be no choice."

Sarah's shoulders start to heave as her head bends forward, "And who will help us now?"

"There, there now," Pieter says, pulling her close. "We have Margaret now, she works hard."

"Margaret is with child, she will need confinement soon."

"With child?" Pacificus hasn't heard.

"Ah men, no eyes or ears!" Sarah says: "She'll be four months soon." It was half-blind Sarah who had finally broached the subject with Margaret in private. And far from the argument Margaret expected, Sarah had already thought the matter through. "What sort of Christian would I be to throw you out, no, you will stay here and we will raise the *kindje*, you and me." And that was that; they told the men that evening after work and Margaret had been devoted to Sarah ever since.

"A baby; I see. Well, peradventure I could send Mark up to help you prepare the fields this spring," Pacificus says, "and it might be possible for the others to return for the odd day to help."

"We would not ask it of them, you know that," Pieter says calmly as if it were already settled. Pacificus knows it, they must forget these peasant ways altogether if they are to persuade the court that they are high-born. They cannot go with Ludham clay under their nails and eel-oil ingrained in their skin.

Later on that afternoon, Richard, Margaret, Beth and Piers sit patiently – Piers least so – as Pacificus tells what he has come to say. Richard and Beth keep looking towards each other, then to Pieter and Sarah for affirmation. Pieter's lips are pursed shut, Sarah is busy with preparations for the meal, a little too busy. She will not let them see her face. Richard's chest swells, he looks from his ragged hose to his dirty feet. He has not had shoes this last winter. He will have boots *and shoes.* At the same moment, Beth is guiltily caressing the jaded embroidery on her sleeve, "but how will Sarah cope without me?"

"Margaret and I will do just fine," Sarah does not lift her eyes from paring vegetables.

"But," says Richard, "she'll be careful for the bairn's sake, eh?" He teasingly pats her belly, and she in turn slaps his arm.

"I'll mind the child, and you mind your business; win that tournament and bring a silk bow back for the baby's hair." She gathers up the long brown curls on his forehead: "Tie it just here."

Beth turns to Pacificus, "But surely only Richard is needed?"

"You are the daughter of Sir Cecil Erpingham."

"I am not acknowledged."

"Not yet."

"And you have spoken to him – to my father?"

"I will do so when I have your consent." He takes her by the hand. "My dear, *you* are the last of an ancient line; you will represent our family before the court for this tournament week, and at the masked balls and pageants. And *because* you are the last of the line, the rules of chivalry allow you to nominate a kinsmen as your champion. Your brother will ride proxy for you."

"But why me and not you?" Richard says, "after all, you are her kinsmen too?"

"It is not safe for me to be known, nor my brother. We are sworn – as the king sees it – to a foreign power, it is complicated." Pacificus eye fixes Richard, willing him out of his uncertainty. "Richard Fenton, God has made you tall, swift and strong, and has given you this opportunity. I cannot say if you will fare well or ill, or even if the king will hear your petition; there are no pledges here, just this open door if you will take it. We must do the good we see before us."

A stare long and deep as an ocean passes between them, before Piers finally interrupts, "And me, will I get armour too?"

"You will be your brother's squire, the only one who may talk to him during the contest, the only one who may hand him his lance, and only you may help him if he is unhorsed – or injured. That is if he accepts the challenge."

"Of course he will! Won't you, Richard? For mother, you will?"

Richard, perhaps for the first time in his life, does not look round to everyone else for what he should do. The decision is clear enough, the risks as obvious as the prize. His mother would not allow him to do it if she were here, but she isn't. The decision is his.

Richard looks to Pieter, "With all my heart, if you will give your blessing, sir."

It is only now that Sarah stops her work. She turns to see Pieter stretching his long, boney legs before the hearth. His jaw is cocked forward like it always is when he is deep in thought, but eventually he lifts his head and sits straight. Tears run in rivulets down the creases in his face. "So proud of you all, so proud. And though it feel like having the skin pulled from my bones, even so I see that God has – "

Sarah wheels round and exclaims, "Pieter!" as if to make him pause and think what he is committing the lad to.

"Whisht, woman. I know, I know." He purses his lips and shuts his eyes hard, "I would not have you take up arms for your faith, and nor would my sister." Sarah lets out a sigh of relief and is about to say something, when Pieter holds up his hand again, "but to defend your family is another matter, ja, this monk has taught me this much, and no man should forbid it. Yes, you shall have my blessing, and my prayers daily."

Two hours later Simon's reaction is somewhat different. "You did *what?*" He had not taken the news well. "And without my knowledge or consent!"

Pacificus paces Saint Peter's churchyard at Horning where they are having it out. The wind has changed to the east and there is the promise of rain. No one is within earshot.

"I wanted to be sure Lord Geoffrey would consent – and the children too, for that matter, I did not think you would mind."

"Just typical of you, Hugh! Get an idea and run hither and yon without taking a thought for anyone! I'm not a child, you know. And – and – and how exactly do you think Beth can be decreed my legitimate issue, pray?"

"It is all very simple; we draw up a trust deed, and have your oath witnessed by Prior Thomas – "

"The prior!"

"Yes, of course. And besides, your vow of betrothal to Elizabeth Fenton – that is your intention to wed – prior to the conception of her child, is tantamount to marriage in the church's eyes anyway."

"And Beth, and Richard *Fenton*?"

"We will take Mistress Fenton's maiden name, Barrett, so: *I, Sir Cecil Erpingham, do acknowledge Elizabeth Erpingham, daughter of Elizabeth Erpingham, née Barrett, as my legitimate heir and successor.* Something like that, it's all in the wording. We'll get a lawyer to help, or better yet, Brother Aloysius. The herald will not question it with me standing over him. You forget, I am helping the bishop organise the lists. I will see that they are all right."

"Aye, *and us?*" Simon leans heavily against a gravestone, folding his arms and eyeing Pacificus suspiciously. "What is my daughter to say about her father, her uncle? We cannot ask her to lie."

"She will be a gentleman's daughter; she may say *or not say* what she wishes – and you forget, she has a ready wit."

"Well, I still say you take a terrible liberty – and risk too – and I don't like it."

Not for the first time this week, Pacificus is prising open deep wounds. "Brother, it is for us to make good where we can – face the past, set straight what we may. She has chosen to own our name – "

"She has chosen pretty dresses, as you well know! And he, the romance of the tilt yard over the drudgery of an eel-catcher's life – filling their heads with armour and masque balls – I know you! But better a living dog than a dead lion, Hugh."

"And *dead* is what their mother will be, think on that, will you. Besides, you do them no credit. They understand the risks, but have chosen to stand by their mother. That is noble, knightly. You should be proud of them. And Simon – what of her? What other chance is there now, to save her life?"

Simon bows his head and sighs, it is the words about *standing by their mother*, whether calculated or not, that have taken the wind from him. "*I am* proud, believe me," he says quietly, "and would God I were more like them."

"Aye, I know – but Simon, the past is another country, you are confessed. There is no need to dredge up old sins. You must – we must – move on. You will consent, won't you – sign the papers?"

There follows a long pause. Simon looks out towards the river, then back to the marshes. He knows what he ought to say, but the tears welling in his eyes resist every insistence, every call to honour. "She is all I have in this world."

"Do you think I do not love them too – her, Richard and Piers?" Pacificus takes his arms, his eyes searching his brother's. "But these children do not belong to us. They came to us not for our asking, nor for our ownership. And rough-hew it as we will, brother, there is divinity in all this. I know it, though I cannot fathom it – know that God sent them here for a purpose, and we must not hinder it."

Simon is nodding, he knows it too. He will consent, even knowing it means she is unlikely to return to Saint Margaret's marsh. That piece of paper, that affidavit, is her ticket either to the gibbet or to a prosperous marriage, but not back to Ludham, not back to him. If Lord Hastings does his work well she'll be the finest woman at court during the pageant week, he thinks, and that by a long shot – she has all the grace and vivacity of her mother, the same fair countenance and lively wit. Only pray God that the king does not take a liking to her.

25

Tempered Steel

Vincit qui se vincit
He conquers, who conquers himself

The more Sir Geoffrey de Hastings thinks of his challenge, the more he warms to it. He stands in his library at Bindringham, his feet irreverently on the desk, his eyes cast across the lawn towards the moat, his mind many miles away – many years away to be exact. He remembers his youth, replaying old scenes, imagining if he had done things better – a fool's game. He snorts every now and then with delight and embarrassment – what a impudent rascal he had been! So many jests, tussles, ventures had he forgotten – or at least kept from the immediacy of necessary memory – until this son of Erpingham had chosen to lard his pride with unexpected flattery. It is true that he was keen with the lance, and no weakling with a broadsword either, but he was never the best. To be the best takes more than mere skill, or the providence of the heavenly bodies; to be the best you must on top of all these excellencies desire the wreath with an abandon verging on the suicidal. You must stick your courage to the lance and hold it there, scorning the two tonnes of death that thunder against you – never turning your head, nor removing your eyes until death's lance has passed. He was always too sensible a man to be the best, he had loved preferment more and so had jousted just enough to be favoured by the king's father, God rest his iron soul, but not so much as to lose his head.

A log in the grate rolls onto the hearth and he stirs abruptly to save himself a smoky room. He kicks it back under the chimney and then crouches to lift it with the tongs. These children, he thinks, firebrands plucked from the flames. It strikes him as a ludicrous thing that he of all people should be helping to rescue Anabaptist heretics. The sheer irony of it sets him into a perverse chuckle. Beyond that, he knows there is something noble and good to be done, some virtue hard to be articulated but solid. He does not glance at the portraits of his own children, though he can feel them watching him. They come here very seldom now, and then only for money. Familiarity breeds contempt, he thinks in a more cynical moment, and, of course, *children.* My poor Katerina, she would be so sad to see what we have become as a family - this great distance passed between us. He glances up to the portraits. I do not blame them, I was the same at their age. The acorn never falls from the old oak, and besides, my long absences on state business spoiled them. We are both to blame, but probably me more so.

Sir Geoffrey shuffles over towards the rather stiff portrait of his beloved Catherine. Ah Katerina, it is now I wish we had ventured a few more shillings and had Master Holbein paint you. He barely recognises the woman on his wall, it could be anyone. But one thing he does know; she would have approved of him helping these heretic children; she was like that. And what could be better for him, than to have young people about the house again? He straightens up, using a thick pile of unbound books to help him. When he is finally upright, he looks down at them; some of them should be bound with hard covers; he thinks, particularly Thomas More's History of Richard III. Thomas understood Richard. Tyrants are all alike.

They arrive on the afternoon, soaked to the skin from the frequent showers. Pieter holds the reigns of his cob Tinky and the three new arrivals jump out of the cart onto the road by the gatehouse for the day is cold. Two retainers with the Hasting's livery appear reluctantly from their post. There is no device on the surcoat, only an oft-repeated gold floral design on a burgundy background. The Hastings' device, a maunch gules on a gold field, appears on the lapels of their cloaks, which the men brush aside to reveal their steel: "Go on now, we'll have no beggars here – be gone or we'll fetch the watchman."

Richard feels he ought to say something but Pieter speaks crisply and clearly: "Please fetch your master quickly, and tell him I have come on behalf of the monk Pacificus; tell him that."

The younger of the two cast a glance over the young people "And if he is busy?"

"Then we will wait here, I must see him before I release these young people to him."

The master is sent for and to everyone's surprise he comes to the gate, without his coat, in a matter of minutes. The thing pleases Pieter, for he sees warmth in the eyes of the other. He had not intended to leave his seat, but on seeing the greater age of Geoffrey de Hastings, Pieter nevertheless gets down in deference and removed his hood.

"Ah, the Dutchman! I was hoping you would come. Are you all so tall?" Hastings says.

"My Lord, forgive me, but I could not leave them until I was satisfied that you would be kindly inclined towards them."

"Hah! And you are sure of that now?"

"That I am, sir; three score years and ten trains a man to read others. These are my wards."

"My lord." Beth curtsies, but it is hard to look elegant with a soaking dress. The hem audibly slaps the ground like a wet fish when she bends.

"My Lady Elizabeth," Hastings says, raising her hand to kiss it. "The half has not been told me; *enchanté.*"

The retainers take the cue and bow quickly. Piers grins from ear to ear at the sight. He attempts to point it out to Richard, but Richard brushes his hand away just in time for his own introduction.

"And this is valiant Richard." Sir Geoffrey waits eagerly for the reply.

"In truth ,my lord, it is perhaps too soon to say."

"Are you afraid? Of the training – the tournament – I mean."

Richard looks uncertainly towards Pieter and then back again; "Aye sir, right in my boots." He speaks firmly and holds the old man's gaze with his own. "That is, if I had any."

"And yet you will still do it? For – " he pauses " – for honour?"

"No, my lord, for my mother, and for the injustice done her."

Hastings smiles. "It is as fair a commission as anything in the old poetry." He takes Richard by the arm. "Don't dwell too hard on silly things like boots and hose, they are two a penny; it is mettle we shall need for this business."

"And I'm Piers! Pacificus says that I'm to be his squire." He beams at the old man in such a way that the dimples in his cheeks recall something of those former childish features which seem to daily slip away.

"Does he indeed?" Hastings says, "And do you think you will be able to help your brother up when he is in full armour?"

"Oh, yes sir! I'm always helping him up, and I can mend things too – like your doublet, my lord; I could mend it on the elbows where it is worn."

"Piers!" Beth gasps in horror, but Lord Hastings bursts into uproarious laughter.

"By my oath, I had forgotten how much mirth young people bring to a house! Young man, you may fix my doublets and darn my stockings all you like."

Pieter clears his throat. "I stay too long by you; I'll be going."

"You will not take some food?"

"I have plenty, my lord."

"Yes, of course, well, I'll get my men to collect your baggage."

"It is just this bag sir," Richard says, holding up a sack.

"Yes. Well, Hobbs will deliver it to your rooms."

Pieter kisses Richard, Piers and Beth in turn and blesses them as if he might never see them again. He savours their long embraces, and then turns Tinky round towards the king's highway. When he is out of site, Beth shoots Richard a wide-eyed glance, *rooms!*

On entering the hall, Lord Hastings apologises that he no longer keeps enough servants to assign them one each. They are shown to their rooms by Hobbs, the older of the two retainers from the gate. He is missing an ear and has a scar halfway down a bristly, square jaw. He answers nothing to Piers' excited chit-chat and Richard's questions, but leaves them at the door to their room with a solemn nod of his head.

The lads pause awkwardly and glance at each other, then find the resolution to enter the huge, oak paneled bedroom with its roaring fire and sizeable four-poster bed.

Beth has an adjoining room with more feminine decoration, though the paper showing apricots and pear motifs is now peeling under the embossed plaster ceiling. When it was hung nearly a decade ago, at Sir Geoffrey's granddaughter's insistence, it was the latest thing – and a necessity when trade slumped with Catholic Europe after the king's break with Rome, and hangings like this became harder to obtain. But the damp is hard to remedy on these north-facing rooms and Sir Geoffrey's family visit so seldom now that the rooms are not often aired. She is waited on by Hannah, a maid about her own age, and though the rooms are adjoining, Beth bathes separately – so much hot water, just to herself! She and Hannah do not talk much at first, for the relationship is uncertain, but Hannah tells her this has been his Lordship's daughter's room originally. There are, as she puts it, "dresses to spare in the wardrobe, and his Lordship says you should wear what you please – and if none please you, we should send to Norwich for a tailor."

Meanwhile the mute attentions of Hobbs are replaced by Jenkins – a slight man with a pinched face, no chin and eyes weary as a judge and watery as a fish. He lingers in the doorway, and is only too quick to tell Richard and Piers that he usually only serves his Lordship. Not quite taking the meaning, Piers beams at him. "Well, good for you Jenkins, and isn't he a nice man? He says I can darn his stockings and sew his sleeves, if I want."

From the look on Jenkins' face you might have deduced he had just been told his deceased mother was being exhumed and gibbetted: "When his Lordship is home he wears what he finds comfortable." The wide-eyed look of effrontery turns sour. "And he doesn't like people meddling with his affairs."

Before Piers can say anything more Richard steps between them and enquires where they might dry their clothes. Piers says he will rig up a drying rack near the fire, but Jenkins cuts him short. "No, young sir, there is no need. I will remove the articles and bring something suitable when you have bathed."

When they are finally alone, Piers bursts out laughing. "What a face, looks like it's been through Sarah's mangle."

"Shhh, will you? He might be listening!" Richard casts a glance across at the windows, the heraldic crests on the friezes and the plasterwork on the ceiling. "Did you think it would be this grand?"

"No, it's bigger than those houses in Antwerp – makes Hamberly's place look like our woodshed! I can't wait to explore the park. Pacificus says they have their own tilt yard for jousting – can you imagine it?"

"Just remember, Piers, to behave like Pacificus told you – watch and learn."

Piers agrees, and soon they hear the creaking on the stairs as Jenkins returns with their new clothes: clean woolen stockings and hose, linen shirts and thick, tanned doublets more threadbare than his Lordship's. "These," Jenkins says, speaking through his nose, "are for the field and for the yard, when there is no company – you may mend these," he says to Piers, "as you wish."

"Now, gentlemen, rise when a lady enters." Lord Hastings is easing himself from his chair by the fire in the withdrawing room. The brothers have well-nigh forgotten that their Beth is a lady as well as just their sister. She has chosen an overgown of black-on-green floral silk, trimmed with bands of black velvet and fur at the cuffs. Kirtle, cap, chemise and belt are all embroidered with lace or silk brocade, but not jewelled like two others she had seen. For the first time in a long time, Piers is silent. Lord Hasting bows: "Like this, gentlemen, right arm sweeping gently back, feet thus, left arm thus, head tilted thus, and eyes attentive – then averted in deference – like so. The brothers try and Beth tries unsuccessfully not to laugh.

"No, Piers. You may look a little but then avert your gaze."

"But why?"

The old man welcomes the question and, as he speaks, goes slowly through the process again: "Because in the first instance, woman to us is the most beautiful thing God has made – "

"She is very beautiful," Piers mumbles, "but what if she weren't?"

" – therefore you may look on her and thank God. And in the second instance, you look away and so admit that she is not a treasure to be possessed like gold or silver – and even if you hold her heart as a man does a wife, then it is with open hands, for she is God's creature first. And we doff our caps and bow, for her lot has been a hard one since the fall. Now try again, both of you."

They do so, this time with marginally more success. Beth curtsies too, and with such ease in her new gown that Lord Hastings claps his hands together, "My dear lady Elizabeth, I believe we'll have less trouble with you than your brothers!" He rests a bony hand on Piers shoulder. "Though fret not Piers, we have several months ahead of us, and we shall put some weight on this brother of yours, and learn how to live, work and breathe these new ways. And we shall train those whiskers on his lip into a proper *moustachio!* But now let us eat before those hose fall from your waist."

And so begins their education in etiquette. That day they eat mainly venison, which seems a staple for the household. Jenkins serves them in the small dining room with a view over the deer park beyond the moat. Lord Hastings says that they will ride everyday, learn to hunt, use various firearms and even falcon. But then adds, "when the yard is cleared, of course." But only as though it might need Jenkins to take a broom to clear leaves and cobwebs.

Richard particularly must near enough live on horses from day to day, and when reins are not in his hand, a sword must be. "Many a joust will be settled with steel. I will show you how to bring your opponent to ground and hammer him to submission, or at least Hobbs will."

"He doesn't say much," Richard remarks.

"He has no tongue." Seeing the children's aghast faces, he adds, "It does not do to be too free with your opinions in our modern day, as I'm sure you already understand. At least he never used his hand to write anything seditious, for I don't know what I would do without a swordsman of his skill."

No more is said about Hobbs that day, but Hastings – who insists they all call him Sir Geoffrey – turns the conversation to Beth's training. "I have taken the liberty of sending for my niece Mary, the daughter of my sister in Napoli, an accomplished young woman. Perhaps too *Italianate* in manner and dress than I would like, but doubtless all the more pleasing to the English court fir it."

Beth speaks more properly and demurely than Richard has ever know her to, "I hope I have not brought her away from an important position."

"What, Mary? No, no, she was lady-in-waiting to a minor Medici, but her mother wanted her back here before some amorous but penniless Florentine claimed her affections – it's anything for romance over there – and besides, it is very likely that the Pope will have Francis and Charles invade England soon – but don't say I said so – and we don't want her mistaken for a spy."

Beth replaces a bread crust on her plate, swallows, and says, "I shall look forward to making her acquaintance."

"Spoken like a lady! I'm sure you will take to each other famously."

Whatever Sir Geoffrey might have said about riding in the park every day, when they rise the next morning the brothers are told they must first prepare the tilt yard. Sir Geoffrey tells them at breakfast that Hobbs will see them there, and that they are to wear their oldest clothes, but says nothing more.

Venturing out, they find a crisp morning but with no sign of frost and the wind stilled. Peaty smoke from the estate cottages lingers in long trails at a certain height about the thatching. The tilt yard, behind the estate buildings and cottages, has long fallen into disuse; the wood railings and seating – mostly broken - have fungi growing from them, and the ground is knee-deep in the dried grass and weeds from successive year's of uncut growth. When they arrive, they see Hobbs on his own, wearing only a shirt and hose, holding a mattock, a shovel and a long rake in one of his square fists. He is waiting near the dividing rail and beckons them with a gesture of the head. Hobbs hands Piers the mattock, and Richard the rake, and then sets off towards the far end of the yard.

"Don't like the look of this," Piers says.

"Shush! Just follow and do what he wants – for mother, remember?"

They follow and soon see what is intended. Hobbs digs a layer of growth and soil away to expose the sand that once cushioned the falls of Sir Geoffrey and his sons, and perhaps many more knights going back even further. Once they are shown the sand underneath Hobbs goes back to digging, and the brothers follow suit. Piers swings the mattock to break the surface, Hobbs uses his powerful shoulders to force the spade under the debris and to lift it up, and Richard drags it, and the remaining soil away into piles. The work is painstaking and slow. Within the first hour, both brothers are sweating profusely, steam rising from foreheads and backs into the sharp air. By the end of the first morning their hands are blistered and backs aching as if they'd never done a day's work in their lives – which is not the case. Pieter made them work hard, but he himself is aged, slow and no hard taskmaster. Back at the cottage this sort of heavy work would have had the help of Pieter's cob, Tinky. At one point Piers starts to say so, but Richard silences him with a stern look.

By next morning both of them feel as if they have been beaten with clubs, and roll out of bed to the dismal knowledge that the yard is only one-third cleared.

Beth, who has been reading, binds their blisters and tries to be encouraging even to Piers. Sir Geoffrey suggests an application of vinegar, and he adds cheerfully that Hobbs used to swear by his piss as a sovereign remedy for blisters, though he himself has never tried such a treatment.

The brothers work on the yard morning and afternoon for another five days, eating their midday meal there, returning only in the evenings to see Beth and Sir Geoffrey. The exercise does nothing for their manners, for they eat like horses, and sleep like kings. Sir Geoffrey will not hear anything against Hobbs, that he drives them too hard, or that he is sullen. "No, I trust Hobbs to know what is best – he has his ways you know." They're in this together, Piers thinks. He's right, of course.

By the end of the week their hands are hardened and their backs stiffened like steel. Piers, who all week is also made to carry every barrelful of debris to the dump, is ruddy like a damson. At first he can manage only a barrow three-quarters full, but gradually his legs are strengthened to take more. By the end of the week he can lift a full load piled high. The raking tests and tears the muscles of Richard's belly, but as he goes on, they become hard as iron.

In the second week, just when they think they are ready to don peplum doublets and go hawking, Sir Geoffrey announces that Hobbs has decided the railings and barriers in the yard are unsound. The brothers glance at each other across the table. They see another week of toil ahead, and they are right. Trees must be cut with axes, sawn and split into rails, all carried from the park by hand to the yard. Hobbs insists that Richard does his fair share of the work, and never lets up on him. If it's not the saw, it's the adze or draw knife.

His upper arms receive no rest day on day as the trees are cut, split and shaved into shape. And in all this Hobbs takes a lusty part too, working on and on like a mill; face riven and cracked like an old saddlebag, eyes as resolute as the blue-grey flint of the barn walls. He does as much work as both brothers together. His corner-gaze is always on them, his hand ready to instruct them in the use of the tools, and yet he never once smiles with his mouth or eyes. They work when he works and break when he breaks; that much is established the week before, when he dragged an exhausted Piers back to his feet and made him carry on. Quite naturally he becomes a source of intrigue to the brothers – his mute displeasure, his acrid sweat, his indifferent manner. Whenever he answers nature's call, Piers prods his brother to watch whether it is true what Sir Geoffrey had said. But they never see him piss on his hands for all that. "Perhaps Sir Geoffrey meant that he drinks it," Piers whispers under his breath.

They fix the new posts and rails in place, and then set about fashioning the pell training post, and the quintain. For the pell they select a young oak. Richard, adept by now, reduces it to a ten-foot post of about twelve inches girth. It is set into a four-foot deep hole, dug and back-filled by Piers. Upon this post, they will attach various objects over the months, and Richard will practice his strokes on it unrelentingly, using a long oak baton, whale bone or sword – the same strokes he has been hardening his body to deliver, working with the axe and mattock.

The quintain, another oak post with a revolving cross-beam, has a shield at one end and a sandbag as counterweight at the other. Hobbs has them fix it by the guardrail late one evening, working on after sundown to get it in place.

The day after brings welcome rest and relief: Sunday. Attired in their best clothes alongside Sir Geoffrey in his and the servants in theirs, they attend the small church at the centre of the village.

All eyes are on them, the little children chatter, the maidens admire's Beth's dress with little nods and whispers behind their hands. Beth had wrestled with her brothers about whether they should go or not. The week before they had been to the first Mass they had heard in a few years. Some Anabaptists would not have done so – Pieter for example – but their parents always had.

"What they did, they did as unto the Lord," Pieter had said one night, "there is no disgrace in that. Did not Naaman the Syrian say he would really be bowing to the Lord when his king leant on his arm at worship in the temple of Rimmon? But let each decide beforehand for himself, for the time will surely come."

It had come, and the three of them felt easy enough as they stood with Sir Geoffrey at the front before the altar rail. Richard spends some time looking at the fresco of Saint George slaying the dragon, and contemplating his own appointment with destiny. To the left of the dragon, just above the chancel arch, is the king's daughter, chained ready for the dragon to eat. The paint is peeling around her hair and dress, but Saint George's lance strikes true, piercing the creature's throat. Dear God, he thinks, Mother would be much affrighted – nay, and sore displeased – to think of me with a lance and a dragon for her sake! Still, it's not her choice, it's mine. He looks again from the maniacal eyes of the dragon to the steely piety of Saint George. I know Piers could do it if he were older, but me?

Beth observes him from the corner of her eye, sees the muscles - hard as knots - flex at the base of his neck above the neckline of his chemise, and the uncertainty in the wideness of his eyes. She reaches and takes his arm, waits for the muscles to relax before giving them a reassuring squeeze, then glowers hard at Piers who is picking his nose, again.

An hour later they are leaving the churchyard and heading back to the hall. Sir Geoffrey is quiet today, there is something on his mind. When they pass through the gatehouse, Hobbs tilts his head in the direction of the courtyard. They follow his ominous stare to see two carriages and eight chestnut mares resting at their reins.

"Here already." He sighs, then turns to Beth. "I had been hoping for another week at least."

"Who is it?"

"My niece. With company it seems – unless the second carriage is for her wardrobe, which I suppose is possible."

26

Arise a Knight

Dimidium facti qui coepit habet
He who has begun, has the work half done

"Uncle Hastings!" Mary de Hastings bustles through the open doorway followed by footmen carrying baggage of every description. Poor Jenkins, deferentially bent low as a croquet hoop, gets a face full of silk as she pushes past.

"Mary," Lord Hastings steps forward with open arms. "Little Mary."

"*Maria*, please uncle! Mary sounds so plain." A flurry green silk and purple taffeta sweeps across the hall.

"The roads!" She exclaims, laying an effected hand upon her ample *décolletage* - a bosom which the farthingale has elevated into a horizontal platform for storing pearls. Heaving once more from under her taut bodice the ample brunette repeats the words, "The roads! Upon my word, the roads, uncle! Simply terrible! I know not how you travel at this time of year, how you even live here, really I don't; I thought we'd never get here. Poor Simpson had to dig us out two-and-twenty times. I thought I would lose my wardrobe. Ah – " She wheels towards Beth " – and these must be the relatives of your friend Erpingham, wasn't it? Yes, that was it. And very pretty too, I begin to be jealous – "

Sir Geoffrey seizes the brief opportunity while she draws breath, to interject, "Yes, quite so. May I present Lady Elizabeth's kin?"

Richard and Piers give their names and bow as they have been taught. At this, and their courtly manners, Maria turns her head aside to sniff at the thyme pomander attached to her wrist, "Upon my word, you never said they were so handsome!"

And then in a trice she slaps her uncle on the chest with her glove: "I suppose this is all a ploy between you and Father to get me to forget my Giovanni? Well, I won't! There, now I've said it, and it's made me flustered, come Lady Elizabeth, let us retire to my *camera da letto*; men are such cruel creatures!"

She leads Beth up the stairs, cloak and all, followed by the eyes of all and servants under the weight of baggage. When they are safely ensconced behind the deep, oak door of the bedroom, Beth offers commiserations over Giovanni. But to her surprise, Maria backs up against the door and giggles, "Him! Just a boy – a pretty one I grant, but I care not a groat for him; only it is good for my father to think so."

"Your father?"

"*Leveraggio!* You know, *il sistema di leve? La influenza?* Oh Elizabetta, how little you know men, and how much I shall have to teach you – of the *Ars Amatoria*! Leverage; last resort of the weaker sex." She walks Beth solemnly to the bed where they sit as she continues the first of her lectures. But gone now is the affected girlishness; Maria is quite herself again – calm, calculating and clever. "My dear Elizabeth, I knew from the first glance that you were innocent in these things and I should help you where I can. Men like to think they are in control of their wives and daughters; this is a well-known fact, they cannot help it. And so long as it may be a thought and not indeed reality, then we may all live peaceably and both have what we want."

"You – you make it sound like they are at war." Beth is no fool either, but allows the supposition of innocence to pass unchallenged, not saying what she thinks; that it is only the rich who have leisure for such folly – the poor family stands shoulder to shoulder against the ravages of poverty and caprice of *Fortuna*.

"Oh, but it is indeed a kind of battle."

"And your Giovanni?"

"Ah!" She gasps dramatically, "Dear *Giovanni Bernabe Angelo Fragoso Umberto* – such a divine face he has, and such eyes!"

"And such a name!" They both giggle.

"Yes, Fragoso means strawberry, can you believe it? They do not stint in munificence, take it very seriously in fact, but be that as it may and despite his divine looks, Giovanni would be as good as any penniless youth – and a good deal better than most – to inflame my father so that he will offer me almost anything I want in this miserable, cold island."

"And what is it that you want?"

"Ah, you have found me out, for of that I am not sure just yet, but I shall look about me in London and think on it well."

She glances about the room, speaking now in a more expectant tone. "In the meantime I shall make Father suffer anguish at my pining until he yields like Samson. Ha! Perhaps I shall like your brother Richard – has he a fortune? But here am I, talking of only myself; what of you? I see from your hands that your life has not been devoted solely to embroidery."

Beth at first tries to cover the hands she thought she had kept so well from view, but then she opens them. The ingrained staining amongst the calluses will wear out in time. It is senseless to hide them now. "Does it shock you?"

"My dear, I have lived in Florence, nothing shocks me. You may count on my discretion. Uncle Hastings said little to me but that I might be of some use. Verily, he seemed so guarded in his words that it peeked my curiosity so I came all the quicker. So say on."

Beth tells her as much as she dare; the leprosy of her father, the incarceration of her mother and their quest at the tournament.

Maria listens, hand on chest, enthralled by all. "Oh my dear Elizabeth! It's like something from Chrétien or Boccaccio – how perfectly extraordinary! We must do what we can for your mother. Oh my dear, I know not what to say to you. It is unspeakable, you poor dear creature. The king is not given to clemency, I am told, that he grows irascible with age and ulcers. But there is more than one way to get round a king. Come my dear, do not look at your hands so. You are of a noble and ancient house and you shall hold that head high – only thank God I am here to help you."

In the morning, the day being dry if overcast, Sir Geoffrey takes them all out hunting in the park with goshawks, and again in the afternoon, with hounds. He says that they have worked hard enough and that now is the time for a little sportive diversion. The park is mostly beech plantations with pockets of oak on the higher ground, and the occasional welcome glade.

Hobbs sees to it that Richard has the type of destrier he will ride at the tournament, a sulky warhorse named Hammer – broad as a mill and built like a forge. It takes Richard all his energy to master the creature, which itself affords Maria much amusement: "How seriously he takes it all – see how his cheeks flush."

Richard says nothing in reply to her coquettish teasing, but anyone can see he doesn't like it. Hobbs doubles as Hastings' falconer. He rides with other ruddy-faced retainers, jingling with the bells of the hooded gyrfalcon they hold. "It is the biggest of the falcons," Sir Geoffrey says, "and a fine hunter too."

Maria will not handle the hawks. "Let them play their games," she says to Beth, "we have other matters to discuss."

But the brothers enjoy working with the birds, especially Piers, who looks every inch the page with his falconer's purse swishing about his belt as he swivels erratically to follow the progress of his hawk. When his bird brings down a hare, he is almost wild with excitement. Richard notices Hobb's approving smile at the bird's prowess, for it was a feisty hare.

The afternoon is even better in Richards and Piers' estimation. The dogs are brought up by other men, bloodhounds for their noses, greys for their speed. Sir Geoffrey checks the thick collar on his favourite bitch: "There m'lady, we won't have any boar goring your throat, will we?" She basks in the attention, but is eager to join the pack when the horses stamp their feet for the chase. They eventually corner a boar near a rocky outcrop in an oak glade. The creature's screams are hideous, loud above the fearless yelps and lunges of the dogs. Sir Geoffrey and Richard dispatch it with bolts from their crossbows, Hobbs making doubly sure with his spear. They strap the boar to Richard's horse. It takes four of them to get it up there. Later, they bring down two red deer, before returning contented to the house.

At nightfall they enjoy the spoils of the hunt, and each other's company. Beth begins to like Maria; not because she flirts with Richard – though he doesn't notice – or fusses over Piers as her "bambino', but that she has never treated her ill, or mentioned again their existence on the marsh. She is even forward with Hannah, including her with an easy air, into all sorts of matters that shouldn't be spoken of before servants. Maria is a bad influence, Beth can see that much, but she has a tender side too and seems, at least for now, to be devoted to the Erpingham and Fenton cause. They share a bed, and though she sees Beth reading her heretical Bible, she never derides her or threatens to tell her uncle. In fact, on one occasion she even expresses curiosity, for the idea of reading contraband material seems very romantic and mischievous to her, though she takes it no further. For of this, as of many continental intrigues, Maria knows a great deal more than she lets on.

Richard starts his training the day following. Sir Geoffrey is pleased by their work in the tilt yard, and says so repeatedly. For the next two weeks the days settle into a routine; Richard and Piers cut wood before breaking their fast, then Richard rides and target-jousts until lunch, the afternoon being given over to sword training and hunting.

The initial results are not encouraging; Richard is too wooden in the saddle and his lance bounces up and down like a willow wand. "God help us all," Sir Geoffrey says to Hobbs as they lean on the new rails, "bolt upright in the saddle like a bloody venetian. You've got some work to do here Hobbs – keep at it man."

Richard blanches under the pained glances at the edge of the yard. Every look, every missed ring or shield and every fall crushes the confidence he had had the week before. They are trying to turn ten years of training into near enough ten weeks. Hacking at wood is one thing, this is quite another. He is wearing Hobb's old almain rivet, a half suit of armour with no cradle for the back end of the lance. They keep saying, sometimes none too convincingly, that his new suit of armour will make all the difference. After another hefty fall, and lying on his back winded once again, Richard is praying desperately that they are right.

One wet spring afternoon, Pacificus brings Will Short to measure Richard for his own armour. His son Tom has come too, and Mark's half-sister Margaret, for a cart was needed to carry all the equipment, and one more aboard was no great matter. Pacificus is riding Percival again, for the prior has hurt his leg in a fall.

Beth runs to them at the outer gate, and in turn Margaret runs to her. They only clasp hands, Margaret gazing wide-eyed and avowing she won't soil Beth's velvet gown with her dingy marsh weeds, but soon the two young women are all but running to the tilt yard to see the brothers. This whole scene is observed by Maria from an upper window.

"Wait 'til Richard sees you – how long can you stay? And the babe –

how is the babe? You shouldn't travel, but oh, it is so good to see you, and I've so much to tell!"

Then, rounding the yard she exclaims, "Richard! Look who has come!"

Richard rides towards them, his hair rising and falling with Hammer's heavy gait. At first he does not dismount, but just beams down at them from the saddle. His sister chides him and he is soon down with his gloves off, offering a courteous welcome. They talk about Pieter and Sarah, the cottage and livestock. Beth does all the talking, firing questions at Margaret who remains uncharacteristically demure in her one or two word responses.

In a pause, Richard gets a word in to ask: "And you, Margaret? You are well I see, and the child?" He points to her belly, which is now unmistakably rounded.

"It goes well," she says, nodding and looking to the ground, "and I please the mistress a little more day by day, though she gives me less and less to do!" She glances at Richard and smiles.

"And nor should you do more during your confinement." Richard says, adding, "Everyone knows that."

"But there is much to do this time of year, as you well know – "

"And Pieter can do it," Richard chides, "I mean, he can with Pacificus and Mark's help when they are able to come."

"And does he?" Beth butts in.

"Does who?" Margaret says.

"Mark, does he come to help?"

"Sometimes, when he can."

"And is he well?"

"Yes, why would he not be?"

"No reason," Beth says quickly, "but I am glad – that he is well, in health – and useful about the place." She swallows and is thankful to see Piers approaching. "Ah! And look, here is Piers to say hello. Come, greet Margaret – and pull your hose up."

Will and Tom Short bring their cart round to a small smithy in the stable yard, where they will be making wax moulds of Richard's limbs. Pacificus talks through the progress with Sir Geoffrey and observes Richard working the destrier about the yard.

"He has flanks like a four-mast carrack."

"Well, we feed the lad plenty."

"Not the lad – the horse!" Pacificus turns to see the old man chuckling. "I'm serious; Richard's legs stick out like oars, he'll need another. He should have Prior Thomas' charger Percival – more biddable too."

"I take it you mean the horse!"

"The prior will not mind, if a benefactor of the abbey needs it, and will ride in the tournament, and – " Pacificus casts an eye at the burly destrier in the yard. "He'd welcome a chance to master this horse of yours, just as soon as his leg mends."

"And if Richard is unhorsed and the horse is forfeit, would your prior be so happy then?" Sir Geoffrey says.

"That I will not contemplate for now, nor should you, my lord."

"He's no natural in the saddle." Sir Geoffrey warns.

"You yet have ten weeks, have faith."

"When will the armourer be ready for a fitting?"

"By Corpus Christi, which falls late this year, end of June."

"Unless our sovereign lord abolishes the feast along with all the others. I hear Henry has given a dispensation that we need not observe the Lenten fast this spring, for there are no fish in the sea."

"His first act as Pope!"

"It's the finger of God, that's what it is, no fish in the sea, mark my words." Sir Geoffrey glances across to the ominous clouds pouring across the eastern sky, "Is it true that Anabaptists and sectaries will be given ten days to leave the country? For this is what I hear is to be read out next Sabbath in all churches." Pacificus nods with that stern grimace which means he's digging his heels in about something. "Hugh?" Sir Geoffrey gives him a fatherly stare, "You are going to tell Beth and the brothers, aren't you? It's not too late for them to take a different course. Ah, I see, you will not! Hugh, this is a dangerous game you play, my friend."

"I don't see what is *not* dangerous right now, and anyway, it is not certain yet what they really are. And even if they were, they are safer here."

"Really? You're not just saying that for your own sake?"

"My sake?"

"I had forgotten what it was to have young people in the house, they fill a void." He lets the last words linger, but Pacificus is too defensive.

"My lord, if they travel abroad, the Lutherans and Calvinists will flay them, burn or drown them. No, I say, they are better here, for there is no safe place for them while this madness lasts; 'tis their best hope."

"Their best hope is to be won to the truth faith," Sir Geoffrey kisses a crucifix that hangs loose inside his doublet. "They took the sacrament on Sunday last, you know."

Pacificus does not answer this straight away, but eventually he breathes out hard and long, letting his cheeks fill with air. "And what pray is *that* in these days - *true faith?* Will we cling to Rome, hoping all her corruption will be made white as snow? By my oath, you say these Anabaptists are fanatics, and perhaps they are, but at least their hands are clean!" With this, Pacificus raises his own hands slightly. "They may have no place to lay their heads, but at least they may sleep with a virgin conscience."

"Take care, Hugh! I know you Erpinghams have Lollard blood in you! My own grandfather – God rest him – used to warn us against 'Sir Thomas Erpingham and that damned heretic Wycliff,' and now here we are come full circle."

Pacificus tries to interject but Sir Geoffrey persists. "Take care I say – and this is all I ask, for your father's sake – that you know exactly *for what cause* you rebel, before you say too much to others."

"Aye, and there's the rub, for surely I know not what I'd reform first – myself I suppose – but, dear God, who can do even that much?" The tightness in Pacificus subsides and he raises his head toward the sky.

Sir Geoffrey continues as if he had not heard. "I say it as a friend of your father, and yours too I hope." He lays a paternal hand on his drooping shoulder. "Ah lad, I would that you could find some peace, only be wise; some threads once pulled unravel the whole garment; do not damn the church to justify yourself. You Erpinghams are stubborn as any Tudor, so just be sure, that is all I say. You know the monk William Letton was burned in Norwich this month, I suppose."

"Should have kept his mouth closed." Pacificus winces and then pinches the bridge of his nose, wiping the journey's dust from his eyes. "Perhaps I should too. Will we have war with the emperor?"

"Our friend, de la Pole, will persuade the Pope no doubt, but whether he can persuade Charles and Francis to mount a campaign, well, of this I am less sure. Perhaps he will, perhaps it would be best. I cannot say. The king has dealt a mortal blow to England as it is. I am a torn, Hugh, that I am."

Invasion? Pacificus ponders the dread thought for a moment. No, he thinks, that ribbon of water between us and them is a mocker of generals, *condotierres* and land armies, makes everything twice the cost and thrice the risk. After a morose pause, in which both men observe the abyss which is before their nation, they shake their heads, thanking God that they will likely be dead soon anyway, and then walk arm in arm to the yard. They talk about preparations for the tournament in Norwich. Pacificus tells of his planning with the bishop, and the various expressions of torment present on Old Norfolk's face when Rugge gives the estimates for the ever-expanding budget. Sir Geoffrey chuckles. "I wish I had been there, truly I do."

Pacificus steps over towards the centre rail and takes Hammer by the reins. Richard removes his helmet, revealing a crestfallen face. "I am trying, but – "

"But nothing, young knight, you fare well for a beginner." He yanks the horse's head down and slaps its shoulder. "Now listen, I will leave Percival here when I return tomorrow, and take this plough horse to cheer Prior Thomas. Keep running at the rings until..."

"But I cannot keep the lance straight."

"Your new armour will have a lance cradle – "

"That's what *they* say, but even so, my body is all over the place."

"Yes, I see that, so put the stirrups more on the ball of your feet and absorb the rise and fall in your knees. Keep the lance higher and bring it down little by little as you near the quintain. That's good practice, cradle or no." He steadies the restless beast with another stiff tug.

"Richard, away with that face, I'll have none of it. You would not be here if I did not know you could do it; remember that."

By late afternoon, Will Short is ready to take the casts of Richard's legs and waist. Maria and Beth are told to leave. "It would not be seemly for ladies," Sir Geoffrey insists. But Margaret is not thought to be in danger and so stays to help. Richard is exceedingly ticklish, and Tom's application of hessian and plaster onto his bare skin causes him to double up. It takes a stern word from Tom's father, and an even sterner word from Margaret, to eventually calm him down. She sends Piers straight outside, for he is partly to blame for it, always prodding and making merry. In the end it is she who applies and smooths the plaster about his calves and loins, and him too embarrassed to say anything as he stands and lets her do it. Only on one occasion does he let out that sort of pent-up sigh of a man whose mind is elsewhere. She looks up from his thighs where she is working and says to him with characteristic directness: "Richard Fenton, you will ride and vanquish all at Norwich, and win your mother too; now trust in God – and hold still!"

"It's getting hot." Richard says.

"Aye. Plaster's curing, ain't it, father?" Tom says.

"That it is, won't be long now lad," Will says. "Go fetch me the razor Tom goes out to the cart, thrilled to see a look in his father's eyes that he has not seen since he was a small boy, since the Greenwich days.

Margaret, who cannot sit idly by for anything, even proves a help with the razors. They must cut through an inch of plaster but not past the hessian lining into the skin. "You'd better let me do it, better a woman's hands than a blacksmith's. I'm a good seamstress, you know."

"Well miss, you'll need to be if you go beyond the hessian."

Will gives her the scalpel and tells her to keep to the lines he has drawn in charcoal. He waits with bated breath as she goes to work, only breaking the silence when she nears his groin. "Peradventure, a little slower round there, that is if you want him to sire you any more children."

Margaret snaps, "It's not his! It's just mine."

Will raises an apologetic hand, "Oh, I'm sorry miss, only you seemed so…so…well, it doesn't matter, only in that case perhaps you'd prefer not to – "

Her hand is trembling now and her cheeks flushed with embarrassment. She dares not look up at Richard. "Yes, perhaps I ought not." But no sooner are the words said than she feels his hand on hers and his voice say softly, almost lightheartedly, "There is no need, she is nearly finished. And look, she has not hurt me yet; let her finish. Only, be gentle with me, maid." She still does not look up, but rather arranges her lips and nods slightly. He shouldn't call me that; he should say it as it is. Later that night, while she is eating in the servants' hall with Will and Tom, she silently thinks on it all. She hears the sounds of revelry and dancing upstairs, the stamping of boards, the sounds of a lute every now and again drifting down the corridor. But then her lips and eyebrows tighten. Richard is kind, she thinks, but he's an innocent fool. Nevertheless, she attends him the next day when they cast his torso, head and arms; attending him like a widow would a corpse, all the time fighting her own battles with rejection and cynicism. Before the mask is made, Richard talks of life back on the marsh, the work he misses, Pieter and Sarah. She says nothing, which he doesn't notice, but she's scolding him inside. You'll never come back to us, Richard Fenton; don't you know that yet?

"He's in good shape, I'll give you that my lord." Pacificus observes Richard working over the pell training post. "He swings that broad sword like a fire poker!"

"My dear Hugh, you may thank Hobbs for that. He has his ways, you know!"

"As do you. I should like to see him spar with Hobbs; you say he is an able swordsman, this retainer?"

"He is. Very."

"But with a war sword, I mean, not one of these Spanish rapiers?"

"Yes, you will see him. Hobbs...Hobbs!"

The swords are brought and Hobbs puts on an even older, rustier rivet than the one he has leant Richard. The two of them spar, Hobbs going easy for Richard's sake, Richard striking high forehand and back, as if he were still chopping wood. When Hobbs does retaliate with counter thrusts and attacks, Richard is easily thrown by the aggression.

Pacificus steps in with advice during their respite. "Very well, masters. Now Richard, hear you this; you will doubtless be the lightest on the field and for that you must be the hardiest and fittest. Master Hobbs will teach you to absorb – with your sword, not your armour – the worst any knight can throw at you."

Pacificus takes Richard's sword. Standing close and speaking more softly he says, "And when their brief strength is spent, you will step forward and lay such blows on them as Saint Michael's strength will give you."

He beckons Hobbs. "Come, Hobbs and I will show you." Hobbs looks uneasily towards Lord Hastings; the monk has no armour. But Sir Geoffrey nods to him.

They stand apart from the others, who watch agog. Piers sits up high on the side rail, eyes out on stalks. Pacificus is weighing the blade and loosening his wrists. "A few small strokes if you please, Master Hobbs, until I give you leave; then you may bear down on me like a wild boar."

After three peremptory strikes Pacificus is happy, for this much he loves; the intimacy of aggression, arm for arm, steel for steel, mettle for mettle. Let the paper princes of Europe glory in the *combat à plaisance*, blunted blades, goblets of wine and fine ladies; give him *combat a l'outrance* any day – make a man feel alive. With a fierce glint in his eye, he shouts, "Right, man; give me your fury!"

Hobbs now flies at him with a raft of fast, heavy blows, the speed and ferocity of which causes Piers to fall from the rail. Pacificus catches each one high and near the hilt. Hobbs comes again, this time with twice as many strokes and sparks flying. With confidence now that this strange monk can defend himself, he lays blows even towards his head.

Sir Geoffrey is clasping his beard and mouth; this could go very wrong. But Pacificus holds his ground, thus denying Hobbs the advantage of putting the weight of a forward step into each new blow. By the third onslaught it is clear even Hobbs is weakening, and it is now Pacificus that steps forward with counter blows, after a few of which he ceases and turns to Richard. "Did you see, Richard? Step forward to receive the blow high before it has gained force, and let it run to your hilt where you are stronger. Deny him ground as soon as he weakens, and then move in when he is spent." After a few breaths he adds, "And remember, it will be strikes on the armour that get you points, but by all means hammer him into the ground if you can."

He thanks Hobbs and takes him by the arm. "I am not as fit as I should be master. Train him hard; he must learn to attack a man as he attacks the pell post."

When Pacificus is walking across to the stable for Hammer, Sir Geoffrey questions him about the need for sword training. "Surely most of the knights of quality will only be jousting? If he will appear before the king, then surely jousting will be enough?"

"I have my reasons, Sir Geoffrey, but I'd prefer to keep them between me and his page for now." He looks over to Piers, who is stroking Percival at his stable door, and he gives the lad a knowing wink. "Short says he has all he needs for now. Let Hobbs work the lad hard, but mind he takes no injury. He says you will see they are shod well for Rugge's Italian masked ball; you will let me know the expense, that I may reimburse you?"

"There is no need. It will be my gift, and my niece will see Beth shines like the star she is."

"Aye, but not too bright; the king still seeks a wife, remember."

"No, Cromwell is working on a German or Flemish alliance, you need not fear for her in that regard, though there are plenty others that her brothers will have to watch for."

"No doubt!" Pacificus takes Sir Geoffrey by the hand. "Well then, until Corpus Christi!"

"God speed you, brother, by God's grace we'll be ready." Aye, by his grace.

"Fare you well, brave knight," Margaret says to Richard from the back of the cart, her tone bravely cheerful. "Don't forget that ribbon for the baby's hair!" She cannot come again for the fitting, nor to the joust for she will be too near her time for travel. Between now and their next meeting – if indeed there be one – she will undergo the uncertain crucible of childbirth, and he the hazards of the tournament.

Richard smiles broadly and approaches the side of the cart, resting his hands on the rail. "That I will, Moll; a blue one for the bairn, and a green one for you too."

Margaret reaches her hand to lay it swiftly on his knuckles. "You bring me nothing but yourself in one piece, you fool!" Shaking and squeezing the top of his hand, she says: "Work hard and win." And then, looking to Piers: "and you keep him safe, you monkey!"

"And you too Moll, God keep you safe, and the bairn, we will pray, won't we sister?"

Beth approaches with Maria, but cannot come too close to the cart for Maria has made her wear a bulbous, pink, Venetian-patterned gown with tied-on sleeves, that show the chemise beneath. Her hair, artfully interwoven with pink ribbons, frames her face in soft waves escaping from her small, draped cap. She wants to go forward to embrace the woman who she feels intuitively is her sister, but dare not for the dress' sake, and something else – the call of her new station, or perhaps Maria's voice in her head, or her more vain self? She is uncertain, still lingering in the two worlds, not wholly claimed by this new one, so flounced with gilt edges and pearl brocade. She fears it will change her, make her untrue to those she loves. She fears this new world and all its pleasures will be stronger than her too. She and Maria curtsey and Beth tries to say with her eyes what her body cannot. As the axles creak under the first pull of the horse, she steps forward awkwardly and says, "of course we will pray daily. God speed and deliver you, Margaret."

Before mounting the cart himself, Pacificus detains Maria as

Richard, Piers and Beth follow slowly to the moat gate. "Lady Mary, I see you have dressed your friend very fine for the afternoon."

"Ah, brother," she observes him with a quiet, yet penetrating eye. "Don't say it. You think I will turn her against her peasant friends."

"You must help her shine at court, not just in vesture but in wit and manners. But I pray you, respect her past, for her future is yet uncertain."

"For you all, I hear."

"Yes, my lady, as you say, *for us all.*"

Maria sighs. "You need not chide me, and I think you do her disservice besides, for she is stronger, and more loyal than you give her credit for. If anything, she will have *me* in woolens and living in a hovel as a heretic outcast 'ere long, never mind aught else."

She catches his look of genuine surprise, then waves her pomander at him provocatively. "Yes, and there is no need to look at me like that. I know what Uncle wants of me. And you need not fear; she will have more book learning than Margaret More before we are finished – and much more *savoir faire* – not that she needs it, with a face and figure like hers, curse her. So leave her with me, and we will be ready for when the court comes to Norwich."

"I thank you for your goodness, my lady." Pacificus bows deferentially, but not too low, for he cannot as yet discern whether she is toying with him.

"Ah, *la mia cavaliere*, I think you know that I am not so dull as to be virtuous: as they say, *bonitas non est pessimis esse meliorem*; but I shall be loyal to my Elizabetta, that I shall!" She flutters her eyelashes and flirts her linguistics his way. But it is all to no obvious avail; she can see this monk is like a rock. So she adds in self-defence, "But listen to me prating on about my virtues, when your party has moved down the king's highway to Norwich! You must away *mon frère* – or should I call you *monsieur*? You are so intriguing!"

He does not yet have the answer to that question. "Adieu, my lady." Pacificus bows.

27

To Norwich

Damnant quodnon intelligunt
They condemn what they do not understand

The warmth of spring brings the promise of a good planting season. It makes up for the dire situation with the sea fishing. Perhaps providence or Fortuna smiles on the Tudor court after all, Pacificus thinks as he paints the doctors of the church on the Ranworth rood screen – perhaps I am fool to even look for portents and omens at such a time as this. He is attempting to paint Augustine's face and wishing he had more of Master Holbein's ability to delineate character. How would Augustine read the times? He lived through the collapse of civilization too. His *City of God* was a firm enough literary response. He stayed with the north African church when he might have fled, and died even as the Vandals were battering down the gates of his city. And what about me? On what hill shall I die? For what, or whom? His mind is never far from the children and their mother.

Further north at Bindringham, the Fentons fair as well as the weather. Each has a birthday within these summer months; Piers turns fifteen, Richard seventeen and Beth eighteen. The early garden blooms shoot forth in the borders and the rosebuds multiply in profusion at the walls and trellises near the moat. Beth's reading and love of verse similarly blossom under the late spring and early summer sun. Her delight is to escape the world under an arbour or behind the topiary figures in the outer gardens. There she feasts on romances, epics and even some religious texts; all in English, for as yet her Latin is small. Often she is dreaming of romances of her own; to be loved as her mother had been, to be the mother of many children that all remained small, and perhaps even to write as Margaret More had done.

Richard lives on Percival or at the pell training post throughout most of the spring and summer. When he sleeps, he still holds the lance, the sword or the reins in his dreams. He grows strong and fast as the weeks roll along, and so too does Piers. The second fitting of armour, a full nine days late, has to be done in the dead of night, without Pacificus present. It shines among the torches like a blue-black beetle, and Richard, who has to be woken from sleep to try it on, feels as though he is still dreaming, that even as he puts it on he is becoming as immortal as Theseus or Achilles. He rubs his eyes, runs his fingers along the curves, rivets and hinges, savours the smell of oil, relishing the gleam of glory.

Will Short laments that Richard cannot see the armour's true glory in the light of day; the acid etch, the bluing, the full effect of the gold inlay. Richard assumes this is an artist's rhetoric, but in Norwich he will see for himself. Master Short is apologetic for the delay – it means Richard will not be able to prove the armour in practice – but his face has the look of a man wholly content. He doesn't need Hobbs and Sir Geoffrey in their nightcaps to tell him what he already knows inside; this is the finest work, perhaps the best, he ever will create.

Richard is not the only one who must undergo the rigours of fitting. Maria, Beth and even Sir Geoffrey and Piers must be measured, pushed, poked, pressed and pinned by the tailors who seem to carry an entire mercer's warehouse compressed into two wagons. Walter Tailor is none too pleased to see that most of his work will be alterations of Maria's farthingales to suit Beth, and that his vast stores of silks and brocade cannot be unloaded at Sir Geoffrey's expense. He is a busy man, don't they know, much in demand among the nobility; it might be a long time before Norfolk will entertain the court again. Sir Geoffrey humours him with regard to his, Richard and Piers' outfits: lush green, blue and brown velvet doublets and cloaks with ornate edgings – all selected at Maria's insistence. "I will not be seen at court with a ragtag bunch of provincials – you especially, Uncle! I have had quite enough of that abroad."

Sir Geoffrey is notorious in the Italian courts for his insistence on appearing at state occasions with all the unkempt appearance of an Athenian Stoic. But today, mostly for the sake of the young people, but also for his departed wife's sake, he bows to their eager evaluations and comparisons with such a smile that Tailor can almost hear the gold angels clinking in his purse.

Maria herself is determined to outdo them all, even to outshine the ladies of the bedchambers and royal closet; she will wear a silk dress over her farthingale in so intense a shade of blue that it is well-nigh purple. "My dear child, it might cause offence, to assume the purple, so to speak," Sir Geoffrey says when she appears on the landing barefoot, wearing it. "We are not the Howards, you know."

"Tush, Uncle, we may not be the mightiest of cedars of Lebanon, but our roots are deep." She swishes this way, then that, rather provocatively, while Hannah tries in vain to gather a loose thread from the hem. "Besides, the king *likes* boldness and sport."

It irks her that he does not answer, but she is soon distracted by Beth giving some instructions to the tailor of which she does not approve. "My Elizaveta," she says in a patronizingly regal tone as she sweeps back into the bedchamber: "*everyone* has the low neckline!"

"But it shows the kirtle and chemise. It is not meet; I feel undressed."

"Perhaps my lady would appreciate the modesty of a partlet? We have sheer or opaque." He shows her a shimmering material and she lays it around her neck and *décolletage* .

The tailor coos encouragingly: "Ooh, yes my lady; it shows the treasure within the veil, the hidden woman of the heart. Oh yes, most comely, most fitting!"

"No!" Maria exclaims, "I say, she shall look like a Genevan!"

"I like it well Master Tailor," Beth pronounces, examining herself in the glass and quite unperturbed, "and if peradventure you might add some velvet or silk to the edging, then it would cover my shoulders too."

"Velvet ruffles with silk edging, my lady, would be most becoming." Tailor is conscious again of the clink, clink as coins drop into his purse.

"Forsooth, sister! Prithee, hear me!" Maria stamps her feet and smacks her own gown with both hands. "If I had your shoulders I would consider it a sin to hide them away! Besides," she continues more softly, seeing Beth's lips tighten in determination, "the young men at court expect a little something for the adoration we merit from them. Be guided by me, prithee; you are innocent in this."

"Aye, and shall remain so. What folly you speak, Mary? A man who adores me for my body alone is not worthy of me. Every woman has shoulders and paps, as every man knoweth right well. So what advantage is there, to render unto him what he has not, by conquest and covenant, a rightful share in."

"Avaunt, you talk as if you are giving away your flower, but I know that look of yours, that stubborn pride. If you insist on having all things your own way, then you shall find fine company among maiden aunts in their flea furs, for surely I shall not be able to introduce you to royalty!"

"Ladies please!" Tailor begs them, "do not argue thus, this is but one of many gowns we must remedy before I take my leave."

"Indeed Maria, as the good tailor says, we have a good many others, as there are days and feasts for the tournament, and I shall let you have your way on most of those."

"Oh, well! Be it as you say," Maria huffs, but in the twinkling of an eye has diverted her attention to ideas for the tournaments and pageants. "Master Tailor, the cuffed sleeves on this other dress – no, not that one, my scarlet one. Yes, if that is for Lady Elizabeth, too – they are too wide; take them in, or else pleat them. And I want to show her wrists if not her shoulders; and I would that you also so arrange it that we may see the decorated over-sleeve attached to this kirtle here."

The tailor scratches notes like a mouse at a floorboard, yet Maria hardly waits for him as she swirls around the bed matching chemises and dresses, caps, hoods, girdles and carcanets. "This must be tucked into the stomacher, and this train gathered up to display the kirtle, for you will agree the fabric is too good to hide – that is, if my fair sister doth not much mind it?"

Beth holds her peace in this and other minor decisions, biding her time against the real possibility of genuine battles later. But, as the afternoon wears on, there is only one other minor skirmish; and that over the sleeves of gowns to be worn at the tournament finals. Beth insists that hers be puffed and cuffed in the traditional way, and will not be persuaded by Maria, who proudly instructs the tailor (still halfway through congratulating Beth on her reserve and taste), "Well, I'm sure I shall not go anywhere looking like someone's grandmother! I shall insist on *la tromba* sleeves."

She is delighted at the tailor's vacant stare and enlightens him, "Forsooth man, *la tromba* – Italian for trumpet? When were you in London last?"

He says he has been very busy, and in the end she has to draw them for him by steaming the window pane. It appears they are well named;

the cuff voluminous and billowing like the end of a trumpet. "They are the very latest in Florence and Cadiz, my dear fellow; you should be more informed if you would prosper!"

To which he bows humbly, suppressing the almost overwhelming urge to ask, 'but with these, how shall my lady eat?'

The Norwich road gets busier as the small cavalcade from Bindringham nears the towns of Hoveton and Wroxham. Piers and Richard ride with Hobbs, while Sir Geoffrey and the ladies are shuffled, stacked and jostled nicely in the carriages, with a separate baggage carriage coming after. The day is hot, even for July, but a breeze from the coast brings welcome refreshment.

They are not the only worthies on the road this day, for the tournament has attracted a crowd in holiday mood; the roads are lined with townspeople and folk come in from the country, all eager to see a knight or a fair lady. Among the many to be seen, not the least are Richard and Piers riding proud and even stern under the Erpingham green banner, with its escutcheon within an orle of silver martlets and the motto *Aut Vincere Aut Mori* – conquer or die. Very apt.

The carriage in which Sir Geoffrey and the girls are sitting draws to a halt on the outskirts of Hoveton at about noon. Beth looks out of the window to see Richard and Piers have dismounted and are talking to someone. She cannot hear the conversation for Sir Geoffrey is asking whether it is a lunch stop, and then bemoaning the fact that the king has banned the use of the noonday Angelus bell. "Devilish inconvenient, not to know when it is lunchtime; though I dare say if we kneel and say our prayers, niece, we shall still win a hundred days off purgatory. What say you?" Maria declines distractedly, still straining to hear and see.

Beth sees Richard taking the hand of the stranger while a small crowd look on, and then she sees that the stranger is Pieter. Beth reaches for the carriage door but then draws her hand back to her bodice, now white and soft as a lily. Maria, craning her neck further on observing this impulse and hesitation, also sees who it is. After only a moment's pause, she says: "Go to, sister. If you need to stretch your legs and take a breath of fresh air, we will wait."

Beth glances only briefly at the kindly face of her friend. "Yes, I think I shall," she says quietly, making up her mind. She unlatches the carriage door and walks carefully towards them. Pieter is still holding Richard's hand as they speak, and Piers is holding the old man's arm, as Beth joins them.

"Ah, Beth!"

She can smell the eels from here, mixed with the all-pervading tinge of the foldyard.

"Pieter, you should not have come."

Richard releases his grip, leaving Pieter to stand awkwardly wringing his grey cloth cap, like a chicken that refuses to die. Where can he look, what can he say now to these finely dressed people he so suddenly only half-knows?

"I did want just to see you kinderen, though not so much kinderen any longer, ya. I – er – forgive me."

"Forgive you?" Beth exclaims. "No, no! I did not mean that – only, you will be so busy without us – there is too much for you to attend to at home." She smiles, embarrassed wanting so much to tell him all that is in her heart. Oh, look at his dear face, she thinks, was ever a man too good for this earth? It is Richard who breaks the awkward pause. "And Sarah? And Margaret? Is all well with them too?"

He nods, then admits sheepishly, "They think I am at Coltishall." He smiles suddenly. "Margaret is big as a barrel of shrimps! Ja, any day now. Any day."

They make further small talk, but the distance even now after a few months seems like an ocean. Sir Geoffrey and Lady Maria look on but tactfully do not join them. Eventually, Pieter says he must go. Richard gives him a feather from his velvet beret. "Tell Margaret that I have not forgotten the baby's bow. You will tell her, won't you?"

"Ja! Ja! But go now, my lad, before I embarrass myself."

Richard doffs his cap once more to Pieter, sweeping low in a bow of unaffected esteem, before turning away to where Hobbs is holding Percival. For the first time ever, he notices something like a smile on old Hobbs's lips. Soon they are once more upon the road, Richard and Piers looking back to wave farewell to Pieter.

Two minutes later the old eel man is still standing motionless as a heron, still holding his cap clutched against his breast with both hands and with his mouth slightly open in silent prayer.

Sir Geoffrey's man, Jenkins, has gone ahead to open up the Hastings family's house on Bishopsgate – a grand but musty old property held in the family since it was first built in Edward Longshank's reign. The limestone carving is worn on the west now, from centuries of prevailing wind and rain, but inside and around the central yard the elaborate stonework is in reasonable condition. Sir Geoffrey regales them with his childhood memories of the place, when his grandfather had often entertained there. "Hah! We used to get up to some wicked pranks, God bless my soul! One Christmas, my brother and I cast the bird muck from that parapet up there, down onto Bishop Goldwell; a very serious-minded man indeed, but we hid back against the wall – a vine grew there then – and my father, who knew it had to be us, made up some tall tale to cover his embarrassment!"

The ladies rustle in their silks through the long corridors to the bedchambers overlooking the river and cathedral. Jenkins is flustered for the house is understaffed and despite his best efforts, the strong afternoon light shows only too clearly the unsettled dust in the air. But the house is wonderfully cool, and has a faded magnificence despite Maria's scathing comments about the architecture.

"You know, I suppose," she says to Beth, while Hannah is hanging up their farthingales, "that the Duke of Norfolk chastised my uncle for having such a wretched old place right in the middle of Norwich? And do you know what he said? I say, do you know what he said?"

Beth turns from the bay window, "No, prithee, tell me."

"Indeed, he had the cheek to tell his grace – right in front of the king, no less – that he did not favour the Italian school of architecture."

"Oh," Beth says absently, looking past Maria to where the shafts of light strike the brown jacquard curtains over the four-poster bed. The way the deep folds obscure the light, and the overall subterraneous gloom of the room, remind her of the watery grave she almost had on Barton broad. She remembers also – nay, cannot forget – her encounter with Mark, his lips, the whites of his eyes, his hair mingling with hers in the half-light. She wonders whether he will be in Norwich helping Pacificus and the bishop.

"Elizabeth! Elizabeth!" Maria's imperious insistence brings her back to the present. "What is it? Why do you touch your lips in that way? Have you not heard me? I asked you what you thought the king told my uncle for his recalcitrance."

"Oh, Maria – my apologies; pray do tell me."

"The king says that he likes it well and would not be thought a second-rate prince by any other prince in Europe, to which my uncle says that, speaking for himself, 'the classical form and the *Umanista* application of it, are so strict in symmetry and proportion that it forces men and their needs behind its rigid façades, in a way unbecoming to a Christian civilisation.' Well, I can tell you, no prince likes insolence, even from his father's friends, and seeing he could not answer, had Sir Thomas Heneage escort him out."

"Oh! Poor Sir Geoffrey," Beth says.

"Poor Sir Geoffrey, nothing! Flaunting his opinions as if he were the last word on style – and near enough challenging the king too!"

"But an opinion honestly held?" Beth looks in appeal to her friend, though she sees that Maria does not really care as much as she protests.

"Tosh to his opinions – and don't look at me like that, for you know I love him too, but women must be practical even if men cannot be. It will be doubly hard for any of us to find preferment at court, but – " Maria's face suddenly lights up in one of her impish smiles "– I for one am not afraid of a little hard work, neither am I devoid of charm, or so I am told. But, oh, how hot it will be! Hannah, be sure to remember my fan. It is not polite to blush too much; we must stay cool."

Beth moves to the bed and picks up the gable hood with pearl drops that she had planned to wear that evening: "These hoods will not help."

"Indeed they will not!" Maria starts to model her tresses into a ball about her ears. "So let us follow the Etruscans and Spaniards. Let us have Hannah puff our hair about our ears, drawing it back just so, into a braid – or perhaps even a wrapped twist at the nape."

"Or – or – " Beth says, surveying her own blonde hair in the glass and angling her head to let the tresses fall where they will on her shoulder "let us wear it loose, as do first-time brides, in token of their virginity."

It is a comment innocently made, but almost straight away, Maria looks back to the bed linen so that Beth may not read her expression, "Well, of course you may be as rustic as you wish, but I shall wear mine up." And then picking up the bonnets and gable hoods, "Here, Hannah, take these away will you?"

"How does that feel now; looser in the shoulder?" Richard angles the sinuously curved steel and soundless hinges about his shoulder. He is at the back of Will Short's smithy in the castle yard. Will and Pacificus look on with satisfaction, their eyes shining like men showing off a new horse for the first time before friends. The low afternoon sun slanting through the forge picks out the etching, rivets and gold inlay. Pacificus can see in Richard something closer to the ideal image for Saint Michael than he – or perhaps even Dante – had yet imagined. Richard moves with ease, for this whole suit weighs less than Hobb's almain rivet. He straightens his arms and makes the thrusting motions he will need to wield a sword. His face says it all; Will Short is not asking for words, anyway.

Then a shuffle in the doorway, and a swirl of the smoke hails the entrance of another. From the silhouettes Richard makes out Tom Short and behind him another – a woman.

"Turnkey says we must be brief, brother," Tom whispers to Pacificus, "or it is *his* head that will roll."

"We will be; my thanks to him." Pacificus had not been optimistic when he had made the request, and now he's kicking himself for not having the others present.

"No need," Tom says, moving aside to let the woman approach. "He says it is for her sake, and he don't want no groat for it, neither."

"Well, ma'am, we'll leave you with your son." He has seen her earlier that week and made up for the manner of their last parting – and also discussed this unexpected turn of events.

Elizabeth Fenton's eyes do not search long through the smoke and dust before she sees her son. And when she at last does single out the burnished knight at the back of the shop she cups her mouth. Two and a half years have passed since she was torn from her children. How could he have become such a creature in so short a time? It is all as the monk has said; her frustrated, little boy has indeed become a man – nay, a knight to boot. Could it be? Could it really be her little Richard? Yes, the eyes and hair are his, but since when such a broad and manly jaw? Of all the losses for which she had prepared, this loss of a boy to manhood was not one that she had imagined. And it is this vision that now rushes to her, and holds her with a mighty embrace that squeezes the very breath from her.

From outside, where the others now wait, great heaving sobs are heard, and in the privacy made for the two of them, they stand for some time as ones that dream, though cannot speak. Pacificus, waiting by himself, and gazing beyond the walls to the sky, acknowledges silently in his heart, 'Yes, for a certainty, I have wrought at least one right thing in my life in helping these Fentons. But how strange a providence to have inadvertently salvaged something of myself too.'

He remembers yet again the haunting words that have been with him since the Lincoln and York rebellion. They are what Cicero asked Atticus in a letter; "Should a man risk himself and all that he loves against a tyrant?" Today Pacificus nods his head and whispers, "Yes, and amen; rend kingdoms too, if it need be so."

Elizabeth gently quizzes her son without letting him go. "So it is true? You will enter the lists for me?" She whispers with eyes shut, her hair trailing across her face, stuck fast by the tears and gold as the gold on the breastplate.

"I will, Mother."

"Oh, Richard, I do not ask it of you, you know that."

"But I owe it, Ma." Richard says. The *debt of Coriolanus* Sir Geoffrey had called it.

"Owe it? No my son, your life is before you, and I am not afraid to face death if it is God's will."

"But we must try the king first."

He is amazed at her lack of resistance. The truth is, she could have added that death looked more welcome than another year in a cell, and her health is not what it was; but she will not burden him with her problems. It should not be that way round. So she asks him about the tournament and how the others fare. Their painfully inconsequential conversation is cut short by Pacificus warning that the turnkey has sent for her. She wishes Richard Godspeed, peeling his hands from her and kissing them, also letting her hand gently touch Pacificus' scarred wrist in thanks as she departs. He sees the way Richard is breathing and the shuddering of his shoulders. He steps towards him and lays a firm hand on his shoulder.

"That is so you remember why you hazard death tomorrow, but do not think over-much on it now, for we have work to do." He raises Richard's arm until it is level with his chin. "You are sure it does not pinch now? Good. Well then, we must get you back to Sir Geoffrey, for it is nearly sundown, and everyone else will be ready for the masque."

While Richard is being dismantled by Will and Tom, Pacificus goes back across the castle yard to enter the prison. He is shown to Elizabeth's cell where he finds her at her chair, arms folded across her stomach.

"Pardon the intrusion – "

"No – prithee come in, brother." She rises as he enters the cell, but the warmth of her greeting and thanks – veiling as they do the lines of grief – soon turns cold when she understands the reason for the visit. After a preamble about Richard and the others, Pacificus points to her best green gown where it hangs by the window. "When you are called to appear, and it may be soon, be sure to array yourself and your hair as best you may – this gown is comely."

"What, trap him with my comely features?" Her head moves back in disgust.

"Madam, that is not exactly what I mean."

"Oh, I think brother that *it is.*"

"Why must you always misunderstand me?"

"Why must you always tempt me to save myself at any cost?"

"*There!* Forsooth, you do it again! What cost?"

"You would have me offer my body, my face, my hair as atonement for my heresy; I will not."

"I merely meant that God has given you many natural blessings – "

"*Natural blessings,* you have been cloistered too long, that you exaggerate so."

"Believe me madam, I do not." He pauses self-consciously when he realises he has been cornered into paying her a compliment, then quickly rejoins, "And – and – and if you would but heed me in this – for whatever else you may think of me, I am still a man – then you will receive a fairer hearing by His Majesty."

"Yes, while the aged and ill-favoured among my sect – those who have nothing worldly to titillate the eyes of a judge or sovereign – may go to the gibbet without mercy."

"I am not asking you to deny your faith, or betray yourself, but once I saw you wear yonder gown with your hair up, to minister to the poor of this prison, and the turnkey said – him not me – that you looked like a queen. Now then, what harm is there in appearing thus before the ruler God has placed over England?"

Her shoulders slump as the fire goes from her; the turnkey is going soft, she thinks. "My hair was up to avoid the lice."

"Well, it was comely all the same. Perhaps you could pray on it?" He sees from the resignation and almost a smile that she is not beyond persuasion. He is right, but neither is she beyond giving as good as she gets. At the moment when he might have expected a nod, or a softer answer, Elizabeth asks him, "And all this you have done for my daughter – "

"My niece."

"Yes, your niece and my sons; is it solely for them, or is this not partly for your family, the great Erpingham name?"

For my family name? He thinks, has she really not guessed yet? He clears his throat uncertainly, "I have no family, there is no male issue. The name dies with us."

"And does this not sadden you?"

"I chose my vocation, I ask not for sympathy."

"It is not what I asked."

"What would you have me say, that it grieves me? Yes, oft it does. But that changes nothing."

"If the monasteries do fall, you *could* marry." She lingers on the word.

"Me? Who would have me?" He searches her for a reaction but finds none. "And to what end? To raise up offspring? Our estates were mostly forfeit after Bosworth. No one will miss the Erpinghams."

"I do not think that is true." This she says with real feeling, but in her next words – almost to compensate for revealing her heart – she adds, "Besides, you could make a living from your brushes."

Her impish eyes – so like her son Piers – bring him at once out from his melancholy, and a broad grin grows across his face. "Cruel

Madam, 'tis right cruel! Will you not at least let me feel sorry for myself for a few moments, mocking me as you do?" But when their laughter subsides, his face clouds over once again. "This will be our last meeting before – " he pauses awkwardly, clenching both fists " – that is to say, I shall be very busy this week."

"I understand," her voice is serene and resolute, though somewhere in the last syllable, and the way she clenches her fingers, he can sense her vulnerability. "And you know that with all my heart I thank you for your kindness to the children and to me." Her hands separate edgily and reach forward slightly. "Perhaps we could pray together, you and I?"

"I – I cannot confess you," he says reflexively.

"No, I know, but peradventure we might beseech God for a blessing for each other? For we may not meet again in this life."

"But I have not my prayer book."

"Surely you may pray without one?"

"Yes. Of course."

When he joins his hands together and closes his eyes he does not see her approach, only he feels the rustle of her gown on the straw and nearness of her by the warmth of her breath. He dare not open his eyes but merely recites a form of words that are as familiar to him as his own scars, "*Gloria Patri, et Filio, et Spiritui Sancto. Sicut erat in principio* – "

But as he finishes the sign of the cross she catches his right hand, and then his left, turning the palms over in a form of supplication. Her hands feel so delicate, yet so assured that he does not withdraw them, nor yet open his eyes.

"Come, I will show you." She half-whispers, half-speaks the words, still holding his hands.

"Our Father who art in heaven, hallowed be thy name. Sovereign Lord, I thank you for this man and for the kindness we have received from you at his hand. Lord, you alone know the anguish in his heart..." At this point he feels his hands go limp – it is like that time with the bees all over again. "Lord, you alone have the power to redeem and heal, to give this man rest. So Father, please have mercy on him and glorify your name in his life."

Here she pauses, and he does not know what to do. "You are to say "Amen"," she schools him, though really she wants to brush the lone tear from his cheek.

Pacificus nods and manages a croaking "Amen', but still will not open his eyes; because he doesn't want the moment to cease, and for shame that she will see the overflowing of his tears.

"And now you are supposed to pray for me too."

"Oh...uh...I see."

"In our own tongue!" she adds playfully.

Then quite to her surprise, he revolves his palms and takes hold of her hands in his. "Lord God, I ask thee to bless this thy handmaid." His hands now squeeze hers tight. "And strengthen her." He heaves a shuddering breath as he feels her hands hold his tighter and tighter, "and grant her favour in the king's sight, if it please you. God please, *please, please*, through Christ Our Sovereign Lord, Amen."

He has no faith for his prayers, not after so many defeats, but somehow he has hope for her, that God would save her for her children's sake. How could he not at least hope for a God like this. They stand there a moment longer, the two of them alone in that cell, both heretics, both tossed ships, both savouring for one last, brief moment the shelter of the other.

But eventually it is time to weigh anchor and sail out across the bar. She steps back quietly towards her window and table, he unconsciously massages his hands. He could have written a third-rate sonnet at that moment, for he feels that a part of his soul is now standing six feet from him. He would write as much if he had a pen and not be ashamed of it either – what a strange witchcraft and madness is this thing men call *eros*. She is smiling, with a sublime radiance that seems to pour out of every part of her skin. He'd write that too, by heaven he'd write a hundred lines on just that light, God forgive him. She says with a smile that she'll make an Anabaptist of him yet, but he hardly hears it. Sweet heavens, what a face this woman has. I could look at it for a thousand years. He knows now how Adam felt when waking up to the rest of his life that morning; "She shall be called woman."

28

The Masquerade

Nosce te ipsum
Know thyself

Sundown, and the torches are lit in profusion like rows of flaming sentinels on the sides of the lawns and walkways at the bishop's palace – *Palazzo Rugge*. Yes, the bishop is pleased with the effect, and doubly so with himself as he surveys the milling *magnati*, and the dainty damsels in their masques and silks fluttering about the terraces in the twilight. Under the neoclassical staging, built specially for the masquers, sit a great mass of musicians, led by a swarthy singer with curly ginger hair, and a lute that Rugge suspects is out of tune. Music is not really his *forte*, but every detail must be right for the king who definitely does have a good ear for pitch.

The bishop eases some cool evening air under his collar, his ruby ring chaffing his pockmarks as he does. Should have had more faith in the English weather and worn something lighter, he thinks. It's unseasonably close for this time of day, the ermine-trimmed sleeves are making his hands swell. God's oath, my ring feels as tight as a terrier in a warren – *though we esteem our present afflictions not to be compared to the glory that shall be revealed.* Speaking of which, His Majesty is fashionably late as ever – and who is that talking to Pacificus? Ah, it must be them.

He moves closer to the western end of the terrace, passing the unmistakable aldermen of the guilds, and their equally gilded wives all fawning and flirting behind the safety of silk, velvet and sequinned masks. The bishop is intentionally unmistakable too; the ornate, crimson dalmatic; the pelican-beaked mask. I suppose the pelican motif will be lost on our sovereign, he thinks, too busy plucking the heart out of the monasteries to un-feather his own breast for his people.

After passing the commercial patricians, he begins to feel a strange yearning in his soul. At first he thinks it is the Burgundian wine, but then like a flood he remembers the last time he dressed up for pleasure, the days of his tender youth, when he had been plain old Willy Rugge from the backwater village of Repps, up-river from Thurne, not two miles from Saint Benet's. He and his friends would dress up, don masks and go "guising' – as they called it then – about the villages and farms. Could he have imagined he would end up a bishop? Even now he stands amazed at it, and is not unmindful that he owes the church – and the church alone – a great debt for it, one he intends to repay with interest if he can.

Pacificus catches his eye and, feeling summoned, leaves Richard, Maria, Beth and Piers at the maze entrance, ascending the steps to the terrace.

"Who, pray, are those young persons?" The bishop does not take his eye off them even as Pacificus approaches.

"Lady Maria Hastings, my Lord."

"And?"

"Lady Elizabeth Erpingham, and her half-brothers, who represent her – "

" – at the tournament, yes man, I have seen the lists. But what I want to know is why I saw it first there?" He finally honours Pacificus with a look, though it is the one he usually reserves for scurrilous deans and tradesmen. "Can't think why you didn't come to me first, I've done my best to conceal you and your brother, but this sort of thing cannot go unnoticed. I take it she's *his* bastard, not yours?"

"Aye, my lord." Why ask, when you already know?

"And this half-brother of hers, Richard is it? Who's his family?"

"No one important, my lord."

"Really, *really*, well it's all most irregular – "

"It is legal my lord – "

"*Most irregular*, and don't interrupt me."

"But my lord, the rules of title – "

"Yes, *the rules of title* ad infinitum, but all this smacks of a sort of base Genevan egalitarianism. The duke's in a rage, and the king won't like it either – "

"His Grace?"

"Oh yes, says if everyone's mother's cousin's widowed aunt can enter the lists, then it'll weaken the vitality of the nation's blood. He said he'd put a stop to it – thought *I* was up to something, the braggart."

The bishop takes Pacificus' shoulder in a firm grip and turns him away from the terrace, at which point Pacificus sees a man, head and shoulders above the crowd, looking intently their way. Pacificus marks the costume for reference: scarlet doublet under a full-length black cloak, hooded but with a golden Roman mask; probably a close-bearded Mars or Jupiter from the look of it. He is looking at me surely, he thinks, at least he does not look away when I stare at him. It is so hard to tell with these masks, even so Pacificus feels a movement in his gut, and thereafter finds it increasingly hard to focus on the soft whispers of his master, the inimitable, relentless bishop.

"But of course, *we* know that it is not me *but you*, and I will tell you now that you do not fool me, though I cannot see at present what this is all about – what game you are playing – and please don't bother to deny it – if I find out the slightest evidence that you have acted against *my* interest in this, I *will* cut you loose – *cut you loose, do you hear?* However regrettable, and painful as it may be, I *must* have men loyal to the abbey, the bishopric, the church, before other gains or ties. Dear God, man, you've turned out contrary! *Why*, I cannot fathom, after all I've done for you. They say some men cannot forgive a favour, but be that as it may, I'll not repay in kind. And I'll say, as a friend – whose power to protect you from your enemies is not inexhaustible, nor as great as it once was – think carefully about your priorities, about *the rock from which you were hewn*, be wise while there is yet time."

Pacificus nods minimally but, even as he does, he again catches sight of the hooded stranger staring from the crowd towards them. The torch flames pick out the mask, the eyes in blackest shadow, like a wraith. But beyond he also discerns the pattern of other gold masks, other hooded robes – perhaps five or six. He feels a chill in his neck, a weakness in his knees. Who is this? Why are those enormous sloping shoulders so familiar?

"Well, have I made myself clear?" The bishop sees Pacificus has not been listening, he has even followed his eyes into the crowd.

"Aye, my Lord, for sure, but that man there, the tall one with the hood – "

"Is no concern of yours."

Pacificus eyes widen in a flash. "God's blood, it's Prior Robert from Hickling isn't it? You've got him *here!*"

"Hold your tongue, man!" The bishop takes Pacificus briskly by the wrist. "Sir Robert Aeyns, aye, *Sir* Robert, has returned to his country seat in Suffolk, and has a damn sight better claim to joust tomorrow than your brother's dubious progeny."

"Joust! But they tortured and murdered a man in cold blood, within the abbey precinct – "

"Listen to me!" The bishop screws his fist around Pacificus' sleeve and tugs at it, eyes boring into him from behind the mask. "Have you heard *nothing*? Even if it were proven, he's mine to deal with under canon law, and what I say *is* law. So steer clear of him and don't meddle in my business."

"Your business?" What are you up to this time, you old fox?

"Have you not been listening to me?" The bishop's grip intensifies, and with one more tug says, "*Do not*, I warn you, cross me on this. Let it drop."

The sound of a trumpet interrupts them from beyond the turrets of the palace, somewhere back in the courtyard. "It is His Majesty, I must away. But you – " the bishop releases his grip only to jab a well fleshed finger in Pacificus' chest, " – you remember what I have said."

"Heigh-ho, methinks the king doth arrive – pinch your cheeks Beth, you look cold!"

"No indeed, it is more that I am affrighted by so many people." She looks lamb-like towards her brothers, while Maria starts to gather her train. Maria has talked non-stop, a full half hour before Pacificus comes to them, comparing the virtues of Tuscan and Umbrian gardens to the bishop's. "Oh, the fontana of the Villa d'Este, the arbours of the *Arcadia dei pastori Antellesi!*" On and on, babbling incessantlylike one Cardinal d'Este's fountains and usually ending in some spiteful barb about the paltry efforts of the bishop; how thin the hedges are, how lackluster the sculpture and ham-fisted the topiary. "Well, it is no matter; we are here now and we shall have fun." She opens her fan to add, from behind it, "And *look* you, we are being pursued."

"Those two men?" Beth turns to the side. "They have been staring at us."

"At you, I fancy, not me, and who other than the duke's son, Henry, Earl of Surrey? Can't hide a ginger beard like that behind a mask."

"And with him? The tall one?" Richard asks, stepping protectively between them and the now advancing strangers.

"Oh, him!" Maria observes the protruding, bald forehead and long beard through the flutterings of her fan. "It'll be Tom Wyatt. They're thick as thieves those two, call themselves poets."

"Poets?" Beth says.

"*Exactly*," Maria replies, "but don't let that put you off; they're both catches, even if they'll not wed you."

The men approach, led by the earl and followed by a small party of hangers-on, finely attired men and women. Richard observes that Henry Howard is a head taller than him and broad too, though with bandier legs. The parts of his face visible are sallow as porcelain, his eyes showing mirth within their hazel orbs but with no noticeable feeling or depth. He guesses him to be no more than twenty or so. Wyatt, whose masque is a slim, black affair which looks handmade, makes no attempt to appear congenial or engaged by the event. He mainly gazes off to one side after he has looked Beth up and down, and like his friend, stands *contrapposto*, hands on hips as if they were posing for a portrait.

"Why sir, do I know thee?" Maria says with warmth, meeting his eye as she curtseys.

"Come, Lady Mary, no coyness from you, if you please. Who are your friends?"

"My lord, this is Lady Elizabeth Erpingham, and her brothers." Beth curtseys along with Maria this time, Richard and Piers bowing as one.

"And you, sir? Do you joust tomorrow?" The earl cocks his head back in order to look more fully down his long nose at a possible minor contender for the laurels which he himself means to win the next day. And not without good hope either, for he is an able soldier with a ready sword – proved most infamously in the bloody suppression of the northern rebellion. His policy on the subject of civil unrest – shared with none but his own dark, aesthete heart – is that if a poet is to be free to write, he must do so with a life uncluttered by worldly distraction. Civil unrest *is* distraction, and not something you want to travel north to deal with twice. And so, with all the simplicity of youth, he decided to have his men kill as many as they could – slash and burn, teach the bastards a lesson. The whole thing has hardened him, Wyatt has told him as much – the Stoic is turning Epicurean; from the spirit to the flesh. But hardness has also brought deadness to his poetic art; though Wyatt has attempted to rekindle his friend's muse by just now pointing out this maid with her hair worn long, appearing as an almost ethereal platinum in the mix of moon and torch light. His friend had agreed, she did seem transcendent and angelic, but he has long since passed from holding beauty at arm's length for its own sake. Now he must possess it too, consume it.

"Aye, my lord," Richard says, and then because he is riled by Howard's turned-down lips, "and win too, if it please God."

"Please God? It'll take more than prayers." He wants to pour out more scorn but does not wish to lose the favour of the sister.

"But enough of that, for the day will declare it. What I wish to know is whether I might enjoy the favour of Lady Elizabeth?" He reaches to bring her hand to his lips. "Whether she would give me a token to ride with tomorrow?"

Beth feels the warm, moist lips on her fingers, and the soft prickle of the ginger beard. "My lord is very kind, but I fear he is right; prayers and even the favours of ladies are poor substitutes for manly valour on the field – "

"My lady?" The earl looks up suddenly from her fingers with his head angled in flirtatious surprise. Surely she is toying with him, testing his wit for the chase. "I have never yet been unhorsed – "

" – nor yet have I," Beth adds icily, removing her hand from his and joining it piously with its fellow at her womb, "but it is no matter in this regard."

"Then I should like to see you in the saddle, anon!" He sees Piers and Richard bristle from the corner of his eye, but still presses on, though this time in a whisper for her ears alone, "An unbroken mare oft-times needs a willing stallion to break her." His hand hovers in the position where it had held hers, though by now the fingers show signs of withdrawal; he has not the patience for protracted courtly love.

"Why my lord," she responds, coolly, "what a silver tongue you have."

"Aye lady, and you a ready one; are we not evenly matched?"

"By no means, for you are matched already, and if you wish for a trinket, sir, you should ask it of your wife or child, not me." The earl draws himself fully upright, the whites of his eyes showing more visibly now through the mask. "And this is your final answer – *to me?*"

"Your Grace must not be so offended. Was it Ovid, no, it was Horace, who said poets were too delicate. Howsoever, that is my answer and any further one you may have from my guardian, Lord Hastings – "

"Or," Piers adds rather too audibly, from the corner of his mouth, "from my brother on the field tomorrow."

The earl glances sharply both at Piers and then at Richard, but still unsure who may have heard the insult. "Erpingham," he says eventually as if it were something on his shoe, and then to Maria, "I shall watch for you. You must forgive me Lady Mary, I am needed with my father and the king on the dais." He feigns a bow and walks swiftly away, barking for his fawning *entourage* to follow – which they do all except one, a fine lady who peels away a few moments later.

In the meantime Maria remonstrates, "Well! There's a fine way to deal with an earl! You might as well announce that we'd prefer a nunnery to being at court!"

"But you told me I am an equal of any gentle person here."

"Yes, but that was because – " Maria brings her fan back up to her mouth for there are other young men near, " – you were so nervous. I never thought you'd lecture a sporting earl on his conjugal responsibilities!"

"He insulted our sister," Piers says simply. "Deserves a hiding, if you ask me!"

"*We're not asking you!*" Beth, Maria and Richard say almost simultaneously, with Maria continuing swiftly: "*A hiding?* He could summon twenty thousand men at arms in a trice; what can you do, you churlish boy? If his father dies tonight, he'll be the most powerful man in England after the king! How do you not know that even now he is not ordering your harm – our harm – *fool?* And well he might, for he was ever a choleric youth; redheads always are."

"He may not have heard Piers," Beth says. She sounds apologetic and a little anxious, and is unwilling to admit to her little brother how much she admires his candour and integrity.

"He got the full meaning!"

The voice comes from behind them all, and they spin round to see who has been eavesdropping. It's a brunette of Beth and Maria's age in a rose coloured velvet gown, intricately ruched and gathered, puffed upper-sleeves, and tightly drawn to accentuate her waist. She wears a gold lattice-work partlet studded with the most enormous pearls Beth has ever seen, and a matching caul tilted far back to expose her chestnut hair. And most stunning of all, at least to Beth's eyes as a needle-woman, is the embroidery at the edges of the square-necked chemise beneath the partlet, decorated with dropping pearls too, as if pearls were as cheap as sequins. "The *full* meaning," she repeats with glee, lifting her masque, "and my cousin is in a king's rage about it!"

"Catherine!" Maria says, letting her fan fall to its string and taking her friend by the hands.

"How now Maria, you look in health and I don't think I enjoyed anything so much in the last year as your letters from Florence." And then under her breath, "and how is *dear Giovanni* now you are gone, does he write and pine away *pour la collaboration horizontale?*"

"Hah!" Maria takes Catherine aside privily. "No more than your music teacher; men are all talk and promises, all fingers and thumbs. How goes it with Sir Francis, is he here tonight?"

"Alas, no. Grandmother got wind of us and engaged herself a new secretary." She pauses, crestfallen for a moment, but then replaces her red-sequined masque. "Still, no matter, there are more fish in the sea – talking of which, you must introduce me to your friends?"

"But of course." Maria turns back to the others. "My friend Lady Erpingham and her brothers, may I present Lady Catherine Howard?" They bow and curtsey, observing all formalities, Lady Catherine showing particular interest in Richard, who seems to be all the more desirable to her because his eyes and general manner are so far from predatory; though in reality his interest is rather taken at that moment by the sight of the king, the bishop and their graces, the dukes of Norfolk and Suffolk, all appearing with a fanfare on the colonnaded staging.

"Aren't their estates fast to her cousin's lands, the Boleyns at Blickling?" Lady Catherine is just starting to rattle out her enquiry when the crowd breaks into a rapturous cheer. Glancing round they all now see their corpulent sovereign, decked head to foot in gold silks, with white ermine trim.

"Look at the size of him!" Richard whispers to Piers.

"He's a target you can't miss," Piers mutters back, "might need a bigger horse though."

"Well, you won't mistake him in a crowd," Catherine says, "and upon my honour, what does he think he looks like?"

"I think it is the golden masque of Apollo," Maria says, "see the harp."

"Then Brandon must be Hermes," Catherine says, "though the winged helmet looks like it was made for a smaller man – what say you, Bess?"

But far from sniping, Beth is for a moment awestruck that she is but a hundred yards away from a sovereign prince, nay, and a king of England too. In that breathless inter-regnum of thought and feeling, she forgets to even reply, dumbly gazing towards the dais, to the vision of shimmering, anointed majesty. She feels that she could burst into tears at the beauty of it – not him so much, but *it*, though she couldn't explain why.

Maria, seeing her expression, remarks, "Come, take your brother's arm, the wine has gone to your head. Let us proceed to the banquet hall. The party will not be long here, for the night chills draw on, and besides we'll beat the tradespeople to the buffet – you know how those merchants' wives always stuff themselves – they have no discourse, nothing else to do with their mouths!" Maria and Catherine take Richard's arm and head towards the palace, leaving Beth to make do with Piers, who pats her hand reassuringly. "I wonder if they will have any eel?"

Lady Mary de Hastings need not have worried for her stomach's sake, for there is food in abundance, the bishop has seen to that. As the servants help them wash their hands at the entrance to the great hall, their senses are caressed by a thousand tempting aromas from the dishes proceeding up from the kitchens in the hands of esquires. These pans, kettles, skillets, cauldrons, bowls, platters and terrines are placed ceremoniously on the tiered buffets, a series of stepped wooden shelves adorned with rich drapes. Maria lets Catherine take Richard on ahead while she quietly explains to Beth and Piers from which shelves they are permitted to take food, and which shelves of the buffet are for the higher nobility.

The Great Table reserved for the king's party is set on another dais at the head of the room. Spread with a white cloth, it is decked with every imaginable golden and silver object that the bishop could get his hands on for the occasion; plates, goblets, even statuary.

But also before the dais, in the centre of the hall, about which all the uncovered tables are arranged, there stands another smaller stage arranged at Pacificus' suggestion, who knows as well as anyone the king's love of hunting. This centrepiece represents a newly clipped lawn, surrounded with large peacocks' feathers and potted shrubs, to which are tied eglantine, honeysuckle and Sweet Williams. Edging the lawn are terrines formed into animals; stags, hinds, boars and hunting dogs. Around them are coloured jellies in the form of swans, peacocks, and pheasants; all adorned with their real feathers! Then at each end, outside the green lawn, sit two enormous pies, each on its own stand, surmounted with smaller pies, to form a crown. The crusts of the large ones are silvered all round and gilt at the top; each containing a whole roe-deer, a gosling, three capons, six chickens, ten pigeons, and one young rabbit.

As if all this were not enough, there is yet one more marvel to which the eyes of all guests are drawn. For on this mock lawn is a cage-like fortress, covered with silver foils, which rises high into the centre of the hall. Inside it several live birds are enclosed, their crests and feet being gilt in silver. And on its gilt tower, four banners are placed, two bearing the arms of the dukes of Suffolk and Norfolk, the upper two bearing those of the bishopric and the king. This much had been Rugge's idea, *his little gesture,* for which he had not sought advice, yet again – *plus apparent posteriora eius.*

Beth, Piers and Maria promenade about the room, as others are doing, admiring the delicacies and decorations. Once out from under the minstrels' gallery they can hear the full effect of the lutes and harps.

Pacificus is observing them all carefully from a discreet distance, and watching the other guests too – most especially the Hickling brothers, or knights, or whatever they now are.

Maria takes them first of all to the staged buffet, saying that her uncle Lord Hastings has kept them so rudely of late – on naught but venison and hare – that she would happily be the bishop's mistress, if he entertained like this once or twice a year. "Why look ye here," she says, teasing a finger about her lips, "our first course; a civet of hare, and a quarter of stag which looks as if it had been a whole night in salt. For these I thank him not, nor much for these stuffed chickens, and this loin of veal – though they will please the guildsfolk, no doubt. No, what I wish for are these last two dishes of gilt sugar-plums, and pomegranate seeds covered with – what, pray? A German sauce, I suppose, yes, that must be it."

Beth agrees, though her attention is more distracted by Lady Catherine leading Richard about the other side of the hall, all the time whispering in his ear and giggling. She is only too glad when the servants begin to seat the guests, and Lady Catherine is taken to the Great Table. They are seated at the second table with Sir Geoffrey opposite them, who keeps saying how busy and noisy it all is, and how tired he feels. "I don't see why they have to invite so many people all at once, I'm sure it makes the air miasmic."

They are called up table by table for the different courses, Piers and Richard nudging each other to see how much the king and Brandon can pile onto their vast golden platters. They avoid Henry Howard, though they cannot but be aware of his malevolent stare directed their way from time to time. The bigger problem for Richard and Piers is to pace their eating, for no sooner has the first course gone then the next arrives. This second course comprises of a spit roasted roe-deer, a pig, surrounded by six large salmon cooked in parsley and vinegar. And then the guests all turn as one as they smell the courses that arrive prepared with powdered ginger; a kid, two goslings, ten chickens, as many pigeons, six young rabbits, two herons, two leveret, a fat capon stuffed with sage and onions, a wild boar and four chickens covered with yolks of eggs and sprinkled with powder de Duc – a spice which nearly makes Piers retch when he incautiously tries a spoonful.

For the third course, the esquires bring out silver platters of wafers and darioles; jellies part white and part red, representing the crests of the main guests, though the King's Beaufort lions are too small to be recognisable. The fourth course is cream – again with Piers' hated spicy Duc powder, covered with sugared fennel seeds; a white cream, cheese in slices, and strawberries, gauges, apricots and plums stewed in rose-water.

By this stage only Maria is still eating anything more than a spoonful. Piers remarks that it was no wonder everyone was so fat if they ate like this every night.

But even they are not quite finished, for yet the fifth course is shortly after presented, though this is entirely composed of spiced wines, preserves, fruits and various sweetmeats. These pastries, first presented at the Great Table, are shaped as stags and swans, upon whose necks hang pendants of the King's coat of arms.

Both Maria and Beth note how the king sends the pendants from his pastry down the table to Lady Catherine Howard. He's had too much wine. Old Norfolk, deep in his owned thoughts, notes it too and unpeels his lips to reveal a thin smile. Maybe he'll have another niece as lady-in-waiting, just as soon as Cromwell can secure a new queen. At the present turnover in the royal chamber anything is possible these days – the Howards could start all over again after all that business with little Anne. Who knows, maybe Kat's got what it takes to go further.

"Dancing, Norfolk?" The King bellows across the table, rousing the old Duke from his dark machinations, "I want to see you up man! Do you some good. And that niece of yours, pretty little thing. She could dance with me, what think you?"

"Very good, your majesty." But, he thinks, first we must make that business with the music teacher disappear.

Dancing follows the last course, after a brief intermission for the privy. The musicians strike up a galliard to which the king and his party respond with good humour, taking the floor with all decorum and summoning the second table to join them.

"Oh splendid, some gentle exercise," Maria says. "Come, let us not keep His Majesty waiting."

Richard, Piers and Beth exchange nervous glances as they try in this moment to remember anything Sir Geoffrey or Maria taught them at Bindringham. "Go too lads," Sir Geoffrey says, "It will all come back to you when you are up there." They venture forth, gingerly taking their stand amongst the great circle of nobility and in full view of the assembled gentry. The Earl of Surrey's eye is on Beth yet again; the wine has made him reconsider. But so now is the king's, who eagerly awaits his opportunity to get a closer look as the dance progresses, which it does with every pivot, every step, every clap, every swirl, every swapped partner; on and on until finally, hypnotically, rhythmically, inevitably, she stands within the spinning orbit of his golden majesty.

Under his Homeric costume she sees what she least expects – a real man. The king of England and France, though tall as an oak, is a mortal, breathing, sweating man. He wears pearl drop earrings that bob up and down when he jogs and jigs. She can hear the rustle of silk too, see the thin purple veins that course from his nose across wine-flushed cheeks, and eyes beady as frost-dried conkers behind the mask; watchful, hungry – hopeful even. He thrusts his hands forth like a child who grasps the world as a right, but expects little from it all the same. She feels his hot, moist skin folding over tight rings, smells the wine on his breath, and sees where it has run down his beard onto his lace-top chemise.

He pulls her closer yet, as he ought not for the dance's sake, nor for the guests who look on with eyebrows raised. She cushions upon his belly as one might alight on a sphagnum-covered pool on the marshes; it gives a little as liquid is displaced, and he roars with laughter at her expression. Beth eases herself away and continues with the moves; two steps back, cast away and clap.

Apollo then circles his Aphrodite as if she really were a hind in the chase, and then in a circle back the other way. Then clap, turn to next partner – thank God – while the lutist misses his notes and the lyres play on for merry England. But the king has not forgotten the moment. He likes a rose just in bud, loves the purity, eternity and all that lies between. And all this business with the opaque partlet obscuring her breast; a tantalising gamble, he thinks, but very effective – might send for her later. But ah, that ready Howard girl is just down the line; now there's a girl who looks like she can please a man – God's oath, look at her move, the minx!

Beth is inexpressibly relieved when the dance is over; neither she nor Piers join in the more sedate pavanne or almain that follow. Maria and Catherine stay up for every dance going, basking in the favour of men, particularly those who should know better. They know their window is short, their enticements fleeting. If they are to net a worthy sire, then nights like tonight will not come again in Norfolk while they are still in their flower – or at least in the appearance of their flower.

Richard dances the pavanne, and very gracefully too, Maria afterward comments. He persuades his sister to stand up for the closing almain for he knows she enjoys it, despite her mild protests. By now the king has retired to the dais with Charles Brandon for more wine, yet Beth finds herself once more pirouetting opposite another Goliath, though she does not know it is Sir Robert Aeyns, former prior of Hickling. But Pacificus sees it, watching carefully from the shadows. Is he doing it to warn me? Has Rugge put him up to this? If he so much as lays a finger on her.

He will not sleep well this night for the waters are muddied and he cannot fathom the bottom.

29

The Tournament

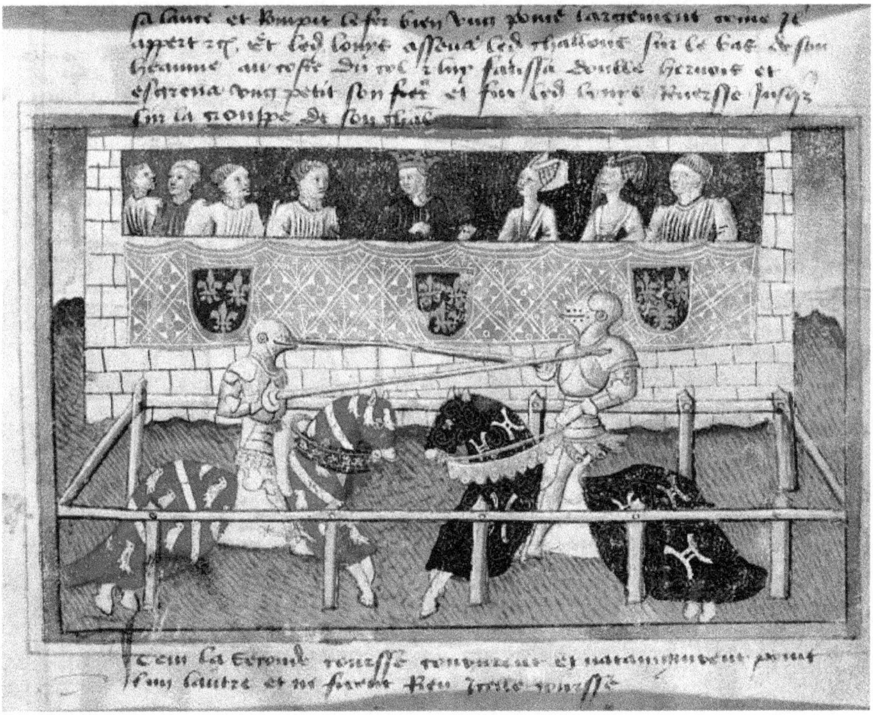

Aut vincere aut mori
Either to conquer or die

"Out of my way! *Busy*, you say? We'll soon see about that!" Pacificus looks up from the table where he is working, as he hears the thunder storm advancing down the corridors of the palace. The voice's cockney edge is unmistakable: Cromwell. It is the morning of the tournament and he is overseeing the lists with the novice Mark and the herald Fitzroy Stevens, making sure Beth's lineage is secure on the record, and scrutinising Sir Robert Aeyns' credentials just in case. But there is nothing obvious, or even curious, except that his mother was a minor princess from Martenburg. But there is no more time to think on this, for louder and louder come the heavy tread of some irate person towards the bishop's antechamber doors. These fly open like the shutters of a hundred-gun man-o'-war, and in walks Baron Cromwell.

"All right! Where is he?" He barks at the three figures he espies silhouetted against the window in the sharp morning light.

"My Lord Privy Seal!" Fitzroy Stevens says, bowing more out of sheer terror than respect. Pacificus and Mark follow suit.

"Your master. Rugge. Where is the ungrateful turd?" He shouts, planting two pugnacious fists on his hips like the massive stone groin-vaults on the ceiling at Lincoln's Inn. "Is he through this door here? Answer me, coxcomb!" A wrong word now and you might get to eat one of those fists.

Fitzroy is about to answer when Pacificus steps forward, dismissing the others and telling them to close the door behind them. When they are alone, or rather while they are still leaving Cromwell snaps again, "Well?"

"I am sure my lord bishop will as ever be honoured to receive your Lordship right here, if I may be permitted to locate him for you."

"Oh, I bet he will! You're all in this together, aren't you?"

"In what, my lord?"

"Don't play soft with me, monk! It doesn't suit you. You knew what he would preach at Mass this morning."

"My lord, I am not privy to his preparations, and was not present to hear his homily. I went to first Mass, for my time is taken up with the tournament, as you can see. Perhaps there has been a misunderstanding?"

"Aye, that is a pretty way of putting it! He insults His Majesty with a homily about the old ways of bygone Christian kings, of Charlemagne, the might of Christendom – and her impious detractors! God's breath, if I had been there I'd have dragged him from the pulpit myself. As it is, Brandon says His Majesty was already in a foul temper because his leg has flared up from all the dancing, and now this sermon against parliament's ruling on *only two candles on the altar*, and on the loss of the "virtues of the old world", the "great spiritual pageant of former times"! Christ's blood, were ever words less advisedly spoken? Has he lost his mind? Has he forgotten who put him here? Dear God, he's dug himself a hole this time; I'll have his liver!" Cromwell sees from the monk's scrunched eyes and pained facial expression that he genuinely had no knowledge of it.

"I knew nothing of it, my lord, but if you wait I will fetch him anon."

Cromwell's matchlock-ball eyes are searching Pacificus' face, and then all at once he knows him. "I know you! The monk from the prison – the Fenton woman."

Pacificus observes Cromwell give a millisecond glance to the tapestry. Perhaps he is remembering her rejection of his suit, and her rejection of his version of *the faith*. "Aye my lord, she will be tried by the king this very day."

"Indeed? Another of Rugge's ideas I suppose. And has she mended her opinions?" His face is still hard as granite but there now comes a little hope and tenderness into his tone.

"No, my lord."

He sighs. "Then there is naught I can do for her."

"Perhaps you might speak with the king? He could cancel the hearing."

"Did she ask for this, or do you?" Cromwell waits as Pacificus rubs his knuckles in the long pause that ensues. Eventually Cromwell speaks again, this time with a soft, dry throat, "I think we should respect her decision." He straight away cups his mouth, shuts his eyes, removing the hand only to speak through gritted teeth, "Damnation, I'll see what I can do. But, you – go to it; fetch me your master."

These look familiar, Pacificus thinks. Two iron-faced retainers stand guard over Rugge's private study, the dark one with the smoking fire. He espies the livery on the shoulders; they are Aeyns' men. In fact, they are both former Hickling monks, now clad in grey cloth hose and doublets, and full length riding cloaks; longer than needful for the season. They block his way, hands on hilts, and eyes with a cold resolve that he marks as unusual in all but the most hardened veterans. He notes their calculating gaze upon him as he approaches.

"You can't go in." One talks, the other tilts his head to assess the threat of a concealed weapon, stepping aside to allow himself space to deploy his own should the need arise. These men know their business. They know both how to weigh up another man and how to handle themselves too. And something in the intense seriousness, the dilated pupils and shine of clammy foreheads, signals to Pacificus a high state of nervous tension. Why so overwrought withal? He keeps his distance in case either should snap.

"I see." He hears raised voices through the door. "Prithee then, tell the bishop that the Lord Privy Seal, yes, Baron Cromwell waits upon him in the withdrawing room."

"B-Baron Cromwell?"

"The same." Ooh. That got a reaction. Are they expecting an arrest?

"Follow me." The retainer knocks at the door and leads Pacificus in when summoned. Pacificus eyeballs the second man as he passes him. "Warm day, is it not?" No reply. The smell of burning ash logs meets his nostrils with the waft of the door, and through the shafts of light, he sees Rugge sitting behind his desk, shrunken slightly, with Aeyns standing over him on the other side, his bear-like frame leaning over it, knuckles down. The unseasoned ash hisses quietly in the grate, and the smoke curls like a serpent around them both.

"I spoke my mind; moreover I spoke the truth," the silhouetted Rugge says, his words hissed out fast and low, but still discernable to Pacificus as he enters the sepulchral gloom "He cannot see what is before his eyes, *will not* see it. I have had him all wrong."

"Then we are agreed, are we not, as I said all along, there is only one course left to us?" Aeyns is waiting for his answer as his man reaches his side. He prompts in a lower voice, while the bishop's hand dithers with a writing reed, "My lord bishop! We are agreed on the final step, are we not?" And then with anger to his man, "Yes, what is it?"

After the low mumbling of the retainer, Aeyns shoots a look at Pacificus through the door as he had done that first day they had met. "And how long has he been there?"

"Just come, my lord."

"And is he alone – Cromwell, I mean?" The retainer looks back to Pacificus, who answers the question for him.

"I believe so."

Aeyns looks back at the bishop. "Then you pacify him bishop, and leave the rest to us. It's what we trained for, and *we'll* not fail."

Rugge nods and says, with a capitulation reminiscent of a failed mercer before his creditors, "*Deo volente*."

"Agreed, but just keep Cromwell busy." Aeyns says with the smile of man receiving his dinner. "And him?" He gestures towards Pacificus.

"Its alright, he is with us." Rugge looks uncertainly toward him.

"Very well, if you are sure. For we must away."

"Oh... yes, *tempus fugit*, Robert. Oh, but be sure to use the cellar exit, won't you?"

Aeyns snatches up his leather gloves from the desk without another word, leaving with his men through the small door to the left of the fireplace. A moment later Rugge and Pacificus are alone together, and the poor man does not know what to do with this hands; one minute they flutter about his folios on the desk, the next they are folding, clenching, almost wringing. He bites his knuckle then says, "Now brother, what is all this?"

"Cromwell."

"Ah yes, he is come up from London – but has he seen His Majesty yet?"

"Aye, my lord."

"I see. Then he comes to chastise me, like the good Vicar General that he is – "

"My lord, you have asked me not to interfere with Lord Aeyns, and I have not – please hear me out, and do not rise so at me – for I feel an ill portent by his last words to you, that you are being forced entirely against your will into some course of action that you may regret – "

"Brother – " Rugge for the first time in months seems tender, even if still brushing him away.

"I pray, hear me my lord, for if you will confide in me, as once you did, then peradventure I might help you - repay your kindness to me."

"Brother, I am touched by your loyalty; it quite makes me regret my harsh words to you last night."

Pacificus can see this is sincere, but with every moment, every new thought and word, Rugge regains his old composure and with each second, his false affection and guile, until he is fully back – cogs, wheels, endless calculations, weights and balances, a man playing his grandest hand in the game of history. "So much do to," he murmurs to himself: "But howsoever, *alea iacta est.*" Rugge drifts in his thoughts. *Infortuna Minor* has dealt him this hand, and he is resolved to match it with his mettle. He does not trust Pacificus anymore, he will not risk divulging his plans to him, though he dearly wishes he could at such a time as this. All that is left is to follow through. Rugge spreads his fingers wide on the desk, takes a deep breath, then says, "But look you; we are keeping the Lord Privy Seal waiting, which we should not."

A healthy south-westerly lifts the city's usual stench away from the green under the castle, where the tournament is laid out like a mystery play, all fluttering tent canvas and banners in crimson reds, ochre and apricot yellows, Sienese oranges; set amid the verdant greens of an English summer.

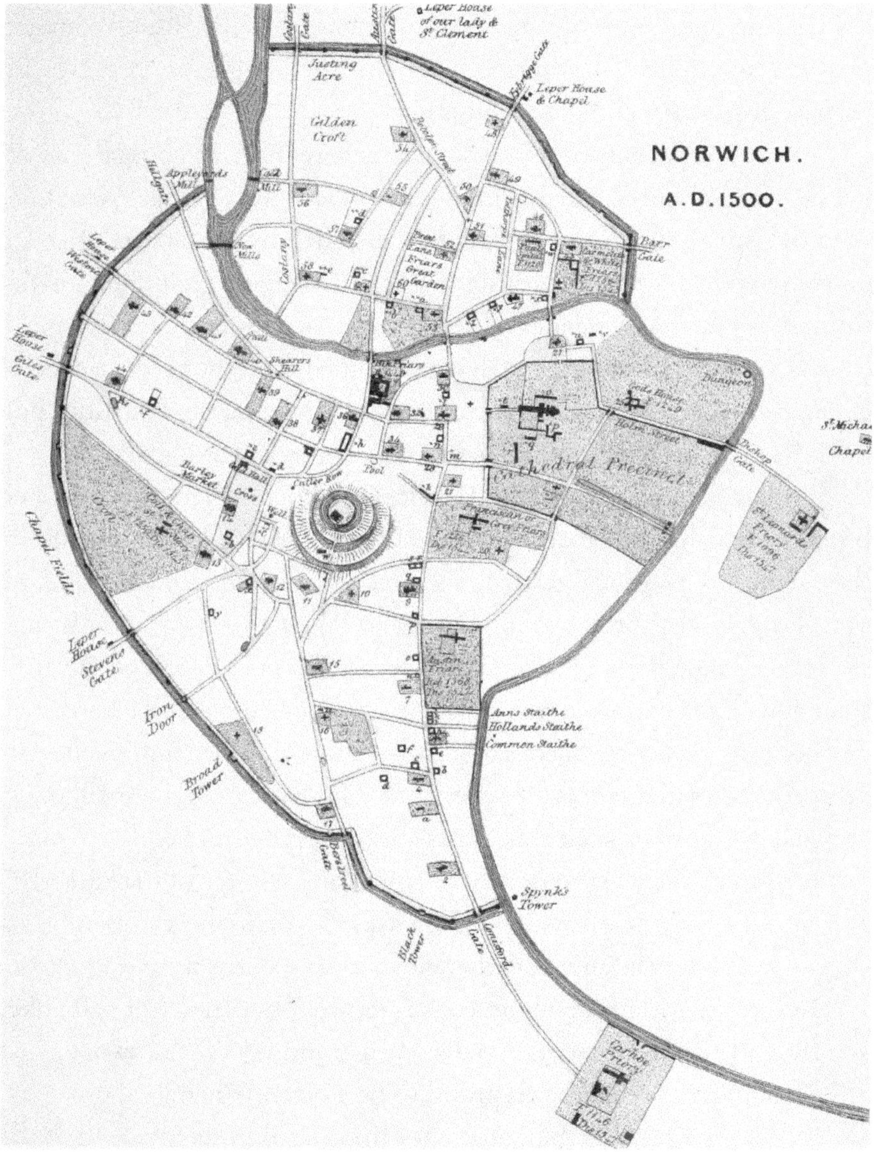

The crowds are blithe, bawdy and bellicose this Saint Swithin's day, rejoicing in their free ale and pork scratchings, staggering from shop to shop, stand to stand, looking at things they cannot afford mostly, and milling slowly towards the tournament grounds where jugglers, jongleurs and bears perform for them. The king himself will ride in the joust – is this alone not cause to celebrate? Some of them – the aged, the infants and the more optimistic among the maids and younger widows, line the street awaiting a view of the knights as they process with all customary pomp and fanfare.

From the moment Tom Short clears a way from Bishopsgate on to Palace Lane for the Erpingham party, there is a crowd surge. Who is at the head of this handsome cavalcade? Unsullied by the smears of court or commerce, there's something about this valiant champion in his shining new armour, slender and upright, that reminds even the most cynical of their imaginings of King Arthur, before nobility had been debased to social status. Lady Elizabeth Erpingham, new blossom put forth from an ancient root, rides proud and graceful at his side.

She has chosen against Sir Geoffrey's advice to ride next to her brother on a chestnut mare, rather than behind with Lord Hastings in the carriage. Her velvet gown is the green of the Erpingham standard that flutters in the breeze above them, *Aut Vincere Aut Mori* it reads, and the learned take note, for it is rare to see such a pure vision of chivalric splendour. In full armour but for his helmet, the sight of Richard that day not only makes the hearts of all who know and love him swell with pride, but stirs in the breast of every man and woman in the spellbound crowd, a memory of what this fair isle was supposed to be.

"Is this not the daughter of that Erpingham, scourge of the Saracen?" An aged guildsmen of Saint George asks his drinking companion as they stand under the short overhang of the king's tavern.

"No, his niece," his Aylsham cousin replies, "but they were all alike, goodly Yorkists as I remember – lost their standing after Bosworth."

"Sweet Mary, it makes you proud to be a Norfolk man!"

"Aye, a sight to make blood run hot in these old veins."

"Right enough," the other says, "I've never seen armour of the like neither, not even on the duke."

"Speak for yourself, I meant the Lady Erpingham. By Saint Winifred, cousin, she's the finest thing I ever beheld – with beer in me or without."

Piers, who is walking in front with the heraldic shield raised high on a pole, gives both men a cheeky grin. Tom Short – similarly grinning ear to ear – is clearing the way and trying to make sure as many people as he knows see him. One old woman crosses herself, younger ones find tears in their eyes for no reason. Even the younger men sense a swelling in their chests at the sight of Richard's earnest, vulnerable face. If he had been riding with the Duke to Flodden the effect on them could not have been more dramatic. For of all the strange and uncertain things of the modern world, this at least they recognise and know to be right, to be honourable, to be ineffably true. On one or two occasions Richard, Piers and Beth catch each other's eyes, each expressing the wonder in which they are alike swept up. Why had they been so stripped in that darkest of hours; first of parents and home, then of their siblings? But then again, why had they, above all the dejected beneficiaries of these modern times been elevated to this point. Their jubilation on this journey, their inexpressible joy in the love that binds them, radiates from every part of their faces. And yet, even for all this, Beth feels somehow in awe of her brother; it is as though at some deeper level, he were altogether more than a mere mortal that day; as if he represented justice itself, nay righteousness, as if this, her brother, was even now being transformed before their eyes into some sort of divine metaphor to answer the dissolution of the age – that God was somehow speaking again.

Word passes from one to the next, and tavern to tavern; that a family is present who might be cheered for without compromise, who might be believed in. For these Erpinghams are not tainted by the suppression of the monasteries or any violation of the people's religion or holy days. They have been busy serving God, grinding Suleman's bones, while Becket has been turned from saint to heretic, and his shrine dismantled. The restless rich, well represented at the tourney today, have been complicit with the king in amassing of power, privileges and palaces for themselves while the institutions of the poor were pillaged. *Lilies smell worse than weeds as they are dying.* In some senses the choice became easier when the gloves came off, and the masks fell. They think they can just move on, that it will be business as usual. *But what the axe forgets the tree remembers.* Mallory had it right, when the round table is finally sundered, you must choose either Mordrid or Galahad. And this Galahad cannot have been party to the recent evils that have befallen the realm. For one thing, he is too young and for another, just look at that earnest face. Perhaps the lady's champion is a holy knight himself? He has the look of Saint George about him.

This effect on the mass of people could never have been engineered by Pacificus or Sir Geoffrey, but they are nonetheless gratified by the result. For the bishop and duke may be out to win the king, but the king is out to win the people. And the people – even more than free ale and pork scratchings – love the romance of chivalric honour; the triumph of virtue (preferably someone else's) over tyranny. It is the answer to that deep longing, a fragrance of a dream that they only just now remember.

The tumult reaches a climax as the cavalcade nears the tournament grounds, trumpeters heralding the knights' arrival, from wooden turrets above the stands and staging, all bought cheap from someone known to the duke, and last used at the Field of the Cloth of Gold.

The stands are crammed with the best people of the city, dressed in their finest clothes and silks from those odd lands beyond Yarmouth. The town bailiffs, burghers, knights of the shire, lieges, villeins, serfs are all present. Men and women, young and old; all have come it seems, and are all cheering, thumping, stamping and shouting out their approval – this is better than a good burning. The contenders process clockwise about the ground with their squires or pages coming before and trying not to get trampled by restless steeds as the crowd-noise reaches a crescendo.

As the bells ring out and the crowds cheer, the Lady Elizabeth, with the Hastings family, sits on the edge of her cushion, her throat dry as June thatch, and her clammy hands held tight together lest anyone see them shake.

The king and Charles Brandon – the two men who ostensibly have challenged the mass of knights – will sit the morning out in the royal box, only entering at the finals to vanquish the two winners of each side. The king will then face Brandon who will respectfully fall at the first lance, and thus equity and poise will be maintained and everyone happy – that is the plan, at least. After a standing or mounted presentation of contenders before his majesty, the knights are dismissed to the stabling yard, and the pages sent to see the lists.

Piers returns crestfallen but Richard does not notice his face, for the day is already warm and he is holding Percival as Tom damps him down with cold water. Richard is thinking about the scowl and derisive words flung his way by Henry Howard, the Earl of Surrey just now in the tournament parade; something about it being scandal for men of honour and rank to go up against peasant boys. A calculated remark that found it target in Richard's breast.

"It's not right." Piers says.

"What isn't?"

"We don't get to joust against the king until we pass Brandon."

"Well then, we'll pass the duke, won't we?" Richard says between short breaths, the growing knots and jitters in his guts trying to get the better of him.

Another shadow enters the stable, Pacificus, in a hurry. Piers moves towards him, but the monk puts out a hand to forestall it, for he has urgent matters on his mind. "Listen carefully. Do not, I pray you, be concerned about your placing, for I have arranged the lists thus. It would not help your suit to unhorse your sovereign in any event."

He checks about the yard to make sure no one else is listening before continuing, "You must distinguish yourselves, that is all; I ask no more. Watch out for the Earl of Surrey, and bring Brandon down by all means if it is God's will, but if you would *win* the king's favour, then let him *win you*; understand?" They nod. "And Piers, you have those things I said you should bring?"

"I have."

"Good, now remember why you are here, Richard. Keep your head down as long as you dare, unhorse your man if you can, use body blows only, the king looks ill on head shots; never mind the points, he thinks them cowardly and unmanly."

'Pacificus – " Piers starts.

"Let me finish. There is another matter afoot today, something I want you to watch for."

He tells them of the near presence of the ex-Augustinians and the bishop's strange behaviour. It is possibly his and their last meeting at the tournament, and they must be watchful in the yard, sending any word of mischief to him directly.

He leaves them in haste, but not before taking Percival quietly by the nuzzle. "Well now, you old rascal; we've come some miles you and me." He strokes his neck, looking straight into the destrier's huge, plum-like pupils. "Tread steady today, old friend, and mind this lad for me; bring him through safe."

It takes but a few minutes to complete three lances of a joust, and the morning passes in a whirl of splintered ash, clattering hooves, cheering crowds and the odd spot of rain. Richard and Percival have broken nigh twenty lances before they find themselves facing Henry Howard. The Earl's amphibious eyes bulge as the bout is announced. He is firstly amazed that the Erpingham champion is still in the lists, but then secondly affeered of the real possibility of an impending embarrassment. With darkest resolve of heart and deathly pallor of visage, the young earl summons one of his retainers. *This cannot stand.*

Richard's pallor, on the other hand, is anything but deathly. "Give me a drink Piers, this is thirsty work. How are we looking against the earl?" Piers, who always had a head for figures, says they have both done well thus far, though the Earl had accrued more points by reason of his head shots; a broken lance on a helmet being worth two points, whereas one broken on a chest is only one. "I see," Richard says, after a long explanation, "but none of that matters if I knock him down, right?"

Piers grins, "Yeah, that's right, so knock him down. The crowd seem to like it that way anyway!" Piers is right. The mere sight of Richard back so soon from unhorsing Sir Stephen Beaumont sends the crowds into wild shouts and cap-throwing. The king is not unmindful of it either and sends for the Lady Elizabeth to join him in the royal box. When Sir Thomas Heneage, Henry's Groom of the Stool, arrives with the request she looks helplessly towards Sir Geoffrey, who merely nods his consent with such amiability as you might think she were being asked to take a turn about the garden with a maiden aunt. Inside though, he's praying – in English. And so is she. Maria squeezes her hand as she rises, whispering, "Remember you are the equal of any Tudor or Beaufort." The crowds see her pass along the wooden terrace and up the stairs to the royal box, and they cheer the more. The duke and his niece, and then Lady Catherine in her turn all move aside as Beth is shown in by Sir Thomas. Norfolk's expression, not graced by nature to be much more than a malevolent scowl in its natural position, is, at this time, about to contort into something approaching apoplexy. His day is going from bad to worse. First, Rugge has created havoc with his accursed sermon, and the duke can feel all too keenly Henry's suspicions that he may have had a hand in that. But then also the king's repeated criticisms of his son the earl, throughout the morning. "Another helmet blow, by my oath," the king would roar. "What's he afraid of, eh, Norfolk? Cannot he joust like a knight?"

The duke could at best reply, deferentially, "He jousts to win, your Majesty." At which the king would crane his neck to the side and speak from the corner of his mouth to Charles Brandon, "Boy's got a face like a fish." To which the Duke of Suffolk, a man affable if a little slow witted, would be obliged to give a hearty laugh. "By my oath, Majesty, he hath that; and a capon's legs, and a mouth tight as a rat's arse." And thus they would amuse themselves in circles. Even Cromwell, who sits behind Beth, grunts at the merry jests from time to time. But he barely sees the jousting from behind the king's bulk, but he does not mind. Besides he's seen too much of real lances in war to let the *La gaîté et la gloire de chivalrie* beguile him. He's thinking, counting, assessing more weighty matters than this. He's twisting the ruby ring that the king gave him, this way then that on his chubby finger, as if he were wringing Rugge's ungrateful, papist neck – he's not turning out well, that one. And the duke of Norfolk, who indeed may not have laughed at all since the last heretic burning, does not laugh one wit at any of the day's proceedings. Under his cloak, he is rubbing his amulet harder than ever, as if he could rub out the last three years. And now look, he thinks, glancing to his left, this Erpingham-nobody is being summoned to replace his niece on the stool in front of his majesty. It all bodes ill.

"Dear God, Brandon," the king says, recovering himself from a belly full of laughter, "you have a poetic turn of phrase, man; more than young Wyatt and Howard put together. Aha, Lady Erpingham, come sit here and let me see you. Catherine, you run along."

She bows and the king stands to greet her, his eyes merry, his cheeks flushed with the French wine. She sees that under his red cloak he is wearing his arming doublet ready for the joust, and also his lower armour; greave, cuisse, sabaton and mail gusset. She swallows hard and then curtsies, feeling her knees almost refuse to bear her up again.

"You must sit with us Lady Erpingham." He points to the stool where she sits obediently. He is just in her right field of vision, but she is fully within his, and he doesn't care what old Norfolk thinks of it. Dear Christ, look at her neck! It's like ivory – and that hair, was ever gold so fine as this?

"Your brother has jousted well this day."

"Thank you, Majesty."

"Let's hope he can bear himself as well under the earl's lance; keep his head, so to speak."

She gazes down the yard to where Piers is steadying Percival, Richard staring straight back at her, waiting for the king to give his consent.

"And a fine suit of armour, Majesty, must have gold to spare in Norfolk," Brandon adds.

"Yes, indeed. Is it from my almain workshop, my lady?"

"No, Majesty, from a local armourer."

"He should be at Greenwich with my almains, that blueing is as fine as my own suit." Then, over his shoulder: "Forsooth, bishop, what other secrets have you hidden away in this city?"

"Secrets, Majesty?" The bishop, from the back of the box, hastens to say: "No secrets, just loyal servants. I can seek out the man, if you wish."

"Do that, but come, let this bout begin, or I shall not get to answer the challengers at all."

Piers feels a large hand on his shoulder, just at the moment he is about to step out with the lance for Richard. He turns to see a man liveried in the earl's blue and yellow chequered shield, topped by the grim face of one used to dirty business. "If you would serve your knight truly, young page, you would do well to warn him he should not joust *too* well this day, or else displease my master, who is not a forgiving man."

For a moment, Piers is too overcome by the sickly feeling that rises in his gut to say a thing. He feels his tongue tied with fear and it is only later, after the man leaves him, that his full anger is roused enough to vow silently that he'll bring some kind of mischief on that earl.

He hands the lance to Richard, who is breathing heavily. "A man from the earl?"

"Came to wish us well."

"Really?"

"No, but he'll wish he had when his master is vomiting his inwards into his helmet; now come on, fix your visor tight."

The reeve raises the flag when he sees the king's finger, after which signal visors are locked in place over the bevors and the lances must be raised. "Go to, Percival," Piers whispers, "smooth and straight as an arrow. All set brother?" Richard nods, his eyes never once leaving off the earl's breastplate, his own heart near thumping against of his own.

Pacificus climbs the stand to get a better view of his family's champion. Stirrups on the balls of your feet, lad, that's it. That's it. Come on. Looking at him now, a blaze of gold, silver and blue, set against the deep green of the horse's covering, he thinks he couldn't have chosen better. God speed him and keep him from harm.

The flag rustles then drops and the spurs are applied. Percival lurches forward, as eager as any there to spread thunder across the stands. Within seconds they are at full speed, the lance in the cradle, the head down. The earl is high on his stirrups, rising and falling steadily, lance high. Richard takes one last breath and braces his stomach for the encounter. The next he knows his head is thrust backwards by a hard, connecting, spine-crunching helmet blow. He is bent backwards in the saddle, looking up at the sky. The crowd are booing and a moment later Piers is shouting at him and leading Percival back to the other end. His head spins, throbs and sings with noise and inertia, but he is nonetheless cheered to see his lance splintered. "What happened?"

"You gave him a nice dent in his breastplate, but you mustn't let him have your helmet again, I thought he'd knocked your head off. Is their blood? No, good. Come on. He's getting ready again." A minute later and the flag is barely down before the earl is thundering back again for a perfect repeat performance. This time the impact pushes Richard's helmet back and to the side, and he really does feel for a moment as if his head has been separated from his body. The torn muscles and crackling vertebrae in his neck leave him paralysed in the saddle until Piers arrives, "Richard, Richard!"

"Leave me," he wheezes, "give me a minute, and I shall be well."

Beth is now standing in the box, her hand clasped to her mouth.

"Why does he not withdraw his head?" the bishop says.

"He's making sure of his aim," Brandon replies, "lad's got balls of steel, eh, Majesty?"

The king is nodding. "It's knightly, is it not? I like him well." Brandon and Heneage agree, though they have no doubt at four points to two how this round will go.

When the crowds see Richard moving again, they break into a cheer and from the stands damsels throw flowers they had been saving for the king. Piers sees Pacificus giving him a nod as they pass, Richard is too busy eyeballing the earl, who passes with a dismissive gesture of his hand.

The last lance will tell all. Piers is pleading for Richard to aim for the earl's head, give him a taste of his own medicine. But Richard will not compromise his suit with the king; for it is his majesty he must win, not a mere tournament, if he would save his mother. Isn't that what Pacificus said? He may yet unhorse him and gain three points, if God wills it.

The earl has seen Henry's scowl from the royal box, and he knows what is thought of him, and said of him, when his uncle is not in the closet or privy chambers. But he won't change his merciless prosecution of the tournament for God, let alone take lessons in chivalry from some hypocrite like the king. The flag is barely raised, let alone lowered, and he is out of the stall, lance down. Brandon remarks on it but, as the duke says, it would not look good to accuse a senior noble of falsity. "I will chastise him later," the duke offers. God's thunder, all this Howard impudence, Brandon resolves to chastise him himself, in the next round.

Richard gets away but his lance is barely in the cradle before the impact comes. Again the groan of the crowd; again the view of the sky and the splinters of flying ash-wood littering his narrow field of vision; again the spinning disorientation, the dizziness. But also this time the thud of the earth and the muffled clatter of armour, the smell of horse manure, the sideways glimpse of the board signaling; seven, three. It is over. He is fallen.

The earl canters to the royal box to receive some courtesy from the lady present. Richard tries to rise but the fall has winded him. He feels tears of injustice and rage welling up within; he did everything just as they said, yet God favoured him not. Amidst his own grinding teeth and humid visor, he hears the sure steps of his brother behind him.

"Come on, up now; it is not over." Piers is tugging at his shoulders but Richard is too angry to cooperate.

"Leave me be, it *is* over."

"It is not. Get up!" Piers unhinges his visor and looks in with his urgent, purpose-bent eyes. "Get up quickly now; you can still have him."

"What?"

"Pacificus says." Another heave on the weary shoulders. "Now, get up."

Because it comes with Pacificus' authority, Richard cooperates. "Says what?"

"Take this over there, and point it in the general direction of that Howard pillock, and leave the talking to me."

"Take what? What are you talking about? What is that thing?"

Piers is removing Pacificus' own family broadsword from its suede covering. "This. Now, come on! He stands between you and mother; let's have him."

Richard seizes the blade and follows Piers unsteadily under the barrier,until they are alike standing near the earl, whose eyes are nearly popping from their sockets.

"What is this, great heavens, this outrage!" The duke seethes from his corner.

"Prithee," the king says, "what favour may we do for your champion, Lady Erpingham? His page looks to have a request to make of us."

"I know not, Majesty, peradventure we should let him speak?" She looks pleadingly at Piers, who returns her stare with his most impish smile. He cannot blame her for not knowing what will come next; though for himself, it is something he has been anticipating for weeks. The whooping crowd falls silent as Piers motions theatrically with his hand – he was made for this. The king sits forward. Piers bows.

"Your most noble Majesty; your Graces and Lordships." Then, turning with raised hands to the crowds, "and most loyal subjects of the most magnificent kingdom on God's earth!" The crowd erupts with delight. The king is amused too. "Her Ladyship's champion is not vanquished yet, for he disdains to call blows to the head as fit sport among men of gentle birth, but more the preserve of foreigners - nay, of Frenchmen!"

The Duke of Norfolk mutters *una salus victis nullam sperare salutem* into his beard, with a petulant sarcasm intended to scorn the king's mirth, but Henry is too busy listening to the blusterings of the Duke's son, the beleaguered earl of Surrey

"The round is finished," the earl says, "the blows have gone to his head – "

"Ah! He fears the cold steel! Rightly so – "

"I do not, impudent wretch, and certainly not that relic!"

"Aha!" Piers says, raising Richard's sword arm, "He fears the sword that rent the skulls of many a Frenchman at Agincourt in the hands of the great Sir Thomas Erpingham, and the English steel that made

Suleman himself tremble with fear in the hands of his legendary descendant; Norfolk's dearest son, Sir Hugh Erp-ing-ham!" The crowd are on their feet instantly at the sound of the name, the noise deafening. This is what they came for. Above it all comes Piers' last cry, "Majesty, let us have sat-is-faction!"

When the cheering and whistling have abated, the king, with little persuasion, declares it fitting to have the matter settled by the Frankish preferments of lance *and sword* together. "What think you, Brandon?"

Brandon thumps his gauntlet on the knee, "By God, yes!"

"Very well, the duel continues," the king says, "but the joust is forfeit only if the earl yields."

"Yields?" The earl spits into his visor while reaching for his rapier from the page. "By God, I'll cut the rascal to ribbons!"

"No, not that Spanish dress piece," the king bawls, "Damn it, get him a proper sword too!"

The bishop looks sideways to where Pacificus is standing by the lower rail. He has overseen this behind my back, all of it. The rascal has played the king like a puppet where I could not, though – he sighs inwardly – it will not matter any more, not after today.

One of the earl's retainers rushes out with a cavalry sword of about the same proportions as the one Richard is hefting now from hand to hand, appreciating the feel of it.

"A fine mount, my lord," Piers says, looking to his next challenge. The earl will doubtless run Richard down with his charger. "Attached to it?" The earl does not deign to answer this youth, contenting himself for now with promising himself revenge on him later.

"I only ask, my lord, because if you need the safety of a horse, well and good, but it would be a shame for my noble knight to disembowel such a creature at first blow, for want of a little manly valour on your part."

The nobles within hearing distance can scarce believe their ears. Did he really just say that? The king is snorting, the duke is asking what was said; just as well he missed it. But Piers is far from finished. He's looking at his fingernails and speaking casually, "For as you are well aware my lord, we minor nobles would dearly value such a prize – that is, if we won it today from you – value it very dear as a whole animal, more than just for feeding to dogs. It would be a knightly gesture indeed if you would spare us the chance of such a prize, if you would descend to this turf of mortals." And then, for the earl's ears only, "if, that is, you be man enough now your henchmen aren't here to do your dirty work!"

The earl's nostrils flare as the broadsword is passed to him, though in his anger the poet has quite lost his tongue. "By God, you will be flayed when this is over, mark you. Both of you and that pretty whore of a sister. Flayed alive, y'hear." And then, with no warning he springs from the horse and rushes upon Richard with raised sword, and hoping that a back glance might sever the page's head from his miserable shoulders. But Piers is quick, and too used to avoiding the wrath of his sister to be caught by a man slow in armour. He is under the barrier in an instant, leaving the two combatants alone before the world. Richard, true to all his training, absorbs the many furious blows of his opponent, who lashes stroke after stroke, six, ten, fifteen times; raining them down like canon fire, with great shouts of breathless anger. But Richard parries every blow, catches them high as he was taught, only once stumbling slightly under the weight and speed of the onslaught, and only once allowing a blow to glance off his armour. Richard thrusts up a guard to meet every stroke, giving the earl the requisite fifteen of so feet of advance but no more.

The frequency drops, and the grunts lengthen, Richard invites more by his lowered guard until the earl has no more. Richard can almost hear the silent thoughts of Pacificus and Hobbs: now Richard! Now! NOW! Take him down. Three big breaths and then he lets the earl have each swing of his taut frame; step, bang, step, bang, step, bang, just like working over the pell training post or splitting wood, only more fun. Richard moves the earl's blade to the side with a mighty swing and then spins his whole body 360 degrees to catch him again unawares. The earl feels it like a sixteen-pound hammer on his upper arm, a surge of pain coursing through his whole torso. He cries out as the metal of his pauldron dints, and sparks fly. But this is only the beginning of Richard's attack. Perhaps if the earl had not been so eager to maintain his ground, he might have used retreat as a strategy to recover himself. But he holds his adversary in such contempt that he will not yield an inch when so many are watching. Yet with his left guard so compromised and his arm in shock, his debilitated counter-attack is easily brushed aside by his adversary. The earl crumples under the sheer weight and speed of the blows, landing thick and fast as they do all over his whole body until his very fine armour is dinged and dented from top to toe. At first he will not yield, even when he's on the ground. He drank too much and too late with Wyatt and some ladies, and he's been too much at verse and too little at the pell-post to offer serious resistance to this lithe upstart. So, in spite, and knowing Richard will not strike him on the ground, he regains his breath there, before finally rising. He tries to distract Richard with an insult: "Varlet!" – all the time aligning, and then lunging a direct thrust aimed between the joints of his armour at the groin. Richard jumps back so that the blade only just catches his cuisse and mail gusset. The crowd sees it and so does the king, but Richard doesn't need their sympathy; he's swinging for England now, and does not stop until the earl is lying on his back with his blade under his foot again. The crowd like it right well; they'd see more of this if they could, and this knight looks like he could do it all day.

The earl looks up to catch the glint of Richard's sword at his throat, and hear the king's voice calling him to 'yield and have done.' He complies with no good grace, even turning his back in surly fashion on the royal box. He storms away with not another word – not even when Piers, now holding his horse, calls after him, "Faith, my lord, there is no hurry! You may keep the armour, if indeed you can get it off!" The earl's vambrace falls from his lower arm, the rivets smashed and broken – he kicks it away in front of him, hearing as he leaves Piers' performance as he addresses the king: "My noble Majesty, your royal Highness, the armourers of Surrey or Greenwich – or wheresoever the earl spends his hard-earned angels – should be pilloried and burnt along with the heretics, or at least sent to Norwich in chains to learn how to make armour befitting a true knight."

The earl is now at the far gate, kicks his vambrace again, this time nearly out of the hands of a long-suffering retainer who had stooped to retrieve it. "I'll have that boy's tongue," he mutters. "Damn him, I'll have his heart on a platter!"

But if he had only known, he would not have devised trouble for Piers, for it has been Piers' playful oration alone that saves Howard from royal displeasure; for the king is too shaken with laughter to afterwards consider the slight. And when his eyes finally do clear, and he lets go of his splitting side, the king points straight at Piers. "I should have this rogue at court! He makes better jest than my fool Will Sommers, eh Brandon? By Jove, bishop, what other treasures have you tucked away? Armourers, maiden ladies, knights – and now pages with more mirth in one little finger than half the fools at court. How do men call thee lad?"

"Piers, Majesty; brother of my Lady Erpingham."

"Well, Piers *Majesty*, you have a ready wit, sir!" Then, turning back to Beth, "Does he not, my lady?"

Beth cannot quite believe that the king of England and France is – rather like her father and mother used to do – lauding her brother's wit, which up until two years ago had been the bane of her life. She beams at him below, proud of him beyond belief and he back at her. "Aye, Majesty; a ready tongue withal..."

"Well young squire, perhaps I shall send for you yet." And while Piers bows low with a flourish, the king turns back to the duke: "What think you of that, Norfolk?"

The duke has near crushed the holy amulet he has been clutching within the breast of his doublet; this has been a very bad day for his house. Even so, or perhaps because of it – for this man is a survivor if he's nothing else – he bows stiffly at the king's right side, whispering as he turns his face away towards the far corner where Cromwell sits like a bored judge, "As ever, your Majesty is a fine judge of fools." The king perceives the snipe at the Lord Privy Seal and heaves an exasperated sigh, "Dear God, Norfolk, not today, man! We are at play today."

Then, to Piers, "Well sir, His Grace the Duke of Suffolk is off for his horse; and you had better take your knight back to *his*, for I warrant he'll not be on it long when Brandon hits him."

30

The Trial

Fiat justitia ruat coelum
Let justice be done though the heavens fall

"He's built like a siege ram," Piers whispers up to Richard, "don't let him near your chest or you'll end up on your back, or in Calais!"

"Yes, I know."

"And they say he never misses – "

"Yes, *I know*," Richard kicks his feet out impatiently, "now finish those catches on my leg, then leave me be."

"All right, but I was just saying, that's all."

Tom brings the lance and Piers puts it into Richard's hand. The

Duke of Suffolk is ready, relaxed; jesting at ease among his retainers. This behemoth fears nothing born of woman that comes at him by horse. Why, he even married the king's sister privily and walked away unharmed, though lighter of pocket. It would take the weight of a millstone hurled by Atlas to have him out of those stirrups. These cowering thoughts fix Richard rigid in his saddle. Come now, long breaths like Hobbs said.

He has been at it all morning and is tiring, as much from nerves than anything physical. The flag is down, and now a trumpet call too. Percival snorts and lurches forward at Richard's spur and Piers' slap. "Go on, *en avant!*" Piers shouts after him. The ground shakes under his hooves, the sand shudders, thunders and jumps like winnowed grain. thighs clenched for dear life, Richard grips the reigns and pushes Percival's head forward. "Now!" he shouts, raising his lance to the cradle and taking a last breath like a man going under for the third time. The rail passes like a mammoth serpent, or a great rope bringing an anchor up from the sea; at the other end speeds the shining mass of Duke of Suffolk, closer by every dreadful second. Three, two, one, *bang!* On impact Richard feels as though an anvil has been dropped on his chest. Brandon's lance explodes into a thousand pieces and Richard jolts back a foot in the saddle, nearly loosing his stirrups altogether. He cannot breathe for a moment and feels an immense pressure in his head. He looks to his own lance, still intact. There is no pain in his arm; he never even made contact. The return journey seems longer than usual. Brandon passes him with a merry tilt of the head, but Richard is still winded and trying to recover his poise. Back at the stall he gives Piers one of his steady, serious looks; eyes fixed, lips pursed.

"I cannot stay upright with another of those; get my belt."

"What?"

"Just get it, Piers."

"But why?"

"Bind my waist to the horns of the saddle."

"But his lance could pass right through you – "

"The armour will hold. Just do it will you, we have no time."

A few minutes later and it is done. All near enough to see understand the meaning of it, and those that don't are told soon enough. A tremendous hush descends around them. The brothers exchange a last glance. Piers breathes out uneasily, jesting that Beth will be wrath with him for it. Richard cannot quite find his smile but mutters a dry-throated *thank you*, before the visor is fastened shut. The flag, the trumpet, the jolt, the hooves and once again the wind whistling through the slit in the visor – and then, oh so soon, he feels the crushing weight of impact. His head is back and spine twisting, and for a moment all is black. When vision returns, he comes to with a great great roar of agony. Through the gasps and hisses, he manages to turn his helm far enough to confirm the worst; a section of Brandon's shattered lance has passed between the joints of Richard's armour through his shoulder. The crowd are both cheering and groaning at the sight. Richard hears one man saying he can see wood sticking out of his back and covered with gore. Is it true? It certainly feels like it.

With blood flowing freely down his breastplate, and then his thighs and even Percival's shoulders, Richard slowly makes his way back. Piers sprints down the yard to take the reins. He finds Richard slumped slightly in the saddle and gasping in pain.

Behind them at the royal box, Beth is out of her seat and straining at the front rail again: "He must have a physician!"

"None may attend but his squire, unless he yields," Heneage says.

"Then he must yield!"

"Lady, he may not wish to," Heneage replies, while scratching some egg from his best blue velvet hose. "To prevail is knightly, after all." Pacificus, who is outside the box yet near enough to hear the remark, takes his eyes momentarily off Richard. Did he hear that right? Oh the irony! Sir Thomas' own brother John *yielded* quickly enough to Captain Cobbler in Lincoln before escaping to London - took *the oath of honorable men* with all the falsity of his class. And the only matter in which these Heneages have *prevailed* at all is the accumulation of monastic properties which they got for a pittance. Pacificus' morose introspections are cut off sharply by Beth's next outburst.

"But he must be made to! Your Majesty, you must command it!"

"Must, Lady Erpingham? Every man is the sovereign of his own soul and destiny in the tilt yard."

And then she, seeing the blood running down her brother's back-plate, retorts: "But surely, you overrule all England in matters of doctrine and conscience, why not here too at a mere game?"

At this Cromwell emerges from his slumber. He has heard this voice, this spirit somewhere before – perhaps even seen the face. In fact, he'd just been thinking about Elizabeth Fenton and how he might help her. He looks at Lady Erpingham's profile, then across to where Pacificus is standing observant as a hawk beside the royal box – and the cogs of his lawyer's mind start ticking and clicking, grinding the grain of fact and circumstance like a slow but steady mill. The king is struck dumb for a moment, shocked by the near *lèse majesté* of this girl's imperious enquiry, and feeling the full impact as her words like a lance enter his soul; honour was everything to him once. In fact, before reading Machiavelli's *Il Principe* - gifted to him by Cromwell, no less - he had loved integrity above all. Caught in these thoughts, the king broods – fingers withdrawing into his fists, then shrinking back into his voluminous sleeves.

It is Heneage who speaks first. "My lady, you forget yourself before the king. It is the heat, no doubt, and the sight of blood. Let me take you to get something to drink at the dining tent." It is tactfully done, and the king, moving his lips left and right in an odd sort of indecision, lets them leave with nothing more than the motion of his finger.

Meanwhile the crowd is nearly all hushed, but for a few drunkards quickly silenced by the others. Pacificus and Hobbs both push their way to the stalls. They cannot talk or touch Richard while the joust lasts but they quickly collar Piers.

"He must forfeit the round so we can get treatment for that wound this minute. Tell him. Go now!"

But a moment later Piers is back, shaking his head. "He won't do it, even though one of the duke's men offered an honourable withdrawal. Even so, he won't do it. He says he'll finish."

"Ah! Stubborn youth!" Pacificus says, turning his head aside in frustration. But his gaze falls on the Erpingham standard raised proud on its pole. *Aut Vincere Aut Mori – conquer or die*, indeed. He tears the banner away from the pole, and hands it to Piers. "Very well. Loosen the pauldron and then get him *on the ground* – listen to me – on the ground, sitting. You got that? Take the wood out carefully but quickly, then bind this round and round as tight as you can, it is a flesh wound at least, and no artery, else there would be a fountain. For this mercy at least we may give thanks. Have you got all that? Good, then be at it." He throws the material at Piers, who loiters a second longer with an uncertain expression that makes Pacificus ask, "What lad? What is it now?"

"He wants to know how to win. He's...he is in distress about it."

Pacificus buries his head in his hands momentarily. Things were going so well, he should have known it could not last. He was mad to lead them into this at all. Brandon has four points, nothing but an unhorsing will turn the tournament for Richard now. But just as these thoughts pass through his mind, he feels Hobbs hand and hears the slur of his tongue-less voice.

"Here. Hith'im here." The words are not clearly discernible, but his hand is pointing to his side, and he motions how Richard should thrust the lance. "Of course," Piers says, "Brandon has a back-stop saddle, so if we hit him on the side, take the lance from the cradle, Hobbs? Is that what you mean, move to the side, like this...? Now it is Pacificus who is speechless. After looking intently at Hobbs one moment more, he sees Piers nod and start back to Richard.

When finally on the ground, Richard insists on taking the wood out himself. He tries not to cry out, but that is little use. It feels as if every bit of the wood is barbed, every bit of it taring at the sinews and ligaments in his shoulder. Each cry, is echoed and magnified by a sympathetic crowd, until at last the shards of lance are pulled from his body. Piers then applies the bandage, and shares Hobb's plan, "come in wide and knock him off sideways."

Richard, facing skyward, eyes tight shut and gasping under the treatment, whispers desperately over him, "yes, yes, of course. But does Pacificus really think we have a chance? It is for our mother, Piers, our mother, her last chance."

"Yes, of course he does, he is waiting to see Brandon in mid-air. Now come, onto your feet. Can you stand? I will help you."

Richard groans, the colour drained from his face, as he finally opens his eyes. "Hits like an anvil, and in the same place too each time, I swear it."

"Really?"

"Yes, on the heart, I don't know how he does it – "

"Probably because he's done this every day for forty years, but, at least you know which part of your body to move at the last moment. I mean, you don't have to be an idiot all your life!"

"What do you mean?"

"Roll your shoulder right back, let it glance off, then let him have it under his left shoulder like Hobbs says. Now come on, up with you, the crowds are restless."

As he gets to his feet using Piers as a prop, the crowd goes wild, cheering, stamping their feet and thumping the rails. Richard does not even register it. Visors, stirrups, lance, flag, trumpets, feet, faces, sleeves, banners, sunlight, then the lurch of the horse one last time. His shoulder is stiff as a board and he begins to wonder how he will ever move it. Brandon comes on steady as an ox, lance raised and only rising and falling an inch or so with the motion of the gallop. Richard eyes the tip as it comes once more to his breast. He then lifts his own lance from the cradle to draw it back, angling it more across his chest. It is heavy, but this is his good arm and he holds it as steady as he can – following the tip towards his adversary's chest. Up down, up down; Brandon's lance is at Richard's chest. He rolls his shoulder back awkwardly, rotating his upper body back, then left. Brandon's lance connects but glances upward over his shoulder. It makes his armour plate scrape and sing. And on his way back up Richard twists his torso hard left, thrusting his lance under Brandon's left shoulder. It is not elegant but the lance does connect, and from that moment onwards the *fait accompli* is all but accomplished as the competing forces of horse flesh and steel reach their impact. If only Richard can keep hold of the un-cradled lance, and as long as Percival does not dissipate the tension by giving to the right, then Brandon will be prised from his war horse like a clam from a rock. The next half second will decide the matter, but within half of that Richard's shoulder is fit to burst. His right hand feels stretched by two feet, muscles screaming, ligaments taring. Percival never deviates an inch from his course, and eventually Richard's hand gives under the strain. It shoots out of his hand but the lance guard catches on the leaf of his gauntlet and, in so doing, holds for that vital last moment of full impact. The lance flexes, creaks and then finally shatters at the middle. For a moment Richard is blinded by a great crack and explosion of white timber. Where is he? Where is the Duke? And then through the splinters he see what could only have dreamt; Brandon, all sixteen stone of him, lifted sideways from his saddle and coursing id-air towards the royal box. In the blink of an eye it is all over and the Duke is clattering in a solid heap of steel and groans upon the sand. The crowd cannot quite believe what they are seeing, nor can the king, nor Richard and Piers for that matter. It is so unscripted, that for a moment no one seems sure whether to cheer or not. Only Hobbs breaks the inertia by slapping Pacificus hard on the back, cheering incoherently, and waving his arms.

The grin that passes between them is sheer, unbelieving joy. As they look back across the yard to see how Richard is faring, Pacificus wonders how it is that God hides himself sometimes more than others. He releases the thought like a prayer, saying inwardly to his own heart, that on days like this he is content not to know the answer.

Richard is appearing once more before the royal box. That scrawny lad, Pacificus thinks, that minnow I rescued from the marshes, just toppled one of the sturdiest knights in Christendom! It is a good thing that miracles don't happen everyday, I'd never sleep at night. Surely the king will reward him, make him a favourite, whether he's an entitled noble or not. Such a show as this should win a royal boon. Brandon is up, winded and staggering a little, but otherwise taking it all with an easy grace. The king is saying something, the Lady Elizabeth and Piers are at Richard's side. He'd go himself but dare not risk it. He catches Piers as they come back to the stabling area: "What did he say, his Majesty, what did he say?"

"He said "what would ye that I do for you?" That was all."

"And Richard? What did he say?"

Piers' eyes follow his brother and the horse, "He said nothing for he was crying."

"Crying! What, did you not then speak for him?"

"I tried and then Beth tried, but the king would not let us."

"Was he angered?"

"In no way, he was much moved withal. I saw his tears in the king's cheek, myself," Piers scratches the fluff on his chin pensively, "The king said he will consider the matter when he has attended Mass, had something to eat, and Richard has had the wound properly seen to by His Majesty's own physician. And that is where he is now, as you see."

"Yes, I see it." Pacificus gazes after the bloodied-yet-victorious knight being led away with an almost reverent awe. Even after Piers has led Percival back to the stable, he stays there, looking on still. He then remembers something he had not thought on since the day he stood before the Holy Roam Emperor in Konstanz, all those years ago as a young man. It was that Lancelot was said to have been *the meekest man and the gentlest that ever ate in hall among ladies*, but also, *the sternest knight to his mortal foe.* And when he had been elevated amongst his peers for these virtues, he *wept as he had been a child that had been beaten.* Pacificus' heart is suddenly pierced within him - a great, yearning, bitter-sweet and hope-filled yearning that almost makes him want to cry out. Oh, how he had wanted to be Lancelot in all the best things, only to become like him in the worst. And, oh, how he would dearly give his all that Richard never fall as he and Lancelot fell. God keep him.

There is no sermon at this second Mass, which is a good thing for everyone. Pacificus stands by a pillar near the entrance to the

Chapter house, and on seeing him there, Cromwell joins him and they converse in whispers.

"I have heard Mistress Fenton is being brought up from the castle even now, to be tried by the king after Mass – in there." He points towards the chapter house, the light bouncing off his emerald ring to cast a green streak on the white stone pillar beside them.

"Before the king's dinner?"

"The bishop did not think to tell you obviously."

"He did not. Things are – " he pauses to find the right word " – strained between us at present."

"I see." But Cromwell isn't really listening, his mind is elsewhere, though when he does come back his whisper is emphatic enough for Pacificus to catch the stale small beer on his breath. "A word, monk, and prithee hear me." Sweet Mary, even when he whispers it's like a cold fist in the belly. "I have done my arithmetic and looked into matters, and I see what you are about. There is little that stays hidden for long in these days. Then is not Lady Erpingham your daughter and Elizabeth Fenton her mother? And are not you thereby in truth Sir Cecil Erpingham? Is that not so? Answer me briefly for it matters not a groat either way to me today, but it may save her if you deal truly with me. You and she were lovers, am I right?"

"In truth all you say is correct, but that I am not Sir Cecil, my lord."

"But then I cannot find reason for your involvement, your attachment to her, to them."

"My lord, I dare not say – "

"Say it, for I swear you have few friends now!"

"It is a family matter."

"You, a Fenton? Well are you? Speak it." He drives the question hard and fast for he trusts a man under pressure to answer with his eyes. "No, then what? You, you – " Cromwell's eyes sidle towards the stained glass for a millisecond, sallying briefly into the upland territory of stories he heard so often when he himself was a soldier in foreign lands. "Sweet Mary, I am standing in front of Sir Hugh Erpingham! – here, but, what?" His gimlet pupils bore into Pacificus, for once dumfounded – surely he would be taller, Cromwell thinks!

"My lord, I swear by Saint Swithin that I am here only as you see me this day."

"I see," Cromwell shelves his astonishment momentarily, "and the bishop, what's his game, pray?"

"I…er – my lord, I have every reason to be loyal to him, but my conscience is now uneasy, that peradventure he has unwittingly fallen under the power of a noble who plans some mischief or other this very day."

"Yes, Sir Robert Aeyns, so-called former Prior of Hickling, he is known to us. What, do you think I spend all my energy at Augmentations counting relics from your precious monasteries? There is much of this mischief afoot at present; many little wars on many fronts. But I cannot arrest a man, especially a man of noble blood, without evidence. Can't have more martyrs. Do you know what he plans?"

"No, but it must involve the king, or at least the court in some way. Why else here and now?"

"Yes indeed, and you do not suspect me in this plot?"

"No, my lord, you are known as a loyal man."

"Ah yes, of course, I kept troth with Wolsey, even to the last, like you with your precious bishop, but the world has grown grey since then, and my hair with it." Cromwell's eyes sink just a little, before the ghosts flee and the dark fire once more ignites them.

"Your bishop has played a fast game these last years, and the only reason he was not on the gibbet last year after the rebellion was because I might need him later. You may choose to remain attached to him, that is your business, but I would not make my bed there if I were you. Now, this business with Elizabeth Fenton. I will speak to the king after Mass; you fetch your niece and her brothers, we'll see what can be done."

"Yes, my lord. Thank you."

"And one more thing; His Majesty, I know, would like to meet you – use you perhaps, for I have heard him speak oft of you – "

"No, my lord. If it please you, let Sir Hugh Erpingham remain at sea somewhere between the Venetian fleet and the Barbary coast. It is better that way, and it is all I ask."

"I see." Cromwell's lips purse and his head nods slowly, giving way in a manner that he seldom has done for years. "Very well. If it had been any other man I would have commanded it, but howsoever – " He trails off at this point as a new thread enters his mind – thoughts of the *Ars Amatoria*. He starts again very slowly, " – *howsoever*, if today turns out in Mistress Fenton's favour, you might think of taking her to wife – "

"To wife!" Pacificus' speaks louder than he meant in his astonishment, but then draws back to a whisper again. "To wife? And my vocation?"

"I wouldn't plan long-term in that direction." He watches the monk's eyes like a heron watches turbid water, before adding almost affectionately, "Believe me, I tell you this out of thanks."

"For...?"

"Today I have received an answer to something that has perplexed me greatly. When she did not return my suit, I thought it was on my account, but now I see it was on yours. I mention it for what it is worth. A man lives but once."

"Let the accused speak for herself, bishop, upon my word she looks like she hath a tongue, nay a prettier one than thine."

A half hour later Elizabeth Fenton is standing before the king – and, because of the occasion, virtually the entire Star Chamber – who have all been lectured for ten minutes by the bishop on the evils of continental reform, and the threat to the king's majesty and the peace of the realm *et cetera, et cetera.* The king is not amused, in fact, worse, is hungry. With every growl of his stomach, his eyes and mouth harden. He'll have this business transacted in ten minutes, and no more popish sermons.

"Come hither, woman. Speak."

Elizabeth Fenton is wearing the dress Pacificus asked her to, and looking every wit a damsel from some tower in one of Henry's childhood storybooks. The green of it matches the green of the Erpingham arms, still clearly seen bloodied and tied about Richard's arms when he arrives with his siblings halfway through the king's words. Piers and Beth alike would have run to her out of impulse, but even so, for all their dreaming and planning, she seems to them like a ghost returned from the grave. Did they ever really believe they would see her again with their own eyes? Yet here she is, but oh, how thin and white. She looks at them ravenously, but for only a moment; she will not trust herself to gaze longer. The king insists on his answer, leaning forward in what was once Bishop Nykke's favourite oak dining chair. "Well?"

"I am, and ever was, a loyal subject of your Majesty." Her voice is faint and hoarse at first because her throat is so dry, but she soon swallows, licks her lips, and summons up her courage. "Neither have I spoken against the royal prerogatives with regard to the state, nor uttered any seditious slander such as the bishop made mention of."

Cromwell is whispering in his ear, but he is brushed off like a fly, "Yes, Tom, yes, yes, I'm not blind."

He takes his eyes from the prisoner, looking to Lady Erpingham and Richard, beckoning them forward. "I am told, lady, that you have somewhat to ask of me; for I say your champion has won at least half the tournament this day. What would you?"

For those watching, the king's eyes now soften in a way that few have ever seen before – it is all his chivalric passion aroused, by God, he thinks, he'll make an example of this family, give them what they want if its in his power.

Beth's heart thunders erratically against the bars of her chest, and she near enough needs her champion's arm to make it into the large space at the centre of the chapter house, where they join their mother by the central pillar. Elizabeth chances one more look as she approaches. Can this be my little Beth? I spent half my life trying to forget the life I might have had with Cecil, and then here she stands, my own daughter, a lady adorned in silk and brocade, jewels and pearls, yay, standing before the king of England and having his royal favour. It seems like only yesterday that Beth was reaching out her hand as they would walk up the lane, or even sitting at table. And now look at her, it is too marvelous.

The bishop's eyes however, are not so favourably framed, but turn sharply towards Pacificus, who he sees standing in the shade of the entrance arch. What is this? I have arranged a little trial, a little pageant to show fealty to the crown, perhaps highlight where these reforms will take England, and what? I am to be denied even the simplicity of this, Pacificus? Oh, I know you are behind this, my own Judas, my Ahithophel, *et tu, Brute?* Yes, feel the heat of my eye upon you, for soon you will feel the heat of my displeasure; damn you, you will.

"I – we ask this day, Majesty, no more than you may show mercy to our mother." Beth's hand trembles as she makes a faint gesture towards the accused, and a sharp gasp runs about the vaults, arches and corbels of the chapter house. Rugge's face is a picture. He'd been sharing a prison with Pacificus' sister-in-law, and never known it. It's that moment when you begin to be unsure whether you are the dog or the tree; the one with the hammer and nails, or the one being crucified. The latter day Haman begins to examine his crosier, chasuble, tassels, the sleeves of his alb; indeed, anything to keep himself from finding the king's sudden gaze.

The king sits right back on his cushions, making the oak hinges squeak. "Well. That sets the cat among the pigeons, eh bishop?" He claps his hands, as if in a very merry jest, waiting now for the tittering to die down. "You know, my lady, I would have given you back the estates my father took from your grandfather if you had asked it – and who knows, perhaps I may yet if your kinsmen unhorses me too this afternoon, eh Brandon?"

"But, if it please your Majesty, we would not ask for land, only – "

"Yes, I know – your mother. The Lord Privy Seal has spoken to me about you, and I suppose you're of the same mind, young knight? Or would you prefer riches and lands instead?"

Richard's mouth is open like a fish and his head shaking slowly. When words do come, it is from Piers stepping forward with his green velvet beret in hand. "Nor I, Majesty."

"Nor you, page? And is she your mother too?"

"Yes, Majesty."

"Then a remarkable woman she be, and one worthy of the king's mercy, eh bishop?"

The bishop, with a supreme effort, forces the scowl from a beetroot-purple face. "Majesty, all England knoweth right well that you are a gracious and merciful sovereign, but – "

"And so I am, and so this woman shall receive a grant of my largesse, for verily her son hath fought like a true knight this day, wrought mightily with word and lance, and so she shall be set fr – "

But even as the pronouncement is upon his lips, old Norfolk is on his feet, knees cracking as he does so. If there is any way to wreck the plans of the Lord Privy Seal, or hurt these upstarts that have used his nephew so ill, he will seize it.

"Majesty, we have one and all received lavishly from the bounty of thy mercy; it is well known and noised abroad. And there is no man of warm blood in here, nay in the realm – " Except you, thinks Cromwell and Henry at the same time. "No man I say, who would not see this woman reunited with her family, if she repent her heresy – for it is treason against your Majesty. She says she has not offended you in matters pertaining to the state, but she may well offend in *praemunire*. Does she confess you as the true head of the church? Will she take the sacrament? Majesty, I would not that you be taken advantage of." The Fenton children look one to another, crestfallen, in disbelief and horror. Someone should say something, someone should help them.

"Thank you, my lord Norfolk. Your concern for my welfare is touching. I am sure this woman is every wit as penitent and pious as you and the bishop here." The king forces his ruddy cheeks upward with an unpleasant but short-lived grimace, then turns back less patiently to the accused, asking, "Well? How do you answer, madam?"

Elizabeth gazes long and steady at the king with eyes full of perception, though not impudence, and not in any way defiant. They are of an age, he and she, within a year or so. She has seen him only once in public before this day, and that was near twenty years hence. But her impression then was the same as it is now; that his eyes are too small in that rectangular lump of flesh, bone and curls that sits on his shoulders like a half-shaven rump of a Gloucester sow. They look out on life so narrowly, as if the world at all times and places were set to conspire against his happiness and dignity, that she reasons they must belong to a shrunken heart. This she thinks in an instant, as if in remembrance. But in the remaining seconds she is weighing up her beloved duty to her children and to her faith. For she has already prepared stout and eloquent answers to just such a question, but that was in her cell, and without her family at her side, looking now towards her. She does not meet their gaze, she dare not, nor respond to Piers' whispered prompts as the seconds pass.

"You see Majesty, she denies your headship by her silence." The duke triumphantly resumes his seat.

Cromwell bristles and pushes his sleeves back impatiently. "She denies or confirms nothing, she has said not a word."

"And how long should his Majesty wait?" The bishop comes to the duke's aid, gazing piously towards the ceiling vault.

"Madam?" The king closes his ears to them all, and holds out his hand to welcome her response. But still she does not speak, and every passing moment reinforces the likely outcome that she will not do so, perhaps cannot do so. Here is another Thomas More. And for all their sympathies, Cromwell and now even Pacificus are glad that she has not, for they know what she must say. Looks cross between them, Pacificus' hands unconsciously rubbing the scars on first one wrist, then the other; old, old wounds these.

As the silence extends, her children hold their breath, looking first at her, then down at the floor, willing her to answer. They have done so much to win her this freedom. What is happening? Will she not take it – for their sakes, at least? Piers, who cannot hold his tongue at the best of times, is almost beside himself; lips mumbling, wetting, whispering. She must not see him, dare not hear. Would it be such a sin just to say it and not mean it?

Her thoughts stream and merge in cold currents before her eyes, *loved not their lives till to the death, …not yet resisted unto blood, …overcame by the blood of the lamb and their word of their witnessing.* That old Wyclif Bible, that old Lollardy never leaves your head once it gets in. *If any man will come after me, let him deny himself, and take his cross, and follow me, …he that shall deny me before men, I shall deny before my Father that is in the heavens.* Round and round until she bites blood out of her trembling inner lip and feels the bitter taste of iron run round her tongue and hot down her throat, though she cannot swallow, or even think any more.

"Oh, Christ's blood!" exclaims the duke. "I am with the bishop; how long must we wait? Verily, she hath a tongue as fast as More's! How long, prithee?"

Then out of nowhere, before anyone else can add their verdict, Richard casts himself before the king on bended knee. "Until Michaelmas, your Majesty!" Then recovering composure, for he does not himself know whence the words come: "Just until Michaelmas. If we have found favour in your eyes, then hear our request that our mother be given until then to answer thee."

The bishop, the duke and one or two others begin to scoff and tut, but Piers and Beth are in haste to join their brother on the floor, and thus prostrated hold forth their petition. The king at this moment is too full of wonder and amusement to process the claim. He closes both lips over a handsome ruby ring, pondering how he may respond to such a winsome suit.

But he need not have worried, for as ever his faithful Thomas of Putney is on hand with his Cockney wit and lawyer's nous. "But of course, Michaelmas! Fitting and just; for when the bailiff or reeve of the manor call their tenants to bring account after harvest, should not His Majesty receive word also?"

The duke is about to speak but the king is on his deliberate feet, moving his square-toed shoes within inches of the Lady Elizabeth, quite disregarding her silent mother. He raises her by the right hand, the limestone dust transferring into the crevices of his palm.

He looks her kindly in the eye and, remembering her sharp words to him at the tournament, says so none else behind can hear: "Let it be as you have asked, for am I not a merciful sovereign?" He lingers near her and Beth returns him stare for stare. "And a man too? But I pray you lady, do not put words into your mother's mouth – or force her conscience. So you see, as in the tournament, so here too, *and thrice more in the affairs of the heart*, the king is subject, as any fool, to the rules of the game."

Here he pauses, his warm breath mingling with hers and his eyes wandering to her heaving breast. He could happily stay here a while longer; there is something about this quiet, defiant, yet unbroken beauty, that would be worth the taming. But by and by he draws himself up and says, this time so all can hear, "So, the accused shall present herself and her answer, and her daughter, at court on Michaelmas Eve, where she may plead."

Then quietly, to Beth: "As, my dear, may I – plead for a heart that has captivated a king with beauty, charm and maidenly virtue." The king turns to face the men on their cushioned chairs, "I have spoken. Let it be recorded and enacted. And now bishop, let me at my dinner, for I'm damned if I must joust on that paltry repast you gave me this morning!"

31

The Assassins

Ut sementem feceris ita metes
As you sow so will you reap

"You have seen nothing?" Cromwell says, as he moves alongside Pacificus amidst to post-lunch bustle in the tilt-yard.

"No, my lord, but I have seen his retainers; the two that stand by and another two out of their liveries, garbed as farriers, near the king's stabling tents."

Pacificus peers round the corner from the stabling yard to the tilt yard, where Sir Robert Aeyns is making a clean sweep of the knights of the shire. Crunch; the splinters of white ash spin in the sky, and the clattering thud of yet another noble backside on the sand brings Sir Robert yet closer to facing the king. "Could you not just arrest him?"

"What, without evidence, and while he carries all before him?"

Cromwell pushes the beret up on his brow, revealing a red line beaded with sweat. "There would be an outcry, and the king would have my guts too, if we found nothing substantial." He will not tell this monk, but it is not Aeyns he worries about so much as the duke and the bishop. They might be in this together. An arm's length assassination perhaps, then placing papist Mary on the throne with Norfolk as regent, and Rugge as...hmmm...archbishop? Yes, he'd like nothing better than to knock Cranmer off his perch, restore the old superstition, have both our heads on Tower Bridge. Perhaps this Sir Hugh Erpingham is in it with him? Yet he did not hide his concern from me, there are wheels within wheels here. Wish I had more of my own men with me.

"Do one thing for me monk, for I see the king is leaving the box for his armour and horse; set those Fentons to watch this stable yard, and you the king's tent, for surely I would be suspected if I am seen near either. I'll wait in the royal box; from there I can see both gates. If you or they signal to me, I can dispatch the master-at-arms forthwith. Blount is a loyal man. Keep faith with me in this and it shall go well with you and them and their mother. Anon!"

All is arranged; Hobbs, Richard and Piers watch Sir Robert come and go from his various victories, but so far he appears to have nothing other than the tournament on his mind. He is greeted and served between bouts by one of his two retainers, one acting as squire, another hovering near the gate. Pacificus surveys the situation carefully. He can feel danger - the very air is scorched as with gunpowder. He wills himself to breathe calmly, to moisten his dry mouth, to restrain his heart from breaking through his ribs. *What, when, how and who?* God, I wish I had more time, and more men too.

He walks swiftly towards the other end of the tournament ground where the royal tents are situated, adorned in crimson, yellow and gold trim. The lions of England flutter overhead, and so too are the billowing clouds of an ominous sky. The king has already left; he waits, mounted, ready to enter the lists, yet the farriers have not moved. The applause is almost deafening, even from here. Pacificus is nervous at leaving the others so near Aeyns and his men; he has a bad feeling of unpreparedness amidst multiple traps. It is not how he has ever liked to work. He stands by a cook tent admiring the meats and fowl that hang on iron racks, keeping a close eye on the two farriers from that vantage point. What have they got in that tool box, or under those thick leather aprons? He can imagine all sorts of scenarios, but assassination is the only option that meets all the facts.

For a moment he is taken aback by the bishop's audacity – staggered even. It is a bold hand to play even from a man like the bishop. The thought flickers in the recesses of his mind like the final flare of a spent candle. It is that perhaps the king's death would end all this bloodshed, and that with this regicide, all the old traditions and festivals and institutions would miraculously return. Had he not thought of doing so himself in those dark days after Robert Aske's death? But even as this dying flame illuminates his imagination, Pacificus applies his fingers to the wick. No, though it might help me, I will have no part in that. What kind of monarchy could anyone hereafter submit to with true troth, if regicide were always so near a possibility. And what foundation would the insurrection of so few be for the tenure of their future polity? No, I'll have non of it. In my gut I know it has been right to help these Fentons, but to murder a king, even this one – or to stand back and let others do the dirty work - no, I will have no part in it. If God allows Henry's reign to blunder on even after eighty thousand men could not change the royal mind then, if nothing else, this murder would be against the Almighty's plan, though I understand it not and like it even less.

But – Pacificus brings his fevered mind back to the scene he now surveys – why the two locations? Are there multiple targets, or multiple sites offering opportunity? Unlikely with so few men, and besides, if the king falls that is enough to achieve the bishop's aims; who else would matter after that? Pacificus quickly assesses what Cromwell must have seen twenty minutes before: one target, two kill sites; one primary, one secondary. But which is which? He looks steadily at the farriers, remembering them as monks in his own cloister – dear God, what a world! They are feigning laughter and jollity but their ready hands and furtive looks tell a different story. He thinks of them in comparison to Aeyns, and the retainers he met earlier outside Rugge's smoky room. *Think, man. What would you do if you were Aeyns?* Might he let these two carry out the deed instead of himself? No, not he, it would run counter to the cogs in that bold Norman forehead of his. These farriers must be the fall-back; he's the goose, by God. In the arena, that's how he'll do it, in front of them all. *But how?*

Pacificus cannot see the means, not in his mind, nor in his experience. A matchlock, a wheellock, a crossbow, a tipped lance? The tilt yard is too uncertain a place, surely. Perhaps easier if you wanted to die in the act as a martyr yourself, but if you would live? Aeyns does not seem the sacrificial sort, too full of himself to contemplate defeat at any level – no, he's no martyr that one. No, he'll do it and expect to walk away, but how? How damn it, how?

He feels his pulse quicken, the blood coursing hot in his veins. The time for thinking is past. It no longer matters how, *the thing is*, and *is now*, happening at this moment – the trumpets are sounding for the king to ride. Two sharp breaths through flared nostrils - alright GO! Pacificus moves out from behind the meat stand as if to go towards the gate, and the farriers recognise him at once. Their faces drop like stones – they have been warned about him – and now they look at each other with uncertainty. The thinner of the two goes not for the box, but the hessian matting at his side. They are thirty feet away and evidently determined to not let Pacificus reach the gate. There is no more time. He roars out to the hascals standing sentry on the king's tent: "A plot! A plot! Look to it! Assassins! Rally to the king!"

These two men, midway between Pacificus and the farriers, call out and raise their matchlocks but before either can fire they feel the swift punch of crossbow bolts in their chests. Their weapons fall, one going off with a plume of smoke. The king's retinue, some thirty of them, scatter for their tents or any other cover. The assassins are reloading and looking sharp as foxes at the clearing smoke, as well they might for they have been told that this monk will waste no time. They see him amidst the haze of smoke, going for the fallen matchlock, but are not prepared for the almost immediate yellow flash and the crunch o lead ball on bone. One assassin, the one Pacificus judged more able to make a swift shot, feels the ball shatter his upper ribs and enter his lung. It is like having a lead stake driven through him at one blow. He will rise no more. John Blount, captain of the bodyguard, has drilled his hascals to always double-powder the shot, calls it his crowd stopper. The assassin crumples, gasping on the ground as the breath leaves his body, looking up like a lamb as Pacificus rushes his fellow conspirator and dashes his brains across the yard with the matchlock butt. Not that the monk even stops to see the effect of the second blow, for anyone can recognise the sound of a broken skull, the hollow thud giving way to gore. Pacificus is already running towards the gate, yelling like a madman, "A plot! Stop the joust!"

John Blount has not heard the shots amid the roar of the crowds, but recognises the bishop's aide running and shouting in his direction, the skirts of his habit whirling and the dust flying in clouds from the beat of his sandals.

"Let him through! Let him through!" he bellows at the hascals blocking his way. "What is it? What ails thee, man?"

"There's a plot," Pacificus urges him breathlessly, "For God's sake, man, the king must not ride!"

But the king is already halfway down the yard, a shimmering mass of speeding steel, juddering in his saddle like so many lead-filled cooking pots. Aeyns is out to meet him too, lance angled and sure, and behind him at the yard gate, his other two retainers – watched carefully by Hobbs, Richard and Piers. Sir John, a veteran of Bosworth, who has now served the Tudors for the greater part of his own three-score-years-and-ten, does not even ask for details, nor flinch from the shock. He motions to Cromwell who is standing like a sentinel in the royal box. Cromwell does not return the nod, but goes straight to barking at others.

"It's the lance my lord, the lance – " Pacificus gabbles as the moment of impact approaches, but the old eagle is not listening.

"Secure the gates!" he bellows at his son, Sir George who, unlike his father, is velveted and feathered like a man who has grown up in court, as indeed he has. But even despite the foppish affectations, the young man obeys without question, starting with three hascals round the back of the main stand.

In frozen horror Sir John and Pacificus watch the titans clash in the arena to a near deafening eruption from the crowd. They see Sir Robert's lance glancing from the king's oversized besagew, the extra steel originally intended to cover the platelets between shoulder and chest, but in Henry's case enlarged to shield half his left chest – and a good thing too, on this occasion. Pacificus sees Aeyns' lance bend and flex as it glances; it does not splinter. Thoughts spring to his mind like a volley of matchlock fire. It is the lance, it is! See how even a brute like Aeyns struggles to hold it straight; the thing is heavy, maybe twice the weight of an ash lance – perhaps green oak, yes that would do it, strength with flex. And the crown? He can't see for the end of the lance is still shaking as Aeyns thunders towards them. But when he does see it, Pacificus grasps Sir John's wrist, "Look you! The crown is clay, with steel beneath!"

Sir John orders his men to prime their matchlocks but Aeyns sees Pacificus and the commotion at the gate, and so wheels his horse and makes to charge the king once more. Two matchlocks discharge to their left, but at fifty or so yards the effect is uncertain; one enters through the steel into his riding arm, the other merely glances off the thick plate on his back.

There is no time, Pacificus thinks, there is no time. He dashes into the arena before Aeyns can spur his horse to speed. What is he going to do? He hardly knows himself, only he knows that the power to act brings responsibility. All those years, trying to forget, to let the world pass by his abbey, his church, his rood screen – his Adullam's cave. It was Rugge who first dragged him back into the world of incarnate action – or was it the Fentons? – he can hardly tell now. But he has seen the indifference of passivity and the evil that always floods in to fill that vacuum, and he'll not be party to it anymore.

Before he knows it, he's level with Aeyn's ankles and just in time to jump and take hold of the saddle horn before the destrier has taken stride. Through his helm Aeyns does not at first see what has happened, only he feels the pull at the saddle. But once he realizes, his steel gauntlet is hammering on Pacificus' head, face and shoulder. As they gain pace, the monk's feet start to drag on the ground, terrifyingly close to the thundering hooves, inches from the rail. They gather momentum towards the returning king, who, because of the barrier and his high visor has not noticed anything amiss. Aeyns still has his lance arm free and can easily make a pass with or without a monk clinging on to his side. This time he'll aim away from that reinforced besagew – he need only make a flesh wound for the steel tip is poisoned too. And the monk, he thinks? Crushed between the Antichrist and a true soldier of Christ, a fitting end. Aeyns digs his spurs without mercy into the horse, closing the gap. Once his feet are gone, Pacificus finds it impossible to do anything but hang on, and use his free hand to fend off such blows as he may. But after only a few yards his left hand is losing grip, his fingers feel brittle under the relentless pounding of hooves and fists. His right arm is vainly grabbing at Aeyns' armour; if he could just grab it, grab something to pull on, but it's no use, and even if he could get a grip he'd not be able to affect the position of the lance. Aeyns is a machine, right arm fixed like a siege ram. Forty yards to go. Snorting horse flesh, dirt flying. Thirty yards, the clatter of mail, the roar of the crowd. Twenty, fifteen, ten. In the moment before impact Aeyns stops spreading Pacificus' nose across his face, and sets his reins. Pacificus sees through the blood that he's damned whichever way this goes; crushed between them if he holds on, or crushed underfoot if he lets go. Five yards, a lance's distance almost and he finds his right hand slipping onto Aeyns' foot. It is then he remembers the beserkers of old who disembowelled knights' horses under them. Fixing his fist round Aeyns' heel, he rams the spur into the flank of his horse; scarring and screwing the spikes until they rip the flesh ragged in the tender parts. The animal, in sheer fight-or-flight, takes to the air; bucking and kicking out like a thing possessed. Pacificus is thrown like a mannequin into the path of the king's horse, but rolls free before its arrival.

Aeyns is nearly thrown but, by some devilry of his own, maintains the saddle. The lance is cast aside. He looks behind but the king's men are in pursuit of him now, and the king safely behind them. For a fantastic, breathless moment, Aeyns raises his visor and makes his calculations. He glances between the gate and king, the king and the hascals. *Damnation!* Aeyn's face is boiling with rage and his right hand is now brandishing a long cavalry wheellock that he had kept concealed in his saddle. His horse wheels and rears. It is too late. *Damn that monk.* The king is lost to him and the sensation of obdurate failure is something so new, so intolerable that he growls like a mad dog. All this he does while fixing his gaze and the wheellock on Pacificus. He is near enough and would dearly love to pull the trigger, but he knows better than to waste his only shot. Instead, with a great shout, he spurs the horse about and on towards the far gate. A moment later he is gone.

Meanwhile in the stabling yard, Hobbs and Richard go to the aid of two of Cromwell's men in their attempt to subdue Aeyn's retainers. At first Aeyn's men appear to put up no resistance, but that is a ruse to lure the guards closer. Once within range, they seize the matchlock barrels pointing at them and open the guards' throats with concealed knives. It happens so quickly that Richard and Piers have hardly had a chance to move before the guards fall to their knees, clutching their throats and vainly trying to stem the gushing off blood. Richard and Piers stand aghast as the sight while Aeyns' men are retrieving their weaponry. Hobbs however, piles in like the bulldog he is, closing on them with sword and buckler, wounding one of the men within his opening strokes. Richard and Piers are soon at his side, Richard with his father's sword, Piers with a pikestaff grabbed from the stable yard.

"Stay behind me!" Richard says.

"I will not," replies Piers who is at his brother's side and now waving the staff in the direction of the grim-faced assassin holding Hobbs off with his rapier and a foot-long basilard with swept hilt.

Hobbes gestures for them to spread out, and tries to shout as much with the half of the tongue left in his head. "Spread out! Watch him – HIM!"

It's too late. These men know what they're about, and at that very moment, Hobbs' guard is lifted by one and breached by the other. The steel enters his gut and kidneys like a cold cramp. The wounded assassin goes for a kill stroke while Hobbs is doubling, but Richard smashes his blade away and up-cuts with such a stroke across the man's face that he doesn't even cry out before death finds him. On seeing this, the second man rushes for the stables and slams the door. The boys give chase but Richard is too slow in armour and Piers, having just seen the sharp end of a sword an inch from his own head, knows he cannot face this man alone, or at least not with just a sharpened pole. Richard tries the latch but it is locked. Behind the door he hears the clatter of hooves. This was a planned escape route for the assassins. Doubtless they have a way out. Partly relieved not to face another swordsman, the brothers return to find Hobbs failing fast. Piers goes straight down to him on his knees. Hobbes cups Piers' chin tenderly. "Good boy." Are the words that Piers makes out, over and over, as the pallor of Hobbes' face turns that ephemeral grey that he remembers in baby Samuel's as they laid him in the coffin.

Eventually Richard too kneels beside them and raises Hobb's head. He doesn't know what to say, this is beyond words. He tries to lay his hand on the wound to stem the flow, but Hobbs catches it and shakes his head, gesturing the futility.

"No!" Richard grips Hobbs' hand. "No! no! We must try."

"Shh," Hobbs says, cheeks smarting and momentarily closing his eyes with the pain. But when he opens them again, the brothers see that his stare is like the sun bursting the clouds in the midst of an autumn shower. "A knight," he says firmly, "a knight." Hobbs brings Richard's hand to his lips and kisses it.

"Hobbs! Hobbs! Oh, good God, no!" It is at this moment that Sir Geoffrey arrives. "Oh man, oh no, no, man; have they done for thee too!" And then shouting into the arena: "A surgeon! Bring me a surgeon! Oh Hobbs, dear God; not thee, not thee!" He falls on him as an equal, a father even. There are tears a-plenty but no surgeon, and no priest either, for all focus and tumult is on the king, who is quite unscathed.

Pacificus arrives to see Sir Geoffrey saying the *Paternoster* over the dying man. He completes the circle gladly, and it does not seem a hard thing for Hobbs to give in to the weakness and tiredness that now sweep over him like a damp January draft. He'd never had a family of his own to speak of, but to die surrounded by men he esteems, who love him more than he knew, is enough for him, and more than most men could claim after longer lives. His last word is "happy'. After that it seems that he breathes to take a breath that never comes. Pacificus stoops and closes his eyes, as he has done for many other fallen men he'd called brothers.

"Follow me; the king is asking for you." Cromwell is the first to find Pacificus at the yard. Hobbes is being carried away and he is standing alone when he hears the voice at his shoulder.

"Master Secretary. Did they stop Aeyns?"

"No." Cromwell screws up his lips and nose, as he always does when he's chewing on a hard matter. "The dullards on the gates were too slow, and two of my men are now dead. It's a mess."

"Yes, and Lord Hastings has lost his man at arms – "

"Regrettable, but never mind that now; the king would speak with you. Can you do something with your face?"

"My face?

"Clean it up man, and get someone to fix your nose. You are to stand before His Majesty."

"Oh, I see."

"I came for you myself in case you – perhaps after all this – would consider revealing yourself." Cromwell tilts his head to better read the monk. "Opportunities like this rarely come; he will raise you this day if you told him who you are, I know it. England stagnates to putrefaction for want of a noble that the people could look to, a general against our enemies – "

"My lord, you forget I am a Benedictine, pledged to serve Christ." Pacificus looks at him, incredulous, does this man never stop?

"You are pledged to the pope more like, that is fealty to a foreign power, and you should watch your tongue."

"I desire naught from any prince in Europe, let alone the one who has hounded and slain my brethren, and taken from the poor their last hope for the bitter winters ahead."

Cromwell begins his usual diatribe against the corruptions of the clergy, but Pacificus isn't done. His blood's up now and so he lets it all out with a vehemence that even silences the Lord Privy Seal. "So, there were some monks and abbots worse than their profession, but would you argue that the guilds and the nobility will somehow be better than theirs? God's oath, almost to a man they live for filthy lucre, their god is the mammon of unrighteousness. You think you can destroy the habits and keep the haloes? You think that I will be party to this? That I will supplement what is lacking in the nobility, as if I could anyway? Look you, I will see the king, yes, I will see him, but I want nothing, nor any more talk of who I was. That man died in the Great Siege and I am all that is left."

"Ah now Tom, is this the monk?" The king is sitting in his tent on a French couchette of red silk. Norfolk and Rugge are barred entry, which has put Cromwell in high spirits. Sir Thomas Heneage is fluttering about talking to well wishers who appear in the tent doorway. Charles Brandon sits on a separate couch with a blonde courtesan rubbing his shoulders.

"Yes, Majesty; Brother Pacificus of Saint Benet's Abbey."

As he bows low, Pacificus' back stiffens in spasm, "Highness."

"Well, brother, you acquitted yourself this day like a man. I am told you felled two more papist conspirators outside this very tent. Brandon here thinks you must be a saint – *or else a knight.*"

Is he jesting, or has Cromwell already told him? Pacificus cannot tell. He glances around the room to check their faces before lowering his eyes toward Henry's pantoffle slippers once more. "I - er, well that is to say, a man plays many parts in this life."

"What did I say Hal?" Brandon interrupts with a jollity wholly unfitted for the occasion, "what did I say, eh? Every saint has a past."

"And every sinner a future, I know it." The King says, bending forward towards Pacificus and resting one hand on the arm of the chair and fixing his other elbow on his knee so as to prop up his head. "But I would hear it from you brother for I warrant he has noble blood and a knightly bearing. Speak man for thyself."

"Majesty, they say of Arthur that *here in this world he changed his life.* If it please you, I will not speak of what is past but rather that I am, as you now see, a loyal subject of your Majesty and a lowly brother seeking salvation for his soul, absolution for his past – and no more."

"Ha – Majesty!" It's Brandon again. "He's got more balls than most knights in this realm. Raise him, Henry, and give him the garter, like I said."

"It is in my gift..." The king offers the words tentatively, as on a golden platter, gauging what he assumes is his suppliant.

"Your Majesty is very generous, but I have taken vows – "

"Vows? Come man, I am your sovereign."

Pacificus glances up, trying to appear humble. Is the king even aware of the irony? He broke his own vows; took an axe to his own marriage and then an axe to the monasteries. Does he think we are all the same as him? "But my vows were to God." This he says a little too quickly, so he adds tactfully, "I desire no more than that your Majesty be in health, and do the will of God."

Brandon slaps his knee. "Oh, *fortiter in re, suaviter in modo - Gentile in manner and bold in deed!* We have a rare one here, Henry! What's to be done?" What, indeed?

As it turns out there is quite a lot the king will do, for it is a matter upon which he mulls a good part of the night. Pacificus' mention of Arthur has particularly exercised his mind in the small hours. His own dear brother Arthur, dead these thirty years, is what exercises him most. All his father's plans for his firstborn's kingdom come readily to mind – a new Camelot, a new Arthurian age. One Christmastide beside a roaring fire, he even remembers his father reading those last lines from *le Morte d'Arthur* to them both. "Yet some men say in many parts of England that King Arthur is not dead, but had by the will of our Lord Jesu into another place; and men say that he shall come again, and he shall win the holy cross." What happened to all that hope? Henry recoils and shudders at the remembrance. A malign vapour brought forth a plague, *that is what happened.* Within weeks Arthur lay dead in Ludlow while the oil of youth was still on him. He was buried in Worcester under the banners of Cadwaladr and Brutus of Troy, and with the broken staves of office of Sir William Uvedale, Sir Richard Croft and his household ushers thrown into his cold grave with him. What an end, what pathos. Henry had wept for days. They had been raised mostly apart, yet Arthur had been everything to the ten year old upon whose head the crown had so suddenly and heavily sat. He had never picked up the Arthurian romances again after that day. There would be no second coming of Arthur, no Camelot - just him. His mother had tried to comfort the king, give him another heir, but had died in childbirth. The gentle hands that had taught him to hold a reed and to write, lay still and cold as marble. There would be no other prince now, just him. The memory had been hateful to him - survivor's guilt, men call it. He swore to be no tyrant as his father had been, not to deflower maids or cast out widows. Children promise all manner of things before they know what the world is. For all that old Skelton had catechised him, he knows he has become most of what he hated in his father. And it is always in these hours before dawn, so far away from the comforting words of a fawning court, that Henry fights off the accusations of conscience and the recriminations of a history that was intended but never came to pass. The monk's words have stirred him and he will speak to him.

When morning finally comes, the King appears before his retinue and tells them what he intends. He will not stay in Norwich for the week as planned, but return that very day to Newmarket and thence to London. He has heard that Lady Erpingham's champion and his garrulous page hazarded their lives for his safety too, and that Lord Hastings lost a man in the fray. They will all, including the monk, escort the king on horseback beyond the city gates. Cromwell sees good publicity, Sir John Blount sees dangers, but is satisfied if the king will wear a breastplate under his robes. They depart the bishop's palace after taking wine on the terrace. The bishop is there to bid them adieu. Cromwell has been to speak to him, let him know what he knows, letting him know who now pulls the strings. Reforms will be swifter from now on in Norfolk, that is for sure. The Duke of Norfolk rides with the royal cavalcade, *but behind the Erpinghams* – a humiliation he bears manfully. Lady Elizabeth wears emerald green velvet and is adorned with every pearl that Lady Maria can find. "I would have worn these myself," says she, "but I shall be behind with Uncle, and – well, you shall be next to the king not I, and I won't have him going back to London thinking we in the provinces have no style. Yes, yes dear, you can keep your blessed kirtle how you will, you'll never die a widow now you have the king's attention – you might even be queen."

Beth accepts the pearls. "A queen! Why Maria, what an imagination you have. The king could have but one use for me, and that he shall not."

"Then see to it that you receive no money, only gifts small and those only through others. And, remove no item of clothing in his presence, nay not so much as a hairpin – oh, how jealous I shall be; you at court after Michaelmas and I languishing in Norfolk."

She rides on the king's left, Richard flanking her with the blooded Erpingham standard flying freely above their heads alongside the king's Beaufort pennant. Richard is sober in countenance; the blood-letting and cauterising of the shoulder wound have each taken their toll. He feels as though he could sleep until Saint Crispin's day, but holds his head high, even so. To the king's right rides Pacificus and beside him

Piers, grinning ear to ear. Ahead of them and on every side, ride the king's hascals, stern as stone, weapons drawn.

When they pass under the palace gates, the king points up to the statue of Sir Thomas. "See, my lady; your ancestor smiles today, methinks." From this point on, the streets down towards the castle are thronged with people of every rank, all wild with glee to see the king's champions. Cromwell is right; in one afternoon these Erpinghams have near saved the monarchy from all the unpopularity of three years of reforms. The king waves and makes pleasantries to Lady Elizabeth in between his casual gestures to the crowd. He wants to know whether she could get used to this. She says she couldn't. He laughs it off – mind, today he'd laugh anything off, except perhaps a matchlock ball. For that, Pacificus is looking at every open window, every balcony, every turret. It would be so easy, he thinks, and yet for all his searching, the demoniac face of Robert Aeyns is nowhere to be seen. Cromwell, who observes the monk's tight vigil, shouts forward above the din: "I have looked him up."

"Who?"

"Aeyns, of course. His mother was from Livonia, he was a Teutonic knight on her account, and very effective from what I'm told. Went missing after their Grandmaster Albert of Brandenburg turned Lutheran, and exchanged the order's Prussian possessions for a duchy under his uncle, King Sigismund of Poland."

"And the knights?" Pacificus knows them by reputation; every man of them thought himself equal to a prince – and a cruel one at that.

"The Livonian knights took it wrathfully as you could imagine, and swore a terrible revenge on the Lutheran princes, and – as they put it – on all other Antichrists."

"You knew all this yesterday, didn't you?"

"I know all sorts of things, but look to yourself, man. You have bruised his heel, I warrant he shall bruise your head 'ere long, that is, if we don't get him first."

"Tom!" The king has left off his attentions to the Lady Elizabeth.

"You and your schemes! Let the man alone while he rides at my side. For it is soon time that we shall be parted from them." And then leaning back in his saddle, he jests, "Come monk, I would speak with you anon. And you, Tom, spend a little more time waving and wooing to the crowd – you have need of friends down here."

"Your majesty?" Pacificus spurs his horse to the king's side.

"And how is your nose today? Don't answer, I can see for myself." There is a brief pause in which Henry says yes, then coughs awkwardly. Pacificus can see two small yellow marks on the king's breaches where his ulcers have transgressed the bandages beneath. "Look, there is something I want to say. You spoke of Arthur yesterday, how he changed his life in this world. I have been thinking on it somewhat in the night season - thinking on it, and you and I and also, Sir Gawain's green baldric. Do you remember that telling?"

"The sash given by the Green Knight?"

"The very same. See you, I make no window into your soul, monk. Your past is your own affair today. That much I owe you, in a debt. But I did take note of what you said yesterday, and your visage - the way you looked at me. Don't think I am insensible to the plight of my people. We have all done much we would amend. But for all Arthur could do, yet the table was still broken, and for all Gawain might have hoped to do, he still failed in the matter of adultery. Mark you that, his other virtues were no less real just because he failed in the matter of women. Are you and I better men than them? I think not. Remember too that Arthur made each knight of his table wear that green baldric to remind them likewise of their clay feet. So judge me not harshly, monk, nor thyself. Leave all to heaven. There is only one righteous and that is God. All flesh is as grass. Each of us follows as we may, falteringly and probably, and most wrongly in the places where we thought ourselves most right. Think on that, and also, think on my offer, which still stands. I can't get Cromwell to tell me ought about you and I am too weary now of intrigues anyway, but the offer still stands. Ah, good, there is the city gate at last."

When they have finally passed through Saint Stephen's gate a halt is called and the crowds fall silent and expectant. Under the shade of the gate the king presents a gold and sapphire brooch to Beth, a gilt dagger to Piers and a German rapier hilt to Richard. He says he looks forward to seeing them again soon after Michaelmas, under a better star. They are all still mounted. The Fentons smile, nod, and bow their heads. Even Piers is unsure if he should speak. There is an awkward pause where the king arranges his gloves and nods one last time to Beth. "But what," he says then, "shall be done for the man whom the king delights to honour?" He asks this looking at the Fentons, and repeats it under the dull echo of the flint and mortar in the gateway. He twists his velvet bulk the other way and catches Norfolk and Cromwell's eye. "What shall be done, eh?"

The duke looks as if he has a suggestion, but Brandon shouts "What, Majesty? Tell us."

The king turns back to Pacificus. "I tell you, that man shall wear the king's own ring, a life for a life, so all the realm may know that in Norfolk the king has loyal subjects that *love not their lives unto the death*, but serve and protect their anointed king."

Henry removes his glove in full view of them all and prises a gold and ruby ring from his index finger. This he gives to the monk with a straight look, closing his fingers over it. "For thy troth and valour. You may send it back if you ever hath need of my help."

Cromwell observes them, thumbing an almost identical ring that the king gave him the year before. He thinks Thomas More may have had one too, Wolsey too for that matter, for all the good it did him.

The king's gaze falls upon the slums beyond the city gate and moves the conversation on accordingly. "Now monk, Baron Cromwell here tells me that in Geneva there are no poor beyond the walls, but that all their ilk are lodged in garrets at the centre of the city; he thinks we should do better than all this here." He waves a hand at the ragged shacks, torn coverings, and the thin columns of smoke barely struggling above the stench. He has spoken without much thought, though he has phrased it as if he expected a reply.

Pacificus remembers Brother William Beccles, almoner of Saint

Benet's, and all his woe of recent years. He remembers the blue fingers, the black mouths, the biting cold, fresh graves of young and old, the haunt of crows pecking at the fresh soil all through early spring. "Well he might, Majesty, for winter approaches and without the monasteries – " Cromwell is scowling at Pacificus so much that he catches himself and stops mid sentence.

The king is not after advice; he brushes Pacificus away with, "Yes, but *the poor ye shall always have with you.*" And then, blithely, "Did not Our Lord say as much – but tell the bishop to see these people fed this winter; do something useful." With that all done, the king retired to his coach and leaves with his cavalcade for Newmarket, and the rest return, as did the disciples after the ascension, to the city.

32

The Setting Sun

Di maiores, di minores
The greater gods; the lesser gods
(i.e. men of eminence, the men of merit)

"Yes, of course they will come with us." Sir Geoffrey is standing with Pacificus and Maria in the chancel of Saint Giles, Norwich, after Hobbs' funeral. Maria says it is unthinkable that they should go back to a hovel on the marsh, when they could be the toast of county society. Sir Geoffrey nods a tired grey head. He will have Hobbs interred back at Bindringham, he thinks. Lady Maria is talking on, but Pacificus is listening more to the parish women – the ones who attend all funerals here – as they inspect Cranmer and Cromwell's new Great Bible, finally complete and now chained to the desk. They clutch their primers tightly to their breasts as they prate against it. What, will they soon have all divine service in the language of the costermonger and alehouse? *Over their dead bodies! Whatever next?* They say they will not even stay to hear it read at Mass, the priest will have no part of it, and that some even say Bishop Walter de Suffield, who founded the hospital, can be heard at night turning in his grave because of it. One hatchet-faced biddy even says she feels faint just standing near it; she needs air, it's likely bewitched! Her friends take her by the shawl and rush her out, as if she were a catch being hurried to the quayside.

On their way, they pass the Fentons in the porch. A physician from the Great Hospital, of which this church is a small part, is examining Richard's wounds. The middle-aged herbalist wrinkles his nose until all its dark hair sticks out. He says he would have used balsam to clean the wound; medicine is changing, ligatures and cauterising have had their day. He's desperate to share other new things he learnt at the university *à Paris*, but Beth presses him to speak plainly. It is healing, he admits with evident disappointment, but – hope enters his voice – there is still a chance of rogue splinters causing pestilence. They should watch for a fever.

Back in the chancel, Pacificus is still not listening to Maria. He's gazing at the black eagles on the embossed ceiling, painted in honour of Anne of Bohemia when she married Richard II. As he considers the cold hinterlands beyond the low countries, with their spires sharp as frosted pines and dialects guttural as scraping boots, his thoughts return to the Teutonic knights and Sir Robert Aeyns. A shiver runs down the lower part of his spine. He knows that look; the bear robbed of her cubs – he'll be back for sure. He is however, happy that the Fentons will be cared for, and advises both Richard and Sir Geoffrey to beware the Earl of Surrey. "He'll not move for a while, but he will eventually, and remember, he is at court and you are not. To have a seat at the king's table usually means that at least you are not on the menu. But you may well be, so keep your heads down."

He does not say much at all in parting to them after that, and what he is thinking he cannot discuss in front of Sir Geoffrey or Maria. He thought this would be the end of a complete story, not a chapter unfinished. They may go and visit their mother at the castle jail, he will not. For these stirrings in his breast, so deep and encompassing; he knows from his experience in Italy, *oh, what a mocker they are of men's vows.* Henry can say what he will about Gawain, but Pacificus thinks he is a match for such temptations. But, thinks he, a man may think he is stepping in a puddle only to find himself in up to the waist. Poets and troubadours may need their muses, Dante his Beatrice, Petrarch his Laura, Botticelli his Simonetta Vespucci, but monks need sense, and not that sort of inspiration. He groans slightly. Why will God make it so hard for him to complete his vows? Why can he not stop thinking about her. He takes his leave of the children with warmth, though each one can feel something hollow in the victory that they have achieved here.

He will see them at Lammas Day in a few weeks, but for now, he must beg his bishop's leave to return to the cloister. He has two broken fingers, probably a few ribs too, eyes as black and blue as a swallow's back, joints and humours all out of kilter. He has left Mark constructing a scaffold at Saint Helen's so he can finish his pictures before the autumn festivals. He wants to be back there, away from all this, wants to hide in his paints, his tinctures, his ochres, his saints. Only when he paints is he outside of time, released from some of the pain of being himself. Well, that and being with her.

The bishop will not see him but gives him leave to return with letters for Prior Thomas, and like Uriah, who carried his own death warrant to Joab, so Pacificus suspects these will in some way seal his own fate. He visits Simon at the lazar house before descending the causeway to the monastery. Simon has had a fever flaring on and off this last week; it comes in the dry summer weather, yet one more thing he picked up in the Mediterranean.

"It gets worse as I get older." Simon wheezes, "I never had your constitution, brother."

"Just feels that way; you said the same last year."

"Yes – because it was as true last year as it is this, now give me your arm. Jesu, your face is a picture, don't tell me; the joust. We have heard. So much for living quietly!" He struggles from his cot and motions to the door. He wants to speak where they cannot be overheard, wants to know all the details. They have *all* heard about the joust. People look at you differently when you've saved the king from assassination. Lazar, monk and lay-brother alike fall back in respectful titters. Men are fickle; a year or two back they suspected him of Bede's murder.

Pacificus walks with his brother past the crumpled and crumbling inmates of that twilight half-world. As they head up the lane on the small rise from which they can see the river curl west towards Wroxham, Hugh is minded again - having been away for a while - that Saint Giles really is the world in truth, without silk or face paint. He remembers Fra Marcantonio and the friars minor in Assisi and all that happened to him there. God help us, we are all lepers. He tries to steady Simon taking his arm, but in truth his ribs ache so much that he is of little use. The evening sun runs through it and them, a flood of orange with bursts of yellow, like light out of time, bouncing from the back of your skull and making the memories live again. For a moment they could be standing, as they had done many times, at the prow of a ship returning through the straits of Mehmet or on the western bastions of their island home. Those days seemed like one long summer that would never end, yet it did, and so would this. They talk briefly of old times, but soon Simon returns to the events of Norwich. Was she radiant? Who showed an interest? Did she say she would visit? How did her mother seem to you? He explains that she will be sent to London for a final hearing at Michaelmas, to which Simon immediately responds, "then what is to be done?" Pacificus answers all his questions apart from the last; for this he has no fixed resolution.

As he gazes on the iridescent curls of light, he remembers again those words: *you never step into the same river twice.*

"Tell the Prior his horse is returned safe and sound – and bring him oats." The stable hand obliges as Pacificus rubs Percival's chin, saying gently, "You've earned it boy." Pacificus lingers under the horse's warm breath, holding his saddlebags and staring up at the abbey bell tower. The last of the evening sun makes the fish-scaled lead roofing look like a flaming artichoke, or pewter dragon's scales. The monks are responding to the Vespers bell, doors opening and shutting everywhere, as they have done here for nearly a thousand years. The life, the parish, the office – Matins, Prime, Terse, High Mass, None, Vespers, Compline, Nocturn – on and on like a great mill, turning yet under its own weight, even when the wind has died back. It is still, even now, unthinkable to him that all this should stop. He leaves the stable and proceeds up the small rise towards the abbey, feeling the sun on his neck. Ah, the setting sun, of course, he thinks, now walking slower and slower as if to savour the last rays, and almost as though he could keep the flame forever if only he could go slow enough. This is how it must feel for a man facing his last winter, if say, an ague is set in and the physicians give no hope. The miasmic vapours of winter will take you this time for sure and so this will be the last summer you will see. Oh, how you would will each leaf to remain on the branch, each flower to remain in bloom. And oh, how you would envy those young and feckless around you who took so little thought for summer's passing. One summer will be my last summer too, Pacificus concludes as he reaches the abbey door. Pray God, I will ready to face him.

"The blackites are still green here. I told you we were too early." Moll snags her dress climbing out of the bramble ditch. "And there'll be no sloes to speak of either, for aught I can see."

"It's what you get with all this rain – but mind – be careful not to overdo it." Sarah stands on the bank with Moll's swaddled bairn, a sturdy babe with a shock of auburn hair. He is three days old and feeding like a prime porker. It is Molly's first time out of the house in a week, a triumphant sortie to show him off to the world. Pieter and Sarah attend her. Childbirth is a different kind of pain, and motherhood, a different kind of happiness than anything she has experienced before. Sometimes she feels she will burst, it's written like lightning all over her face. She is wearing a woolen skirt, and one of 's Beth's cotton shifts, with the sleeves rolled up. Her freckles and cheeks are aglow in the afternoon sun, and her hair billows and furls across her face as a small cavalcade is heard and then appear down the lonning.

"Quick, it is the sheriff, to the woods!" Sarah says. Pieter, increasingly deaf, is still pottering in his barley field nearby. Gus looks up from his wanderings amidst the brambles, sneezing and pins his ear to the breeze, but does not bark as he usually would.

Margaret pauses on the verge of speaking, her lips moving without sound. They are gentlefolk in travelling clothes, she thinks, but not the sheriff's men. Her right hand rises to her breast and grasps the air. *It's them!* She knows it is!

Three horses draw on at a canter – just the three Fentons. Richard leads, his left hand in a sling under the cape. Piers is waving like a windmill and standing high in his stirrups.

A minute later they are embracing, all talking at once. "*Mijn kinderen, mijn kinderen*," Sarah keeps repeating in between lavish kisses. Margaret lets Richard embrace her with his strong right arm, but not for long. "So, you survived after all and came back in one piece." She is looking down and speaking with an awkward haste. She is saved from saying anything more when Gus, who has no such restraint, begins jumping up for Beth, and almost spooks the horse before she can get down. None need say too much, mostly it is just the embraces of family affection. Pieter is the last there, bottom lip trembling, long fingers limp with. "*God zij geprezen*," he mutters through his tears, "*God zij geprezen*, we are together again."

They pass the child between them. "What will you call him?" Piers asks.

"Richard," Sarah says, hands on hips, 'Ya, ya, Richard – can you believe it?"

Richard tries to catch Moll's eye, but she will not meet his, shrugging away the moment. "As good a boy's name as any." She ruffles the baby's hair. "Now come, let us go inside and fetch some ale, big Richard looks none too well."

Sarah is awkward at having them back in the cottage. She will not settle, keeps moving utensils, and sacks and loose herbs about the place. She's sorry for the smell of smoked eels, and she'd meant to take the innards to the pigs before she'd gone out. Pieter however sits in his usual chair, grey eyes taking it all in. He can hardly imagine such a picture, much less add to it. He strokes his upper lip as Piers regales them with the week's events – and to think he never even knew them three years ago.

The talk of the trial is less frivolous. "The king wants them to appear at court, especially Beth," Piers says.

"The king took a shine to you, then," Margaret says. "I thought he might."

"Aye, but as a mistress, not a wife," Beth says, smiling when she sees Sarah nearly keel over. "But I'll not go, and mother will not recant – says we're not to ask her to, either – so there's an end of it...an end..."

"There child, do not fret thyself, God will judge aright." Pieter would take her in his arms as he used to, but he would not dare spoil that pretty riding cloak. She looks as though she finds it impossible to believe him, so he adds, wagging a grandfatherly finger, "Has he not thus far?"

"But nothing has changed," she replies.

"It has. Almost everything has. Trust in God and you'll see. What does the monk say?"

Margaret sees Richard cast his eyes towards the dirt floor, Piers looks towards the window with compressed lips. Beth distractedly makes excuses for Pacificus; he was unwell from his fall, melancholic about relations with his abbot, but she will not voice their darkest fears that he has given up. Richard is feeling too weak right now to do more than keep from sinking into despair himself. But Piers knows what he'll do; he'll get her out before Michaelmas, even if it's just him and Richard.

They will not stay for dinner, they are expected to rejoin Sir Geoffrey's party. Richard wants to know if the livestock are in health, the eel traps yielding a good catch, and if they have help enough for the harvest. He says it meaning he will come down to help if they are short-handed, but standing there in his finery he knows it sounds more like charity. He walks back into the cottage to say his farewell to Margaret. She is feeding the baby under her shift, the folds in his chubby legs rubbing on her lap, as he half-struggles, half-snuggles into her.

"He's a good feeder," she says awkwardly, still getting used to feeding one Richard, and having another about the farm looking like a lord. "You don't mind?"

"No." He hovers in the doorway. "Does it hurt?"

"This? Of course not, it's nice." She checks her chemise to make sure that he can't see too much, and then points to his shoulder. "Does that?"

He nods, and then they both speak at once, both to say how glad they are that the other is well. They laugh and he looks to the floor. "I am glad to see you happy, Margaret." He catches her eye with a smile.

She blushes. "Call me Moll; everyone else does."

"We will be back for Lammas, in a week or two." His gaze wanders about the cottage; though all is orderly, it looks strangely shrunk and congested to him now. "You will make Pieter send for me if he has no one else to help with the wheat? I mean it. I will come straight away."

"Not with that wound you won't; you need rest – and no dancing with the ladies!"

"Stop it! You know there's no – well, I mean, it's quiet up there."

"With that gay lady, Maria? I doubt it!"

This she mumbles down at the baby, but he hears it all the same, and smiles. "Why Margaret, you sound vexed – "

"I am not, indeed, and you should not say so! Only, Piers said some things, you know, teasing you, and so I tell you as – well – as a sister, that you should be careful." He tries to interrupt, but she persists. "Or she'll break your heart; she will, too. Now I've said my piece and you can do what you want." A stunned silence follows her words and Moll regrets saying quite so much. She sighs and says repentantly, "Go on now, the road is long enough."

Richard doesn't mind her scoldings, in fact he finds the artifice of court ladies, like Maria, tedious and wearing by comparison. With Margaret, yes, there is a barb to her defensive wit, why wouldn't there be, but on the other hand, she is so unaffected and transparent. Richard has always abhorred doubleness, has always liked to know where he is with people.

He goes to replace the velvet beret on his head, but realises he has unwittingly crumpled the pheasant feathers, and he cannot use his other hand to straighten it for the pain in his shoulder.

"Give it here," she says. "Looks like that bird well and truly had its neck wrung!"

He approaches sheepishly and hands it to her, averting his eyes from looking down the neck of her chemise. "Look at the poor thing!" she says, smoothing it on her lap with her free hand. "Maybe that's what they mean by crushed velvet – it's a wonder you managed to get baby Richard's blue ribbon here in one piece."

"I don't think I'll ever make a proper gentleman." He says this to make her smile but she senses the sigh under it.

"You're their equal and better, Richard Fenton, and you know it right well. Here, kneel down and I'll knight you with the blessed thing." He kneels down near her presenting his head. She fights the overwhelming urge to run her hands in his hair, to push a loose piece behind his ear. Why do those we love always have to go away – it is an unbearable pain that heaves now in her whole being. She reaches for the beret and with his help, sets it straight.

He looks at the babe's eyes, and remembers Samuel and James at that age. "He is a beautiful child, Margaret."

"That he is! Now, best get going or you'll miss your dinner – and mind that shoulder on the road. Plenty of ruts after that rain and if the horse stumbles - oh what am I doing, I sound like Sarah more and more by the day. Avaunt Richard, get you gone!"

Lammas Eve comes soon enough for them all. Richard has made good recovery in the intervening weeks and the wound is well healed. He rides ahead of Sir Geoffrey and Maria, close to his sister as they pass Horning on the high road to Saint Benet's. Sir Geoffrey, whose family have for a long time been benefactors of the abbey, will be guest of honour at the celebrations this evening. But for now he is just glad the rains have held off for their journey and Maria has agreed to come without a fight. For she hates the abbey; with its lack of company, meagre fare, damp fires and fusty accommodation. Though of late he has noticed a calm, almost a contrition, come over even her, which pleases him. It's that Beth and her heretic Bible, he says to himself; she'll have us all wearing black and dancing Geneva jigs 'ere long.

Even before they reach Saint James' Hospital and the lazar colony, Beth spies a ragged figure standing under the great beech trees. Simon has had her letters but found it hard to write back at length, for a distemper in his hand is causing a steady shake of the wrist. As she approaches the rise of ground, he no longer sees the little marsh orphan he had once known, but a beautiful and graceful noblewoman, occupying a saddle as if she had never known any other way of life. She is the only thing he has that seems to be worth anything now. He falls back from the road and bows to them as they pass. This Pacificus has arranged for safety's sake, he fears their discovery as much as anything else.

"The Lord bless you, sir, this fine feast day," she calls to him.

"And thee too, my lady. And thee too." They have arranged to meet later, but for now he has to stand and watch them go, continuing down to the causeway where the harvested marsh hay has filled the Dutch barns to bursting. It is all winter fodder for cattle or for thatching corn stacks. Along the dykes men and women can be heard with scythe and song, clearing mud and weed for the transport of next year's harvest, and cutting rye grass for finishing thatched roofs, as they do year on year, world without end. Richard and Piers know how it feels, so does Beth; up to your waist in mud all day – but better do it now when the water is warm and the growing season is closing, than wait six months and not even get your boat down to the dyke.

At this same moment, a mile or so south, Pacificus is packing up his brushes. Mark is taking the last of the scaffold out, the upper work is done. He stands on the slab under which he has buried Saint Helen's reliquary. The ground has compacted and it has sunk half an inch. It is no matter, and the events that brough the sacred bones here seem far off now.

Pacificus notices the church warden, Robert Holdych, looking earnestly towards a statue of the Madonna now silhouetted in the west window. He is leaning his old frame on the antiphonal lectern, and he looks troubled. Pacificus calls to him but he does not answer. The crooked old soul, as good a hoary-headed saint as any parish could boast, is holding a pen over the sizeable antiphonal, and muttering darkly to himself.

"Robert, friend, what ails you?"

"Oh, brother, I did not see you. And, peradventure, best you did not see me, for what I am about to do."

"About to do?"

"Oh, it is grievesome to me, it is." Holdych raises arthritic fingers to cover his protruding and bald forehead, "I must remove the service for Saint Thomas Beckett with my quill, or Sir Christopher will have me before the parish council."

"Sir Christopher is a priest who likes to move with the times." Pacificus could put it stronger but he won't stir up strife in the parish; it always comes back on you in a small community.

"I wouldn't be so vexed, but that he knows it was given to the church by my grandfather John Cobbe – oh, many many summers before I was born. Mother said he sold two fields to have it done. It was his legacy, she said – to the church, like."

He waves his quill away so that ink drips on the rushes, "Oh, I know it's not as fine as some, and perhaps we will never more sing the Mass for Beckett, but to spoil the handiwork of holy men seemeth awful wrong to me. I would as soon hurt a babe."

Pacificus is caught off guard by the strength of emotion that arises in his breast at these words. He has witnessed so many abominable acts in the last three years, this should pale by comparison, but it does not. He controls his breathing a moment, then he takes the reed from Holdych's trembling fingers. He gazes down at the book of nigh-on three hundred vellum pages, illuminated with gleaming colours and gold leaf, burnished with agate. He wonders if at another tide of history, men will tear down his paintings, outlaw his angels, his saints. He looks again at the Beckett page. The work is well done – from Norwich he thinks.

"Allow me to do it, Robert," he says. This is work for a murderer, not a peaceable man in his dotage. He marks a large, but faint X through the whole page. "There, the deed is done, and it is still legible if *di maiores* change their minds. Good day to you, friend."

"Sit, man." Prior Thomas leaves off his vellum accounts. "The painting is finished now?"

"Almost." Pacificus moves towards the stool at the long oak table in the abbot's hall. "Sir Christopher decided he would rather have Saint Agnes than the Baptist, even started to sketch it out with my own paints while I stood there. Verily I think he would have finished it too if he had not found it harder than it looked."

The prior snorts in derision. "The man's a coxcomb, and I only say it for I know you can keep a secret or two, or three, I suppose now." He stares hard at Pacificus. "It's been a rough few years."

After a pause, Pacificus says, "Yes prior, it has that." And then after another, "but Percival is doing well, I hear."

"Ha! Misses the action, I'd say, and I hunt so little these days. He was made for the tilt yard and field of battle or I'm not a judge of horse flesh." He stares out across the marsh to Norwich from the windows, half-dreaming, half-dreading what he must do next. "A fine boned stallion, that. Look you, I won't keep you long, and what I relay to you now is for none but your ears alone, and God knows I would rather not be telling you, either. I have hard decisions to make this winter Pacificus, hard decisions, but not regarding you." He is speaking so quickly and vaguely that Pacificus thinks they are riddles.

"Frather Prior?"

"Those letters you brought me from the bishop – aye, those ones." The prior rises from his desk and walks, hands on hips, to the window, breathing hard through his nose. "We are finished here. I never thought I'd say it, but it's true."

"Suppressed?"

"No, the only one in England not to be, but it's as good as. The bishop will keep the abbey *in commendam* with twelve brothers on site for the upkeep of divine worship." He turns and looks at Pacificus. "*Just twelve.*"

"And the bishop does not wish me to be among the twelve?"

"You have displeased him, I presume – though do not tell me anything I need not know. I am telling you this perchance you would like me to choose Mark to be among those who remain. He is a useful sort of lad as I remember."

Pacificus shakes his head, "He has no true vocation; it was his father's choice. No, let him go home – at least he has one. He'll not blame you, and I think he'll make a better squire than his father or brother, at any rate."

"Yes," he says vaguely. "Yes, I see."

"Thomas, I have not thanked you for your kindness this long while, but it is in my heart. Will you be all right here?"

The prior has turned back to the window, but Pacificus sees him nod. "There'll be little time for hunting now, I warrant." The prior covers his view of the marshes with two upraised and penitent hands. He is weary.

"You'll be the only Benedictine prior in the country," Pacificus ventures a little well-meaning humour, but the prior does not respond. "Did he say anything else?"

"Yes, yes, he wants the same rent – £585 a year and his panelling sent to the palace." He points at the oak panels depicting the scenes from ancient myth, and then exclaims, "Sweet Virgin, of all the times to mention his damned panelling!"

"Are you not better going back to your own family?"

To his surprise, the prior winces to avoid his tears. "I don't think my brother would like that somehow. And this you might find odd, but I don't think I could ever leave this old place while I had the chance to stay. I've been here most of my life, came as a nine-year-old oblate – nine years old. Memories, you see. And you, where will you go?"

Strange as it may seem, Pacificus had not thought of it before. The realisation of it hits him between the shoulder blades like a sharp arrow, the image of a ragged man wandering the lanes, alone, cold. But then, and this is for him the epiphany, comes a different image – of Pieter, of Sarah, of Richard and his niece, and of course, Piers. And he is able to answer the prior without any reaching for words: "I have friends."

These things Pacificus thinks on that evening in the refectory during the celebration dinner. Half the village is present for the Lammas festivities. The guests stream in from the abbey cloisters in a candlelit procession. From his window seat Pacificus can lean back to see the children dancing on the abbey green with unlit tallow candles, waving cobs of Lammas bread and queuing for the apple bobbing. He looks on their sun-burnished faces, listens to their laughter, sees the whites of their teeth distort in the glass. Brother Aloysius knows about the changes, frets that this really is the end of the world. Perhaps it is. But certainly this is the last Lammas day they'll see, he thinks; they'll not be here next year. As the guests are called to stand for the prayers, he can see that the sun has almost dipped completely behind the trees near Saint Helen's church. It seems to go down so slowly for so long, but then falls off the western horizon with such resolute speed that Pacificus takes his fingers away from the glass and raises his eyes skyward in supplication. The skies are so clear this evening that he knows it will be a cold night to come.

Lady Erpingham, the Fentons, Lady Maria and Sir Geoffrey sit at the top table with the prior. Squire Hamberly is there too, but down at the end, much to his chagrin. Hamberly knows who they are now, how they won the tournament and the king, and so for once he's keeping his head down.

Later in the meal Beth, who is slowly caressing the scar dealt her by Miller, glances down the table at Hamberly. Their eyes meet for a moment and she wonders at him. Was he really their enemy? Were they really fighting him, Miller, the justices, the earl of Surrey? Or were they all – these busy and important men – unwitting accomplices in a greater story? Seen on this level, she begins to pity him. He, on the other hand, cannot hold her gaze long, partly for the guilt he smothers and partly for his maxim; that a capon is best eaten hot. Pacificus finds

Richard after the meal and arranges a meeting on the morrow. "You must come ready to make hard decisions," he says.

"About Mother?"

"About everything."

33

Decision Time

Ars longa, vita brevis
Art requires time, and life is so short

"I did not think ever to be here again." Beth wraps her arms about her as she looks at the bell tower door in Saint Helen's church. "It seems such a very long time ago."

Richard lays a hand on the tower door handle. He suddenly feels very young again, and afraid. Piers is near the altar, remembering his little brothers, now gone. Samuel's toothy smile, James' irascible belly laugh. But there is not long to relive their memories, for Pacificus arrives with Simon, Mark, Pieter and Margaret.

"I've had a look round the building, we will not be overheard here while the village makes merry at the hall." Pacificus walks down the nave, fingers flickering in his sleeve like a moth in a curtain fold. "Come everyone, to the choir."

There are general greetings, yet a reserve evident to, partly because of the clandestine nature of the meeting. Why the secrecy and why here? And why is the monk looking at us thus, so furtive and uncertain? Mark watches as Beth's lips move as she talks to her father. Her nose downward slightly when she uses words like, what, when, why. She sees him watching her and saying nothing. He has the same look in his eyes as in the refectory the night before; wide open like a lake. They have hardly spoken since the incident at Barton Broad, and neither has he been this close to her, now she is a lady.

She curtsies. "How now, Mark?"

"I'm well, my lady, and all the better for seeing you in health." When he bows his head she can see where Brother Jerome's razor has chaffed his skin at the renewing of his tonsure. He feels her eyes on him, feels the coarseness of his habit compared to the refinements of her velvet and embroidered bodice. Love is cruel, he thinks. But then, so is life uncertain.

Pacificus calls them again to comedown the nave away from the door. He expects them to comment on his work on the rood screen but no one does, they are too busy with each other. An odd mix of pilgrims, he thinks.

"Come Pieter, have this seat, you others gather round, I have something to tell you."

"I see that Sir Geoffrey is not here?" Moll says looking about.

"He must be innocent of what we will discuss, and neither must you tell him Piers, even if he were to ask it of you. We owe him that much. I will speak to him later."

"Speak about what?" Piers says.

"About your mother for one thing, and her religion for another."

"Her religion?" This time it is Pieter who raises his head.

"Yes Pieter, her religion, your religion; this dream you have of a country where a man might worship as he chooses; where the church cannot have recourse to the state's power for the enforcement of her will in matters of conscience. Yes, *that* religion, if that is what you call it."

Simon clears his throat, and says, "Brother, have you called us here to argue again?"

"No, Cecil." He almost breaks into full laughter at the thought of their many verbal battles over the last two years. "No, quite the reverse. I called you here to see how serious you are; whether it is just an ideal as Plato would render an ideal – a pretty idea – or indeed a dream that you would put your backs into, your futures."

"You mean – "

"Yes, brother," Pacificus says, laying a hand on Simon. "It means I have thought about it for many long hours, and I cannot see a way for a religion or a state to survive or prosper without that separation whereof you spoke."

"You mean – build a new society?" Simon says.

"Aye. Something like that."

"In England?" Beth says.

"No, not here, somewhere else."

"Another country?" Beth stares in amazement. "You mean – leave England?"

"Dear niece," Pacificus says, "What did you think rescuing your mother would entail? For you know she will not recant and must burn if we do not act. Did you think you could all live at Bindringham, or on the marsh? There will be a price on the head of each one of you – not just hers. You have enemies and so do I. The bishop, for one, would as soon serve us up to Tyburn, as he would salt his eggs and meat. I know him. No Beth, if we can get her out, then we must flee England."

"And if all our sect left England?" Pieter again, this time his lips turned down like a catfish.

"I do not say all, Pieter, but I say these must go, or else face arrest, and sentencing."

"And has it not crossed your mind that it is God's will that their mother should wear a martyr's crown?"

"Predestined, you mean? Like the Genevans think? That I cannot say. All I know is that God has given us freedom to act in this world for the cause of good, and here too I have felt his hand – a divinity that shapes our ends, so to speak – and a narrow path ahead that may yet work to his glory, if we dare take it. Did Christ not say that if we are persecuted in one city we should flee to another? Is that not so? Verily it is. God used Moses' staff, the one he had to hand. And so with us, I fancy; we have wits and connections – and these." With this he taps his feet on the pavement.

"Prithee, what do you mean, you speak in riddles." Beth lays a hand on Pieter's shoulder, and casts an enquiring glance at the slab.

"What twist of providence bought us a means of bartering with the emperor." He crouches, laying a hand on the stone as he whispers, "Saint Helen's bones. I have buried them here. This is something he wants, enough to ensure our passage to anywhere in the world. I for one cannot believe that God hath not ordained this."

"You mean...very far away?" Moll folds her arms and furrows her brow. "Never more to return?"

"Margaret, God's plans are different for each of us; I cannot see all of my own path, let alone yours, only that it leads far from here, likely to the New World. But not, I say, just for ourselves, to escape the fire. Not that, but peradventure to so bring a dream alive that it will last into generations unborn. You can see that, can't you Margaret? For little Richard – and on to his children and grandchildren?" Moll is quiet, her mouth ajar, eyes staring intently at him. She does not know whether he is in earnest, or delirious.

"J-just us?" Richard says.

"No, we will have to contact others on the continent as we pass though; my old friend Christopher, his family and friends from the

Yarmouth jail perhaps, if they still be alive – he has a fine legal mind, and that we shall need."

"You would become an Anabaptist, Hugh?" Simon says.

"Would you love me more if I were?"

"Well I – "

"I may come as a Lutheran or Genevan – or a papist, nay even an atheist – and how would that hinder the pilgrimage? So long as we are agreed to have freedom to worship and convert as our conscience prompts us. Don't you see that? Can't you see this is what God wants?"

"Well, yes, I think so. But how would we travel, it is so far?"

"The emperor would send us."

"Send us? He hates all Protestants."

"He need know only what we tell him. Besides, we have the reliquary to trade, *and something else, too.*" At this Pacificus lays down his best card, his eyes twinkling with mischief. "One more piece of information came my way in Norwich, without which I would never have made such plans. I heard the duke complaining that the emperor has made a man I know – Antonio de Mendoza – Viceroy of New Spain."

"Mendoza!" Simon exclaims.

"The very same, and as you well know, this man owes me his life. He will never stop us moving north across the frontier. In fact, he'll see to it that we are not harassed, I know he will."

"And we will farm?" Richard says.

"Yes, and hunt," Piers adds.

"And be no more afraid of kings, dukes and reeves." Pacificus looks down and opens his hands. "I will not make light of this, for it may not be an easy life. But if we run – and we must – then let us at least feel we have made something of our trials, something the world might one day look upon. This much only I can see, and oft-times my thoughts condemn me for reaching so far; yet I have confidence in God. He has not made these hands only for painting – " he indicates the rood screen with a self-effacing gesture of the hand " – but for adventure, new worlds and the high seas – *ars longa, vita brevis*. Anyway, I for one will not stay around here to be sport for the bishop or old Norfolk. I will surely sell my life dearer than that, *Deo volente*, for I perceive that God still has work for me to do. But – " he tucks his bottom lip under his teeth with an earnest nod " – let each be persuaded for themselves."

A silence falls on them all, as they try to write themselves into this fantastical story. Richard and Piers would be happy wherever they went, if only their mother and Pacificus were there. Moll sees Richard's eyes, full of wide skies and oceans, and knows his mind straight off. She is torn between scorning his simplicity, and admiring his brazen nerve. Men are so infuriating; both he and the monk are dreamers. They will need good women with English nous about them if they are to survive. For this cause, and for her child, she is minded to go.

Beth, however, can at first only think about what answer Pieter and Sarah might give. And also all that she herself will be leaving behind. She is appalled to be first thinking of pretty dresses at a time like this. She disdains the thoughts and forces them far back in her mind. But even so, it is a heavy price that confronts her, and she cannot tell how much she would pay it on account of her mother, and how much on account of her faith. Perhaps this mingling of loves and necessities is God's doing? Perhaps life is always like that. One thing she knows is that to attend more Masses and feign the old piety will not do. What others may do or have done, she – with all the eagerness and scorn of youth – cannot do again. For her own conscience, yes; but also for those she now counts as her fellow dissenters, hounded, flogged, disemboweled, drowned, and dispatched with sword and fire in every country in Europe. Can she live at ease while they suffer torment? She will not, for how could she face them, or her Lord? There was a time not so many weeks ago, before the trial, when she pictured herself living with her happy family in the old Erpingham estate. Must she become a noblewoman only to give it up? Yes, and it is a little thing, she repeats to herself often - a very little thing. Still, as ever the spirit is willing, *but oh the flesh!*

Simon is already a stranger and pilgrim on the earth. When a man has nothing, and barely even his own skin, it is a small thing to move, if that is, he would not jeopardise their progress, which he thinks inevitable.

Pieter still grips his stick, his face fast in its stern grimace as he grapples with the proposition. He has already fled persecution in one country, he knows what it is to have *no enduring city* in this life. He will not say anything now, only wait to speak to his sister. Mark, on the other hand, already knows what awaits him the year following, for Pacificus has told him what the prior has said. Like the Fentons, he would not now be separated from Pacificus, even though he might enjoy an easy life under his father and older brother. He looks to Beth; it will be a hard life for her, he thinks, or for any woman. She may not accept me, but that's as maybe; at least I should be near her, and see that she is protected. This last thought quite surprises him as it settles like an autumn leaf into his mind. It is at once the noblest, yet most desperate resolution he has ever made, and he knows it. He tightens his lips and breathes hard, at which point her eyes meet his, and he quickly looks away. What must she think of me, fool that I am? I saw the way she looked at Father last night. We all but destroyed her family, and because of us she must now flee England. They agree to meet again and give their answers.

In his coracle on their return journey, Simon does his best to dissuade Pacificus from taking him with them. He highlights the added difficulties of travelling with a leper. But his brother will not hear of his objections, besides which his mind is on other things. He is sculling in an unsteady rhythm towards Saint James' jetty, trying to decide what he will tell Lord Hastings, and what he will not.

Pacificus finds Sir Geoffrey on the abbey green, watching two ravens harass a buzzard somewhere over Saint Margaret's marsh. He knows about the meeting, and knows not to ask about it too. He trusts the monk, and even on this his birthday, there are bigger issues in the world than the loneliness of an old man.

"You know Hugh, I find myself always adjusting to my new age."

He catches Pacificus' eye, his own chestnut eyes dark and shiny as wet otters. "I have never been this old before, and life seems so very brief to do all one would like. Three score years and sixteen, can you fathom it? It feels more like thirty."

He wants to talk, as so many old men do, and Pacificus is happy to listen. In truth, the monk has come to hold in much affection this flawed noble who has brought so much upheaval to his own life, and that of the monastery. They talk about the harvest, the increasing coldness of the winters, and – as ever – the break-up of the monasteries. There is news daily now, trickling in with every trader, every wherry or cart; which house is pulled down this week; who has purchased an inner city convent for slum tenements; of Lord Such-and-such who bought a whole site, roofs and all, for a country retreat; or who got the land for a song because he thought the ruins would make a picturesque folly. Pacificus hates rehearsing the catalogue of horrors, he always feels worse for it; they both do. Eventually they stroll to the fish ponds in silence, staring down at the beaten walkway, then at the carp on their permanent patrol.

"I wanted to thank you."

"And I you." Sir Geoffrey does not take his eyes from the fish. "You'll be leaving soon I imagine?"

Pacificus nods. "I -er, out of the love I bear thee – "

"Yes, yes, I understand, I must not hear aught that I should not. Will I see you again?"

Silence. Pacificus is running his lips across his teeth, surprised at the lump in his throat. After all that has passed, he feels as close to Sir Geoffrey as he did to his own father – closer, if anything – and will miss him very much.

"Ah. No need to say it. I see how things stand." The cogs turn and the beard is caressed, he's no simpleton. "Then Hugh, I pray you will let me speak my mind again on one small matter. I would not – that is to say, you should not – feel bound by your vow of celibacy, if you are released from the house of your convocation. I say it as a man who has experienced great felicity in marriage, and I – "

"Sir Geoffrey!"

"Let me finish, dear boy – "

"But you forget my age."

"What? You can only be – what, fifty or thereabouts? Verily the best years if I remember. No, my boy, be guided by me in this; you have given the first issue of your strength to the church, but there is no reason why your latter end might not be fruitful in other ways. Be guided by me in place of your own father; take a wife."

Pacificus, caught off-guard, then catches the mirth in his eye, and waves him shamefacedly away. "Away with you, as if anyone would have me!"

"Somehow, I don't think that will be a problem. And you may have more success in bringing her back to the true faith than Cromwell's flames." He sees more than he says – it is very much the ambassador's bag – to observe people, to read them.

"But...but ...What made you think...?"

"Never you mind. I'm not as blind as I am old, you know!" One look from the condemned woman towards the monk as she passed out of the cathedral chapter house had been enough to persuade Sir Geoffrey of the true situation. He has been around long enough to know that look. He places a tender hand on the monk's wrist. "Only, suffer no guilt because of your vows, that is all I meant to say. Life is too short for regrets – I should know."

There is silence between them. And after it has passed Pacificus arranges with Sir Geoffrey about letters for Ambassador Chapuys. "It regards the bones of Saint Helen, and other matters." He will not say what.

"Say nothing more! Only let me know if there is aught you need." The old man taps his nose meaningfully, but then with a long sigh he looks up into the pale, late autumn sky. "The swallows are gathering early to flee south, I see. It will be another cold winter in England."

"Yes, I think so, and I thank thee."

Sir Geoffrey takes him in an embrace, kissing his forehead in benediction, "Fare you well Hugh, and God speed you; God speed."

"Will you go?" Beth is mounted in the abbey stable yard, close to the abbot's lodge. It is the morning of their departure back to Bindringham. She and Mark have a rare moment alone together.

Holding the bridle, he takes a deep breath and summons up his courage: "Aye. If *you* will, Beth." He looks her straight in the eye for any sign of encouragement.

"And if I do not?"

The mare pulls at the reins, but Mark holds her steady, turning to stare pensively out to the clouds on the western skyline. "I should go all the same."

It is only now that she smiles, smiles as if she had just swallowed the sun, "Aye Mark, and I too." She has no time for those pining knights from her mother's stories, overconsciously chivalrous, yet sentimental. She wants a man she'd be happy to follow; one who needs her in the right way. "And your family?"

The freckles stretch on his cheek, "I don't think they'll be coming."

"Anon, you know what I mean."

"They will not understand; well, you know my father – " He stares now at his feet. "He has understood very little, and never me at any rate. But howsoever, I shall make up with him as best I may. Truth told Beth, for the first time in my life I begin to see what I was made for. It sounds daft, but there you are."

"Oh, it does not; not at all." She looks down at him, her lips just open enough for him to see, and dream. He asks her about the others and she says they are all agreed to go, except Pieter and Sarah, as yet.

Pacificus sees them to the gate, along with the prior and sub-prior. The morning is chill enough for shortness of breath. Prior Thomas pays Sir Geoffrey great attention; he will need friends in the years to come. Pacificus walks between Richard and Piers. "Keep your wits about you – yes, on the road, but also at Bindringham. You have real enemies now." He is woken often these nights with visions of that Teutonic knight, standing over his bed with a poleaxe raised to strike.

"You too," Piers says.

"Aye, well look to it, then, you young cockerel! Do not let your sister from your sight, and mind you are here again at the appointed time. We'll have work to do!

34

Old Nykke's Tomb

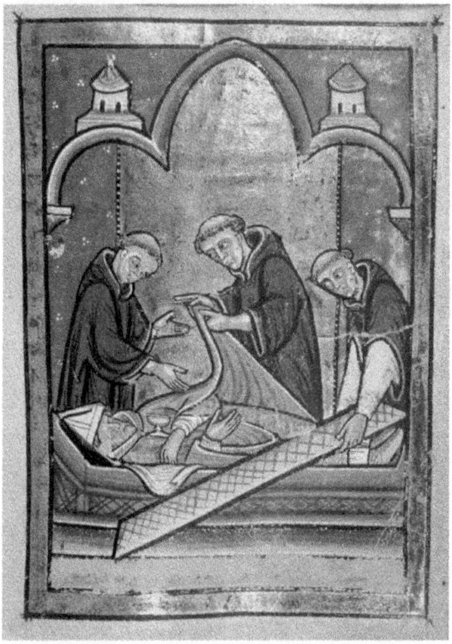

Corruptio optimi pessima
The corruption of the best is the worst

"He says he needs them, and you should take them with the accounts to the palace before the Michaelmas synod." Prior Thomas hands Pacificus the books and vellum scrolls.

"Augustine and Aquinas?" Pacificus examines the gold lettering on the spines. Does he now turn his mind back to spiritual matters?

"Yes, just what I thought, but he says he's debating Thomas Watson in public and wants to bury him – you know the bishop!"

"Oh aye, nothing if not thorough. Watson?"

"Heretic Calvinist; he wants to argue about predestination – good luck to him."

"And the bishop asked for me in particular?"

"Yes, I told you he wouldn't be angry with you long." The prior is busy at his desk, doing all the things he hates – accounts, reports, discipline. The very thought of the Michaelmas synod brings him out in a cold sweat, even a full six months before. "Oh, brother – prithee, remember to put in a good word for me when you're with him, will you? I've taken on the work of chamberlain and sacristan in anticipation of next spring. A few are spitting feathers about it. He might hear rumours, but you could pave the way, so to speak."

"A large bundle! Looks like you're dragging a corpse." Pacificus greets Simon under the chestnut trees on the Wroxham road at the first light of dawn. "I thought you had vowed poverty too?"

Simon drops a lumbering sack at Pacificus' feet, "Our regalia."

"Our old regalia?"

"Well, just the surcoats and cloaks, seemed a shame to leave them, but they're heavy enough."

"Our regalia!" Pacificus repeats with something akin to shock.

"Did I not tell you I'd kept them under my bed."

"I told you to destroy everything except Father's sword."

"Seemed a shame."

"It was a shame," Pacificus says, reaching down to the hessian sacking and patting it. "Everything was."

It was their mother who had wanted their knightly attire, but she died before their return and keeping them seemed an unnecessary risk. "Still, no one saw it and it hardly matters now."

He heaves the bundle onto Percival's back and then goes to help Simon up too. "Come, give me your arm. I don't mind the walk."

Once Simon is seated, they both instinctively look back from the rise towards the abbey; grey as the ashes of a dying fire, the odd ember of light still glowing in the refectory windows, and trails of thick chimney smoke rising straight then dispersing laterally across the marshes.

"Said your farewells, have you?" Simon asks.

Pacificus shakes his head, it's hard enough to leave yet another self behind, let alone the men who had become brothers. "I gave brother Gerald my best shoes, to stop him belly-aching."

Simon's laugh trails off into a coughing fit. "There's one I will not miss – or perhaps I will."

They know they ought to move on but cannot resist savouring this last glance. Not all sweet, Pacificus thinks, but it was their home for over sixteen years when it seemed there was nowhere else in the world for them. Hard to think it will all end here on this little silt bank called Cowholme; a system of life that has lasted nearly as long as the Roman empire. Celts, Saxons, Danes, Normans have all passed and gone, but in the end she was destroyed by her own children, God forgive them. He draws his winter cloak about him, trying to comprehend it all, but he cannot, though he is sadder to leave here than he was to leave Rhodes. The poor are even now gathering at the gate for alms. A straggling line of the halt and lame, the fatherless and widow, moving like penitents towards the outer gates. Brother Porter will be wrath at so early an imposition, and William Beccles the almoner will be wringing his hands and heart again, for another winter like last one is promised. The poor are ever with us, but will the almoners be?

"Will Sarah be all right?" Pieter nods, his hand firm on the worn wood of the skiff's tiller. "Don't you mind her, Piers, it is just her way." And then, after a pause, "She would only say more if she loved you less."

They are passing Thurne mouth on their long passage to Norwich.

Piers has said little since they left the cottage an hour back. He doesn't understand why Pieter and Sarah would not come with them to this new world, or how they can be so insistent that God wants them to stay. Old people are strange to him, but for all that he feels happy that Pieter will help them take back their mother. He's come a long way, this pious old Anabaptist. He's always said that a man must never be too old to learn, and so it is. It can even be easy being the victim, he had said to Sarah a few days before when they argued about him going to help them free their mother. "Tends to fear, to laziness, ja, you may look like that sister, but I know, I know – sometimes we must disobey men's laws to obey God's. Think of the Hebrew midwives who disobeyed Pharaoh, eh! I will go, and God will help us – you'll see." He will discharge his care of the Fentons by seeing them on that boat from Yarmouth to Calais, God help him, he will not fail in this. The others, including Mark, sit silently and watch the morning draw on, geese bickering and the small hamlets slipping away on their right and left. Mark points out a faint huddle of grey bodies massing round the bell tower of Saint Edmund's Church, downstream of Thurne. "Lepers looking through the squint hole, they are," he says to Beth and Margaret. Simon sighs. "I used to go there myself one time, try to catch sight of the sacrament, like those cripples at Siloam – until Christ came, that is – aye, until he came."

Mark doesn't want to look on the other side of the boat, for he might see his old home beyond Ranworth Marsh, and lose resolve. But Beth is already looking that way. She can see the small wood to the right of South Walsham where she knows her childhood home still nestles. Richard,is looking at it too. He remembers the trees he climbed, the dens he built, remembers the boy who trod the lane to South Walsham school with books, slate and candle in hand, and tears sometimes in his eyes. What a long time ago. What a lot of water has passed under the bridge since then. He puts one hand on his sister's shoulder, and another on Piers' knee. It's all right for her to cry; he too thought he'd grow old there.

"Oh, it's you, brother! Bless me, the nights draw on, do they not?" The palace porter, Able Wisbeck, hurries Pacificus in. "Your 'orse is seen to by the boy, all right, is he?"

"I came on these two wet feet, old friend. The roads begin to be clarty again." He smells the comforting spice of wood smoke. "Indeed these feet would gladly spend an evening by one of your fires."

"Ha!" Wisbeck's riven features light up with delight, eyes becoming almost twice the size. "We keep good fires here – not like at your abbey, least so's I'm told. Come in, come in. I'll take those, brother."

"Books for the bishop, is he in?"

"That he is, though he's in a peevish temper. Wouldn't 'ave his food, wouldn't 'ave no wine, neither – all a-jitter he is."

"Well, perhaps I should leave these and come another time."

'No, no brother; he was most particular to know when you arrived, I'll go tell 'im now, while you get your feet by that there fire."

Wisbeck wanders into the south passageway with his candle, staggering every now and then to one side. His eyes are not good, the poor old rascal. Pacificus rests a weary hand on the overmantel and stares down into the spitting grate. He lets the flames near his toes until the steam comes off his boots. He knows he shouldn't, but his feet are like ice. It will be my last meeting with him, this; I used to think him a man above men not so many years back. But these are times that find out men, myself included. We have no reason to be proud, none of us.

He thinks of Robert Aske, that he shouldn't have given him the *misericordia*. Isn't this why the world and the church have gone so foul, that we have all done such foul things with good intentions? What does old Pieter say? *The greatest crime and surest treason, to do a wrong thing for the right reason.* Wise old bird is Pieter, wiser than Rugge by half as it turns out. He feels his stomach tighten with the thought of facing his old mentor, as if all his own father's rejection was yet still alive in him. He trains his eyes to follow the cracking in the new plasterwork above the fireplace. New last year and already looking old. They have laid it too close to the green oak which has dried and shrunk there by the fireplace. You need new wine for new wineskins. He looks back to the doorway and rehearses what he will say, what he will not. Eventually he sets his teeth then mutters, "Just get it over with."

He can still hear doors opening and banging somewhere in the south wing. The sound of deep voices find their way to his ears along the oak floorboards. More than one person talking, a scuffle of feet on stairs. More doors opening and shutting, opening and shutting. And then the doddery steps again of old Wisbeck with his candle.

"I give him the books I did, and he says you're to meet'im down in the cathedral chantry – got summat a show you, he says." He shakes his head almost confidentially. "A peevish temper he has, born under Saturn or Mars, that one. Anyways, best not keep his lordship waiting, brother; he'll be crossing the green, if you hurry."

Wisbeck's last words about the fire being here when you get back are lost to Pacificus, for his mind is deep in thought, in suspicion. A moment later he himself is on the green, walking swiftly. The moon has risen, almost full tonight, and the gusting clouds speed over it, now illuminating the trees and cloister buildings with lead silver light, the next minute, plunging the old world into darkness and obscurity. He sees the flapping robes of the bishop – if indeed it is the bishop – entering at the north transept. He looks round but does not wait, or even leave the door open. Pacificus feels his blood quicken; there is something strange here. He reaches the transept doors, placing a hand on the peripheral stonework of the opening, held back from entering by the gnawing flutter in his gut. Is this how Theseus felt entering the Minotaur's labyrinth? He knows the place will be deserted, for it is long after Vespers. He has every reason to suspect this man, and he knows the old dog is capable of devilish cunning.

Pacificus screws his courage to the task, lips closed like a usurer's purse, nostrils flared wide as hell. He opens the ironwork as softly as he can. The door gives way with a loud creak, and then after the echo fades into the darkness, he sniffs the air. He smells incense but no taint of beer, garlic, sweat – of men. He draws the basilard from his sleeve, and removes his cowl to wrap it round his left forearm. If there are men waiting in the shadows left or right of the door, he'll give them a run for their money. He waits for the clouds to cover the moon, listening breathlessly to the inward sounds from the threshold, and when darkness comes, he slips through quickly, clearing the niches near the door and moving into the open space of the transept with swift steps.

All is deathly quiet within, the vaults rising high above him, the moving shafts of moonlight streaking from left to right through the clerestory windows. He slips the dagger into his bolstered left sleeve, and walks on silent feet to the end of the transept. He stares left and right, then left again; a dark form lingers among the shadows in the chantry aisle. It is Rugge, it must be. What is he doing standing there in the dark? Why doesn't he call me?

Pacificus stares out into every inky recess around his field of vision. Nothing moves, nothing breathes, there is no sound of the abrasion of approaching feet against the pavement or robes swishing against each other. But there are so many shadows, so many hiding places. And left of the chantry aisle are curtained chapels and alcoves, a veritable plethora of hiding places. Pacificus approaches the solitary figure, walking well clear of these, letting his fingers drag reticently over the diagonal grooves cut into the Norman pillars. The bishop has made no sign that he has heard the silent figure approaching him but when Pacificus is fifteen feet away, he begins to speak as if it were all as normal, though in the intonation Pacificus notes a breathless intensity and maniacal fervour. Pacificus covers his nose, for suddenly a foul and guttural stench of decaying flesh is all around him.

"He was an unbending man, was the late bishop. Hard and twisted as old hawthorn, full of thorn and brier too, as you well know. Ruled us at Saint Benet's like Beelzebub himself. And that last visitation!" Rugge casts round at Pacificus, though all that can be seen is the black voids in his eye sockets. "Nearly sent him to an early grave. You wouldn't have thought two pieces of missing silver plate and a monstrance would matter that much to anyone – thought he'd have the sub-prior flogged for it in Chapter, let alone fined."

Pacificus now sees that Rugge is standing next to Bishop Nykke's tomb. It is set into the ground and so stands only a foot from the pavement. Tonight it is lower still, for the lid has been removed almost clean off and is resting against the further side.

"It made him enemies, I know." Pacificus strains his ears for any sound behind him.

"Many indeed." Rugge is peering into the gaping hole of the vault. "He hunted heretics with the same love that he hounded and humiliated the abbeys and parishes in his see."

There is a pause after these words, and Pacificus is not sure how to answer. The bishop stands still, staring into the grave, seemingly unaffected by the smell. Why is this tomb opened? Is it an exhumation because foul play is suspected? Surely not after all this time.

"My lord, you once said to me that you feared he had been murdered."

The bishop stares round once again with his bottomless black eyes, and speaks matter-of-factly. "Oh, I know he was. It's not difficult to relieve a blind man of four score years, the burden of life, of having to breathe. Why a woman could do it with a pillow – *anyone could.*"

"You have suspicions ?" Pacificus tries to interject, but the bishop does not hear.

"The problem with Nykke was that he could not adapt to the times, he would never be moved on a point of principal. He'd have rotted in Marshalsea when Henry locked him up – aye, and let all the monasteries and parishes be pillaged and rot too – rather than say he was anything else except right. You cannot reason with a man like that, cannot deal with him."

Rugge looks up to the patterns and fast shadows on the windows, and lets out a long sigh. "Oh, there is a wind that shakes the barley, Pacificus, a wind that breaks hawthorns and oaks but leaves willow and birch still standing, for they have sap and flex in them. Nykke would have damned us all. Still, it's done now; we cannot go back."

"My lord, I do not take your meaning?" He means about old Nykke but Rugge's thoughts have already moved on.

"Do you not? Oh. I thought *you* would, at least." The black eyes are on him again. "I have always felt my life was for some greater purpose, more than just the abbey; felt it in my bones since I was a novice. And these times – devilish times, too – are moved by men who know how to act, and do act, like Cromwell and all his demoniacs. I think you understand that much, or at least you should. You used to see things as I did – once."

"My lord, you know I am very grateful for your many attentions and preferments but – "

"Enough, man! There are bigger issues at stake here than merely us, you or I, or old Nykke here. No, we fight against hell itself – and we must fight fire with fire, believe you me, that much is clear. No, 'tis nothing personal, we do what we must for the holy Mother Church, that is our calling. There is no room for faltering sentiment."

"My lord?"

"You, me; we have gone our separate ways, at least you have. Yes, I am wounded by it all, but there's nothing for it. You have that Erpingham blood in your veins, I have Christ's. You have chosen, I bear you no ill will, I cannot judge you ill, for I have never walked in your shoes, never been of a natural nobility – no, I cannot condemn you." He lingers on the words, glances once into the tomb and then back again – his words now harder: "But neither can I let you jeopardise our work any more: *he that gathereth not with us, scattereth abroad.*" Rugge turns away from him, saying, "No, Christ shall judge you."

"My lord?" But even as the words leave his mouth he feels the vice-like grip of a broad man's arms binding him about the chest like a hooper's band.

"Didn't hear me did you, little man? Bishop talks a good shop." The voice is Sir Robert's, and he is not alone; his accomplice moves round to the front to secure Pacificus head by the hair and jugular. It's the man who killed Hobbs. He can feel Aeyns' hot breath in his ear, and his feet struggle to find the floor as he is heaved back. His ribs compress to bursting and yet still they wait for a word from the bishop.

"Are you confessed, Pacificus?" The bishop's voice is dry and quiversome like Abraham's might have been when he offered up Isaac. The coward is still looking away. "Are you in a state of grace, my son?"

When no answer comes, the bishop hastens away from the execution scene. Pacificus cannot answer because he is flailing unsuccessfully with his forearms, and

hissing, spluttering, gasping through what is left of his windpipe, now nearly ripped from his throat.

"That's right, that's right, Hospitaller! Full of piss and wind, aren't you? Just like the rest." And then to his blank-faced companion, "go on, stick him – but in the right side, so the blood goes into the tomb."

The right hand releases his jugular but is back with expert precision and speed, the moonlight glinting off the steel of his knife with its skinner's hook on the back of the blade.

"That's right, my little artist, 'tis the blade we did your friend Filcher with, and did he scream? Had to stuff his nuts in his mouth to shut him up. But don't you worry, we've not got time to serve you up proper, besides the bishop pleaded for you to have it quick and easy, which I think a bitter shame after what you did to us, Judas."

The blade is angled towards his neck, but he keeps twisting his head this way and that to avoid it. By now he has no more breath, and feels his lungs will explode. A terrible, heavy dizziness is coming over his mind.

"Damn it, he won't hold still," the other says.

"Well, cut him right across the throat then," Aeyns says, as the blade is re-angled, coming closer and closer in small practice swipes. "I think we'll have your head clean off in just a moment, and swap it with old Nykkes, make a bishop of you – for, by my oath, you've been little use for anything else. Go on, do him now."

Pacificus moves his forearms one last pathetic time to fend off the inevitable last slice. It is then he feels the basilard dislodge from where he had stuffed it into his left sleeve. He joins his hands and draws it in a trice, taking the handle and yanking his own

head back. The other man's hand is still grasping his hair, and the backward movement causes him to overbalance forward where the knife is waiting to slide easily into his chest. He tries to pull away but he is so close that Pacificus' left hand grips his doublet, drawing him onto the blade until it enters his heart.

"What?" Aeyns cries out at his companion's death pangs, a shrieking cry which reverberates about the lantern tower. But before he can say more, Pacificus is pushing the dying man away and bringing the blade down into Aeyns' thigh. It sinks into the sinew and flesh; not far but far enough for him to be released and tossed away like a sheaf of reeds across the stone floor. With a roar of pain and rage, Aeyns draws his rapier and descends on Pacificus where he has fallen against a pillar. The first thrust is parried only partially with Pacificus' bolstered sleeve arm, and his upper arm is badly slashed; the second meets more successfully with the basilard. He moves Aeyns to one side with it, then leaps towards the dying accomplice to recover his sword. He pulls it clear of the sheath just in time to rebuff five or six more thrusting flashes of moonlit silver. In this darkness it is no more than guesswork, Aeyns' huge form often obscuring what little light there is. He would dearly like to have been carrying De Blanchfort's old carrack sword - black bladed piece for blackest work on nights like these. But this is better than nothing, he thinks, as he gives a few passes to test the weight and balance.

Pacificus moves clear of the body, keeping low and ranging with his basilard and rapier. If Aeyns would show any timidity, the least sign of hesitation, he'd move on him and stick him like the pig he is – but there is no weakness, just a relentless, sure advance, blade work in all directions at a speed that would stave off rain. And every few seconds he lunges forward like a tiger, in a manner and speed astonishing in a man of his size. In this darkness, the first Pacificus knows of the thrust is that it has pierced his habit and entered his flesh. Other times, the blades find him like a blind man's stick and they exchange blows. On and on he comes, panting like a bull, breathing out threats about what he'll do to various organs of Pacificus' anatomy when he has him on the ground. The intimidation is working, for Pacificus cannot remember when he has ever felt so outmatched. If they go on much more like this, he knows it is only a matter of time. He needs a plan, a change of format, and so in his retreat, Pacificus leads Aeyns to the confinement of the spiral stairs that join the colonnade to the triforium. Aeyns follows him up with oaths, his bulk not so nimble here where his shoulders scrape the walls and his blade speaks on the stonework. He fends off Pacificus' stinging jabs from above, and the sparks illuminate his bloodied face – at least one jab has pierced his cheek. Even so he forges ahead until they are both staggering on the walkway above the choir.

Here in the open again, he comes on like a fury. "That's right! Run away like you did at Rhodes, the great Sir Hugh – like the caitiff we all knew you were."

Their blades cross. "We left – " Pacificus breathes at him " – because the islanders pleaded with us." He tries to close with him, but is repulsed with such violence that he falls against a pillar near the precipice. His head cracks against the Caen stone and he loses his rapier, which clatters somewhere to his right.

"Coward! You would have licked Suleman's silk slippers to save your neck, bring shame on Christendom, and then you skulk back here to England to paint pictures as if there were no dishonour. I should have shot you straight like the dog you are, rather than waste my blood and steel on you. Get up! Come on! On your feet, coward!" He raises his sword to plunge it into Pacificus' heart, but as he does so the sweeping clouds obscure the moonlight and they are in complete darkness for that fateful moment. Aeyns is still pursuing his thrust, and Pacificus drops down so the blade misses his heart but pierces his shoulder near the neck, passing right through to the stone as through tender beef. It is withdrwan in the same second but this Hughbarely feels, for at the same moment he is reaching for Aeyns' left flank with his left hand, sticking him in the thigh again with his dagger hand. The shock of the basilard straightens Aeyns long enough for Pacificus to heave him toward the precipice by the cloak. The darkness Hugh cannot know if he is gain his goal or not. Aeyns slashes wildly again to where he thinks the monk should be and in so doing loses his poise.

The re-emergence of moonlight reveals for one last macabre moment, the open-mouthed shock of a face registering complete disbelief, plunging from this world into the darkness of the world below with barely another sound. It is Aeyns, and when he hits the pavement the noise is more like a loud whip than the sack of potatoes he imagined; but after that, there is no more. It is over.

Pacificus quickly grabs his own shoulder and neck. The cold, shivery, wet sensation and searing pain leave him hissing and deliberating for a moment or two. In departing, Aeyns took his rapier with him. Now all that remains is to stem the flow of his own blood. It stings like hell and his neck and chest are now warm and wet with blood. He's expecting it to spurt out, from experience of similar wounds he has seen – in which case he has only minutes to live in any case. But no, it is only flesh and sinew cut, no main artery. He manages to bind it with his cowl, then takes a moment to gather his wits.

"My lord bishop!" Rugge's face is a picture; looks like a man who has suddenly lost all his clothes in the street. "But? What? I er – "

"Aye, no ghost bishop. Those butchers who now lie covered in their own blood in old Nykke's tomb - they are ghosts now for sure."

"It was all his doing! Sir Robert wouldn't let me save you while you knew all you did – I swear it."

"Enough!" He levels the blade at Rugge's eye, though even now Pacificus is so amazed to be alive himself, and so grateful to be spared, that he'll not have more blood for the sake of vengeance. Besides, he now cares so little for the schemes of his one-time mentor that he pities Rugge's weakness, disdaining his wretched hubris too much to do more than just say his piece and depart. Boethius is right enough; the reward of the wicked is their increased wickedness. God punishes sin with sin. Lawlessness unto lawlessness. Look at him now, the wretched villain, already one foot in Virgil's hell with those who had "all purposed great deeds and got their own way." Pacificus leans over the study table and slams Aeyns' skinning blade into the woodwork.

"That is to remind you of the men who were murdered in your name; aye, your name, bishop – not Christ's."

"But Pacificus, I, I, I never – "

"Ah, hush now will you? Enough! Hear me this once!" The bishop is used to so speaking above people that Pacificus thumps a fist on the desk. "Enough, damn you! I never betrayed you out of any ambition of my own, or for my family. After the northern rebellion failed I was a spent man – as was the cause – and you would have seen it, if you'd but had eyes. Christ does not ask for our swords or want them, in that much the Anabaptists are right. We placed a sword of steel in the bride of Christ's hands – you, me, Cromwell, all of us – and we made England pay for it. You and I have acted against the gospel commands, we sacrificed conscience for ambition, yoked the devil to gain – what, pray? Naught but a crop of desolation. That much I know now, and so will you."

"Me?"

"Yes, I grant you your life back this night, that you might find repentance and true faith in Christ, and that you use your influence no more to fight against God, but serve and strengthen God's people as he shows you. D'you you hear me? *I am granting you your life!*" Pacificus raises his hand to stop the wide-eyed bishop interrupting. "Are you hearing me? Good, then hear on. You shall be a shield to those Lollards, and other dissenters of which you may hear. When you sit in the Lords next February, you will favour the bill proposed, seeking the restoration of the Sectaries and Anabaptists who were exiled this year."

"Brother, you seem well informed – " The bishop re-establishes his posture on his chair. His facial muscles relax, for he now feels his life is safe.

"That I am – Sir Geoffrey has kept me so. But don't you look so at ease, for I swear if you do not use your utmost influence – or if any more harm come to me or my family by you – then I will send that letter you wrote to the lawyer Thomas Moyne – "

"Moyne?"

"Oh, aye – I kept it as surety, for I've known you a long time, and it is enough to hang you. I give you my word, Cromwell will have it, if you do not do as I say. You will not see me again but I will be watching you, be sure of it. Break this charge and you shall be broken. God help me, you *will* be broken."

35

Michaelmas Eve

Una salus victis nullam sperare salutem
The one hope for the doomed, is to give up all hope of safety

"They're closing the gate." Mark rejoins the group at the back of Will Short's forge in the castle yard.

"Then let us stay quiet and out of sight." Pacificus crouches under a workbench feeling very old and ill-humoured. Bruised, pierced, battered and bandaged with poultices; he knows he will need the long voyage just to recover from the wounds he now has - that is, if all goes well tonight. The women have tended his wounds with such remedies and cures as can be found in the shambles, but he charged them not to be seen in the main part of the city, lest they be recognised. By now, he thinks - or hopes - they will be approaching the unguarded section of wall with the weapons. He and Richard will have to work fast to retrieve them while the guard is being changed. "Are you ready?" he says to Richard.

Richard nods and they head out into the dusk, leaving Mark, Piers and Simon at the forge. Will and Tom are still working at the front, keeping an eye on the castle yard. Their shop has a rear staircase to the walls, so it is ideal for the night's work. Richard's heart is in his mouth, thumping louder than his feet on the worn limestone steps. The night is still, but not too cold. The wind has blown itself out, leaving an unnerving quiet over the city. He reaches the wall-head first; no sign of a watch. He gives Pacificus the hand signal that all is clear and they move to the parapet.

"No, the other end," Pacificus whispers, "I told them the other end of the wall by the keep. Come on, quickly now."

They move swiftly and silently toward the part of the wall where the steps mount towards the keep, and below them they see the squat forms of Beth and Moll with their bundles. Good. Thank God. When they arrive above that point Pacificus makes Richard secure the rope to himself before letting it down. One slip of the wrist and the whole night will be over before it is started. Moll and Beth tie their bundles to the rope end, giving a tug to signal they are finished. Richard and Pacificus together haul it hand over hand, hand over hand; always looking and watching, always listening and praying. Pacificus is mainly using his right arm, for the left is weak from his wound. He can see the women heading back down the bank in silence. They do well to be away from this place, and their trails through the dewy, ungrazed banks will hopefully complete their deception. For Pacificus' plan is to relieve the turnkey of his keys, Elizabeth Fenton of her fetters, and then feign an escape over the castle wall by rope, all the time hiding out at the forge until the gates re-open in the morning. And while the city gates, streets and London road are searched, they will smuggle her away in the dung cart to Dragon Wharf where Pieter will be waiting to take them to Yarmouth the next night, and from there with Toppes' Pelican to Antwerp. It's not the best plan he ever made, and he could have wished for a little more time at the prison, to watch the movements from outside. But things are as they are, and he knows the balance of any campaign is with the Lord of Hosts; so he is content to let it be.

"Easy now as they come over, lad. Quietly now, gently, good, that's right."

They handle the hessian bundles with care, one for each man's back, and are soon away back down the steps. Back in the cover of the forge, Simon primes the matchlocks with wad. These are more for show, for deterrent and wounding if need be. They don't expect to use them, but as Simon himself had said, "a stern word and a matchlock will sooner get you what you need, more than just a stern word." He's been coughing again, but has told no one about the blood as yet. He is apprehensive too, more about meeting the woman he abandoned with child, than the danger of rousing the sheriff's men at the guardhouse. He sits by himself, chapped fingers trembling over the steel, checking the locks, the wicks, keeping other thoughts at bay. Not long to wait now, the guards usually take a turn of the walls when they come on duty, before going to their card games. The slow hum of coals and occasional gust of the bellows are the only sounds now. Piers squats like a squirrel under the bench, the whites of his eyes looking skyward through the opening. Richard fits his sword belt, and tries to make sure no one sees that his hand shakes like a wet dog.

Eventually they hear the new guard on the wall, the coarse joking, the tread heavy as clay, scraping along the flags like foot-worn travellers.

"Were you ever afraid?" Richard says, "In the siege of Rhodes, I mean."

"Half to death," Pacificus says without hesitation. "At the sight of two hundred thousand men, anyone would soil his breeches. I know I did."

"You did?" Simon speaks finally.

"That I did, brother, but I was too weak and vain to tell anyone, especially you."

"Me?" He wished he had.

"Well, I knew you were inclined to believe the myth of the *paladin invincible*, I didn't want you to think less of me. I was a hypocrite, and I am sorry for it now."

"What was it like?" Piers says. "You never spoke of it before."

"What? Being scared enough to shit myself, or the siege of Rhodes? Oh. Well, it was as bright a day as we ever saw, just two days after the feast of Saint John. I was up at the English Langue – where we lived – when I heard the cry go up from the watch that finally he had come."

"Who?" Piers and Richard say in unison.

"Mustafa Pasha, Suleiman's brother-in-law."

"On his own?" Piers waits, breathless for the story.

"No, not quite. When I looked over the north wall of the fortress I counted over a hundred galleys, and there were another three hundred vessels off the coast – dare say such a thing will never be seen again while the earth lasts."

"Oh. Not alone, then' Piers says.

"Not one wit," Simon chips in, "he had a hundred and twenty thousand men and a further sixty thousand Balkan peasants for labour – like locusts from hell they were. And a week later Suleiman himself arrived with more fresh troops so the artillery could keep up their bombardment of our landward fortifications day and night, week on week with infantry attacks in between, all through the late summer."

"But the Langues of Provence, Spain and England held their positions," Pacificus continues, "but then on the fourth of September two huge gunpowder mines exploded under the bastion of England, bringing down twelve yards of wall which filled the moat. It must have seemed to Mustafa that his god had sent him a perfect way into the bastion."

"Oh, no!" Piers is spellbound. "What did you do?"

"It was our section of wall," Simon answers, "we were sworn to defend it."

"The Turks rushed to the gap like flies to meat, but we English brothers under Fra Nicholas Hussey held an inner barricade, and we were soon joined by the Grand Master Villiers de l'Isle. It was hot work, I can tell you. We regrouped and sallied forth on the heathen, driving them back and capturing the Turkish standards."

"You took them Hugh," Simon says.

"No more than the brothers who fell in the rout."

"But was that the end of it?" Richard asks.

"How could it be with a breach like that? No. Twice more Mustafa repeated his assault on the damaged bastion of England and twice more the English brothers drove him back, helped by some Germans, who had rushed through the town to aid us. The Saracens lost over two thousand men during these assaults and Pasha himself had to be dragged away by his own men after all around were fleeing. He decided to risk everything on a final assault and on 24th September, watched by Suleiman from a hillock, they came at us and the bastions of Spain, Provence and Italy with everything they had. Wave after wave of Turkish infantry followed, skies as black as hell with the powder, the gunfire shaking your ribcage until you thought your innards would collapse. They came to the walls, fighting us with matchlock and scimitar. The bastion of Spain changed hands twice that afternoon, and the sea beside the Italians was red with blood. We had only about two hundred dead and less than that wounded, Mustafa lost three thousand that day."

"So you showed him, didn't you!" Piers says.

"Didn't care, with the numbers they had. Life was cheap for the sultan - less people to pay or feed. They had plenty left, all still out there - I can see them now, spread over the land like the plagues of Egypt. Sulieman was enraged and paraded his entire army to witness his brother-in-law Pasha shot to death by arrows. He spared him only after one of the elders pleaded for his mercy."

"Nice brother!" Piers says, looking at Richard, who in turn is looking to the back stairs of the forge where they too will soon be going to face their fates on the battlements. He wipes sweaty palms on his hose and nods.

"Aye, well that is the way with them," Pacificus says grimly, "Anyway, Suleiman was about to pack up and raise the siege when an Albanian deserter was brought to his tent, claiming we had lost so many men they could not face another assault. So he appointed a new commander, Ahmed Pasha, an elderly engineer, who resumed the barrage on the walls, which were by now badly damaged in many places with nobody left to repair them. Some Turkish slaves escaped and began to burn the town, but they were soon rounded up and executed."

"And it was then," Simon adds, "at the end of September, that a servant of the Prior of Castile and Grand Chancellor d'Amarel, was caught shooting messages into the Turkish camp. After torture, he implicated his master and Andrea d'Amaral was solemnly degraded from his vows in front of the whole order – "

"Doesn't sound very harsh ' – " Richard says, his sense of justice inflamed.

" – and beheaded for treason," Pacificus adds. "All October and November the barrage continued but weak though we were, we beat them back."

"November! Could you not get word to the heads of Europe?" Richards says.

"Yes, many times but – " Pacificus's voice trails off, for he can still scarce believe the truth of it.

"They were busy fighting each other," Simon explains. "Still, we were not the only ones in trouble. Suleiman's army was weakened by exhaustion, disease and famine. He couldn't go on fighting all winter, so he made a fair offer to the townsfolk: peace, their lives and food if they surrendered the city. But threatening to put them to the sword and under slavery if he had to enter by force. The Grand Master was obliged by the island's leaders to accept a three day truce in mid-December. But it did not go well. The locals demanded further assurances for their safety and welfare from Suleiman, and that's when he swore by the beards and graves of his ancestors to have all their heads. He ordered his men to begin the bombardment of the town again. By the 17th of December the bastion of Spain fell once more, after that it was only a matter of time before the whole city went."

Pacificus rubs a hand over his face and hair. He can feel the sweat all over just at the thought of it.

"Was there really nothing you could do, having come so far?" Piers says.

"Some wanted to fight on," Simon looks cautiously at his brother who is staring intently towards the light of the forge, "death rather than dishonor, but the ramparts and walls were mostly rubble by now. To continue was suicide. On the 20th of December the Grand Master asked for a fresh truce, and this time we got good terms for us and the islanders, better than we had hoped for. On the evening of the 1st of January, 1523 we marched out of the town in parade order, to the sound of a lone trumpet blast; banners flying and in full battle armour, and the drums beating a regular tattoo. We departed in fifty ships to the Island of Crete, the last crusading state, defeated and homeless."

"And you came back to England?" Mark says.

"Aye, we came back, I for my body, him for his soul, and so you see us this day, for the rest you know."

"They're at cards, me lads; Father says you can do what you will now." It is Tom Short at the cloth partition, face eager and fearful.

"I thank you, Tom," Richard says, "we are in your debt."

"Ha! Well, master, the devil may pay for ought I care, father has a commission from the king now thanks to you, and we'll be away soon anyway." Tom takes one last look at Pacificus. "But go easy on Turnkey Salcot; he ain't a bad'un at heart, and he's been gentle to your mother, Master Richard."

"He'll suffer no harm by us," Pacificus says. "Now on your way, young squire, and look to your father."

"That I will – God speed you!"

After these farewells, Pacificus says to Mark, "You remember your part? Wait 'til Piers sends that arrow, then off to the wall with the rope, and over you go – do not look back, not for anything. Rejoin the womenfolk at the warehouse and stay still 'til morning. You understand?" Mark nods, and Pacificus cups his cheek in one hand, "Then God speed you, lad." Then to the others, "We make our prayer to God for the defence of true justice; we owe no man harm here, so aim low if you must, and by God's grace we will leave this place alive with your mother unharmed. Brother, are your legs troubling you?"

"Stiff from all this tarrying, give me your hand and let us away."

Piers holds his father's bow and basilard, Richard the matchlock and sword. Each stare to the door of departure with uncertain eyes – hands moist on their weapons, breaths pent, lips pursed. A moment later they are on the stairway to the wall with Simon staggering and panting behind them. He wears again the black garb belonging to Mark's father, with the ebony mask. But this time he cannot walk far without a support, and his breathing is hideously constrained by the time they arrive on the wall. They pass in silence to the foot of the keep, letting him regain his breath, then mount the steps towards the door. These upper chambers hold a great hall and the one-time royal quarters of that first Henry, with a parlour, bedrooms and a chapel. Most rooms here are now cells – one had been Rugge's three years back – but they are also the jailer's lodgings too. Pacificus listens at the door as they all glance about them. From this vantage point the city lays spread beneath them, unsuspecting in slumber. Pacificus sees the Erpingham gate and the cathedral spire. He wonders what the bishop is doing this night, if he has taken seriously the chance for amendment - unlikely, but it was worth a shot. He can hear no sound at the latch but the scratchings of the rats and chatter of women. It's time to move. One, Two, Three - the doors swings slowly open.

Pacificus is first to enter the deserted and unlit corridor. Piers almost barges past him, for he knows his mother will be in the first cell on the right. In a trice he is whispering at her door and his eyes light up like a primed matchlock when her voice reaches his ears.

"Piers? Piers?"

"Yes, Mother! Here to set you free!"

"What, you? But who – "

"Do not fret, it is all arranged; Pacificus and Simon are here."

"Simon? Who is Simon?"

"Do you not know? Pacificus' brother; he is just coming in now – he was a knight too."

But even as he gabbles his almost incoherent greeting, she is echoing, "His brother? But Cecil is dead! Did Hugh not say as much?"

Her bewildered questioning is cut short by Pacificus' voice, "Keep the noise down. Look to it! You two guard this door, Richard and I will get the keys. Quietly now." The sound of their quick steps fade on the other side of her door, leaving the whispering of Piers, and awkward shuffles of another near him. Elizabeth's hands and ear are fixed to the weathered oak, and her heart quickened suddenly that her prayers for freedom should be answered in this way. But her right hand also begin the scrunch into an uncertain fist as she imagines what is waiting for her behind that door. Could it really be? The man who inflicted the deepest possible wound on her is now but inches from her fingers. She recoils from the wood. "Cecil?" The restless steps stop, but no answer is forthcoming. "Is...is that you, Cecil?"

"That's his name, and Mama, you should have been there when Miller tried to take us off the ship; he stuck him like a goose!"

"Cecil?" she says, ignoring her son now, her voice belying her urgency.

"Come, Simon," Piers whispers, "will you not say aught to my mother?"

But Simon shoos him away with a wave of the hand, turning to the wall, then again back to the door. Tonight he faces all his demons, every one of them. Every sinew screams that he should run. The door is there, the stairs. He is no man's slave to have his past dragged up again. Are all men's actions ripples that go on forever? Must all sins be present in the universe, unforgotten? Why, in Christ's name must he be involved in the restitution of his past? Would it not increase Christ's glory to attend to all things with each sinner *in absentia*? Dear God, there she is calling my name again; now I know how Adam felt. I'd be anywhere else in the world, right now. Where in hell is Hugh?

Pacificus holds a wheellock to the head of the lad who acts as servitor and watchman for the Salcott quarters. He was slumped asleep on a low bench by the outer door. "Your master in, is he?" The wretch never heard them coming and even now has the look of a man who is unsure whether he wakes or dreams. "Come now, to your feet, and knock for your master."

"Are – are you going to shoot me?" He abandons his cudgel on the floor, backing along toward the door.

"That I will, if you do not ask Master Salcott to open to you: in a plain voice – a plain voice, you hear?"

"Aye, I'll do it, that I will and gladly, only keep your finger shy of the trigger. I am my mother's only son, and she relies on me."

"Then do as you are bid, or she'll be on the parish."

He raps his knuckles soft, then at last hard on the double oak doors of what was once the great upper hall of King Henry, son of William the Bastard.

"What is it, Elfric?" A woman's voice from within. "Can'st thou not leave the master alone while he is at meat?"

"No Sal, I must speak with him. He will want to know it."

She tuts but does not argue. Within a minute there are more steps, heavier ones, and the clank of keys. "God's blood Elfric, I gave you this work to save my legs at eventide!" The turnkey's voice, rich and full as a chestnut tree sounds through the keyhole as the doors open. "But I perceive you would have me up every hour and see your mother starve: what is it? Oh – " The door now opens, revealing a small antechamber constructed for his use. Salcott is forced back in at the point of a gun. "Brother, it is you!"

"Yes it is, who else were you expecting?"

"Well, they said there would likely be a rescue party but – "

"They?" Pacificus feels that shudder, a sudden sinking feeling in the pit of his stomach, such as a man might have who begins to see that he has been strung along in a chess game.

"Why," Salcott whispers, "the Earl of Surrey has come with twenty men."

Pacificus eyes narrow like a fox. He twists Salcott's collar tight round his throat and buries the gun into his temple, "what?"

"Catch him an Erpingham, so I heard him say." Salcott starts to shake and sweat, but he nevertheless controls his speech to a whisper: "Now, dear God, brother, you and me's had no cause for falling out, and you must go now if you would escape, for they are here!"

It is even as he says this that a young retainer with Surrey's livery appears in the corridor beyond Salcott, as if to call him back. But when he sees Salcott hauled up against the door by a Benedictine monk, and then finds himself staring down the barrel of a wheellock, he lets out an unmanly shout, and hastily retreats out of sight, summoning his fellows.

"The keys!" Pacificus tightens the collar.

"The earl has them – I swear it. They knew you were coming." The sound of twenty sets of boots in the corridor causes Salcott's eyes to bulge wide as eggs. "For God's sake, brother, go now while you can." Thud, thud, thud, like a giant millipede, like the infidels pouring over the walls, the force of numbers against the right, the spirit of the hive over against the cause of justice. Pacificus lips and fist are tight as stone – to come so close. For a second longer he tries to find a way to seize control of the situation, not to retreat, not to see darkness triumph. He feels Richard at his elbow, hears the infernal march of injustice reaching their own end of the corridor.

He lets out a roar of impotent rage, unleashing a flash of fire power towards the corridor to stem the tide. The ball ricochets from the stone lintel with a spray of sparks. Shouts, stumbling, a halt of steps. "Lock the doors, Salcott!"

Richard and Pacificus bolt back down their own corridor to where Piers and Simon are waiting with weapons raised.

"What was it, where are the keys?" Piers says.

"No time to explain, we must go – now!" Pacificus shoves Richard past him towards the outer door. "Take your brother, find Mark and get over that wall, I'll help my brother get down."

"Without Mother?" Piers says.

"The earl and twenty men have been lying in wait for us, now go before you are taken too."

Even so, Richard has to near drag Piers away. At one point he clings to the handle only to hear his own mother pleading with him to go. Down the corridor Simon hears the grinding of iron hinges.

"Not enough time," Simon says to his brother, taking his sword from the scabbard and placing it within reach on a ledge. He flexes his sword arm, and then loosens his clothing. He should have seen this coming. Under his travelling cloak he is wearing his Hospitaller surcoat, the white cross showing near luminescent in the scant light. "I will hold them here; you see to those lads."

"You cannot hold them; now come." Pacificus takes his arm. "Brother, enough foolishness, this is not the way."

But Simon shakes him loose, gaze fixed steadfast on the bend round which the earl's men are about to arrive. "*Aut viam inveniam aut faciam* – find a way or make one. Did you not used to say that, too? I will hold them long enough. Hugh, for God's sake let me do something right in my life! Go! Please, just go! It is alright to leave me this time. *Please.*"

"What?" But slowly Pacificus begins to nod with understanding. He will not sully this sacrifice with remonstrance, only make it worthwhile by looking to the living. He savours the last glance. "Then God be with you, my brother, my friend," he says, "you are a knight of true valour, do not doubt it. Fare you well." They embrace then a moment later Pacificus slips through the outer door and is gone.

Simon hears the door shut, feels the waft of night as he stands alone. He hears her voice again in the darkness, calling him. But there is no time to talk, the rattle of boots grow to a pitch that seems to shake the very walls. "I pray, madam, that you forgive me."

Elizabeth cries back, "I do, Cecil! I do!"

He feels the pulse of life in him more strongly than at any time since the great siege. "This time," he repeats to himself, "this time." He will not run this time, even if all the furies should breach that corner, he will not run. No, he thinks, this time he has something he loves enough to die for, and so finally, he is ready to live. The first three men around the corner almost crumple into one another when they see the surcoat on the man standing silhouetted by the arrow-slit window. It is the sight of him that buys Pacificus and the others the most time of all. A holy knight, a paladin of almighty God is no ordinary thing to these homegrown household toughs, who in their hearts despise their role as the earl's thugs, and could think of nothing better themselves than to fly the standards of liberty against the infidel. Even the most ignorant of these men know the tales, the miracles, the myths, the Chanson of Roland, Ariosto's *Orlando Furioso*, Mallory's *Morte* etc. They know they are set to catch some Erpinghams, could this be Sir Hugh? He might have been an apparition, or else a spirit for aught they knew, and if it were not for their captain, the duke and the other men behind them, they might well have run away, or dropped to their knees.

But the eral is their bacs and in their ears, pressing them to the task. And when the fighting starts it is over in less than a minute. First Simon's matchlock brings down their captain, followed swiftly by swordplay at close quarters, which sees four more fall badly wounded. Sir Cecil Erpingham, for all his condition, has lost little of his expertise with a blade, though his limbs are by no means as swift as they were. Even a few moments later, with seven balls lodged in his own body, three of them in the gut, he is still a match for any one of them, fighting like a man inspired, aflame. Only in their twos and threes do they finally bring him to the ground among the slain.

They trample over him on their way forward, the clatter of boots close to his ear. He tries to trip the earl up as they descend the steps but his leg will no longer move. Outside he hears his brother's voice urge the lads to hurry on the ropes, then the thud of matchlocks, then the whistle of arrows. He smiles at the thought of Piers with his beloved bow, and prays that God will spare them.

The earl gives a shout as one of the arrows misses his head by an inch and embeds heavily into the door oak. Surrey does not see Piers, but he does recognise the monk. "Charge him! Charge that monk while he reloads! Go to it, man, damn you," he shouts at the forward soldiers, the first of which gets a thick head when Pacificus belts him with the matchlock butt, sending him spiralling onto the roof of the forge below the wall. While Piers joins Mark and Richard on the rope, Pacificus drives Surrey's retainers back two at a time, his sword swinging and singing through the matchlock smoke. Aim low, he had said, but now he will take their heads from their trunks, every one of them, if they do not retreat to the steps. Back, back you braggards. Which one, he thinks, which one of you pierced the body of my brother? He fights the thought away. They're boys, not men these caitiffs, selected by the poetic earl for their comely looks, not fighting spirits. They give way to his tempestuous advance like scattering poultry. He swings again and again, this way and that, like Achilles grieving with every blow for the death of Patroclus. He sees the earl racing down the steps to meet him. Good, I'll have those fishy eyes on a plate, the coxcomb. But then he sees the men higher up priming their matchlocks. No time. I cannot waste Cecil's sacrifice, I will not. His eyes meet the earl's for a fleeting second. He sees the whites of them, sees his rapier ready, but then he, with one last glance to the matchlocks, runs in the opposite direction, back to the rope.

"Coward!" the earl shouts, trying to get past the four men in front of him on the narrow walkway behind the wall. "Out of my way. Coward, come back and fight!"

Pacificus chooses not to hear. The earl would be dead by now if he had stayed, but so would he, by those matchlocks. He extends the cuff of his habit so that the rope will not burn him on the rapid decent. He is over the wall like a ferret, the earl and his men swiftly now arriving at the wall-head.

They level their weapons over the parapet only to receive a volley of matchlock shot and arrows from the bushes at the base of the castle rampart.

"Cut the rope, you fools! The rope! The rope!" The earl screams in fury, then over the wall, "You will pay for this, monk! I'll burn your monastery to the ground – hand over the lot of them! Do you hear me, monk? I know who you are now, damn you! I will burn your abbey, by God. Burn it and cast each stone into the marshes!"

Pacificus lets the rope out at almost a free fall, boots scraping on the stone, sending mortar out in a spray of dust. When at last he hears the twang of the rope, he is already more than halfway down, already falling. He lets out a small and rather unmanly yelp at first, then buttons his mouth and stomach for the impact. He hits the steep embankment and rolls forward like a ragdoll, pain shooting through his legs, then his head. He's tumbling down the bank, amid a hail of matchlock shot; the deep boom above, the thud, thud, thud all around, as ball after ball embed in the earth near him. One ball passes through his calf muscle, though he hardly senses more than a nick. The wound on his neck reopens as he rolls shoulder over shoulder. The half-torn ligaments and muscle scream through his whole body like shouts of rioting madmen in confined city streets. But soon he has rolled out of sight, if not beyond range of the matchlocks. His body comes to rest under the scrub of hazel, gorse and ash at the base of the ramparts. He hears the voices of the boys, but he feels himself slipping and spinning away from them. His head becomes lighter and lighter, the voices echoing through his skull and out again. He hears his name, but at first he cannot speak. It is Piers, shaking him. And the shaking works, the dizziness eases. He moves in one sudden jerk onto his elbows and knees, as if to spring up, though he cannot.

"We ran from them – you made us run away!" Piers' voice is trembling with a sort of pathetic, adolescent rage. His hand is on Pacificus' arched back, half-steadying, half-shaking, twisting the course woolen cloth with his white knuckles. "Why did you not fight them?"

But Richard pulls him away. "Stop this. We'd all be dead by now. There were over twenty of them, not including the castle guard." He drags Piers' hand away. He wants to ask about Simon. The question is on his lips but he dare not. "Pacificus, are you badly hurt?"

Now, there's a question. Pacificus is groaning, and while doing a rollcall through his members, finds his right leg feels like wood. He knows what it means.

But Piers is not finished. "He said we would rescue her, that's what he said. But we ran away, just like they ran from Rhodes – "

"Enough – " Pacificus straightens to his knees.

"You said that we should never fear or run if our cause was just, and now you – "

'PEACE," he roars, grabbing Piers by the tunic. "Have done, now!" He shoves the lad aside and says to Richard and Mark, urgently, "Get thee hence before the gates open. Take the back streets through the shambles to Blackfriars, salute no man."

"But you – " Mark goes to help him but he is rebuffed.

"I need to bind my leg, I will come another way and meet you there; just go quickly." He sees their silhouettes lingering, and growls through his growing pain, "Go."

Back in the castle keep, lives ebb like a nib tide retreating fast off the salt marshes. Simon is left alone to see a black pool of his own blood running on the stairs, every now and again catching a line of silver light from the window. His head feels cold and numb, and lighter by the minute. He closes his eyes only to hear her voice again. She is in his head, like a whisper above the groans, gasps and coughs of these other wounded men that lay around him. He hears his name, "Cecil? Are you still there, Cecil?"

He turns his head a fraction to see that he has fallen at her door. "Elizabeth?" He speaks softly through the gap.

"Cecil, I am here."

"Elizabeth..." His faint breath releases her name like a free vapour. "You raised a fine daughter, and fine sons too."

When she hears him at the base of the door, she drops to her knees and whispers, "Are you badly hurt?"

"A very fine young woman, our daughter, is she not?"

"Yes, yes she is." She tries hard to curb her emotion for his sake. "I am glad you have known her."

"Aye, me too – very glad." He gasps, for the blood now fills his chest. "You will tell her how proud of her I was, how much I loved her, won't you?"

"Yes, Cecil, I will; of course I will," She slides her fingers along in the narrow gap beneath the door, pushing her hand under as far as it will go; he feels her touch his hair. "She...she is so very like you."

He reaches her fingers with his own. "Like you, I think – like you."

"She is willful – the Erpingham spirit and stubborn pride – sometimes we worried." Her voice is filled with mirth tinged with regret. "Your brother told me all about you – at least he told me about Simon the leper – said what you did for her, how you saved her – not just from Miller, but you read the Bible with her – "

" – saved me more like." At these words she hears his breathing decline to the gurgling and bubbling of the end. She can discern the words, "Pray for me," because she is so near, and so she recites Psalm 23. In his own mind he repeats the words like a man reaching out with all his being to grasp the golden rungs of a celestial ladder; shepherd; leads me; refresheth my soul; banquet for me; cup runneth over; goodness, mercy, follow me; the Lord's own house, forever. And ever. She listens for his breath when she finishes but there is none, he is gone. She remains caressing his hair for some time, all she can reach; her last rites to the dead, this man she had too briefly known.

"Why stand ye upon it," Pacificus bawls again, "Go!"

Mark and Piers drag Richard to his feet. He is reluctant, obstinately so, but they harry him to the edge of the copse and thence across the track to the tenements flanking the northern edge of the castle ramparts. Leaving him seems to them like abandoning their last hope. Hugh sees it in their eyes but, thinks he, it is a night for dying withal - hopes, dreams, family, youthful fancies and idols, all things die in this world and face corruption. They were wrong to look so to me. It is a s well they become disillusioned now, than reach my age and not have learnt the lesson. He watches their forlorn faces fade into the darkness and so he is alone again - just him and his maker.

Mark, face set, thoughts grim, leads the Fentons through the shadows, silent and sorrowful. The night watch will not visit this district – he'd be mad to, and besides there is nothing the city fathers wish to protect in this corner of the city. They reach Blackfriars within minutes, and encounter no difficulty there, nor in the rest of the brief journey to the warehouse.

Back at the castle rampart, Hugh takes a whole minute to emerge from the blackness that befuddles him. He mechanically binds the leg, and then – whether from the loss of blood or darker portents of the mind – returns to the ground in a hunched huddle of breathless distress. He thought he had realigned his narratives – that is, his understanding of how to work the Almighty into bringing success to his own labour – but now the great, looming Goliath of doubt and failure are assailing the ramparts of his own castille. Why does his God have to b Yahweh, the God of the slaves and dispossessed, rather than Zeus, the god of success? No wonder the pagans preferred the latter - they wanted a power that was on their side. *Not this - this!* He buries his face into the turf, dribbling and hissing as if his head might explode with the pressure, his eyes from their sockets. His stomach twists in the gall of bitterness and anguish. What does he want of me, *what?*

He has never known what it is to covet death until this moment. Cecil gone, his sisters, his mother when his father was too broken to attend? How many has he, the eldest son, sent on ahead of him? Why is he alone alive? What use now is he? What remains to hold him here? The church? It is not his church now, if it ever was. England? Dear God, what has that become now but Augustine's *magna latrocinia* - a great brigandage - a means for the state to transfer the wealth of many to the few? So what keeps me? These young ones, my niece, their mother? Yes, thrice yes, I have loved them – do love them. Like a drowning man loves driftwood I have, but what of it? Have I helped them, really helped them? Has not God overthrown my best efforts to help them, to rescue her? Is not my life still based on a myth, a lie? Ah, surely if he is the champion of widows and orphans, then he fights in ways I cannot understand, nor ever will. Better that I am gathered up to him, for I am no help here.

He does not weep, nor feel much at all now. He has not helped them, that is all he knows; his best was not needed, *that* he feels. His life has had no point to it at all, unless you count the point of a two-edged sword – a work of destruction, the lowest point a man can descend to. He has proved it; his whole life has, and it is enough for him. "No better than my fathers," he mutters, curled in a foetal position on the dewy sward. "No better." And there he lies, side on, hearing the slow, even breaths of a man tired of battle. He does not hear the drawbridge raised, the clattering hooves, the march of steel, the yellow blaze of torches. Neither does he fear for the children, or their mother. There is a God in heaven, he will do what is right. Yes, he may choose to use us, even the conceited and the fool, yay, even donkeys in Balaam's case, but what right have we to boast or lay claim to his will? He might equally use a devil from hell, or Cromwell, or the king to rescue a widow, to right a wrong. Were not Nebuchadnezzar and Cyrus recorded as his servants too? I am tired. I am tired, oh God, I am so tired.

The soldiers pass round him, torches reflecting on the wet bark of trees, swords prodding into the bushes. He is, as he thinks, within their fullest view, and yet he continues to lie in mute resignation next to his hawthorn bough – his own guard. At least two men stand at times within a foot of his head, yet never discover his body beneath them. When they give up the search and leave for the tenements, Pacificus starts to wonder if he had not been all the while dreaming. He had given himself up, not to danger of death so much as to the vulnerability of absolute dependency, and at that point found succour. A miracle? A sign? He will not dare think it, but wrenches his body from the earth by support of his friendly hawthorn. He is alive, still. And from that place, his grinding struggle along the sewerage culverts to their lodgings, this is the gossamer thread of thought that drives him on; he is still alive. Like Jacob, limping from the fight with the angel of God, Pacificus staggers on through the shambles and back alleys, leaning on house walls, street after street, all the while daring to hope just one last time. He'd always wanted to see just how much he could take. Now he is finally finding out.

"Moll, quick, he's here. I don't believe it. He made it back." Mark opens to him, pulling him into the cellar where their baggage is stored, going back to look up and down the street, but nothing stirs – Pacificus has not been followed. How could that be? How could that possibly be? Moll is instantly at his side with water and bandages. "He stinks like a sow's tail; help me get his clothes off. I'll get some soap – just hold him, and put this on his neck to stop that blood."

Moll, quick and efficient as a terrier, is back down the stairs in a moment with more water and soap. "All we got," she says. "Come on man, you can at least loosen your own girdle!" Pacificus submits to the ordeal, too exhausted to raise a finger now, let alone an objection. More than once she chides him for not responding to her questions, but he remains silent. Mark too is uncharacteristically inactive, brooding and quiet. It is only after he is half-clothed again and with a mouth full of ale and a morsel of bread that

Hugh can finally pull enough threads of his own inner self together and relate to his surroundings.

"The others?"

Mark sits on a windowsill, though from this cellar he can barely see street level, where the dawn gains her slow conquest of the night. He does not answer, but merely keeps cupping and rubbing his mouth and chin, in a nervous manner.

"The others?" Hugh senses trouble and asks again, louder this time, his connection to the present thickening with every second.

"Gone." It is Moll who replies from the stairs, where she sits nursing the babe.

"What?"

"Gone," she repeats. "Gone to the duke, to escort their mother to London, to plead her cause before the king."

He lets out a long groan in affirmation, sinking further back onto the sacks on which he sits.

"Piers wouldn't wait when you didn't come," she continues matter-of-factly. "He said you'd given up, that they should look to it themselves. Richard wanted to wait longer, but when you didn't come, Piers got dressed up like a little lord and made Richard do it too."

He groans again, but she chides him: "Well, she is their mother after all. They have the king's good opinion, and they were not recognised at the castle, they said. And for all they knew, you been taken – or worse."

"But you stayed?"

"Yes, we stayed – " She starts with her usual scolding comeback but then pauses. He has found her out, and Mark too; *they stayed. God reward them for their troth, they deserve better.* Moll's sharpness has alarmed the baby and so she speaks to the child in a mother's voice, not to him. "Yes, little peasecod, we stayed for that ungrateful old man; someone had to, and look precious, he's here now..." Her voice trails away.

"Did they do the right thing?" Mark walks towards the sacks, then back to the window. "I mean, will they be safe with the duke?"

Pacificus does not answer. His eyes are settled on the rafters where the morning light highlights the cobwebs. He looks where the caught flies are struggling or entombed in their silken chains. At the centre there are no spiders to be seen; they wait in the corners, by the ceiling joists, watchful, out of sight.

They have been gone an hour at least, and he cannot reach them now, even if he wanted. But even so he feels no gnawing anxiety, only an unexpected and unfamiliar peace – awkward to him because it is so alien. Mark repeats the question, but still gets no answer - only he observes the almost luminescent gaze on his master's face and senses that something is about to change.

36

Michaelmas

Ense animus major
Courage is greater than the sword

When the dawn light reveals Pacificus' face, Mark knows – really knows – that his master is not the same man he was the night before. All that usual tension in his brow is gone. Still the lines of age, but gone the deep furrows above his nose, and that tight-lipped expression that made him look like a man in pain - someone to fear. But now all is serene in him, at rest. Mark wonders at it, that for the first time he is not just a little afraid of him.

Moll, picking at her shawl, is still sitting on the stairs – fretting about Richard, where he is, what he is doing. She has not noticed the monk yet, not seen the new light about him. Pacificus is unaware of giving any impression to others; he only knows he feels different. He examines his hands, feeling the sleeve of his linen chemise slip back to reveal his arms – pale, he thinks, like Piero della Francesca's resurrected Christ. The scars are still there, but neither they, nor the memories, feel like lead weights on his heart as once they did. He looks again at his hands, where paint still clings to the crevices of his fingers and under his nails. He looks at his scarred wrists, still the same. He is himself, he thinks, this is the same body. He takes a deep breath and feels like he could, for the first, sleep deeply and peacefully for a thousand years.

Mark is asking again about the others, whether they should not go to find out if they are safe. Moll is muttering that they wouldn't listen to her. Both their voices sound far away, like the chattering of insects. But they are both brought to silence when he finally asks, "What day is this day?"

"What are you about?" Moll chides him. "You know full well it is Michaelmas day."

"Michaelmas day..." he says, "so it is." There is a pause, while Mark looks uneasily at Moll and she at him. But Pacificus has the attention of them both when he adds, "No ill shall come to them on Michaelmas day, though old Norfolk decree it, and his son the more so. No, there shall no harm come to them this day."

"Brother?" Mark says slowly, always uneasy when he sees Pacificus smile.

"Do you know what our sub-prior will be reading at Chapter this day, Mark?"

"No."

"If I am not much mistaken, he shall be reading chapter seven of Benedict's rule on humility – how appropriate – and later from the prophet Daniel, "And at that time shall Michael, the great prince who stands guard over the children of my people, arise," and then further down, that "they shall be delivered." So if I be not mistaken, and I believe for the first time in my life that I am not, we shall see something today, Mark. I feel it. I used to wonder if Michael would fight for us when we were up north, him or any other of the angelic host. He did not, but the angels will come to our aid today."

"How can you say that?"

"I know not, but I tell you it is true, I feel it in me. All those times I painted my Michael at Ranworth; I thought I did him such great service with my brushes!"

"You did. It was a fine painting – Sir Geoffrey said so."

"But look you, Mark; one angel destroyed all the firstborn of Egypt; one angel the great hosts of the Assyrian army. Have I been so blind all my life? For I swear if I had known the strength of God, nay the strength of the least of his host, surely I would not have used my sword to defend him."

"He's not well," Moll says, getting up and coming to lay a hand on his brow. "Got something from the sewer, that he has."

"Margaret!" He takes her hand and kisses it. "Sweet child!"

"Mad as a bag of ferrets, he is," she says, looking back to Mark. "Look at his face. He's cracked, he has."

"I have been mad, girl, that's for sure – all my life; and all Christendom has too, but not any more."

"I see. So...what are you going to do? Sit here and think of angels?"

"No, I shall go to meet them as they come forth."

"Now hold on a minute!" Mark says. "You were recognised last night – all Norwich will be looking for you." Mark comes to crouch where Moll is still reluctantly holding his hand. "They will come from the castle fully armed. And we? Well, you have that old sword, a matchlock – "

"God has no need of our swords, Mark. Haven't you been listening to me?"

"Oh, this is fine!" Moll says. "And with what, pray, will you face the duke's son and his troop? Your pious words, eh?"

"Oh, Moll," he tries unsuccessfully to stop her from pulling away. "Listen! What did God tell Moses to use?"

"Oh, my saints above! Moses is it now?"

'Moll, what did he tell him to take? Come now, Moll."

"What he had to hand, but you – "

"Aye – "

"Oh, this is foolishness."

"And the more foolish the better, that none may boast."

"And what *you* got then? Even that chemise isn't yours. What have you got?" Moll has pulled free and stands over him with an accusing finger. "Bet you never gave that a thought, did you? Men are all talk!"

For a moment he feels a pang of doubt sparked by her words. He has lived three lifetime's worth of action, one thing he always feared was being a man of words – a play actor, a windbag, a braggart. What has he got? He is *persona non grata* at this moment, that much is true. He can never go back to the cloister. The chemise is an old one of Sir Geoffrey's – which means that it is near threadbare. He has naught but his name – his old name, Hugh of Erpingham. He leans back again, placing his hands on the half-filled turnip sacks. He could say that he had the sacks too, or did they have him – a metaphysical enquiry he is too tired to pursue right now. And what else? His left hand is resting not on a turnip sack but something softer; it is Simon's baggage, and he knows what is inside. From this knowledge, the threads of an idea begin to weave into a plan on the loom of his mind.

Three things he has; his name, his old surcoat and cape, and these humble turnip sacks. With these random pebbles from the brook in this, his Valley of Elah, he will face his Goliath.

"Mark, Moll, you must hearken unto me carefully, for we do not have that much time." He pulls one of the sacks towards Mark. "You take these – all of them, and the neeps in them too – down to Toppes Yard; aye, Toppes yard – you know it. You tell him from me – mind you use the name Pacificus – that if he loves his life and his business, he will allow you to load a small cargo of turnips onto a boat that will arrive at about the time of the Angelus bell."

He hears Moll muttering that there is no Angelus bell now, and then also Mark objecting, "But – "

"No "but", Mark, he is our only safe way past the city wall. And if he won't do it, ask him whether he would rather that than be burned at Smithfield for smuggling heretics to Antwerp, and heretic Bibles back again – aye, tell him that from me and see how helpful a man can be."

"But, how…? I can't carry these! There must be nigh on a ton of them!"

"Oh, I don't know lad – use your wits! Borrow a horse and cart, do what you have to; get Toppes to lend you one, even."

"And where will I meet you?"

"Meet us on the Surrey Street side of the Convent of Notre Dame, but first find Pieter at Saint Matthew's staithe beyond the gates, and tell him to meet us at Dragon Wharf just as soon as he can – we can still make that tide at Yarmouth."

"Right; cart, horse, Toppes, Pieter, Dragon wharf, Notre Dame." Mark numbers off the order of things on his fingers.

"Aye, and be in the trees with the cart, keeping well out of sight – we shall be in haste no doubt."

"We?" Moll says.

"The Fentons and me. You will join Mark after you have done one simple thing for me."

"Oh, yes? What?"

"You have a mouth on you, girl?"

"Some have said so." She tosses her hair back over her shoulder.

"And you know most of Norwich?"

"The bad ones mostly."

"Good, then you shall tell them, aye them and anyone else you see."

"Tell them what?"

"That, I will tell you as you help me dress."

The duke does not receive Lady Erpingham straight away, for the hour is early, even for him. It is unusual that they should call on the palace, but understandable given the unusual situation. He half-expected them sooner, for all Norwich knows he and his retinue are taking the heretic mother of the tournament champion to the Tower of London on their way to the final Privy Council sessions of the year.

It is a story followed even by the gentler folk of the town. The duke has not yet been told of the trouble at the castle, and when he does at last appear to greet them he pays more attention to his mastiff.

He leaves them to break their fast alone in an antechamber, and they do not see him again that morning until his manservant comes to the gallery, to tell them the duke is already waiting in his carriage, impatient to leave and meet the cavalcade at the bridge of the castle keep. Beth, who has been deathly silent all morning, takes a deep breath, looks at her brothers and says: "Come; let us not keep His Grace waiting."

The second footman assumes she will be travelling in the duke's carriage and so leads her there. The old man scowls but Beth ignores him, gathers her skirts and climbs in. The footman shuts the door carefully, wishing her a pleasant journey. Norfolk grunts, and then on an afterthought reminds the footman to feed Festus only lean beef, and no swimming in the lake. He turns to Beth saying almost apologetically, "Chews the rushes; they get in his gut and make him liverish."

A few miles along the road, the old man's eyes alight all at once into a sort of feverish rapture. They flare up with life in the very retina so that for a moment, she can almost see the man he once had been. Old age has made him slower, but no less wily. He has remembered something important; a thread, a plot, a means to an end – his own ends of course. He leans forward, saying, "I could not make you out at the tournament, not at all. My niece Catherine says you are a lively girl with a ready wit, but too straight for court. Ah-Ah! Please let me finish!" He raises the smallest, boniest finger on his right hand so as not to release his amulet, looking her up and down as if he were inspecting a horse. "I will say this much, the king likes you and has mentioned you twice in my hearing since the tournament. As does my son Henry, but you could do better than him. And if you would be..." he pauses briefly, the fatherly benevolence increasing in every crease of his grey face: "...be guided by me – work with me, so to speak – it may yet be possible for you to prosper at court, perhaps even save your mother, if you really want that."

"To be the king's wife?"

"God, no!"

"I thought not."

"What? And this affects your answer?"

"It does not, for it would be "no" in either instance; for one thing I prefer my head where it is."

"You seem very sure of yourself for a – "

"I am a nobleman's daughter." At this point he tries to laugh her out, but she raises her voice over his. "And I will marry where I choose, and certainly I will not become the king's concubine, or a spy for you, of that much I *am* sure."

"Nobleman, indeed! You have no money, no protector – no one, nothing. You should think very carefully before throwing in your lot with misguided virtue; the wine of youth is but a short draft - but a little of the *collaboration horizontale* never hurt a lady's chances..."

"This is no doubt how you counselled your nieces Mary and Anne, and whether they should have turned you down or no, I shall leave to Your Grace's wit to decide, only you may be assured that I shall heed you not – and I wish that you speak not of it again."

He calls her a foolish child, reiterates again his view of her position, grunting about 'no money, no protector, no future, nothing.' These he says more to himself; no further conversation passing between them on the short ride to the castle. The morning sun has given place to drizzling cloud from the coast. The cobbles of Saint Giles' street

glisten as the droplets fall light as air. Richard and Piers ride behind, liveried retainers fore and aft, baggage carts in the rear. Neither will admit the cavernous void in his own gut, not with others looking on. Piers feels physically sick at every turn, every new view of the castle. Richard is recognised by a loud-mouthed costermonger on the edge of the fish market.

As the townsfolk fall back respectfully to make way for the duke's carriage, they too recognise Richard. Of course, they say one to another, it is Michaelmas day. Soon word spreads in the adjacent guild halls and among the clerks in the accounting offices to the east of the markets. And hot on the heels of this news – while it is still upon tattling lips and titillating bored minds – more news comes, more incredible than the first, more like a fairy tale. Within the space of half an hour, the city is in more of a stir than ever it was even for the coming of the king.

The castle proper, as of Norman times, is built on a hillock formed by three mounds of decreasing height, the castle being on the highest. Each level is artificially separated by ditches, the dug-out soil added to the ramparts, accentuating the definition of the three distinct areas. Each part had been fortified with crenelated walls and joined by connecting drawbridges. The lowest and biggest section has been overtaken by merchants' houses, with space for a market of considerable size. On all sides, the houses of the wealthy and successful surround the marketplace, the location being set well up from "the lower town', with its damp and miasmal vapours.

The duke's cavalcade draws up in the market square, waiting for the castle watch to open the portcullis to the upper citadel, from which the earl and his troop will appear with the prisoner. A crowd has already gathered, but not just the inquisitive merchants and their wives and servants, for there now stands many others of humbler station. They alike fawn and shout, "God bless your Grace," as he passes them, though the duke makes no acknowledgment of their existence. He knows they are hoping to glean some scattered coins from his Grace's largesse, and he won't have it just yet. Let the wretches wait - let them earn it when this woman is brought forth. For the crowd know well that for all her vaunted beauty this Anabaptist heretic woman is no friend of the duke; no friend to social order. Worse, they saw her children put the duke's son to scorn at the tournament – the gracious duke, who might even now give them something for their bellies. And so without a twinge of conscience this wretched crowd about the ale houses forget every high thought that they may have felt at the tournament, and would trade it all now for a groat from their oppressor. And well they know how to win the duke's pleasure; to show that his enemies are theirs, if they might just see a coin, any coin.

For this and no other reason do they now gather about the

drawbridge, throwing rotten vegetables, mud and such missiles as their blackened fingers can find, when Elizabeth Fenton is brought forth from the castle. At first Beth does not know what is happening, for her carriage is angled downhill, but she soon guesses by the unholy grimace on the old man's face, that it is her mother to which the jeering is aimed. Piers and Richard cannot believe their eyes. Their mother is in a stationary tumbrel, such as are used to take condemned prisoners in open view to execution – the earl's doing. Her simple travelling coat of coarse grey wool is soon covered with mud and besmeared with rotten matter from flung vegetables. Stones strike her arm, thigh and head. As she falls, shrieks rise that she is "the devil's whore', and worse. Still no money. The soldiers give space for this, and the earl, riding to the rear clad in a magnificent, vermilion doublet and cloak, makes no sign that they should stop – particularly when he sees Richard and Piers spur their horses to her aid. The air is still thick with flying missiles – verbal and otherwise – as their horses clatter up the cobbles towards the side of the tumbrel. A soldier tries to prevent Piers breaking through their ranks, but gets short shrift from Piers' boot for his trouble.

As they come near their mother, the crowd hushes; toothless mouths open, sinewy arms half-raised with something to throw. The young men are either side the cart when their mother sees them, and she struggles upright again. "Oh, my boys! Why ever did you come?"

"To go with you to London." Richard replies.

"To plead with the king." Piers adds.

"Ah, no, you must leave me – it is not safe! Look to yourselves, and your sister."

"We will not leave you, Mother." Piers says.

"No, you must Piers – you must!" Her face appears all the whiter for the splatterings of mud and filth. "Hearken now – you must."

The earl passes Richard without looking too long, but whispers to the captain as he goes by, "I think it sore wrong for the people not to have the chance to display their rightful indignation against this criminal, just because her bastards flank her."

The captain, an Aylsham man named John Ditcher, does not quite grasp the import of this at first. "My lord, shall we move on?"

But the earl insists through gritted teeth: "Let the crowd continue, 'till they be done, fool!" When the man still hesitates, he repeats again: "Let them continue – here – give them this." He drops his entire stock of groats into Ditcher's hand, silk purse and all. The man's eyes are wide in disbelief for he has never seen the earl so charitably disposed before. But he is soon to his business when the earl murmurs again, "Now, you fool! Do it now!"

Ditcher speaks to his soldiers, and they to the crowd, who at first do not respond for disbelief. To pelt a criminal is one thing – a civic duty even – but to assail two young gentlemen seems as near blasphemy as they can imagine. But shown the earl's coin, hard currency, they go at it heart and soul, mothers even sending their children to run for the dung the horses' drop. Richard and Piers call out for them to stop, but they take no heed. A small rock coated in horse muck grazes Richard's cheek and he cries out, "Have you no shame?" He feels the hot tears of youth spring readily to his eyes.

"Show us your coin, lad," a tall man shouts. "Show us that, and we'll have shame enough."

"Nay," another less enlightened and more ragged man says, "let thyself be ashamed for standing up for't devil, a curse on thee and his whore."

Richard's hand reaches for the sword but his mother chides him quickly, "Do not shame me, nor disgrace yourself. Am I not to drink the cup he has given me?"

"Mother – "

"You should not have come," she says again, and then with the pained breath of heartfelt pity, "Oh my boys, my poor boys, you must leave me!"

While the hail of debris continues, the earl pulls alongside the carriage to look in at the door and address his father. When he sees Beth he is pleased – that much is written in his eyes and smile; pleased as a child that thinks it has found what it dreamed about. But he is not so confident without Wyatt at his side and his father present, and certainly not when his conscience smites him concerning the abuse of her mother. He stammers, trying vainly to find the tone and words with which to address her: "Why, my Lady Erpingham, I... er...I – "

But it is too late, she has seen her brothers pulling their steeds tight about the tumbrel, seen the excrement, the rocks, heard the abuse and the sniggers of the soldiery. She will not sit with Norfolk now for all the gold in Cathay. Friendless, penniless, she will show him. "Let me out!" She flicks the door catch and kicks it open with such force that the furthest edge hits Surrey's horse hard on the nose. The creature rives back from the source of pain and in so doing crushes the earl's leg against the carriage. She does not hear his cry, does not even see him, for she will be with her brothers, her mother, her family. Rushing through the ranks of retainers and soldiers she comes upon the open patch where they are, butt of the scorn and contempt of the whole world. There is barely an unmired part of their clothing, their hair, their faces – only dirt and blood. Blood running a surreal bright crimson from their heads and hands, down their faces onto the sides of the cart. The boys shield their mother as best they can, but Piers has taken three rocks to the head and he is now about ready to fall from the horse that sidles and rears, itself now wounded. Into this hysterical screaming, frenzied mob, Beth runs with her usual cool passion. She sees the boys, the crowd, the guards, the captain, even the purse. But he – the captain that is – does not see her until she has snatched the thing from his hand and is throwing the groats far and wide. The destitute wretches scatter like rats, pleased with the payment and now not caring from whence it came. The whole din and clamour is gone in an instant. As Richard straightens up, the foul mud and shards of pottery fall from his coat onto the cobbles. She rushes to the side of his horse, only to see her mother supporting Piers who was bleeding badly. "Help him, help him someone. Will someone help him?"

At the same time as Elizabeth is crying for help, merchants standing more cautiously with their households outside their properties, begin to point in the other direction and call to their neighbours with alarm. From their vantage point they can see a new crowd approaching. From within the two exit gateways – one leading south to All Souls, the other west to Saint Peter's – this new throng of jostling, jubilant bodies, comes pouring forth and separates across the market area. And at their head, quite distinct from everyone else, for he is the only one on horseback – and that because he cannot now walk – is a lone figure clad in the black surcoat and cloak of a Hospitaller knight with a face stern as granite. All round his horse are working men who have left off their labour; carpenters, masons, farmers, wherrymen. Not young men, rabble rousers, drunkards or whoremongers, but men who have lived through hard times, through broken dreams, seen themselves turn out to be less than they hoped – but now, like old Will Short had done, have caught a glimpse of what they wanted to be once and still might be yet. These rugged and bearded men, with their caps, aprons and rolled sleeves, had been boys once – boys who knew who this rider was and what he stood for; knew that light trumps darkness, that good prevails where good men see that it is so.

They had heard a girl tell that Sir Hugh Erpingham was returned to Norwich, one man alone at Bishopsgate, she had said, come to see the city he had shed his blood to protect, and come also to take his brother's wife away from unjust men. Moll had been distressed that she managed to tell so few people, and is now amazed to see the leaven spread through the whole city. Is there a man of them still left at their trades? They reach from wall to wall, and even down the alleys, and still they keep coming.

The rider moves at as slow a pace as is possible, rhythmic, plodding like the march of time, the mills of God. He does not look back, he does not look to any man, nor even talk to them. Closer and closer he comes toward the duke's cavalcade, nearer to the deciding moment. Piers comes round in his saddle enough to point down the square and say in an almost childish whisper, "He has come."

"Yes," his mother replies, hope rising once more in her breast, "yes, he has."

"Who," Beth says, "who has come?"

"Pacificus!" Richard whispers, never taking his eyes off him.

"Say not 'Pacificus'," his mother corrects, "thine uncle, Sir Hugh Erpingham, has come."

The duke and the earl are not slow to line up their men's matchlocks, and train all their steel on the advancing sea of human aspiration and hope. The duke is no stranger to war, it is how he rose in the late king's esteem – but not on odds like these. There are maybe two thousand men here – perhaps more – against his fifty; would to God they had time to retreat to the keep. But this has happened so quickly, look at them all! His bones shake like a man afraid to meet his maker, spitting out broken Ave Marias every other second to calm his nerves, which will not be steadied for anything now.

But when the rider stops within thirty yards of the carriages, he sees first the earl's fishy eyes near pop from their sockets, then those of his father. Both Howards mutter internally as one, "It is the monk," like men cheated of their purses in a market. The duke musters what courage he can, garnering most of it from the sheer outrage of being cornered by this man who he had always suspected of something mischievous. The bishop, that wretched fool! Does not nonsense always draw folly after it, like flies on – but suddenly even *his* mutterings are cut short by the voice of the rider.

"ENOUGH!" It is not the duke he addresses, nor the earl, but the common soldiers, for that is all the duke's power is – hired swords. "Enough," he cries raising just one hand to quell the cheers and the voices that shout his name about the rooftops. "Enough," his voice pierces the heart of all assembled like the cry of a king calling men to battle. "ENOUGH!" Yes, enough of it all, returns every heart in the silence; the oppression, the mockery of justice, the realpolitik of Machiavelli, these new, slower ways of enshrining avarice and destroying the nations.

"Yes, you know me," Hugh says, addressing the line of matchlocks, "and the stories about me, though most be stretched a good deal. But I tell you this – " using his good leg, he rises high on his stirrups and then points far away to the south, " – I am but the least of men, nay dust and ashes, compared to the valiant knights I knew who spilt their lifeblood on Saracen ground to keep Christendom free to worship the true God!" This the crowd approves with deep-throated mutterings and amens. When they are done, he bellows with fierce, unaffected rage, "But is this what England has become? Was it for this – this den of usurpers and usurers – for which the flower of the European nobility, aye, my brother and myself with them, gave our bodies as a living shield against the tyranny of the heathen? *For this?*" He points at the carriage and then to the tumbrel, "*This!* To return home and find our families dispossessed, our kin abused by unjust men – "

At this the duke raises his empty, nasal voice: "It's the king's law."

Hugh heeds neither the man nor his words. " – using unjust laws, I say" he bellows over him, "framed by weak men for their own malice and malignity!" The crowd groan and murmur. "Is this how my brother is to be repaid? He who died as a Christian in the service of the weak - is the mother, yay, the mother of his only child to be treated thus? A woman, who has in no wise wronged the king." Again the stamp of feet and guttural disapproval of a thousand voices. "Is she to be taken to a stake at Smithfield or Tyburn for the sport of Londoners? If so, Your Graces, then two thousand Norfolk boys will know the reason why!"

The crowd suddenly erupts, every boot stamping and shaking the very earth under them. Moved by the memories of this woman's son at the tournament, who had been all the talk of the taverns and workshops in the intervening weeks, and now doubly so by the appearance of their own Hugh de Erpingham, who is to them the very memory of heroism. "Aye!" every man of them yells, "We shall know the reason why!"

When the noise subsides, the duke is saying, "You will break the king's peace? The laws of – "'

"Oh, aye, there may be a law in Westminster, your Grace, and let them look well unto it, but there is also the higher law of God which all just men know right well, and I appeal to this today with the good will and troth of these honest men. Stand aside, you soldiers; let me pass. I mean you no harm."

But the earl shouts to them: "Heed him not! He is an imposter! Do not lower your matchlocks."

Hugh leaves the mass of bodies at his side, the horse taking him slowly but surely into their circle. He bares his wrist. "I am Sir Hugh Erpingham, and these scars are from the Barbary galley where I served six months at the oars."

"Liar!" the earl shrieks. "Infamous liar!"

Seeing the restlessness of the crowds, the duke growls, "Henry," hoping to curb the folly of his son. Norfolk has not survived this long by hotblooded impetuosity – a wise man knows when he's beaten.

"Would you see my back too, boy?" Sir Hugh looks him level in the eye. "For I bore the lash too."

"The back of a charlatan, or a convict! Men, do not listen to him!"

"Henry, be silent for once!" His father growls again.

"He is no holy knight, I will fight you myself, sir!" The earl snarls impetuously, lips curling back from his teeth in rage. His adversary is but a horse's head away and approaching him.

"Hah!" Hugh smiles and looks him full in the eyes, while he rides even nearer. "You forget, I saw you at the tournament against my squire. *And if the footmen have wearied thee, how shalt thou race against horses.*"

"What!" The earl bristles as his horse takes a step back.

Hugh continues his steady approach. "It is in Jeremias, chapter twelve, and that," he motions easily toward the crowd, "is the swelling of the Jordan."

"What!" The earl bleats again, this time less certainly. But, at the same moment, they both hear a voice from inside the carriage, husking like November winds across the barley stubble: "Henry!" The old fox has seen his son's hand fingering the hilt of his rapier. "For God's sake, Henry," he says, appearing now on the step with sweat running down his face. "Obey me, damn you, and hold thy peace." This is how whole earldoms have been forever lost, You must pick your battles.

Hugh rides alongside the earl without again looking at him but merely remarking almost casually, "Order the bonds be loosed from my brother's widow, and you shall live out your youth."

A trickle of saliva from the earl's open mouth finds its way along his downy beard and onto his doublet, as he turns to his father. The old man snaps, "Prithee shut thy mouth, son; and do what he says." Then, waiting no longer on Surrey, Norfolk snaps at the captain, "You there, man! Have the woman unfettered." The captain steps to it and the duke returns to his carriage without another word. He knows no soldier will shoot Sir Hugh Erpingham, not with half of Norwich watching, nor perhaps even without them. They would be torn to shreds by the mob. The matter stands on a knife edge. But it is less of a hardship than his son yet understands. The wily old goat smiles inwardly. For as he always says, it is the one who laughs last that laughs loudest. Let them laugh now, he will have them followed and cut down before the day is done and this crowd will forget it all soon enough.

The earl stares lamely after his father, but says nothing, or if he does it is not heard by Hugh. For now his eyes and ears are for the woman in the tumbrel. He does not see Piers' grin, nor hear Richard greet him softly, nor even smell the stench of them, though he does say, "I beg you boys, forgive me last night – I knew not what I said." They nod silently, and Beth goes to Piers' side to steady him and ride with him, for he is still unstable.

"Of course," Richard says, moving aside to give Hugh's horse access to the rear of the cart, where the captain is removing the chains.

For once Elizabeth is not the one with ready words. She lifts back the grey woolen hood as a bride lifts away a veil. "You came."

"I did." Hugh has looked at her so many times before in her prison cell, but never like this – there are worlds in those eyes of hers, he thinks, whole worlds – new worlds. "And, by your courtesy, will you come with me, madam?" He holds forth his hand. There is no telling with her, he thinks, she might want to be a martyr still.

"I do – I mean, I will," she says, recovering herself. And then, relaxing her shoulders and releasing a pent-up breath, adds softly, "If it please you, my lord."

"Ma'am, it pleases me right well." And so too does it please the multitude who cheer and toss their caps into the air as she takes his hand and sits easily across the front of his saddle. "Better than Gower or Marie de France?" he whispers near her ear.

"No, not quite," she says, twisting round to look into his unshaven face with its weary lines, "Not yet, my lord."

She places one hand upon his, and Hugh's hands tremble on the reins, so much so that the horse moves backward, mistaking the command. For Hugh does not yet know this woman, though right now, for the first time in his life he is aware – and painfully so – of holding a weight of treasure too heavy for a man to carry. A burden beyond even the aid of Michael, for what do angels know of these labours that mortals bear? And he, Hugh, too long trained and armoured in the defence of citadels to remember how to scale them himself – what can he do now but stare. And what ramparts are these, and what siege works may he employ? He has more to learn than even he can guess on this Michaelmas day. The anticipation of discovery is more than three new worlds, as he sees it today, even as he looks upon the future with this woman in his arms. And how those arms tremble at the thought.

Hugh turns Percival to the duke's window. "I pray your Grace will rule a little more justly – nay, mercifully – after this day, that you may deserve the good will of these men."

"A rabble," mutters Norfolk from his corner cushion, where he sits like the cornered fox that he is.

"Free born Englishmen, your Grace, and men that in no wise worship the setting sun – for this day they have heard their own voice. You tell them they do not need the monasteries, for your own ends; soon they will decide they have no need of you – nor of your son either – you may depend on it."

Hugh does not wait for the reply; by the time he has finished speaking he is already halfway back to the crowd. He smiles at the young man, Robert Kett, who at one point had held Percival's reins on the way through the town; a yeoman farmer of Wymondam with a dense thatch of brown hair, eyes that see more than most, and believed for better things – for no other reason than his brief conversation with this knight. For he laid his griefs before Hugh: the enclosure of the commons, the spread of sheep in croplands and many other grievances. He had not thought the knight was even listening until, he felt a hand on his shoulder just before they had reached Norfolk's carriage, and heard the voice saying, "You ask, where is the God of Elijah, Robert, do you not? But heaven answers – aye, lad, answers you; where are the Elijahs of God?" He had said no more after that, but now as Hugh salutes him, and the crowd is parting for him like the waters of the Red Sea, Robert Kett feels once again the fire in his belly. Life will be different now. The crowd closes after the three horses and soon they are obscured amidst the raised hands and caps.

Old Norfolk dispatches riders from the south and east gate, though Hugh is too much master of the situation now to be caught by them. But the duke also dispatches the remaining men in twos to gather the sheriff's men from every court and guard room, with orders to cut off every city gate, every staithe - in short, to turn the city inside out if need be. The monk called Pacificus of Saint Benet's, and the heretic Fentons, will be brought back for a reward of five hundred gold angels – or a whipping if they are allowed to slip away.

Hugh and the Fentons are only five minutes hard ride ahead of their pursuers; down Saint Stephen Street, cutting hard left before Westlegate through the alleys towards the convent of Notre Dame. They find Mark and Moll amongst the trees in the graveyard, sitting on a double axle wagon with Toppes' own insignia next to the Saint George guild livery on the side. Hugh compliments Mark on the acquisition, though only as he is leaping from Percival, helping Elizabeth down. But his wounded leg nearly gives way, and it is she who helps him up onto the wagon and into his sack. Moll helps Richard, Mark helps Beth, and Piers is helped tenderly by his own mother for once; tucked into his sack as she used to tuck him into his truckle bed. He smiles through the mild concussion, for it something similar to his dreams, now all but forgotten, so many nights that first winter without her. In no more than five minutes the four fugitives are tied in their turnip sacks, huddled among seven other sacks bulging with real turnips.

Mark takes the reins and sets his cob's nose towards Ber Street. Sir Geoffrey's horses are tethered behind the cart, and Moll sits up at the back on the hindmost turnip sack, with her feet resting on another – which in actual fact happens to be Richard's back. The cobbles on Thorne Lane are broken up and, in some places non-existent. Through the rutted tracks and back alleys, Moll leads them the most circuitous, yet safest, route to Rouen Road, from which point the Dragon Hall and their staithe lies little more than a stone's throw away. They finally pass through the seclusion of Saint Julian's Way, an alley so narrow that the cart axles scrape the lime mortar from the walls.

But when they come out on King's Street, Mark and Moll see that the duke's men are already arriving to guard the staithes – and where better? For the east side of the city is butted by the river and has no defensive wall or gates. Ten of the duke's men bar the way to the wharfs, with the same John Ditcher as their headsman and captain. They are searching those who pass through, inspecting goods, talking to the women. Mark sees Ditcher smiling before ever they get near in the queue, but cannot understand why.

"What are you carrying, lad?" Ditcher scratches a purplish growth amongst the stubble under his jaw.

"Turnips. J-just t-t-turnips." Mark's nervous grin is too ready, and draws the attention of another young brave.

"T-t-turnips you say, and w-w-where are they b-b-bound for eh?"

"T-Toppes' Staithe," Moll says, pointing to the insignia on the cart, "if you can read as well as you stammer!"

"Oh, is that so?" He comes closer to Moll's end of the cart, staring her up and down. "Well, you're a lively one, girl, but what would old Toppes be doing trading turnips? Run out of worsted cloth?"

Moll, all the while eating her apple, has never for one moment lost the ready tongue that was the bane of her childhood. She swallows her mouthful and says with a dry smile, "These ain't for trade, lover boy, they're for the poor. Alderman Toppes is a goodly Christian, or ain't you h-h-heard?"

"For the poor!" The man's lip curls, as he takes a knife from his belt, stabbing it randomly into the sacks on his side of the cart.

"Well, we can't all have venison like the duke's men, can we?" Moll tries not to flinch from her teasing discourse but Captain Ditcher, looking on knowingly from the side, sees there begins to be no more breath in her. A few women in the crowd like her last comment and start to laugh, calling the soldier "sweetheart', and asking if he will share his meat allowance with them.

After a few moments of this, the other soldier's cheeks flare red and he shouts above the din, "Enough, wench! Off your sacks! We'll search the lot of them!" He is halfway to jumping on the wagon, when he feels a hand pull him back to the street. It is his captain, John Ditcher, "Your zeal does you credit, George, but we have more important work today than chastising girls and forking turnips. Come, now; leave this to me and look to that next cart coming."

George is not happy, his eye twitches a little at the corner, but he has to obey, grabbing his matchlock from where it is propped on the back of the cart and storming off to the next one without another word. That done, and the other soldiers busy elsewhere, Ditcher approaches Moll and says, "My girl, we are here today to capture criminals and injurious persons, or so I am told. Well, I see naught here but good English turnips, aye, good English neeps, and Norfolk ones at that." He places a hand on the side of the cart, and smooths it up and down the timber, eventually patting it and saying, "God speed you all."

Shocked though he is, Mark does not wait for a second invitation to pass through the gate, and he leads the cob on. But Moll, facing backward anyway, looks steadily at the strange expression on Captain Ditcher's face as they clatter through the archway and out of sight. And Ditcher himself stands watching long after they have gone. He'd have recognised that destrier anywhere, but he would not have said anything about it today – not on Saint Michael's day. Good Norfolk neeps, indeed!

Alderman Toppes is looking for them from his upstairs window, and when they finally roll in through his archway, he is there to greet them. He rubs his hands like a man not quite in his right mind, ushering the cart all the way to the staithe, shooing off his staff and glancing back incessantly towards the archway. Moll can hear her babe crying in the boat, and she jumps from the cart to get to him.

"Make haste, now; take it to the water," Toppes says, hurriedly leading his old cob. His nervy-twitchy glances increase dramatically when he hears the turnip sack speaking to him, but even then, he could not be more obliging, if by any means he might just get this monk and his turnips clean away from his staithe. Hugh instructs him where to return each horse, saying particular attention should be paid to the destrier Percival, and that the prior and Sir Geoffrey will repay him for his troubles. To all of which Toppes says he has no interest in payment, only that he keep his head firmly upon his shoulders and hear no more of the business.

Before he is loaded by Mark and Pieter, both Hugh and Richard find themselves being sniffed at through the hessian. That familiar half-grunt, half whiney - the sound of a horse only pretending to be uninterested.

"Ah, it is you old friend," Hugh says. "Fare thee well, Percival. Would that I could take you with me, but go to, now, and look unto your master. He shall have need of a solid friend this next year, if ever a man did." It is only moments after he is placed in the boat that he also hears the scratchy patterings of Gus on the decks, and feels his breath when he sneezes at the dust in the sacking. Ah, Hugh smiles, stupid dog!

At this point, six feet away, Richard feels a dam of emotion burst in his soul, releasing as it does great flood of tears. It is partly through relief at being here – becoming aware from this vantage point of what he has escaped – and partly because horses have that way saying so little yet knowing so much. This horse he had ridden at the tournament, the one who had borne him patiently while he was a frustrated beginner, and the solid flanks and musky breath recall Hobb's patience and Sir

Geoffrey's unearned kindness – what Pieter called Sir Geoffrey's 'grenade', grace. Richard reaches two fingers through a hole in his sack and strokes the horse's nuzzle, repeating his thanks over and over, hoping that Sir Geoffrey will hear it, and that Hobbs will know from wherever he is now. Then he feels Mark's hands about his elbows, and hears old Pieter's voice at his feet: "Come now, young master, ja, 'tis time we were away." They heft him with some effort into the boat, Pieter reflecting on how much Richard has grown since the night that the scared little lad arrived at the cottage on the marsh.

As Pieter leads them out into midstream, they hear Toppes shouting for his men to take away the horses. Their last link with the old world goes trip-tropping across the yard, their hooves sounding higher and lighter, the further they go. Pieter unfurls the sail, and says it is a fair wind. They jostle among the wherries and other boats as they pass the main wharfs. Many will be bringing hay into the city for fodder, and straw for bedding and many others are back-hauling manure to fertilize the fields. They even hear, on two occasions, the sounds of the duke's men searching boats still tethered to the staithes. They pass unsuspected within feet of the men searching for them. The good Norfolk neeps pass unnoticed. Further and further downstream they go, imagining in the close confines of the sacking the familiar warehouses, inns and hovels that hang on the river's every bend like limpets on curling seaweed. Once they reach the confluence of the Yare and Wensum, far enough into the country that only sheep can be heard above the flap of the sail, Pieter says that it would perhaps be safe for them to speak.

And so it is that Hugh finds himself, as at so many other times once more in conversation with this woman. She is imprisoned this time, not in stone, but in thin hessain sacking and only a foot away from his face. He has been listening the last half-hour to her breath gently rise, gently fall. And he fancies when the boat is turned just right that light pierces the hessian veil and thinks he has caught a glimpse, and she thinks the same; they each wonder if the other can see or not. When the silence breaks she says she can hardly imagine she is free from her cell, that she is like one who dreams – mind, they all are. He listens, and thinks he could listen to her forever. Piers is gently asleep, and Moll is sitting on the gunwale near Richard's sack, feeding the babe.

"Moll?" Richard's voice is low, and he is hoping his mother cannot hear him above her own conversation.

"Yes."

"I am sorry for leaving you this morning, only – "

"Don't speak of it now," she says, but then thinking she had sounded too tender, adds, "but don't do it again, either."

After a pause, and the flap of canvas, Richard replies, "I won't, Moll."

Mark is tying ropes and busying his hands in any other way he can. The sack with Beth in it lies silent, listening to the others and, though he does not know it, for him. Every now and again he sits close to where she is, gives a little cough or sniffle, hoping she will speak to him. He could speak to the girl with the bare feet from the eel-catchers cottage, but hardly this Lady Erpingham, the one who turned the king's head. Today he is not sure what she is, or who, or what she is to him. And to think he had once amused himself long ago at Mass by pulling the hair that fell from the back of her coif! Eventually he hears her shift position slightly and so says, "Beth, I'm so glad all is coming right."

"I am too, Mark." She says it in a husky whisper, for she has said nothing for so long.

"I thought last night we were all done for."

"I had to go, they would not have got far without me – or with me, as it seems." After a pause she adds, "Thank you for rescuing me – again."

"Go on with you! It was hardly me."

"You know what I mean," she says.

"Well, you are safe, and we are all on our way to a new world."

"I shall be glad of a little less adventure," she says, "and to think how I used to hate the quiet of the farm; always wanting masque balls, fairs and dances."

"And now..." He hesitates. "...now, you would be happy to settle down?"

"Yes," she says vaguely, for she is trying to imagine all that they must pass through first; the emperor's court, the voyage to New Spain, then

Viceroy Mendoza's court, and then to where? She cannot even imagine yet. "Yes, eventually Mark, and you?"

"Yes. I would like a farm – a quiet farm, with a family. What normal man would not?"

"I would like that too."

"You would?"

"Yes, but Mark – " as she says it, his hearts falls until she adds " – d'you think they have chickens in the New World?"

"Great big ones, I'd say, that lay golden eggs."

She laughs and so on they go, she talking to him, Moll to Richard and Hugh to their mother; sharing their hopes, their dreams, their naked selves. New worlds, and worlds upon worlds.

And all the while Pieter listens to them from the helm, wondering what a strange hand there must be on the tiller of history and what a strange boat that must be. Strange, yes, but today he senses anew that the destination of that great voyage is not to everlasting tyranny, but to righteousness, joy and peace. He came to these lowlands to escape persecution in his own land. He had prayed for naught but a little peace after long years on the sea. He had sought the last place where men would find him, yet even from here his God had wrought something marvellous to behold. That those frightened, shivering children who came to his door all those years back should now be leaving England to found, if he can believe it – and he scarcely can even now – a new country, well, it is all too marvelous. This monk can conceive of nothing on a small scale; in contrast to himself, who seems afflicted with the opposite plight, having no ability to imagine anything so large as a free church, let alone a free nation. And yet has God not used both in the weaving of his subtle threads? For he can imagine a free home, and see how the Lord brought him these kinderen to shelter and flourish there. So why not use this man, this monk who wants to paint a bigger picture than a thousand rood screens; ja, why not a free country – why not a free continent? He chuckles into his beard. Let God do what pleaseth him.

By morning they are moored up just downstream from Chedgrave Marsh near the Berney Mill. They have slept out of their sacks under canvas, but with daylight comes the risk of being spotted. From here to Yarmouth is but a mile or two across Beyden Water, and even now the tide is covering the great flats around it. Soon it will be deep enough for them to cross, and for Captain Cobb to weigh anchor in Yarmouth once more for the continent. Piers observes Pieter, now standing motionless as a heron on the bank and looking across Langley Marsh towards Yarmouth. From here he can see Burgh Castle in the morning mists, and even the wall-heads of the old Roman fort below it. But beyond that is Yarmouth, and beyond that, no more Fentons, no more Moll or the babe, no more Pacificus, even. He feels a hand on his shoulder, it is Piers. And as he looks around he sees all eyes on him.

"I wish you were coming too," Piers says, "and Sarah."

"Ah Piers, no tears lad," he replies. "We will all meet again one day, at the Last Trumpet."

Elizabeth joins him on the bank and caresses Pieter's beard with her right hand. "I have no words for my thanks Pieter, you know that."

"Shh, now, who would not take in orphans?" He looks round at them all, and they at him. "To see you safe is all the thanks I need." But then he catches, from the corner of his eye, a duck dabbling in the water the nearby rushes. And because his mouth hangs open a little, as it does when he is between sentences, she encourages him to speak on. "There are many things, as you know that I will not see now; weddings, homes, your children grow – " Here again he hesitates, and for good reason, for never was there a man who more respected the sanctity of another's free will before heaven. But she urges him again, and so do they all. "This is a new day; for me, yes, but especially for you. Today you sail from your homeland to a new life." He is speaking into his beard, "I had not thought to ever mention this before, but if you have chosen the religion of your parents – to be an Anabaptist, and if – if, I say – you were at some later time going to be baptised, then it would gladden the heart of this old man to see you do it here, on your last morning in England."

"And Moll?" Richard says quickly, not wanting her left out.

But when he looks at her, he sees she is smiling too, and holding up her baby. "Was baptised before I went into labour, wasn't I."

So now it is just the Fentons again, though each stands alone in making the choice, as their mother explains. But the thing does not seem so great a request to them as it does to the old man. In their own way, each has already come to love the simplicity of Master Tyndale's heretic book, and after all their adventures they need no persuading that they are sinful creatures in need of washing and new life. The water, amber in the morning light, is cold as ice. Yet each in turn wades out midstream after Pieter, and he hears their confession of faith before immersing them in the water, as is the custom of his sect, and the oldest tradition of Christian faith.

When they are standing on the bank again, huddled in blankets and the embrace of their mother, looking as if they'd just swallowed the sun, Hugh sees the eel-catcher still motionless in the water, still like a heron on the hunt. Their eyes meet for a moment, but Hugh looks away, way down across the shining Beyden Flats to the east, the source of the light. He has been here before, registered every objection - not least the font water on his unknowing head as a babe. It seems such a small thing to do, too small even to him, who would more readily defend a citadel, lead an army, save a king. Even as he tries to push the thoughts away, he remembers the pride of Naaman, whom Elisha sent to wash seven times in the Jordon to cleanse his leprosy, but who would not do it. What did his servant say? "If the prophet had asked you to do some great thing, would ye not have done it? So why not this small thing?" Jesu, we great men and our great deeds – the greater the man, the greater the deeds. How we must stink to heaven; and none more than I, who have waded openly in blood, will I not now wade in water too? He remembers again the bees, how they felt in his hand, how his heart yearned to be free, forgiven, clean. And not just clean, as if that were not enough for most, but the promise of a new life. Dear God, and then again under the castle walls did he not die a death that night? Was that not baptism enough, there in the sward – must he now find common cause with these despised outcasts? No, he sighs, lying in sward is no baptism, what did old Cobb say? *Them that's born to hang are safest on't water.* He stairs again at Pieter, then at the river, then to the exultant skies and hears finally Cecil's voice one last time whispering in the reeds: *you never step in the same river twice.*

TERRA DE
NOREMBERGA
LAGO D'ARCADIA
L'ARCADIA PROV.
GVADALPE. PR.
CICORA
PR.
La florida scoperta
capo de l'arena
c. S. Helena
Rio de santa
Helena
c. secco
Cabo de la crus
LA FLORIDA
Bermuda
Lucaia
Bahama

PART FOUR - 1539

- EPISTOLOGY -

Sic transit gloria mundi
So passes away earthly glory

Vol. I. P. XIV

The East side of the ABBEY GATE of St. BENNET's in Norfolk.
Sumptibus Societatis Antiquariæ.

37

Epistolary

- LETTER ONE -

Fragments of a letter from Lady Maria de Hastings to Elizabeth Erpingham. Circa August 1540

My dearest Beth, how astonished I was to receive your letter after so long a time, and how happy Uncle and I were to hear that you are all well, and verily seem to thrive in this new world of yours. (Section of letter damaged or missing)

... As I am sure you have heard, (or have you?) our king was married to the sister of the Duke of Cleves this Epiphany last. And then soon after Candlemas, Lady Katherine and I travelled by barge with the newly-weds to Westminster for the revels, though anyone could see the king looked as miserable as sin. Katherine's uncle said even then the king wanted an annulment, and she might yet be queen. And that is how it turned out, for Cranmer annulled the marriage this July and now, two weeks gone, the king married my friend at Oatlands. Then on the self-same day – and many rejoiced at it – Cromwell himself was brought to Tower Hill where he suffered many strokes of the axe, for the butcherly executioner very ungodly performed his office. So he who made the nations tremble is no more, and that only weeks after being given an earldom, yet so suddenly attainted by parliament, and arrested in the very council chamber. It was all the duke's doing. To have Cromwell gone and his kin accede to the throne, in one day, verily it must have put a smile on even *his* face. As to the things you asked about the monasteries for Sir Hugh – or do you now call him Pater? Or Abraham, seeing your mother is with child? I confess I found him an intriguing fellow. But to the news he asked of; the last abbey – Waltham – surrendered this spring, at the same time as the reformers Barnes, Jerome and Tom Garret were hung, drawn and quartered. But do not think only your sort of heretic are treated thus, for these days most men of conscience have it so. Soon after you left us, the abbots of Glastonbury, Reading, and one other, I think it was Colchester, would not surrender their houses and so were hung, drawn and quartered too. Poor Uncle was heartbroken, for they were all university friends of his.

(Section damaged or missing) ... And yes, verily I am behaving myself as I should, and doing most of the things you command. My father has quite given up hope of marrying me into wealth and status, and has settled for just wealth, which suits me well enough. And so, learning from your true humility and long-suffering, I shall bear the burden as well as I may. Apparently, my intended is a wool merchant from Lincoln, a widower with two children, but sensible – at least, according to father, who as you know hopes to rebuild his London house on the saving of a dowry. Still, if he be kind, and rich, then I shall be happy enough, even if it is so very far from London; though I confess that even being at court has lost its lustre, for there is so little jollity here and I see little of my friend now she is queen. Some better

news for you that I forgot to mention, is that my uncle prevailed somewhat with his friends at court this Candlemas gone, having success he believes mainly on your account, for the king now knows the true identity of a certain monk, and was sore vexed to have lost him to foreign parts. In short, the new proclamation regarding the Laudable Ceremonies straitly charges us not to treat the sacrament, nor candles, water, bows, hallowed ashes and the like as more than tokens and outward signs. But also this, that will the more interest you, the proclamation ends with the pardoning of all Anabaptists and Sacramentaries, though methinks you should still have to recant if you would return to England, which verily I long for, for I so miss your sermonising, and I fear I shall not be half as good as I ought, Beth, without you to chide me. Howsoever, do write me again if you have leave and tell me more of this man, Mark. You say he was at one time a novice at Saint Benet's, but little else. Is he witty? Does he behave himself as a gentleman? And what of your handsome brother and Margaret – was she that lively maiden who came to Bindringham that day? And how can they have a child over one year already? Was he not as virtuous as he appeared? If not, then I shall have hope for myself. Oh Beth, I wish you would give more detail, surely this farming life gives you time for writing? And tell us more of these native peoples. You are all very brave, my dearest, and these lice, they have sound fearful – do take care. Your ever affectionate and devoted friend, Maria de Hastings.

LETTER TWO

Fragments of a letter from Maria Shackleton (née de Hastings) to Elizabeth Erpingham. August 1549

...are in health and do prosper. John has bought us a comely little townhouse, near Whitehall, which was sore expensive and really too small if we want to entertain as I hope to. The children grow, but our little Elizabeth, your namesake, was taken of a distemper this Corpus Christi. We laid her next to my mother at Bindringham, but the very heart has gone from our home. John was so melancholy that many feared for him too, but this new house in town, the growth of his trade there, and news that I am with child again has done much to cheer him, and me with it. He is a good man, Beth, and I wish that one day you could meet him, and my growing brood, as I wish to meet you and yours, though I can hardly imagine it now, you being a world away. I think you shall have to learn to speak German, Dutch or somesuch with all these settlers joining you. You say there are no jails and magistrates, but I cannot imagine they are all such saints as you.

Howsoever, I am glad to hear all your doings, though how you do with so little help, I do not know. Thank you for the locks of hair and the seeds, they are treasured, and as for these fruits that grow in the earth like our turnips, could you send them next time, or would they be too costly? We could wish for one of your summers too, for ours have been too wet even for sheep, at least John says so, and that the trade has suffered for it. But worse, the summer has been a tempestuous one for uprising and strife over land enclosures – and the new prayers, which we now must say in English. Fifteen counties had disturbance, first in Cornwall, though the Cornish are ever warring over something, but then also in Norfolk where twenty thousand men led by Robert Kett occupied Norwich, and refused the king's pardon. The rebels could not be moved for two months until Warwick came, and afterward three thousand were slaughtered and Kett hung from the castle wall, as they did with that lawyer Robert Aske at York. There is news of the bishop too. He was blamed somewhat over his handling of Kett's rebellion, as it is now called, but also had accrued such liabilities that my father said he should have been glad to have traded the bishopric for the clearance of his debts, which verily he did. One of the bishop's servants penned a very ill ditty, but I thought your stepfather would like it well.

"Poor Will, Thou Rugged art and ragged all,
The Abbey cannot bless thee (since ye sold the roofs and walls)
To keep a palace state, and a Lordlie hall,
Best repay thy debts and return to cell.'

But of course as you know, he has no cell to return to; the last monks left Saint Benet's five years hence. Uncle, who is now very frail, says the site is dilapidated and cannot be restored, and that the new bishop will renovate the abbey farm at Ludham for his country residence. Much stone, even grave stones, were taken for the duke's palace in Norwich, who by the way, survived the king by a whisker, though his son the earl did not. Both were arrested for treason after the earl had the Confessor's coat of arms augmented with his own. The earl was beheaded and his father, the duke, was to follow him to the scaffold nine days later. But on the very morning, would you believe it, the king himself died and so he was spared, the old fox. (The rest is missing.)

LETTER THREE

Exert of a letter from Sir Hugh Erpingham to Elizabeth I after her accession to the throne of England circa 1559-1560

To her most serene highness Elizabeth Regina, This letter I have sent when I heard of your accession to the throne of England and France, as one who, though many thousands of miles away, was once close to your family, knowing your mother and aunt from their infancy, for that our family lands were fast to theirs at Blickling. Indeed, there was aforetime a hope, on my father's side, for a union between our two houses, which came to naught when my brother and I joined the English *langue* of Hospitallers on Rhodes. The men who delivered this letter will well attest this fact, that both he and I defended the citadel in the great siege on that Island, after which time and during the sojourn of our order, I returned to England in much vexation of mind and heart, whereupon I took orders under Abbot William Rugge at the Benedictine house of Saint Benet's of Cowholme, Norfolk. I am also he who rescued your father from the tipped lance of Sir Robert Aeyns at the great Norwich tournament more than twenty years ago. And it was upon this occasion, Majesty, that your father the king did give me this ring which I now return to you in plea for my brothers and sisters of our like faith who both do suffer want and persecution as evil-doers, but do in no wise wrong your majesty, or the people of thy realm. They, called formerly Lollards, Winklers, Anabaptists and many other names of derision, seek only to live according to the gospel among the nations of their nativity without hindrance of a state religion, be it ever such a perfect one. For they believe that it ever was of the earliest times that the church was composite with society, though not coterminous with it, and as such it flourished under Christ's hand.

And, Majesty, if ye will bear with me a little, I will plead the more that this is borne out by the very early church fathers like Tertullian and others, and is seen clearly in this Epistle of Diognetus:

'Christians are not distinguished from the rest of humanity by country, language, or custom. For nowhere do they live in cities of their own, nor do they speak some unusual dialect, nor do they practice an eccentric life-style....While they live in both Greek and barbarian cities, as each one's lot was cast, and follow the local customs in dress and food and other aspects of life, at the same time they demonstrate the remarkable and admittedly unusual character of their own citizenship. They live in their own countries, but only as aliens; they participate in everything as citizens, and endure everything as foreigners. Every foreign country is their fatherland, and every

fatherland is foreign. They marry like everyone else, and have children, but they do not expose their offspring. They share their food but not their wives. They are "in the flesh' but do not live "according to the flesh." They live on earth, but their citizenship is in heaven. They obey the established laws; indeed in their private lives they transcend the laws.'

I do not ask for the rending of ecclesiastical bodies from the civil magistracy, for even though I judge it right and prudent, I have not faith that it is a plea you can readily hear, nor indeed answer. But rather, my plea, Majesty, is that you suffer them which do by conscience dissent from the religion of the state to do so without fear of the sword or flame, if indeed it be that they do not in anywise offend the other laws of thy realm. And I pray thee, let those who tell your Majesty that this leniency will tend to the end of religion be not thought overwise, but rather let the soft tilth of toleration, and the sweet rains of religious liberty be the legacy of thy reign, doing that which no other prince in Europe has yet done, and thus bequeath unto thy subjects the rights of freemen before God in matters of conscience, and that thou entangle not thyself in the mire that eclipsed the reigns of thy father, brother and sister.

I, Hugh of Erpingham, formerly called Lord, though now verily called *The Aged*, came to the New World during the reign of thy father to lay hold on that vision of liberty insomuch as it was wanting in Europe. We thereby did journey many months with Francesco Vazquez de Coronado into the interior of this vast continent. He, on behalf of his sovereign did spy out the location of Cibola, the fabled Seven Cities of Gold, whereas we sought, after the call of our divine sovereign, *a city whose builder and maker is God.* He did not find his city, but in departing from him, we found ours and so have learned to live unmolested in this land among its native peoples. Yes, and we sojourn even unto this day in peace, not just between men of diverse religious convictions, but also the heathen, and in such sweet concord that we would verily wish it for our brethren in Europe. And so I, if I have found favour with your Majesty, do hold forth this one hope to youward, and do pray unto my God that you will consider these words, and so act wisely, that the Lord God will bless thy reign and find you faithful at the end.

by the grace of Our Lord Jesu,

Hugh de Erpingham

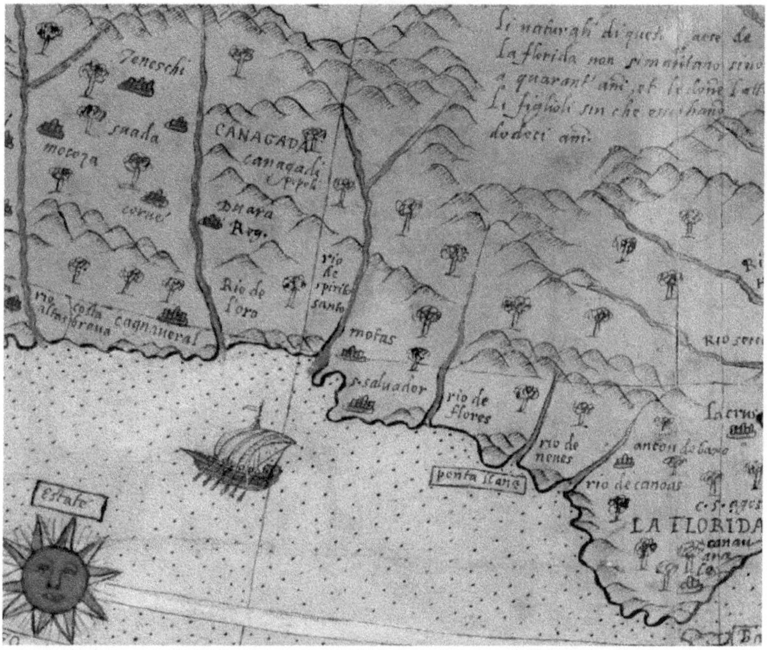

FROM 14TH CENTURY FEMALE MYSTIC, JULIAN OF NORWICH:

"In my folly, before this time I often wondered why, by the great foreseeing wisdom of God, the onset of sin was not prevented: for then, I thought, all should have been well. This impulse [of thought] was much to be avoided, but nevertheless I mourned and sorrowed because of it, without reason and discretion.

"But Jesus, who in this vision informed me of all that is needed by me, answered with these words and said: 'It was necessary that there should be sin; but all shall be well, **and all shall be well, and all manner of thing shall be well.'**

www.ingramcontent.com/pod-product-compliance
Lightning Source LLC
Chambersburg PA
CBHW021823090426
42811CB00032B/1998/J
* 9 7 8 0 9 5 6 9 4 2 7 9 1 *